UNCOVERING *the* TRUTH ABOUT

MERIWETHER LEWIS

Praise for *Uncovering the Truth about Meriwether Lewis*

"Informative and fascinating reading. Thomas Danisi's research is impressive. He is to be congratulated for bringing to light so much hitherto unknown Lewis material."

—James J. Holmberg, curator of manuscripts,
the Filson Historical Society, Louisville, Kentucky

"Danisi's skillfully substantiated insights will be the basis for all future study of Meriwether Lewis's life and times. Includes a treasure trove of original documents, many never before presented to the public."

—Glen Lindeman, retired editor-in-chief of Washington State University Press
and editor of Martin Plamondon's *Lewis & Clark Trail Maps* (3 vols.)
and Alan H. Hartley's *Lewis & Clark: Lexicon of Discovery*

"Thomas C. Danisi's research is both wide-ranging and deep, much of it in hitherto overlooked sources. The result is a wealth of new information about a major figure in American history."

—Michael J. Brodhead, Professor Emeritus of History,
University of Nevada, Reno,
author of *Isaac C. Parker: Federal Justice on the Frontier*
and editor (with John S. Tomer) of
A Naturalist in Indian Territory: The Journals of S. W. Woodhouse

UNCOVERING *the* TRUTH ABOUT

MERIWETHER LEWIS

Thomas C. Danisi
Foreword by Robert J. Moore Jr., PhD

59 John Glenn Drive
Amherst, New York 14228-2119

Published 2012 by Prometheus Books

Cover image: Portrait of Meriwether Lewis by Charles Willson Peale, ca. 1807
Independence National Historic Park
Jacket design by Nicole Sommer-Lecht

Inquiries should be addressed to
Prometheus Books
59 John Glenn Drive
Amherst, New York 14228–2119
VOICE: 716–691–0133
FAX: 716–691–0137
WWW.PROMETHEUSBOOKS.COM

16 15 14 13 12   5 4 3 2 1

Library of Congress Cataloging-in-Publication Data

Danisi, Thomas C., 1951–
    Uncovering the truth about Meriwether Lewis / by Thomas C. Danisi ; foreword by Robert J. Moore Jr., PhD
        p. cm.
    Includes bibliographical references and index.
    ISBN 978–1–61614–505–7 (cloth : alk. paper
    ISBN 978–1–61614–506–4 (ebook)
    1. Lewis, Meriwether, 1774–1890 2. Lewis and Clark Expedition (1804–1806).
3. Explorers—West (U.S.)—Bibliography. 4. West (U.S.)—Discovery and exploration. I. Title.

F592.7.L4D37 2012
917.804'2—dc23

                                                                            2011037540

Printed in the United States of America

Dedicated to my parents:

Jack Francis Danisi and Mary Henrietta Kelly

Meriwether Lewis
August 18, 1774–October 11, 1809

That brave soldier, that amiable and excellent man, over whose solitary grave in the wilderness I have since shed tears of affliction, having been cut off in the prime of his life, I hope I shall be pardoned for consecrating this humble note to his memory, until a more able pen shall do better justice to the subject.

—Alexander Wilson
American Ornithology

CONTENTS

ILLUSTRATIONS

FOREWORD

by Robert J. Moore Jr., PhD

There are many biographies of Meriwether Lewis. In fact, two years ago, Thomas Danisi, the author of this book, cowrote one of the most incisive and well-documented biographies of the man, simply entitled *Meriwether Lewis*. Cowritten with John C. Jackson, it was also published by Prometheus Books. Why, then, is another book on Lewis's life necessary?

The present volume is not a standard biography, but rather a series of vignettes that illuminate turning points in the eventful life of Meriwether Lewis. It is based on an almost overwhelming body of new historical research, most of which was conducted since the 2009 biography was published. In the course of conducting this research, Mr. Danisi has mined many collections and archives throughout the United States, his sources ranging from medical records, legal and court documents, military records, and newspaper reports, all compiled to further augment the emerging portrait he is providing of a very complex and misunderstood historical figure. In addition, Mr. Danisi has consulted with many experts in the legal, medical, political, psychological, and military fields to ensure that his interpretations of historical events, documents, and personalities are reasonable and accurate, even from a specialist's point of view. In my over twenty years' experience as a working historian, I have rarely encountered a researcher willing to put in the time and expense necessary to ensure that each fact presented is checked and double-checked for accuracy. Where Mr. Danisi expresses an opinion as a historian, he is careful to base it on the historical evidence, and if an opinion cannot be backed up by existing facts, he has very graciously dropped it rather than publish an unsubstantiated viewpoint.

In a biography of any person, there are crucial moments in which decisions are made that affect the remainder of their lives. In some instances the subject of a biography is aware that the decisions he or she has made are momentous, in others they find only in hindsight that seemingly trifling choices resulted in major consequences. This book focuses on such choices in the life of Meriwether Lewis; some decisions were made in full awareness and others were made out of necessity or in considering the question at hand to be of trifling importance. Some of the quandaries presented here may be familiar to those who have read about Lewis's life, while others will be surprising. Each of the episodes contains new, never-before-seen scholarship that puts these turning points in a new light.

Take, for instance, the well-worn story of the court-martial of Meriwether Lewis, which took place when he was a young ensign in the army. In 1795 Lewis was arrested for being intoxicated and for challenging a superior officer to a duel. Historians have based their treatment of this event on an original document, a two-page summary of the trial, which briefly lists the charges and the verdict, in which Lewis was acquitted with honor. The account of the incident in this book is based on the actual court-martial trial transcript, a document thought to be lost for more than two hundred years but discovered by Mr. Danisi in his extensive search for evidence pertaining to Lewis's life story. The transcript allows for a fuller examination of the episode, providing details regarding the exact nature of the charges against Lewis, eyewitness accounts of the events, a profile of a vindictive superior officer making the charges, and Lewis's able conduct of his own defense at the trial. This information had not yet been discovered two years ago when Mr. Danisi's first biography of Lewis was published.

Mr. Danisi also provides new information regarding Lewis's role in the famous expedition of 1804–1806. Why did Lewis not keep regular journal entries, as Clark and others did, during the course of the expedition? Lewis is often criticized by historians for not doing so, and the absence of journal entries has been grist for all kinds of suppositions about Lewis and his mental state on the journey westward. As Mr. Danisi demonstrates in this book, Lewis was busy with a myriad of duties that prevented his journal keeping for extended periods, while he kept copious notes of other kinds.

Readers of Mr. Danisi's *Meriwether Lewis* are aware that his theories about Lewis's death on the Natchez Trace in 1809 are unique and unconventional—but persuasive. Because so many historians have dismissed Lewis's death as a suicide, they have searched for signs of mental derangement in Lewis throughout his life. They have unfairly taken every unusual incident, every instance of behavior that does not seem "normal," and placed it under a microscope, with the ultimate conclusion that these many and often unrelated sets of circumstances led inexorably to suicide.

Things as minor as an early court-martial and not keeping journal entries on the expedition are listed with Lewis's inability to find a wife, his delay in reporting to Saint Louis to take up his duties as governor of the Upper Louisiana Territory, and his inability to prepare the journals and scientific notes of the expedition for publication as harbingers of his eventual suicide. The problem is that so many historians examine the end of Lewis's life and work backward to formulate their hypotheses about the man, rather than starting at the beginning and working forward.

Mr. Danisi takes issue with these interpretations in this book, finding new evidence to support fresh conclusions about many aspects of Lewis's life. His own theory about Lewis's death is based, as many readers will know, on the fact that Lewis was a long-term sufferer of malaria, a common malady on the frontier at the time, but one which, either because it was a different strain of the disease or because of the physical constitution of the victim, affected Lewis more strongly than others.

The author plows into original medical records, never before examined in connection with this story, that chart Lewis's disease and the medicines prescribed for him during the final two years of his life. He examines Lewis's financial health during these latter years. He also delves biographically into the lives of two men often implicated in his death by conspiracy theorists who believe that Lewis was the victim of an assassination plot. The two men, James Neely and Gilbert Russell, gave accounts of Lewis's death that have been challenged by historians. These chapters not only vindicate these historical figures, but also clarify errors and suppositions about documents attributed to them, and provide much new evidence to support quite different conclusions about their role in the days and weeks leading up to Lewis's death.

With this book, Mr. Danisi provides readable and intriguing final thoughts on the death of Meriwether Lewis, presenting his own unique theory with new clarity and drama, incorporating the perspectives of physicians, virologists, psychologists, and others, resulting in a wholly new and very thoughtful investigation of this much-debated topic.

Readers with an interest in early American history, the Lewis and Clark Expedition, frontier medicine, and the makings of myth and legend in the writing of popular histories will be fascinated by what Mr. Danisi has to say and overwhelmed by the evidence he brings to bear on his topic. So much conjecture and so many ill-informed conclusions have been made about the life of Meriwether Lewis that readers owe themselves the pleasure of turning to a well-documented book such as this, written by a historian who follows the evidence to reach his conclusions (rather than letting personal theories guide his interpretations). In the course of finding out about Meriwether Lewis, the reader will also acquire a better understanding of the times in which he lived, a young America just finding its place in the world and establishing a western frontier for defense and future expansion.

This book of turning points will inevitably spur internal and external discussions about the "what ifs" of history and of Meriwether Lewis's life. Luckily, the book itself remains wedded to fact rather than supposition and is a testament to dogged historical research and its application to popular biography.

—Robert J. Moore Jr., PhD
July 2011

PREFACE

Discovery is a fascinating word because it is a combination of two human faculties: intelligence and emotion. The act of discovering frequently occurs in tiny steps; most times it is imperceptible, particularly in the field of historical research when sifting through a mountain of clues over a period of years. Eventually an element of truth emerges and the process of fact building begins, brick by brick, which slowly and deliberately can obliterate a longstanding debate or theory. In the past fifty years, when writing about one controversial historical figure, Meriwether Lewis, the element of truth has become quite elastic, which makes verification extremely difficult because the documentation may be missing or it was never there to begin with. But at some point, historians have a duty to the subject matter to cite the proof or to abandon the story altogether. In Lewis's case, that decision-making process has been broken for a long time, which has resulted in his almost complete deconstruction as a historical figure.

Bernard DeVoto, a venerable historian, stated in the 1950s that speculation is a requisite and, when "properly controlled, inference and conjecture are valuable tools of history; in fact, history cannot be practiced without them."[1] That rationale now imperils Meriwether Lewis scholarship because inference and conjecture have not been properly controlled, and the dearth of historical material, or at least the material repeatedly used by researchers, has led to speculation rather than informed historical writing. This alteration has created a two-fold problem. First, any new claim about Meriwether Lewis, no matter how ridiculous, is published because of the intense and continuing interest in his life, but particularly the fanatical fascination with his dramatic death. And second, reputable historians are not objecting to these unsubstantiated claims, demanding that some reasonable and authentic documentation be produced to prove them. Put simply, the Lewis landscape is littered with the carcasses of fictional animals, which have covered up and buried the life of Meriwether Lewis. Historians must turn away from preconceived assumptions and metaphysical speculations and turn toward life—*the actual life* of Meriwether Lewis—and learn from that.

Arriving at this conclusion was not done hastily, because in this book several new and authenticated discoveries that have revealed a completely new aspect of Lewis are discussed—including his actual thoughts and feelings about specific incidents. For the first time in two hundred years, we learn that the young Lewis was not intoxicated, as claimed, when he first joined the regular army at Fort Greenville, and that he did not challenge any superior officer to a duel. These two events of his early life have been used by some historians to support some of the faulty reasoning behind his death, a death that some speculate was caused by alcoholic consumption, depression, and serious lethargy.

Then there's the crazy notion that Gen. James Wilkinson orchestrated Lewis's death, which has been completely misinterpreted from a well-known historical document referred to as the "Gilbert Russell Statement." The author, origin, and meaning of this mysterious document are finally proven in this book with the inclusion of handwriting samples. There are also chapters on how Lewis and Clark acquired the Missouri River map that they relied upon for the first fifteen hundred miles of their 1804–1806 expedition, and background on the physician who attended to Lewis in the immediate postexpedition years in Saint Louis, confirming that Lewis was sick with malaria—a familiar and chronic physiological illness.

My recent Meriwether Lewis biography was backed by twelve years of research, although there was so much information that not all of it fit neatly within the pages of a standard biography. Some of the chapters in this book expand upon that research. For example, William Simmons, the accountant of the War Department, a frighteningly "by the book" public servant in Washington from 1795 through 1814, ruined the lives of many military officers by his frequent quibbling, delay of reimbursements, and utter refusal to settle accounts in a timely manner. One chapter demonstrates how Simmons created Lewis's fiscal problems in 1809, although in the past historians have blamed Lewis for the mismanagement of his territorial and financial affairs.

One chapter explores Lewis's introduction into the topsy-turvy world of greed and thirst for prime land in Spanish Louisiana, and how land speculators duped Lewis prior to his expedition in 1804 into believing that the Spanish officers and inhabitants were the greedy ones. When Lewis returned as governor, these same individuals, whom he had previously helped, were actively undermining him.

Another topic that has received much attention focuses on Lewis's four hundred missing journal entries and the fact that Lewis's failure to keep a regular journal during the 1804–1806 expedition has been branded by historians as being irresponsible and negligent. A chapter of this book analyzes the historical evidence to present a balanced view of Lewis's contributions to the expedition. Historians have also criticized Lewis for his failure, while territorial governor of Louisiana, to carry on a proper and regular correspondence with his superiors. Lewis informs us in an important letter that some of his mail had been lost, but it is apparent that someone was working behind the scenes to delay it. We also discover Lewis's aptitude on an esoteric topic referred to as "on-land navigation."

A very recent point of historical controversy examined here is the role of Maj. James Neelly, the Chickasaw Indian agent who cared for Lewis in his final days, which has gained much prominence through a television broadcast on the History Channel. The recent discovery of court documents mentioning Neelly by name suggests that Neelly was not present at Grinder's Inn on the morning of October 11, as he said he was, and was instead in a courtroom in Williamson County, Tennessee. If this claim is correct, then much of the established orthodoxy about Lewis's death and burial, based on Neelly's testimony, may be untrue. This is another iteration of the deconstruction process, another pet theory allowed to parade as authoritative research because little documentation has been uncovered or published about Neelly. Yet as we discover from new research presented in this book, Neelly was indeed Lewis's companion in the final days of the explorer's life.

Within this book is a wealth of information drawn from newly discovered primary source materials, which are faithfully reproduced verbatim and without correction, making this volume an important collection of hitherto unpublished documents by and about Meriwether Lewis. Among these are documents relating to Lewis's court-martial, his real estate transactions, his long sought-after account book entries, transcriptions of letters he sent to various persons, and letters about him and his death. Finally, Lewis's controversial death is revisited, with key aspects that contributed to his demise given more focus and depth.

This is an exciting time for Meriwether Lewis, and because of an extraordinary twist of fate or luck, two hundred years later, this new documentation restores the reputation of a man who successfully governed the Louisiana Territory and who led the iconic expedition of 1804–1806.

ACKNOWLEDGMENTS

Asking the right questions at the right time is grounded in scholarship and intuition, and equally important is addressing those questions to individuals who know how to answer them. This progression is the starting point for an equally simple paradigm—teamwork, which often begins invisibly, but inevitably becomes truly useful. I am deeply appreciative and grateful toward these individuals and institutions that helped with this lengthy process.

Martha Riley, librarian at Washington University School of Medicine, Bernard Becker Medical Library, Rare Book Department, provided extensive assistance on eighteenth- and nineteenth-century medicine; Philip Skroska, archivist from the Rare Book Department, for his suggestions regarding the endless reels of medical microfilm. Of equal weight, and what I have come to claim as my alma mater, is the Missouri History Museum. Since 1976, persons from this revered institution have assisted my research, and I thank Emily Troxell Jaycox, Molly Kodner, Dennis Northcott, and Carol Verble. The museum's library staff, Edna, Jason, and Randy, have given loads of time searching through the shelves.

I am especially grateful to Daniel N. Rolph and David Haugaard from the Historical Society of Pennsylvania in Philadelphia, whose extensive holdings on Gen. Anthony Wayne also included the original 1795 Meriwether Lewis court-martial proceedings. I am equally appreciative to Charles Wise and Rhonda Chalfant from the Pettis County Historical Society and Museum in Sedalia, Missouri, for allowing me to access Dr. Antoine Saugrain's medical ledgers and to photograph the pages of Meriwether Lewis's malarial treatment. I am also indebted to Sue Presnell from Indiana University's Lilly Library, which holds the Jonathan Williams papers, who assisted with the original Gilbert Russell Statement and other pertinent documentation, and to Melanie Bower from the Museum of the City of New York, which holds the Samuel Latham Mitchill papers. Mitchill, a Washington official, wrote daily to his wife, Catherine, describing Meriwether Lewis, Thomas Jefferson, and other historical figures.

Several Missouri institutions helped with strategic historical documentation, such as the Missouri State Archives, the Saint Louis Mercantile Library at the University of Missouri, the Civil Court Archives for the City of Saint Louis, the Jefferson National Expansion Memorial Library, the State Historical Society of Missouri, and the Supreme Court Library of Missouri. There were also institutions that assisted from afar: the New York Historical Society, the Kentucky Historical Society, the University of Virginia's Small and Alderman Libraries, the New York Public Library, the Tennessee State Library and Archives, the Williamson County Court Archives, and two academic libraries in Saint Louis, Washington University's Olin Library and Saint Louis University's Pius Library. Special mention to Susan Snyder from the Bancroft Library at the University of California, Berkeley, for her kind permission to republish the James MacKay archival map from the Louisiana Papers collection, and to Carolyn Doyle for granting permission to reprint the article from the *Western Historical Quarterly*.

My historical study evolved by drilling deep into a source that is so pervasive that it remains invisible most of the time: Google's digitization of out-of-print books. For the scholar, researcher, and student, this easy and quick aid is a formidable educational tool and one that I thanked every time I didn't have to go somewhere to read a book or obtain permission through interlibrary loan. This courtesy also applies to many smaller institutions like the Ohio History Online Portal, Cornell University Library: The Making of America, and the Wisconsin Historical Society, which publishes valuable online historical information.

These resources are only contributory when ably utilized, and much gratitude is owed to a tiny legion, a small "think tank" of individuals, who helped with the organization of a gargantuan amount of documentation. Robert J. Moore Jr., Lewis and Clark historian and author, grappled with numerous historical, textual, and technical aspects of the manuscript, and because of his guidance and editorial recommendations, the complexity of the project was less daunting. I wish to thank R. Mark Buller, a formidable researcher in the sciences, whose editing skills sharpened the focus of the subject matter, and Jeanne M. Serra, whose legal/medical expertise helped to hone my research when hunting for clues on Lewis's malarial condition and to build "brick by brick" dynamic presentations.[1]

I am also indebted to coauthors John Danisi and W. Raymond Wood for their expertise. John Danisi assisted with the final chapter, which required a logical, organizational structure to simplify the arguments surrounding Lewis's death.[2] The chapter on Lewis and Clark's route map contained numerous details, and I thank W. Raymond Wood for helping me set the record straight, and for also agreeing to be a coauthor when I was an unknown historian at the time.[3]

There is also a ring of individuals who assisted with special services: Caesar A. Cirigliano, who gladly researched historical legal documentation from Tennessee;[4] Professor Nancy Durbin of Lindenwood University, my eighteenth-century French translator; Bob Shay, who took a dull graph and redesigned it into a fascinating timeline of Lewis's life, created the map of Lewis's "Final Journey," and who also livened up most of the illustrations in the book; George Huxtable, for his remarks concerning on-land navigation; Lorna Hainesworth, for her timely contribution on the Cumberland Gap; Andrew Janicki, expert model maker of Fort Greenville, who provided much information on the Ohio forts; Patrick Riley, who provided information about persons connected with General Anthony Wayne and Fort Greenville; Jill Schriewer, for her statistical analysis on the Meriwether Lewis correspondence; Tony Turnbow, for sending the Williamson County Court minutes documentation; Zoe Lemcovitz and Catherine Lemcovitz, aka Mrs. Z., for their comments when reading early chapters; Jay Buckley for endorsing my research on Lewis's physical illness; Bill Gleason, for his encouragement when I first began to research history; and T. Melodious, Inc., for loaning out its chief audio designer to research and write early American history for the past thirty-five years!

Additional appreciation to the Lewis and Clark Trail Heritage Foundation, which supported my research on Meriwether Lewis with a grant in 2004; to Jim Merritt and Wendy Raney, the former editors of the foundation's scholarly journal, *We Proceeded On*, for publishing several of my articles; to Barb Kubik for her assistance with the foundation's grant and for other helpful suggestions. Special thanks to Lewis's descendants, Jane Sale Henley and Ann Sale Dahl and to Saint Louis chapter of the Lewis and Clark Trail Heritage Foundation members Jerry Garrett, Bev Leer, Patti Malvern-Frick, and LuAnn Hunter for their encouragement over the years.

I also laud the efforts of Prometheus Books, and specifically Steven L. Mitchell, editor-in-chief, for publishing American history. The staff at Prometheus has been both exemplary and highly accommodative with last minute details.

Lastly, and in retrospect, I have recently acknowledged a penchant for tracking down historical clues, which seems to come under the purview of one word: curiosity. It was ignited from an early age, and I thank my parents, Jack Francis Danisi and Mary Henrietta Kelly, for supplying the spark.

Cantonment Greene ville November 6th 1795 — [handwritten]

Cantonment Greene Ville November 6, 1795 —
At a General Court Martial this day
convened pursuant to a General Order yesterday of
"for the trial of such prisoners as may be brought
before them" —
Major Shaylor – President

Captain H. Lewis -		Capt. Marts
Lieut. Polhemus -		Lieut. Steele
Lieut. Bissell -	Members	Lieut. Sterett
Lieut. Webster -		Lieut. Strugh
Ensign Johnson -		Ensign Swain
Ensign Rand -		Ensign Dodd

the following proceedings were had

Ensign Meriwether Lewis of the 4th Sub Legion in arrest appeared for trial, and [handwritten]

Ensign Meriwether Lewis of the 4th
SubLegion in arrest appeared for trial, and
challenged Capt. Marts, Lieutenants Bissell
Sterett and Webster from sitting as members
on his trial —
Ensign Rand, challenged on the part
of the United States —
Captain McRea, Lieutenants Diven
and Freemer, and Ensigns Richmond and
Scott returned vice those challenged
appeared —
Captain McRea, Lieut. Diven, Lieut.
Freemer, and Ensign Richmond challenged
by Ensign Lewis —

First page of Meriwether Lewis's courts-martial proceedings, held at Cantonment Greene Ville on November 6, 1795. (Anthony Wayne Papers, General Orders of Court-Martial, May 1793–October 1796, vol. 50, folio 49–91, Historical Society of Pennsylvania, Philadelphia, PA.)

Chapter 1

DEMANDING SATISFACTION: THE PERILOUS TRIAL OF ENSIGN MERIWETHER LEWIS

September 1795 found Meriwether Lewis, a young ensign (a rank later abolished by the army and called "second lieutenant" instead) stationed at Greenville, Ohio (about seventy-five miles north of Cincinnati, Ohio) with the US Army or "Legion of the United States," commanded by Gen. Anthony Wayne. Victorious over the consolidated Indian tribes of the Ohio River Valley, who fought to retain their lands in the face of intense pressure from American settlers, the legion won a great victory at Fallen Timbers in 1794 and forced native chiefs to sign a peace treaty ceding their lands in 1795. With the warfare over and the treaty signed, the legion settled into the boring routine of camp life. Soldiers groused and cursed as they went about their daily routines of fatigue duties and drill, and officers, especially junior officers like Lewis, had a difficult time keeping the men in line while fighting their own ennui. Friction was commonplace among enlisted men, between officers and enlisted men, and within the ranks of the officers themselves.

But despite this dull period in the life of the legion, and the frictions it caused, it was still somewhat surprising when a young officer, Lt. Joseph Elliot, charged Ensign Lewis with being intoxicated and for challenging Elliott to a duel. Challenging a superior officer to a duel fell under the charge of "conduct unbecoming an officer," which led to Lewis's court-martial trial in November of that year.

Lewis's indictment came from an officer who was highly respected. Lt. Elliot's credentials alone seemed to spell disaster for Lewis. In August 1795, Gen. Wayne commended Elliot for providing a great firework display, probably before the signing of the Greenville Treaty.

Head Quarters, GreenVille, 9th August 1795 The Uniform industry, and Professional Knowledge of Lieutenant Elliott, of the Corps of Artillery & Engineers, have not escaped the Notice and Grateful Approbation of the Commander in Chief. The ingenious formation, Judicious Arrangement, and Brilliant display of the fire Works, on the Evening of the 7th Instant, cannot fail of making an indeliable impression upon the Minds of the Savages, not only of the Day, but also of the Principles and Conditions upon which the UNITED STATES of America gave Peace to all the Hostile Tribes of Indians, North West of the Ohio—and adopted them as Children.[1]

A year earlier, Elliot had charged an enlisted man—a Sgt. Chase—with disobeying orders. This charge landed the sergeant before a court-martial; the verdict stripped Chase of his rank and demoted him to a private sentinel.[2]

Then, in late September 1795, Elliot charged Ensign Lewis with intoxication and issuing a challenge to a duel.[3]

Head Quarters, GreenVille 16th November 1795

At the General Court Martial whereof Maj. Shaylor is President, begun on the 6th, and continued by Adjournment untill the 12th Instant, inclusive—Ensign Merriweather Lewis, of the 4th Sub Legion, was tried upon the following Charges exhibited against him by Lieut. Elliott, Viz't—

1st Charge—A direct, open and contemptious Violation of the first and Second Articles of Seventh Section of the Rules and Articles of War—

Specification. 1st. In presuming on or about the 24th of September last to use provokeing Speeches and Gestures to Lt. Elliott in his own House

Specification. 2d. In presuming on the same Day to send Lieut. Elliott a Challenge, to fight a Duel—

2d Charge—Conduct unbecoming an Officer & a Gentleman to Lieut. Elliott on the 24th September.—

Specification. In abruptly, and in an Ungentleman like manner, when intoxicated, entering his (Lieut. Elliotts) House on the 24th September last, and without provocation insulting him, and Disturbing the Peace and Harmony of a Company, of Officers whom he had invited there

Which being stated to him, he Pleads that he is not Guilty thereof—.[4]

It was probably a mixture of honor, intelligence, and mortification that caused Lewis to vigorously deny the charges, but it was the fact that he was ready to defend himself and refute the charges that showed tenacity.

The proceedings of Lewis's military court case file had never been located and were presumed to be lost.[5] What has existed for scholars to examine is a summary document from the National Archives, which briefly describes the specifications and charges of Lewis's misconduct.[6] Furthermore, in the absence of more expansive data, historians have unkindly and critically speculated about Lewis's actions, which have become for them the precursor or template of his alleged moody and intemperate behavior.[7]

Fortunately, after years of intense research, the original court-martial case has been found among the Anthony Wayne Papers at the Historical Society of Pennsylvania.[8] The court-martial transcript is about forty handwritten pages and contains a tremendous amount of new material regarding the young Lewis. One can only imagine the stress of this event on the young officer, who was arrested and put in confinement—the court record does not state where he was confined, but undoubtedly, as an officer, this arrest embarrassed and shamed him.[9] The Meriwether Lewis who later led a successful transcontinental exploration and administered a territory a third the size of the modern continental United States emerges in his ability to surmount obstacles—he took advantage of the time to prepare his defense, preserve his honor, and save his career.

Beginning his military career as a volunteer in the Virginia militia, Lewis was so impressed with the "mountains of beef and oceans of whiskey," that he continued serving in the military.[10] But when the twenty-one-year-old joined the Legion of the United States as an ensign on May 1, 1795, due to what he called a "Quixotic disposition," his mother already knew that he would forego his duties to oversee the family's Charlottesville farm. Joining the legion in peacetime was supposed to be easy, but there was inner turmoil among the ranks of officers, a hatred and contempt possessed by Gen. James Wilkinson toward his commanding officer, Gen. Anthony Wayne, and the fort was rampant with illness at various times of the year.[11]

Since William Clark was also serving, as a lieutenant in the Legion of the United States at this period, there has been a lot of speculation by historians about how his presence might have affected the outcome of the trial and whether he and Lewis had yet become friends. Descriptions of fort life at Greenville are numerous and have been compiled from journals, diaries, military orderly books, and court-martial papers. While some diary entries contain information about William Clark, and Clark kept his own diaries, none mention Meriwether Lewis. One of the more puzzling questions in Lewis and Clark literature concerns when the two men first met. Clark accepted a position as quartermaster in the Fourth Sub-Legion in August 1794, right before the decisive Battle of Fallen Timbers, and Lewis joined the regular army, in the Second Sub-Legion, on May 1, 1795.[12]

The summary document of the court-martial at the National Archives states that on November 16, 1795, Ensign Lewis was an officer of the Fourth Sub-Legion. Historian Stephen Ambrose suggested in *Undaunted Courage* that the sub-legion transfer (from Second to Fourth) occurred because Lewis "quite obviously could not continue to serve in the same outfit as Lieutenant Elliot," and thus, Gen. Wayne transferred Lewis to Clark's Chosen Rifle Company to avoid friction between the two men between the time Elliot brought the accusations and the date of the trial.[13] That made perfect sense as a speculation, but records show that on September 24 Elliot was an officer in the Third Sub-Legion.[14] The answer instead lies somewhere between May 1 and September 9, 1795, when Lewis transferred to another battalion. The court-martial transcript dated November 6, 1795, shows that Ensign Lewis was already in the Fourth Sub-Legion by that date.[15] Lewis and Clark had to have met prior to September 9, because on that day, Clark received orders for a secret assignment that would keep him occupied and away from Greenville until the very eve of the court-martial.[16] On September 10, Clark and seventeen men departed Fort Greenville on a reconnaissance mission to meet with Spanish officials and demand an end to intrusions on American soil. Clark reported back to Greenville on November 4, and Lewis's trial commenced two days later. In all probability, the battalion transfer occurred because of Lewis's keen expertise in shooting a rifle, which caught Clark's attention.

Gen. Wayne, as commander in chief of the legion at Fort Greenville, perused every court-martial trial verdict and sometimes changed the court's decision based on preference or using the officer's reputation to teach the enlisted men a lesson. Wayne was irritated with officers who used the court-martial system to settle personal disputes instead of working it out among themselves, and some abused the system repeatedly, according to military law historian Bradley Nicholson, because of their "personal malice and resentment—and without any regard to the benefit of the service, or to the Honor of the Legion."[17] Lewis would specifically remind the court of this mandate during his trial:

> The Commander in Chief further observes that he hopes in future the times of the Officers will not be taken up, or their feelings tortured by hearing and recording charges and proceedings, which only tend to disgrace the orderly books of the Legion. Can any doubt, but what the Commander in Chief, was induced to make those observations from the most noble motives truly worthy of himself . . . the good of the service.—The reputations of the Officers of his Corps. An anxiety that they should distinguish themselves as gentlemen, men of honor, men who are ever as willing to unsheath the sword in redress of private injuries, as public rongs. Also that the records of this noble Tribunal, a Tribunal which ought to be held sacred to honor and justice among military men, should not be disgraced with charges fostered by malice and dictated by spleen.[18]

Lt. Elliot had caught Ensign Lewis on a technicality, that he had violated the officers' honor code. That was a serious problem that military historian Bradley

Nicholson clarified: "Behavior unbecoming an officer and gentleman served as a vague catch-all for undesired behavior by officers." Nicholson pointed out that "the Articles of War never defined conduct unbecoming an officer" and, by keeping the term undefined, "effectively left regulation of officer's behavior up to self-definition and self-enforcement."[19] What seemed like an open-and-shut case against Lewis was now showing cracks.

Prior to the first day of the trial, Lewis requested that four members of the court be removed. These members had some conflict of interest with Lewis that he felt could jeopardize his reputation.

> Ensign M. Lewis had objected to four members of the Gen. Court Martial appointed to try him, viz Capt. Marts, Lieut. Sterett, Lieut. Webster and Lieut. Bissell—The Commander in Chief was made acquainted with the circumstance and directed that four other members should be detailed to supply their places on the Court.[20]

Courts-martial were governed by the Articles of War, familiar to each soldier because they were read to every man as part of his enlistment procedure and once again four times annually to the assembled companies on the parade ground. The Articles of War specified two types of courts-martial, a *general* and a *regimental*. A general court-martial was formed to hear cases of a capital nature—that is, cases for which the death penalty might be invoked, or, in the case of Lewis, a case in which he might be cashiered from the service. It was composed of from five to thirteen commissioned officers, with the Articles stressing the necessity of having the full complement of thirteen officers serve if at all possible. Only a general court-martial could hear cases involving commissioned officers. At this time, there was no jury in a general court-martial; the officers appointed to hear the case were the judges and jury, making the composition of the court extremely important to what the verdict might be.[21]

For a man who had, as far as we know, no experience in a military court, the young Lewis showed great skill. He served as his own defense attorney, assembling his case, calling witnesses, and preparing his summary arguments. His first act of legal diplomacy came in bumping potentially hostile officers from the court and then smoothing the waters:

> I hope none of the gentlemen I have objected to have felt themselves hurt on the occasion—I also feel myself disagreeably situated to be obliged to make my objections known which respect the last members which I have objected to—But I trust they will excuse me knowing my reputation is at stake and the obligation is from the order of the Commander in Chief and not from myself.[22]

Far from blemishing Lewis's record, as some historians have maintained, the full trial record shows instead that Lewis was a young man of great resourcefulness and intelligence in the handling of his case.

Once the trial started, Elliot's witnesses told their version of the events of September 24, 1795. On that evening Elliot was hosting a convivial party for a small group of officers in his quarters. Lewis arrived during the course of the party accompanied with a Mr. Rand, interrupting the group with his knock at the door and requesting a private conversation with one of the attendees. Lt. Diven said that Lewis asked to speak to him on the porch of the officer's quarters:

> [T]hey stepped aside, opened a door which leads to a platform projecting towards the Park—they left the door on a jar perhaps about half open—Doctor Carmichael got up and pushed too the door with his foot—Mr Elliot replied,—that was perfectly right, as he or they (alluding to the Company) did not wish to hear their conversation—in a short space of time the conversation of the gentlemen on the platform became so loud that we heard the sound of their voices.—Mr Elliot rose saying "this is wrong" and opened the door and addressed himself to Mr Diven "Sir you are my guest you were invited here pray do take your seat gentleman (addressing himself to the others) I am sorry that you came to my house to settle your disputes"—Mr Lewis turned into the house and appeared to be very much hurt and answered Mr Elliot "that he did not come to his house to settle his disputes nor had he any dispute with Mr Diven that he wished to settle"—more conversation of this kind perhaps past on both sides . . . and Mr Elliot mentioned that he wished them to sit down and take a glass of brandy and water and say no more on the Subject.[23]

Elliot confronted Lewis in a room packed with his guests and embarrassed the ensign.

> Mr Elliot warmly said that his house should be sacred that he would not suffer any disputes to be settled in it while he was master of it . . . but that his favor would be open to any gentleman officer at any time in a respectable decent way—Mr Lewis and Mr Rand in consequence of the second conversation immediately went down stairs—In a few minutes Mr Lewis came up the stairs again—the company were seated round the table—Mr Lewis stepped up towards Mr Elliot and addressed himself . . . "Sir I am now perfectly cool I consider myself to have been insulted in your house and by you Sir—as an officer and a gentleman I wish for Satisfaction, in two hours I will see you"—Mr Elliot replied "Very well Sir"—Mr Lewis then descended the stairs again.[24]

Another witness, Dr. John F. Carmichael, surgeon of the Third Sub-Legion, filled in more details about the event. As in civilian courts, witnesses in a military court do not hear the testimony of other witnesses. According to Carmichael, Lewis, accompanied by Mr. Rand, first knocked on the door and waited a few minutes outside before entering the house.

> I dined on the day . . . with Mr Elliot—after dinner Mr Lewis and Mr Rand came into the room and called Mr. Diven from the table. They and Mr Diven went out . . . leaving the door half open behind them—some interesting conversation appeared likely . . . and, to prevent my hearing it, I shut the door—for which Mr Elliot thanked me and observed that he never wished to hear any thing like disputes or controversies . . . he soon afterwards got up . . . went to the door and invited the gentlemen to walk in and requested Mr Diven to take his seat . . . he observed to the gentlemen that . . . in his house . . . it was not the place for settling disputes . . . that they could be settled else where—that he wished his guests and such gentlemen as came to his house to enjoy themselves. During this conversation Mr Elliot invited the gentlemen to take some brandy and water—Mr Lewis made some apologies—that he had no intention of quarrelling or disputing in his house—he appeared much agitated and withdrew—a few minutes after he returned to the room and addressed Mr Elliot "Sir I am now cool, I consider myself insulted in your house—I therefore call upon you for satisfaction as a gentleman—I will call upon you in two hours." He made a slight bow and withdrew—Mr Elliot answer'd "very well."[25]

The court asked Carmichael if Lewis was intoxicated, but Carmichael could not confirm it:

> I am not sufficiently acquainted with him to determine—he appeared agitated but I did not then know the cause—previous to his leaving the room the first time, he appeared to have some difficulty in expressing himself and shed tears.[26]

Carmichael testified that a half-hour later, a friend of Lewis's spoke with Elliot and wanted to resolve the situation, but Elliot said, "I don't know you as a friend to Mr Lewis nor do I know Mr Lewis as a challenger untill he sends a challenge in writing." Lewis's friend left and returned with a note, and when Elliot opened and read it, he exclaimed, "Sir what does this mean?" Lewis's friend said that Lewis wanted to fight him, but no type of gun was stated. He then said the duel was set for the next morning. Elliot rose and stepped toward the table where some books were lying, took up the Articles of War, and said, "Sir this is the way I will fight him—I will arrest him for a breach of certain articles of War naming them."[27]

Lewis had signed the note and a copy was handed to the judge and read aloud. "Sir: Your treatment to me as an officer and a gentleman obliges me to call on you for satisfaction . . ."[28] Presumably the person who spoke with Elliot was Lewis's second, but Lewis later stated that Capt. Marschalk misinterpreted what he meant by satisfaction because there was no mention of a weapon. Clearly, in Lewis's day, any mention of the word "satisfaction" was equated with a challenge to a duel, but according to Lewis's testimony in his own defense, he disagreed, stating: "That the word sattisfaction is vague, and may be given in a variety of forms each sufficient to do justice to the feelings of a gentleman, cannot be denied."[29]

Lewis argued three points as he presented his defense. The first concerned the true meaning of the note entered into evidence. The second was to ask why Elliot resorted to charging him with a crime instead of working it out. And third, and most important, he had to convince the court of his brash stupidity and innocence of knowledge about the *code duello* in this matter. The transcript of Lewis's testimony is about ten pages long and provides a detailed description of his intentions and actions. A court scribe imperfectly wrote as Lewis addressed the court tribunal:

> I have been accused of having directly and pointedly challenged Mr. Elliot, I deny it from this presumption, that a challenge should both mention fighting and the implements of War with which to fight, before it can amount to a direct challenge, such as the Rules and Articles of War take cognizance of—We find nothing decisive or printed as having come from me contained in the testimony either of fighting or arms, which I conceive as the only principe constituant [principal constituent] parts of deweling [dueling]. Mr. Elliot has informed you in his testimony that he received that note as a challenge to fite a diewel [duel], provided that note had come from me in his construction of that note, or an explination of it by another to be a proof of my intentions by no means I conceive—If the gentleman from his frantic immagination has construed the vague word Sattisfaction into a loaded pistol intended for his execution; without having any other resources, am I to be accountable, or punished for his frenzy? I trust not or perhaps my stripes might be many. Is any presumtive proof, or the mear opinion of any person as to the intention of the note to justify so harsh a sentence as that of dismissing me from the service of my country.[30]

Lewis believed that Elliot should have reasoned that they were both gentlemen and that the two could have settled the matter privately.

> As to the business of settling personal disputes in a private manner I conceive it is intimately connected with the former (viz—Self Defence) for he who is willing to settle his own private disputes, need not call upon the Publick for her protection in the one cace, or pester trybunals in the other—He who acts differently sets up in opposition to the oppinions of all that vallue their reputations as millitary men,

as well as the customs of all armies that have exhisted to the remotest ages, and will no doubt, for his unexampled vanity be rewarded with their contempt.[31]

Lewis said that he believed Elliot wanted to teach him a lesson, but cleverly diffused this motivation by making reference to Elliot's prior pattern of accusations and by playing upon Gen. Wayne's stated dislike of frivolous courts-martial being instigated by his junior officers:

> I observed in the first instance that this business was designed and mallicous, in justification of which, I will observe to the Court, that immediately I was in confinment, proposals were made to the gentleman of leaving it to refferees, who should determan upon honor, who had been the aggressor, and how far, and also the method and manner of the accomidation. this might . . . have done justice to the feelings of both without the trouble of a Court Martial. But in order to put his favourit scheme in . . . practice, or from a contintiencious knowledge of the ballance being much in my favour, he proved refractory as he has done in every other instance.[32]

Lewis also brought two other officers into court as witnesses for the defense. He questioned them specifically on the subject of intoxication, which Elliot had charged him with. Lewis believed that the specification of being intoxicated proved maliciousness on Elliot's part, "for it has been proven by several that I was not in the least intoxicated either before or after visiting the house of Mr. Elliot."[33]

Ensign Rand,

Ques. by the Court—Did Mr Lewis make use of any provoking words or gestures—

Answer—I don't conceive that his language was positivly provoking—

Ques. by Mr Lewis—Did not Mr. Elliot, addressing himself particularly to me, observe that no gentleman would come to his house to settle his disputes, after being informed by me that it was no dispute I came to settle . . .

Ques. by the Court—Do you know of Mr Lewis having challenged Mr. Elliot to fight a duel that day?

Answer [:] I do not—

Ques. Was Mr Lewis intoxicated that day—

Answer [:] I did not conceive him to be in in the least—

Ques by Mr. Lewis—Were you not with me from the forenoon of that day until we entered the house of Mr. Elliot when the conversation happened—

Answer. I was with him from 10' O' Clock I believe until the . . . conversation happened . . .

Ensign Scott testified by saying that "I have known Mr Lewis since Christmas last and have been on a most intimate footing with him ever since—I never saw him the least intoxicated but conceive that he has always conducted himself with the utmost propriety."[34]

Lewis confronted the charge of ungentlemanly conduct by turning the tables and making a veiled accusation against Elliot for the same infraction, inferring that ungentlemanly conduct could be seen in his malicious attempts to sully Lewis's reputation through his accusations:

As to the second charge of unofficer and ungentlemany conduct—I defy not only my Prosicutor but the world to alledg any thing derogatory to the character of a gentleman I wish the gentleman may see his faults, and that he never may on his imagination though this life meet with an adversary so malicious refractory or absurd as he had proven to me.[35]

Finally, Lewis asked the court to find a verdict in his favor. "I also trust that my sword will not only be returned, but that it will be done in a manner which will do justice to the cause in which I have contended."[36] The court promptly returned the verdict, exonerating Lewis of all charges and acquitting him with honor.

Lewis must have breathed a sigh of relief. Indeed, his acquittal must have been a close thing, for circumstantial evidence was certainly strong against him. We will never know what was in Lewis's heart or mind when he demanded "satisfaction" from Elliot and later sent him a signed note demanding the same. Despite his protestations in court, Lewis would have been an unworldly fellow indeed if he had not been aware of the connotations this word carried in American society at the time. Yet his written summation and presentation of it to the court was so eloquent and persuasive that he convinced a bevy of officers that he was innocent of the intention of challenging a fellow officer to a duel, and that the accusations of ungentlemanly conduct against him might have just as easily been leveled against his accuser. This was no mean feat for a young shavetail to pull off. Without the aid of defense counsel, Lewis won an amazing upset in a very tough trial.

The lessons Lewis learned in this court-martial carried through the remainder of his life; for, despite later documented provocations like those he suffered at the hands of Frederick Bates when he was governor of the Louisiana Territory, Lewis never again, so far as is known, demanded "satisfaction" from any man.[37]

Chapter 2

LEWIS AND CLARK'S ROUTE MAP: JAMES MACKAY'S MAP OF THE MISSOURI RIVER

*by Thomas C. Danisi and W. Raymond Wood**

Maps, no less than narratives, are among our most basic documents, and when they are examined carefully they shed great light on the timeline of history and reveal the growth of knowledge as well as the progress of human endeavors. A history without maps is inconceivable.

Thus, a crucial aspect in the planning of the single most important exploration in American history, that of Thomas Jefferson's Corps of Discovery, the Lewis and Clark Expedition, was to obtain reliable maps to chart their route.

How did Lewis and Clark do this?

The answer to the captains' success in finding a viable map of the Upper Missouri River is to be found in the story of cartographer James MacKay, a Scotsman who, based on his extensive trading with the Indians in Canada, and on his proficiency in mapmaking and experience in surveying, had been hired to lead the Spanish expedition up to the Missouri in Louisiana territory.

A superficial look at history would indicate that MacKay was only one small player in the international intrigue of land and economic disputes in the late eighteenth and early nineteenth centuries. It would suggest that the handwriting on the map, in both French and English, proved that John Evans (MacKay's field assistant) and Nicolas de Finiels (a Frenchman who assisted MacKay and others in various cartographic efforts) contributed to the actual drawing of the map—which is now known as the Indian Office Map.

But a cursory look at history, as always, can be misleading. It is true that it was John Evans who, on that 1795 expedition, traveled the Upper Missouri River to the Mandans while MacKay remained in Fort Charles—795 miles above Saint Louis—

and it is logical to think, since it was Evans who explored the Upper Missouri, that he would have been the one to draw the map. Also, there did exist at the time an international aspect of cooperation: MacKay, Evans, Antoine Soulard (surveyor general of Upper Louisiana), and Finiels all assisted one another on cartographic efforts. It is perhaps because of this, combined with Evans's explorations on the Upper Missouri, that historians have denied MacKay's role as the primary draftsman of the Missouri River map. The truth is to be found in detailed detective work.

The story begins in the 1790s. At that time, Louisiana encompassed a huge swath of country west of the Mississippi, and distant European powers lacked the means to populate it or patrol its borders. When Spain took control of the region in 1762, British traders in Canada had already begun establishing alliances with the various Indian nations along Louisiana's northern boundary. These alliances enabled the British to make deep forays into Spanish territory without fear of reprisal. It proved very difficult for Spain to wrest control from the British. Beginning in 1789, a few hunters, including Juan Munier and Joseph Garreau, were the first Spanish to explore the Missouri. Jacques d'Eglise followed a year later. These men reported that the British had been stealing the trade from the Spanish and were underselling them in their own territory. Something had to be done and quickly: the Spanish would have to ascend the Missouri, establish relations with the Indian tribes, and somehow win them over from the British.[1] In 1791, Spain appointed as governor general of Louisiana the Baron de Carondelet. One of Carondelet's first decrees was to throw open the trade to all subjects of His Catholic Majesty Carlos IV. In that year, Spain learned that the British had established a trading alliance with the river tribes on the Upper Missouri, and, if war broke out, the Spanish would lose control of that river. While Carondelet's decree offered advantages, the Indians had already become allied with the British and thus discouraged Spanish traders from going upriver. This development demanded a strategic plan, and, in 1793, a group of Saint Louis traders formed the "Company of Explorers of the Upper Missouri," pooling their resources to finance well-equipped expeditions. While the financing appeared to come easily, finding suitable persons to lead the expeditions proved challenging. The first two expeditions, led by Jean Baptiste Truteau and a man named Antoine Lecuyer, made little progress on the Missouri.[2] However, in choosing James MacKay to lead the third expedition in 1795, the traders found a well-prepared and uniquely talented man.

MacKay arrived in Canada sometime between 1776 and 1777, and for the next five years his whereabouts are unknown. In 1783, the British traders Holmes and Grant hired him. Robert Grant, an experienced trader from Montreal associated with the North West Company, took him to Grand Portage, the rendezvous for Canadian traders on the north shore of Lake Superior.[3] Evidently, James's brother John was also in Grant's outfit, but they separated a year later.[4]

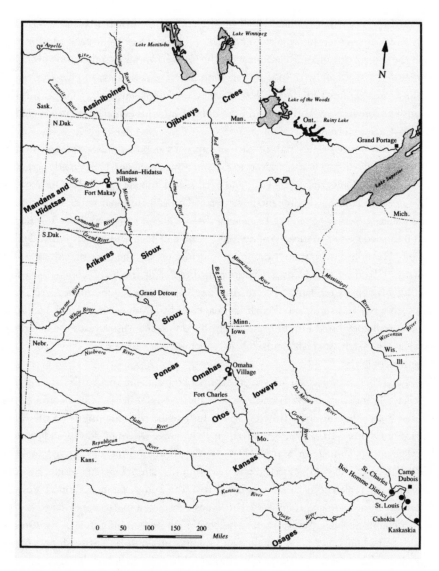

Major features and Indian tribal names in the Louisiana Territory mentioned in the text. (Map © 2003. By W. R. Wood. Originally appeared in "Lewis and Clark's Route Map," *Western Historical Quarterly* 35 [Spring 2004].)

MacKay was released to go to the Saskatchewan River as a clerk, but he was back on the Assiniboine River for the winter 1786–1787. On returning to Grant in 1787, he was given an opportunity to travel overland to the Mandan and Hidatsa villages on the Missouri River.[5] That overland journey was usually made during the winter using dog trains to haul small outfits and bring back peltry and foodstuffs, especially corn. When his contract ended in 1788, MacKay went back to Montreal with the returning canoes. Relations with the Canadian traders soured, however, and he renewed association with his brother, John, in New York City, and began trading in the United States.[6] In June 1789, MacKay met with Don Diego Gardoqui, the Spanish chargé in New York City and presented him with a map, "a su modo" of the British–Canadian trade.[7]

MacKay started a fur-trading partnership with depots in Cahokia, Cincinnati, and New York City.[8] He had arrived in Cahokia by September 1791, made acquaintances in Saint Louis that same year, and established a name by 1793.[9] On May 20, 1793, Zenon Trudeau, lieutenant governor of Upper Louisiana, wrote to Baron de Carondelet, governor general of Louisiana, that he hoped "to see within a few days a well informed Canadian mozo [young man]" who had been trading with the Mandan nation. He hoped to obtain from him information on the British among those Indians.[10] Trudeau and Jacques Clamorgan, director of the Saint Louis–based fur-trading Missouri Company, were so impressed with MacKay's abilities—to make maps, to write and speak the French language, and to trade with a variety of Indian tribes—that they hired him to head an expedition up the Missouri for the company. MacKay then left Spanish Louisiana to conclude his business in New York and Cincinnati.[11]

Two other notable men arrived in Spanish Louisiana at about the same time as MacKay: John Thomas Evans and Antoine Pierre Soulard. Evans had come to the United States looking for a tribe of Welsh Indians he thought might be the Mandans. On October 10, 1792, he arrived in Baltimore, where he stayed and worked for various Welshmen. In March 1794, he departed by boat and landed in New Madrid [present-day Missouri] about two months later. Upon entering Spanish domains, he took the oath of allegiance that the commandant, Thomas Portell, forced on all newcomers. It appears that Evans contracted malaria and stayed with a Welsh couple in New Madrid before he continued on toward Saint Louis. On the way to Saint Louis, Evans became lost and finally turned up at a Spanish post opposite Kaskaskia, deranged from the summer heat. Fortunately, he met another Welshman, the lawyer John Rice Jones, who took care of him on the Illinois side of the river.[12] A month later, Jones introduced him to a Cahokia merchant and court clerk, William Arundel. Evans stayed at Arundel's home until Christmas 1794, when he learned about James MacKay's forthcoming expedition up the Missouri River and left for Saint Louis, hoping to join.[13] It was an inopportune time for Evans to go to Saint Louis. War with Britain was imminent, and explaining to Zenon Trudeau, the lieutenant governor, that he was on a quest to find a tribe of Welsh

Indians must have sounded preposterous to the highest ranking official in Upper Louisiana. Suspicious of British spies entering Spanish country, Trudeau had Evans "[i]mprisoned, loaded with iron and put in the Stoks . . . in the dead of winter."[14]

A few months after Evans was thrown in jail, in February 1794, Antoine Soulard arrived at Sainte Genevieve.[15] The commandant of New Bourbon, Pierre Charles Delassus de Luziéres, knew Soulard because he had deserted the naval service at Martinique, France, with one of de Luziéres's sons. This son had told de Luziéres that the two had not wished to recognize the French Republic as their home and had decided to join the family in America.[16] The commandant of Sainte Genevieve had fears that Kentuckians might attack Louisiana. With no defenses in the village, Soulard volunteered to help and began "directing the works on the fort" according to the "plans and sketches" of a Flemish engineer, Louis Vandenbemden.[17] The work was completed quickly, and Trudeau summoned Soulard to Saint Louis, who arrived there by March 20, 1794.[18]

In August of that same year, MacKay had gone to Cincinnati to conclude his partnership in his eastern business interests with John Robertson. While in Cincinnati, MacKay met with John Rees, or Rhys, a native of Wales, who told him of Evans's quest for Welsh Indians and gave him a small dictionary of Welsh and Mandan vocabulary. MacKay had been among the Mandans in 1787 but "had heard nothing of a Welch tribe." When MacKay arrived in Saint Louis a few weeks later, he "sent for, & engaged for [his] assistant Mr. Evans who spoke and wrote the Welch language with facility."[19] MacKay, realizing that Evans could be an asset to the expedition, decided to employ him as his lieutenant and field operator.

The story of the MacKay map of the Missouri River begins when the first expedition for the Missouri Company, headed by Jean Baptiste Truteau, a schoolmaster, left Saint Louis on June 7, 1794. Clamorgan had provided Truteau with a plan or idea so "that he may know his whereabouts."[20] The north half of this plan, taken directly from MacKay's travels in Canada in 1784 through 1788, was the first of its kind and gave a tactical view of where the British traders had encroached upon Spanish soil.[21] When MacKay first met Zenon Trudeau and Jacques Clamorgan in May 1793, he had shown them this "topographical idea of the Upper Mississippi and Missouri."[22] MacKay had met with Soulard to help produce a map for Carondelet. Trudeau wrote to Carondelet on November 24, 1794, stating that he was remitting some maps drawn by Soulard "among which was a map of the Missouri river."[23]

Trudeau's admission of a Soulard map is interesting; Soulard could not have completed it by himself, because during the summer and autumn months that year he suffered bouts of "most violent fever" and "would have succumbed," except that

Trudeau and his wife took care of him.[24] In other words, being so ill, Soulard, who had not been on the Upper Missouri River, could only have completed a map of the river with MacKay's assistance, because MacKay had visited the Upper Missouri River. Nonetheless, Trudeau recommended that Soulard serve as the surveyor of Upper Louisiana, and in December, Soulard made a voyage to New Orleans, where he was appointed surveyor general on February 3, 1795.[25]

Between January and August 1795, Soulard began surveying land grants in Saint Louis and Cape Girardeau, as well as drafting a large-scale map, "Ydea Topografica," of the Missouri River Basin.[26] The original Spanish map is titled "A Topographical idea of the Upper Mississippi & Missouri that shows the progress of the Spanish Discovery of the Missouri river & the encroachments [or usurpations] of the English companies over the Spanish possessions."[27] The French copy attributes its drawing to Soulard, who completed it in August 1795, though MacKay revised "Ydea Topografica" when he returned from his expedition in 1797.[28] Soulard wrote on December 15 of that year that the map was "corrected by one of the voyagers of the company of discovery," and that he would soon present a map of the Missouri to Manuel Gayoso de Lemos, the new governor general of Louisiana, "much more correct than what I gave you earlier."[29]

Charting a river requires at least two people: the surveyor and the draftsman. The surveyor takes measurements and sketches landmarks like islands, bends in the river, and large trees, recording the field notes in a book, while the draftsman draws a grid and translates the measurements from the field notes into a diagram that represents the river. In 1795, charting a river required taking detailed astronomical observations to determine longitude and latitude, the critical east and west directions. William Dunbar, who lived in Spanish Louisiana in the 1790s, had been hired by the Spanish as their astronomer. Dunbar had advanced the science of astronomical observation further than any of the prominent group of Philadelphian astronomers had during this period by "requiring neither assistant nor timepiece."[30] Dunbar was able to reduce the complexity yet raise the bar for accuracy; however, in 1795, James MacKay knew only one method and, by hiring Evans, it presupposed that an assistant was mandatory.[31]

Near the end of August 1795, the third expedition for the Missouri Company left Saint Louis with a number of objectives: to make a map ascertaining the northern boundary of the province, since no chart had been drawn nor evidence collected that verified the northern extent of Louisiana; to establish forts along the Missouri River; to reach the Mandan in North Dakota; and to find a water route to the Pacific Ocean.[32] Governor Carondelet was so pleased with the possibility of finding a water route that he offered a cash prize of 3,000 piasters to the first Spanish subject who could penetrate to the Pacific Ocean via the Missouri River. He also promised to pay the salaries of one hundred men to guard the forts that MacKay would build along the route of that river.[33] How such a complex expedition with so few resources was to achieve its goal is a mystery, but MacKay, having been assured that the Missouri Company was well financed, embarked upon the exploration.

The expedition arrived at the Omaha village in Nebraska in mid-October and built Fort Charles, approximately twenty miles south of present-day Sioux City, Iowa. The Omaha chief, Blackbird, had the reputation of being both difficult and tyrannical. He demanded daily communication with MacKay. This meant that MacKay had to remain at the fort when Evans left for the Mandan at the end of November. MacKay realized that Evans would have to continue the survey of the river on his own, and so MacKay taught Evans with precision and gave him a comprehensive list of instructions:

> You will keep a journal of each day and month of the year to avoid any error in the observations of the important journey which you are undertaking. In your journal you will place all that will be remarkable in the country that you will traverse; likewise the route, distance, latitude and longitude, when you observe it, also the winds and weather. You will also keep another journal in which you will make note of all the . . . territory . . . lakes; rivers; mountains; portages, with their extent and location.[34]

MacKay also wrote about the accuracy of the observations:

> In your route from here to the home of the Ponca, trace out as exactly as possible a general route and distance from the Missouri as well as the rivers which fall into it; and although you cannot take the direction of each turn and current of the Missouri, since you go by land, you can mark the general course of the mountains which will be parallel to each bank. You will observe the same thing for every other river (landmark) which you may see during your journey, whether river, lake, ocean, or chain of mountains which may effect your observations.[35]

MacKay, in effect, instructed Evans on how to take a detailed set of field notes so that when he received them, MacKay could continue updating the map of the Missouri River. MacKay also reminded Evans that if he ran out of ink to "use the powder, and for want of powder, in the summer you will surely find some fruit whose juice can replace both."[36] Clearly, the man who needed such orders written down could not have been the author of the map.

MacKay also gave Evans a supplemental set of instructions to ensure that Evans's observations, regardless of the distance between them, would remain accurate. He wrote, "As I mean to make Sunday (being a remarkable day) the day for observing the distance of the moon from the sun I wish you to do the same when convenient so that we may be the better able to compare them when you return." He treated Evans as a novice and his student. His instructions continued:

> "I will always make my observations when the sun is on the meridian which will of course give the just time of day. You may draw a meridian line by the north star if you should be a couple of days in one place & if the sky be clear at night if this cannot be you may take it by the compass if you know exactly the variation." He also told Evans not to reveal his plans to anyone, including Truteau, the leader of the first expedition.[37]

MacKay had sent a message to the Sioux before Evans left to notify them that an expedition was en route. A few weeks after Evans left Fort Charles, his party came upon a band of Sioux who chased him for an entire day and were about to overtake him when night fell.[38] Evans returned to Fort Charles on January 6, 1796, although he left again on January 28.[39] It took him two months to reach the Arikara village—traveling seven hundred miles by water and then spending an additional six weeks to talk the Arikaras into letting him journey onward.[40] On September 23, Evans arrived at the lower Mandan village, in present-day North Dakota, and found a fort built by the merchants of Montreal that he named Fort Makay [Evans's spelling]. Carrying a formal notice written by MacKay, Evans ordered several British traders on October 8 to leave Spanish soil. The traders were surprised to learn that it was the same James MacKay, a former trader and friend, who was chasing them out of the territory.[41]

Evans had assumed that supplies were forthcoming, but when none arrived and what he had at Fort Makay ran out, he departed for Saint Louis. MacKay's supplies were also depleted by March 1797, when Clamorgan ordered him to return to Saint Louis. MacKay arrived a few days before May 13. Evans arrived on July 15. Trudeau wrote to Carondelet at the end of May, informing the governor that MacKay had arrived and had already completed a substantial section of the map—the first "three hundred and fifty leagues."[42] When Evans returned from the Mandans, MacKay took the Upper Missouri River data and completed drafting the expedition map. He referred to several documents that were an integral part of the expedition: MacKay's Table of Distances and the journals written by he and Evans.[43] The map employed the French language to designate the names of rivers and locations. Jacques Clamorgan, on October 14, 1797, wrote about the map to André Lopez, the intendant at New Orleans:

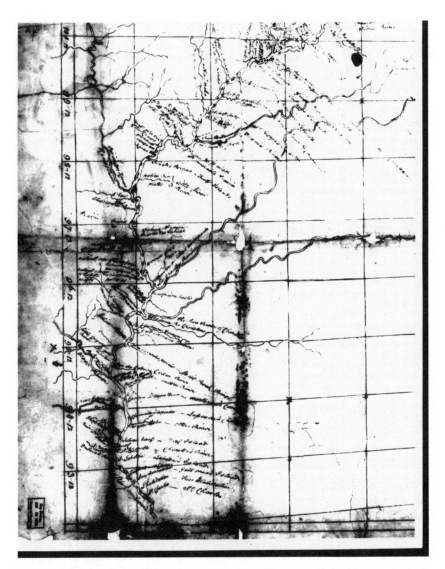

Detail of the lower Missouri River from the Indian Office map created by James MacKay. (Courtesy of Library of Congress, Geography and Map Division.)

I am sending to the governor, the well-chartered map at the expenses and fees of the company. I hope that the company will take back its usual vigor without delay and that it will merit in the future by its zealousness and activity in making discoveries, the bounty of the government.[44]

Two months later, on January 16, 1798, Zenon Trudeau informed Manuel de Gayoso, governor general of Louisiana, that he was sending the river map and "a relación," or record, of the voyage:

> I am enclosing to Your Excellency a relación of the voyage which M. Mackay has made in the Upper Missouri, and the map of the said river, as far as the Mandan nation, made by the same person, which I believe to be the most exact of those which have been formed up to the present, since M. Mackay was instructed in the matter and knew that he had pledged himself to procure this map with careful attention for the government. Up to the present time the government had only [information] intellectually based upon the simple relaciónes of the hunters.[45]

Trudeau wrote again to Gayoso on March 5, 1798, explaining that Auguste Chouteau would deliver another copy of the map.

> I have spoken to you in different letters about Mr. Mackay and this would be a good occasion to let you meet/know him. Even if Mr. Mackay would not ask for the favor of being presented to you, I will take the liberty of asking you to look upon him with interest. I can assure you that he deserves it, and in a few days you are going to appreciate him as I and all persons that already know him do. Can Mackay meet with you to talk about the Missouri? He is the author of the map that Mr. Chouteau is going to give you.[46]

MacKay had suggested to Trudeau that he would make another map of the Missouri more detailed than the one being sent with Chouteau. Trudeau wrote to Gayoso speaking about MacKay and the maps, "He also has the intention [literally: ambition] of continuing to make another complete one, but the expenses will be too considerable to propose them to you."[47] As Trudeau noted, the expenses would certainly have been prohibitive, since the Missouri Company had expended all of its resources on the three previous expeditions. MacKay departed in late March 1798 to meet Gayoso and talk with him about the success of the expedition. John Evans, after completing his work as a deputy surveyor, departed for New Orleans in the beginning of July.

More evidence disputes that either Evans or Finiels drafted the Missouri River map. In 1908, Frederick Teggart discussed an Evans map that came into the possession of John Hay and William Henry Harrison.[48] In late October 1797, Soulard had appointed Evans the deputy surveyor of Cape Girardeau, and on November 7, Evans had departed for the district with surveying instructions.[49] Sometime in May 1798, a flood devastated the district and Evans lost most of his belongings. Intent on going to New Orleans to meet MacKay and Gayoso, he tried to sell his surveying instruments and asked Bartholomew Cousin, the newly appointed surveyor of Cape

Girardeau, to help him with his map and to buy his instruments. Cousin replied that he had no use for his instruments and that his assistant would "send you your . . . chart which I have not divided because I don't remember on what scale it is drawn, nor what is the exact longitude and latitude of any plan on it. . . ."[50] In the meantime, Jones gave the incomplete chart to John Hay, who had the means to complete it.[51] Hay had been a British trader and had a merchant store established at Cahokia under the name Todd and Hay. Events that were to thrust the map into the limelight began to converge: in January 1801, Jones was appointed attorney general of the Indiana Territory and moved to Vincennes, the capital.[52] When William Henry Harrison, governor of the territory, was apprised of the expedition in 1803, Jones sent the map to him. Harrison wrote to William Clark on November 13, 1803, informing him that he had the map copied and "now send it to you by Post rider."[53]

On November 26, 1803, Harrison wrote President Jefferson that he was sending a "map which is a copy of the manuscript map of Mr. Evans who ascended the Missouri river by order of the Sp. gov't further than any other person."[54] He wrote to Lewis on January 13, 1804, that he was sending him a map, which was a copy of the copy from Harrison: "I now enclose a map of the Missouri as far as the Mandans, 12. or 1500. miles I presume above its mouth. It is said to be very accurate, having been done by a mr. [*sic*] Evans by order of the Spanish Government. But whether he corrected by astronomical observations or not we are not informed."[55] The map was indeed incorrect. MacKay had given Evans a raw copy, a template of the map, because he believed Evans had the ability to complete it.

Before MacKay went to New Orleans, Finiels drafted a map for him. In fact, he and Finiels assisted each other, which has not been fully understood because the dates of their mapmaking overlap. They both produced maps during 1797 and 1798: MacKay from May to December 1797; Finiels from August 1797 to June 1798. Finiels arrived in Saint Louis on June 3, 1797. He had been hired in Philadelphia to oversee the building of defenses at Saint Louis. But Carlos Howard, the military commandant, refused to employ him. Howard had no explicit order from Carondelet and believed that Finiels, an artillerist engineer, was not as competent as Louis Vandenbemden, a fortifications engineer.[56] Finiels decided to embark upon a private mapping project during 1797–1798.

Finiels refers to a map completed in mid-1798. *"La carte de cette Riviere que j'ai dressée en 1798 sur les memoirs ds/des Mess./Messieurs MacKay et Evans donnera une notion trés exacte de la partie de son cours que l'on peut regarder comme la mieux connue jusques apresant."* ("The map of this river that I drew up in 1798 [based] upon the accounts of Messieurs MacKay and Evans will give a very exact notion/idea of its [the river's] course which one can regard as the best known up to the present").[57] The Finiels map, which measures ten feet long and a yard wide, shows the Missouri River for more than eighty miles west of its mouth.

This map is Finiels's greatest achievement, a colossal, unauthorized, and personal project: mapping the central Mississippi Valley. His idea for it was likely due to MacKay's arrival from the Upper Missouri, replete with fresh data regarding the expedition and Soulard's "Ydea Topografica," as well as the fact that Soulard possessed the surveying measurements for many of the villages. In terms of artistry and accuracy of detail, Finiels's map of the central Mississippi Valley stands apart from any other produced in the history of North America.[58] Even now, Finiels's hand translates an ancient time into a living one. The map details Saint Louis, Carondelet, Prairie du Pont ("Prairie of the Bridge," now Dupo), Cahokia, River Des Peres, Chouteau's Pond, the Commonfields, Cape Girardeau, Sainte Genevieve, and New Madrid. Tiny red squares represent houses, and he depicts each field under cultivation, the hills, and the green-tinted Mississippi River. The breadth and majesty of this map argue for the amount of time and concentration Finiels took to complete it.

The time necessary to complete this map precludes the idea that Finiels could have also drafted a Missouri River map laden with all the complexities of a course of 1,510 miles. But surprisingly, Finiels describes another map that he drafted in 1797 near the Bon Homme Creek on the Missouri River. From the French manuscript of *"Notice sur la Louisiane Supérieure"* ("An Account of Upper Louisiana"), Finiels states that he made a map for MacKay—not the Missouri Company: *"C'est sur ses memoires et sur ses relevés que j'ai dressé pour lui en 1797 la derniere carte du Missouri."* ("It is upon his written statement and upon his account that I drew up for him in 1797 the latest map of the Missouri.")[59] Finiels's attempts to make a distinction between MacKay's Missouri River map (a version of the Indian Office map) and the one that he drafted for MacKay that was of an unnamed district; thus the appellation "latest map of the Missouri." The map is titled *"Plan ideal de las habitaciones del riachuelo bon homme cuyos tierras no se hallan aun apeadas,"* or "An ideal map of the habitations of the Bon Homme creek whose lands have not been delineated [up until now]."[60] It was a proposed plan of the district subject to approval by the governor and soon to be given the name Saint André. Trudeau forwarded the map to Gayoso on February 28, 1798, adding his description of the progress of the new settlement:

> I am sending you a small ideal map of the American's habitations, situated on the shores of the Missouri and the Bonhomme creek. Part of these are already established and in all of them they made the corn harvest last year; currently we are working to construct a mill over that which belongs to Lorenzo Long, who has brought in (for this) black stones and very intelligent workers, such that I have no doubt that this place will be prosperous before two years, for a distance from seven

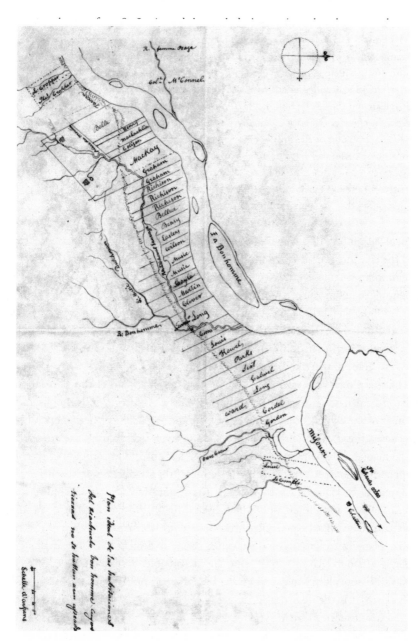

The Bon Homme Map. The district of Saint André was located south of Bon Homme Island on the Missouri River. This map covers about twenty-three air miles of the Missouri Valley and locates tracts by owner, houses, springs, rivers, and the river bluffs. (Photo courtesy of the Bancroft Library, University of California, Berkeley: catalog M–M 508, box 5, #516, MSS.)

necessity of appointing there a trustworthy person as Commander and who can correspond with me at least in the French language. I propose to you Mr. James (Don Juan) MacKay who has already held from your predecessor the title of Commander of the forts which are to be constructed in the Upper Missouri, he is well known as an intelligent and prudent man and the only one who speaks the French language among those who hold lands in the said place and that you can have confidence in his fidelity and it is equally well that the above-mentioned Mr. MacKay be named captain of the militia company that needs to be formed out of the said inhabitants. And as I have expressed to you, the commanders of the town of Ste. Genevieve, New Bourbon and Cape Girardeau have a compensation of 800 pesos yearly, the others equally deserve it and among them Mr. MacKay. I find that it is appropriate that you appoint him to that which I propose to you.[61]

MacKay's interest in the area of this plan came naturally. Once he had completed the chart for Clamorgan in October, he began looking for a place to live. The Bon Homme settlement attracted him probably because it was in need of a commandant.[62] Therefore, he set himself to making a plan of the district with Finiels's assistance. Like Soulard, in 1795, when Trudeau proposed him as surveyor general, MacKay also demonstrated his abilities to the lieutenant governor. Evidently, the idea worked. MacKay had already chosen the location for the tract he was asking Trudeau to grant him. Trudeau agreed, granting MacKay about 3,700 acres near the Bon Homme Creek on December 23, 1797.[63] MacKay's plan of the Bon Homme district is a small-scale map, illustrating houses, rivers, islands, hills, lot sizes, and the names of the owners of lots. This map is unique to MacKay's heritage; however, when comparing it to Finiels's Mississippi Valley map, a recognizable feature stands out: the manner in which the rivers are drawn. The shape and contours of the Mississippi and Missouri Rivers, and the rendering of their sandbars, are so similar that they appear to be made by the same hand. To the untrained eye, the technical skills between MacKay and Finiels would have been difficult to ascertain, but it was their artistic treatment that helped solve who drafted which map. Unaware of the Bon Homme plan, historians have mistakenly credited Finiels with the drafting of MacKay's Missouri River map.[64] But an identifiable design element exists on MacKay's Missouri River map and on the Bon Homme plan that does not appear on Finiels's map: it is the fleur-des-lis drawn by MacKay on the north arrow. This element, an unconventional map symbol, assisted in the recognition of his maps.

When MacKay began as commandant at Saint André in November 1798, he continued surveying while handling all civil and criminal matters in the district.[65] Five months earlier, when Gayoso appointed Charles de Lassus as lieutenant governor, he told him that MacKay merited his special attention. De Lassus was instructed to help MacKay fulfill his duties and to pay particular attention in "obtaining the most rapid and exact information concerning the intentions of the traders from Canada in Spanish territory."[66] In 1802, François Perrin du Lac allegedly made a voyage up the Missouri and produced a map that he ambiguously credited to "*un ancien traiteur de la riviére des Illinois. . . .*"[67] Historian Annie Abel's claim that Perrin du Lac was referring to Jean Baptiste Truteau as the ancient trader gave rise to an arduous debate over MacKay's expertise in the ensuing decades.[68]

One of Meriwether Lewis's primary goals when planning the expedition was to find the most up-to-date maps of the Missouri River, and he had obtained several of them before arriving in Saint Louis, including one by Aaron Arrowsmith and another by David Thompson. On December 8, 1803, Lewis arrived in Saint Louis without William Clark but accompanied by two interpreters from Cahokia, John Hay and Nicholas Jarrot. Lewis met with Charles de Lassus, the lieutenant governor, who had become suspicious about the expedition because Lewis presented a French passport instead of a Spanish one. De Lassus told Lewis that if the papers had been in the name of the Spanish king, there would have been no difficulty granting the expedition access to the Missouri. De Lassus needed time to write to his superiors in New Orleans and ask permission; he told Lewis he would have an answer by the spring of 1804. Lewis "agreed to wait" and said that he would spend the winter on the east side of the Mississippi.[69]

A day later, Clark and the remainder of the corps made their formal entrance in Saint Louis. "Under Sales & Cullers," Clark noted, they put ashore where "hundreds Came to the bank to view us." Clark was surprised to see some of his old friends from Vincennes and Kaskaskia. While Lewis remained in Saint Louis tending to business affairs, Clark "proceeded on" to find a site where the group could establish the temporary encampment.[70] Lewis had asked de Lassus if he could meet with individuals in Saint Louis who might be able to help him with the geographic information of the country. Although de Lassus granted permission, Lewis wrote that, while the inhabitants were eager to help, "every thing must be obtained by stealth." Furthermore, Lewis stated that everything underwent his examination and "you may readily conceive the restraint which exists on many points." For example, when Lewis met with some merchants, he reported that they were all afraid of de Lassus, especially the inhabitants, who moved more "as tho' the fear of the Commandant, than that of god, was before their eyes. . . ." Even some of the wealthiest had been jailed for slight offenses, which "has produced a general dread of [de Lassus] among all classes of the people." Antoine Soulard, surveyor general of Upper Louisiana, had agreed to let Lewis copy government information from the 1800 census, but when he realized that Lewis was going to copy the whole document, he expressed extreme fear. Soulard became so agitated that Lewis desisted and wrote "if it were known that he had given me permission to copy an official paper . . . it would injure him with his government."[71] Although full of trepidation, Soulard did help Lewis, but he failed to obtain the genuine map of the Missouri River. If Lewis and Clark were to depend on MacKay's map for the first part of their journey, it was absolutely urgent to meet with him.

But de Lassus had only granted the Americans access to Saint Louis, and MacKay, commandant of Saint André, wrote that his district was a "long journey" from there. Finiels believed that a trip to Saint Charles by water took about two days and Saint André was almost nine miles further west.[72] Delays continued to hamper Lewis, and now the most important person in Upper Louisiana lay out of reach. If the Scotsman were truly an expert, then they probably would meet often to strategize and make maps, yet it could be the height of summer before they departed.

Jefferson believed that the transfer of the country would take place at the end of December, and Lewis had relied on that information. Henry Dearborn, the secretary of war, had approved a journey up the Missouri in July 1803, and when Lewis wrote to Jefferson on October 3 from Cincinnati, he confirmed that he would "make a tour this winter on horseback of some hundred miles . . . on the South side of the Missouri." He also thought that he could prevail on William Clark "to undertake a similar excurtion through some other portion of the country." Lewis had hoped that when he arrived in Saint Louis, Louisiana would have been transferred to American soil, so that by February or March 1, he would have procured additional information about the country that would further attest "to the utility" of the expedition. In a letter dated November 16, Jefferson cautioned Lewis to revise his plans because he believed by the time Lewis arrived in Saint Louis, the Missouri River would begin to freeze. He thought that Lewis should remain at Cahokia or Kaskaskia for the winter and gain the necessary information he had requested months earlier instead of taking an ambiguous trip that might incur Spanish opposition and be "exposed to risques," which Jefferson wanted to avoid at all cost.[73]

In the meantime, Clark found an excellent site for the military encampment opposite the mouth of the Missouri River and named it Camp Dubois. Apparently, the site was well-known to the local population too, and after Clark had landed at the bank, several canoes of drunken Indians managed to camp near him. In the following days, Clark noted Indians paddling up and down the Mississippi who undoubtedly alerted villagers at Portage des Sioux of the American encampment. Portage des Sioux, located on the west bank of the Mississippi, was the closest Spanish settlement to Camp Dubois, about five miles up the Mississippi. Samuel Griffith, an American farmer from Portage des Sioux, visited Clark on December

16, 23, and 24. Clark ordered John Shields to accompany Griffith to purchase dairy items and Shields returned on Christmas Day with "a cheese and 4 lb butter."[74]

Jefferson had sent another letter repeating his orders to Lewis that he should not enter the Missouri until spring, to which Lewis had already indicated his compliance in his December 28 letter. Still, the most essential part of the expedition, examining an accurate map, was out of their grasp. Deciding not to wait any longer, they implemented a plan that has remained hidden for two centuries. Lewis and Clark dispatched Private Joseph Field up the Missouri to locate James MacKay and invite him to Camp Dubois. Field traveled "30 miles up" river to Saint André, where MacKay was commandant.[75]

The journal entry on January 10, 1804, reveals that the historic meeting between Lewis and Clark and MacKay was kept secret. Lewis and Clark ordered Field up the Missouri regardless of the subtle illegality. While de Lassus had granted access to Saint Louis, where he could monitor their activities, he certainly did not intend for MacKay to reveal government information. Yet, would the Saint André commandant accept the invitation? If he did, he would have to evade telling de Lassus. And if he brought the official map of the Missouri River, a classified government document, that, too, would be illegal. But MacKay took the risk because he needed a job. He learned in September 1803 that the United States had bought Louisiana, and he had informed a Kentucky congressman that becoming an American citizen would deprive him of his office and salary.[76] By handing over the genuine map to Lewis and Clark, updated with an additional five years of river information, MacKay would demonstrate his allegiance to the new American government.

The journal entries preceding January 10 were brief, and Clark does not mention when he sent Private Field to locate MacKay. Field probably left on January 7, the same day that Clark began drawing a map of the Missouri River "for the purpose of correcting from the information which I may get of the countrey to the NW."[77] It may have taken Field until the morning of January 9 to find MacKay, who had witnessed the signing of a warranty deed at Saint André. Later in the day, MacKay went to Marais des Lairds (Bridgeton, Missouri) to witness and authorize other documents and then went to Portage des Sioux. The portage was a thin strip of land, a peninsula between the Missouri and Mississippi Rivers north of Camp Dubois.[78] After surveying some lots at Portage des Sioux on January 10, MacKay made his way to Lewis and Clark's headquarters at Wood River.[79]

As Field returned to Camp Dubois, Clark watched the private cross the Mississippi "between the Sheets of floating Ice with Some risque. . . ." Suspicious that Field took too long to return, Clark questioned him about the trip and was told that it had been impossible for Field to cross, for "the Ice run so thick in the Missourie."

That took time. Clark also didn't like the fact that Field had remained "so long" on the Missouri where he likely was recognized by the inhabitants. Field allayed Clark's fears by saying "that the people is greatly in favour of the Americans." Field returned at 1:00 p.m., and MacKay arrived at camp some time thereafter.[80]

The meeting probably was long. Due to the winter weather, the afternoon hour when MacKay arrived, and the fact they needed much time to discuss the intricacies of a river map written in French, MacKay stayed overnight and possibly longer. Clark's journal entries for the next two days were short; he continued to complain of being ill due to the severe "Ducking" on January 9 and indicated that Lewis may have left the camp late on January 12. By January 21, Clark began making detailed calculations based on the distances from Camp Dubois to the Mandans, from the Mandans to the Rocky Mountains, and from the mountains to the Pacific.[81]

Finally, de Lassus received official word that Louisiana had indeed been sold to the United States. On February 21, he wrote to Capt. Amos Stoddard, the American military official who was to oversee the transfer of the country, and informed him that they should meet. They agreed to the dates to transfer ownership: on March 9, Spain would transfer the country to France and on March 10, France would transfer it to the United States. By March 21, Lewis and Clark had traveled up the Missouri with Spanish Osage Indian agent Pierre Chouteau and Charles Gratiot, a wealthy landowner. Sometime in the spring of 1804, Lewis and Clark drafted a new map based on previous maps made by MacKay, Soulard, Chouteau, and on information gleaned from traders. That map was sent to President Jefferson with Chouteau, who later accompanied an Osage Indian delegation to Washington in July 1804.[82]

The convoluted history of the map of the Missouri River as high as the Mandan and Hidatsa villages is an important but overlooked detail of the march of the Corps of Discovery. The background of James MacKay and the contribution of his invaluable map shows a curious international progression to what is usually regarded as a strictly national enterprise. It was a transplanted Scot with a history of British service who, at personal risk, provided the link between the preceding Spanish and fleeting French regime to the United States' assumption of authority in Louisiana. Lewis and Clark's predecessors had already carefully laid out a third of the landmarks that the expedition's members would note in their journals—landmarks that had been named by French voyageurs nearly a century earlier, and that, indeed, persist as toponyms (though often in English translation) to this day.

Chapter 3

INTRIGUE, MAYHEM, DECEPTION

W hen Meriwether Lewis and William Clark first arrived in Kaskaskia, Illinois, with a skeletal crew of expedition members on November 29, 1803, Lewis met several individuals from the Indiana territorial government.[1] Unknown to Lewis, the purpose of their meeting was procuring lucrative positions in the newly bought Louisiana territory. While historians have described the "Louisiana Purchase" many times, an essential part of the story has been missing for more than two centuries, leading to a misinterpretation of the facts.[2] How Lewis was swindled in late 1803 requires some explanation and a short history on how the Americans acquired Louisiana.

Louisiana, the territory encompassing the Mississippi River and its tributaries, was claimed by the French in the seventeenth century. The portion of the territory to the west of the Mississippi, but including the "Isle of Orleans" and the city of New Orleans, was passed to the Spanish in 1762, prior to the end of the French and Indian War, to ensure that it did not become a possession of the British in the war settlement. The French under Napoleon wanted Louisiana back in 1800 as part of a scheme to revitalize Caribbean sugar cane interests, using Louisiana as a granary to feed Caribbean slaves. The revolution begun by Toussaint L'Overture in Haiti, coupled with yellow fever, doomed Napoleon's scheme, and by 1803, strapped for cash in the face of impending warfare with Great Britain, Napoleon was willing to sell it to a willing buyer: the United States. Louisiana was important to the Americans not for the lands west of the Mississippi, but rather because it contained New Orleans, and with it the right of free passage down the Mississippi, allowing Ohio River and Illinois farmers to take their goods to market. The territory, sight unseen, had cost the nation about fifteen million dollars, and having bought it, President Thomas Jefferson wanted to explore it. Jefferson's dream of cross-continental exploration had once been an ambition of his father, Peter Jefferson, and Thomas had tried to inaugurate at least four expeditions, all of which failed, prior to his presidency. He believed that a small military scouting party with expertise in the sciences could comprise an effective exploration team, and he appointed his private secretary, Lewis, as expedition leader. But before Lewis stepped into Louisiana, other events transpired that would shape his future.

The Northwest Territory was a prize of the American War of Independence, which extended the reach of the United States to the east bank of the Mississippi. Many Americans on the east coast were eager to exploit or homestead these new lands, some of which were divided into land grants as rewards to Revolutionary War veterans. Resistance from consolidated Indian tribal groups prevented easy settlement, however, and it was not until the signing of the Treaty of Greenville with the Indians in 1795, coupled with the clarification of national boundaries in the Jay Treaty with Great Britain of 1794, that the area was truly ready for settlement, and it was soon divided into the Indiana and Ohio territories.

Jefferson learned in the latter half of 1802 that Spain had secretly retroceded Louisiana to France. On October 16, 1802, top-ranking Spanish officials at New Orleans closed the port to Americans bringing goods from the north in reaction to reading about the retrocession. The Spanish intendant at New Orleans, two days later, issued a proclamation canceling the American right of deposit at that city. He pointed out that the treaty of San Lorenzo, signed by the United States and Spain in 1795, called for the right of deposit to last three years. The three years were long since up, Europe was at peace, and he must consequently close it until the king at Madrid should order it opened. The proclamation was a bombshell. Western trade was based on the free deposit at New Orleans, and the economic health of thousands of people depended on it. On the afternoon of October 18, two American flatboats reached the city and tied up, as usual, at the muddy batture just above the town, but were forbidden to land. Recalling the proverbial toughness of the men who handled the flatboats, the official who forbade their landing did not go unguarded. The news of the closure swept back up the river and created a storm of controversy. Demands for action were made and a letter published in the *Kentucky Gazette* that stated that "the reptile Spaniards" acted "in a hostile manner . . . with degrading remarks that the people of the United States have no national character."[3]

Forbidding Americans access to New Orleans was in direct conflict with the 1795 treaty of San Lorenzo between Spain and the United States, which allowed Americans the right of import and export without paying a tariff.[4] This event led Jefferson to send his diplomats to France to buy New Orleans. At the end of February 1803, Napoleon sold Louisiana to fund his war chest in Europe, and by July 1803, the news of the Louisiana Purchase had spread to the east side of the Mississippi River.[5]

Speculation ran the gamut in the Indiana Territory, which was located east of the Mississippi; some said that the territory would be extended to include Louisiana.[6] A sliver of the Indiana Territory population eyed Louisiana in a different light altogether, and speculators hoped to acquire precious tracts of mineral land. The mining country in Upper Louisiana around the district of Sainte Genevieve held an abundance of lead ore, more pure than in the United States, and since lead was used in the manufacture of ordnance materials, the most potentially lucrative portion of the new territory was directly across the river from Kaskaskia.

A flurry of activity began in the Indiana Territory in the summer of 1802. John Rice Jones, the attorney general, invited the US War Department to locate a military camp on his land in Kaskaskia, for free. The War Department accepted his "liberal and patriotic proposal," and by autumn a military company of about fifty men, commanded by Capt. Russell Bissell, occupied a piece of his land.[7] Six months later, another company of troops was sent out to Kaskaskia under the command of Capt. Amos Stoddard, who would preside over the transfer of the territory.[8]

Many American citizens did not want the United States to buy Louisiana, and some members of Congress voiced their concerns that the Louisiana population had no idea of a democratic government. They viewed the French and Spanish inhabitants as an ignorant people because they had lived under a monarchy.[9] President Jefferson agreed that "our new fellow citizens are as yet as incapable of self government as children."[10]

Other viewpoints were also expressed. Too much was at stake, according to the citizens of Knox, Saint Clair, and Randolph Counties, in the Indiana Territory (today's southern Illinois), who petitioned Congress, claiming that lands on the east side of the Mississippi were poor and limited while the new lands on the west side were far more attractive.[11] While petitions galvanized attention on a particular problem, a more intensified approach emerged when Indiana Territory officials put themselves on the line and pitched a specific and alarming cause. Indiana territorial judge Thomas T. Davis was the first to report land fraud in Upper Louisiana on October 17, 1803. From Kaskaskia, Davis wrote to John Breckinridge, a Kentucky senator, asking him for the appointment as governor of the new territory, and explaining the land fraud issue in a roundabout way:

> You were very friendly in procuring me this Judgship; but as I expect a Division of the Territory to take place . . . I must ask the favor of you to nominate me to the President as Governor to the new Territory. I am persuaded that my General Acquaintance with the people & the country will render the appointment popular. The United-States will be greatly imposed on by the Spanish Officers who are to this Day Granting large Tracts of Land to individuals & Dating them back so as to bear Date before the late Treaty. Some Deeds are made to men who have been Dead 15 or 20 Years and Regular Transfers to appearance to the present holders—the frauds are numerous & Americans chiefly Concerned.[12]

John Rice Jones also sent a letter from Kaskaskia the following day, but sent it anonymously to Albert Gallatin, President Jefferson's secretary of the treasury, which was subsequently printed for Congress and later included in the *American State Papers*.

> You have no guess how the United States are imposed on by the Spanish officers, since they have heard of the cession of Louisiana: grants are daily making for large tracts of land and dated back; some made to men who have been dead fifteen or twenty years, and transferred down to the present holders. These grants are made to Americans, with a reserve of interest to the officer who makes them; within fifteen days the following places have been granted, to wit: forty-five acres choice of the lead mines . . . the iron mine on Wine creek, with ten thousand acres around it . . . the Common touching St. Louis . . . and many other grants of ten, fifteen, twenty, and thirty thousand acres. . . . I could name persons as well as places.[13]

Isaac Darnielle, a lawyer from Cahokia, also wrote to Breckinridge in October and believed that Upper Louisiana was to be joined with the Indiana Territory. Darnielle opposed the plan: he felt that a majority of designing men had been appointed to the Indiana government and "occupied places sufficient to give them influence over the Ignorant and uninformed part of the people." They could be elected to places of primary importance in the government of Upper Louisiana. He also warned the senator that John Rice Jones was "capable of natural and acquired abilities . . . a man of bad character . . . ."[14]

The following month, President Jefferson wrote to Gallatin about the land problems in Spanish Louisiana:

> There are a great number of Americans in that territory whom Spain attracted thither by the bait of concessions fifteen or twenty years ago, and who will have profited by the facility of the moment to acquire land for but little. Many adventurers from the east bank will also have made purchases, and in those wildernesses, possession is a title that the law can not easily contest.[15]

In the meantime, Kaskaskia became the headquarters for Jones and Davis, who awaited the arrival of President Jefferson's point man, Meriwether Lewis. The purpose of Lewis's landing at Kaskaskia was to gather supplies and to enlist soldiers from Bissell's and Stoddard's companies for the western expedition. On December 3, 1803, William Clark departed upriver while Lewis remained behind to meet with Davis and Jones.[16]

Davis had just returned from Upper Louisiana and was confident that there would be no opposition to the United States taking possession. The two informed

Lewis and Stoddard of the land fraud issue, and Jones departed at the end of November to uncover more details in Sainte Genevieve. He returned to Kaskaskia at the beginning of January and met with Lewis and Stoddard.[17]

> During my stay in the Illinois, I discovered that a scheme of iniquity had for some-time been practicing on the . . . Spanish side of the Mississippi to defraud the United States of a considerable quantity of land. The method . . . was to make large grants of land to individuals dated above three years ago. . . . Information hereof had been made some weeks since by Capn M. Lewis to the President and by Capn Stoddard of the Artillery who has received orders to take possession of St. Louis & appointed commandant there. . . . I have therefor little doubt but that proper pre-caution will be taken to invalidate these iniquitous and fraudulent grants.[18]

Ten days into the new year, Stoddard sent a disturbing report to President Jefferson. He claimed that Zenon Trudeau, the former Spanish lieutenant governor of Upper Louisiana from 1792 to 1799, was the mastermind behind the land fraud. Jones had tangible proof that Trudeau, who had lived in Saint Louis, was "induced by the speculators to sign a number of blank sheets of paper which were used as the basis of large land claims."

> The Attorney General of the Indiana Territory, who, a few days since, visited the Louisiana side, has given me some information which I think it my duty to com-municate.
>
> Attempts are now making to defraud the United States [of] . . . nearly . . . two hundred thousand acres of land, including all the best mines, have been sur-veyed to various individuals in the course of a few weeks past. All the official papers . . . bear the signature of M.—the predecessor of the present lieutenant-governor. . . . This state of things has suggested the possibility of a successful fraud; and the progress of it will probably turn out to be this: M . . . who was cer-tainly authorized to cause surveys of land to be made to settlers has been prevailed on to put his signature to blank papers. It is now five years since M.—was com-mandant of Upper Louisiana, to which these papers appear to be antedated.[19]

The Stoddard report revolved around one event that occurred in 1799 and resulted in a monstrous land speculation scheme in the Sainte Genevieve mining district. To this day, no one has discovered how Jones acquired this damaging infor-mation and for what purpose. It not only condemned Trudeau but also ruined the reputation of several Spanish officers with the incoming American administration. What has not previously been uncovered by historians is that the Stoddard report was influenced and contrived by two avid land speculators and partners, Moses

Austin and John Rice Jones, who were "joint claimants" in the largest and most profitable lead mine in Upper Louisiana from 1798 to 1812.[20] Furthermore, the blank sheets of paper known as the "Trudeau concessions" originated with Austin in 1799, although we are led to believe that the emergence of those blanks occurred in 1803.[21]

Austin and Jones concocted this scheme to deliberately freeze the mineral land wealth in Sainte Genevieve. The reason why they did this is because they did not want the Sainte Genevieve *habitants* to acquire mineral land concessions and wanted the lead mines for themselves and for their American friends. A time lag preceded the news of both the retrocession and the sale of Louisiana, which caught Upper Louisiana residents unaware of their circumstances, and at the beginning of September 1803, the so-called landgrab in Upper Louisiana exploded.[22] The landgrab was initiated because the habitants feared that the American government would not honor their simple system of conceded lands and petitioned the commandants for surveys.

The largest amount of surveying occurred in the Sainte Genevieve district and included ten mines of varying size that had been worked intermittently for years, owing to deadly attacks from the Indians.[23] Although working the mines was perilous, the miners had no choice, since mining lead was their sole (and very lucrative) occupation.

Most of the habitants lived on and cultivated a part of their land concession, but the process of having a land grant confirmed or completing a title under the Spanish involved several steps. A *habitant* had to address the commandant of the district, either orally, because many of the inhabitants could not write, or in writing, in what was commonly known as a petition or *requête*. The requête was a letter of introduction detailing the petitioner's accomplishments and goals as well as a request for title to the desired land. Depending upon the commandant's recommendation, the lieutenant governor would then approve the requête. In other cases, the inhabitant did not petition the commandant, but simply stepped onto a vacant tract of land and acquired it. The lieutenant governor told the inhabitants that "their best titles were their axes and hoes," which was the only proof needed to show cultivation or habitation.[24]

The next step was to have the land surveyed, which in almost all of the concessions was not performed because it cost more than the land was worth. Completing the title involved taking the papers to New Orleans, where it passed through four to seven offices, to have it recorded.[25] In the history of Upper Louisiana, only eleven concessions had a complete title.[26]

Historians have presented an alternate account of what transpired a few months before the transfer of Louisiana—that Spanish officials conspired against the American government and doled out the royal domain to friends, relatives, and to them-selves.[27] In reality, the habitants' livelihood was at a stake—they lived a meager exis-tence, at the poverty level, and bartered in furs and grains. They worked their land, extracting minerals or selling produce. When Upper Louisiana officials became cog-nizant that the United States would be their new sovereign, they realized that the habitants were in jeopardy of losing their land concessions, since they had no papers that verified ownership. It was at this moment in time that Austin could see that the mineral lands that he had selected might fall into the wrong hands. Austin and Jones decided to create a diversion that has not been understood until recently.[28] A few paragraphs of explanation will bring their scheme into focus.[29]

In the year 1797, Moses Austin, a successful Virginia miner, found that he was competing with the lead coming out of Spanish Louisiana. He decided to travel to Sainte Genevieve and assess an opportunity for greater employment and profit. Sainte Genevieve lies across the Mississippi River from Kaskaskia, and it is where Austin first met John Rice Jones, who offered to accompany him as his guide and inter-preter.[30] Upon their arrival in the mining district, Austin verified that the purity of the ore was superior to Virginia lead. In addition, it was cheaper, more abundant, more enriched, and was also untaxed. He decided to move to Sainte Genevieve and become a Spanish subject.[31]

Austin formed a partnership with Jones and the commandants from Sainte Genevieve and New Bourbon on January 26, 1797.[32] The partnership was necessary in order to be granted land in the Spanish country, otherwise the commandants would have opposed the grant. Austin had also promised that he would bring thirty American families with him and that they would also receive land concessions.[33] Austin was granted three square miles of mineral land, 6,085 acres, and provisions were made to dispense those land concessions to his followers. In July 1799, when a new lieutenant governor took office, a survey had not been completed for Austin, nor had the orders of surveys been obtained for Austin's followers.[34] This was because five of Austin's followers had yet to ask for the acreage, since they had not decided where to locate their land concessions.[35]

The surveyor general of Upper Louisiana, Antoine Soulard, asked the outgoing lieutenant governor, Zenon Trudeau, to leave with him eight blank but signed land concessions "to be delivered to . . . Mr. Austin's followers."[36] Saint Louis is ninety miles from Sainte Genevieve, but in 1799 it took weeks to arrive at that location. Soulard gave the concession blanks to an officer who was traveling to Sainte Genevieve to deliver them to Austin so that he could complete the names and quan-tities.[37] A few months later, Soulard and Austin met and Soulard noted that Austin had signed his name to five of the petitions instead of the petitions being signed by his followers. When Soulard called his attention to it, Austin said that some of his followers were absent from the country. This was not possible, since Austin already knew which followers had come with him from Virginia. In the fall of 1803, Soulard requested that Austin make the survey payments, but Austin remarked that his people were not satisfied with the concessions. Soulard then asked Austin to return the concessions, but only five were delivered.[38] Austin retained three of the blanks.[39]

A few weeks later, Jones showed them to Lewis and Stoddard during their meeting in January 1804. Jones passed along his version of the land grant situation in the new territory to President Jefferson on February 11, 1804.[40]

> [F]rom the Information of Capt. Lewis, who I had the pleasure of seeing at Cahokia a few days ago appears not to be true. Some part, perhaps the whole of the Information contained in the "emancipated american," has I doubt not, been communicated to you by Capt. Lewis, who informed me of his Intention of doing so—For fear it has not I take the liberty of enclosing a newspaper, wherein that piece has been inserted, for your perusal, and of assuring you that, from the best Information I could obtain on the spot, it does not in the least exaggerate the conduct of the late Spanish officers, and that the charges alledged against them, can most, if not all of them be substantiated.[41]

After meeting with Jones, Lewis asked Stoddard to procure a knowledgeable person to report on the history and production of the lead mines. Stoddard recommended Austin as "the most experienced and judicious man on such subjects then on that quarter." Austin wrote a dissertation on the lead mines of Upper Louisiana, which accompanied the message sent to the president in November 1804 that was read before Congress.[42]

After the United States took control of Upper Louisiana, Austin received select appointments and became famous as a mining entrepreneur.[43] He was never prosecuted because the extent of his fabrication of land grants was unknown. Jones, too, received lucrative positions in the Indiana territorial legislature. The Jefferson administration also passed a law to limit the number of grants by declaring that no land could be granted after the date of the treaty, which was signed on April 30, 1803.

Although historians have lauded both Austin and Jones as true-blooded Americans, the facts counter this praise and furnish proof that they were the actual conspirators—not the Spanish officers—in a wide-ranging landgrab that preserved the most lucrative, mineral-rich portion of the new territory for themselves.[44]

When Lewis recommended Austin to Jefferson, Austin was appointed a judge at Sainte Genevieve and, upon publication of the lead mine dissertation, he became an instant celebrity and mining expert. He presided over a kingdom, actually a fiefdom, that was at the center of the "mineral wars" in Sainte Genevieve, where two opposing mining competitors, Moses Austin and John Smith T., battled for land rights from 1804 through 1808.

When Gen. James Wilkinson arrived in Saint Louis in July 1805 as governor of the Louisiana Territory, he tried his best to allay factional spirit, but territorial officials like John Rice Jones, William Carr, and Rufus Easton stood behind Austin while Wilkinson defended Smith T. by unseating Austin as a judge. Party politics escalated, and within the year Wilkinson was ordered to another hot spot in the United States, New Orleans. By 1806, the Austin faction had caused the elimination of five of the top positions in the territorial government—governor, secretary of the territory, territorial judge, attorney general, and a recorder of land titles. It was precisely at this moment that the Lewis and Clark Expedition returned to Saint Louis. A few months later, President Jefferson appointed Lewis governor and Frederick Bates secretary of the territory.

Bates, who had arrived in Saint Louis in April 1807 to take up his duties a year before Lewis's arrival, served as acting governor during that period. Within the first month of arriving in Saint Louis, Bates traveled to Sainte Genevieve and visited Austin. Bates was so enamored with him that he promised to buy a farm in the area, and he appointed Austin's brother a judge as well as electing several of his friends.[45]

When Lewis arrived in Saint Louis in 1808, he observed the situation of the French-speaking habitants as well as the newly arrived Americans in conjunction with the Americans who had arrived—and prospered greatly—during the Spanish period. There was no doubt that Americans like Austin and Jones had profited from their legacy of having been in the territory before the American purchase and acquiring land under the Spanish, as well as from their later connections with politically powerful Americans who had ensured lucrative government positions, power, and contracts. When Lewis reassessed the recommendations he had made as a newcomer to the territory in 1804, he must have realized that he himself, through his writings, may have set off the mineral wars, and he immediately began dismissing the Austin clan from the bench.

The persons that Lewis appointed to the vacated positions embarrassed Bates and galvanized the Austin forces to thwart Lewis's intentions to bring peace and harmony to the district. Bates, who had faithfully and regularly apprized Lewis of events in Saint Louis up to this point, was angered and appalled by the governor's swift reprisals. In Bates's view, "Affairs look somewhat squally since the arrival of Gov. Lewis. Mighty and extraordinary efforts are making to restore to office some of those worthless men, whom I thought it my duty to remove." Bates believed that public sentiment had approved of his conduct and that animosity in Sainte Genevieve had subsided. He feared that Lewis's actions reignited the "Demon of Discord," that "will again mount the whirlwind and direct the storm."[46] In fact, it was Bates who became the demon who secretly allied with Austin to topple the Lewis administration.[47]

While very little Lewis documentation has been uncovered describing how the Sainte Genevieve mineral wars affected him, he wasted no time asserting his authority by convening the territorial judges and replacing previous appointments made by Indiana territorial governor William Henry Harrison and Bates. Lewis began the formal process of enacting, revising, and passing territorial laws, and in the space of ten months managed to write, authorize, and implement about a hundred of them.[48] One law that was immediately passed was meant to curb lawlessness, "regulating riots and unlawful assemblies," and was directed at Austin and his associates, who had previously menaced others who tried to survey choice mineral tracts near his lands.[49] Frederick Bates had appointed John Perry as justice of the peace, but about six months later Governor Lewis revoked his commission:

> Complaints of violence and a contempt have lately been exhibited against you, and so conclusively supported, as to render it highly improper, that you should be longer continued in the discharge of public duties. When an Officer acts in direct opposition to the best and principal objects of his appointment, and perseveres in that opposition, after being warned, cautioned & admonished, it is surely time to inform such misguided Officer, that his services are no longer required.[50]

Lewis replaced Perry with Austin's brother, James Austin.[51] That appointment appeared to be a huge blunder, but Lewis had something else in mind. He wanted to corral all of the malcontents, including their leader. Lewis had received depositions from various miners in the area "in relation to a riot" that had recently occurred where members of the Perry family, who were intricately linked to Austin's thugs, were "principally concerned." Lewis castigated James Austin for permitting it to take place:

> It would appear to me, from the evidence which has been transmitted, that it would be the duty of a Justice of the Peace to issue his process for the arrest of the offenders. You will therefore be pleased to review the subject, and compel the execution of your warrant, by the aid of the militia of the neighbourhood, if necessary. The delinquents should be bound in heavy penalties to keep the peace . . . or . . . should be committed to jail.[52]

The Austin thuggery was no match for Lewis's military expertise. The riot had occurred because the rightful owners of the mineral land were prevented from taking the mineral from their property. Lewis asked James Austin to complete an estimate of the lead, which had been gathered on US land adjacent to Moses Austin's tract. Lewis then elaborated via Moses Austin what was in store for James Austin if he did not comply:

> After an account has been made of this estimation, you will permit the proper owners, that is, the persons who have dug and raised it, to take it away. And if any resistance be made by any armed force, the militia, are to be called to your assistance, and in the event of a continued forcible opposition, they are hereby ordered to fire on the lawless Banditti, employed in the resistance.[53]

Surprisingly, the rioting ceased immediately. While Lewis lost the battle in 1804, he later became aware of Austin's deceitful practices and was eventually able to curb them. But Austin still had a confidante implanted in Governor Lewis's office.

President Jefferson and his secretary of the treasury, Albert Gallatin, appointed a committee to oversee the grant process in Saint Louis, a board of commissioners who would make recommendations for confirmation or rejection. Their recommendations brought about congressional legislation and oversight to record, hear, and dispose of all land claims in Louisiana through a series of land boards. The Upper Louisiana board of land commissioners was comprised of five men who presided over the hearings, which began in 1805, and for several years they met at various towns to record claims and testimony. One of the five members was Frederick Bates, who had been appointed in a dual capacity as recorder of land titles and as a land commissioner. Bates could set the pace and direct what land titles would be favored over others.[54] The board of commissioners functioned under the US Treasury and received orders from Gallatin himself, but Bates allowed Austin to influence his decisions. Austin wrote to Bates, "I have to tell you that you are to consider & receive what I write as given in strict confidence." Austin wanted Bates to examine the commissioners' books and to take such extracts as would answer the intentions of the party. They were to be taken from time to time and in such a way as not to give alarm to the commissioners. It was also hinted that if the extracts could not be obtained in any other way, a friend in court would furnish them.[55]

This was an abuse of power, and Bates, who served in three official capacities besides territorial secretary/acting governor, had been entrusted by Gallatin to oversee this important transfer of ownership among the claimants. In that role Bates had principal duties; the duty of loyalty, the duty to act in good faith, and a fiduciary duty to act to the best of his ability. For Moses Austin, the penultimate speculator, to ask for and obtain confidential information created a direct conflict of interest in the execution of Bates's duties.

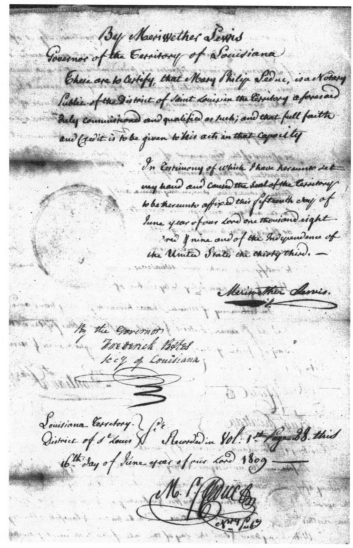

Meriwether Lewis and Frederick Bates attest to Marie Philippe Leduc's appointment as notary public of the District of Saint Louis "duly commissioned and qualified as such; and that full faith and Credit is to be given to his acts in that capacity." Bates's principal duties included the duty of loyalty, the duty to act in good faith, and a fiduciary duty to act to the best of his ability. As secretary of the Louisiana Territory and recorder of land titles, Bates usurped this pledge to his country when he covertly assisted Austin, a major speculator of mineral lands in Sainte Genevieve. (Pierre Chouteau to War Department, June 14, 1809, C562, Leduc's appointment, RG 107, M221, roll 20, frame 6255, National Archives and Records Administration.)

Bates aided Austin and delayed the confirmation of grants for years. This type of thievery was clearly beyond the scope and governance of Lewis and cannot be associated with the territorial government. The results of the board of commissioners culminated in a decision-making process in 1812 that Gallatin soundly rejected; he "suspended the issuing of patents" to land grants and dismissed the board.[56] Divided into a mind-numbing tabulation of forty-nine groups in five classes, the claims took years to resolve.[57]

During this prolonged delay, the primarily French-speaking claimants were forced into selling their land for a pittance to provide for their families, and as English-speaking settlers moved into the area, they became squatters, and "conflicting land claims led to a large volume of litigation in both state and federal courts" for the next fifty years.[58] Confirmation delays deprived the claimants of their land at a crucial time in their lives.

Luke Lawless, a lawyer who defended many land grant suits, took up the cause in court in 1830, stating that the habitants had been assured of their vested rights in the Louisiana Purchase Treaty, which had not been honored, constituting a breach of faith on the part of the United States:

> Many of those inhabitants were meritorious servants of the Spanish crown, and had an undoubted right to its future protection. This right, of course, became forfeited by the transfer of their allegiance to the United States, and there then remained . . . no other fruit of their allegiance to Spain than the grants already made to them . . . and which they were justified in supposing were virtually confirmed by the treaty under which they became American citizens. It is to be regretted that this reliance on the faith of treaties has not been confirmed by the event. Already twenty years have elapsed, and grants made for services rendered are still unconfirmed. A confirmation at this day cannot repair the mischief and injustice of this long delay; for what can compensate twenty years of human existence wasted in disappointed hope and galling penury? The decree may restore to the injured claimant possession of his lawful property, but it can do no more.[59]

Without the means to profit from their land to support their families, the claimants were penniless in a new economy that used specie money instead of depending on a barter system. Claimants and officers alike were treated with indifference when it came to having their grants confirmed, and historians have assigned blame to them instead of understanding the core issue:

> The great difficulty the land claimants had to contend with, was the imputation of fraud cast upon their claims: the instructions of . . . Gallatin . . . appear to have been founded upon a charge of that nature, and show the imperfect knowledge had

at that early day. . . . By those instructions, the whole burden of proof was thrown upon the claimant, and a failure in any one point decided the claims to be surreptitious. . . . It was further required to show the legal authority of the officer making the grant; this, in no instance, could be done, as the law of the country was the will of the sovereign, known only through the acts of the officer who represented him.[60]

Austin and Jones were privy to information that they chose not to disclose to Lewis and Stoddard. They instead garnered special attention for being obstructive whistleblowers, and their malicious efforts set about a long and protracted battle for the habitants to acquire titles to their land concessions. The concessions were large, which aided in the belief that the land had been misappropriated, but the rule had been established many years before the Louisiana Purchase because

[t]he small number of the first emigrants to Upper Louisiana, and the warlike character of the surrounding tribes of Indians, compelled the pioneer settlers to establish themselves in villages, and to cultivate but small tracts in their immediate vicinity. Anticipating, at some future day, that their numbers would be sufficient . . . in extending their settlements, they applied to the authorities and obtained grants for more remote tracts, which they looked upon as the future homes of their families, and some remuneration for the many dangers and privations encountered by them in making their first establishments in the country.[61]

In 1873, Congress confirmed one of the last Spanish land grants in the old Upper Louisiana district. It had originally belonged to Moses Austin.[62]

Chapter 4

THE MISSING JOURNAL ENTRIES: FACT OR FICTION

For the past fifty years, historians have utilized a psychological reading of Meriwether Lewis's behavior in an attempt to explain why he missed four hundred days of writing journal entries. They blame him for being lax and lazy, even absent-minded, because he ordered William Clark and several expedition members to write journal entries instead of doing the task himself. Historians believe that Lewis's lethargy contributed to irresponsibility, which prevented him from writing consistently, but new evidence proves the opposite: his duties required multiple entries in other journals. This evidence also suggests that Lewis was not psychologically handicapped, but of sound mind, and that historians have imposed unrealistic expectations and unnecessary demands upon him.

Lewis's responsibilities for the expedition's success originated with President Thomas Jefferson. In his confidential message to Congress in January 1803, Thomas Jefferson announced a bold initiative with the yet-to-be-named Lewis and Clark Expedition. The president had hidden its costs between the paragraphs of a congressional bill that funded the establishment of trading houses near tribal villages. His plan was simple, and he regarded the Missouri River as key to opening the western trade.[1] Since 1787 Jefferson had intended to make Alexandria, Virginia, the place of deposit for furs, but George Washington had grander plans and suggested suitable locations further west along the Illinois and Wabash rivers "as the most abundant in furs."[2] In his message, Jefferson framed the expedition in terms of profitability and its usefulness to the public to galvanize Congress into accepting a deeper US trading partnership with Native Americans. And he initially envisioned opening the trade from the Pacific to the Atlantic by employing a unique emissary:

> An intelligent officer with ten or twelve chosen men, fit for the enterprize and willing to undertake it, taken from our posts, where they may be spared without inconvenience, might explore the whole line, even to the Western ocean, have con-

ferences with the natives on the subject of commercial intercourse, get admission among them for our traders as others are admitted, agree on convenient deposits for an interchange of articles, and return with the information acquired in the course of two summers.[3]

This became the template for the Lewis and Clark Expedition. Congress was funding a deft army corps experienced in light scientific training and "for other literary purposes," to extend the commerce of the nation. Jefferson must have spent some time pondering the wording of the message in order to weave the necessary components of an intricate expedition into it, and at the very end he made one final request to elicit support from congressional members who favored the undertaking.

The interests of commerce place the principal object within the constitutional powers and care of Congress, and that it should incidentally advance the geographical knowledge of our own continent can not but be an additional gratification.[4]

At the date of his message, Jefferson was also president of an exclusive organization, the American Philosophical Society, which represented American and European scientific-minded individuals who believed in the advancement of the sciences as a literary pursuit. His private secretary, Lewis, was a budding pupil of the society and "incidentally" was "the intelligent officer" who possessed the expertise and ability to accumulate the scientific and geographical aspects of the expedition and to later convert the vast, cumulative data into print.

Congress approved the bill on the final evening of the congressional session, and Lewis departed Washington soon thereafter for Philadelphia to acquire more training on a variety of subjects that would aid him on the expedition. But by the summer of 1803, Lewis realized that the roles of leader and manager of the expedition required the talents of two men and thus invited a longtime friend, William Clark, to be his cocommander. Clark had relevant army experience, which suited him perfectly for the assignment, and when Lewis informed the president, Jefferson excitedly wrote to Henry Dearborn, the secretary of war: "I have the pleasure to inform you that William Clark accepts with great glee the office of going with Capt. Lewis up the Missouri." Dearborn's reply matched Jefferson's elation. "Mr. W. Clark having consented to accompany Capt. Lewis is highly interesting, 'N adds very much to the ballance of chances in favour of ultimate success."[5]

The Lewis and Clark partnership provided a balanced combination of expertise in scientific matters and in the handling of a group of men. Having approval from the top officers in the nation meant that the division of responsibility was germane to the command. Managing a boat crew, a troop of soldiers, and daily affairs was best left to Clark's prior experience in the army. Clark had joined the army in 1791, and by the time Lewis signed up at Fort Greenville in 1795, Clark had been appointed a lieutenant, commander of his own rifle corps, had fought in the decisive Battle of Fallen Timbers under the leadership of Gen. Anthony Wayne, and had made several important military excursions down the Ohio and the Mississippi.

An important aspect of Clark's military career was having the experience to write journal entries. The details known of his early military career are a result of his written record. Clark was the type of person who understood the necessity of maintaining documentation and duplication of records. A dire requisite of expedition duty entailed a tremendous amount of journal writing maintained principally by Lewis and Clark, but augmented by several other expedition members, too. Lewis implemented redundancy in journal writing because he understood the importance of preservation, diversification, and perspective. In making a trek across the continent into lands unknown to Americans, "amidst a thousand dangers and difficulties" from rampaging animals to possible Indian attack to falling from a cliff or drowning, the expedition's records had to be preserved even if the lives of one, several, or all of the explorers were snuffed out.[6] Having several expedition members writing in journals enhanced the chances of success; however, historians have been critical of Lewis in this regard because they believe that he was shirking responsibility and putting undue strain upon William Clark as the principal journalist. That reasoning is based upon unrealistic expectations about what was possible for the success of the expedition.

Jefferson created the template of the expedition and selected Lewis to lead it. He wrote specific goals, which revolved around a scientific and literary model and which comprised four handwritten pages in his typically small writing style.[7] The president had placed absolute reliance on Lewis's abilities, and the depth of his range was nothing short of astounding. As far as Jefferson was concerned, Lewis was already a natural scientist who was ordered to use "instruments for ascertaining, by celestial observation, the geography of the country." He was to "explore the Missouri river . . . by it's course and communications with the waters of the Pacific ocean . . . for the purposes of commerce." He was to take observations of latitude and longitude at the mouth of the Missouri and "especially at the mouths of rivers, at rapids, at islands & other places & objects . . . that they may with certainty be recognized hereafter."[8]

Jefferson devoted a page to describing what was necessary for Lewis to take observations on, a half page to learning about native American commerce and customs, a page concerning soil, vegetable productions, animals of the country (known and unknown), "mineral productions of every kind . . . more particularly metals . . .

salines" and their temperatures, climate, and thermometer readings. Finally, Jefferson emphasized that Lewis was to find whatever means necessary to deliver "a copy of your journal, notes & observations, of every kind, putting into cipher whatever might do injury" if stolen.[9]

Lewis secured other pertinent information from members of the American Philosophical Society in Philadelphia—in the form of refresher courses in Indian ethnography, botany, zoology, geography, astronomy, ornithology, minerology, meteorology, natural history, and medicine, and he was also given assistance in comprehending and maximizing instrument readings.[10] Jefferson placed special emphasis on the need for accurate measurements for longitude and latitude and told Lewis to compare and test those measurements from time to time with others residing in the United States. Today, a complex science centers on celestial navigation and sextant accuracy, and modern-day experts wonder who assisted Lewis in Saint Louis.[11]

That distinction goes to Capt. Amos Stoddard, who arrived in the Illinois country in June 1803 to assist Lewis and Clark and to oversee the transfer of the country. Stoddard's expertise when reading latitude and longitude measurements was outlined in his first report about Upper Louisiana. Destined for a newspaper in the Atlantic states, it was an exacting reflection of the type of reporting specified in the instructions that Jefferson gave to Lewis:

> The south boundary of what is called Upper Louisiana, is on the Mississippi, in lat. 36, N. just below the village of New-Madrid, and 75 miles below the mouth of the Ohio. From that boundary to the Shining Mountains or to the sources of the Mississippi and Missouri, is about 2078 miles: and the width of the territory in question, between the Mississippi and the Rio del Nord or North River, is 692 miles. Hence you will perceive, that in Upper Louisiana is contained 1,437, 976 sq. miles, or 920,304,640 acres. It is suggested, however, that the line between North of New Mexico and Louisiana . . . begins on a ridge of hills near the mouth of the Rio del Nord, in lat. 26, 12, N.; that this ridge extends, parallel to the river, to the source.[12]

Stoddard had begun writing a book detailing various observations and aspects of Upper Louisiana and expected to publish it the following summer, but by 1806 he still had not completed it. In November of that year, he requested a transfer to Saint Louis because "I have been three years engaged in compiling an account historical and descriptive, of Upper Louisiana—and without a short residence in that territory, I cannot complete it."[13] Six more years were to pass before Stoddard published it.[14] Lewis has been criticized for the shortcoming of not publishing the expedition journals within a reasonable time, but completing personal projects was a lengthy process and required much patience when one had other pressing official duties to perform on a daily basis, as governors and military commanders did.

Criticism has also been leveled at Lewis for not making daily journal entries. This criticism was first introduced in 1904 by the historian Reuben Gold Thwaites, who claimed that "[w]hether the missing journal entries (441 days, as compared with Clark; but we may eliminate 41 for the period when he was disabled, thus leaving 400) are still in existence or not is unknown to the present writer."[15] In the present day, historians Gary Moulton and Paul Russell Cutright have taken Lewis to task for saddling Clark with this duty when Lewis should have been writing daily. Moulton says that there were gaps in Lewis's journals that lasted months while Cutright called them "hiatuses" and speculated that Lewis was just plain lazy in not adhering to Jefferson's dictum.[16] Moulton said that the gaps in Lewis's journals were numerous and extensive.

> They include missing days from the trip on the Ohio and Mississippi rivers from September 19 to November 11, 1803, a nearly complete lapse from May 14, 1804, to April 7, 1805, only spotty entries from August 26, 1805, to January 1, 1806, and a final hiatus from August 12, 1806, to the completion of the expedition. The last gap can be explained by Lewis's being partially disabled from a wound; in contrast to other lapses in writing. . . . One might also include the period from November 28, 1803, to May 14, 1804, during the winter in the St. Louis area, a time for which no Lewis journal is known. Clark at least kept a rough diary during that time. In all, from May 1804 to September 1806, there are over four hundred days of missing entries by Lewis during the expedition proper.[17]

Because of the large blocks of missing dates in the daily journals, Moulton and Cutright sidestepped the issue by claiming that there were most likely missing expedition journals. That theory makes sense if Lewis had been an absentminded subordinate who conceivably misplaced or lost the other relevant journals compiled by others on the expedition, but these historians were privy to Lewis's full writing output. They chose not to reveal what Lewis was doing on the days when he was not writing journal accounts on the occurrences of the expedition and the behavior of its individual members. Stephen Ambrose has a completely different view, theorizing that Lewis was depressed, which prevented him from writing daily.[18]

What these historians ultimately claimed was that Lewis was not as competent as William Clark, and they arrived at this conclusion based on Lewis's mysterious death three years after the expedition. The speculation on the cause of his death and the charge that it was a suicide has led to an avalanche of criticism against him based on the supposition that he was a manic-depressive, addicted to pills and alcohol, and that he ultimately possessed a "flawed character." In order to prove this theory and support the idea that Lewis was capable of, and indeed predisposed to, suicide, they have to go back through his life, searching for "evidence" in any quirky, strange, or inexplicable episode for the character flaws that they argue led to his downfall. The missing journal entries supply them with evidence for this purpose. According to Moulton, Cutright, and Ambrose, the hiatuses in Lewis's journal-keeping prove that Lewis was deficient and neglectful of his duties as outlined by President Jefferson.

An examination of the dates on which Lewis did not write journal entries, coupled with an outline of what he did accomplish during those periods, will perhaps provide an explanation that will exonerate Lewis from these charges. The gaps in the first group of dates are longer than in the second group, but all the gaps are important nonetheless.[19]

May 21, 1804	to	Sept. 15, 1804
Sept. 18, 1804	to	Feb. 2, 1805
Aug. 27, 1805	to	Dec. 31, 1805
Aug. 13, 1806	to	Sept. 23, 1806
Feb. 14, 1805	to	Mar. 15, 1805
Mar. 17, 1805	to	Apr. 6, 1805
Aug. 27, 1805	to	Sept. 6, 1805
Dec. 2, 1805	to	Dec. 31, 1805

Moulton explains that these gaps suggest "a larger pattern of negligence."[20] Cutright, an expert on Lewis's naturalistic activities from May 21, 1804, until April 7, 1805, seems to think that Lewis should have been on the boat writing notes that would duplicate Clark's work instead of accumulating and labeling new species of plants. Cutright describes the level of expertise needed to dry and press plants:

> The job of pressing plants is not as simple as it sounds, even under optimum conditions of warm, sunshiny weather. Since they contain moisture, they require continued attention until fully dry, which means regular exposure to air and transferring to dry paper for many days running. During the periods when Lewis botanized most actively . . . he may well have had three or four dozen specimens (or even more) to attend to daily . . . but there was more to it. . . . Lewis had to supervise their transport and take every precaution against loss to rain, flash flood, fire.[21]

Interestingly, the historians do not acknowledge how much time it took Lewis to collect, dry, label, and store the plant specimens. They have essentially graded Lewis within the narrow context of whether or not he took time to make daily journal entries, seeing this activity as being of more importance than all others, and believe that the other time-consuming chores, outlined and ordered by Jefferson, were no excuse for not performing in the area of journal keeping.

For the entire time of the alleged eleven-month gap of May 21, 1804, to April 7, 1805, Lewis was engaged daily with chores having to do with the collection and preservation of flora and fauna, and working diligently to preserve new specimens and catalogue and label assorted minerals and animal furs. Lewis dated and recorded activities for many days, not in a daily journal but in small books specific to these tasks. For the dates May 21, 1804, through April 7, 1805, there is an alternate or separate amount of data that Lewis collected, per Jefferson's orders, that runs contrary to what historians have claimed. In fact, in the gaps that they cite, they completely ignore the chores and duties that fully occupied his waking hours.[22] According to Lewis's botanical collection, he was engaged in scientific work with plant specimens on the following specific days from May through November 1804:[23]

May:	10, 22, 23, 25, 27 (3), 29, 30
June:	1, 3, 14 (2), 15, 16, n.d.
July:	13, 15, 17, 18, 20, 27 (7), 29, 30
August:	1, 2, 4, 10, 17, 25, 27
September:	1, 2 (3), 4, 5, 8, 12, 15 (2), 18 (2), 19 (2), 21 (2), 22
October:	1 (2), 2 (4), 3 (2), 12, 15, 16 (2), 17 (2), 18
November:	16, 17

Ten specimens were undated. The dates that are in parentheses indicate that Lewis found more than one specimen on that day and wrote about it. And, according to Lewis's mineralogical collection, he was engaged on these days as well:[24]

May:	30
August:	1, 6, 17, 20, 21, 22 (6), 23 (4), 24, 25
September:	1, 2, 4, 5, 8, 10, 12, 15, 17, 18, 19, 21
October:	2, 3, 12, 14, 16, 17, 18, 22

Close to 119 days of the missing four hundred have been accounted for in this one gap, and this number does not take into consideration all of Lewis's small notebooks. In addition to science, much of his time during the autumn of 1804 was taken up with diplomacy, as the Americans officially notified Missouri River tribes of the change in government from Spain to the United States in official and repetitive ceremonies. The period also involved a week of tense encounters with the Lakota people, which would have disrupted any scientific work.

Lewis also posted a weather diary and charted four conditions every day: state of weather at sunrise and at 4:00 p.m., and the state of the wind and sunrise at 4:00 p.m. He also took regular observations of the sun for navigation, not to mention the failed attempt at coursing the transit of Venus.

Lewis stopped making entries from October 23 until November 16 because Lewis and Clark arrived at the Mandan villages in present-day North Dakota on October 24, 1804, and for the next few weeks they were entertained by the Mandans, gave out medals, delivered talks, and went looking for a suitable spot to build a fort, which was begun on November 4. During the remainder of the month, they saw scores of Mandan and the completion of the fort. Lewis recorded meteorological observations in his "weather diary" for the months of October and November and astronomical observations for three days in November.[25] On the thirteenth, Lewis took a pirogue with some of the men to the Mandan village to find stone for chimneys. Six days later, he met with the Hidatsa and returned to the fort on November 27.

By December 7, the weather had turned extremely cold—Lewis recorded 42 degrees below zero on the eighth! With the completion of the fort, they began to think about having to stock it with meat for the winter, and on December 9 Lewis took a detachment of men on a Buffalo hunt. He stayed out all night in the bitter cold. The next morning they were curious about the temperature and Gass recorded that they made a test with "proof spirits," which "in fifteen minutes froze into hard ice." Clark also went out in December to hunt buffalo and deer and brought back the meat on sleds.

Once winter set in, Lewis set to work reviewing his notebooks on flora, fauna, mineralogy, and botanicals. During the coldest months he compiled, labeled, and stored a prodigious number of his specimens, readying them for shipment in April to Saint Louis and eventually to Washington.[26] Some of the articles shipped on April 5 included 108 botanicals, 68 mineral specimens, 15 skeletons, horns, skins, insects, stuffed birds, and 6 live animals.[27]

In the month of March 1805, when the night sky was filled to the brim with stars, Lewis took various astronomical readings.[28] These readings essentially guided the Lewis and Clark Expedition westward, although historians have separated and minimized these necessary chores from his daily regimen. On April 7, the expedition ventured forth into the unknown, which Lewis confirmed when he wrote in the journal that "we were now about to penetrate a country at least two thousand miles in width, on which the foot of civillized man had never trodden."[29] On his thirty-first birthday, he displayed a wider range of emotions, exposing his introspective side and taking a personal inventory of himself. In his estimation, he "had as yet done but little, very little indeed, to further the hapiness of the human race, or to advance the information of the succeeding generation." Little did he realize then that the success of the Lewis and Clark Expedition would fill inquiring minds to the present day. He also criticized himself for being indolent, a characterization so contradictory because, as leader of the expedition, he had performed diverse scientific pursuits and had completed them.[30]

For the years 1805–1806, Lewis continued with his various collections and integrated with his weather diaries the discovery of more plants and the uncovering of a bounty of minerals. For the months from January to November 1805, he found twenty-one more specimens, but in 1806, the western part of the nation afforded many learning opportunities.

March:	13 (2), 26 (3), 27 (2)
April:	1, 8 (2), 10 (2), 11, 12, 14 (4), 15 (3), 16 (2), 20, 22, 25, 30, 17 (4), 29 (2)
May:	6 (2), 7 (2), 8 (2), 17, 20 (2), 27, 29 (5)
June:	1 (2), 5 (3), 6 (3), 9, 10 (3), 12 (2), 14 (2), 15 (4), 16 (4), 23, 25 (2), 26 (2), 27 (4)
July:	1 (3), 4 (2), 5, 6 (3), 7 (5), 8, 9, 12, 17, 20 (2), 22, 28
August:	10 (2), 17 (2), 27
September:	8, 14, 21, 12

These dates bring the number of entries to 136 from January to November 1805 and from March to September 1806, with a grand total from the start of the expedition on May 20, 1804, of 255 notebook entries.

In July 1806, besides summarizing every day and evening with weather and wind specifications, he also jotted down other information apart from the discoveries. On July 1 he reported "a species of wild clover with a small leaf just in blume." Two days later, he wrote about turtle dove eggs, and on July 5, after recording the temperature, he described pigeons and how cold the temperature had become.

Perusing this new data has exposed a new trait: Lewis was a chatty diarist! In fact, when examining these weather diaries a new side to his personality emerges. Lewis took the utmost care with his observations and injected a literary aspect/component to them. On July 8, he wrote that in the morning a heavy white frost blanketed their camp and that it was very cold the night before. He wrote specialized information in the weather diary for these days: July 1, 3, 5, 6, 7, 8, 9, 10, 11, 12, 16, 17, 23, 24, 25, 26, 28, 29, 30, 31.[31]

In July 1806, Lewis and Clark headed in two different directions. Lewis led a group to the Marais River looking for its northern reach, but on August 11, Pierre Cruzatte, an expedition member, accidentally shot Lewis, mistaking him for an elk in the bush. Despite the severe injury and having to lay face down in a boat, Lewis's writing output did not suffer; he assembled a weather table on August 12 and continued making weather observations until the end of the month.[32] Taking into account all of his weather diaries and notes from October 1805 through August 1806, Lewis wrote about 270 descriptions, which greatly exceeds the "400 missing journal entries."[33]

One strategic piece of information that the critics fail to address is that the expedition was mounted for several purposes, and that Lewis, as commander, could delegate tasks and make decisions about who did what type of work and who kept what types of journals. He divided the tasks of managing science and managing men between the commanders, and this could be extended to the type of journal kept by each. Clark's journals contain some scientific information, but are mostly, let's face it, the adventure narrative; they are more akin to military orderly books than scientific journals. All of these experiments and duties kept Lewis busy with the scientific portion of the trek, but we can't ignore that his diplomatic responsibilities with the Indians were an important distraction as well.

The question is not so much why he didn't keep a diary like Clark's as a duplicate, but rather why, on those days when he did so, did he keep a diary at all? If it was for the duplication, then why weren't the scientific records themselves in the separate little notebooks duplicated, and, indeed, why were they scattered in individual notebooks in the first place?

The loss of items like the answers to the Indian queries posed by Dr. Benjamin Rush could have been avoided if these things had been duplicated or if they had been copied into journal books. The loss of the plant and animal specimens and information was every bit as important as the potential loss of the narrative of the trek. Even enlisted men on the expedition who were literate could have been detailed to do the monk-like copy work necessary to ensure duplication of scientific and/or narrative journals, at places like Fort Mandan and Fort Clatsop, but this was not done. Have modern scholars merely jumped to the conclusion that Lewis tried to follow Jefferson's order about duplication? Or was the effort needed for such duplication just too overwhelming in the overall scheme of making the expedition a success?

Questions about Lewis's role on the expedition will hopefully swing the other way now that the puzzling weight of the missing journal entries has been solved, and the need to inquire further into Lewis's supposed recording gaps has come to an end. He was actively engaged in the enterprise of collecting and collating his discoveries, one of the major purposes of the expedition. In light of this newer research, the time has come both to review his participation in the colossal undertaking of gathering new specimens for science and to give him the credit that he deserves.

Chapter 5

THE HOMEWARD BOUND
JOURNEY*

O n September 23, 1806, members of the Lewis and Clark Expedition
stepped out of their boats on the Saint Louis riverbank. Their long voyage
of discovery was over and the comforts of home and prepared meals awaited them.

The date of their arrival is confirmed by a letter that the wealthy Saint Louis
resident John Mullanphy wrote that day. His short, excited note was rushed across
the Mississippi River to catch the mail rider, going east:

> Concerning the safe arrival of Messrs. Lewis and Clark, who went 2 years and 4
> months ago to explore the Missouri, to be anxiously wished for by every one, I have
> the pleasure to mention, that they arrived here about one hour ago, in good health,
> with the loss of one man who died. They visited the Pacific Ocean, which they left
> on the 27th of March last. They would have been here about the 1st of August, but
> for the detention they met with from the snow and frost in crossing mountains on
> which are eternal snows. Their journal will no doubt be not only importantly inter-
> esting to us all, but a fortune for the worthy and laudable adventurers. When they
> arrive, 3 cheers were fired. They really have the appearance of Robinson Crusoes,
> dressed entirely in buckskins. We shall know all very soon, I have no particulars yet.[1]

Mullanphy's hearty letter, with its air of praise, congratulation, and wonder-
ment, was published in *The Palladium*, a Frankfort, Kentucky, newspaper, on
October 4, 1806.

The small, muddy Saint Louis village the Corps of Discovery had passed twenty-
eight months earlier had changed greatly during their absence, as new Anglo-
American residents arrived, intent on making fortunes for themselves. By 1806, the
prime topic of conversation involved property rights. When Lewis and Clark had
first arrived in Saint Louis, almost three years earlier, the inhabitants were fearful
that their property would be lost in the changeover of governments as English land
law replaced that of the French and Spanish. And their fears proved partially correct—

President Jefferson and his treasury secretary appointed a board of commissioners to hear land claims and to decide upon them. The territory was split in two between those who could afford to live without land and those who survived off their land. Rufus Easton, a territorial judge, believed that the land record books kept under the Spanish regime were in disarray and asked Captains Lewis and Clark to evaluate them. They agreed with Easton that the old books contained "innumerable erasures and forgeries."[2]

Territorial property rights did not prevent the explorers from relaxation or attending celebrations, and for the three weeks that they were in Saint Louis they discharged expedition members, sold surplus equipment, and hired several persons to accompany delegations from the Mandan Nation and the Osage Nation to Washington. President Thomas Jefferson anticipated major changes in the fur trade, which would result in jobs and opportunities for industrious young men. At the Cantonment Bellefontaine factory, located eighteen miles north of Saint Louis, the assistant factor George Sibley wrote an enthusiastic letter regarding his expectations.[3]

> Perhaps nothing of so great importance has ever happened (as respects the Commercial interests of the United States, & particularly the Western Country) as these discoveries. It would be useless for me now to enter minutely into the subject, the limits of a letter would not allow it. Suffice it to say that in a few years the most Rich & Luxurious field for Young men of spirit and enterprise will be opened. Then we shall see floating down the Missouri, valuable cargoes of merchandise: I need Say no more, this bare hint will be sufficient for you to build on for weeks & months. I cannot predict what effect these things will have on my fortunes, tho' certain it is they will have a material one. It has been hinted by Captain Lewis, who it is supposed will have the management of our Indian Affairs . . . that several trading houses will be established by Govt pretty high up this river & the Mississippi, next Spring.[4]

Lewis and Clark departed Saint Louis on October 21, 1806, and proceeded east with Clark's slave York, Sgt. John Ordway, interpreter François Labiche, Osage Indian Agent Pierre Chouteau, and the Mandan and Osage delegations.[5] Prominent among them was the Mandan chief, Sheheke-shote (or Big White) who invited Lewis and Clark to build a fort in the Mandan country during the winter of 1804–1805. This part of the trip must have been exhilarating for the persons traveling with the explorers. The pinnacle of western exploration lay with just two men amid a select group headed to Washington, and for the next three weeks, what kinds of incredible stories did they tell? Did anyone have the sense to write and capture those experiences on paper? Part of the entourage was going home, the others were traveling to the seat of the American government to share in the festivities. Pierre

Chouteau thought the trip to Washington, DC, would take about forty days, based on his previous escort of an Indian delegation to the capitol.[6]

A page from the "Registers of Letters Received by the Office of the Secretary of War." Pierre Chouteau, Osage Indian agent, informed the secretary of war in letters 203 and 209 that the Indian delegation that he was leading from St. Louis to Washington had arrived in Lexington, Kentucky, on November 16, 1806. On December 7, he wrote from Pittsburgh that it had been snowing for a few days and that the delegation would have to "proceed to Washington in sleighs." (Registers of Letters Received by the Office of the Secretary of War, Main Series, RG107, M22, roll 3, p. 46, National Archives and Records Administration.)

In 1806, there was only one land route that headed east, which was a post road. Most traveling was still accomplished by boat, but the Lewis and Clark entourage traveled by land, probably due to the cost but possibly so that Clark could be reunited with his family before proceeding on to Washington. The group arrived about November 10 at Louisville, Kentucky, and three days later at Frankfort.[7] The entourage split at this point: Lewis and the Mandans headed south, Clark and York went to Fincastle, Virginia, to visit the Hancock family, and Chouteau, leading the Osage delegation, continued east.[8]

The Chouteau party stopped at Lexington, Kentucky, on November 16, and Chouteau wrote that he and the Osage would proceed by way of Pittsburgh.[9] On December 7, when Chouteau arrived there, snow had already fallen, and he wrote that they "will have to proceed to Washington in sleighs."[10]

Lewis took a detour that has escaped the history books until now. He added a trip that delayed his arrival at Charlottesville by traveling to the Cumberland Gap. President Jefferson was unaware of the trip. He had written to Reuben Lewis, Meriwether Lewis's brother, on November 2 "informing him he might hourly expect his brother" at Charlottesville.[11] Instead, Lewis took the route from Frankfort to Harrodsburg, where he met with the Wilderness Road, then to Danville, which took him south through Barbourville, Kentucky, and then to the Cumberland Gap.[12] Lewis arrived there about November 20, 1806, but it is not known if it was to complete a duty, an errand, or to enjoy a leisurely activity.[13]

It is known, however, that Capt. Lewis was to conduct an interesting business while in the vicinity: surveying the Cumberland Gap to settle a border dispute between Kentucky and Tennessee. In a letter written in 1810, local resident Arthur Campbell detailed Lewis's activities for the benefit of Governor Charles Scott of Kentucky:

> [C]aptain M. Lewis returned from his travels to the Pacific Ocean, that he halted two days near this place (Cumberland Gap, Knox County), on one of which he was requested to make celestial observations, with his astronomical instruments, in order to find the true latitude of the Virginia, or as it is commonly called Walker's line, run in 1779. The captain with his usual complaisance acceded to the request, and made the usual observations and calculations, by which it appeared, that the line run in 1779 was several miles too far north.[14]

What led Lewis to perform such a task or how it evolved is a mystery, but perhaps he was just being agreeable: "The captain with his usual complaisance acceded to the request." Or, since he was quite familiar with using a sextant to take astronomical readings, he believed that he could be of service.[15] The story takes an interesting and detailed turn.[16]

The Cumberland Gap is situated at a point where the states of Virginia, Kentucky, and Tennessee come together, and it was the only way then to traverse that portion of the Appalachian Mountains. In July 1749, the council of the province of Virginia authorized Dr. Thomas Walker to survey 800,000 acres along the southern border of Virginia, now southeastern Kentucky. During his survey he encountered an area that he called Cave Gap, a notch about 1,000 feet deep into Cumberland Mountain, which game animals, particularly bison and deer, used as a means of traveling through the Appalachian Mountains.[17] Native Americans followed this game trail, too, as they moved from one hunting area to another.

In 1779, Dr. Walker accepted a commission on behalf of Virginia to run the state line between Virginia and North Carolina west through the Cumberland Gap and, ultimately, to the Mississippi River. Walker never physically surveyed that far, stopping at the Tennessee River at the 36° 40' parallel of latitude instead of the agreed location for the dividing line at 36° 30', which was more than twelve miles north of the true latitude line.

Kentucky became a state in 1792 when Virginia ceded its western lands to the federal government. In the intervening years between 1779 and 1792, several legislative acts passed by Virginia and North Carolina accepted Walker's survey line, but after Tennessee, which had been created from the western lands ceded by North Carolina in 1790, became a state in 1796, controversies arose. Kentucky and Tennessee passed legislation concerning the shared border in 1801 and 1803, but no real agreement was reached on the placement of the boundary line.

A week before Lewis arrived at the Cumberland Gap in 1806, he made sure that his instruments were working correctly:

> Captain Lewis in a conversation further mentioned, that he had taken the latitude of the junction of the Ohio with the Mississippi, with the same instruments and on the same spot Mr. Ellicott took the latitude, with his much approved Zenith Sector, and on calculation he found their observations to agree.[18]

When Lewis arrived at the Cumberland Gap, he was invited by Col. Arthur Campbell to ascertain Walker's survey line, the dividing line between Kentucky and Tennessee, which was thought to be in an incorrect location. Over the course of a few days, Lewis assessed Walker's line and then issued a survey certificate and made a report.

> This day in compliance with the request of certain gentlemen, I undertook to settle the latitude of a line usually denominated Walker's line, formerly dividing the states of Virginia and North Carolina. The position selected for this observation was near the habitation of a Mr. E. Walling, two hundred yards south of said line, and about two miles distant from Cumberland Gap. The instruments used in this observation were a Sextant on the most approved plan, with a reversing Telescope for an eye piece [sic], and a good micrometer, and artificial horizon, in which water

was used as the reflecting surface. With these instruments, I took the meridian altitude of the sun's lower limb, and calculated the latitude; from which it appeared that the place of observation was in North latitude 36° 38' 12 1–10; if, therefore, the charters of the states of North Carolina and Virginia call for a parallel of latitude at 36° 30' N. as a boundary between them, the line of Walker is nine miles and 1,077 yards North of its proper position. . . . This statement, I have given to Colonel Arthur Campbell, at his request, to be presented to the public view, in any manner he may think proper.[19]

Lewis's role when taking astronomical readings on the western expedition of 1804–1806 was complex, but he tackled the Cumberland Gap project in record time. Lewis departed the area and arrived home in Charlottesville, still accompanied by the Mandan delegation, on December 13. On December 22, after making the rounds with his family, he sent a bill to Secretary of War Henry Dearborn for $52, describing the expense as a "charge of certain Mandan Indians & for other public purposes."[20] His cousin James Gilmer kindly put up the money and Lewis gave him a receipt. After spending Christmas Day with his family, he set off for Washington and arrived late in the evening of December 28, where he found a warm welcome at the presidential mansion. Chouteau and his delegation had arrived at the capital on December 20.[21]

On December 30, Lewis met with an old friend, New York congressman Samuel Mitchill, who had invited Lewis to dine with him at his Washington lodgings. The physician, scientist, and professor of chemistry admired Lewis's astronomical and other scientific attainments and he admitted, years later, that he looked upon Lewis "as a man returned from another planet." On that day also, President Jefferson welcomed the Mandan delegation to Washington, saying, "I take you by the hand of friendship," and then reading a three-page speech that paid tribute to Lewis: "I therefore sent our beloved man, Captain Lewis, one of my own family, to go up the Missouri river, to get acquainted with all of the Indian nations in its neighborhood." The following day, Jefferson gave an address to the Osage, welcoming them "to the seat of Government," and praising them for taking the journey, which was "long and fatiguing . . . to become acquainted with your new brothers of this country."[22]

On New Year's Day, the citizens of the capital traditionally came to pay their respects to the president, but this was a special occasion and they came to catch a glimpse of the colorfully dressed Indian delegations. Mitchill paid his compliments to Mr. Jefferson at the president's house on the Palatine Hills:

> While I was looking round and meditating what to do with myself, the Miss Johnsons . . . expressed a desire to be escorted to the side of the room where the

newly arrived Indians were. I at once became their pioneer and showed them the King and Queen of the Mandanes, who with a child of theirs, have come from a journey of about 1600 miles down the Missouri to see their great Father the President. His majests were gaily dressed in a regimental coat, &c, but his Consort was wrapped in a blanket, and had not the smallest ornament about her. She resembled exceedingly one of our Long Island squaws. There was also another Mandane woman there, who was wife to a Canadian White man, that acted as interpreter. She had two children with her. We also looked at the five Osages and the one Delaware warriors. . . .[23]

A testimonial banquet in Washington, DC, had been delayed until William Clark's arrival, but finally was held in his absence on January 14, 1807, and attended by the citizens of Washington, several officers of the government, members of Congress, and strangers of distinction including Pierre Chouteau, the French translator Pierre Provenchere, the Mandan chief Sheheke-shote, and his personal interpreter Rene Jusseaume.[24] The newspaper *The Sun* faithfully reported the event:

> Capt. Lewis was received with the liveliest demonstrations of regard. Every one present seemed to be deeply impressed with a sentiment of gratitude, mingled with an elevation of mind, on setting down, at the festive board, with this favorite of fortune, who has thus successfully surmounted the numerous and imminent perils of a tour of nearly four years, through regions previously unexplored by civilized man. After partaking of the gratifications of a well spread table, the following toasts were drank, interspersed with appropriate songs and instrumental music.[25]

In the early part of the entertainment, poet Joel Barlow presented "elegant and glowing stanzas" on the discoveries of Capt. Lewis, which were recited by John Beckley. Throughout the evening, many toasts were offered up on a variety of topics: the people; the Constitution; the president of the United States; Congress; Washington; Franklin; Columbus; the United States; the red people of America; the council fire; science; union; peace; the militia; the army and navy; agriculture, commerce, and manufacture; and the District of Columbia. The descriptions on these topics were well-explained. Science "animated by the enterprize of the American mind, has made the desert to blossom and the wilderness to smile." And regarding agriculture, commerce, and manufacture, "their interests, like those of the independent sovereignties they enrich and unite, are one and indivisible."[26]

After seventeen toasts on national topics, one was given on "Lewis's retiring."

> Capt. Meriwether Lewis—Patriotic, enlightened, and brave; who had the spirit to undertake, and the valour to execute an expedition, which reflects honor on his

country. Capt. Clark, and the other brave companions of Capt. Lewis—Their patriotic and manly perseverance entitles them to the approbation of their countrymen. The memories of captains Cook, Bourganville, and other cicumnavigators, whose perilous enterprises and indefatigable labours have so much enriched the world in the science of geography.[27]

The evening "proceeded on," and toasts were expressed by Capt. Lewis, Joel Barlow, Gen. Jonathan Mason, Robert Fulton, Thomas Mann Randolph Jr., George Clinton, and an anonymous person.[28]

The next morning, Capt. Lewis addressed Congress regarding the compensation due to the members of the expedition. At the opening of Congress, Jefferson briefly detailed the journey of the Corps of Discovery. He recommended additional compensation to show "that Messrs. Lewis and Clarke, and their brave companions, have, by this arduous service, deserved well of their country."[29]

Lewis promptly delivered a roster of the men, which included their ranks and his remarks on their respective merits and services. Secretary of War Henry Dearborn transmitted the list of the officers, noncommissioned officers, and privates who formed the party to Congress. He believed that the expedition met "with a degree of boldness, perseverance, and judgment, and success, that has rarely, if ever, occurred, in this or any other country." Dearborn recommended that each of the men receive double pay and a grant of 320 acres, which they could locate on any surveyed land now for sale in the United States. Lewis received 1,500 acres, and Clark 1,000 acres, which did not set well with Lewis, who felt strongly "that no distinction of rank so noticed as to make a difference in the quantity of land granted to each," and that there should be "an equal division" of the quantity granted.[30]

Weeks passed as Congress deliberated on the various types of compensation. Finally, on February 20, 1807, the House resumed its discussion regarding double pay for all expedition members, but Rep. Matthew Lyon believed that double pay amounted to more than $60,000, and coupled with the land grant, compensation could exceed that sum three or four times. He believed that the companions of Lewis and Clark "might go over all the Western country and locate their warrants on the best land, in 160 acre lots."[31] On February 28 the House deliberated late into the evening before passing legislation bestowing double pay on members of the expedition and a grant of 320 acres each in the Territory of Louisiana at the rate of two dollars an acre.[32] Lewis and Clark received 1,600 acres each. The Senate passed the bill on March 3.[33]

In addition to a worthy compensation package for the band of explorers, Jefferson had been grappling with the myriad complexities of a new territory and finding a suitable and trustworthy candidate to administer it.[34] Jefferson and his cabinet saw a potential solution to their dilemma in the appointment of Lewis as governor of the Louisiana Territory. They believed Lewis's return to Saint Louis would restore confidence in the US government and its intentions in the new territory. On February 28, 1807, President Jefferson issued an order nominating Lewis as governor of the Louisiana Territory, which the US Senate confirmed two days later.

Secretary of the Treasury Albert Gallatin recognized that Lewis would be busy for several months settling expedition accounts and submitting his final report in Washington, then traveling to Philadelphia to arrange for the publication of the journals. He urged Jefferson to appoint a secretary of the Louisiana Territory who would govern in the interim. Jefferson appointed Frederick Bates to the post, a man who already was familiar with territorial politics, land claims, post roads, and business affairs from his residence in the Northwest Territory at Detroit.[35]

Lewis remained in Washington completing his obligations. He had to commit all of his expedition expenditures to paper, and the treasury accountant at the War Department, William Simmons, had a reputation for being manic in the pursuit of details. The expenditures were complex, and it took time to locate and tabulate the innumerable ledger items. The total cost had risen to $38,000, a ten-fold increase from his original estimate of $2,500 in early 1803.[36] A final accounting could not be made because receipts had still not arrived, some vouchers had not come in for payment, and others had not been credited. That time-consuming paperwork delayed other pressing matters, like his detailed treatise on Indian trade relations, which affirms that Lewis was in control of his faculties.[37]

Lewis finally departed for Philadelphia the first week of April. Historians have wondered why he took so long to leave the capital, but new information shows that Lewis was sick with malaria. President Jefferson had written to Charles Willson Peale on March 29 and informed him that he was leaving for Monticello within a week and that "Capt. Lewis will set out about the same time for Philadelphia."[38] Lewis hurried under an already impossible deadline and was burdened by the responsibilities of his troubled official post as governor. Lewis intended to distribute the specimens he had collected throughout the expedition to those who could help him evaluate them and arrange for expert assistance in compiling a narrative dealing with the natural history of the expedition. In addition to that challenge, he had just a few months to compose a narrative of the great adventure, for he realized that at least two of the enlisted men who had made the trip had kept journals of their own and were interested in publishing them. In Saint Louis, after the return of the expedition, Lewis had given Pvt. Robert Frazer permission to publish his private journal. Now Sgt. Patrick Gass was planning to publish his scribbled notes as well, beating the "official" version of the expedition to bookshops across the country and becoming the first detailed glimpse into the hardships, adventures, and accomplishments of the trek.

Lewis intended to do more than merely publish the raw field journals. He intended to produce a synthesis of the journals coupled with precise descriptions of the natural history specimens that he had collected, giving a comprehensive description rather than a mere day-to-day account of adventures like Gass's and Frazer's publications promised to do. Lewis asked Alexander Wilson, the celebrated ornithologist, to make some drawings of the bird specimens that were brought back from the expedition. "It was the request and particular wish of Captain Lewis, made to me in person, that I should make some drawings of such of the feathered tribes as had been preserved, and were new."[39]

Lewis outlined his intentions with printer John Conrad. From what must have been a rudimentary description, Conrad worked out an estimate of the cost at the beginning of April 1807 at $4,500, and he developed a revised proof of the prospectus.[40] The prospectus described a narrative of the voyage in the first volume, with a second volume devoted to geography, Indians, and the fur trade embellished with a number of plates. A third volume would be confined exclusively to scientific research, principally in natural history, under the heads of "Botany, Mineralogy, and Zoology . . . including a comparative view of twenty-three vocabularies of distinct Indian languages," and of course, the great map of North America.[41]

The prospectus was published in the *Philadelphia Aurora* on June 16, 1807.[42] The following morning, Lewis and his friend Mahlon Dickerson accompanied a party to Peale's museum to see a stuffed monkey and other exhibits.[43] During the time that Lewis spent in Philadelphia, Dickerson's record paid close attention to the ladies they visited. During a hot June and July, Dickerson and Lewis visited a number of homes that may have sheltered eligible daughters. The young women might have been impressed by Lewis's southern manners, but parents may have observed that his future lay in a frontier French town of uncertain respectability. Additionally, a governor's lady would be, in the view of jaded upper-class Philadelphians, meeting rustic strangers, dirty linen Frenchmen, Spanish scoundrels, and even Indians.

Lewis returned to his family home in Albemarle County on November 3, 1807, and wrote Dickerson to arrange for the education of his half-brother John Marks. Lewis then talked of romance, noting that "his little affair" with Anne Randolph was short, perhaps due to the fact that she was "previously engaged."[44] The references that Lewis made about his disappointed overtures did not entirely mask shyness—Lewis may have met the 16-year-old Letitia Breckenridge or her younger sister Elizabeth—and in the November letter to Dickerson, Lewis revealed that his heart remained in Philadelphia.[45]

At the end of November 1807, as he returned to Saint Louis to assume his duties, Governor Lewis's entourage included his brother Reuben and John Pernier, the free mulatto valet whom Thomas Jefferson sent along to look after Lewis.[46] There were wagoners and horse handlers to deal with who hauled the governor's papers, the wardrobes of the two young gentlemen, and household furnishings necessary to make life bearable in Saint Louis. Lewis carried with him the heavy documents of the exploration of western America, which was a constant reminder of what he needed to complete for the publisher. Would he have any time to complete the journals in addition to governing the most challenging territory of the United States?

The slow-moving wagon gave the brothers time for conversation and to check on the lands that belonged to their mother and their half-brother John Marks, which appeared to be secure. But Lewis's holding on Brush Creek in the Ohio Military Reserve, a land grant descended from his father's service, was in doubt, and Lewis was resigned to losing the greater part of it. When they reached Lexington, Kentucky, on January 14, 1808, the citizens gave Lewis a huge party "in testimony of their regard and respect for him."[47] By mid-February they arrived in Louisville to find that William Clark had been there as late as the third of the month. They had failed to intercept him on the road as he traveled east to his wedding.

Lewis found an opportunity to write to their mother while Reuben set out in a flat-bottomed boat with the baggage and carriage, accompanied by Maj. Hughes, Mr. Cox, and Pernier. After descending the Ohio for 320 miles, they disembarked on the west side of the Mississippi River and covered the next 165 miles by land. Lewis expected to leave the next day, traveling overland by way of Vincennes (Indiana) and Cahokia (Illinois). After a dizzying year of business, he arrived in Saint Louis to begin his tenure as governor on March 8, 1808.[48]

Chapter 6

Preserving the Legacy of Meriwether Lewis: The Letters of Samuel Latham Mitchill*

S amuel Latham Mitchill (1764–1831) was known by various titles: doctor, senator, professor, representative, and husband. An avid and prolific letter writer to his wife, Catherine Akerly Mitchill, some of his most beautiful and descriptive letters were about Meriwether Lewis. He worked seven months a year in Washington, DC, and the other five on North Hempstead, Long Island, a seaside nook a few miles from New York City. Mitchill spent his personal hours at home working as an editor, analyzing chemistry formulas, and tending to his wife, Catherine, and their two daughters.

Information about Mitchill was difficult to obtain, and it was only because I was eager to enliven and dig deeper into the story of Meriwether Lewis that I have this information at all. Historian John Jackson said that unless new information was presented in our coauthored *Meriwether Lewis* biography, it would not be worth writing. I had already spent four years tracking clues and facts on Lewis's long-standing physical illness, but finding additional new information felt like a daunting task.

I thought of Mahlon Dickerson, a close friend of Lewis's. Perhaps there was more about him that historian Donald Jackson had failed to uncover. However, the Dickerson Papers were in New Jersey and I guessed that a lot of money would be spent for a small return. I considered other friends of Lewis and his brother Reuben. I thought of many individuals, but most did not have a known "collection of papers," and the rest did not write about Lewis.

About the time that I started to worry about uncovering some truly new material that would reveal the personal side of Lewis, a faint thought persistently reminded me of a Frederick Bates letter. Bates had been the territorial secretary of the Louisiana Territory and Lewis's archenemy.[1] A month after Lewis's death, Bates had written to his brother, scoffing at Lewis because "he had been spoiled by the elegant praises of Mitchell & Barlow."[2] While familiar with Joel Barlow's ode to the Lewis and Clark Expedition, I had no idea of Lewis's connection to Mitchill.[3]

Years earlier, I had found a couple of letters praising James MacKay's explorations for the Spanish.[4] Those letters were printed in the *Medical Repository*, the leading scientific journal founded and edited by Samuel Latham Mitchill.[5] The more I dug, the more I found, and in October 2004, I made a trip to the Museum of the City of New York to examine the Samuel Latham Mitchill collection.[6]

I made a chronological wish list of his letters because, in the event that it would be difficult to read his handwriting, I had to prioritize what I thought were the most important years.[7] Within moments of putting on the white gloves and opening the December 1806 case, I learned that his handwriting, thankfully, was readable.

It was well-known that Lewis arrived in Washington, DC, after the completion of his western exploration, late in the day of December 28, 1806, so I started reading the letters beginning a few days before.[8] Initially, they offered no mention of Lewis, but the Mitchill letter dated December 30 revealed exciting news:

> Capt. Lewis has reached this place after the performance of a journey across the Continent of North America, quite across to the Pacific Ocean, and back again. The distance is computed to be considerably more than three thousand miles across. He and his party went away from Washington in the Summer of 1803, and . . . got no farther than Kahokia on the Mississippi, and wintered there. The ensuing spring, he reached Mandane, near the great Bend of the Missouri and passed the cold season at that place (1804–5). Thence he proceeded westward, and crossing the Northern Andes . . . travelled before the Vigorous Weather set in, as far as the Ocean, near the mouth of the Columbia River. Here he remained during the inclement part of 1805–6; and as soon as the spring was far enough advanced . . . he started for home. And here, he is . . . in good health & spirits. I feel rejoiced on his own account; an account of Geography & Natural History; and on account of the Character and Honour of Country that this expedition has been successfully performed.[9]

Mitchill must have been near or in the presidential mansion when Lewis arrived, for this letter was three pages long and filled with details of the expedition and other interesting events going on in Washington for the holiday festivities. Mitchill biographer Alan D. Aberbach described President Jefferson and Dr. Mitchill as having the curiosity of little children and said they "listened for hours as Lewis reported on his tale of hardship and success."[10]

Mitchill had become a member of the legislature of New York in 1790 and was elected to the US House of Representatives in 1801. He became a senator in November 1804 and remained in that capacity until 1813, when he decided to return to New York and attend to scientific pursuits.[11] His first observation of Thomas Jefferson occurred about a month after Mitchill's initial arrival in Washington:

> He is tall in stature and rather spare in flesh. His dress and manners are very plain; he is grave, or rather sedate, but without any tincture of pomp, ostentation, or pride, and occasionally can smile, and both hear and relate humorous stories as well as any other man of social feelings. At this moment he has a rather more than ordinary press of care and solicitude, because Congress is in session and he is anxious to know in what manner the Representatives will act upon his Message.[12]

For the twelve years that he resided in Washington, Mitchill wrote almost daily to his wife. She visited him infrequently—with two daughters it was difficult to make the trip from New York to the nation's capital.[13] In March 1806, she made a trip to Washington and had an awkward encounter with President Thomas Jefferson. At the conclusion of a church service in the House of Representatives, she accidentally stepped on his toes and was "so prodigiously frighten'd," she told her sister, "that I could not stop to make an apology, but got out of the way as quick as I could."[14] Catherine's letters to her sister also described the latest news. In August 1807, she wrote that her husband, "Sam," had accompanied Robert Fulton on the maiden voyage of his steamboat in New York harbor. "An ingenious piece of workmanship," Catherine remarked. She was surprised how fast the steamboat moved through the water "with the tide against her."[15]

Catherine lived in a wondrous and fortunate time and enjoyed the additional benefit of being married to man with a consuming hunger for knowledge. A witty friend once stated, "Tap the doctor at any time, he will flow."[16] The House of Representatives referred to him as the "Stalking Library," Thomas Jefferson called him the "Congressional Dictionary," and to his admirers he was known as the "Nestor of American Science."[17]

He first encountered Lewis when he was the "Master of Ceremonies" at an assembly on December 21, 1801, and formally met him at a dinner at the presidential mansion in January of 1802. Jefferson had "generally a company of eight or ten to dine with him every day. The dinners are neat and plentiful, and no healths are drunk at table nor any toasts or sentiments given after dinner." At this first dinner, seven were invited, and the "[p]resident and his secretary, Captain Lewis, completed the party."[18] By April 29, Mitchill had become a select member of the dinner party of regulars. Afterward, Mitchill said that he accompanied Lewis into the "[p]resident's Council Chamber," and "saw two . . . Busts of Indian Hatuary, lately found near the Mississippi. I did not know until I saw these that sculpture had advanced so far among the Native red-men of North America."[19]

Mitchill wrote some of the most interesting descriptions of Lewis later, and he never lost an opportunity to write a review in the *Medical Repository* regarding Lewis and Clark's accomplishments.[20]

Legislative historians have struggled for years to understand why there were no written records of the inauguration of what today is called the Lewis and Clark Expedition. All that exists in the congressional files is mention that Jefferson delivered a secret message to Congress on January 18, 1803, and Congress approved a ten- to twelve-man expedition on February 26, 1803.[21] Discovery of Mitchill's letter to his wife dated January 31, 1803, finally enhanced those records. He began with:

> My Dear Kate: I write you from a secret conclave of Congress . . . the House of Representatives is now setting with closed doors. The Galleries were cleared a little while ago to receive a confidential communication. After receiving it, a Debate arose whether it ought to be considered as a secret any longer or whether the Injunction of Secrecy should be taken off. And that discussion is now going on. So I thought I would write you, my dear, a few lines to let you know . . . something about this Political Secret, was I not restrained by my own decision because I have just set down after making a Speech against taking off the Injunction of Secrecy. You must however not imagine any thing about it, nor pretend to suppose that a secret expedition is meditated up the river Missouri to its source, thence across the Northern Andes and down the Western water-courses to the Pacific Ocean, and that the reason of keeping it secret is that the English and Spaniards may not find it out and frustrate it.[22]

Mitchill had sworn to secrecy, probably on a stack of Bibles, but could not help himself and told his wife anyway! What a treasure for the Lewis and Clark archives. On January 11, 1807, Mitchill dined alone with Lewis and wrote to his wife:

> During the expedition, communications . . . and productions of the country were . . . forwarded to the President. Where that mode of intercourse was not possible, the articles collected were . . . brought home by the adventurers in person. They achieved so much, that I told Lewis . . . shortly after his return to Washington, when he dined with me, I looked upon him . . . as a man arrived from another planet.[23]

Five days later Mitchill sent Catherine an elaborate letter. A short excerpt follows:

A few evenings ago, I went to the Presidents House to see the specimens of Natural History brought by Capt. Lewis from Louisiana, and his Map of the regions he has visited between the Mississippi and the Pacific. He has several non-descript animals. . . . He has brought with him the seeds of many plants; and shewed me several presses . . . in fine preservation. These make an instructive herbarium of the Regions to which he passed. . . . But his Map of those parts of North America is the most instructive of his bounties. . . . The distance from the Source of the Missouri to its junction with the Gulf of Mexico is computed to be more than 4000 miles and it runs the greater part of this distance without a Cataract.[24]

On February 18, 1807, Mitchill met William Clark at one of Jefferson's dinners.

After the adjournment, I went to dine with Mr. Jefferson. There I found Capt. Clarke the traveller to the Pacific Ocean. He is a fine-looking soldierly man, and very conversant with the North American Indians. My seat at the table was between the President and him. So of course I could converse, by turns, with each. I improved the opportunity to inquire of Capt. C. concerning the manners and Customs of the native tribes he had visited on the Missouri.[25]

It is almost indescribable how the Samuel Latham Mitchill papers have augmented and expanded the record of Lewis and Clark's "bounties." They originated with one man who was easily Thomas Jefferson's scientific equal and who excitedly shared them with the scientific and geographical community. Descriptive letter writing is a disappearing art. Some corners of the past remain dark and unknown for lack of such letters, while others are illuminated and brought to life because of a single dedicated correspondent. Some faithful letter writers, such as Mitchill, are located in important places at crucial times in history and record exciting facts and observations mixed in with the more mundane descriptions of family life and personal incidents.

Chapter 7

OBSERVATIONS AND REMARKS FROM LEWIS TO DEARBORN IN 1807: AN UNKNOWN LETTER REVEALS AN *IN ABSENTIA* GOVERNOR IN CONTROL*

One of the exciting things about conducting historical research is that on almost any topic one chooses to investigate there is always the possibility of the discovery of new information. This information can take many forms. It might lie in associated or even previously unrelated manuscripts or records that make reference to the same events or individuals one is studying. Even more exciting is the occasional discovery of a previously unknown, misplaced, or overlooked manuscript relating directly to the subject matter of the historian's investigation. During the many years of exhaustive research needed to prepare for my recent biography of Meriwether Lewis, I ran across many such pieces of information. One would think, after two hundred years and the close scrutiny of so many authors, researchers, and historians, that the bones of the Lewis and Clark story's skeleton would be picked pretty clean. However, this is not the case, and there may be even more material still buried in voluminous archives, libraries, and attics yet to be discovered.

The subject of this chapter, in fact, is a letter that was hidden in plain sight within one of the best-known collections in the world—the National Archives in Washington, DC. One of the essential sources for the Lewis biography was the examination of surviving military records of the period. Short of purchasing all of the microfilm necessary for a thorough look at these records, I decided in November 1998 to visit the National Archives, Central Plains Region Branch, in Kansas City, Missouri, which had a complete set. After two days of examination (punctuated by giving up my seat every half hour to genealogists), I photocopied about three hundred pages, but after returning home and reading through the material, I found that I had not secured all that I needed. I realized then that it was foolhardy to waste so much time driving across the state of Missouri, staying in a hotel, using timed microfilm readers, and then paying for photocopies.

From the letters that I read in several reference works, like the *Territorial Papers*, I realized that a serious study of Lewis warranted the purchase of the necessary microfilm, both for initial research and for later reference. The National Archives published a microfilm resource catalog, which was helpful in determining what to buy.[1] The guide did not indicate specific locations of any individual Lewis letters— it was just a microfilm guide of the governmental record groups listed by year.

Clarence Carter, editor of the *Territorial Papers*, cited numerous documents in the National Archives as references, so it appeared that his footnotes could be followed on the microfilm rolls; however, it was not that easy. While the documents were located on the microfilm, more often than not, they were out of sequence by date. That meant that instead of using the fast forward or reverse button on the microfilm reader to speed through the process, I would have to turn the microfilm roll by hand and painstakingly look at each frame. At first I was annoyed at the glacial pace of this type of investigation, but when I began to discover new or at least unheralded documents, my mood began to change. In the very first batch of microfilm that I received, I found an 1808 letter from Denis Fitzhugh to James Madison, forwarding a bill of exchange from Lewis for $500, which had been allocated for Joseph Charless's printing press in Saint Louis.[2]

By 2004, I had amassed an extensive library of National Archives microfilm. I had also implemented a new personal standard for advancing a microfilm roll—with my index finger, frame by frame. As each day passed and I continued to discover a cornucopia of new information, I grew increasingly anxious about how I was going to be able to remember, much less find, where all the facts were stored—in notebooks, photocopies, and other primary and secondary sources. The scale of the research was becoming enormous.

The old stand-by index card method, or the newer method of placing categorized notes in a word processing file, were both unsatisfactory. As I was lamenting to a friend the way in which I was slowly becoming immobilized and overwhelmed by huge amounts of information, she suggested a novel method—to use a spreadsheet to create a database completely searchable by columns. It took nine months to enter the microfilm information into eight columns of data, which eventually totaled 3,600 entries. Despite the enormous amount of time and effort it took to create it, I found this database to be highly efficient when trying to locate tiny pieces of strategic information or just helpful in following the history of a given topic. Additionally, the database made it easy to copy the exacting endnotes that are the foundation of this chapter, the Lewis biography, and the rest of this book.[3]

Carter incorrectly cited some important letters and other historians copied his mistakes, so inspecting the microfilm became a mandatory exercise that eventually led to the discovery of the Lewis letter featured in this chapter.[4] On February 18, 2003, I had received two rolls of National Archives microfilm from the M222 series. The descriptive pamphlet for this microfilm stated, "On the 34 rolls of this microfilm . . . are reproduced letters, with their enclosures, that were received by the Secretary of War . . . but, for one reason or another, not registered." The pamphlet writer continued, "The letters are arranged by year and thereunder alphabetically—most by the initial letter of the surname of the officer, but a few by the initial letter of the subject."[5]

Placing roll 2 on the spindle, I began to advance it slowly.[6] Categories from A to K held nothing of importance for the biography, but at frame 0555-58 under the letter "L," there was a listing for "Expenditures in Capt. M. Lewis Expedition to April 1805." At frame 0571, a Capt. Bruff wrote Gen. James Wilkinson that he had succumbed to the ague (malaria) and could not report for some time. At frame 0657, Lewis addressed Henry Dearborn, the secretary of war, in a letter dated October 1806 at Saint Louis, apologizing for signing a large number of drafts. This section of the microfilm details much business concerning expedition members and some supplies.[7]

The following day I reached frame 0772. William Clark had written on May 9, 1807, about his participation in a treaty and council with the Yankton and Teton nations. At frame 0974 Rodolphe Tillier, the factor at Bellefontaine, wrote that illicit traders were telling various Indian nations that Spain would regain Louisiana and expel the Americans.

Reaching the end of the reel, I started to rewind the film by hand. At frame 0952 I noticed something peculiar under the "S" category, which stood for "secretary of war." The letters were from officers in the field detailing expenditures or asking for monetary relief. One letter did not have a date. I continued backing up the reel, but stopped and thought to myself, *that letter looks like Lewis's handwriting.* When I returned to the frame, I was surprised. It was indeed a letter from Lewis, and one that I had never before seen.

[page 1] Observations and remarks of M. Lewis on the several subjects embraced By the inclosed communications which were referred to him by the Secretary at War.— I think it would be well in answer to Genl. Clark's letters of the 18th of May and 1st of June—to instruct him to contract for the runing gear and stones of a horse-mill to be prepared in Kentucky, transported to St. Louis and delivered to Mr. P. Chouteau for the use of the Osage nation—also to engage a discrete Blacksmith to reside at the

Osage Village for the purpose of reparing their arms and impliments of husbandry, provided such promises has been made them by our government.—

This smith should be engaged for the term at least of two years, and to be held risposible for his conduct to the Superintendent of Indian affairs as the Agent for that nation—stipulate with him that he sall be furnished with a set of tools, have a Cabbin and shop built for his accomodation and allowed   dollars per year as his wages (with this perquisite of certain stipulated prices which being agreed on he may have a right to exact from the Indians individually for the services he may render them either [page 2] the compensation from the Indians to be received by him in peltries or fur at their option and at the rate of $1.25 per lb. for beaver $2— for a buck and $1 for a doe skin.—it might be well to instruct Genl. Clark to settle with and pay Mr. P. Dorion the amount of his wages and the accounts of expenditures he has transmitted, and to confine the future expenditures of Mr. Dorion to such objects and to such amounts only as he, Genl. Clark shall think absolutely necessary to the public service—Mr. Dorion having been ordered to reside among the Tetons is worthy of approbation, as is also the course Genl. C. has taken with rispect to the deputation from the Yanktons & Tetons—.

I think it would be well to instruct Genl. Clark to take measures for the recovery of the Osage prisoners, should your letter reach him previous to his leaving St. Louis and if otherwise to inform him of your having in such case confided that duty to Mr. Bates—it might not be amiss to suffer Genl. Clark to engage the blacksmith of whom he speaks for the service of the Saucs and Foxes, provided he can be obtained on moderate terms.—

[page 3] In answer to Mr. Bates's letter of the 15th of May, it would be well to inform him that Govr. Harrison had been instructed to make every exertion to recover the Osage prisoners in his territory, and request of Mr. Bates, in the event of Genl. Clark not being at St. Louis, to use his exertion for the same purpose among the Indians of Louisiana—inform him also that Genl. Clark had been instructed to contract (furnish) for the Horsemill which had been provided the Osage—on the subject of the Horse-mill and Blacksmith that have been promised the Osages.—

I think it would also be well to instruct Mr. Chouteau to make compensation to the Osage for the horses which were purchased from them by Lieut. Pike and Wilkinson—to inform him of the measures taken in order with a view to provide the Horse-mill and Smith for the Osages and request him to communicate this information to that nation in order to satisfy them for the present—inform him of the measures taken relative to the Osage prisoners, and request that also to be communicated to them.

[page 4] It will be necessary to write to Govr. Harrison fully on the subject of the Osage prisoners. I am convinced that it is much more in his power to obtain them than any other . . . officer in that quarter, as it becomes more immediately his duty as those prisoners are among the nations in his territory—as a matter of general policy it appears to me that it would be well to mention to Mr. Bates, Genl.

Clark and Govr. Harrison on the subject of recovering these prisoners, that nothing should be given to the individuals preparing them for their delivery, and that it would be better to give double the amount to the chiefs of some of their more powerfull neighbours to compel their delivery than to redeem them by purchase from their owners.

—M. Lewis

The first page of a recently discovered letter written by Meriwether Lewis to Henry Dearborn, secretary of war, July 1807, making various "observations and remarks" regarding Louisiana territorial affairs. (Meriwether Lewis to Henry Dearborn, July 2007, S1807, RG107, M222, roll 2, frame 0952, National Archives and Records Administration.)

Titled "Observations and Remarks," Lewis's letter was written at the end of July 1807 to Henry Dearborn, who was not in Washington at the time.[8] Lewis's letter consisted of a lengthy answer to many questions on Indian relations and Indian trade posed by Dearborn in referencing two letters from William Clark (dated May 18 and June 1, which were received at the War Department on June 29 and July 7) and a letter from Frederick Bates, the acting governor (dated May 15 and received on June 29).[9] Dearborn either forwarded the original letters to Lewis along with his own queries, or had the Clark and Bates letters transcribed and enclosed so that Lewis could read them. In reading all of these letters it must be borne in mind that Lewis was at the time the governor of the Louisiana Territory, even though he had not as yet returned to Saint Louis to take up these duties full time.[10]

We know from other sources that at the time that Lewis answered the Dearborn letter, he had recently traveled from Philadelphia to Washington. Lewis departed Philadelphia on July 21 and arrived in Washington a few days before a meeting with William Simmons, the accountant of the War Department.[11] We do not know if Lewis took a night coach, which would have taken two days from Philadelphia, or rode a horse, which would have taken four more days to reach Washington.[12]

Interestingly, Lewis was not idle in Philadelphia from the time of his arrival on April 14 until his departure three months later, as some historians have claimed. Lewis employed individuals to draw botanical illustrations and scenery for the publication of the journals, met with publishers and printers, paid newspapers to run his ad for the journals, began editing the journals, and prepared additional material for another volume. He also attended three meetings at the American Philosophical Society, having become a member in November 1803.[13]

In light of this new letter, I believe that he also was writing his treatise on the business of Indian trade in the Louisiana Territory titled "Observations and Reflections," which when complete numbered twenty typed pages. Donald Jackson, editor of *Letters of the Lewis and Clark Expedition*, contended that Lewis wrote the greater part of this treatise before he departed Washington in August 1807. This letter proves that Jackson was correct.[14]

The letter itself is clearly thought out, pragmatic, lucid in its detail, and refers to specific topics that involved William Clark, Pierre Chouteau, and the Indian agency. Clark's letters of May 18 and June 1, to which Lewis was responding, brimmed with territorial business.[15] Foremost on Clark's agenda were the frequent visits of various Indian nations and how to deal with them. Since Spanish colonial times, Indian tribes had arrived in Saint Louis asking for gifts of food, clothing, and shelter. Nothing in this respect had changed, although Jefferson had conveyed to Lewis, when on the expedition, that he should invite as many tribes to Washington as he saw fit. Soon the news of the Indian delegations led by Pierre Chouteau, Amos Stoddard, and others made its way back to the Louisiana Territory, and the leaders of Indian nations heard that the "Great White Father," in Washington was generous indeed.[16] This prompted a huge influx of Osage Indians into the town of Saint Louis. Clark's May 18, 1807, letter stated that "[t]he Great Chief and about 120 Osarge [sic] Warriors left this place three days ago; they were here for some time."[17]

Clark's letter opened by stating that he had made arrangements since his arrival in Saint Louis "to send the Mandan chief to his Town in Safty." Dearborn had instructed him to use no more than sixteen soldiers because there were few remaining in Saint Louis, and barring that, Clark could entice traders going up the Missouri River with exclusive licenses. This is exactly the strategy that Lewis employed a year later.[18] Under this arrangement, Clark obtained an additional escort from a private trading outfit and also a returning delegation of Sioux Indians. Clark feared that the Arikara might prove hostile to the group and felt that the larger party, about 101 adults, would help to deter them. Two other large companies of traders and trappers set out from Saint Louis on May 1, intending to trap in the Rocky Mountain area for a period of two to three years. A smaller outfit also departed Saint Louis in March; historian John C. Jackson believes that it was led by John B. Thompson, who was bringing supplies upriver to John Colter. Thompson and Colter were members of the Lewis and Clark Expedition.

Clark also spoke in detail in his letters about various Osage complaints, the most prominent being that they had been promised that a mill would be built at their village and that a blacksmith would reside with them. These complaints were not to be taken lightly, as the Osage were the most powerful tribe on the lower Missouri River and a potential American ally. The tribal leaders also complained that James Wilkinson, son of Gen. James Wilkinson, took seven horses and promised to pay for them, which had not been done.[19] Indian nations from the eastern side of the Mississippi had taken some Osage prisoners and had returned only a few.

Clark informed Dearborn that a Sauk had murdered a Frenchman at the mouth of the Missouri. He had dispatched Nicholas Boilvin to the Sauk nation to demand that the chiefs deliver the murderer. To the west the Spaniards had assembled an Indian conference and informed the nations that the Americans were untrustworthy. From the north came word that the British had formed a new trading company with Montreal traders to encompass the entire fur commerce of the region. Clark believed that the new company could injure the trade that the United States was trying to establish. The furs and peltries would fall into the hands of the British and various Indian nations and local Creole merchants would be deprived of the means of supporting their families.

Pierre Dorion, an Indian subagent, showed up in Saint Louis with a large band of Sioux who had been invited to visit the president in Washington. Clark had no instructions on the subject of these sudden appearances of Indian tribes and wanted Dearborn to enact some policy to guide him in the future. Clark did not want to reject the Indian tribes because their friendship was important to the stability of the region. He decided to give them about $1,500 worth of presents, which would "give their bands an exolted opinion of the Paternal affection of the President to all the Nativs who seek his protection."[20] Dorion had not been paid since Gen. Wilkinson appointed him to his official position in 1805 and demanded that Clark pay him. While Clark refused, he felt the necessity of giving the Sioux the presents. Having resided with the Sioux for close to thirty years, however, Dorion's influence in keeping the Sioux at peace was paramount. Clark asked Dearborn for additional money so that he could pay Dorion. Clark closed the letter by stating that the militia of the territory, as well as their arms and ammunition, were deficient.[21]

Clark also sent Dearborn a letter dated June 1, 1807, which was almost a repetition of the May 18 letter. Boilvin had returned from the Sauk nation without the murderer but was promised him in due time. A Mr. Ewing, who had been sent to the Sauks in May 1804 to teach them farming, had been recalled, and it was Clark's job to inform him. The Sauks also wanted a blacksmith, and a Saint Louis farmer had offered his services.

Bates's letter of May 15 did not add any new information, but one can discern that he did not want to become involved in the Indian business.[22] While that was his intention three months into his tenure as territorial secretary, he also believed in free trade for American citizens. When Clark departed Saint Louis in August 1807, Bates began issuing licenses to trade without restriction.[23]

In response to Clark's letters concerning the Indian business, Lewis was on point. He laid out detailed answers and told Dearborn what should be done. His answers regarding Dorion, the blacksmiths, Governor Harrison, and Bates's role after Clark's departure show that Lewis was in command of the Indian business. On August 18, 1807, Henry Dearborn copied Lewis's words almost verbatim to Clark and Bates, reminding us that Lewis was held in great esteem even at the highest levels of government.[24]

This newly identified Lewis letter affords us a glimpse of the man during a period in mid-1807 from which we have little surviving written evidence. This lack of information has caused some rather wild speculation by some biographers, imagining Lewis reveling in a life of at most debauchery, or at least indolence, during a period when he was expected to travel to Saint Louis to take up his duties as territorial governor. The letter shows Lewis exercising his duties as governor *in absentia*, answering crucial questions regarding the territory and the future of the United States on the frontier that could not be addressed by Clark, Bates, or Dearborn. The letter presents a picture of a clearheaded administrator delayed in the east by duties other than those of his post, but one who would be quite ready to assume those duties upon his arrival in Saint Louis.

There may be other letters still out there, undiscovered or unrecognized, that will provide more insight into the Lewis and Clark story. Just as we should go through microfilm frame by frame, the discovery of these letters, if they exist, will also be a slow and painstaking process, but a highly rewarding one for scholars and enthusiasts.

Chapter 8

MERIWETHER LEWIS'S LAND WARRANT: AN UNTIMELY REWARD*

Looking back in time, we often are able to identify the mistakes of our predecessors. When the Corps of Discovery returned from its epic journey, Congress bestowed upon each member a tract of land in the Louisiana Territory. Although a seemingly benevolent and well-deserved gift, it was impossible for any member of the corps to benefit from this land gratuity because very little of the Louisiana Purchase had been surveyed and none of the acreage had been platted on a map to differentiate private from public land.

On January 2, 1807, a congressional committee convened to assess the compensation for Meriwether Lewis and William Clark and "their brave companions for their late service in exploring the western waters."[1] Willis Alston, chairman of the committee, asked Secretary of War Henry Dearborn for a roster of the men, which Lewis provided on January 15. Dearborn proposed double pay for each member of the Corps of Discovery, a grant of 320 acres to each of the thirty-one enlisted members, 1,000 acres to Lt. Clark, 1,500 acres to Capt. Lewis, "and that each one should have permission to locate his grant on any lands that have been surveyed, and are now for sale."[2] Lewis was emphatic that no distinction of rank be made between he and Clark, preferring "an equal division of whatever quantity might be granted to them."[3]

The House deliberated on the bill for several weeks, and on February 20, a heated discussion followed:

The bill grants land warrants, which may be either located or received at the land offices in payment of debts due there, at the rate of two dollars an acre. The bill grants these persons 24,960 acres. A motion was made . . . to strike out so much as permits the receipt of these warrants at the land offices in payment of debts. . . . It was contended that double pay was a liberal compensation, and that this grant was extravagant and beyond all former precedent. It was equivalent to taking more than $60,000 out of the Treasury, and might be perhaps three or four times that sum, as the grantees might go over all the Western country and locate their warrants on the best land, in 160 acre lots.[4]

The House of Representatives recommitted the bill eight days later and sent it to the Senate, where it was revised and approved on March 3. Lewis and Clark each were granted 1,600 acres, the enlisted men were given 320 acres each, and the grants could be located only on the public lands west of the Mississippi. Double pay was authorized for all.[5] The grant came in the form of a certificate known as a land warrant, which was an authorization to receive a quantity of public land at an unspecified location. The actual selection of a tract of land lay more than a decade in the future.

At the time of the reward, public land on the east side of the Mississippi sold for two dollars an acre, while on the west side of the river, public land essentially was worthless. This was because public land had not been surveyed, and until boundaries separated the public from the private land, the public land could not be sold. The first appointment of a US surveyor in the Louisiana Territory occurred in July 1806, but the business of surveying the territory languished until 1816 due to insufficient manpower and Native American hostilities.[6]

Corps of Discovery members who remained in or returned to Saint Louis after the expedition could do nothing with their 320-acre warrants. In November 1808, Territorial Secretary Frederick Bates bought land warrants for about $300 each from seven members of the expedition: John Collins, George Drouillard, Patrick Gass, Hugh McNeal, John B. Thompson, Joseph Whitehouse, and Alexander Willard. Bates ran an ad in the *Missouri Gazette* at the end of March 1809 to sell two warrants and in August, attorney William Carr exchanged a slave for one warrant and was delighted with the deal.[7]

That same month, Lewis and Clark were forced to sell their land warrants. In March 1809, Clark paid for two shares in the Missouri Fur Company and Lewis advanced payments to take Mandan chief Sheheke-shote home. Three months later, the War Department sent letters with refusals to pay Clark's expenses related to the Indian agency and Lewis's for Indian presents. That left Lewis and Clark in a fiscally tight and embarrassing situation, and they turned to their land warrants to bridge this economic shortfall. Lewis decided to tender the warrants at the land office in New Orleans and that may have been the initial reason why he intended to travel there.[8]

Lewis left Saint Louis on September 4, 1809, and arrived at Fort Pickering terribly ill eleven days later. As Lewis recovered over the course of nearly two weeks, he switched plans and decided to travel on horseback to Washington. On September 17, Lewis wrote about the warrant in his account book:

> Then enclosed my warrant for 1600 acres to Bomby Robertson of New Orleans to be disposed . . . for two dollars per acre or more if it can be obtained and the money . . . deposited in the branch bank of New Orleans or the City of Washington subject to my order or that of William D. Meriwether for the benefit of my creditors.[9]

Capt. Gilbert Russell, the commander at Fort Pickering, stated that at Lewis's request, he sent Lewis's land warrant to Thomas Bolling Robertson, secretary of the Orleans Territory and a land commissioner. Lewis hoped that Robertson would be able to sell the warrant, but it was returned due to insufficient cash.[10]

Lewis's warrant remained with his mother for a dozen years. Members of the expedition who did not settle in the Louisiana Territory, but rather resided in adjacent territories in Alabama and Mississippi, were able to assign and redeem land for their warrants.[11]

In 1821, the Lewis family hired a Richard Searcy as its agent to facilitate selling the warrant, but he ran into many obstacles. In 1826, Searcy explained the difficulty to the commissioner of the General Land Office:

> I have heretofore informed you that I was the holder of the warrant to the late Governor M. Lewis for his western tour. . . . This warrant was placed in my hand for the purpose of being sold . . . which I have been endeavoring to do for the last five years, but owing to the inconvenient size of the warrant and other causes I have yet been unable to make any disposition of it. Besides the refusal of the Commissioner of the General Land Office to issue certificates in smaller amounts which would have facilitated its sale the land officers here have been reluctant at having any thing to do with the claim . . . the receiver of Public Monies at Little Rock refused to receive it at more than $1.25 an acre . . . notwithstanding the letter of your predecessor . . . directing it to be received at $2.00 an acre. From the above causes the representatives of Govr. Lewis have already suffered considerable loss by being so long kept out of the value of the warrant. The claim has repeatedly been offered for sale at from 10 to 20 percent discount and more. . . . This warrant was granted to a meritorious officer for valuable services rendered to his country.[12]

20th CONGRESS,
1st Session.

H. R. 282.

APRIL 28, 1828.

Read twice, and ordered to be engrossed, and read the third time to-morrow.

Mr. Isacks, from the Committee on the Public Lands, reported the following bill:

A BILL

For the relief of the legal representatives of Meriwether Lewis.

1   *Be it enacted by the Senate and House of Representatives*

2   *of the United States of America in Congress assembled,* That

3   the act, approved the third of March, one thousand eight

4   hundred and seven, entitled "An act making compensation

5   to Messrs. Lewis and Clarke, and their companions," be, and

6   the same is hereby, so extended, as to allow to the legal repre-

7   sentatives of Meriwether Lewis, deceased, the right of enter-

8   ing any of the public lands of the United States, subject to

9   entry at private sale, to the amount of the residue of the war-

10   rant of sixteen hundred acres, issued to said Lewis, by virtue

11   of said act, which has not heretofore been satisfied; or of

12   applying the same in payment for any such public lands, in

13   the same manner, and at the same rate, prescribed by said act.

Almost twenty years after his death, Meriwether Lewis's family had to obtain congressional approval in 1828 in order to tender his 1,600 acre land warrant. It was awarded to the explorer in March 1807 for his discoveries on the expedition, but owing to the "inconvenient size of the warrant," it was impossible to sell. (House of Representatives, 20th Cong., 1st sess., A Bill for the Relief of the Legal Representatives of Meriwether Lewis, House Resolution 282.)

Searcy received no satisfaction. The following year, the Lewis family pressed Congress to intervene, and on April 28, 1828, the Committee on Public Lands reported a bill "for the relief of the legal representatives of Meriwether Lewis," which asked that Congress allow Lewis's legal representatives

> the right of entering any of the public lands of the United States, subject to entry
> at private sale, to the amount of the residue of the warrant of sixteen hundred acres
> . . . which has not heretofore been satisfied.[13]

Congress finally approved the bill on May 26, 1828.

Lewis eventually was reimbursed for his public service, and his family enjoyed a fleeting glory. It is tragic that he never shared in the realization of 1,600 acres of the immense wilderness that he explored and set on the way to development.

Chapter 9

WAS GOVERNOR LEWIS'S CORRESPONDENCE INTENTIONALLY DELAYED?

I n an age where computers and cell phones carry instantaneous messages around the world and overnight shipments of letters, parcels, and goods is fairly cheap and commonplace, it is difficult to imagine a time when correspondence between some of the major cities of the United States took months rather than seconds. Even the vital correspondence of a frontier governor like Meriwether Lewis was subject to the same difficulties of transport as the mail for any person living in the mid-Mississippi River Valley. The following information is centered on proving that some of Lewis's mail, specifically correspondence that included monetary instruments, appears to have been intentionally delayed and perhaps tampered with. While the identities of certain individuals who had access to the mail is known, modern historical detective work has yet to uncover the culprit or culprits, leaving this a fascinating story that, at least for the time being, has no real conclusion.

When Saint Louisans sent correspondence to officials in Washington, DC, the mail took about thirty-eight days to reach the capital. Surprisingly, when Governor Lewis included monetary instruments in his correspondence, like a draft or a bill of exchange, delivery took more than twice that time. Drafts and bills of exchange were two different monetary instruments during Lewis's time, while today the terms have the same meaning. What they knew as a "draft" appeared to have ready value and was used much like a check today, but in Saint Louis, where specie money was scarce, the value was exchanged in goods. A "bill of exchange" only had ready value after it was sent to the government for approval and reimbursement.

In order to explore the mystery of Lewis's delayed mail, it will first be essential to understand how the mail was collected and transported in the early nineteenth century. There were two collection points on the west side of the Mississippi, one at Saint Louis and the other at Fort Bellefontaine eighteen miles to the north. The mail from the fort was carried to Saint Louis, then taken by boat across the Mississippi and deposited with the Cahokia postmaster in the then-Indiana Territory (today's State of Illinois). From Cahokia, post riders formally carried the mail over the post roads to Washington. The use of the term "road" is a loose one, as many of these routes were merely glorified paths. No system of highway maintenance or construction was yet in place west of the Appalachians, and road maintenance in western Virginia and Maryland was rudimentary at best. Arduous routes included river crossings, many without bridges or ferries, and passage through the mountains. In 1804, delivery time from Saint Louis to Washington, DC, averaged about a month, yet was dependent on weather conditions. Winter in the wilderness was hazardous and spring rains made traveling treacherous due to flooding. The opportune time for the regular delivery of mail occurred before the temperature dropped below freezing and after the spring rains.

Post riders carried the mail in special leather saddle-bags that were locked with keys that only postmasters possessed. Delaying a post rider or tampering with the mail was a Federal offense. Riders had to endure severe extremes of temperature and weather as they rode their routes, relaying the mail from one rider to the next between individual post offices as the mail slowly worked its way from one town to the next. These mail riders, although perhaps spiritual kin to the Pony Express riders of fifty years later, were unlike the Pony Express in that there was no time constraint or record to beat; they were only obligated to do their best to move the mail in a timely and efficient manner on to the next post office and one step closer to its ultimate destination.

Once the mail arrived at the capital, it was taken to a central government post office, where a clerk recorded it in a ledger, assigning each piece of mail a document number, alphabetically by surname of the sender, and numerically in the order of its receipt. For example, when one of Governor Lewis's letters arrived in Washington on September 8, 1809, it was given the document number L-328: L for Lewis and 328 for the 328th piece of mail with that surname letter designation that had arrived in that year.[1] The number was not sequential for each piece of mail received by the government for a calendar year, nor was it sequential for each piece of mail received from an individual sender, but instead was sequential for each piece of mail for a specific letter designation. The clerk then briefly described the contents of the letter and its point of origin. Before sending it to the proper department, the clerk then wrapped it in a cover sheet, on which he wrote the date, a thorough explanation of its contents, the number of the document, and when it was disbursed by the clerk to the proper official.[2]

Saint Louis, August 18th. 1809.

Meriwether Lewis, — relative to his transactions in public Office; — stating that he is on the point of departure for the Seat of Government. — suggests the expediency of continuing Mr. P. Chouteau as Agent to the Osages, — at least for some time to come, — and transmits Copy of his Bond & Receipt for certain public Property confided to him. —

L-328(4)

Recd. Septr. 8th. 1809.

Typical cover sheet for incoming correspondence, designated L-328. On August 18, 1809, Governor Lewis sent this letter from Saint Louis to William Simmons, the accountant of the War Department. This letter is regarded as the most pivotal piece of correspondence of Lewis's career because he had to defend his decisions as governor "relative to his transactions in public office." (Meriwether Lewis to William Simmons, August 18, 1809, L328, RG107, M221, roll 23, frame 8501, National Archives and Records Administration.)

Mail delivery increased dramatically with the transfer of the administration of the Louisiana Territory from France to the United States and the need for an increased number of Federal officials to govern this vast land. This process started six months before the transfer of the Louisiana Territory with the arrival of Capt. Amos Stoddard in Kaskaskia to begin his tenure as territorial commandant. The transfer of the territory occurred on March 10, 1804. In October of that year, the postmaster general appointed Rufus Easton, a lawyer from upstate New York, who had already arrived in Saint Louis, as Saint Louis postmaster.[3] From August 1803 to September 1804, the average time for official letters to reach Washington was thirty-nine days.

1803

sent	received	author	doc.#	days
Aug. 26	Sept. 20	Stoddard	S-20	24
Sept. 9	Oct. 14	Stoddard	S-96	28
Oct. 11	Nov. 20	Stoddard	S-106	39
Dec. 4	Jan. 3	Stoddard	S-115	30

1804

sent	received	author	doc.#	days	description
Jan. 10	Feb. 20	Stoddard	S-140	40	
March 17	May 1	Stoddard	S-149	45	
Apr. 2	May 18	Stoddard	S-186	40	
Apr. 4	May 15	M. Lewis	L-144	41	prior to the expedition
May 18	July 7	Easton		50	Saint Louis postmaster
May 25	June 26	Stoddard	S-172	32	
June 3	July 5	Stoddard	S-175	32	
June 16	July 28	Stoddard	S-189	43	
July 7	Aug. 25	Bruff	B-204	48	Saint Louis commandant
Sept. 9	Nov. 1	Stoddard	S-217	53	

In July 1805, when Gen. James Wilkinson arrived in the territory as governor, there were clashes with the habitants, immigrating Americans, expatriated Americans, and Saint Louis officials regarding territorial policy. It is reasonable to assume that these conflicts might contribute to a lengthening of the time for mail delivery to Washington, and yet they did not. On January 6, 1806, Gen. Wilkinson wrote five letters to the War Department, which arrived on February 20, and on January

7 and 8, he wrote two more, which also arrived on February 20, suggesting that mail went out once a week.[4] The average transit time for the recorded official territorial correspondence of 1806 to reach Washington was thirty-seven days, except for letters dated February 10 and August 15 by Pierre Chouteau, the Osage Indian agent, which took much longer.

1806

sent	received	author	doc. #	days	description
Jan. 6	Feb. 20	Wilkinson	W-15	45	
Jan. 6	Feb. 20	Wilkinson	W-16	45	
Jan. 6	Feb. 20	Wilkinson	W-18	45	
Jan. 6	Feb. 20	Wilkinson	W-19	45	
Jan. 6	Feb. 20	Wilkinson	W-20	45	
Jan. 7	Feb. 20	Wilkinson	W-14	44	
Jan. 8	Feb. 20	Wilkinson	W-17	43	
Feb. 10	May 24	Chouteau	C-105	103	draft, $2,486
Mar. 6	Apr. 12	Tillier	T-12	37	letter
Mar. 25	May 7	Ewing	E-39	43	draft for wages, agriculture teacher, $500
Mar. 28	Apr. 28	Wilkinson	W-63	31	letter
Apr. 24	May 24	Tillier	T-18	30	letter
May 12	June 20	Chouteau	C-119	39	letter
May 12	June 20	Chouteau	C-120	39	draft, $400
July 15	Aug. 9	Chouteau	C-143	24	letter
Aug. 15	Nov. 10	Chouteau	C-187	86	draft $50
Aug. 21	Sept. 19	Chouteau	C-157	28	draft, $189

The Lewis and Clark Expedition arrived at Fort Bellefontaine after their voyage of discovery on September 21, 1806, and two days later returned to Saint Louis. Capt. Lewis began discharging the men and also sent five letters to Washington with drafts ranging from $49 to $300. These letters took between thirty-five and forty-five days to reach Washington.

1806

sent	received	author	doc. #	days	description
Sept. 27	Nov. 1	Lewis	L-72	35	draft, $300
Sept. 27	Nov. 1	Lewis	L-73	35	draft, $49
Sept. 27	Nov. 3	Lewis	L-74	37	draft, $220
Sept. 27	Nov. 3	Lewis	L-75	37	draft, $300

sent	received	author	doc. #	days	description
Sept. 24	Nov. 8	Lewis	L-79	45	draft, $272
Oct. 10	Nov. 15	Clark	C-188	37	returned his commission
Dec. 2	Jan. 14, 1807	Browne	B-165	43	letter

In 1807, the delivery time of letters mailed between January 5 and March 23 averaged forty-three days, but when William Clark arrived in Saint Louis as Indian agent for the territory, he included a bill of exchange in his June 8 letter, which took five months to arrive in Washington.

1807

sent	received	author	doc. #	days	description
Jan. 5	Feb. 18	Hunt	H-180	44	letter
Jan. 10	Feb. 4	Stoddard	S-244	25	letter
Feb. 10	Apr. 2	Lucas	L-121	50	letter
Feb. 23	Apr. 10	Saugrain	S-285	45	letter
Mar. 10	Apr. 27	Tillier	T-82	47	letter
Mar. 23	May 7	Browne	B-217	45	letter
May 6	July 29	Bates		84	letter, secretary, Louisiana Territory
May 9	June 19	Hunt	H-234	41	letter, commander, Fort Bellefontaine
May 15	July 7	Bates	B-245	53	letter
May 17	June 29	Bates	B-246	43	letter
May 18	June 29	Clark	C-280	42	letter
May 23	July 4	Hunt	H-242	52	letter
May 25	July 4	Chouteau	C-283	50	letter
May 28	July 13	Tillier	T-91	46	letter
May 30	July 7	Bates	B-251	38	letter
June 1	July 4	Bates	B-250	33	letter
June 7	July 13	Chouteau	C-287	36	letter
June 8	Nov. 2	Clark	C-338	146	bill of exchange, $500[5]
June 16	July 22	Boilvin	B-256	36	letter, sub-Indian agent
June 22	Aug. 3	Clark	C-293	41	letter
July 10	Aug. 17	Hunt	H-260	38	letter
July 18	Aug. 26	Clark	C-312	39	bill of exchange, $200
Sept. 30	Nov. 9	Bates	B-304	40	draft, $300

When Clark departed Saint Louis at the end of July 1807 to wed Julia Hancock, the arrival time of the mail became regular once again.[6]

1807

sent	received	author	doc. #	days
Sept. 1	Oct. 9	Chouteau	C-324	39
Sept. 28	Oct. 30	Bates	B-297	32
Oct. 31	Nov. 27	Tillier	T-119	27
Nov. 7	Dec. 5	Hunt	H-317	28
Nov. 28	Dec. 30	Hunt	H-331	32
Dec. 10	Jan. 29, 1808	Tillier	T-135	50

Lewis arrived in Saint Louis on March 8, 1808, and the delivery of his mail lagged far behind mail sent by others, especially letters Lewis posted that included monetary instruments.[7] The letters dated April 15 and April 25 took eighty-one and ninety-eight days, respectively, to make the journey.

1808

sent	received	author	doc. #	days	description
Feb. 7	Mar. 23	Bates	B-405	46	
Feb. 12	Mar. 23	Chouteau	C-458	40	nine drafts, $1,104[8]
Mar. 31	May 5	Lewis	L-24	35	draft for Delauney, $300.55
Apr. 8	May 14	Kimball	K-9	36	letter
Apr. 15	July 5	Lewis	L67	81	L67-L70, four drafts[9]
Apr. 25	Aug. 1	Lewis	L-97	98	bill of exchange, $213[10]
Apr. 30	July 5	Kimball	K-20	66	letter
Apr. 30	July 12	Kimball	K-24	73	letter

Lewis had been in Saint Louis a little more than two months when the pattern of delayed delivery began to increase. Of the nine letters written by Lewis between May 12 and July 8, 1808, which included drafts, five took greater than fifty days between posting and delivery.

1808

sent	received	author	doc. #	days	description
May 12	Aug. 8	Lewis	L-102	88	draft, Sub-Agent Dorion, $184.96
May 15	Oct. 7	Lewis	L-341	145	draft, Pierre Chouteau, $440
May 20	July 12	Lewis	L-78	53	draft, James Reid, $266.63
May 28	June 20	Lewis		23	draft, Peter Provenchere, $18
May 28	July 1	Hunt	H-90	34	letter
June 1	July 1	Saugrain	S-153	30	letter
June 5	July 12	Bates		37	letter
June 16	July 8	Lewis	L-303	23	draft,
June 24	Aug. 1	Lewis	L-98	37	draft, Wilkinson & Price, $419.83
June 25	July 22	Clark	C-133	27	letter
June 26	Oct. 6	Lewis	L-339	102	draft, William Christy, $1,488
July 1	Aug. 8	Lewis	L-101	38	draft, no amount given
July 6	Sept. 5	Lewis	L-326	60	draft, Christy, $43.25
July 8	Aug. 16	Hunt	H-144	38	letter

Two letters with bills, one from Clark dated August 13, 1808, and the other from Lewis dated August 26, 1808, deviated from the regular pattern with transit times of 190 and 225 days, respectively. Delayed payments could easily strap the sender financially, since the sender was advancing payment to others using his own personal credit.

1808

sent	received	author	doc. #	days	description
July 16	Sept. 2	Lewis	L-121	47	letter
July 16	Sept. 2	Hunt	H-149	47	letter
July 30	Sept. 2	Hunt	H-151	33	letter
Aug. 13	Sept. 21	Lewis	L-125	38	draft for $271
Aug. 13	Feb. 20, 1809	Clark	C-411	190	bill of exchange, storekeepers, $350[11]

Aug. 15	Sept. 26	Clark	C-199	41	draft, Price & Wilkinson, $228.25
Aug. 18	Sept. 23	Clark	C-196	35	letter
Aug. 20	Oct. 7	Lewis	L-135	48	letter
Aug. 20	Sept. 23	Clark	C-197	33	letter
Aug. 26	Apr. 14, 1809	Lewis	L-264	225	draft, Andrew McFarlane, $156
Sept. 24	Feb. 28, 1809	Lewis		157	bill of exchange, John Rice Jones, $140

A disconnect between correspondence and payments affected them. Between October 6 and December 31, 1808, five Clark letters containing drafts or bills of exchange took an average of 105 days to reach Washington. Clark raised concerns over the issue in a letter to the secretary of war in November 1808 when he mentioned previously sent vouchers: "please to inform me if you have received the public vouchers which I sent from this place last August. The distance and uncertainty of the mail, created some anxiety on this subject."[12]

Three 1808 Lewis letters with vouchers in them took an average of 128 days for the journey. When Lewis's November 28 letter arrived in Washington, the contents were missing. It was a draft for $500 that was to be taken from the governor's salary.[13] That meant that Lewis had already allowed the payee to debit his account at a store. In this particular case, Lewis did not become aware of the missing contents for at least six months. The store sent in a voucher for payment, and the clerk in the accountant's office held the voucher waiting for Lewis's draft.

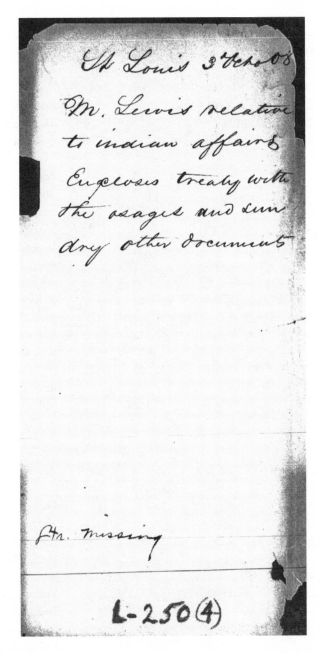

Dated October 3, 1808, and designated L-250, a War Department clerk noted that the letter from Governor Lewis was missing. (Meriwether Lewis to Henry Dearborn, October 3, 1808, L250, RG107, M221, roll 23, frame 8437, National Archives and Records Administration.)

1808

sent	received	author	doc. #	days	description
Oct. 3	Mar. 20, 1809	Lewis	L-250	143	draft, part of letter missing
Oct. 6	Dec. 2	Clark	C-290	61	draft, Tillier, $983
Oct. 7	Apr. 14, 1809	Lewis		189	draft, Wm. McFarlane
Oct. 12	May 15, 1809	Clark	C-515	208	draft, Lisa, $500
Oct. 17	Dec. 5, 1809	Clark	C-291	49	draft, Mason, $843.33
Oct. 18	Nov. 14	Clark	C-264	26	letter
Oct. 30	Nov. 28	Clark	C-284	28	letter
Nov. 10	Dec. 21	Clark		41	letter discussing vouchers from August
Nov. 17	Apr. 29, 1809	Clark	C-525	132	letter and draft
Nov. 18	Dec. 21	Clark	C-313	33	letter, transmitting vouchers
Nov. 28	Jan. 19, 1809	Lewis	L-199	52	contents missing, draft $500
Dec. 31	Mar. 16, 1809	Clark	C-1808	75	bill of exchange, $526

1809

sent	received	author	doc. #	days	description
Jan. 26	May 11	Clark	C-456	105	
Feb. 6	Apr. 13	Clark	C-486	66	bill of exchange, Kerr, $700
Mar. 7	July 1	Lewis	L-299	116	bill of exchange, Benj. Wilkinson, $1,500
Mar. 7	May 1	Lewis	L-273a	55	bill of exchange, Benj. Wilkinson, $1,000
Mar. 7	May 1	Lewis	L-273b	55	bill of exchange, Benj. Wilkinson, $1,500

Mar. 7	May 4	Lewis	L-276	58	bill of exchange, Benj. Wilkinson, $1,000
Mar. 7	May 4	Lewis	L-276	58	bill of exchange, Benj. Wilkinson, $1,000
Mar. 7	May 4	Lewis	L-276	58	bill of exchange, Benj. Wilkinson, $1,000
Mar. 17	Apr. 26	Clark	C-496	40	bill of exchange, storekeepers, $1,007.08
Mar. 25	June 13	Clark	C-544	80	bill of exchange, Heath, $700
Apr. 20	May 26	Tillier	T-266	36	letter
Apr. 27	June 8	Tillier	T-1809	42	letter
May 1	Oct. 7	Lewis	L-340	130	bill of exchange, William Thomas, $220
May 13	Oct. 7	Lewis	L-295	118	bill of exchange, P. Chouteau, $500
May 15	Oct. 7	Lewis	L-341	115	draft, Chouteau, $440

From January to August of 1809, letters written by Lewis and Clark containing drafts or bills of exchange averaged eighty-four days to arrive in Washington, whereas all other correspondence not relating to monetary issues averaged thirty-three days. The thirty-three-day transit time mirrored the average of thirty-seven days for all listed letters (except the two Chouteau letters) posted in 1803, 1804, and 1806. Taken together, the evidence suggests that someone was specifically delaying Lewis's and Clark's correspondence. In one instance, an important Lewis letter dated July 8, which included vouchers, was never delivered to Washington.[14]

1809

sent	received	author	doc. #	days	description
June 14	July 8	Chouteau	C-562	24	letter written by Bates
June 14	Sept. 22	Clark	C-621	100	bill of exchange, McKeever, $1,307.82

June 16	July 8	Bissell	B-535	23	letter, Fort Bellefontaine commander
June 16	July 8	Lewis	L-303	23	draft, Chouteau, $1
June 16	July 8	Lewis	L-302	23	draft, Chouteau, $81
June 20	Aug. 21	Clark	C-606	62	bill of exchange, Morrison, $735.16
June 25	July 21	Clark	C-580	27	letter
June 26	Oct. 6	Lewis	L-339	103	draft, Christy, $1,488.76
June 30	Aug. 4	Clark	C-594	35	bill of exchange, J. Phillipson, $750
July 1	July 21	Clark	C-581	20	letter
July 4	Aug. 21	Clark	C-603	47	bill of exchange, storekeepers, $1,318.71
July 6	Sept. 5	Lewis	L-326	60	draft, Christy, $43.25
July 8	undelivered	Lewis			letter with vouchers
July 9	Sept. 22	Clark	C-691	77	draft, Chambers, $163.50
July 15	Aug. 18	WD		34	from Washington to St. Louis
July 23	Aug. 25	Lucas	L-322	33	letter, territorial judge
July 29	Aug. 18	Bissell	B-555	19	letter
Aug. 1	Sept. 1	Bissell	B-560	30	letter
Aug. 2	Aug. 25	Boilvin	B-559	23	letter
Aug. 2	Aug. 25	Bissell	B-558	23	letter
Aug. 12	Aug. 25	Bates		19	letter
Aug. 12	Sept. 1	Chouteau	C-612	19	letter, Bates's handwriting
Aug. 17	Sept. 8	Bissell	B-565	21	letter
Aug. 18	Sept. 8	Lewis	L-328	20	letter to Simmons/ secretary of war
Aug. 26	Apr. 14, 1810	Lewis	L-264	230	draft, James McFarlane, $156

Lewis departed Saint Louis on September 4, 1809, for New Orleans, on his way to Washington, and Clark followed three weeks later. Frederick Bates, the territorial secretary, then took command of the territorial government. After Lewis's death in 1809, William Clark had a mountain of duties to perform that prevented him from returning to the territory until July 7, 1810.[15]

It is difficult to identify the person or persons who might have contributed to the delay of Lewis's mail. Lewis certainly had enemies who understood how to financially strangle his progress, but they would have to have been living in or near Saint Louis and have had regular contact with him. One important piece to the puzzle is how the mail from Saint Louis reached Cahokia, which was the terminus for all incoming mail delivery. In March 1808, Territorial Secretary Frederick Bates wrote to a printer in Vincennes, Indiana, regarding forms for commissions and trading licenses, "if the Post Rider can be prevailed on to bring them to Cahokia."[16] Lewis wrote to Clark at the end of April 1808, "I have reason to believe that . . . letters and valuable papers which I dispatched by the succeeding mail, remained at Cahokia several days."[17]

There are a few leading suspects who may have tampered with Lewis's mail, and Frederick Bates, Rufus Easton, Rodolphe Tillier, and John Hay top this list, but there is no definitive proof at this time linking any of these men to the deeds in question. Most historians would pick Frederick Bates, the territorial secretary, as the most likely suspect. Bates believed that he was a better administrator than Lewis and talked ill of him almost every time that he wrote to his brother. A particularly angry confrontation between the two men occurred at a Masonic celebration at the end of June 1809 when, according to Bates, Lewis challenged him to a duel. Bates declined, and from then on they had an agreement to steer clear of each other.[18]

Besides being the territorial secretary, Bates was also a member of the board of commissioners as the recorder of land titles. The board of commissioners was a federally appointed board assembled to hear and record land claims. Bates was absent from Saint Louis for long stretches of time because the commissioners frequently traveled to distant parts of the territory, and when they met in Saint Louis, most times it was at Fort Bellefontaine. After Lewis's arrival in March 1808, Bates took a 1,200-mile trip, "performing a circuit" as a member of the board of commissioners, departing Saint Louis on May 27, 1808, and returning on August 12.[19] During this absence, two of Lewis's letters dated June 26 and July 6 were delayed for 102 and 60 days, respectively. For the remainder of 1809, Bates was busy recording land claims into ledgers and completing a report due by January 1810 to Albert Gallatin, secretary of the treasury. Bates also had to meet weekly with the commissioners at Fort Bellefontaine, where they held their meetings.[20] The necessity of completing the report and traveling the eighteen miles to and from the fort was rigorous and would have demanded a large portion of his time, thus making it very difficult to believe that Bates was the culprit.

Rufus Easton, the Saint Louis postmaster, was also a territorial judge and lawyer. Easton had been a friend of Thomas Jefferson but lost his judgeship when he had a confrontation with James Donaldson, the attorney general of the Louisiana Territory. Donaldson accused Easton of taking advantage of a poor habitant on several occasions, and Easton, infuriated, beat Donaldson with a cane in a crowded courtroom. At the time of the delayed mail, Easton was one step away from having no job at all in the territory. He may have had opportunity, but a motive was lacking.

There were two persons who had better reasons to delay the mail. The first was Rodolphe Tillier, the factor at Fort Bellefontaine, and the other was the Cahokia postmaster, John Hay, a former British agent.

In 1808 the Fort Bellefontaine trading factory was moved 250 miles up the Missouri River and Tillier lost his job; however, Tillier believed Lewis had instigated his removal.[21] Tillier needed a job, so he openly complained to his superior, John Mason, superintendent of Indian affairs, that Lewis had used public money to fund a private venture, namely the Missouri Fur Company. While Tillier's contempt and actions toward Lewis gave him a motive to steal the governor's mail, he would have been unable to carry out the deed, as he resided at Fort Bellefontaine, located eighteen miles from the Saint Louis post office.[22]

What Tillier lacked is a direct connection to the mail, to which John Hay, the Cahokia postmaster, had unfettered access. Hay began his career as a fur trader in 1791, having left Detroit a few years earlier. When he arrived in Cahokia he opened a merchant store with Andrew Todd, a well-financed partner who resided in Montreal, and called the business Todd & Hay.[23] Todd became a secret partner to Spanish interests, putting up a sizeable chunk of money to fund the establishment of a fur company based in Saint Louis and appointing Hay as his agent.[24] The Spanish lieutenant governor granted Todd "the exclusive privilege of trading with all the Indian nations" of the Upper Missouri region.[25] But within the space of a few months, Todd contracted yellow fever and died in New Orleans, and Hay was left to pay Todd's creditors. To do that, he needed the books from the Spanish Fur Company in Saint Louis, so under the pretext of conducting a meeting, he stole the books and fled to Cahokia, making himself a fugitive, an example of his true character. Hay became the Cahokia postmaster in 1799. When Lewis arrived in Cahokia in November 1803, he selected John Hay as his interpreter when he met with the Spanish lieutenant governor in Saint Louis.[26] Whatever bad business Hay previously had with the Spanish was behind them, and the conference between Lewis and the lieutenant governor went smoothly.

Prior to the departure of the Lewis and Clark Expedition in the spring of 1804, Hay helped Lewis by drafting a copy of the MacKay/Evans map, an essential piece of cartography depicting the Missouri River, which was based on the journeys of James MacKay and John Evans and drawn in 1797.[27] This was the map that Lewis and Clark referred to for the first 1,500 miles of their journey. Hay also translated MacKay's journal of the Upper Missouri River, which was in French, and also assisted Lewis and Clark with the assembly of parcels of presents for various American Indian tribes.[28]

Historian Donald Jackson alluded to an aspect of Hay's character, which remained hidden from Lewis in 1803–1804 but gives some indication that his true intentions were not always honorable. When Lewis and Clark returned to Saint Louis from their explorations in late September 1806, Lewis wrote to President Jefferson to describe the trip; surprisingly, a copy of this letter arrived in Canada before it was delivered in Washington.[29] Jackson believed that Hay intercepted the letter at Cahokia and forwarded a copy to the British in Montreal. The letter was a summary of the cardinal discoveries made by Lewis and Clark on the expedition to the Pacific Ocean. It was of major value and consequence to the British. John Hay may have been involved in sending the letter to Canada, but because there is no evidence, this is mere speculation.

It is not clear from the research who might have tampered with Lewis's mail and it is also not the intent of the author to condemn any historical figure without definitive proof. While much historic documentation exists in the Saint Louis record today, information that would lead to specific persons who disagreed with policies implemented by Lewis and Clark enough to tamper with their mail has not come to light.

Chapter 10

GOVERNOR MERIWETHER LEWIS'S FISCAL HOUSE OF CARDS: A CLOSER LOOK

T he young United States was not a wealthy nation. Prior to the gold strikes in Georgia in the 1830s and California in 1848, little of material wealth had been found within the nation's boundaries. Relying almost solely on commercial import duties and tariffs for income, the nation had a handful of fledgling industries and no power to tax individual incomes or business profits. The nation also had a huge debt to repay, which it had incurred during the Revolutionary War. Due to the controversial fiscal proposals of Alexander Hamilton, the new federal government had assumed the debt of the Continental Congress and the individual states. It had borrowed money to pay off the international debt while settling on maintaining a perpetual internal or national debt and funding the government with secure bonds.

Of all the costs borne by the early treasury, it was the army, which had swelled in size to drive allied Indian tribes from the Ohio River Valley that drained away the lion's share of the nation's paltry fiscal resources. Representative Albert Gallatin, a member of the House Committee of Ways and Means and later the secretary of the treasury under President Thomas Jefferson, believed that "military expenditures unnecessarily exhausted a nation's resources."[1] To that end, Gallatin sought the reformation of Treasury Department procedures and a severe reduction in the size of the military. Since the inception of the federal government in 1789, army or War Department officials had assessed the military budget, but Gallatin wanted a more rigorous process for overseeing and handling its administration.

Congress passed legislation in May 1792 creating the Office of the Accountant of the War Department, which made the War Department subordinate to the US Treasury Department in fiscal matters. This office "was authorized to settle all accounts and expenses of the War Department" and report from time to time "all such settlements for the inspection and revision of the accounting officers of the treasury."[2] This crafty congressional maneuver placed a unit of the Treasury within the War Department and effectively "tied the hands of the Secretary of War."[3] The accountant's office assigned to the War Department had complete autonomy and was housed in a separate building with six clerks. The first accountant, Joseph Howell (of which little is known), retired in less than three years. President George Washington appointed William Simmons of Philadelphia, then chief clerk, as the new accountant in April 1795.[4]

By an act of 1798, Congress separated the Navy from the Army Department, giving an accountant to each. Besides adding a messenger and another two clerks to the accountant of the War Department's office, Congress increased its duties to purchase arms and munitions and to oversee the finances of the Indian Department.[5] From then on, the secretary of war's sole fiscal responsibility was to provide the department's budget, while the accountant's office strictly adhered to the settlement of incoming bills. The procedure for settling the accounts was simple; once the accountant finalized the vouchers for reimbursement, he made out a warrant for the settled amount, signed it, and sent it to the secretary of war for his countersignature. If the account could not be settled, the accountant sent a letter to the authorized officer discussing the discrepancy, and the exchange continued until an agreement was reached. If the account still met with resistance, legislation had been provided so that the accountant could send the disputed account to the comptroller for review. After 1802, the accountant stopped transferring the challenged expenditures to the comptroller, because it delayed payment for months, and decided to settle them himself.

The government accountants were the watchdogs of Gallatin's policy, and Simmons was scrupulous in his attention to detail as well as in familiarizing himself with all of the congressional acts relating to military law and procedure. The process by which an approved expenditure incurred by a military officer in the line of duty received reimbursement was arduous: it depended on the complexity of the account, sending the required documents to the accountant's office, waiting for settlement, and then receiving payment. The amount of time this bureaucratic exercise took could span up to three months, which was counterbalanced by local merchant conditions and the availability of specie money.

Various monetary instruments used in the regular course of business passed between the accountant and military officer-clerks, and terms such as warrants, vouchers, drafts, and bills of exchange were the subject of conversation. The accountant regularly employed warrants and vouchers. Warrants were authorizations signed by two parties validating that a transaction was legitimate, while vouchers were receipts showing the value of what was purchased. A draft was a sort of promissory note issued by an officer to a merchant for goods received, while a bill of exchange was a delayed transfer of money. Thus, a draft appeared to have ready value and was used much like a check today, but in Saint Louis, where specie money was scarce, the value was exchanged in goods. A bill of exchange only had ready value after it was sent to the government for reimbursement.

The scarcity of specie money was a serious problem and one that Lewis and Clark had to bear on their own through the use of drafts and a plethora of IOUs, which regularly circulated throughout Saint Louis. Clark wrote several times to the secretary of war explaining the dire necessity of having money available to pay for incidental expenses and was forced to authorize trips to Louisville to obtain it. Clark wrote to the War Department in 1808 that a "[g]reat demand for specie by the different offices of gov't. military agents & near the place is the cause of cash being very scarce and compels me to receive the money whenever I can get it and give bills—in several instances I have been obliged to send to the different towns near, for cash: and at two different times to Louisville; which is too great a risque, to bring silver (as a great portion of the country is yet a wilderness) and no bank notes to be procured."[6]

Thus, officers who were appointed to positions that interfaced with the accountant's office were ill-equipped in the field, where stupendous amounts of paper or ledger transactions were necessary for consistent tabulation. If the figures were not correct, then the onus was placed on the officer's abilities when he sent bills in for payment. In the interim, the officer ran a deficit and sometimes used his own money to bridge the shortfall. What happened in many cases was that the accountant disagreed with the bill and returned it for review, and sometimes this happened repeatedly. But the cruelest part of the review process was invisible: if Simmons refused to settle the account, the disbursing officer was responsible for the difference, which came out of his own pocket.

In February 1799, Simmons infuriated a Capt. Samuel Vance, who had been trying to collect payment on a longstanding account. Vance, a veteran officer of six years, acted as paymaster, and a soldier in his regiment made a claim for clothing to the secretary of war. Simmons objected to the settlement and returned the papers without cause. When Vance met with him he asked Simmons to give him a reason why the claim was returned. Simmons believed the claim had been fabricated, what he called "a rascally one," and that "the papers he now presented were insufficient." This led to a heated confrontation between Vance and Simmons, during which Vance called Simmons a villain. Simmons felt "grossly insulted," and took great exception to this treatment of an "executive in the duties of his office."[7] Simmons had Vance arrested and subjected him to a court-martial. While Vance was exonerated for any wrongdoing, Simmons's reputation was made as one to be feared.

Meriwether Lewis had met Simmons as early as 1797, when Lewis served as the army paymaster in Detroit, and a year later when he served on the recruiting service.[8] While these duties placed Lewis directly in Simmons's purview, Lewis, a master of mathematical detail, had no problems with the accounting system during those years.

When the United States purchased Louisiana in 1803, the scope of the accountant's duties increased enormously because a myriad of jobs and official positions had to be created and appointed to administer the new lands. Forts would have to be built to protect the hundred thousand inhabitants, and territorial administrations would have to be created to govern and establish laws. Indian agents were hired to conduct business with the hundreds of Native American tribes on the west side of the Mississippi River, factories (official government trading posts) were established to facilitate the Indian trade, and a vast network of new opportunities was formed to serve a growing country.

The transfer of the governance of the Louisiana Purchase was divided into parts as a consequence of its size and the lack of infrastructure. Gen. James Wilkinson oversaw the American transfer of Lower Louisiana in New Orleans in 1803, and Capt. Amos Stoddard presided over the transfer of Upper Louisiana in Saint Louis in March 1804. Once the American government took control of Louisiana, the first task was to assess the existing military fortifications, and both Stoddard and Wilkinson reported that new forts were necessary. Forts required a multiplicity of supplies, materials, and purchases, which required authorized contractors to deliver a constant stream of goods on a regular schedule.

Stoddard's report recommended building a new fort eighteen miles from Saint Louis, to be named Fort Bellefontaine, and an important facet of that installation was hiring a trustworthy contractor to supply meat and other essential foodstuffs. The secretary of war hired T. & C. Bullitt in October 1804, months before the fort was built and when the troops were still using the old fortifications in Saint Louis as their encampment.[9] The fort was completed in December 1805 and Bullitt, who had been delivering provisions in Saint Louis during construction, switched delivery to Fort Bellefontaine. Bullitt began sending bills for payment, but at some point Simmons refused to reimburse the contractor, and after repeated review over a number of years, Simmons began to ignore letters and bills from the contractor. By that time, the contractor had ceased doing business with the War Department but he continued to fight for reimbursement.

In November 1810, the comptroller of the treasury reviewed the case and could not understand Simmons's refusal to reimburse Bullitt. Simmons said that he would not pay because Fort Bellefontaine was not specified as the installation for which provisions were being procured in the original agreement. He was correct on that one point, but Simmons also argued that Henry Dearborn, the secretary of war, had fixed the price of incoming supplies. Gabriel Duvall, comptroller of the treasury and a lawyer, reminded Simmons that Dearborn had not consulted the contractor because he resided in another state and had made a decision "ex parte, and in justice ought to be considered as open to examination."[10] The comptroller immediately paid Bullitt.[11]

Simmons's rationale was not based on any legal footing but on faulty empirical reasoning. Importantly, there was no government entity or immediate superior who could force him to transfer contested accounts to the comptroller, even though legislation had provided for it. When Lewis returned from the expedition to the Pacific Ocean, Simmons required that Lewis present a formal accounting of the expedition expenses, but the intrinsic details of the expedition, namely the journals and notebooks kept by expedition members, paled in comparison to the extrinsic ones, which were the innumerable ledger items recorded by the clerks in Simmons's office.[12]

Lewis met with Simmons during the summer of 1807, but Lewis was too busy to track down incidental receipts when other important duties competed for his attention. Simmons wrote to Lewis when he was in Philadelphia that summer and said that he was going to suspend payment of Lewis's account until his arrival in Washington. "You will therefore do well to bring with you any papers or documents which may relate to your expenditures on the Expedition, so as to explain such of the charges as may require it." Simmons said that the charges for subsistence to the men required the authority of the secretary of war.[13] Simmons had no idea of the complexity of the business side of the expedition, nor did he care. He was simply trying to subtract money that the government owed Lewis.

When Lewis did not arrive by the appointed time, Simmons forced him to comply by dispatching another letter on July 31 raising the subsistence topic again; "I conceive it would be proper, before I finally close the account to be laid before the Secy. of War for the approbation of the President of the United States."[14] When they finally met on August 5, Lewis had difficulty producing paper for every transaction, and unbeknownst to him, Simmons back-charged those amounts, reporting that Lewis owed the government $9,685.77! Even though President Thomas Jefferson provided Lewis with a carte blanche letter of credit for expedition expenses in 1803, Simmons reported this egregious amount, which was printed in a Treasury publication for debtors. Lewis was expected to pay the overage within three years or a suit would be filed by the government.[15]

Abstract, continued.

NAMES.	Capacity or Rank.	Place of Residence.	Balance due 30th Sep. 1807. (Dollars. Cts)	Balance remaining due. (Dollars. Cts)	REMARKS.
Hughes, Thomas Hooker, John W.	late captain, late United States' factor,	not known, Tellico, Tennessee,	31 38 20 84	31 38 20 84	dead. Balance on settlement, 2d quarter of 1798. for provisions received by him from the contractor in 1798. Special report directed, &c.
Hughes, Daniel	lieutenant,	in service,	3,514 19	3,514 19	the greater part of this money was advanced for provisions purchased for the troops on the failure of the contractor, and for which said Hughes will be entitled to a credit, when he furnishes accounts.
Horton, John Hurley, Daniel	late lieutenant, contractor for furnishing timber,	not known,	40 45	40 45	amount arising on running account, while recruiting.
Hammond, Samuel	late colonel commandant in Louisiana,	Washington City,	80	80	no accounts rendered. Special report directed, &c.
Jones, Abraham	late cornet,	not known, not known,	139 400	139 400	dead. Reported specially to the treasury 4th February, 1804.
Irvine, Callender Johnston, Francis Kalteisen, Michael	late Indian agent, late captain, late captain,	Philadelphia, not known, formerly of Charleston, S. C.	388 57 100 1,537	388 57 266 1,537	balance on settlement. dead. Advanced in 1806 and 1808 for recruiting. dead. Accounts rendered to the pay-master of the army, but not yet adjusted. This sum will be accounted for.
Lee, William A.	late lieutenant,	formerly of Virginia,	430 33	430 33	dead. Reported specially to the treasury, 23d December, 1803. Insolvent.
Lee, William A. Lawton, William	late captain, late surgeon's mate,	Ditto, formerly of New York,	500 301	500 301	ditto ditto Insolvent. this is a balance of public money which he embezzled and for which he was cashiered. Special report directed, &c.
Lewis, sen. Samuel	late a clerk in the war office,	Philadelphia,	2,565 55	2,565 55	this is a balance of public money due by him, for which he was imprisoned and afterwards liberated by an act of Congress.
Livingston, John W.	late lieutenant,	formerly of New York,	330	330	dead. No accounts received at this office. Special report directed, &c.
Landais, Lewis	late lieutenant,	not known,	56	56	advanced for recruiting. No accounts rendered to this office.
Leybourn, John Lee, Thomas A.	do. do.	not known, not known,	141 6 612	141 36 612	balance on settlement 22d May, 1807. advanced for recruiting. Account rendered and sworn to, but no vouchers; it could not therefore be settled.
Lamkin, Peter Lyon, Matthew Lawrence, Thomas	late contractor, late pay-master militia.	not known, Kentucky, New Jersey,	208 29 61 7,795 69	208 29 61 7,795 69	balance on settlement 3d quarter of 1800. balance on settlement 2d quarter of 1803. He has never forwarded the receipts of the individuals who performed the service.
Logan, James	late ensign,	not known,	310	333 45	advanced principally for recruiting. No accounts rendered.
Lucket, John R. N. Lewis, Meriwether	lieutenant, late captain.	in service, formerly of St. Louis, La.	300 8,749 36	242 9,685 77	advanced principally for recruiting. amount arising out of advances made him to pay his detachment, who accompanied him to the Pacific ocean, per act of Congress of 3d March, 1807.
M'Mickle, John	late ensign levies,	not known,	20	20	dead. Advanced by the late pay-master general and commissioner of army accounts.
Miller, William Meigs, Return J.	late ensign, late military storekeeper,	not known, Highwassee, Tennessee,	70 50	70 50	no accounts received at this office. advanced on account of his compensation. He states that he has accounted for this money).

After Meriwether Lewis's return from the expedition, Williams Simmons, the accountant for the War Department, reported that Lewis had not submitted all the receipts from the expedition and owed the government $9685.77. Lewis's debt was published in a Treasury report titled "Abstract of Accounts on the Books of the Accountant for the Department of War Which Were Unsettled on 30 September 1807 and Which Still Remain Unsettled." Lewis's debt was updated every year until 1810. (*Early American Imprints*, second series, no. 21675, p.12.)

Once Lewis completed his business with Simmons he departed Washington, en route first to the Burr trial in Richmond, Virginia, and then to Charlottesville to pack and head toward Saint Louis. Lewis met with Gen. Wilkinson in Richmond at the trial and probably talked with Wilkinson about the continual squabbles with the accountant. He likely found a sympathetic ear with Wilkinson, who had been ordered by the War Department to attend the Burr trial and to provide testimony, yet Simmons refused to pay the bill for his expenses to do so. Wilkinson explained in a letter to Secretary Gallatin that "the conflict is not between Burr, the conspirator and the United States, but between an injured citizen and a despotic vindictive executive & a military panderer. I am sick of it. . . ." He had spent $160 traveling from New Orleans to Richmond, Virginia, and was "almost penniless."[16]

Two other incidents exemplify Simmons's autocratic reign. For years, Simmons had been fighting with Gen. Wilkinson, and he finally had enough documentation to convene a court-martial hearing in 1808 by claiming that Wilkinson had irresponsibly spent thousands of dollars in a four-year period. The general had allegedly hid the expenses in extra rations and quarters and in forage for horses. Simmons sent the complaint to Henry Dearborn, the secretary of war, who then informed President Jefferson and Caesar Rodney, the attorney general of the United States. Rodney pointed out not only that Wilkinson was a brigadier general, but also that, as the nation's overall military commander, he was entitled to additional awards from the president, and thus, Wilkinson, because of his rank, was permitted to enjoy those benefits.[17]

Simmons disagreed, which prompted Dearborn to send a complaint to the comptroller. What is evident from this exchange is that the secretary of war was, surprisingly, subordinate to the Treasury Department in this matter. Also by virtue of the fact that Dearborn had to explain his position, it is evident that the Treasury Department made the ultimate decision.

> Having understood that the accountant of this department has doubted the legality of an allowance I had, with the approbation of the President of the United States, directed to be made to Gen. Wilkinson . . . commanding officer at New Orleans. . . I take the liberty of stating the facts. . . . In the 5th section of the act fixing the military peace establishment, passed March 16, 1802, the President is authorized to allow the commanding officers of posts . . . additional number of rations, as he shall deem proper. . . . In the compensation Gen. Wilkinson receives by law, as brigadier-general, the usual rations were estimated; but it is presumed that this cannot justly bar him from an extra allowance . . . which, in the opinion of the United States, would entitle any other officer to an extra allowance of rations. This allowance to him for quarters . . . is nothing more than what is granted to all other officers according to their respective grades, although there has never been any law for furnishing officers or soldiers with quarters, any more than for tents or fuel. . . . I . . . have thought it my duty to make this statement to you, to aid in any opinion you may please to give.[18]

The comptroller agreed with Dearborn and passed on a credit to Wilkinson.[19] This unanimous decision angered Simmons, and, incredibly, he turned over Wilkinson's account to a Washington newspaper, going public with the information that government officials had approved $56,000 of public money for frivolous expenditures. Simmons's tirade stated, in part:

> Fellow-citizens . . . your treasury has been plundered . . . by the connivance of the President, the Secretary of War, and the Attorney-General of the United States. . . . [W]ith such facts staring them in the face . . . the democratic members of the legislature . . . have offered the most . . . unqualified approbation . . . of the administration thus . . . sanctioning, countenancing, and encouraging the most gross and abominable fraud and peculation.[20]

Simmons was in a unique position of power, as evidenced by the fact that he did not incur any penalties or censure for this violation of government privilege and releasing internal, nonpublic documents to the press.

Simmons hounded individuals like Wilkinson, whom he believed stole money from the government. He also attacked Gilbert C. Russell's tenure in the army from 1803 to 1810. Capt. Russell, commander of Fort Pickering, is a well-known figure in the literature because he cared for the ailing Lewis in the final two weeks of September 1809 and had wanted to accompany him to Washington but did not receive his orders in time. Russell was from Tennessee and was a friend of Sen. Joseph Anderson, also from the same state. On two occasions, Russell circumvented Simmons by giving his protested accounts to Anderson, who pushed them through channels and ensured that they were paid in April 1806.[21] When a few months later Simmons wanted Russell arrested for defrauding the government, Russell explained the circumstances: "The accountant pretends or wishes to attach criminality to me for receiving pay for the months of October and November 1806 after passing receipts to William P. Anderson of Nashville T."[22] Russell asked Dearborn to make a formal inquiry, and, if his action made an "unfavourable impression," he wanted the secretary of war to make things right, even if it meant his discharge.[23]

Simmons was the ultimate fiscal predator when judging what he thought were erroneous expenses, but according to congressional law, he had no authority to judge *any* account. Legislation provided the accountant's office with the means to send disputed accounts to the comptroller for review, and he would then render a decision. Over the course of Jefferson's administration, the comptroller reminded Simmons several times of that specific rule:

> As the accounting officers of the treasury are authorized to revise settlements made
> in your office, and not to decide on claims in the first instance, it is necessary that
> you should admit or disallow the claim, in order that it may be finally decided on
> in this department.[24]

No matter, every disbursing agent became Simmons's prey regardless of what the comptroller had reminded him. His zeal to force military officers to conform not only to the fiscal laws, but to his sometimes bizarre interpretations of the laws, worsened after the passage of the Embargo Act in 1807, which was an attempt to financially strangle England by ceasing to export or import furs and other goods.[25] The United States suffered greatly under the embargo because England was the nation's chief trading partner during the era. As a result, Treasury Secretary Gallatin tightened budget expenditures and imposed stricter regulations for military and territorial reimbursements. This budget tightening affected Upper Louisiana, a distant territory awakening from fiscal dormancy.

The beginning of Lewis's financial troubles began with the return of the Mandan chief, Sheheke-shote, to his village along the Missouri River in modern-day North Dakota in May 1807, which was about a year before Lewis arrived in the territory. While Lewis was in Philadelphia working on the journals for publication, William Clark had been sent to Saint Louis in the spring of 1807, and his first order of business was the return of the Mandan chief and his family. The genesis of the problem stemmed from the invitation of Lewis and Clark to the chief and his family to accompany them to Washington to meet with the president. The chief returned to Saint Louis in March 1807 to await transport home. Dearborn approved a military escort to accompany the chief, but due to the insufficient number of troops stationed at Fort Bellefontaine, he instructed Clark to use a combination of military and civilian personnel to take the Mandan entourage up the Missouri River.

> You are authorized to draw on this Department, for four hundred dollars, to be laid
> out in suitable articles to be sent with the party, as presents to the Mandan Nations
> . . . you will likewise draw on this Department such Sum as may be found indis-
> pensibly necessary in fitting out the party for the Voyage. . . . Should any mer-
> chants or traders be found disposed to send goods as high up the Missouri as the
> Mandan towns, and will, without delay take measures for dispatching a suitable
> number of men with such goods so that they may be associated with the
> voyage . . . you will afford them encouragement, by granting them licenses to
> trade with the Indians generally on the Missouri from the Ricaras upward: and
> engage . . . for two years at least, no other persons will be licensed to trade with
> those Indians.[26]

Dearborn also allowed Clark to "furnish, each man . . . ammunition for the voyage . . . at the expense of the United States," and also instructed him to recruit as many suitable men to enlist in the army for five years.[27] There were no takers.

One of the Louisiana territorial judges, John B. C. Lucas, wrote to a friend explaining that various trading companies were feuding for the Mandan contract.

> There is a company forming here for the purpose of carrying on the fur trade on the heads of the Missouri, it is all ready composed of eight or nine parties; the funds of the Company amount . . . to . . . $5000, there were at first two or three companies . . . who were all . . . jealous of each other; and whose interest . . . might have led them to mutual injury, after various conferences they have . . . agreed to consolidate their interest into one, it is said that the expedition will take place in the course of next month, the whole party will come to one hundred men, several of the partners are going with the expedition, they will not return for three years.[28]

Clark, adept at discerning tense Indian relations, thought that the party escorting the Mandan chief would encounter hostility somewhere up the Missouri. He believed that the strength of the escort required manpower and cobbled together an impressive number of persons from various groups: a Sioux deputation, two trading ventures, and two military escorts. The Sioux deputation was going to the Yankton Indian village in modern-day South Dakota, while the Mandans would press on to North Dakota. The group totaled 101 adults composed of soldiers, traders, boatmen, interpreters, hunters, Sioux warriors, and from the Mandan nation, eighteen chiefs, men, women, and six children.[29]

The group departed Saint Louis on May 18, 1807, and split up on August 23 when the main party journeyed onward to Mandan territory.[30] The party was attacked on September 9 by hundreds of maddened Arikara Indians, and four men were killed, five wounded, and the rest narrowly escaped to Saint Louis.[31] George Shannon and René Jesseaume were two of the men wounded in the melee; they had accompanied Lewis and Clark, Jesseaume during portions of their 1804 to 1806 journey, and Shannon for the entire trek. On this trip they were not so lucky; Shannon had his leg amputated in Saint Louis and Jesseaume "received two dangerous wounds that made one fear for his life, and which retained him more than four months in Saint Louis, without being able to get out of bed."[32] The cost of the stricken military escort totaled about $6,500.[33]

Pierre Dorion, the Sioux interpreter who accompanied the Mandan party, survived the ambush. Dorion visited Saint Louis in May 1807 with a Sioux delegation and entreated Clark to pay him his salary, which had not been accomplished since his appointment as interpreter in December 1805.[34] Clark was reluctant to pay him because there was a chance that he would quit, and Dorion's role was too important to be vacated. Remarkably, Clark instead gave gifts to the Sioux and urged Dorion to send yet another letter to Simmons.

> I take the liberty of representing to you . . . that my Salary as Sub-agent is barely Sufficient to the maintenance of my family and that the expences I have been compelled to incur to obey the orders of government or rather of persons employed by them cannot be charged to me: I have been obliged to borrow, to meet these expenses, and I am now at the mercy of my creditors: I must then entreat you to give the most prompt orders to reimburse me for the two due . . . amounting to $1061.96 and which have been entirely employed for the service of the Government . . . in my last journey, I ran a risk of loosing my life, having been struck by the Ricara [Arikara] Savages.[35]

Simmons ignored Dorion's plea.[36]

When Lewis arrived in Saint Louis in March 1808, the Louisiana territorial administration had been in neglect for almost three years, a sure sign that large sums of money would be required to fix it. Even Frederick Bates, the most boastful and egotistical official in Saint Louis, and Lewis's territorial secretary, believed that his best judgments for the discharge of the duties of government were so difficult that "I feel that I am no atlas for so great a weight."[37] After only one year on the job, he believed the territory had been an insupportable burden and was relieved that his tenure had ended as acting governor. "It was a task to which I thought myself unequal even before experience had demonstrated the truth of my fears."[38]

This was a really bad omen because Bates, who had been a capable Detroit administrator, had concluded that territorial problems abounded in every sector of Upper Louisiana. The new governor, Meriwether Lewis, would be forced to confront a daunting diversity of territorial issues, which would take varying amounts of money and latitude, and put him in economic peril. The Jefferson administration was oblivious to the most obvious: their star pupil was on a collision course with Simmons's office. Issues that required Lewis's immediate attention centered on language barriers, warring native Americans, trading licenses, bootlegging, property rights, mineral lands, squatters, civil unrest, amending and printing territorial laws, forming a militia, protection and safety, enactment of laws, murders, theft, and hiring Indian Department personnel. The most vexing problem centered on the return of the Mandan chief and his family to their homeland.

Upon Lewis's arrival in Saint Louis, he paid his men from the rewards of the expedition. Lewis had received a load of credit, which amounted to double pay for expedition members and a generous grant of land for each in the Louisiana Territory.

Lewis set about paying some members of the expedition who remained in Saint Louis after their return in September 1806. William Clark, who had been appointed Indian agent for the Louisiana Territory, was due to arrive in Saint Louis with his new bride in June, but pressing matters surrounding Indian Department business forced Lewis to immediately take action, and he paid the Sioux interpreter, Dorion.[39]

A priority vying for reform was the enactment of territorial laws, which would quell civil unrest and murders. The unrest had occurred mainly in Sainte Genevieve, a town ninety miles south of Saint Louis, due to the abundance of lead in the hills to the west, which prompted a landgrab and resulted in the so-called mineral wars. Indian murders had garnered special attention due to selling liquor to Native Americans, which was forbidden but, nonetheless, took place, prompting more hostilities. Beginning in June 1808, Lewis convened the territorial judges and soon began passing a wide range of laws.[40] Once Clark arrived in Saint Louis the division of responsibility between the two fell into the same pattern as when they had commanded the expedition. The administration of the territory began to take shape with military precision.

One challenge that the two could tackle together revolved around safety for the territorial residents. The Upper Louisiana country had always been an unsafe locale due to the large number of tribes in the area and a severe shortage of troops, first with the Spanish administration and then with the Americans. Normally a territory's second line of defense fell to the militia, except in Louisiana few were eager to volunteer. Indian hostilities had been on the rise owing to the ever-expanding American frontier and discontent about American settlements. Saint Louis was a relatively defenseless place, and the subject of one Indian raid. Lewis and Clark's answer to the problem was to galvanize the residents into accepting their militia duties. The perception of an organized militia would have "a powerful effect" upon the Indians, which Clark had hoped would "prevent the intended Blow altogether."[41]

In spite of all these demands swirling about him, Lewis took time off to see Saint Louis and began buying prime real estate in the Saint Louis area. Territorial governors were required by law to own a freehold estate of a thousand acres, and Lewis knew a good deal when he saw it.[42] By the end of July 1808 he had purchased about 5,700 acres for $5,530. One of the tracts had a good source of flowing water and would make "an excellent mill seat."[43] The purchase terms were generous, and Lewis could pay the balance over the next year.

Lewis invited Joseph Charless, a printer from Louisville, to establish a newspaper in Saint Louis. A printer was vital to the territory for publishing national events, advertisements, and the local news, not to mention the compendium of Lewis's new territorial laws. Lewis sent Charless $225 in bank bills and a draft as a loan to establish the printing shop, but Lewis learned that the post rider had drowned in the Little Wabash River and the funds had disappeared. He then raised the exact amount again and sent it to Charless.[44] Another item lost in the rider's pouch was Dorion's payment, which did not become apparent for some time, and when Lewis sent a duplicate bill, he was not reimbursed. This was yet another example of Lewis's lost income, which would diminish his personal wealth and negatively affect him the following summer.[45]

Lewis hired a favorite interpreter, Peter Provenchere, to translate the territorial laws into French, which would then be published and circulated throughout the territory.[46] Provenchere had accompanied the Mandan entourage to Washington. He spoke and wrote several languages, and coupled with Charless's talent, the two could commence proper communications in the town.

In July 1808, Lewis advanced Charless $500 for the purchase of paper for publishing the territorial laws, 250 copies in English and 100 in French.[47] At the end of the month, Lewis gave Provenchere a partial payment of about $71, and sent the bill to James Madison, the secretary of state. At the end of 1808, he paid Charless the balance so that the publication would be ready in the first quarter of 1809. In all, Lewis disbursed about $1,500 of his own money, and after sending invoices for each expenditure with the reasoning behind them, all of them were rejected by the secretary of state's office! This was puzzling because the secretary of state was required by an act of Congress to reimburse governors when they published public laws.[48]

Earlier in the year, Dearborn ordered Lewis to hire several persons to explore the saltpeter caves on the Osage River. He wanted a detailed report on its extent, quality, distance from Saint Louis, and how long it could be worked. Saltpeter was a major component of gunpowder, and the secretary was looking for extensive deposits of the mineral that could be worked for at least seven years. In mid-August Lewis hired two persons to carry out the work, but when he sent the $730 draft for reimbursement, Simmons refused to pay it.[49] This refusal did not make any sense unless Simmons was trying to delay what he believed were unauthorized expenditures.[50] From a strategic point of view, it delayed planning for the defense of the territory.

A new fort and trading factory was to be established about 250 miles up the Missouri River, and the trading facility at Fort Bellefontaine would close in November 1808. About eighty soldiers accompanied William Clark, who would select the site, and the fort would be built beginning in September 1808.[51] Clark, as the new Indian agent of the territory, would officiate at a treaty signing, exchanging American goods for Osage Indian land and offering protection using the fort's resources. What Clark had in mind, however, was seen as being disadvantageous to the Osage, and Pierre Chouteau came to their rescue by interfering with the treaty signing.[52]

A few days before Clark departed Saint Louis, he wrote to Dearborn inquiring about the timing for the second attempt to return the Mandan chief to North Dakota. It would take time to prepare and obtain approval for those plans, and Clark had set his sights on the spring of 1809, since "Govr. Lewis will be absent at that time," editing the journals for publication.

> If the Government does not intend to send a Military Command with the Mandan Chief next Spring, and you think it necessary that arrangements should be made in this country . . . to send him up to his nation . . . if I am to make the arrangements . . . to get him to his Country I must request the favour of you to inform me. That timely preparations may be made by some party so as to let out early in the spring— My former plan has been defeated for the want of a few more regular troops, or a sufficient time for a large company to equip themselves. I think a Company can be formed of Hunters & Traders attached to a few troops who will take up the Indians, if Government should not send a large command into that country.[53]

Clark's letter did not reach Dearborn until September 23, and it took until mid-November before he received the secretary's approval.[54] By late October, Lewis and Clark learned that the Osage Treaty signed at the new fort was refused due to Chouteau's interference, which forced Governor Lewis to revise it and invite the Osage to Saint Louis.[55] This took much preparation and there were two signings, one with the Big and Little Osage on November 10, 1808, accompanied with multiple Indian councils, and the other on August 31, 1809, during which the Arkansas Osage delivered up "200 miles square of the finest country in Louisiana for which they received merchandize to the amount of about $2500." Clark recommended that the Senate ratify the treaty as it would "require five times the amount to effect a purchase of the same tract."[56]

In December, officials in Saint Louis commented that Lewis was about to leave the territory and travel to Philadelphia to work on the publication of the journals. Every time that Clark, Bates, or Lewis mentioned his imminent departure, Lewis was forced to stay and work out another problem in the territory. The time of departure was finally fixed and Lewis wrote his mother that "you may expect me in the course of this winter."[57] Lewis and Clark were relying upon Territorial Secretary Bates to assist Clark, but the plan backfired when he flatly refused. "Mr. Bates has very earnestly requested of me not to impose on him duties in the Indian department during my absence, alleging that it is a subject with which he is wholly unacquainted." Pierre Chouteau's interference with the signing of the Osage Treaty had caused tension between Clark and Chouteau back in September. Lewis wanted Bates to act as a buffer between them, but Bates was not interested. "Mr. Bates is extremely unwilling to exercise the authority of superintendent," Lewis wrote.[58]

While the issues with Bates had finally come to a head, two other events prevented Lewis's departure. The first was the establishment of the first Masonic lodge in Saint Louis, which occurred on November 8, 1808.[59] The second event was unexpected; from mid-November to almost mid-January, Lewis had again succumbed to a malarial relapse.[60] During the times that he was not ill, he composed a long letter to Thomas Jefferson detailing the Osage Indian Treaty. [61] A shortened version was printed in the *American State Papers*, but historians have yet to acknowledge that Lewis was still communicating with the president.[62]

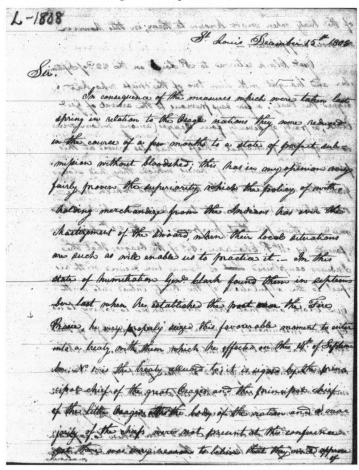

Meriwether Lewis wrote this lengthy letter of fifty pages to President Jefferson on December 15, 1808, explaining territorial affairs and Indian treaties. Historians had claimed that Lewis had stopped writing to Jefferson by July 1808. (Meriwether Lewis to Henry Dearborn, December 15, 1808, L1808, RG107, M222, roll 3, frames 1260–88, National Archives and Records Administration.)

The letter was long and divided into multiple sections, which amounted to fifty pages.[63] Once Lewis regained his strength, the weather turned bitterly cold and Lewis and Clark began to organize the mission to return the Mandan chief, Sheheke-shote, to his nation. It took almost the entire winter to assemble the parties to be engaged in the enterprise, sign papers, and to set deadlines.

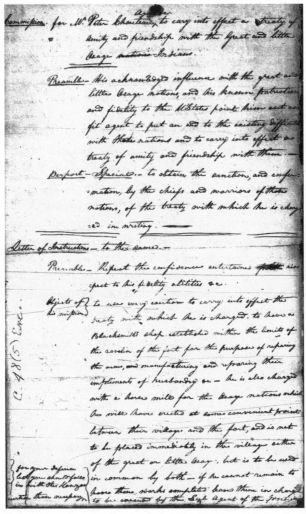

Lewis wrote instructions for Pierre Chouteau's role in the signing of the Osage Indian Treaty. These instructions were included in the December 15, 1808, letter to Jefferson. (Meriwether Lewis to Henry Dearborn, December 15, 1808, Preamble to Osage Treaty, in William Clark's documents from the War Department, February 20, 1810, C48, RG107, M221, roll 35, frames 2307–17, National Archives and Records Administration.)

In his quarterly briefing to Congress in December 1808, Treasury Secretary Gallatin reported that the Embargo Act had strangled the life out of the nation's economy and that government revenue had dropped by $6 million from the previous year and was "daily decreasing."[64] For all intents and purposes, the US government was broke, and he recommended that President Jefferson rescind the Embargo Act.[65] In a frantic effort to economize, Gallatin believed that the War and Navy Departments still had excesses to wring from their budgets:

> It is believed that the present system of accountability of the military and naval establishments may be rendered more prompt and direct, and is susceptible of improvements which, without embarrassing the public service, will have a tendency more effectually to check any abuses of subordinate agents.[66]

The term "subordinate agents" was a broad stroke that included a wide range of government appointees, contractors, and hirelings who had been qualified and vetted by high-ranking American officials. Gallatin's newly found religion of economy served to further embolden a man like Simmons, and it was bad news indeed for military officers and other government officials who expended their own money and were then subject to intense scrutiny over every penny spent.

The election of James Madison to the presidency in 1809 contrasted the politics of two administrations, one departing and the other arriving.[67] Jefferson's model of expansion would soon give way to Madison's model of contraction, but a few days prior to Madison's inauguration, Secretary of War Dearborn stepped out of character and suddenly recommended the removal of William Simmons:

> It was early perceived that the passions, prejudice, general disposition and character of the Accountant of the Department of War, rendered him very unsuitable for the Office he holds; and I should have applied for his removal several years ago, had I not been induced to expect, from year to year, that such an arrangement would have been made in relation to the Accounting Offices of the War and Navy Departments, as would have superseded the necessity of such an application. But of late the conduct of Mr. Simmons has been such in regard to the Head of the War Department as to compel me in justice to that Department and to the Office I have had the honor of holding, as well as to my Successor, to request that he be removed; and I am fully pursuaded that the opinion of the public Officers generally who have been acquainted with his character and conduct accords with mine,—that he ought not to be continued in Office.[68]

For all those unfortunate officers over the preceding thirteen years who had wrestled with receiving reimbursement for expenses honestly incurred in the performance

of their duties and for the benefit of the United States, Dearborn's letter finally condemned Simmons's behavior and his "perplexing incapacity in the settlement of
public accounts."[69] Unfortunately, the letter was an empty threat; if he had only
attached proof, including specific charges, outgoing President Jefferson could have
removed Simmons. Why, then, did Dearborn write the letter? Perhaps in response to
his own guilt of inaction and to alert his successor of the accountant's conduct.

Madison's appointment to replace Dearborn as head of the War Department was
William Eustis, a trained physician who had served four years in the House of Representatives from his home state of Massachusetts, and then as a hospital administrator. It is baffling why Madison appointed Eustis to one of the most demanding
posts in the presidential cabinet, which was reiterated by Treasury Secretary Gallatin when he wrote of Eustis's "incapacity and . . . total want of confidence"
throughout the public service.[70] Eustis had little military experience per se,
although he had been a key surgeon and hospital administrator during the Revolutionary War. The appointment may have been purely political; Eustis was a staunch
Republican in the midst of Federalist New England and had won his races for his
House seat in opposition to John Quincy Adams and Josiah Quincy III, narrowly
defeating both. Eustis began his official duties on April 5, 1809, but had little effect
on the department's accounts payable, not being directly involved in the process.
Simmons communicated with all disbursement officers when settling their
accounts—not Eustis. And even if Eustis had the authority, he knew nothing about
War Department business, being completely unfamiliar with its personnel for the
first six months of his tenure, which spanned the final months of Lewis's governorship of the Louisiana Territory.[71]

In the fall of 1808, Saint Louis officials had been working out the details for the
coming year. At the top of the list was the inadequacy of the mail system where the
Louisiana Territory was a distant point on the rider's trail, resulting in the slow
delivery of important correspondence and reimbursements.[72] Lewis made a formal
complaint to the postmaster general detailing those delays and why improved
delivery was absolutely critical to the efficient administration of the territory.
Gideon Granger, the postmaster general, admitted that he had been "apprised of
several failures," but wintertime was notorious for "deep snow and uncommon high
water," which further hampered delivery.[73] While Granger said that he would
launch a "strict investigation," it would take much time to complete.[74]

The slow delivery of the mail was but a minor distraction compared with one
of the thorniest problems still facing Governor Lewis. In February 1809, Lewis and
Clark devised a new and bolder plan for returning the Mandan chief to his village.
No one wanted a repeat performance of the dead and wounded men that had

resulted from the 1807 attempt on the books of the territorial administration. Further delays in returning the chief and his family would only make the United States look weak in the face of tribal power, leading the Mandans to consider the US a poor trading partner and military ally. On a personal level, neither Lewis nor Clark needed reminders of George Shannon's amputated leg or the complaints of René Jesseaume, the Mandan interpreter, of his shoulder and thigh wounds, even though both men received a salary while they recovered.[75] In hindsight, placing the entire responsibility for the success of the 1807 expedition on Ensign Pryor had been a mistake, and Lewis realized that experienced personnel were essential.

Borrowing an idea from Secretary Dearborn's instructions of March 1807, the Missouri Fur Company (MFC) was formed to take advantage of a once-in-a-lifetime endeavor, funded by the US government. The project set up a fur trade company with the intention of "killing two birds with one stone." The lucrative business aspects of the proposal would draw investors and participants, while the large party of men assembled would be able to successfully fight its way past the Arikara blockade of the Missouri River—if that became necessary. The fur trade aspects of the proposal were enticing because the scheme was designed to propel the company's hunt of beaver beyond hostile territory into the relatively peaceful region of the Upper Missouri.

The MFC sold shares in the company, and William Clark became one of the partners along with other wealthy Saint Louis and Cahokia residents. Lewis felt that Pierre Chouteau, the Osage Indian agent, was the fittest person to lead the expedition, and his experience in the fur trade and with native peoples was equal to the task. At the end of February, plans for the Mandan expedition were laid out and the contract was signed. Lewis wrote six drafts on March 7, 1809, amounting to $7,000, and he explained what the money would buy:

> [T]he said company are likewise bound to raise or organize arm and equip at their own expense One hundred and forty effective volunteers to act under my orders as a body of the militia of this Territory, and to furnish what ever may be deem'd necessary for the expedition, or to insure its success.[76]

In the meantime, Clark wrote to the War Department asking to build an Indian house and storage facility for peltries in the town of Saint Louis, near where Lewis and Clark engaged in daily business matters.[77] At the time, the Indian house was located at Fort Bellefontaine, eighteen land miles north of Saint Louis, which was too far for Clark to manage, but the rates for renting in town were exorbitant. Clark knew that he could save the government a large expense if they constructed and owned buildings for this purpose near the governor's office.[78]

Clark's letter dated January 26, 1809, was addressed to Dearborn, but when it arrived in Washington, Dearborn had resigned and the letter was given to Simmons, who proceeded to dismiss Clark's proposal and criticize him for past expenses:

> Before any authority can be given for erecting the buildings proposed in your letter . . . it is necessary that this Department should be furnished with a partial estimate of the expense—The Expenditures in the Terr. of Louisiana on account of the Indian Department have exceeded expectations; the amount in 1808, was not less than $20000—you will please therefore in future . . . forward to the Secy. of War quarterly estimates of the Expense in your Agency—They should be transmitted in sufficient season to enable him to advise you of his Approbation, before any Bills are drawn on that department.[79]

An important piece of information in Simmons's reply was a new government mandate of quarterly estimates, which contained instructions that Lewis and Clark could not have anticipated and would be problematic due to the inadequate mail system. Clark sent his letter on January 26, and received, on July 1, Simmons's May 11–dated reply. That one communication cycle took five months to complete. The whole idea of quarterly estimates, coupled with the inadequate communication system and lag times, made reimbursement for territorial and Indian Department expenses a long and cumbersome process. Added to this was the wild unpredictability of Simmons and the ever-present possibility that legitimate expenses incurred out of the pockets of government officials would not be reimbursed on some technicality. Although Simmons said that expenditures required the secretary of war's approbation, that was not true either in law or in practice, because the mandate gave Simmons extraordinary power and he became both judge and jury on all War Department disbursements.

As territorial business increased over the next couple of months, an unforeseen event further disrupted Governor Lewis's financial affairs. A federal official in Saint Louis criticized the plan to return the Mandan chief and wrote a formal complaint to his superior, John Mason, superintendent of Indian affairs. Rodolphe Tillier, the factor of the Indian factory at Fort Bellefontaine, gave damaging information in his complaint that enabled Simmons to further disable Lewis's administration.

There is no doubt that Tillier had an ax to grind. When Clark established Fort Osage in August and September 1808, the trading factory at Fort Bellefontaine was relocated, and Tillier's position was terminated. He believed that Lewis had recommended his removal because of an altercation that had resulted in the firing of his assistant, George Sibley, in November 1807.[80] In reality, the factory was moved because Gen. Wilkinson suggested its relocation as early as 1805 to a location close to where the tribe actually resided, and Dearborn had approved the move.[81]

Tillier waited for the change in the presidential administration to inform Mason of his version of Lewis's plan and sent three letters.[82] Tillier supplied trumped-up and inflammatory information to Mason in an attempt to land a new job:

> To represent the present situation of these remote parts of the United States Territory may be of public service, to the wise administration of your Excellency; and can give no offence if founded on Fact & real Truth.
>
> Two years ago an Expedition had been made here under the command of Lieut. Pryor to take back the Mandan Chief & family, it failed on account of being coupled with a private expidition . . . as no inquiries have been made of the real cause, tho' the Public has suffered no fault . . . that it was entirely owing to the Misunderstanding and Mismanagement of the parties of Lieut. Pryor and Chouteau's people.
>
> Last year a War was predetermined against the Osages & all the surrounding savages were invited in grand Council to join the Administration utterly to destroy them, without ever manifesting any plausible ground or reason. . . . I am well informed by one of the principal Osage interpreters that if they did not submit they were threatened to be utterly destroyed from the face of the Earth!
>
> There is an other expedition on foot of about 200 men divided into shares to hunt Beaver in the upper part of the Missouri . . . however it was after designed . . . to bring the Mandan Chief and family home that the Governor promised the company seven thousand dollars if delivered safe. at present it seems by Proclamation of the Governor to be altogether on public account, man'd & officered and paid as U.S. militia. . . . Is it proper for the public service that the U.S. officers as a Governor or a Super Intendant of Indian Affairs & U.S. Factor at St. Louis should take any share in Mercantile and Private concerns.[83]

Tillier was not privy to any discussions between Lewis and Clark, and what he reported to the War Department was a distortion of the facts.

Two weeks later, Tillier sent another letter deploring Lewis's plan, which was "afeared not a creditable one."[84] In his final letter, Tillier baited Mason to forward his version of the events to President Madison.

> I intended to send the enclosed to his Excellency the Pres. After mature deliberation I have changed my mind, & submit to your judgment if the Facts alledged may be interesting to him, or the U. States or if it will be better to bury them in oblivion in either case, disclaim any personal motive of ill will, or interested motive of courting favour at the expence of another.[85]

Mason dutifully forwarded the letter to Madison, which set off a chain reaction of events that ended with the president's approval to reject any other payments above the initial cost of the expedition, empowering Simmons to execute the order.[86]

Lewis's original drafts of $7,000 were paid, but in May he sent three other bills connected to the expedition without including a quarterly estimate. Those three drafts did not arrive in Washington until October 7 and would not be paid in time, which meant that Lewis's liquid capital was greatly reduced. The following is an itemized list of Lewis's transactions pertaining to the cost of the expedition:

1809

sent	received	document	description
March 7	July 1	L-299	Benjamin Wilkinson, $1,500
March 7	May 1	L-273	Benjamin Wilkinson, $1,000
March 7	May 1	L-273	Benjamin Wilkinson, $1,500
March 7	May 4	L-276	Benjamin Wilkinson, $1,000
March 7	May 4	L-276	Benjamin Wilkinson, $1,000
March 7	May 4	L-276	Benjamin Wilkinson, $1,000
May 1	Oct. 7	L-340	William Thomas, $220
May 13	Oct. 7	L-295	Pierre Chouteau, $500
May 15	Oct. 7	L-341	Pierre Chouteau, $440[87]

By this time Lewis had received two refusals for inconsequential sums from the secretary of state and had already returned them to the secretary of the treasury.[88] Not having heard from the War Department, he sent two additional bills on June 16. Those two bills arrived three months before the ones sent in May, which arrived on October 7, 1809.[89]

1809

sent	received	document	description
June 16	July 8	L-303	Pierre Chouteau, $1
June 16	July 8	L-302	Pierre Chouteau, $81

Clark replied to Simmons on July 1 acknowledging that he would begin submitting quarterly estimates and sent a detailed bill with a list of Indian agents, subagents, and interpreters "who received their salary from me . . . authorized by the Secty. of War or the Superintendent of this Territory."[90] When Simmons received Clark's letter, he rejected eight of the twenty-two salaries, which amounted to $1,069.91.[91] That meant that Clark had to pay those men from his own funds until he either had the time to meet with Simmons face to face or appeal the rejection of his request. Simmons explained his position on the matter:

Those appointments have not been authorized or approved by this Department; nor has the expediency or propriety of making them been submitted to the Government; or an opportunity given to determine, whether the appropriations for the Indian Department would justify such an increase in expenditure. It does not appear to be necessary that the expense attending our Relations with the Indians in the Territory of Louisiana, should be four times as much as the whole expense of supporting its civil government.[92]

It must have been infuriating for Lewis and Clark to be reprimanded by a person who knew nothing about Louisiana territorial affairs and who ignored previous authorizations from Dearborn. After receiving a rejected payment from the Treasury Department for a miniscule $18, Lewis waded into the financial depths and wrote to Simmons on July 8 hoping for leniency. This letter, which has never before been published, shows that Lewis was extremely worried over all of his unreimbursed expenditures up to that time:

[T]his occurrence has given me infinite concern as the fate of other bills drawn for similar purposes to a considerable amount cannot be mistaken; this rejection cannot fail to impress the public mind unfavourably with rispect to me, nor is this consideration more painfull than the censure which must arise in the mind of the executive from my having drawn for public monies without authority; a third and not less imbarassing circumstance attending the transaction is that my private funds are entirely incompetent to meet those bills if protested . . . .[93]

By this time, Mason had received the three letters from Tillier regarding the alleged improper federal funding of the fur trade expedition to return the Mandan chief, and he forwarded them to President Madison. Coincidentally, on July 8, Simmons had just received an odd letter from Pierre Chouteau. The Osage Indian agent always corresponded in French, but this letter was written in English; it had in fact been penned by Territorial Secretary Frederick Bates and Chouteau had signed it. The letter was undoubtedly meant to derail Lewis's administration as governor of Louisiana:

The contract . . . transmitted by the Governor, will have given . . . the principles of this arrangement . . . it is as well mercantile as military . . . a detachment of the militia of Louisiana as high as the Mandan-village and commercial afterwards. . . . If my participation in speculations of this kind should excite the surprise of government as inconsistent with my duties . . . I . . . refer you to Governor Lewis, whose advices I have pursued. . . . My agency has . . . been limited to the Osages, and . . . I accompany the expedition, merely in a military capacity . . . and as soon as my command ceases at the Mandan Village, shall return with all convenient haste to Saint Louis. . . . I take the liberty to enclose a Power of Attorney, by which my son Peter Chouteau . . . is empowered to draw in my absence . . . .[94]

Bates had almost certainly concocted the contents of this letter, and the insinuating tone is typical of his writing style. His hatred for Lewis by this point in time was palpable and was a clear motivation for the veiled hints of impropriety: "If my participation in speculations of this kind should excite the surprise of government as inconsistent with my duties . . ." The other part allowed Simmons to judge the legality of Chouteau's temporary lateral move: "I take the liberty to enclose a Power of Attorney . . ."

Instead of merely weighing the ethics of the proposed expedition in light of the insinuations of the letter, Simmons used the power of his office as well. True to character, Simmons decided that Chouteau had vacated his position as Osage Indian agent in order to lead the expedition and so terminated his salary. Simmons then wrote a nasty letter to Governor Lewis, on July 15, that had President Madison's sanction:

After the sum of seven thousand dollars had been advanced on the Bills drawn by your Excellency on account of your Contract with the St. Louis Missouri Fur Company . . . and after this Department had been advised that "for this purpose the Company was bound to raise, organize, arm & equip at their own expence one hundred and forty Volunteers and to furnish whatever might be deemed necessary for the Expedition, or to insure its success"—it was not expected that any further advances or any further agency would be required on the part of the United States. Seven thousand dollars was considered as competent to effect the object. Your Excellency will not be surprized that your Bill of the 13th of May [to pay Pierre Chouteau $500] . . . has not been honored . . . . [95]

Since Simmons had not received a quarterly estimate from Lewis, he rejected the payment out of hand.

Although Lewis hadn't really explained the details of the expedition to Simmons, Tillier and Bates had given the accountant ample misinformation, which Simmons used against Governor Lewis:

In . . . accepting the volunteer services of 140 men for a military expedition to a point and purpose not designated, which expedition is stated to combine commercial as well as military objects, and when an Agent of the Government appointed for other purposes [Chouteau] is selected for the command, it is thought the Government might, without injury to the public interests, have been consulted. As the object & destination of this Force is unknown, and more especially as it combines

Commercial purposes, so it cannot be considered as having the sanction of the Government of the United States, or that they are responsible for the consequences . . . . Being responsible for the expenditure of Public money & made judges in such cases whether the Funds appropriated by the Legislature are applicable and adequate to the object, it is desirable in all practicable cases that they should be advised and consulted when expenditure is required. As the Agency of Mr. Chouteau is become vacant by his accepting the command of the Detachment it is in contemplation to appoint a suitable character to supply his place. Another bill of your Excellency's . . . drawn for erecting an assaying Furnace has not been protected. . . . The President has been consulted and the observations herein contained have his approval . . . .[96]

The military part of the expedition had a designated point and purpose, but Tillier and Bates were emphasizing the commercial and military combination, which ran counter to the use of public funds. Lewis had not explained the plan to the War Department because it had been previously approved and sanctioned by Dearborn in 1807. When Simmons charged Lewis that he had not complied "in all practicable cases," Lewis hadn't been advised of the government mandate of quarterly expenditures until after he sent the bills. The accountant refused five drafts, which amounted to $1,242, in his letter of July 15, 1809, four of which had been preapproved by Dearborn in March 1808.[97]

One can only imagine what Lewis was feeling when he read Simmons's refusal—with each sentence, his administration was unraveling before him. He responded to Simmons on August 18:

Yours of the 15th July is now before me, the feelings it excites are truly painful. With respect to every public expenditure, I have always accompanied my Draft by Letters of advice, stating explicitly, the object of the expenditure: if the object be not a proper one . . . I am responsible; but if on investigation, it does appear to have been necessary . . . I shall hope for relief.[98]

Penned by Jeremiah Connor, the sheriff of Saint Louis, because Lewis was sick with malaria and his shaking hands could not write legibly, Lewis's letter was seven pages and explained, point by point, Lewis's intentions in an attempt to refute the accountant's remarks.[99] Letters of advice had accompanied every one of his drafts since his arrival in Saint Louis. On the last page of the letter, Lewis spoke about missing correspondence that he had sent to Washington to which he had not received an answer. "I have reason to believe that sundry of my Letters have been lost, as there remain several important Subjects on which I have not yet received an Answer."[100] His July 8 letter was never received; two others written in 1808 arrived with their contents missing; others arrived just before his death in October; and one arrived after his death.[101]

Lewis personally paid for the expenses of publishing the laws.[102] On August 29, 1809, he met with the legislature and laid before them an account for printing and translating the laws of the territory in the amount of $1,524.57.[103] The following day the legislature approved the bill, but it does not appear when he was reimbursed, or if Lewis paid Peter Provenchere the $560 owed to him.[104] Provenchere wrote to his father on December 21, 1809, complaining that he hadn't been paid:

> The disastrous death of our last Governor, while he was himself on a voyage from here to Washington, and who was a debtor of Mr. P. Ch. [Pierre Chouteau] of a very consequential sum, has put the latter in such a constrained position that whatever connections were between the two of us, would make it useless for him to employ me as before. I am, then, reduced in St. Louis to working for his elder brother [Auguste Chouteau], work of not enough consequence to fully occupy me. After all this, you can judge what my position is and see that I am really forced to leave St. Louis. . . . The death of Governor Lewis is again a misfortune for me, for because of his influence, I would have obtained something to do, although actually his conduct . . . was disapproved by the government. I lost hope, then, of getting anything.[105]

With expenses piling up and his reputation on the line both in Saint Louis and in Washington, Lewis knew that he had but one chance to salvage his personal honor and preserve his chances for a future career, and that was to go to the nation's capital to explain himself to the president and to confront Accountant Simmons about his unreimbursed drafts. Lewis departed Saint Louis on September 4 with the intent of going to Washington by water, but upon reaching Fort Pickering at the Chickasaw Bluffs on September 15, he rested for two weeks, as he had been stricken with a bout of malaria. Capt. Gilbert Russell, the commanding officer of the fort, took care of him and wanted to accompany Lewis to Washington.

During his stay at Fort Pickering, Lewis had changed his mind about traveling any further downriver. New Orleans had been struck with a malarial epidemic and would be a most unhealthy place to be. Lewis continued overland to try to reach Washington and died on his way there, never having had his face-to-face meeting with the officials who could have cleared his name and his financial health.

The career of William Simmons was not yet ended, however, and his parsimonious and autocratic reign was destined to ruin or end more lives. Dr. John M. Daniel, the hospital surgeon stationed in New Orleans, worried about the outbreak of malaria there, requested of Simmons the establishment of a small hospital. Predictably, Simmons replied that there was no need and that "there is not any other post within the US [containing] a body of troops sufficient to require or justify such an establishment."[106] By November of that year, more than 700 soldiers had died in New Orleans from the epidemic.[107]

At the beginning of 1809, a Capt. Thomas Van Dyke was ordered by the War Department to move his troops to a fort in eastern Tennessee. Simmons rejected the entire amount of a $623 bill submitted by Van Dyke for the relocation. Van Dyke mirrored Lewis's angst when he wrote in August 1809:

> I feel conscious of having exercised my best judgment for the promotion of my countries interest and true good—from the subsequent statement & facts I still hope to impress you with the same belief . . . in addition to those [facts] mentioned it may not be improper to observe, that having a large family to support, & dependent on my pay alone, for that support, my situation will be extremely embarrassed, without my accounts are admitted.[108]

After Lewis died, several Saint Louis residents brought suit against his estate to recover their debts. When reviewing Lewis's lawsuits in 1810 and 1811 and Lewis's estate papers, there was no mention of a debt from the territorial legislature. There were other expenses that Simmons, the secretary of state, and the secretary of the treasury refused to pay, which amounted to about $3,800 out of Lewis's pocket that were never reimbursed. The refusal of these expenses ushered in Lewis's financial ruin, which had started with his trying to fulfill the land ownership requirement of his post through the purchase of extensive land holdings in the territory.[109]

From 1810 to 1812, the US government acknowledged many of the drafts that Simmons refused, and these were paid to Lewis's estate.

A chart showing some of the bills incurred by Governor Lewis later reimbursed by the government:

1808

Lewis's drafts	amount	date paid	description
Nicholas Boilvin	$50.00	1810	Indian agent
Pierre Dorion	$313.70	1812	
Sydall Manley	$500.00		unrecognized[110]
James McFarlane	$459.54	1812	
Peter Provenchere	$71.60	unpaid	translations
Joseph Charless	$1,524.57		territorial laws

1809

Lewis's drafts	amount	date paid	description
Pierre Chouteau	$440.00	1812[111]	

Pierre Chouteau	$500.00	1812[112]	
Pierre Chouteau	$81.00	1812	
William Thomas	$220.00	1812	
James McFarlane	$808.80	1812	
Nathan Boone	$15.00	1812	
J. McDonald	$271.00	1812	
John Mullanphy	$2.25	1812	6 handkerchiefs for Mandan chief
Expedition expenses $8,843.84		1812	expunged from the record[113]

If Simmons had followed treasury and congressional protocol, Lewis would not have incurred these debts, but in the last three months of his governorship, he faced unspeakable anxiety, misfortune, and embarrassment. Simply put, Simmons's unchecked power degraded the life of a great man in the service of his country.

EPILOGUE

William Eustis served as secretary of war until after the start of the War of 1812, when, in the midst of trying to prepare the nation for a sudden war and military defeats on the battlefield, he resigned from office due to public pressure. In 1813, President Madison replaced him with the far more experienced John Armstrong. Armstrong was known to be a tough, no-nonsense, but even-tempered individual, but he clashed often with Simmons. On January 3, 1814, Armstrong brought the nature of Simmons's tenure to the attention of a congressional committee whose mandate was to investigate the abuses that had occurred from the "many defects in the organisation and practice of the Accounting branch of this department."[114] Armstrong wanted the committee to propose a bill establishing that

> the expending departments of the government ought to have ... little ... to do with the settling of accounts and that balances ... due to individuals ... with the United States should be ... found by the Accounting officers of the treasury department.[115]

In the past, the secretary of war was obliged to sign warrants before the accountant fulfilled his duty, which resulted in great abuses against such government officials as Meriwether Lewis, Capt. Samuel Vance, Thomas and Cuthbert Bullitt, Gen. James Wilkinson, Capt. Gilbert C. Russell, Pierre Dorion, William Clark, Pierre Chouteau, Peter Provenchere, and Capt. Thomas Van Dyke. The attorney general prepared a bill according to Armstrong's instructions and delivered it to the Senate, but it was set aside with the comments indicating

> that the provision already existed; that the law commanded reports of Accountants to be submitted to the officers of the Treasury department for examination and revision; that this was obviously and wisely intended as a check upon these reports and that to ensure this end, warrants . . . could not be legally drawn until after such examination and revision had been made, and that otherwise the check upon the haste, the errors or the corruption of Accountants, contemplated by the law would be lost and the provision itself become a mere fiction.[116]

Ezekiel Bacon, the comptroller of the treasury, having received this note from Armstrong, wrote to Simmons and reprimanded him for settling and revising accounts, especially a large one from the deputy commissary of purchases:

> [T]he adoption of such a course of proceedings . . . appeared to be entirely novel in itself, & inconsistent with the whole system of accountability which has heretofore been prescribed by this Department of their own government, as well as for that of the Accounting Officers of the War Department.[117]

Bacon reiterated the various sections in the act of Congress that regulated Simmons's duties, which provided "that the Accountant to the Department of War shall report from time to time all such settlements . . . for the inspection and revision of the accounting officers of the Treasury."[118] Simmons had not observed that provision since 1802 because he thought it wasted time.[119] Armstrong believed that the practice fell "under the head of deficient morals."[120]

Armstrong had met with Simmons and told him that he would not sign any more warrants until each and every account was approved by the Treasury Department. One of the clerks in Simmons's office brought several reports accompanied with warrants to sign, but Armstrong "tore them up with great violence, and put them in the fire," and returned the rest to the accountant.[121] Armstrong then discussed the matter with President Madison on June 29, 1814, explaining that many officers in the government shared his concern and "that I could multiply proofs of this sort of mischief and misrepresentation—from three to three hundred."[122]

Armstrong provided what Dearborn did not—proof. He described an account of one officer where Simmons refused to sign a warrant for $3,500, "and which, after eight journies to this place, would have enabled him to discharge debts incurred in public accounts two years ago."[123] Armstrong also wrote about the abuse that Simmons had waged on Wilkinson for five years and mentioned other accounts.

President Madison wrote to Armstrong a week later, and in a four-page letter described many aspects of Simmons's duties, including the requirement of submitting quarterly accounts to the Treasury, the reason for warrants, what they meant, and their legality and usage. Armstrong thought that the signatures on the warrants were essential to the final settlement of an account, but Madison stated that they only provided authenticity.[124] After Madison replied to Armstrong, the president sent a brief letter to Simmons: "It being requisite that the office of Accountant to the Department of War be placed in other hands, you will consider it as ceasing to be in your's after this date."[125]

Finally, justice had been meted out, but it was too late for a dedicated individual like Lewis. For over a decade, one person with too much power had been able to negatively affect the governance of the country, the administration of the nation's defense establishment, and its mechanism for diplomacy with Native American tribes. How many persons did Simmons flatly refuse to pay, and how many accounts were arbitrarily modified or delayed in the far reaches of the empire? Simmons's office reviewed thousands of transactions yearly.[126] As we have seen, the fanatical machinations of this one man led to the deaths of innocent men from disease, and can be cited as a major contributing factor to the death of the governor of the Louisiana Territory, Meriwether Lewis.[127]

Chapter 11

FROM FORT PICKERING TO NASHVILLE, TENNESSEE: THE FINAL CHAPTER

Since Meriwether Lewis's death in the Tennessee backwoods on October 11, 1809, tremendous interest has fueled endless speculation about how events unfolded during his journey from Fort Pickering (modern-day Memphis) to Nashville, Tennessee. Writers and historians have determined from reading official correspondence that Lewis's demise was somehow intricately linked to Maj. James Neely, the Chickasaw Indian agent who traveled with him. They have also employed a plethora of guesswork to try and discredit Neely, to question the route that he and Lewis took when they departed Fort Pickering, to instill doubt about the events at the homestead of Robert Grinder known as Grinder's Inn, and to assert that the letter Neely wrote from Nashville, informing Thomas Jefferson of Lewis's death, was a cover-up.[1]

Given these accusations from leading historians that discredit Maj. James Neely, it is important to establish who James Neely was as a historical figure, whether or not he actually accompanied Lewis during the explorer's final days of life, and if he was the author of the letter to Thomas Jefferson describing Lewis's death.

Up until the present, James Neely was an easy target for criticism because little information had been found about him. This criticism resulted in a skewed conception of his conduct when he was the Chickasaw Indian agent from July 1809 to June 1812.[2] Recently, a program on the History Channel presented documentation that supposedly placed Neely in a courtroom fifty-five miles away from Grinder's Inn on October 11, 1809, the date of Lewis's demise.[3] This new information and the way in which it was presented might lead persons unacquainted with the details of Neely's life to believe that Neely lied to Thomas Jefferson in his letter about Lewis's death; it might even lead to wild speculation that he was involved in Lewis's murder—or was at the very least an accomplice. If it is true that Neely was in court and not at Lewis's side, the order of events, including Neely's arrival at Nashville on October 18, would be thrown into doubt, exacerbating the mystery of Lewis's final days.

However, as in many other instances involving historical mysteries, dogged research can uncover hitherto unknown sources. A danger inherent in this statement is encapsulated in the word "dogged"; partial research involving single documents taken out of context can often result in worse misconceptions than those that had existed when there was a vacuum of historical knowledge. Thorough research of a topic, approached through traditional and nontraditional types of documentation, can yield new and enlightening perspectives on the past, while half-baked efforts can lead to dangerous misconceptions and false conclusions.

In order to properly tell the story of James Neelly's involvement in the final days of Lewis's life, we first have to examine the development of the Natchez Trace, which ultimately led to James Neelly's appointment as an Indian agent and his timely arrival at Fort Pickering in 1809.

The Natchez Trace was an important wilderness road leading from Natchez to Nashville; it was also known as the Old Natchez Trace, Chickasaw Trace, or the Columbian Highway.[4] It had begun as an Indian trail or a game trail that cut through the present states of Mississippi and Tennessee and wound through land that was occupied by the Chickasaw and Choctaw Indians.[5] According to historian Arrell Gibson, the Natchez Trace served as "a strategic land bridge connecting the Cumberland and Ohio River settlements with the lower Mississippi Valley and Gulf."[6] It had been hewn out of the Mississippi and Tennessee wilderness and was considered unsafe because it "exposed the traveler to dangers of the natural elements, disgruntled Indians, and—worst of all—attack by notorious highwaymen and murderers."[7]

In 1797, the United States government signed a treaty with the Chickasaw Nation, the stated purpose of which was to exchange land for goods, but with the unstated primary goal of opening the Natchez Trace as a major postal route and thoroughfare for travelers. Work on what was then referred to as the Natchez Road-commenced in 1802 and took a decade to complete.[8] In the process of building out the road, large numbers of squatters encroached upon Chickasaw soil. This encroachment led to the passage of laws under the aegis of the US Department of Indian Affairs, which regulated the intercourse and commerce with the tribes. In an effort to prevent squatting, the department appointed an Indian agent to reside among the Chickasaws who would serve as their intermediary and report crimes against them and incursions upon their land back to Washington.

The Chickasaw Indian Agency was established in the Mississippi Territory, near a thriving Chickasaw village called Big Town, halfway between Natchez and Nashville, near modern day Okolona, Mississippi, at milepost 241.4 of the Natchez Trace Parkway.[9] In May 1802, Henry Dearborn, the secretary of war, described the numerous duties and responsibilities of the Chickasaw agent:

The motives of the Government for sending Agents to reside with the Indian Nations, are the cultivation of peace and harmony between the U. States, and the Indian Nations generally; the detection of any improper conduct in the Indians, or the Citizens of the U. States, or others, relating to the Indians, or their lands, and the introduction of the Arts of husbandry, and domestic manufactures, as means of producing, and diffusing the blessings attached to a well regulated civil society: To effect the foregoing important objects of your Agency, you will use all the prudent means in your power. Suitable measures should be pursued for introducing the use of the plough, and the growth of Cotton as well as Grain. A Woman well calculated for the business should be employed in teaching the females spinning and weaving, and other household Arts; the use of Spiritous Liquors you should discourage by precept, and example. . . . You will refer to the Act passed the 30th March 1802 entitled an Act to regulate trade . . . to preserve peace on the frontiers.[10]

These agents also took charge of a subset of responsibilities that related to internal problems, such as insuring peaceful travel through Indian lands, collecting debts, recovering stolen horses, removing trespassers, and capturing fugitives.[11]

By 1808, the Chickasaw Agency was large and contained "a stable, granary, and fodder loft," and still later, "a blacksmith's shop, and shelter to house the spinners and weavers."[12] There were also houses for the Indian interpreter, Indian agent, weaver and instructor of husbandry, blacksmith, and a lodge for visiting Indian dignitaries. James Neelly, the fourth Chickasaw Indian agent, succeeded Thomas Wright in 1809.[13] Wright had succumbed to a severe attack of the ague on August 10, 1808, and at the end of September he died from it.[14] A few months later, in February 1809, George Colbert, half Chickasaw and "chief negotiator" of that nation, recommended Neelly to Secretary Dearborn:

Father if you would be so good as to indulge us, we could recommend an old Gentleman of our acquaintance that is not so fond of Speculation, as our former agents have been, his name is Maj. James Neely but perhaps it may be too forward in us to recommend any person to Government—therefore we will leave it to your superior judgment to send us a good man . . . we would prefer an Elderly man as an agent as young men in the heat of youth may abuse your authority, there has been an instance of that already, in this nation of an agent going wrong, the red people wished to put him right & he threatned us with the Government & the Laws therefore we conceive that an Old is more suitable to do business with red people than a young man.[15]

Colbert's use of the word *speculation* meant other nefarious activities, too: a former agent had established a tavern at the agency to supplement his income by selling liquor, while others were known to engage in private trading.[16] Colbert himself operated a ferry forty miles from the Chickasaw village near modern Tupelo, Mississippi, where the Natchez Trace crosses the Tennessee River.[17] The river was deep at this place, with a rapid current that made it "impossible to ford," and Colbert made a good income from this business—about $2,000 annually.[18]

Having not received an answer from the secretary of war, Chenubbee Mingo, the king or headman of the Chickasaws, followed with another letter to Dearborn explaining the necessity of a Chickasaw Indian agent, the constant trespassing of intruders on Chickasaw land, and the distribution of their annuity:[19]

> Father: after the death of our late Agent last fall we petitioned the Government of the United States to send us an Agent, a good sedate sober man from some one of the old states, & we have never received any answer as yet.—the reason why we did petition for such an Agent, was that some of the individuals of the neighbouring states, are a good deal inclined to land speculation—for instance gentlemin from near franklin Tennessee by the name of Potter & whom we heard had petitioned to Government for this Agency has with some others been in our land hunting old lines, at least fifty miles within our boundary line this makes us believe that were we to have any Agent from any of the neighbouring states they might be guilty of the like Practices . . . our Annuity for the last year has been laying at the Chickasaw Bluffs above twelve months & we are afraid it may be damaged—if the President our Father would be pleased to authorize the officer Commanding fort Pickering or any other person that he may think proper to deliver it to us—we will take it as a particular favour & as an instance of his Parental kindness to his red Children the Chickasaws.[20]

Return J. Meigs, the Cherokee Indian agent, had been assisting the Chickasaws since Wright's unexpected illness and death. He explained the utmost urgency to fill the position of Chickasaw agent in a letter to the secretary of war dated June 12, 1809: in June 1809 he had to remove ninety-three families, all farmers, from Chickasaw land.[21] Although these family groups were compliant, there were others who were an aggressive and feared lot:

> The great length of this frontier & the few troops in this quarter, puts it in the power of lawless characters to impose on the Indians & to put the U. States to considerable expence. Should this disposition to encroach on Indian lands increase, they will perhaps at some future period put the few troops here at defiance. These intruders are always well armed, desperate characters, have nothing to lose; & many of them hold barbarous sentiment toward Indians. They see very extensive tracts of forrest held by the Indians imcullivated, disproportioned to the present or even expected population of the tribes, they cannot purchase lands. They plead necessity in the first instance, & if the land should be purchased of the Indians will plead a right of preemption making a merit of their crimes.[22]

Finally on July 7, 1809, the secretary of war took the advice of Colbert and appointed James Neely as Chickasaw Indian agent at the standard rate of $1,000 annually and $365 for subsistence.[23]

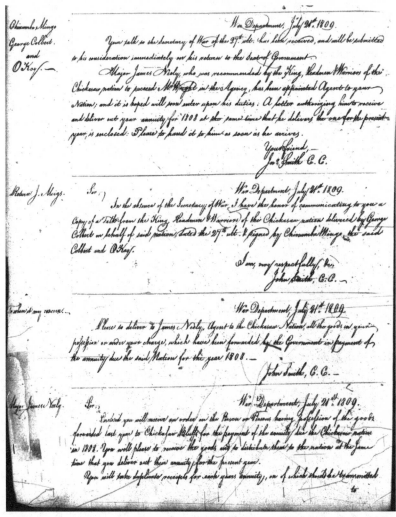

Letter from the secretary of war to the Chickasaw headmen Chinumba Mingo, George Colbert, and O'Koy, appointing Major James Neelly as the Chickasaw agent. (Secretary of War to Chinumba Mingo, George Colbert, and O'Koy, July 21, 1809, RG75, M15, roll 3, p. 3, frame 0019, National Archives and Records Administration.)

Neelly did not receive the news until August 8, when Gen. James Robertson, the commissioner of Indian affairs from Nashville, delivered the commission in person at his home, a few miles from Franklin, Tennessee.[24] Neelly, who held the rank of major in the Tennessee militia, was from Duck River, outside Franklin. During the three years that Neelly served as Indian agent, he remained faithful to his appointment, which is not surprising, since he was closely allied with the regional government in Williamson County, Tennessee. In February 1800, when the Court of Common Pleas and Quarter Sessions was established in Franklin, Neelly was immediately enlisted as a juror in civil court, appointed a juror in the Superior Court, and he collected taxes for Capt. Gordon's Company until his appointment as Indian agent.[25] Neelly's commission also contained an extensive letter from the secretary of war, which included orders to hasten to his post and take command of the agency and buildings. When the former agent, Wright, suddenly died, the War Department routed the annuities due to the tribe to the factor at Fort Pickering, 150 miles northwest of the agency.[26] It was essential that Neelly, when he completed his initial work at the agency, depart post haste to meet with the Chickasaw chiefs, then travel to the fort, meet with the factor, pick up the articles for the Chickasaws, and return to the agency to distribute them.[27]

On July 21, the War Department acknowledged the letters from the Chickasaw chiefs and informed them of the new appointment:

> Maj. James Neelly, who was recommended by the King, Headmen & Warriors . . . to succeed Mr. Wright in the Agency, has been appointed Agent to your Nation; and it is hoped will soon enter upon his duties. A letter authorizing him to receive and deliver out your annuity for 1808 at this time that he delivers the one for the present year, is enclosed: Please to hand it to him as soon as he arrives.[28]

The War Department instructed Maj. Neelly to take possession and distribute the annuities for 1808 and 1809, which covered a vast quantity of materials.[29]

Neelly's first month as agent was packed with chores and travel. The Chickasaw Agency was due south from Neelly's home on Duck River on the Natchez Road, and Neelly arrived there about August 26.[30] The following day he assessed the agency property and reported dismal conditions regarding the office and residence:

> After my arrival at this place I viewed the Public Buildings in hopes to find a Comfortable house to live in but to my surprise I only found the remains of a house that is an old shell, the roof at first was covered with what workmen call lap shingles, there is part of them gone & all the remainder loose, the Sleepers are all rotten & not worth repairing. by the best judgment that I can Collect to view it—the bottom logs of the smoak house are rotten & the kitchen is in a decayed state— from a letter that I found among Mr. Wright's papers from Henry Dearborn Esqr. your predecessor in Office a letter in answer to a letter from Mr. Wright respecting permission to repair or build an addition to the agency house Mr. Dearborn's letter

directs him to make such Economical repairs or addition to the Agency house as he might think proper—I suppose on the strength of that letter Mr. Wright in his life-time had got a frame almost complete ready to be raised as an addition to the Agency house which frame is still lying here unfinished—on viewing the plan I percieve his intention was to keep public entertainment which would have given great umbrage to the Indians as they wish to reserve that business soley to them-selves for the benefit of the nation it is said that Mr. Wright had began the busi-ness & that the Indians would soon have drove him, had not death taken him off. now sir if you forbid it not I think the best plan would be to put up the new frame in place of the Old one—as I cannot think of living in the old one there is no pos-sibility of making it a safe or comfortable house to live in—this I hope you will advise me of as soon as practicable as the season is fast advancing should it not meet your approbation, I must, I suppose, live in a wigwam, Indian fashion—as I expect my board will be high until I get a house to put my family in.[31]

After making his assessment of the agency, Neelly prepared to fulfill his duty to the Chickasaws regarding their annuities, and purchased a government horse on August 30 for $125.[32] He set out first to the Chickasaw village to make introductions and then headed to Fort Pickering to meet with David Hogg, the factor, and take pos-session of the annuities to return them for distribution. Maj. Neelly made good time on the 150-mile journey and arrived at the fort on September 18. There he learned that Governor Lewis had arrived by boat three days earlier, so ill that he required assistance to walk from the bottom of the bluff up the 120 square log steps to the fort.[33]

Maj. Neelly had never met Lewis, but because of a simple act of kindness, his life would be forever changed. Our knowledge of Neelly's involvement with the governor at the time of Lewis's death is based on various letters written to Thomas Jefferson, including those by Maj. Neelly himself.[34] While at Fort Pickering, Lewis changed his mind about his preferred travel route to Washington, deciding not to proceed to New Orleans for an ocean voyage because, as he informed President Madison, of his "appre-hension from the heat of the lower country."[35] Lewis's concern regarding "the heat" was an expression of his worries about malarial fever, which Lewis had already suc-cumbed to in the beginning of August 1809, a month before departing from Saint Louis. Reports from New Orleans stated that the fever was rampant there, and in an era when medical knowledge of malarial fevers was limited, such areas were to be avoided by those coping with the disease. When Lewis arrived at Fort Pickering he was still sick with fever, which is known to incapacitate for several days.

Gilbert Russell, the commander of the fort, thought that he might be able to escort Lewis to Washington. He had been corresponding with the accountant of the War Department over a costly unpaid bill and had asked the secretary of war for per-mission to go to Washington to clear up the matter.[36] Russell waited an extra week

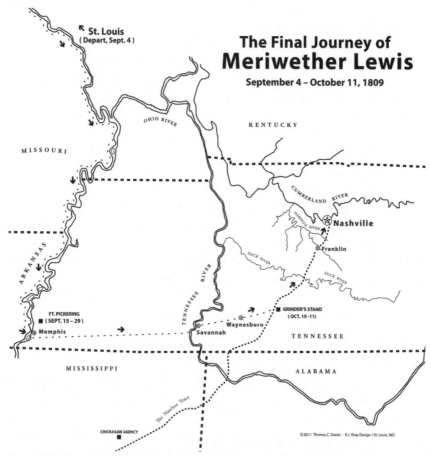

The route that the Neelly/Lewis party traveled from Fort Pickering to Grinder's Inn. Nashville was their initial destination, not Grinder's Stand. It has been assumed that the party rode south to the Chickasaw Agency, then northeast to Grinder's Stand, but that would have taken more than eleven days. (Courtesy of Thomas C. Danisi.)

for the mail to arrive, thinking that his approval was forthcoming from the War Department.[37] When the approval did not arrive, Neelly may have stepped in to offer his services to the ailing governor and hero of western exploration. Russell may have requested that Neelly, as a government employee, accompany Lewis, who was still very ill while staying at the fort. Russell was certainly very concerned over Lewis's condition. Exactly how Neelly's services were offered and accepted is unknown, but on September 29, 1809, Lewis, his servant John Pernia, a hired horsepacker, and Neelly departed Fort Pickering for the Natchez Trace.[38]

Some historians believe that the party first traveled to the Chickasaw Agency before turning north for Nashville, but that would have been physically impossible. Simple math dictates otherwise when considering the standard travel time on horseback of 10–15 miles per day and keeping in mind Lewis's physical condition. The agency was not on the direct route from Memphis to Nashville, and in fact was in the opposite direction. From Memphis to the Chickasaw Agency "as the crow flies" is about 110 miles, which would have been a much longer route over the twisting roads of the time.[39] From the agency at milepost 241.4 on the Natchez Trace to Grinder's Stand, the inn where Lewis died at milepost 385, is 143 more miles, for a total of 253 miles. In a simple calculation of the distance at 10–15 miles per day it would have taken 17–25 days to reach Grinder's Inn by way of the Chickasaw Agency, instead of the eleven days they actually spent in travel.

Additionally, after they departed Fort Pickering, there were complications. Neelly stated that after crossing the Tennessee River, which is located at Savannah, Tennessee, Lewis became ill and the party rested for two days. The direct distance from Fort Pickering (Memphis) to Grinder's Inn is about 150 miles, and given an eight-day spread, only the most direct route would have allowed them to reach their destination. The party probably traveled the route of present day US 64.[40]

The party made their penultimate camp at milepost 375, and on the morning of October 10, Neelly remained behind to look for two horses that strayed the previous night.[41] The party was approaching the area where Neelly lived. Since he was very familiar with the locale, he could have advised Lewis on October 10 about how to proceed until he could catch up and bring the lost horses. Neelly knew that a man named Robert Grinder had accommodations for travelers and that his "stand" or inn was not far—a day's ride.[42]

Late in the afternoon, Lewis and the two others arrived at Robert Grinder's house. In the early morning hours of October 11, Meriwether Lewis died. Maj. Neelly arrived the next day, reporting that "I came up some time after & had him as decently Buried as I could in that place."[43]

Recently, Maj. Neelly's solid two-hundred-year-old account of the events has been challenged by a new interpretation of a historical court document, an interpretation that was aired on the December 9, 2010, presentation of *Decoded* for the History Channel.[44] Tony Turnbow, an attorney who practices in Franklin, Tennessee, and the discoverer of the court document, alleged that Neelly was in a Tennessee courtroom on October 11, 1809, rather than on the Natchez Trace with Lewis. The Williamson County Court document shows that a lawsuit had been filed against James Neelly, who had been ordered to be in court on October 11 and thus could not have been at Grinder's Inn.[45]

Tony Turnbow very generously shared copies of the documents he relied upon in drawing his conclusions. In the preparation of this chapter, the court documents were utilized, as was the expertise of Tennessee attorney Caesar Cirigliano, who practices criminal and civil law in Williamson County today. Mr. Cirigliano's investigation of the documents revealed that Neelly had simply not been ordered by the court to be present on October 11, 1809. The minute book of the county court states:

> Thomas Masterson & Co. vs. James Neelly. Debt $103.44 Dam. $20. . . . This day came the parties by their attor & came also a jury of good and lawful men . . . who being elected tried and sworn the truth to speak upon the issue joined upon their oath. . . . [46]

Cirigliano explained that the county court minutes show that "this day came the parties by their attor"; in other words, the litigants in the civil suit were represented before the court by their attorneys, and the litigants did not have to be present. The legal wording is very exact: "came the parties by their attor," The abbreviation "attor," common at the time, was included in most legal writing from the county court minutes of Williamson County. This wording indicates that attorneys represented the parties at the courthouse on that date. It does not state or imply that the parties *and* their attorneys were both present; it is common practice, observed today as well, to waive the presence of the client in court when represented by counsel in a civil suit of this type.[47]

One other point must be made: How important was this trial to Neelly? Some might feel, from reading the document, that since Neelly was close enough to where the court met at Franklin, about fifty-five miles away, he might have been inclined to drop everything and go to court. However, this would be unlikely considering that Neelly had taken it upon himself to deliver the ailing Lewis safely to authorities at Nashville. Since Neelly would most certainly miss his day in court, how important was his appearance? What would be the ramifications if Neelly did not appear? Actually, nothing serious would have occurred except that he would have lost the case by default and would therefore have had to pay the amount of money for which he was being sued, which totaled $123.44 with damages. Although this was a substantial amount of money at the time, there is no evidence that it would have worried Neelly. And there is proof for this line of reasoning: On July 8, 1805, Neelly was called as a witness in a civil lawsuit. Neelly "was solemnly called but came not." The court levied a fine of $125 unless he could show sufficient cause of his inability to appear and he was ordered to attend at the next court, which was set for January 17, 1806. On that day, Neelly "came not" and had to pay the fine.[48] The case was a civil and not a criminal action, and Neelly was under no obligation to attend, as he had been in 1805 when he was subpoenaed as a witness to someone else's lawsuit. Although his attorney may have ably represented Neelly on the date in question, the court records reveal no further disposition of the case, which may have been dropped thereafter.

These two arguments, while clever in dismantling the impact and seriousness of Neelly's involvement, do not absolve him of wrongdoing and continue to reinforce the idea that he might have been underhanded in some way. The underlying problem with the lawsuit is that no identifying characteristics mark the James Neelly named in the suit. There is no information pertaining to age or date of birth, nor the location where he lived or worked. Furthermore, the discoverer of this document left too many questions unanswered. Who was James Neelly, and was he an honorable or dishonorable man?

As archaeologist and historian W. Raymond Wood ably wrote, "The truth is to be found in detailed detective work."[49] In an effort to corroborate Turnbow's assertion, deep research was conducted to fully understand the inconsistencies. The Williamson County clerk at the time of the Neelly suit was Nicholas P. Hardeman, who also operated a merchant store in Franklin, Tennessee, with his brother. The Hardemans ran a brisk business with many of the locals, including an extensive number of individuals by the name of Neelly. Taking a sample of the Hardemans' accounts from this time period, fourteen Neellys are revealed to have transacted business with the store. The Hardemans made particular identification for four Neellys with similar names: Maj. James Neelly, James Neelly Sr., James Neelly Jr., and James Neelly, Esquire.[50]

The lawsuit papers that Turnbow provided originated from the Williamson County Court files and County Clerk Minutes record book. The County Clerk Minutes record book spans the years from 1800 to 1815 and interestingly contains many entries with the name of Neelly. For instance, on January 13, 1807, there are two separate Neelly entries regarding the repair of a road, which corroborates the identifications in the Hardeman accounts. The entries stipulate the "keeping in repair [of] the public road lately laid from Jas. Neellys to Cannons horse mill . . . ," while the other entry calls for "keeping in repair the public road from . . . N. P. Hardemans land to Duck river ridge . . . to the mouth of Maj. James Neellys spring branch where it enters into Murfrees Fork . . . ."[51]

One court document viewed in isolation should not be enough evidence to dismantle an honorable man's reputation. The fact that four James Neellys were living in the same area at the same time casts doubt upon whether the defendant in the October 11, 1809, lawsuit was even the same James Neelly who was Chickasaw Indian agent and accompanied Lewis from Fort Pickering.[52]

On October 11, 1809, after burying Lewis, Maj. Neelly and party departed Grinder's Inn and made their way to Nashville with Lewis's belongings. It was probably one of the most grueling and tragic weeks of Neelly's life. Within a day's ride and minus two horses, they had to cross another large river and then travel over rough terrain: "Duck River was fordable and once over it the Trace struck boldly into the mountains that made up most of the 50 miles to Nashville. Travellers had to dismount at this stage and get along the best they could on foot through sandy soil that played sad havoc with their feet."[53]

Ten miles from Nashville the Trace crossed the Harpeth River, which was "fifty yards wide" and "the road widened, announcing the nearness of a settlement."[54]

They arrived about October 18 in Nashville, where a small US trading post had been established years earlier.[55] A special agent of the United States, Capt. John Brahan, receiver of public monies, was Neelly's local superior, and Neelly reported the details of Gov. Lewis's death to him. It has been a mystery to historians why Capt. Brahan was in Nashville and not with his company of soldiers. However, it may be of some interest that Albert Gallatin, the secretary of the treasury, had temporarily appointed Brahan to a nonmilitary position. Gen. James Wilkinson even complained to the secretary of war about Gallatin's over-reaching authority in June 1809:

> One of my Captains, Brahan, at Columbian Springs, has been appointed by Mr. Gallatin a receiver of public monies for the sale of lands some where. He has received his appointment & instructions whilst at the head of his platoon. I respect the authority from whence they emanated too much to counteract the intention, & have therefore given him leave of absence without forcing a resignation; but I must believe it is not exactly correct, to take our officers from us without our privity or approbation.[56]

On October 18, 1809, letters were written to Thomas Jefferson and to the secretary of war detailing the tragic news.[57] What has not been uncovered until now is that Brahan wrote not only letters of his own but Maj. Neelly's letter as well. This oversight explains some of the apparent dates where Maj. Neelly was in two places on the same date. While Maj. Neelly was an Indian agent, for instance, Malcolm McGee, the Indian interpreter at the agency, wrote almost all the letters for Neelly, Chinumba, and Colbert. For the first time it makes sense how Maj. Neelly could have been in Nashville on October 18 and also have a letter with that same date written from the Chickasaw Agency.[58]

While it has been thought that Maj. Neelly was somehow a suspicious figure and had possibly lied or attempted a cover-up in regard to Lewis's death, it has now been proven by authentic documentation that he was an ordinary man somehow embroiled in a suspected murder because of errant speculation. At the end of September 1809, Maj. Neelly, busy organizing an Indian agency, trying to do justice to his government appointment and the Indian people who requested his services, volunteered for a thankless assignment that has met with extreme controversy for at least a century, but now, hopefully, has been more fully explained.

Capt. John Brahan wrote these three letters, even though one letter originated from Maj. James Neelly, Chickasaw Indian agent: Maj. Neelly to Thomas Jefferson, John Brahan to the secretary of war, and John Brahan to Thomas Jefferson. (James Neelly to Thomas Jefferson, October 18, 1809, document 33522-23, roll 44, and John Brahan to Thomas Jefferson, October 18, 1809, document 33520-21, roll 44, Thomas Jefferson Papers, Library of Congress; John Brahan to Secretary of War, October 18, 1809, B589, RG107, M221, roll 18, frame 5632, National Archives and Records Administration.)

Chickasaw nation Feb.y 18th 1809

Father since the death of our Agent there has a great many white people came into our country & have settled on our land without our permission

Chickasaw Agency Aug.t 27th 1809

Sir

after my Arrival at this place I viewed the Public Buildings, in hopes to find a Comfortable house to live in but to my surprise I only found the remains of a house that is an old shell. the roof at first was covered with

Malcolm McGee, the Chickasaw Indian interpreter, wrote letters for both the Chickasaw headmen and Major Neelly. These letters demonstrate, for the first time, how Neelly could be present in two places on the same date. (George Colbert to Secretary of War, February 18, 1809, C469, RG107, M221, roll 20, frame 6146, and James Neelly to Secretary of War, August 27, 1809, N94, M221, roll 27, National Archives and Records Administration.)

Chapter 12

THE GILBERT RUSSELL STATEMENT

Various documents connected to Meriwether Lewis, William Clark, and the Corps of Discovery in the form of letters, official reports, and period newspaper articles, have garnered special attention over the course of many years of intense study. One document, intricately linked with Lewis's death in 1809, has received a great deal of notoriety as a result, yet its background is a mystery to historians. Known as the "Gilbert Russell Statement," it is a four-page document detailing the circumstances of Lewis's death, an event that has baffled historians for two centuries.[1]

In 1811, Gilbert Russell, an officer in the US Army, was ordered by the secretary of War to Fredericktown, Maryland, to attend Gen. James Wilkinson's court-martial. The trial was convened because hundreds of soldiers had perished from malaria under Wilkinson's command during the summer and autumn of 1809. Russell provided testimony at the trial to establish Wilkinson's character and, during this same trip, also gave a statement regarding Lewis's death, which had occurred two years previously. Russell had personal knowledge of the events surrounding Lewis's death because he had been the commander of Fort Pickering (near today's Memphis, Tennessee) when Lewis passed through that post in 1809. Fort Pickering was the last habitation where Lewis was seen prior to his death. A knowledge of his actions and behavior at the fort is crucial to understanding the events that unfolded a few days later when Lewis died along the Natchez Trace, en route to Nashville.

What has not been properly addressed by historians is that the Russell Statement is a recollection of the event, not a first hand report, and Russell's version of the story was composed not only from his own experiences, but also from interviews he conducted with various persons who conversed with Lewis at Fort Pickering and knew of events that had taken place along the Natchez Trace and at Grinder's Stand, the scene of Lewis's death. These eyewitnesses to various portions of the story included Maj. James Neelly, David Hogg (the factor at Fort Pickering), and Dr. William C. Smith, the surgeon's mate at Fort Pickering. Russell's recollection was also based upon reading newspaper reports and his correspondence with officials like Thomas Jefferson and William D. Meriwether, the administrator for the Lewis estate.

Top section of the first page of the Gilbert Russell Statement written on November 26, 1811. It has been a mystery since 1811 who wrote this letter and who knew so many facts regarding Lewis's death. It had been assumed by the murder and conspiracy theorists that whoever wrote this letter was either Lewis's murderer or in on the murder. "Governor Lewis left St. Louis late in August or early in September 1809, intending to go by the route of the Mississippi and the Ocean, to the City of Washington; taking with him all the papers relative to his expedition to the pacific Ocean, for the purpose of preparing and putting them to the press, and to have some drafts paid which had been drawn by him on the Government and protested. . . ." (Gilbert C. Russell, November 26, 1811, p. 1, Jonathan Williams MSS, box 6, Lilly Library Manuscript Collections, Indiana University, Bloomington, IN.)

The Gilbert Russell Statement begins :

> Governor Lewis left St. Louis . . . early in September 1809, intending to go by the route of the Mississippi and the Ocean, to the City of Washington, taking with him all the papers relative to his expedition to the pacific Ocean, for the purpose of preparing and putting them to the press, and to have some drafts paid which had been drawn by him on the Government and protested. On the morning of the 15th of September, the Boat in which he was a passenger landed him at Fort pickering in a state of mental derangement. . . . The Subscriber being then the Commanding Officer of the Fort on discovering from the crew that he had made two attempts to Kill himself, in one of which he had nearly succeeded, resolved at once to take possession of him and his papers, and detain them there untill he recovered. . . . [O]n the sixth or seventh day all symptoms of derangement disappeared and

he was completely in his senses. . . . On the 29th of the same month he left . . . with the Chickasaw agent . . . and some of the Chiefs, intending to proceed the usual route thro' the Indian Country. . . . [I]n three or four days he was again affected with the same mental disease . . . .[2]

In the year 2006, historian James Holmberg had difficulty describing the document because he did not know "why the statement was given."[3] Those who suggest that Lewis was murdered in 1809 generally believe that the Russell Statement is a forgery and have suggested two incidents with which it is supposed to coincide: a revisionist version of Lewis's final days, and the identification of Brig. Gen. James Wilkinson, the commanding general of the United States Army, as Lewis's murderer.[4]

The Russell Statement describes the route Lewis took from Saint Louis to Fort Pickering in September 1809. It describes his behavior during that time, his departure to Nashville, and the events leading up to his death on October 11. The statement bears the signatures of Gilbert Russell and a man named Jonathan Williams, another army officer, but neither the text nor the signature are actually in Russell's hand. Russell had penned two earlier letters in January 1810, both sent to Thomas Jefferson, which detailed the events leading up to Lewis's death.[5]

Comparing the handwriting in the two Russell letters of 1810 with this 1811 statement, even a layman can see that two entirely different people penned them.[6] The discrepancy in handwriting led to a presumptuous and controversial conclusion on the part of conspiracy theorists, wherein it was claimed that whoever wrote the 1811 statement possessed such intimate knowledge of so many crucial details of Lewis's murder that he must have been Lewis's murderer—or at least in on the conspiracy to kill him. To the untrained eye the Russell Statement is truly an enigma. Who was its author? Who possessed such detailed knowledge about the circumstances surrounding Lewis's death? Why was the document written? Was the author the long-rumored murderer of Meriwether Lewis?

After searching through many archival collections for clues regarding this mystery, the Russell Statement must be considered as a completely authentic document that represents the viewpoint and experience of Capt. Russell. It is not in his handwriting because it is a legal document—an affidavit, which is a sworn statement administered in a court of law. The evolution of this important document begs for a comprehensive explanation.

Capt. Russell assumed command of Fort Pickering in June 1809.[7] During the next few months he wrote letters to the US secretary of war complaining about the deplorable condition of the fort, frequent sickness, and the inefficient surgeon of the garrison.[8] He reported in August that the ague and fever, known as malaria today, had depleted his troops to the extent that but eight or nine of them were fit for duty.[9] Less than a month later, Lewis arrived at the fort, also extremely sick from the ague, and he recuperated for nearly two weeks under Russell's care.[10] Maj. Neelly, who was appointed US agent to the Chickasaw Nation on July 7, 1809, and was a significant figure in the story of Lewis's death, arrived at Fort Pickering for the first time on September 18.[11] Neelly accompanied Lewis on his overland trip east, eventually arriving at Grinder's Stand, the place of Lewis's demise.

During the two weeks that Lewis resided at Fort Pickering, Russell, much concerned about his condition, wrote to his commanding officer asking for a furlough in the hopes that he could accompany Lewis to Washington. Russell later told Thomas Jefferson that "I had made application to the General & expected [a] leave of absence every day to go to Washington . . . with Governor Lewis."[12] Historians have guessed that Russell was referring to Gen. James Wilkinson, but that is an incorrect assumption.

Wilkinson was stationed in New Orleans during that time, and it took four weeks for mail posted from Fort Pickering to arrive in that city. What actually happened was that Russell received orders to move his company to Fort Pickering in March 1809, and when he did, he sent William Simmons, the accountant of the War Department, an expense account of the trip. Simmons denied the expenses and Russell then asked the secretary of war, Gen. Henry Dearborn, for a furlough to come to Washington and discuss the account.[13] Russell had had a similar problem with Simmons a few years earlier.[14]

When Russell told Jefferson that he requested a furlough, he was referring to the expense account problem. He had hoped that the furlough was imminent but he had only been at Fort Pickering a little over three months, and with his garrison so sickened by malarial fever he could hardly have expected approval to leave his post. However, if true, the request reveals how genuinely concerned Russell must have been about Lewis's condition, knowing that when Lewis continued on toward Washington he would need a reliable protector, perhaps an experienced nurse if he had a relapse, and someone who realized the horrible nature of Lewis's attempts to alleviate his pain while burdened with fever. Since Russell could not leave his post, he had to settle for sending Maj. Neelly as a surrogate to fulfill these roles.[15] Russell, still at Fort Pickering over a year later in November 1810, wrote once again to his superiors and repeated his desire to visit Washington.[16] Perhaps this request also involved the now-deceased Lewis, for Russell had a tale to tell regarding Lewis's final days that he alone was privy to.

Russell's account of his experiences with Lewis during the two weeks at Fort Pickering is corroborated by another, rarely cited, original document in the collections of the Missouri History Museum in Saint Louis. It is a letter written by a man named James Howe to Frederick Bates, secretary of the Louisiana Territory, on September 28, 1809, from Nashville, Tennessee. Note the date; the letter was written thirteen days before Lewis's death by a man who had no particular interest in the matter other than passing along distressing information and lamenting Lewis's condition. Although the information reported is third hand, it is crucial evidence because it was written prior to Lewis's death:

> I arrived here two days ago on my way to Maryland—yesterday Majr Stoddart of the army arrived here from Fort Adams, and informs me that in his passage through the indian nation, in the vicinity of Chickasaw Bluffs he saw a person, immediately from the Bluffs who informed him, that Governor Lewis had arrived there (some time previous to his leaving it) in a state of mental derangement, that he had made several attempts to put an end to his own existence, which this person had prevented, and that Capt. Russell, the [commanding] officer at the Bluffs had taken him into his own quarters where he was obliged to keep a strict watch over him to prevent his committing violence on himself and had caused his boat to be unloaded and the key to be secured in his stores.
>
> I am in hopes this account will prove exaggerated tho' I fear there is too much truth in it—As the post leaves this tomorrow I have thought it would not be improper to communicate these circumstances as I have heard them, to you.[17]

While Russell dealt with problems at Fort Pickering, downriver Gen. Wilkinson was about to become embroiled in a tragic situation that he could not have prevented. The War Department at the end of April 1809 ordered Wilkinson to move the troops in New Orleans up the Mississippi River to Fort Adams and Natchez. Wilkinson did not receive those orders on a timely basis and instead moved the troops twelve miles southwest of their encampment to Terre aux Boeufs due to the impending sickly season.[18] The bilious fevers were strong that summer, however, and overtook the troops in their new location.[19] Consequently Wilkinson was forced to move again but this time lacked boats and supplies, and by November 1809 more than 700 soldiers had died of the illness.[20] A physician caring for the sick troops testified that "a number [of them], in a state of delirium, wandered from their lodgings into the fields and swamps and there expired."[21]

Murder theory proponents claim that Wilkinson orchestrated the murder of Governor Lewis from afar, but moving 2,000 troops to two separate cantonments in succession was an enormous and time-consuming undertaking. The second move proved more dangerous: Wilkinson did not have enough boats to ferry the sick, and the boats that arrived on August 17 from Fort Adams were leaking and "in very bad order and some almost rotten." Lt. Samuel McCormick, who superintended the boats, said that they had to be refitted for service, and several new ones had to be built. "Rudders, oars, masts and sails were made and completed by September 10."[22] Wilkinson personally supervised their repair, attending "daily to urge the progress of it," but in September, Wilkinson was stricken with the ague. Dr. Robert Dow explained that Wilkinson was confined to his bed and "had a remittent fever attended by very violent paroxysms," and did not recover until the end of the month.[23] Dr. William Hood visited Wilkinson several times in September and described the depth of his malarial attack: "[H]is state of convalescence was tedious owing, I believe, to the great anxiety of mind which he then appeared to labour under and then being, incessantly importuned on business."[24]

Word of the massive mortality rate spread quickly, and President James Madison was appalled that Wilkinson failed to follow orders to protect his command. In April 1811, the House of Representatives appointed two committees, one to inquire into the fatalities and the other to investigate Wilkinson's public life, character, and conduct.[25] The House determined that the government possessed enough evidence to put Wilkinson on trial, and President Madison approved the military court-martial to convene on the first Monday of September 1811.

Wilkinson chose a number of military personnel and civilians as defense witnesses, some of whom were well known: Maj. Amos Stoddard, Col. William Russell, Col. Jonathan Williams, Maj. Gilbert Christian Russell, Col. John Bollinger, William Claiborne, Capt. Daniel Hughes, George Mather, and Col. William Wikoff. Brigadier Geneneral Peter Gansevoort chaired as president of the trial, which began on September 2 and ended on December 25, 1811.[26]

Russell testified on three separate days in the same month: Tuesday, November 5; Wednesday, November 20; and Saturday, November 23, 1811. He maintained that Wilkinson's conduct during the years he was in the Mississippi and Orleans territories was exemplary and he also gave a character reference.[27] The significance of the court-martial and its links to the Russell Statement, which was dated during this same period, was not apparent, however, until a crucial handwriting comparison was made. Looking at both the record of the court-martial proceedings and the Russell Statement side by side, one can easily see that they were written by the same person; the man who served as the clerk of the court-martial. There were several scriveners (court scribes) in attendance for the duration of the trial, so it is difficult to determine which of the named men this was; however, the handwriting was indisputably the same.[28] And thus, on November 28, 1811, one of the court scriveners for the Wilkinson trial wrote in beautiful flowing penmanship Gilbert Russell's own statement of the events leading up to Lewis's death.

The top illustration is taken from the bottom section of the last page of the Gilbert Russell Statement, showing Jonathan Williams' signature. The bottom illustration is taken directly from the Jonathan Williams Papers and directly linked to the Wilkinson court-martial. Williams's signature is entirely different from the other handwriting on the two pages, which exempts him from being the author of the statement. There is no doubt that the unique, flamboyant script above the "The" in both illustrations was penned by one person at the trial. The words in the bottom illustration begin: "The Judge Advocate informs the Court that a number of the witnesses, supposed among the most important to whom letters of summons had been sent on the part of the prosecution had not attended, nor had they acknowledged the receipt of the summons." The crossing of the "t's" and trailing off at the end of some of the words in both documents attests to one person's unique and beautiful style of writing. (Gilbert C. Russell, November 26, 1811, p. 4, and September 1–2, 1811, Jonathan Williams MSS, box 6, Lilly Library Manuscript Collections, Indiana University, Bloomington, IN.)

The top illustration is taken from the first page of the Gilbert Russell Statement. Comparing the "G" in Government to the "G" in the middle illustration, the flair of the "G" originates from the hand of a unique writer. The "B" in the top illustration matches the "B" in the bottom illustration. The words "produced" in the top illustration and "promoted" in the middle illustration, with emphasis on the "pr," are almost identical. One person in all three documents, namely the clerk of the court, penned this unique writing style. All three documents were found within caches of the Wilkinson trial. (Gilbert G. Russell, November 26, 1811, p. 1, Jonathan Williams MSS, box 6, Lilly Library Manuscript Collections, Indiana University, Bloomington, IN; Records relating to the 1811 and 1815 Courts-Martial of Maj. General James Wilkinson, RG94, M1136, roll 1, p. 44, frame 0296, and p. 24, frame 0276, National Archives and Records Administration.)

The remaining question was why did Russell provide such a statement during the course of the Wilkinson court-martial? To answer this question, the reader must first become acquainted with a little-known early American organization. The following people, all familiar to Lewis and Clark historians, have something in common: Amos Stoddard, William Russell, Jonathan Williams, Peter Gansevoort, William Clark, Thomas Jefferson, James Madison, Samuel Latham Mitchill, Frederick Hassler, Zebulon Pike, James Wilkinson, and Meriwether Lewis.[29] These persons were all members of the United States Military Philosophical Society, which was founded in 1802 by Col. Jonathan Williams, a grandnephew of Benjamin Franklin.[30] The society's purpose was "to stimulate the collection and dissemination of military knowledge," but Jonathan Williams eloquently wrote a more detailed description of the society's goals:

[T]o preserve for future generations the science which their fathers have obtained by dear experience on fields of glory. . . . It will become an immediate object to join to the institution the most respectable military and scientific characters of our country . . . and it is hoped that knowledge resulting from their honourable experience will be saved from oblivion, and secured among the archives of the society.[31]

The society began collecting important papers written in the field concerning new and ancient fortifications, harbors, floating batteries, or gun boats, boat designs, maps, canals, coast surveys, meteorological observations, barometrical measurements, mountain altitudes, and experiments conducted on musket barrels. The society sponsored publications and endorsed scientific works that gave them validity.[32] There was also the occasional letter addressing future works like the one Samuel Latham Mitchill wrote to Williams at the end of December 1806: "I have just had a conversation with Capt. Lewis, who has just returned from his journey to the Pacific Ocean. He is a very interesting Traveller, and will in due time furnish us with a Book & Map of his Adventures and Discoveries."[33]

At its inception, the United States Military Philosophical Society regularly held its annual meeting at West Point, then in New York City, and finally wherever a quorum was in attendance.[34] By 1811, the society numbered about a hundred members, and a segment of its membership attended the Wilkinson court-martial. How fortunate that the most important person associated with Meriwether Lewis in September 1809 was at Fredericktown in a court of law. Jonathan Williams, who had been called as a defense witness, wrote copious notes during the trial.[35] If you will recall, the second name appended to the Russell Statement is that of Jonathan Williams. Because of his active leadership of the United States Military Philosophical Society and his past inquiries and interest in Lewis's story, it was completely understandable that Williams would want to depose Gilbert Russell, a key witness, on one of the young nation's saddest and most important chapters.

On November 28, 1811, Gilbert Russell recalled the two weeks he spent with Lewis in the autumn of 1809 while the court clerk patiently scribed his testimony. Russell may have been reading from a document that he had previously compiled, which would establish that he already knew that he would be giving a sworn statement to Williams. If we look at the last couple of sentences of the 1811 statement, Russell declares, "His death was greatly lamented. And that a fame so dearly earned as his should be clouded by such an act of desperation was to his friends still greater cause of regret." In April 1810 Thomas Jefferson had replied to Russell's two letters describing Lewis's demise by concluding, "We have all to lament that a fame so dearly earned was clouded finally by such an act of desperation."[36] It is obvious that

Russell agreed with Jefferson's bitter sentiment, and even included a paraphrase of it in his 1811 statement.

One other piece of documentation removes any vestigial doubt of the authenticity of the Russell Statement. The paper that the Russell Statement is written upon and the paper that Jonathan Williams wrote his copious notes upon at the Wilkinson court-martial each bear the identical watermark: *C. WILMOTT 1809.*[37]

Because historians and other readers did not understand the nature of the Russell Statement, why it was written, and from whom the information came, they jumped to the conclusion that it revealed a specific historical figure to be a murderer, or at least to have ordered a murder. This was quite unfair to the already somewhat tarnished reputation of James Wilkinson. Ironically, Wilkinson was unwittingly the catalyst for the circumstances surrounding the creation of the statement, for it was written primarily because his court-martial brought together the various *dramatis personae* necessary for its creation; a witness to history, a person interested in the preservation, through official testimony, of the historical record, and an official scribe skilled in the taking of testimony for legal purposes.

Chapter 13

DR. ANTOINE SAUGRAIN'S TREATMENT OF GOVERNOR MERIWETHER LEWIS

O ne of the most fascinating and instructive recent discoveries regarding the life of Meriwether Lewis was his battle with malaria, which in his time was called "the ague," an incurable and untreatable disease. Few examples of his illness have survived, mainly from the expedition journals and from official correspondence, but also from those closest to him who wrote about his condition. Definitive proof has now been found from the physician who cared for him from April 1808 to September 1809, the full term of his governorship while he was in Saint Louis. This is a remarkable discovery not only because it occurred in the year of Lewis's death, but also because the care was provided by a trained physician who noted on what date he saw Lewis and what treatment he prescribed for him.

Lewis's malarial woes possibly began when serving in the militia in 1795, as evidenced by a letter he wrote to his mother on April 6 of that year in which he told her that he had succumbed to a camp fever. "I have had a pretty severe touch of the disorder which has been so prevalent among the troops."[1] Lewis joined the regular army as an ensign in the Second Sub-Legion on May 1, 1795, and was assigned to Fort Greenville, which was commanded by Gen. Anthony Wayne, overall commander of the US Army at the time. Fort Greenville, located seventy-five miles north of Cincinnati, Ohio, was named for Nathaniel Greene, a personal friend of Wayne and a fellow Revolutionary War officer.

Gen. Wayne won the decisive battle in the Ohio country against the Indians at the Battle of Fallen Timbers in 1794, and a treaty was signed with the various tribes involved at Fort Greenville in August 1795.[2] By this time Lewis had chosen the army as his career and was serving with the entry-level officer's rank of ensign. Orderly books show that Lewis would have been exposed to various maladies at Fort Greenville, the most prevalent being malarial fever or "ague." After the Battle of Fallen Timbers in 1794, Wayne reported that "the soldiery gets sick very fast with the fever and ague, and have it severly." The next day he wrote that "the troops were very sickly" and that "the number of our sick increases daily, provision is nearly exhausted."[3]

But the summer of 1795 was much worse—especially at Fort Greenville—where hundreds had taken ill.[4] The fort was huge, having fifty acres of land within the picket area and a capacity of 4,000.[5] On August 9, Gen. Wayne wrote to the secretary of war, "[T]he sickly season has commenced, & we are totally destitute of hospital stores—bark etc. etc." The "bark" referred to by Gen. Wayne was Peruvian bark, *quina* in the indigenous language, which was a common treatment for the fever and ague (discussed in greater depth below). Wayne had hoped that the War Department would soon demonstrate "the indispensable Necessity of immediately remedying the deficit" of bark on hand in the fort.[6] On September 2, Wayne was most concerned that they had not received any supplies with "the sick list increasing by rapid degrees."[7] In the late summer of 1795, Wayne reported that 120 men were ill in August and 300 in September "and what is truly alarming, there is not nor has there been one ounce of bark in the Medical Stores" for the past six months.[8]

In desperation, Wayne ordered the removal of the hospital "one mile into the open woods, in a pleasant position."[9] This was a commonly-advised form of treatment for epidemic disease during the period, to take men out of crowded, stuffy hospital rooms and get them into a situation where fresh air could prevent the spread of disease and could help them to recover. Additionally, some physicians believed that fetid, putrid air, like that issuing from a swamp, was somehow the cause of the fever itself. This theory was in dispute during the late 1700s, but was the source of the name of the disease, *malaria*, from the Italian words for "bad air." Unfortunately, medical science of the time was not sufficiently advanced to understand that bad air was not a cause, nor fresh air a remedy, for malaria.

On October 5, 1795, Gen. Wayne was at a loss for words when he wrote that they were "totally destitute . . . of Medicine and Hospital stores." He had sent men "to Kentucky to procure peruvian bark," and they were able to obtain twenty pounds.[10] One of his officers reported that out of 1,000 troops, 700 had been ill with the ague and fever.[11] By early November, 336 were still on the sick list, and by mid-month, medicinal supplies had finally arrived.[12]

Illnesses at the fort were common, but the ague was a distinctive disease with pronounced features. From the French term *fievre aegue*, or Latin, *febris acuta*, the word ague "referred originally to any acute febrile disease and especially a fever accompanied by a shaking or shivering fit."[13] At some point in time, ague and malaria became synonymous.

Malaria was likely introduced into colonial America from Africa by the slave trade.[14] It had a complex etiology and was caused by four distinct parasites that were transmitted by mosquitoes. "The fevers caused by these four organisms vary enough in their clinical presentations that different labels evolved for their symptom complexes."[15] The nature of the disease established "long-term chronic infections, in which the host stays infectious to ensure that sufficient transmission . . . can occur to guarantee survival."[16] Because malaria is not a single disease, it went by a dozen archaic names like "autumnal fever," "bilious fever," "remittent fever," "intermittent fever," or, simply, "the ague" in various parts of the country.[17]

By the mid-1750s physicians were writing that the disease was a year-round illness. "From the latter end of January or beginning of February to August, Agues or Intermittents are said to be Vernal; and from August to January or beginning of February, autumnal."[18] Attempting to understand malaria in nineteenth-century America defied medical reasoning because it was episodic or periodic, was not confined in terms of geographic area, was not limited to areas of epidemic concentration (and so did not seem to be spread from one person to another), and was incredibly debilitating and grueling when attacking the patient, but in the intermission of the attack the patient's "memory is almost always impaired or even completely obliterated," followed by periods in which the patient displays no symptoms at all, only to have renewed attacks months or even years later.[19] As delineated at a conference commemorating the three hundredth anniversary of the use of Peruvian bark in 1931, the observable symptoms were laid out in this fashion:

Called ague at a very early period on account of the acute fever, that term soon applied to the more conspicuous feature, the chill, with shaking of the body, in common language ague shakes. Beginning with a feeling of chilliness and with shivering, violent shaking follows. The temperature rises even during the chill, and soon can be felt as a burning heat all over the body, with thirst, nausea, and vomiting, pains in muscles and bones, headache, delirium, and other symptoms. After some hours the fever subsides, followed by profuse perspiration, after which there is a stage of relative well-being, the intermission or remission, according to the degree of freedom from the symptoms.[20]

That degree of freedom might last a day before the suffering continued, as described in an 1801 medical textbook:

[It] begins with the most intense, painful, and irksome cold, penetrating, as it were, to the very bones. After the first paroxysm, in which there is generally great rigor . . . sometimes the teeth . . . by being struck together are knocked out of their sockets. The cold stage can last a great number of hours distressing the patient . . . then a 5–6 hour head ache.[21]

Each attack lasted about twenty-four hours and was repeated every day, every third day, or every fifth day for a number of months and then would disappear only to return a few months later as the individual went into a relapse.[22] A relapse is defined as a "return of symptoms and signs of a disease after a period of improvement."[23] An attack of malaria was most times left vague with very little description in historic documentation. However, there are personal accounts of malarial sufferers in various populations of the time, and tending to them required intensive care instead of the popular notion of dabbing a cool, wet cloth occasionally on a hot forehead. Malarial symptoms often began with a high fever during which the patient writhed and tossed and had to be restrained by being bound to a bed frame. Soldiers residing in temporary shelters were known to abandon their beds and wander into the fields and swamps and consequently drown.[24]

The malaria parasite had the capacity to infect all the peoples of the Americas if the mosquito vector was present. In 1793–94, it affected Upper Louisiana where Zenon Trudeau, the Spanish lieutenant governor who resided in Saint Louis, reported that the entire region in the summer months was subject to severe illness due to the fevers and relapses.[25] But the fever could strike any time of the year, evidenced by Lewis's bout with it on November 13, 1803, when he said that he was "siezed with a violent ague."[26] This was a familiar pattern, and hundreds of military documents attest to accounts of soldiers and officers who had experienced this radical illness. Capt. Amos Stoddard, the US Army officer who presided over the transfer of the Upper Louisiana Territory to the United States in March 1804, reported that the entire local population suffered from intermittent fever.

> The climate in this quarter has frequently been deemed unhealthy. St. Louis is in . . . lat. 38°, 25°, N.—Strangers from the northern States, (such, for instance, as your humble servant,) are sometimes sickly the first season of their arrival. The usual disorders are of a bilious nature. Intermittents, and fevers and agues, prevail at times—but they readily yield to detergent medicines, succeeded by a few doses of Peruvian bark. . . . The warm season usually commences about the 10th of July, and ends in September; and during part of this time the mercury generally rises, in the middle of the day, to 94°, and not unfrequently to 108°.[27]

Stoddard remained in Saint Louis until he led an Indian deputation to Washington in October 1805. About a year later, when stationed in Carlisle, Pennsylvania, he requested a transfer to a post in Tennessee: "It is also very healthy—of such a place I really stand in need, as my frame is still much shattered in consequence of the fever, under which I languished for more than seven months."[28]

In 1808, the Arkansas Indian agent John Breck Treat succumbed to malaria:

> A few days ago . . . a sudden and very severe attack of the Fever seiz'd me and although it only remained eight or ten days . . . I have . . . constantly . . . been extremely ill: almost the whole time confined to my bed from which I now write this—from the emaciated, and feeble state I now am in; it is extremely uncertain when I may become convalescent . . . this is the first month of serious sickness which I have ever experienced.[29]

The disease was continental and not localized to the east coast and midwestern riverine areas, and was probably carried west over trade routes by early European explorers or by ship-borne traders putting in on the Pacific coast. Chinookan and Kalapuyan peoples in the Willamette Valley suffered with malaria at least by the early nineteenth century.[30]

> It first broke out among the Indians near the fort, and spread far into the country . . . And with the natives it proved very fatal, sweeping off whole bands, partly probably owing to their plunging into the water when the fever came on constantly.[31]

They did not understand the illness, and since malaria has its own sweating stage, native logic inferred that "a cure would have been a dip in cold water."[32] Consequently, "maddened by fever, they would rush headlong into the cooling stream . . . in search of relief" and perish.[33]

Fur traders in the 1840s were all too familiar with the disease:

> [O]ne of my Indians began to show symptoms of the . . . fever . . . and the . . . sick native was obliged to lie down in the bottom of the canoe in great distress. When we reached our evening encampment he was burning with a high fever. . . . The darkness and damp, chill miasma of the Willamette soon closed over us, and . . . being unable to endure the pains of fever . . . [he] crawled to the river's brink and tried to allay the burning inward heat by large draughts from the running stream . . . in the morning our patient was a picture of disease and distress . . . by noon . . . the violence of his pains obliged us to put ashore under the shade of some low willows. In a few minutes violent retchings of the stomach commenced . . . and in less than an hour he lay stretched upon the grass . . . a frightful corpse.[34]

These attacks were typically treated with what Gen. Wayne referred to as the "bark." Peruvian bark was so named because it was obtained from the bark of several species of the genus *Cinchona* of the Rubiaceae family that are indigenous to tropical South America. Peruvian bark, also known as *Quina* was long used by the Quechua

Indians of Peru to halt shivering due to low temperatures, and quina-quina indicated "great value," or medicine of medicines or bark of barks.[35] While *Cinchona* was widely used in England and praised in America as a "sovereign remedy" for the ague, Dr. Samuel Latham Mitchill, a prominent physician, found that "the Peruvian bark was commonly . . . ineffectual."[36] This was due to three reasons: there were twenty-five distinct species of *Cinchona*; the content in the bark of the anti-malarial ingredient, quinine, varied in *Cinchona* trees from 3 percent to 13 percent; and its effectiveness varied between individual trees and different parts of the same tree. The alkaloid, quinine, was isolated from the bark in 1823, and the current treatment for malaria still uses its derivative.[37] The grade was established by bark color: red (*Cinchona Rubra*), yellow (*Cinchona Flava*), and gray or pale (*Cinchona Pallida*).[38] The highest grade, red, yielded two alkaloids, quinine and cinchonine, while the yellow only produced quinine.[39] The Spanish, who cornered the bark market, coveted the highest grade for themselves, casting in doubt the medicinal properties of the fifteen pounds of pulverized Peruvian bark purchased by the Lewis and Clark Expedition.[40]

For the bark to be utilized, it had to be pulverized into a powder and made into an infusion or decoction, like a tea, but it had its limitations.[41] When reduced to a powder, whether it was preserved in a box or in closed vessels, it lost "a great deal of its efficacy," unless pulverized for immediate use.[42] The brewing could take as long as forty-five minutes, and the product was so bitter it had to be mixed in a quart of claret, port wine, or brandy, which the patient drank at regular intervals for a number of days. *Cinchona* was not regarded as a "specific" for intermittent or other fevers because the accepted practice of the time revolved around the Greek doctrine that "perceptible evacuation was essential to cure and that a drug ingested as hot tea was counterindicated in a fever."[43] Unfortunately, by the time this treatment began to have some effect, the attack had probably run its course. Continued heavy use could produce serious side effects, including tinnitus (ringing in the ears) and deafness.[44]

The bark was not the only remedy for malaria, as many physicians of the time prescribed calomel, the powdered form of mercury. Dr. Benjamin Rush, one of Thomas Jefferson's medical advisors, relied on calomel exclusively as treatment for malaria and dispensed his own formula, a combination of mercury and jalap, a strong purgative, which came to be known as "Rush's pills."[45] In preparation for the expedition, Lewis consulted Dr. Rush about his illness in May of 1803. Rush specifically wrote: "Directions for Mr. Lewis for the preservation of his health & of those of who were to accompany him," and forwarded those instructions to Jefferson.[46] Rush believed solely in "heroic" medicine and prescribed his own mercury pills to Lewis—and the expedition bought "50 doz. Bilious Pills to Order of B. Rush," which were taken for all sorts of ills.[47] Dr. Rush believed that Lewis suffered from a recurring bilious fever, another name for the ague, but a fever that presented with a malarial character. Lewis dutifully adhered to Rush's prescription, but over the years modified the formula and noted it in his account book:

> Method of treating bilious fever when unattented by Typhus or nervous symptoms—Let the patient take a strong puke of tartar emetic: the second day after a purge of Calomel and Jallop, which should be repeated after two days more, to be taken in the morning, and no cold water to be used that day.—a pill of opium and tartar to be taken every night and after the purgatives. ten grains of Rhubard [rhubarb] and 20 grains of Barks should be repeated every morning and at 12 O'clock.[48]

The most telling feature of this description is the length of time that he devoted to the treatment, and conversely how long the bout affected him. Another name for this disorder was bilious cholic, which could produce "excruciating pain," and often "relaps'd with such violence" that as one observer remarked "baffled the powers of medicine."[49]

There has been a tremendous amount of curiousity expended on why Lewis chose Clark to be coleader of the expedition. It is possible that their original bond was formed as a result of the illness at Greenville in the summer of 1795. On September 10, Clark departed Greenville on a special assignment, ending the period during which Lewis and Clark originally served together in the army, making it most probable that Lewis and Clark began their friendship between May 1 and September 9 of 1795.[50] In August, Gen. Wayne reported that 120 soldiers were sick with malaria at Fort Greenville. That was cause for great alarm because the medical staff, comprised of one surgeon and four surgeon's mates, was wholly insufficient to care for the multitude of sick.[51] Other soldiers and officers were employed to carry out the menial duties, and without hospital stores, one can only imagine the desperate situation confronting Gen. Wayne.

Sickness consumed vast amounts of energy from both the ill as well as the healthy in the form of caretaking. It is quite possible that either Lewis or Clark or both were taken ill during this period, or one or both might have assisted with the care of patients. Being expert marksmen was the catalyst that brought the two together, but illness, and its caretaking counterpart, may have clinched the friendship. By May 1803, Lewis chose Clark as the expedition's cocommander, and upon receiving Lewis's moving invitation, Clark gladly accepted:

> My friend I join you with hand & Heart and anticipate advantages which will certainly derive from the accomplishment of so vast, Hazidous and fatiguing enterprize. You as doub[t] will inform the president of my determination to join you in an "official Character" as mentioned in your letter.[52]

Lewis and Clark were adept at caring for both their men and Native Americans on the expedition and were given the appellation "Captain–Physicians" by modern medical doctor–historians.[53]

The evidence is overwhelming that malaria was a prevalent and formidable disease in seventeenth- and eighteenth-century America. Although historians agree that Lewis became infected with malaria at some point in his life, they dismiss its relevance to the expedition and to his later duties as governor of the Louisiana Territory and author of a published form of the expedition journals. What they failed to appreciate was that once Lewis had contracted malaria, he had it for the rest of his life—it was incurable and untreatable during his lifetime.

As stated in the biography *Meriwether Lewis*, "Malaria is a disease fitted with a hydra-head of painful secondary complications that mimic other conditions like anemia, jaundice, migraine-type headaches, and enlarged liver and spleen."[54] During March 1807, several persons visiting Thomas Jefferson, including Jefferson and Lewis, became ill with a bout of malaria. Historians have characterized this example as a humorous situation where everyone in the presidential mansion caught a cold, but what this really demonstrates is that malaria can imitate many diseases and fool even the most hardened experts.[55] Several persons residing with President Jefferson jointly experienced what is called today a synchronous malarial attack. Malaria can strike in the middle of winter as easily as in the summer months because the parasite depends upon the host's circadian rhythm, which signals the opportune time to proliferate.[56]

On March 2, President Jefferson reported that his son-in-law, Thomas Mann Randolph Jr., had succumbed to a "chill and fever," which lasted four days, and Lewis and others attended to the stricken man. On March 6, Jefferson remarked that he had caught a very bad cold, and on March 11, Lewis wrote that he had been indisposed and took some of Rush's pills.[57] This prompted historians to conclude that everyone at Jefferson's mansion had caught his cold.[58]

The illness that affected several persons at the same time was a classic presentation of the ague. Jefferson complained of a periodical headache, which was his way of explaining the agues in the head that are also described today as a retroorbital headache—a sharp pain behind the eye.[59] Medical historians believe that his periodical headache was a migraine; however, Daniel Drake, one of the foremost physicians of the upper Mississippi Valley, recognized that the periodical headache was a symptom of the ague.[60] Jefferson suffered from relentless headaches, what he "called the Sun-pain," beginning in 1764, and by 1807, they had become a familiar and debilitating malady.[61] Little documentation exists about Lewis's malarial bout, but it disabled him until the beginning of April, when he departed Washington for Philadelphia. Jefferson, on the other hand, was very ill too and wrote how those headaches crippled him. He relied upon the most advanced treatments of the day, using bark and calomel, hallmark remedies for this type of condition.[62] Jefferson was so ill from these frequent malarial attacks that he departed the capital for Monticello to recuperate. It was the third week of May 1807 before Jefferson had recovered; he had actually been sick for almost three months.[63]

Like Jefferson, Lewis continued to seek medical treatment for malaria. When Lewis arrived in Saint Louis on March 8, 1808, to take up his duties as governor, he met with Dr. Antoine Saugrain, a physician and chemist, who began treating him for the disease less than a month later.[64]

Born in Paris, France, Dr. Saugrain began practicing medicine in 1783, and by 1799 he had arrived in Saint Louis and opened a practice. In 1805, he was appointed surgeon's mate at Fort Bellefontaine, and four years he later became surgeon at the fort. It is noteworthy that in 1809 he was also the first physician west of the Mississippi River to use the Jenner cowpox vaccine to prevent smallpox.[65]

The top half page of Dr. Antoine Saugrain's medical ledger for the treatment of Governor Meriwether Lewis. The word quina (quinine) is evident from April 6 to September 19, 1808. The Peruvian bark, quina-quina, was the preferred treatment for malarial sufferers. (Dr. Antoine Saugrain's Medical Ledgers, 1801–1817, 2 vols., Gov. Meriwether Lewis, vol. 1, p. 410, Pettis County Historical Society and Museum, Sedalia, Missouri.)

Beginning April 6, 1808, the illness that plagued Lewis since writing to his mother on April 6, 1795, sporadically returned, culminating in a steep descent into a series of drastic prescriptions that allows us to see, for the first time, Lewis's physical debility. Thirteen years to the day that he informed his mother of a bout with camp or putrid fever, Lewis met with Dr. Antoine Saugrain, and judging from the entries in Dr. Saugrain's medical ledgers, the governor was very ill.[66] On April 6, Saugrain gave Lewis an ounce of quina quina.[67] For the entire month, Lewis battled malaria:

April	6	an ounce of quina quina
	14	two ounces of yellow quina
	27	Glauber's salt (a sodium sulfate described as a saline cathartic).[68]

Lewis was illness-free for the next six weeks, although on June 15 he received a dose of Glauber's salt and on June 18 a vial of "saturne white vitriol," which was a by-product of sulfuric acid, a substance to "check diarrhea."[69] For almost two months following, Lewis was healthy again, until August 30, when Saugrain gave him tartar emetic and two ounces of Glauber salts: it is evident that Lewis had already been ill for a time.[70] Tartar emetic, a combination of antimony and potassium dissolved in water with Glauber's salts, was "an all-purpose depletive," which in "small amounts . . . produced disabling vomiting."[71] This therapy regimen of purging the digestive tract was thought at the time to alleviate the symptoms of malaria, but of course it only made Lewis more sick.

The entire month of September 1808, which mirrored the physical distress to Lewis caused by the same disease a year later, demonstrated (through entries in Dr. Saugrain's ledger) the episodic nature of malaria:[72]

September	3	twelve purgative pills
	6	two ounces of cream of tartar (potassium bitartrate—another purgative.)
	11	an ounce and a half of quina and two ounces of tincture of quina
	19	a tincture of quina
	26	a tincture of quina
October	15	two ounces of Glaubert's salt and a tincture of quina
	24	two ounces of vitriol oil

The bottom half of Dr. Saugrain's medical ledger, dated October 15, 1808, to August 24, 1809. Saugrain continued to treat Meriwether Lewis for the same illness, sometimes alternating the ingredients in the prescription. (Dr. Antoine Saugrain's Medical Ledgers, Gov. Meriwether Lewis, vol. 1, p. 410, Pettis County Historical Society and Museum, Sedalia, Missouri.)

In Lewis's account book, he kept several formulas, one of which he labeled the "best stomachic,"[73] which was a specific for malaria: "1/4 oz of cloves, 1/4 oz of Columbo, 1 oz Peruvian bark, 1 quart of port wine—the ingredients to be well pounded and shook when taken—a wine glass twise or twise a day may be taken with good effect, it is an excellent restorative."[74]

Lewis wrote to his mother on December 1, 1808, stating that he generally shared good health.[75] He also wrote a voluminous letter to President Jefferson on December 15 detailing a number of events from the time of his arrival in Saint Louis to the signing of the Osage Treaty on November 10, 1808.[76] For the remainder of 1808 and into early 1809, Dr. Saugrain's ledger contained a repeat of the same prescriptions:

1808

November 4   one dose of Glaubert's salt

17   two ounces of Glaubert's

December 24   two ounces quina

colombo oil (for vomiting or dysentery)

1809

January   10   an ounce quina, two big [ounces] columbo, one big [ounce] clove

February   4   eleven pills

For about two months, Lewis enjoyed good health and finalized plans for the Missouri Fur Company to return the Mandan chief Sheheke-shote and his family after two long years in Saint Louis. On May 20, Dr. Saugrain gave Lewis a vial of British oil and one dose of calomel and jalap. British oil and jalap were unsavory substances—the first was a combination of the oils of turpentine, linseed, amber, juniper, and petroleum, while the other was a Mexican root and "drastic cathartic" that caused violent intestinal cramping. Calomel and jalap were used together to evacuate the mercury as fast as possible.[77] Up until this time, Lewis had been taking quina quina, his preferred treatment, but Saugrain switched Lewis to a more powerful alternative. This dosage was a poisonous cathartic and the same treatment that Dr. Rush prescribed for malaria and almost everything else.

At the end of May, Dr. Saugrain was appointed surgeon of Fort Bellefontaine and required to make a report on current conditions there, which he described as dismal: "Intermittants are very prevalent in all Seasons of the Year . . . but they leave the Patient in a state of debility. . . . Putrid fevers cause great debility towards the end and have been mortal in several cases."[78]

It was specifically his understanding of the air and damps, in the form of effluvia or miasma—bad air, that led him to describe how the illness pervaded the air and released "noxious . . . exhalations" near Bellefontaine:

> The Cantonment [fort] is situated on a low, flat and Morassy bottom . . . after a Rain the Water having no issue, becomes stagnant, which, together with a neighboring Creek, which is dry during the Summer, occasions noxious and foeted [fetid] Exhalations, injurious to health: as a proof of the insalubrity of the Air of this place, after a Considerable rain, the Sick reports are generally double and often treble.[79]

Saugrain was all too familiar with the summer conditions in the Louisiana Territory, which coincided with Lewis's continued bout with malaria and sick soldiers at the fort and in the surrounding area.[80]

Lewis attempted to write to the secretary of war on July 8, but writing proved to be difficult.[81] Malarial sufferers struggled when writing letters and some took months before they could competently hold a quill. An account written by a traveler to a friend in Saint Louis described his frustration after succumbing to malaria, from which it took weeks to regain some strength. He wrote an almost unreadable letter, to which he alluded, saying, "you will Discover by the shaking of my hand."[82] Interestingly, on August 18, Lewis received a stinging rebuke from the accountant of the War Department, rejecting payment of a draft he had submitted.[83] On that day, shocked beyond description, Lewis did not pen the most important letter of his life—someone else wrote it for him because he was probably in the throes of an ongoing malarial relapse. "Yours of the 15th July is now before me, the feelings it excites are truly painful. With respect to every public expenditure, I have always accompanied my Draft by letters of advice, stating explicitly, the object of the expenditure . . . ."[84]

About a week later, on August 24, Lewis paid Saugrain for purgative pills and to assemble a medicine chest for his voyage down the Mississippi River to New Orleans.[85] This was the trip that Lewis had been planning for a year, to return to Philadelphia and work on the publication of the expedition journals.

Governor Lewis was by no means the only person in Saint Louis who was ill with malaria—the month of August proved to be sickly for many Saint Louis residents, including most of Lewis's friends.[86] This timeline continues to demonstrate Lewis's illness in the summer of 1809:

May	20	a vial of British oil and one dose of jalap and calomel
June	1	one ounce and a half Glauber's salt
	3	two ounces of Glauber's salt
July	10	four ounces of Glauber's salt
Aug	17	one ounce of quina for Porney
	23	for Monsieur purgative pills
	24	to the same, purgative pills[87]

Judging from these dates, it is clear that Lewis preferred quina quina to ingesting calomel, and the argument that Lewis suffered from mercury poisoning has been greatly overstated. Lewis preferred Peruvian bark, then Glauber's salts, and rarely, calomel, to treat his malarial symptoms.[88]

On September 4, 1809, Lewis departed Saint Louis by boat. His intention was to travel to New Orleans and take a seafaring boat around Florida and then sail up the east coast of the United States to Washington. Upon his arrival eleven days later at Fort Pickering, in present-day Memphis, Tennessee, Lewis had succumbed to a malarial relapse. The boat crew informed Capt. Gilbert Russell, the commander of Fort Pickering, that Lewis had made two attempts to kill himself during the trip and that upon his arrival he was mentally deranged.[89] Capt. Russell assisted Lewis up the 120 square-log steps to the fort and put him in his own quarters.

Capt. Russell had first arrived at Fort Pickering on June 9, 1809, and had reported that the fort "was in the most wretched state." Russell summarized the work to be performed from repairing the pickets, the roofs of the officer's quarters, and the huts for the men to replacing rotted floors and building a chimney. By August 26, none of the repair work had been accomplished because his company had been stricken with malaria: "And such has been the unhealthiness of the season that with the Troops I have as yet been able to make no improvement to Fort Pickering—Out of forty eight Officers & men I have sometimes had but eight or nine fit for duty."[90]

Other distressing news followed him when he reported that "four of my best Mechanics" were drown'd a few days ago. . . . My only two Brick layers were drown'd" too.[91] The cause of their drowning could have easily been related to malaria. William C. Smith, the surgeon of the garrison, mirrored Russell's complaints and reported that from the time of Russell's arrival at the fort "sickness had immediately prevail'd here in an uncommon manner." Regardless of his duties, Smith was stricken for five months and "in that time frequently prescribing for the sick, when confined on my bed." He recovered the first week of November but felt that his health was permanently damaged "probably forever . . . under the most obstinate and confirmed complaint of my liver."[92]

Under appalling circumstances, Lewis arrived "to this sequestered and sickly Post."[93] Without skilled workmen or cash, Russell's own quarters were completely dilapidated, and even though he invited the ailing Lewis to recuperate in them, who can imagine their condition? This was the frontier, and rudimentary conditions were the norm, as evidenced by Russell's ending paragraph to the secretary of war: "Unless the Garrison is repair'd before the hard weather commences, which can not be done without a considerable sum of money in its present state the Troops would all die."[94] Conditions were just as unfavorable in Saint Louis at Fort Bellefontaine, but with Dr. Saugrain as surgeon's mate, an expert was at the helm who had seen many diseases and assorted ills on the frontier.

With the discovery of Antoine Saugrain's medical ledgers, a new understanding has emerged about Meriwether Lewis and the frontier life that surrounded him. The prevailing thought concerning Lewis's illness has always been that it was mental in origin, while today, medical testimony from 1809 proves the opposite. Lewis suffered from a physical disease, which tormented him for his entire adult life.

Chapter 14

REVISITING MERIWETHER LEWIS'S DEATH: A NEW PERSPECTIVE

by Thomas C. Danisi and John Danisi*

One of the great American historical mysteries concerns the death of Meriwether Lewis (1774–1809). Did he commit suicide? In the past fifty years, the discovery of letters written at the time of the explorer's last days indicate that he was subject to depression, to bouts of alcoholism, and to mental derangement. Although the prevailing view supports the reasoning that depression drove him to suicide, we believe through studying new finds that Meriwether Lewis, in his adult life, suffered from chronic, severe, and untreated malaria, an incurable disease at that time. In light of this new information, Meriwether Lewis was not stricken with a psychological illness, namely, depression, but rather with a physiological disease, "the ague," which is known today as malaria.[1] A study of Lewis's malaria and the symptoms it produced provides the gateway toward a better understanding of the nature of his death.

HYPOCHONDRIA TIED TO A DEPRESSIVE STATE OF MIND: EXTREME DEPRESSION MADE LEWIS KILL HIMSELF

Most historians have concluded that Lewis's illness was psychological and that he suffered from lifelong depression. They have repeatedly claimed that a pattern of behavior had developed during his life that was consistent with someone who suffered from a mental condition. Historians have arrived at this conclusion based mainly on Thomas Jefferson's testimony, but also from other persons who knew Lewis. Evidence left behind by Lewis's contemporaries described events leading up to his death and discussed his death after the fact in terms of what were perceived as signs and portents that foreshadowed his demise. Lewis's contemporaries have been placed by historians in an order based on the importance of their connection to him and their perceived veracity based on class and position in society: President Thomas Jefferson, William Clark, Capt. Gilbert Russell, Maj. James Neely, John Pernier, and Priscilla Grinder.

When Thomas Jefferson's election to the presidency of the United States was determined by the Electoral College in February 1801, he hired Meriwether Lewis as his private secretary. In 1803, Jefferson appointed Lewis as the leader of the famous Lewis and Clark Expedition, and then four years later, as governor of the Louisiana Territory.[2] William Clark accompanied Meriwether Lewis on the Lewis and Clark Expedition as cocommander and also resided in Saint Louis as Indian agent of the Louisiana Territory during the same timeframe that Meriwether Lewis was governor.[3] Capt. Gilbert Russell, commander of Fort Pickering, cared for Lewis in the last two weeks of September 1809.[4]

Thomas Jefferson, in 1813, wrote the most definitive view of Lewis's death in a biographical letter for the introduction to the Lewis and Clark Expedition Journals. Jefferson knew Lewis's family well, having lived near them in Charlottesville, Virginia. In this letter Jefferson outlined the most damning evidence about Lewis's illness, which has led most historians to conclude that Lewis committed suicide.[5]

Governor Lewis had from early life been subject to hypocondriac affections. It was a constitutional disposition in all of the nearer branches of the family of his name. . . . While he lived with me in Washington, I observed at times sensible depressions of mind.[6]

Jefferson also repeated his view to Capt. Gilbert Russell:

We have all to lament that a fame so dearly earned was clouded finally by such an act of desperation. He was much afflicted & habitually so with hypocondria.[7]

Jefferson's explanation of Lewis's illness was the result of a series of events that culminated in Lewis's unexpected death. On September 4, 1809, Lewis departed Saint Louis on a boat bound for New Orleans, which would take him to Washington.[8] A week later he disembarked at New Madrid with his servant, John Pernier, and went to the New Madrid Courthouse to make out a will.[9] Four days later, on September 15, he arrived at Fort Pickering, the site of present-day Memphis, Tennessee. Capt. Gilbert Russell reported that the boat crew informed him that Lewis had made two attempts to kill himself—and in one of them he nearly succeeded. As Russell assisted Lewis up to the fort, he commented that Lewis was in a state of mental derangement.[10] Lewis remained at the fort for about two weeks, recovering his health.

On September 29, Maj. James Neely, the Chickasaw Indian agent, departed

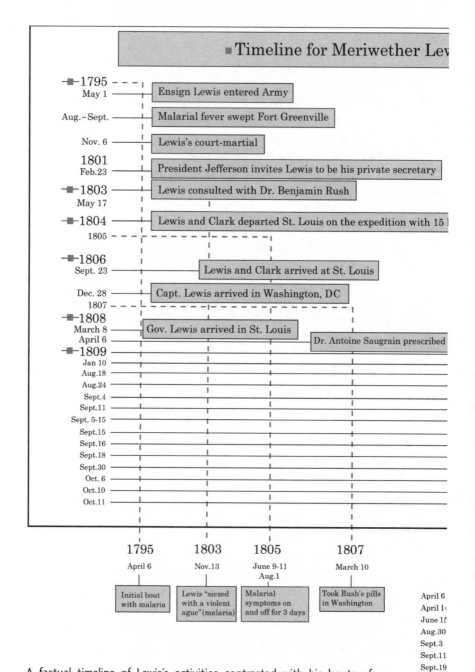

■Timeline for Meriwether Lev

▬■1795 May 1	Ensign Lewis entered Army
Aug.–Sept.	Malarial fever swept Fort Greenville
Nov. 6	Lewis's court-martial
1801 Feb.23	President Jefferson invites Lewis to be his private secretary
▬■1803 May 17	Lewis consulted with Dr. Benjamin Rush
▬■1804	Lewis and Clark departed St. Louis on the expedition with 15
1805	
▬■1806 Sept. 23	Lewis and Clark arrived at St. Louis
Dec. 28	Capt. Lewis arrived in Washington, DC
1807	
▬■1808 March 8	Gov. Lewis arrived in St. Louis
April 6	Dr. Antoine Saugrain prescribed
▬■1809	
Jan 10	
Aug.18	
Aug.24	
Sept.4	
Sept.11	
Sept. 5-15	
Sept.15	
Sept.16	
Sept.18	
Sept.30	
Oct. 6	
Oct.10	
Oct.11	

1795	1803	1805	1807
April 6	Nov.13	June 9-11 Aug.1	March 10
Initial bout with malaria	Lewis "siezed with a violent ague" (malaria)	Malarial symptoms on and off for 3 days	Took Rush's pills in Washington

April 6
April 1
June 1
Aug.30
Sept.3
Sept.11
Sept.19
Nov.4

A factual timeline of Lewis's activities contrasted with his bouts of malaria from 1795 to 1809. It is evident from this model that Lewis suffered from a recurring physical disease.

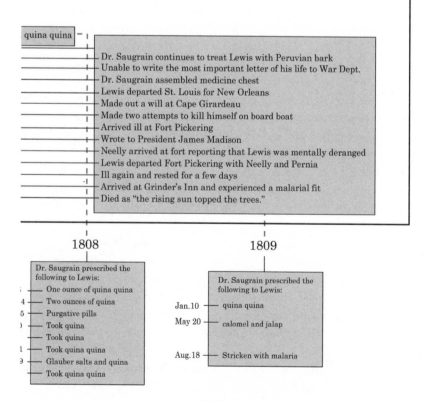

wis's Activities & Illness, 1795–1809

lbs. of Peruvian bark

quina quina

Dr. Saugrain continues to treat Lewis with Peruvian bark
Unable to write the most important letter of his life to War Dept.
Dr. Saugrain assembled medicine chest
Lewis departed St. Louis for New Orleans
Made out a will at Cape Girardeau
Made two attempts to kill himself on board boat
Arrived ill at Fort Pickering
Wrote to President James Madison
Neely arrived at fort reporting that Lewis was mentally deranged
Lewis departed Fort Pickering with Neely and Pernia
Ill again and rested for a few days
Arrived at Grinder's Inn and experienced a malarial fit
Died as "the rising sun topped the trees."

1808

1809

Dr. Saugrain prescribed the following to Lewis:
One ounce of quina quina
Two ounces of quina
Purgative pills
Took quina
Took quina
Took quina quina
Glauber salts and quina
Took quina quina

Dr. Saugrain prescribed the following to Lewis:
Jan.10 — quina quina
May 20 — calomel and jalap
Aug.18 — Stricken with malaria

©2011 Thomas C. Danisi - R.J. Shay Design / St. Louis, MO

Fort Pickering to escort Lewis to Nashville. Neely noted less than a week into their trip "that [Lewis] appeared at times deranged in mind." They rested two days, then two horses strayed from camp and Neely went looking for them the morning that Lewis, Pernier, and the packer continued on to a small wayside inn known as Grinder's Stand.[11] When they arrived at Grinder's Stand on the evening of October 10, Neely had still not rejoined them. That evening Priscilla Grinder made dinner and reported that when she served the food Lewis "walked backward and forward before the door talking to himself."[12] Afterward, Lewis went to his room, Priscilla and her children to hers, and Pernier and the packer to the stable. Before Neely's arrival the next morning, Lewis had died from gunshot wounds.[13]

When Maj. Neely arrived at Grinder's Stand on the morning of October 11, he prepared Lewis's body and then buried him, afterward questioning Priscilla Grinder and Pernier. He then took Lewis's belongings to Nashville, arriving about October 18, and sent a long letter to Thomas Jefferson detailing the trip from Fort Pickering. The letter began with very distressing news:

> It is with extreme pain that I have to inform you of the death of His Excellency Meriwether Lewis, Governor of upper Louisiana who died on the morning of the 11th Instant and I am sorry to say by Suicide.[14]

William Clark, who had been traveling eastward, had the news broken to him in a brutally unfair way: by reading a newspaper account. Immediately afterward he penned his reaction to Lewis's sudden and unexpected death in a letter to an extremely trusted correspondent, his older brother Jonathan Clark, stating that "I fear O! I fear the waight of his mind has over come him, what will be the Consequence?"[15]

Most historians have claimed that it was depression that brought about his death—that is, by suicide.[16] Three historians who have written on Lewis and Clark, Gary Moulton, Stephen Ambrose, and Dr. David Peck, believed that depression caused Lewis's death.

Moulton believed in a strict analysis of Jefferson's statement that Lewis was subject to hypochondriac affections and "that he suffered bouts of depression, which resulted in a "state of severe depression" when he departed Saint Louis.[17]

Ambrose's approach was direct and unwavering: that Lewis's sensible depressions of mind equated to "the same melancholy in Lewis's father, and . . . a malady that ran in the family." He further wrote that his depression was exacerbated by drinking to excess and "suffering from a manic-depressive psychosis."[18]

Peck sided with what he perceived to be Jefferson's viewpoint, that "Lewis had a constitutional/genetic tendency toward depression, which was beyond his conscious control."[19]

Traditional historians such as Dawson Phelps, Paul Russell Cutright, and Donald Jackson have concluded that Meriwether Lewis suffered from depression in its various forms. Dawson Phelps, the most outspoken of the group and a National Park Service historian, stated flatly in 1956 that Lewis killed himself. Phelps based this statement on Lewis's troubled governorship, noting that he was beset with financial woes and agreeing with Jefferson's observation that Lewis "suffered from sensible depressions of mind." Phelps ended his paper with a judgment that still resounds today: "In the absence of direct and pertinent contemporary evidence to the contrary, of which not a scintilla exists, the verdict of suicide must stand."[20]

Paul Russell Cutright believed that Lewis was unstable and based his conclusion on four factors: his failure to find a wife; his intemperance; his delay in furnishing a manuscript copy to publisher Conrad; and the erosion of his long-standing relationship with Jefferson.[21]

Besides depression as the cause of his suicide, there is also the additional claim that Lewis was an alcoholic. Donald Jackson, editor of *Letters of the Lewis and Clark Expedition*, agreed with Phelps, "I am inclined to believe that Lewis died by his own hand," but attributed the act to Lewis's "lapse into intemperance."[22] At the time, Jackson had found a letter that Capt. Gilbert Russell had written to Thomas Jefferson describing this new aspect:

> The fact is . . . his untimely death may be attributed solely to the free use he made of liquor which he acknowledged verry candidly after he recovered & expressed a firm determination never to drink any more spirits or use snuff again both of which I deprived him of for several days & confined him to claret & a little white wine.[23]

Jackson also confirmed his hypothesis by citing Jefferson's reply to Russell:

> [H]e was much afflicted and habitually so with hypocondria. this was probably increased by the habit into which he had fallen & the painful reflections that would necessarily produce in a mind like this.[24]

According to Jackson, the word "habit" confirmed that Lewis suffered from alcoholic depression and that it eventually led to his suicide.[25] True enough, Jefferson used the word "habit," but Jefferson was not using the word to refer to alcoholism, but to hypochondria. Clay Jenkinson connected Lewis's inherited disposition to a "man afflicted with bipolar personality disorder," which "points to melancholia, alcoholism, and suicide" as the likely causes of death.[26] Another historian who is also a medical doctor, Ronald Loge, refuted the hypothesis that Lewis suffered from malaria, and instead, relied upon a strict medical and evidentiary standpoint that "historical retrospective or forensic analysis is unable to demonstrate this."[27]

Other peripheral views concerning Lewis's death are interesting but speculative. Some do not mirror Jefferson's statement but instead concentrate on the events at Grinder's Stand or dismiss facts regarding Lewis's personal history. For instance, Dr. Reimert Ravenolt, an epidemiologist, declared that Lewis had contracted syphilis from relations with Indian women on the expedition and probably died from it years after infection. Ravenholt believed that the escapade occurred on August 13 and 14, 1805, but Lewis had written statements to the contrary.[28] "I think its most disgusting thing I ever beheld is these dirty naked wenches." Lewis's knowledge of the effects of venereal disease was abundantly described throughout the journals: "once this disorder is contracted it . . . always ends up in [decrepitude], death, premature old age." [29] Since Lewis was responsible for the health of his men, and as an officer of the army was sworn to observe protocols through personal example; and since he announced in general orders that his men should refrain from liaisons with native women for the sake of their health and the success of the expedition; and since he personally treated those with the disease, seeing firsthand the aftereffects, it seems doubtful that he indulged in this sort of dalliance.

Another novel theory attempted to discredit Priscilla Grinder and Pernier by suggesting that the night of Lewis's death was moonless, and thus, whatever the two thought they saw, they couldn't have.[30] The theory dismisses the science of photometry, implying that it had no bearing on the night in question—that these two persons living during this time period and in the wilderness could not acclimate their sight to darkness. Photometry textbooks clearly state that a person's eyes will adjust to darkness when leaving an area of bright light (not candle or firelight, which is not bright enough) after twenty minutes.[31]

There are theories suggesting that Lewis was assassinated by thugs at Grinder's Stand or by minions sent by the nefarious Gen. James Wilkinson. Nameless thugs have always been an interesting story line, but with no foundation, and the feeble attempt to tie Wilkinson to the plot is even weaker because he was stationed more than five hundred miles from Fort Pickering.

Other theories came from the psychiatric sector: Howard Kushner embraced Jefferson's description of Lewis's constitutional disposition. He argued that Lewis's father's death invoked "incomplete mourning," where Lewis played catch-up to his "repressed loss," which corroborated the predictable suicide.[32]

Kay Jamison, on the other hand, remained within the bounds of the historian's perspective and took Lewis's own grasp of wonder or lack thereof, postexpedition, to say that "the same bold, restless temperament that Jefferson saw in . . . Lewis can lie uneasily just this side of a restless, deadly despair."[33] If these two positions were really true, Lewis would never have risen from his bed and explored the continent.

Finally, historian Ann Rogers disagreed with the evidence presented in the biography *Meriwether Lewis* that argued that Jefferson's description of hypochondria was a description of a physical disorder. She countered that it was "an outlook, a disposition, a state of mind."[34] Rogers quoted various letters that Jefferson wrote from 1787–1816 using the word hypochondria and maintained Jefferson was referring to temperament and "not diagnosing any physical disease."[35] What she failed to acknowledge is that the eighteenth-century word *hypochondria* did not carry the same definition in modern usage, which she has misinterpreted to be the same. The eighteenth-century word pertains to a physiological complex while the modern term stipulates a mental state where the patient is continually anxious about an unreal physical condition.[36]

HYPOCHONDRIA TIED TO A PHYSICAL DISORDER: THE AGUE (MALARIA) MADE LEWIS SHOOT HIMSELF

Let us return to Jefferson's statement about Meriwether Lewis's condition. It is important to do so because Jefferson was intimately acquainted and involved with Lewis's life and because Jefferson's statement has been used to establish the nature of Lewis's death.[37] Jefferson wrote:

> Governor Lewis had from early life been subject to hypocondriac affections. It was a constitutional disposition in all of the nearer branches of the family of his name. . . . While he lived with me in Washington, I observed at times sensible depressions of mind.[38]

Two questions arise here: What did Jefferson mean in writing that Lewis was afflicted with hypochondria? And secondly, what did Jefferson mean when he said that Lewis's hypochondria had a constitutional source? Surprisingly, the historians mentioned earlier seem to speak about the first question, but they fail to address the second question in an adequate or complete way.

Lewis's "hypocondriac affections" are not to be understood as having a genetic or a psychical source, but, in Jefferson's phrase, a "constitutional source"; that is, an organic or bodily source passed on to Lewis by his family in the form of a "diseased body." As so understood, Lewis's hypochondriac affections, his "sensible depressions of mind," are byproducts, or afflictions, arising from the diseased organs in Lewis's body, notably, the diseased organs in the hypochondriac, or abdominal, region of

Lewis's body. And Jefferson also notes that Lewis's body, in its diseased state, has its roots ultimately in his father: "It was a constitutional disposition in all of the nearer branches of the family of his name, and was more immediately inherited by him from his father."

Jefferson remarks about the intimate relation between the hypochondriac mind and the diseased body. He writes, "There are indeed (who might say Nay) gloomy and hypochondriac minds, inhabitants of diseased bodies, disgusted with the present, and despairing of the future; always counting that the worst will happen, because it may happen."[39] Jefferson's statement is crucial to understanding the nature of hypochondria, which is linked to a bodily disposition or bodily makeup. It follows that we must connect Lewis's hypochondria with Lewis's constitutional makeup, that is, his bodily makeup or disposition, if we are going to understand the full significance of Jefferson's statement.

It is important to note that Jefferson's acquaintance with the word "hypochondria" is not rooted in the modern science of psychology—indeed, it is not rooted in psychology at all. It has its roots in his knowledge of the languages of Greek and Latin, which he studied and mastered. As is well-known and documented, Jefferson was a lifelong student of the Greek language.[40] In 1800 he reminded us that "to read the Latin & Greek authors in their original, is a sublime luxury. . . . I thank on my knees, him who directed my early education, for having put into my possession this rich source of delight." Almost twenty years later, he reiterated his deep passion for reading Greek texts in their original state: "The utilities we derive from the remains of the Greek and Latin languages are . . . models of pure taste in writing. . . . Among the values of classical learning, I estimate the luxury of reading the Greek and Roman authors in all the beauties of their originals."[41]

When Jefferson wrote about "hypochondriac affections," and "hypochondria," we have to assume that he was referring to an organic, or, a bodily condition. But the question arises: What do the languages of ancient Greek and Latin tell us? The word "hypochondriac" comes from the Greek—*hypochondriakos*—and from the Latin—*hypochondriacus*—meaning "of the abdomen" and in the singular form, "hypochondria" or the abdominal region of the body. Jefferson's statement that Lewis was afflicted with hypochondriac affections means he was affected by and concerned with that region of the body. Hypochondriac affections actually referred to the disease, which is hypochondria of pathological proportions, "a complex physical sickness," and that the "hypochondriasis [or hypochondria] that afflicted Lewis was a debilitating complication of chronic untreated malarial fever."[42] In short, Jefferson is informing us that Lewis's concern has to do not only with the abdominal region of his body but also with a disease inhabiting his body.

Jefferson's description of Lewis's hypochondria points to a complex condition, and the root cause of his illness originated from a physiological disease. This syndrome needs to be examined in some detail in order to understand the depth of its meaning. In the usage of the time, hypochondria described a set of physical symptoms. The first part of the word, *hypo*, means "under" and *chondros* means "cartilage," and the compound word referred to the area immediately below the ribs. The anatomical region below the ribs and above the pelvis, called the hypochondrium, included the cartilage, viscera, muscles, and organs located there. When ailments were ascribed to the hypochondrium, the physical illness was known as hypochondriasis.[43]

When Jefferson stated that Lewis suffered from hypochondriac affections, he was referring to a physical locality, the abdominal area or the hypochondriac region of the body. An 1841 medical dictionary explained it in this way:

> The seat of the hypochondriac affections is in the stomach and the bowels. . . . On dissection of the hypochondriacal persons, some of the abdominal viscera (particularly the liver and spleen) are usually found considerably enlarged.[44]

Thus, the hypochondriac region was comprised of some of the major organs in the body that processed blood and filtered toxins: the spleen and the liver. It also included the digestive system, the stomach, and the intestines. As late as 1850, physicians were still calling the abdominal area the hypochondriac region.[45]

In the literature of the time, the hypochondriac region was commonly associated with a lexicon of phrases, including *vapours* and *spleen*, which ultimately evolved into the more recognized term *splenic humors*. Meriwether Lewis included the term spleen in his 1795 court-martial trial: "[T]he records of this noble Tribunal . . . ought to be held sacred to honor and justice among military men, should not be disgraced with charges fostered by malice and dictated by spleen."[46]

The term "dictated by spleen" was associated with physiological pain and covered a variety of ailments like malaise, pain, temper, and disgust, as did the highly emotive, "vents his spleen," or "the spleen of the satirist," or "be thou my shelter from the spleen of vexatious housewives," to the more nasty "a farrago of miserable spleen," or the highly poignant, "his antagonists . . . are not real characters, but the mere drivelling effusions of his spleen and malice."[47] Hypochondriac affections and spleen coexisted together in a time when this sickness was thought to dwell in this bodily region.

One physical disorder that enlarged the spleen and liver was known as the ague. The ague was also tied to physical symptoms known as hypochondriac affections. Some historians have argued that the ague and malaria were unrelated, but today, malariologists have agreed that the two conditions were one and the same, namely, the ague was malaria.[48]

The ague was the name of an old disease, but in the late eighteenth century it was a fever accompanied by a shaking or shivering fit.[49] When persons succumbed to this illness, they referred to it as "ague and fever."[50] Sometimes they only mentioned the ague, and for good reason: it attacked them incessantly for a period of weeks to months and impaired their thinking.[51] At some point in time, ague and malaria became synonymous. The Greeks knew it as intermittent fever, and its familiar presentation began with a fever, skull-splitting headaches, intense chills, and prodigious sweating. The attack usually lasted twelve to eighteen hours, and a period of convalescence followed, during which it could take days for the patient to fully recover unless the sufferer experienced another attack, which could occur every day or every third day for a period of months.[52]

Malaria was known by a dozen archaic names like autumnal fever, bilious fever, remittent fever, intermittent fever, bilious remittent fever, the chills and fever, or, simply, the ague. Those names were used in different parts of the country because malaria is not a single disease but a family of four different diseases caused by four different parasites.[53]

The malarial parasites are microscopic and live in the gut of a mosquito. The bite or sting of the mosquito transmits the parasites into the bloodstream, which then make their way to the liver. The parasites may remain dormant for a time or morph into several stages of maturity until they burst out of the liver in great numbers and invade the red blood cells for nourishment, which triggers the body's defense mechanism to switch on, resulting in the characteristic stages of fever, chills, and sweating.

Once the disease becomes chronic, a reduction of red blood cells is common, which puts a great strain on the spleen, causing it to enlarge.[54] A healthy spleen weighs barely five ounces, but after repeated malarial attacks, the spleen can occupy the entire abdominal cavity and weigh up to ten pounds. The enlargement of that organ has been characterized by patients as a dragging pain in the abdomen.[55]

Untreated malaria can lead to unpredictable, wild, and erratic behavior and has been cited by physicians during the eighteenth and nineteenth centuries, as well as today. When Lewis arrived at Fort Pickering, Capt. Gilbert Russell reported that he was in a state of mental derangement. Dr. Jean Alibert remarked:

> Every paroxysm of [intermittent] fever . . . was evidently marked by a derangement of intellectual functions. . . . The delirium continued the whole day . . . the patient awoke . . . spoke rationally for a few minutes, but soon relapsed again into such a deep delirium that he could scarcely be kept in bed.[56]

Alibert was confirming that the patient he was treating was being restrained. A more alarming reason for the restraint was to prevent a patient from committing bodily harm, a factor that English physician John Pringle noted when describing soldiers who had succumbed to the first stage of the ague.

> There were some instances of the head being so suddenly and violently affected, that without any previous complaint the men ran about in a wild manner, and were believed to be mad, till the solution of the fit by a sweat, and its periodic returns, discovered the true nature of their delirium.[57]

Pringle, a military camp physician for twenty-five years, may not have known the modern term for malaria, but he knew the sequence:

> That a few returns of the paroxysms reduced their strongest men to so low a condition as to disable them from standing. That some became at once delirious . . . and would have thrown themselves out of the window, or into the water, if not prevented.[58]

Aboard the boat, Lewis's irrational behavior had to be restrained, and there is evidence from the modern day to support this claim. In 1995, a *New York Times* writer traveling in Uganda succumbed to a malarial fever and "a friend had to throw himself across my body to keep me from shaking myself off the bed."[59]

Priscilla Grinder reported that after Lewis had retired to his room at Grinder's Stand, she was suddenly awakened in the early morning by the sound of gunshots.

In 1828, Dr. John Macculloch, another English physician tending to chronic and uncured ague patients, wrote about their irrational thinking:

> The patient feels a species of antipathy against some peculiar part of his body . . . or he longs to commit the act by wounding that particular point . . . this very point is the one eternally forcing itself on his imagination as an object of hatred and revenge. And so perfectly insane is this feeling, that I have been informed by more than one patient . . . that there is no conviction . . . that death would follow; or rather the impression is . . . if the offending part could be exterminated or cured by the injury . . . that the patient would then be well.[60]

Lewis's actions in his final hours are consistent with Macculloch's observations:

> There is also a particular part of the body affected by an uneasy but undefinable sensation, such that the mind constantly reverts to it as a source of suffering . . . or a condition of absolute pain . . . always returning to that one point under the same

stage of the fever or delirium. When, as is not unusual, it is seated in the head, it is even distinguishable by a dull pain, or a confusion, or a sense of "buzzing" (for it is described by patients) in one fixed place. . . . I have the assurance of such patients, that the suicidal desire is exclusively directed to that spot, and that while a pistol would be the only acceptable mode, there would also be no satisfaction unless that were directed to this actual and only point.[61]

The unsystematic courses of action employed by malarial sufferers were extreme efforts to allay pain, even if it meant to wound themselves in the head.[62]

These examples mirror Meriwether Lewis's final days. His affliction was real, it was located in the hypochondrium, and he had sought counsel from Doctors Benjamin Rush and Antoine Saugrain.[63]

In May 1803, prior to the Lewis and Clark Expedition, Lewis consulted with Dr. Benjamin Rush in Philadelphia about his illness. Rush wrote eleven instructions for Lewis and prescribed his own pills as a remedy. Rush's instructions and pills signify that Lewis was under the care of a physician. Rush stated that Lewis suffered from a bilious condition, which meant a certain type of fever originating in the liver and located on the right side of the hypochondriac region.[64]

Three months later, on September 14, 1803, Lewis provided more information about his illness. Descending the Ohio River, he wrote that "the fever and ague and bilious fevers here commence their baneful oppression and continue through the whole course of the river with increasing violence as you approach its mouth."[65]

One has to wonder, as Lewis traveled down the Ohio on the biggest adventure of his life, why he wrote about a specific and serious illness. Instead of contemplating future geographical wonders, he dwelled on a grim aspect of his life.

Then, on November 13, when he departed Fort Massac on the Ohio River, he suddenly fell ill and wrote:

Left Massac this evening about five oclock—descended about three miles and encamped on the S.E. shore raind very hard in eving and I was siezed with a violent ague which continued for about four hours and as is usual was succeeded by a feever which however fortunately abated in some measure by sunrise the next morning.[66]

The phrase "as is usual" implies that Lewis suffered from a long-standing illness, and this is today a marker of a disease that is periodic and/or episodic in nature. The original journal entry of this date affords a rare view of this event.[67] Lewis stated the next day that he was entirely clear of the fever by that evening.[68] But he was so weak that he experienced difficulty when writing anything until November 27, which is when he had fully recovered from the malarial episode.[69]

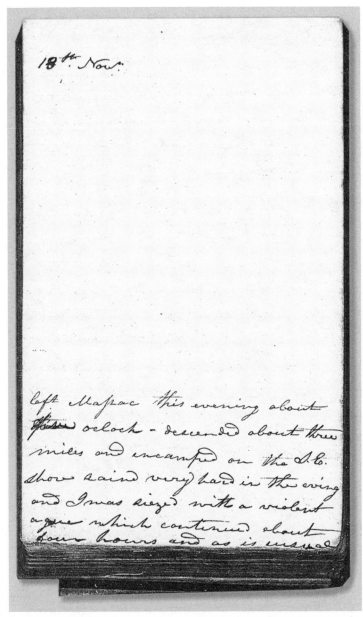

November 13, 1803, journal entry. It is not certain when Meriwether Lewis wrote this entry because the date is unclear. Nor can we determine what time he suffered from a malarial attack. By the fact that he wrote at the bottom of the page suggests that he wrote it after November 13, so that he could write other information at the top of the page. (Meriwether Lewis, November 13, 1803, Eastern Journal, American Philosophical Society, Philadelphia, PA.)

November 14, 1803, journal entry. The journal entries and entry dates from November 13 through November 27 indicate that Lewis could not write well, perhaps due to periods of impaired thinking, which is a hallmark of malaria. (Meriwether Lewis, November 14, 1803, Eastern Journal, American Philosophical Society, Philadelphia, PA.)

Historians have stated that what Lewis experienced was "the ague and fever," which has been equated to a bout of the flu where a person experiences high fever and chills for a short duration. Loge claimed that Lewis "was describing nothing more than a shaking chill—that is, the ague." Because Lewis didn't couch the malarial attack in terms that we are familiar with today—"never recorded a fever relapse"—Loge stated that Lewis was simply talking about a shaking chill.[70] But there is proof to the contrary, and what Lewis described was perfectly understandable to readers of his time.

In the narrowest definition of the ague, it is a shaking chill or an acute fever, and in *Webster's International Dictionary*, it is defined as "a fever of malarial character attended by paroxysms which occur at regular intervals. Each paroxysm has three stages marked by chill, fever, and sweating."[71] Medical dictionaries are more precise. As far back as 1809 the ague and intermittent fever were interchangeable and "known by cold, hot, and sweating stages, in succession, attending each paroxysm, and followed by an intermission or remission."[72]

Dr. John Elliotson in 1842 stated that the "ague shatters the constitution," and he also explained why malarial sufferers abbreviated their descriptions when writing about them:

[T]he common people limit the word "fever" to the hot, or hot and sweating stages; and denominate only the cold stage "ague;"—so that it is common to hear one of the lower orders that has got "the ague and fever," but "ague" properly speaking, includes the whole of the three stages.[73]

When Lewis was on the expedition he had been stricken with malaria several times, but Loge has dismissed this because Lewis "did not have any indication of a malaria-like syndrome."[74] For example, referring to June 11, 1805, which was the end date of a malarial episode, Loge stated that it was "not characteristic of any form of malaria." Lewis's condition between June 9 and 12, 1805, was indeed characteristic of a bout of dysentery and symptomatic of malaria, which is one of the most common features of that disease, and which originates from a derangement of the liver.[75]

June 9

I felt myself unwell this morning and took a portion of [glauber] salts from which I feel much releif this evening.

June 10

I still feel myself somewhat unwell with the disentary, but determined to set out in the morning up the South fork or Missouri.

June 11

This morning I felt much better, but somewhat w[e]akened by my disorder. at 8
A.M. I swung my pack, and set forward with my little party. . . . I determined to
take dinner here, but before the meal was prepared I was taken with such violent
pain in the intestens that I was unable to partake of the feast of marrowbones. my
pain still increased and towards evening was attended with a high fever; finding
myself unable to march, I determined to prepare a camp of some willow boughs
and remain all night. having brought no medecine with me I resolved to try an
experiment with some simples; and the Choke cherry which grew abundanly in the
bottom struck my attention; I directed a parsel of the small twigs to be geathered
striped of their leaves, cut into pieces of about 2 Inches in length and boiled in
water untill a strong black decoction of an astringent bitter tast was produced; at
sunset I took a point [pint] of this decoction and abut [about] an hour after
repeated the dze [dose] by 10 in the evening I was entirely releieved from pain and
in fact every symptom of the disorder forsook me; my fever abated, a gentle perspiration was produced and I had a comfortable and refreshing nights rest.

June 12, 1805

This morning I felt myself quite revived, took another portion of my decoction and
set out at sunrise.

It would appear from Lewis's summary that the chokecherry plant had reduced
the fever and stopped the dysentery but "this is characteristic of the malarial cycle,
suggesting that Lewis's relief had more to do with his fever's natural ebbing" than
any treatment during the time in which he lived.[76]

After Lewis returned from the expedition he had several bouts with malaria,
including March and July 1807 and throughout 1808–1809. But despite these
attacks, Lewis was an active, energetic, and effective governor, which has been little
understood until now. Historians have tagged Lewis as a depressed individual, but
there is no evidence to prove it—being physically ill with untreatable malaria could
be depressing, but actually, Lewis rose above it. From November 1807 until September 1809, Lewis was busily engaged with territorial duties and his letters to officials and friends confirm it.

During the two weeks that Lewis recuperated at Fort Pickering, he had changed
his mind about going to New Orleans for two reasons: he didn't want his journals
falling into the hands of the British when traveling by boat, and he expressed concern about the heat in the lower country.[77] The heat was an expression of a dire
malady. Reports coming from the barges on the Mississippi advised to stay clear of

New Orleans: an ague and fever epidemic was killing the inhabitants and army personnel. By November of that year, more than 700 soldiers had perished.[78]

Lewis then departed the fort with Maj. Neelly, Pernier, and the packer, but after resting at a camp, a week later, Neelly had to look for the horses. Alexander Wilson, an ornithologist and a close friend of Lewis, visited the Grinder family seven months after Lewis's death. He interviewed Priscilla Grinder about the events that occurred on the late afternoon of October 10, when Lewis exhibited a recurrent form of malaria:

> Lewis . . . walked backwards and forwards before the door, talking to himself. Sometimes . . . he would seem as if he were walking up to her; and would suddenly wheel around, and walk back as fast as he could. Supper being ready he sat down, but had not eat . . . a few mouthfuls when he started up, speaking . . . in a violent manner. At these times . . . she observed his face to flush as if it had come on him in a fit.[79]

Lewis was delirious, and Priscilla Grinder, familiar with this illness, knew what it was. When Neelly interviewed her, he reported that Lewis "reached the house of a Mr. Grinder about sun set, the man of the house being from home, and no person there but a woman who discovering the governor to be deranged gave him up the house & slept herself in one near it."

Lewis's actions, on that fateful night, were not unique. It may be an aberration from the point of view of healthy patients, but Lewis was a malarial sufferer. Dr. Macculloch corroborated that the treatment that Lewis performed, shooting himself, had been attempted by others as a remedy and that some of these patients had lived thereafter:

> [T]his particular aberration . . . is well known . . . while I need not do more than suggest one peculiar part of the body which has been often the offending and selected point; the act having been . . . not always followed by death.[80]

In a prior chapter medical evidence identified that Meriwether Lewis had malaria and that he had the same set of feelings and desires displayed by Macculloch's patients. Lewis had a certain antipathy toward his head and liver/spleen and wanted to wound it by shooting it, as if the shooting would cure it. Ultimately he was following Macculloch's description, and was one among those malarial patients who wounded "the offending part." In this scenario, Lewis desired to alleviate his pain but was not trying to terminate his life. The reader must understand that the pain in his head was unbearable and debilitating. As Macculloch pointed out,

"There is also a particular part of the body affected by an uneasy but undefinable sensation, such that the mind constantly reverts to it as a source of suffering . . . or a condition of absolute pain."

Lewis was driven to shoot the offending part because of the absolute pain.

In sum, the ague made him do it. Lewis probably contracted the disease in 1795. He followed a regimen of treatment prescribed by Dr. Rush and later by Dr. Saugrain, and his actions mirrored those of Macculloch's patients. In light of these facts, Meriwether Lewis did not commit suicide. Lewis was suffering from an acute physiological illness, that is, the ague or malaria. As such, that acute illness was the cause not only of his erratic behavior but also the radical and violent actions he performed upon himself in October 1809.

Historians, in the past, have claimed that Lewis killed himself; my conclusion, as a historian, is that Lewis did not mean to kill himself in his malarial attack. Rather, he, by his actions, meant only to treat his absolute pain.

APPENDIXES A–G:
SUPPORTING DOCUMENTATION

Appendix A

DOCUMENTS FROM, TO, AND ABOUT MERIWETHER LEWIS, 1803–1813

1. MERIWETHER LEWIS, JOURNAL ENTRY, NOVEMBER 13, 1803[1]

left Massac this evening about ~~five~~ oclock—descended about three miles and encamped on the S.E. shore raind very hard in the eving and I was siezed with a violent ague which continued about four hours and as is usual was succeeded by a feever which however fortunately abated in some measure by Sunrise the next morning, ~~I then took a~~

2. MERIWETHER LEWIS, JOURNAL ENTRY, NOVEMBER 14, 1803[2]

set out by light at sunrise I took a doze of Rushes pills which operated extremly well and I found myself much to my satisfaction intirely clear of fever by the evening passed Wilkinson ville about 12 Oclock oposite to which is the first or great chain of rocks streching in an oblque manner across the Oho

3. MERIWETHER LEWIS, JOURNAL ENTRY, APRIL 7, 1805[3] (EXCERPT)

Our vessels consisted of six small canoes, and two large perogues. This little fleet altho' not quite so rispectable as those of Columbus or Capt. Cook were still viewed by us with as much pleasure as those deservedly famed adventurers ever beheld theirs; and I dare say with quite as much anxiety for their safety and preservation. we were now about to penetrate a country at least two thousand miles in width, on which the foot of civillized man had never trodden; the good or evil it had in store for us was for experiment yet to determine, and these little vessells contained every article by which we were to expect to subsist or defend ourselves. however as this the state of mind in which we are, generally gives the colouring to events, when the immagination is suffered to wander into futurity, the picture which now presented itself to me was a most pleasing one. entertaing as I do, the most confident hope of succeeding in a voyage which had formed a daling project of mine for the last ten years, I could but esteem this moment of my departure as among the most happy of my life. The party are in excellent health and sperits, zealously attatched to the enterprise, and anxious to proceed; not a whisper of murmur or discontent to be heard among them, but all act in unison, and with the most perfect harmony. I took an early supper this evening and went to bed. Capt. Clark myself the two Inter-pretters and the woman and child sleep in a tent of dressed skins. . . .

4. MERIWETHER LEWIS, JOURNAL ENTRY, AUGUST 18, 1805[4] (EXCERPT)

This day I completed my thirty first year, and conceived that I had in all human probability now existed about half the period which I am to remain in this Sublu-nary world. I reflected that I had as yet done but little, very little indeed, to further the hapiness of the human race, or to advance the information of the succeeding gen-eration. I viewed with regret the many hours I have spent in indolence, and now soarly feel the want of that information which those hours would have given me had they been judiciously expended. but since they are past and cannot be recalled, I dash from me the gloomy thought and resolved in future, to redouble my exertions and at least indeavour to promote those two primary objects of human existence, by giving them the aid of that portion of talents which nature and fortune have bestoed on me; or in future, to live for *mankind,* as I have heretofore lived *for myself.*—

5. MERIWETHER LEWIS, JOURNAL ENTRY, JANUARY 1, 1806[5] (EXCERPT)

This morning I was awoke at an early hour by the discharge of a volley of small arms, which were fired by our party in front of our quarters to usher in the new year; this was the only mark of rispect which we had it in our power to pay this celebrated day. our repast of this day tho' better than that of Christmass, consisted principally in the anticipation of the 1st day of January 1807, when in the bosom of our friends we hope to participate in the mirth and hilarity of the day, and when the zest given by the recollection of the present, we shall completely, both mentally and corporally, enjoy the repast which the hand of civilization has prepared for us. at present we were content with eating our boiled Elk and wappetoe, and solacing our thirst with our only beverage *pure water.*

6. MERIWETHER LEWIS TO AUGUSTE CHOUTEAU, FEBRUARY 11, 1807[6]

This will [be] handed by you by a particular friend and acquaintance of mine Mr. Fleming Bates, late Judge of the Michigan Territory and receiver of public monies at Detroit–.

Mr. Bates has been recently appointed the Secretary of the Territory of Louisiana and recorder of the Board of Commissioners for adjusting the land claims in that territory and is about to establish himself at St. Louis, in order to take on him the discharges of the duties incumbent to those offices.

The Situation of Mr. Bates as a public officer sufficiently shews the estimation in which, he is in my opinion, deservedly held by the Executive of the United States, and consequently renders any further observations in relation to his talents or integrity unnecessary on my part. You will confer on me by making Mr. Bates acquainted with the respectable inhabitants of St. Louis and its vicinity or by rendering him any service which it may be in your power to give him–.

The papers you confided to my care have been laid before the Executive, but as yet I have received no answer on the subject, nor do I believe that any definitive answer will be given or measures taken in relation to the land claims of Louisiana until after the passage of a law on that subject which is now under the consideration of Congress–.

I shall probably come on to St. Louis in the early course of the next fall, for the purpose of residing among you; in such an event I should wish timely to procure a house by rent or otherwise for my accommadation, and I have fixed my eye on that of Mr. Gratiot, provided we cam come on terms which may be mutually agreeable. I would prefer renting or leasing to purchase; in either case the enclosure of the garden must be rendered secure, and the steps & floor of the piazza repaired by the 1st October next– I would thank you to request Mr. Gratiot to write me on this subject and to state his terms distinctly as to price, payment &c, in order that I may know whether my resources will enable me to meet them or not, or whether it will be necessary that I should make some other provision for my accommodation.

My respectful compliments to your lady, Madme Chouteau and my friends of St. Louis and its vicinity, & believe me

—Meriwether Lewis

7. JAMES WILKINSON TO PRESIDENT THOMAS JEFFERSON, SEPTEMBER 15, 1807, RICHMOND[7] (EXCERPT)

Sir

I did intend to transmit you a copy of Capt Pikes report by Governor Lewis, but have been too occupied to fulfil my purpose—I shall have the Honor to Hand it to you at the Seat of Government. . . .

8. MERIWETHER LEWIS TO MAHLON DICKERSON, NOVEMBER 3, 1807, ALBERMARLE[8]

Dear Dickerson:

This will be handed you by my brother, John H. Marks, who visits Philadelphia with a view to attend the medical lectures. I have given him letters of introduction to Wister, Rush & Peal, and have strictly enjoined him to call on you frequently, as for all those little matters of advice, admonition, &c., for which he would have called on me had I been personally present: we both know that young men are sometimes in want of such a friend, but could I believe that he would give you any anxiety on this score I should not have placed him in this point of view with rispect to you; but on the contrary his stability, industry and application hitherto give me the best hopes of him and therefore think I can with confidence confide him to your friendly care.

I have given John H. Marks $60 and a bill of exchange on the bank of the U'States for two hundred dollars more, which I have conceived would be equal to his expenditures until the middle or last of January next; this bill however, is for a part of my quarter salary ending the 31st of December and not payable until the 5th of January 1808: as his expenditures immediately after his arrival in Philadelphia, in making the necessary arrangements for attending the lectures, will be greater than at any subsequent period, he will be in want of more money than he has now in possession before this bill becomes due; if therefore you can with convenience to yourself, advance him the sum of two hundred dollars or such part of it as shall be deemed necessary for his immediate wants upon a transfer of this bill to yourself, you would confer a singular favor on me. After the 1st of January, other arrangements have been made which I hope will furnish him with the necessary means of support; but should any accident happen on this rispect, I trust you will not suffer him to want for any sum under $300, as I pledge you my honor it shall be returned immediately on notice of the advance having been made.

I have enjoyed a great share of health since I had the pleasure of seeing you last, and am now on the eve of my departure for St. Louis. So much for business, now for the *girls*.

My little affair with Miss A—n R—ph has had neither beginning nor end on her part; pr. Contra, on my own, it has had both. The fact is, that on enquiry I found that she was previously engaged, and therefore dismissed every idea of prosecuting my pretentions in that quarter, and am now a *perfect widower with rispect to love*. Thus floating on the *surface of occasion*, I feel all that restlessness, that inquietude, that certain indiscribable something common to old bachelors, which I cannot avoid thinking my dear fellow, proceeds, from that *void in our hearts*, which might, or ought to be better filled. Whence it comes I know not, but certain it is, that I never felt less like a heroe than at the present moment. What may be my next adventure god knows, but on this I am determined, *to get a wife*.

Do let me hear from you as frequently as you can, and when you have no subject of more importance talk about *the girls*. You see already from certain innate workings of the sperit, the changes which have taken place in my dispositions, and that I am now so much unlike my former self, that I speak of those bewitching gipsies as *a secondary consideration*: I sincerely wish my dear fellow, that candor would permit me to say as much with rispect to Miss E—B —y of Philadelphia, whose memory will still remain provokingly *important* in spite of all my philosophy. Have you heard from her? Have you seen her? How is she? Is she well, sick, dead, or married? Oh! I had forgotten you have no particular acquaintance with her; ask your coadjutator T. Rush, and tell me. Adieu. Direct to me at Louisvill Kentucky, untill the last of this month, and after that period forward your letters to St. Louis. Dr. Fothergil perhaps can give you the necessary information.

My best wishes and compliments to all our acquaintances in the city, and particularly to Mrs. Bache and the Dr., Mrs. Sergeants Mrs. Water &c. Believe me your very sincere and affectionate friend & Obt. Servt.

—Meriwether Lewis

9. MERIWETHER LEWIS TO WILLIAM CLARK, MAY 29, 1808

My Dear friend

I had not the pleasure of recieving yours of the 30th April untill the 25th Instant, I wrote to Col. Hunt on the evening of the same day and have made arrangements to dispatch Ensign Prior, one trusty Sergt. & twenty good men, from the cantonment at Belle Fontain to meet you at the Mouth of the Ohio, one french Patroon and four perhaps six, French engages will also be sent with him two large Keel Boats have already been engaged and prepared with necessary stores at this place for the voyage, one of the keel boats which I have employed is extremely well calculated for the accommodation of your goods (as you are pleased to denominate them) but I must halt here in the middle of my communications and ask you if the matrimonial dictionary affords no term more appropriate then that of goods, alias merchandize, for that dear and interesting part of the creation? it is very well Genl., I shall tell madam of your want of Gallantry; and the triumph too of detection will be more compleat when it is recollected what a musty, fusty, rusty old bachelor I am. This Boat then is the same in which Mr. McFarlane descended the Ohio, it is well covered and sufficiently capacious to accomodate the ladies comfortably. Prior will take with him the tools which we deemed necessary such alterations as you may think proper—he descends the river on Teusday next, and is directed, should he not meet with you at the mouth of Ohio to ascend as high as Massac and there wait your arrival. I trust you do not mean merely to tantalize your Neices, I have already flattered the community of St. Louis with this valuable acquisition to our female society. On my arrival here the 8th March I learned that Mr. Gratiot had let his house to one of his sons in law, and that had it not been let I could not expect it for less than $500 per. annum, such rent I never had calculated on giving and consequently engaged another dwelling, I have rented the house of Mr. Campbell on the main Street at $250 pr. annum./ I know not whether you are acquainted with the interior of this house and will therefore endeavour to give you some Idea of it. The cellar is dry, equal in its temperature and sufficiently capacious for our purposes; there are four good rooms on the first floor with a convenient store room or closet and a small office, a Piazza on the East front the whole length of the building, it continues also on the south end and is terminated by the office, on the same floor there is a half passage leading from the centre or principal room to the back yard garden & kitchen; the door of a flight of stairs, leading to the garret, opens in this passage, as with the cellar, the garret is in one common room, but it has a tolerable floor and will be convenient for the servants to lodge &c. the kitchen has two fire places with a good bake oven opening into one of them, a large stable, a good well, a small though well protected garden and a small indifferent out house formerly used for smoking of meat constitute the other appendages of this dwelling. Should we find on experiment that we have not sufficient room in this house, I can obtain an Office somewhere in the neighbourhood and still consider myself your messmate; the garden has been attended to; and I have also enclosed a large garden near this lot, which will furnish us with potatoes, cabbage &c. You know the difficulty of procuring furniture in this country, I have been able to procure but little and that even is not of the quallity I could have wished. I hope you will therefore bring with you a good stock of household apparatus, for should you not want them all on your arrival, they can be readily disposed of.

On the 29th April I wrote to Mr. Fitzhugh and enclosed to him for Mr. Joseph Charless a bill of exchange on the President and directors of the Bank of the United States for one hundred dollars also ninety five dollars in bank notes, and requested him to pay Mr. Charless the further sum of thirty dollars, and to call on you for that amount, or draw on me for the same, these several amounts make the sum of 225 dollars which had been subscribed by myself and others as a loan for twelve months to Mr. Charless to enable him to commence his paper in this place to greater advantage, from Information recieved a few days since, I have reason to believe that this letter to Mr. Fitzhugh one to Mr. Charless and sundry other letters and valuable papers which I dispatched by the succeeding mail, remained at Cahokia several days, and were unfortunately lost when the post rider was drowned about the 15th of this month in the little Wabash, not haveing yet heard from Mr. Fitzhugh I am still further induced to believe that my letters have been lost and therefore I am extremely anxious that Mr. Charless should come forward I enclose the fourth and fifth of my bill of exchange on the Bank of the United States In favour of Mr. Charless for one hundred dollars and must beg leave to request that you will make some arrangements by which he can be served with the further sum of $125. Inform Mr. Charless that I have made no arrangements with any other Printer Publishing the laws of the Territory, but that if he calculates on my encouragement and support he must come forward in person as soon as possible. The Legislature will meet on the second Monday in June to revise the laws of the Territory and will most probably originate others, a printer is absolutely necessary and that there is no time to be lost unnecessarily I know not of any point in the UStates where I concieve a country paper or printer would meet with more encouragement than at St. Louis.

I shall write you by Ensign Prior on Tuesday, but supposing that it was possible that you might not think proper to leave the falls before you recieved an answer to yours of the 30th April I have dispatched this by the first mail since the receipt of it, my sending Ensign Prior immeadiately will also prevent your being detained should you have set out before this reaches you.

Your sincere friend
Meriwether Lewis

William Clark, May 29, 1808
    N.B. Should Genl. Clark have left the falls Mr. Fitzhugh is requested to attend to the part of this letter in relation to Mr. Charless.

—M.L.
—St. Louis June 1st 1808

My dear friend
    I am so much engaged at this moment I hope you will pardon my not writing to you further by Ensign Prior at this moment—he will give you a description of my present situation and my anxiety to see you. My love to the ladies.

—Adieu Yours &c
—M. Lewis
(on the cover it reads: *Genl. William Clark at or near the mouth of the Ohio.*)

10. Meriwether Lewis to William Preston, July 25, 1808, Saint Louis[9]

Your favor of the 11th inst. from Nashville has been duly received.—how wretchedly you married me arrange the subjects of which you treat. I am induced to believe from the date of your letter and the arrangement of the subject matter, that you must have been engaged in compiling toasts for the fourth of July, in which, the great dirth of gallantry among our countrymen has very uniformly consigned the recollection of the fair, to the *last glass*, and the *last haza!*—you have gained that which I have yet to obtain, a *wif*; pardon me therefore for begining where you left off. you run through a sheet of paper about your musty fusty trade, your look out for land speculations without locality or interest in your old friends, a flimsy excuse about the want of money to enable you to come and see us &c &c before you came to the point. then *she is off*, passed—off the hooks,[10] I mean in a matrimonial point of view; bet it so, the die is cast, may god be with her and her's, and the favored angels of heaven guard her bliss both here and hereafter, is the sincere prayer of her very sincere friend, to whom she has left the noble consolation of scratching his head and biting his nails, with ample leasure to ruminate on the chapter of accedents in matters of love and the folly of castle-building. well, I find it an amusing study notwithstanding admirably calculated to kill time, and when I find myself without imployment I will begin again.

—Gamble is a good tempered, easy honest fellow, I have known him from a boy; both his means and his disposition well fit him for sluming away life with his fair one in the fassionable rounds of a large City. such is the life she has celected and in it's pursuit I wish she may meet all the pleasures of which it is susceptible. I consider Miss E—B— [Elizabeth Breckinridge] a charming girl, but such was my passing for her sister [Letitia], that my soul revolts at the idea of attempting to make her my wife, and shall not consequently travel that road in quest of matrimony. so much for *love*, now in order I shall take up *friendship*, then treat of land speculations money making and other matters of minor importance. — . . . In my opinion— Louisiana, and particularly the district of St. Louis, at this moment offers more advantages than any other portion of the U'States to the farmer, the mechanic, inland merchant or the honest adventurer who can command money or negroes. in point of soil or climate it is inferior to none; it is calculated to produce a greater variety of valuable articles for export than any other portion of the continent and those too in great abundance. . . . From Cape Girardeau upwards I do not consider it a good cotton country; saving crops might be made but there is much greater profit to be obtained by cultivating other articles, even as great or greater than can be obtained by cultivating cotton and we are certain of enjoying what we can as there is not a healthyer contry than upper part of Louisiana . . . you would in my opinion do well to come and see us from the Falls of the Ohio, it will only take you a few weeks longer and you can then be a more competent judge, and can make your arrangements accordingly; if you do not celect Louisiana as your place of residence I will wrisk my existence that you will at some future period regret having chosen any other. you have no time to loose. lands are rising fast, but are yet very low; the choice positions/ which I could have purchased when I was last in this country, or about 16 months before my return, at one dollar pr. Arpent I have been obliged to give two dollars for. excellent land can be had within six eight & ten miles of St. Louis at 50 Cents pr. Acre, with a general warrentee as to tittle against all claims except the U'States, and with a condition also that if the lands are not confermed to you that the money shall be returned with interest from the date of the decesion of the Commissions should they decide against the claim . . . I have purchased 7,440 arpens of land for $5,530, all of it lying in the nighbourhood of St. Louis in situations as eligible as I could have wished with an excellent mill seat on one of the tracts. if you would sell that fort of yours within the mountains at half price, and bring your money or negroes with you to this country you might purchase a princely fortune; but to do this as I have before/ told you there is no time to be lost. The Genl. has informed me of the mode he has proposed to you for bringing on your family to this country which I think is the best that can be devised. —

The Indians have been exceedingly troublesome during the last winter and spring, but I have succeeded in managing those on the Mississippi; they have delivered three murderers to a party which I sent with a strong talk to them, they are now under trial will no doubt be stretched. the Osage and others on the Missouri are yet in a threatening position but the arrangements which have been made and the steps we are now about to take I feel confident will reduce them to order.

11. MERIWETHER LEWIS TO MRS. LUCY MARKS, DECEMBER 1, 1808, SAINT LOUIS[11]

My life is one continued press of business which scarcely allows me leasure to write to you. I have consequently not written to you as often as I could have wished. I sincerely hope you are all well tho' it seems I shall not know whether you are dead or alive until I visit you again. what is John Marks, and Edmund Anderson about, that they do not write to me? I am very anxious to learn whether John Marks has returned to Philadelphia or not; and if he has gone on, what prospects he has for the means of supplying himself with money, or whether he is sufficiently supplied already. I am also anxious to know whether May is married or not, and where she is, if she is married and has removed to Georgia I know your feelings on the subject. I hope you will bear this separation with your usual fortitude. I still hope if this is the case that I shall have it in my power to offer Mr. More (Wm. Moore) such inducements as will determine him to remove to Louisiana.

I have purchased five thousand seven hundred acres of land in this neighbourhood, lying in four parsels, one of forty two acres adjoining the town of St. Louis, a second of three thousand acres at the distance of six miles from the town, and the other tracts at the distance of twelve or fourteen miles, all above the town and in situations which I conceive the most elligible in the country in many points of view. The tract six miles distant contains three thousand acres; the improvements area field well enclosed of forty acres a comfortable dwelling house with three rooms, with stables and other convenient out houses; a good well, and a garden of three quarters of an acre well inclosed. there are also three springs within a short distance of the house. The land is of an excellent quality and contains a happy proportion of prarie or natural meadow and woodland. These improvements with one thousand acres of land including them is the consideration I entend giving you for your relinquishment of dower to the lands on Ivy creek. it was my intention to give you a life estate in that property but if you wish it I have no objection to convey it to you in fee simple. This place which I have selected for your residence is in the most healthy part of the country; it is an agreeable situation one with which I am convinced you will be pleased. I have paid about three thousand dollars for the lands which I have purchased, fifteen hundred dollars more will become due in May and twelve hundred more on the 1st of May 1810—to meet these arrangements it will be necessary to sell the Ivy creek lands or at least as part of them, and for this purpose I shall shortly inclose to Mr. Dabney Car[r] a power of attorney to dispose of them. I have been detained here much longer than I expected but hope to get off shortly. You may expect me in the course of this winter.

I have generally had my health well since I left you. I am with every sentiment of filiel affection Your son

—Meriwether Lewis
Mrs. Lucy Marks near Charlottesville, Virginia

12. Pierre Chouteau to Secretary of War, June 14, 1809, Saint Louis[12] [penned by Frederick Bates]

When at Washington in the winter of 1806–7, I was consulted by the late President, with respect to the arrangements which ought to be made for restoring the Mandan chief to his people. I suggested a place and offered my services to conduct the expedition, pledging myself for its successful accomplishment. Mr. Jefferson appeared to approve my ideas, tho' he expressed himself only in general terms, and desired me to confer on the subject with Governor Lewis.

In subsequent conversations with the Governor, my opinions were overruled, and the preference given to a military escort. A young and inexperienced officer was appointed to command it and the party, as you perceive having suffered a defeat, was compelled to abandon the enterprize as impracticable.

The scheme originally submitted by myself has been with some modifications, been adopted by the Governor at whose solicitations, I have thought it my duty to take the command of the Party.—The certain fatigues and probable dangers which must be encountered in this excursion, have scarcely been reflected on by me; for in this, as in every other public transaction of my life a wish faithfully to discharge those duties, which have been familiarized by a long experience, has been my prevailing, and indeed my only inducement.

The contract heretofore transmitted by the Governors will have given you the principles of this arrangement. You will have observed that it is as well <u>mercantile</u> as <u>military</u>. It is a detachment of the militia of Louisiana as high as the Mandan-village and <u>commercial</u> afterwards.

If my participation in speculations of this kind should excite the surprise of government as inconsistent with my duties as an Agent, I beg leave to refer you to Governor Lewis, who advices I have pursued and whose explanations, will, I hope, in my justification. My agency has, of late, been limited to the Osages, and with these tribes the company will have us trading intercourse. I accompany the expedition, merely in a military capacity (as Major Commandant) and as soon as my command ceases at the Mandan Village, shall return with all convenient haste to Saint Louis, unless prevented by ice or other unexpected occurrence.

I take the liberty to enclose a Power of Attorney, by which my son Peter Chouteau jnr: is empowered to draw in my absence, for my compensations as an agent.

13. MERIWETHER LEWIS TO WAR DEPARTMENT, JULY 8, 1809, SAINT LOUIS[13]

Dear Sir.

Inclosed I transmit you twenty dollars in bank bills and return you my sincere thanks for your friendly interference with rispect to my bill of eighteen dollars rejected by the Secretary of the Treasury. this occurrence has given me infinite concern as the fate of other bills drawn for similar purposes to a considerable amount cannot be mistaken; this rejection cannot fail to impress the public mind unfavourably with rispect to me, nor is this consideration more painfull than the censure which must arise in the mind of the executive from my having drawn for public monies without authority; a third and not less imbarassing circumstance attending the transaction is that my private funds are entirely incompetent to meet those bills if protested. —

You will also recieve inclosed the voucher on which the bill of eighteen dollars was predicated on which I shall take the liberty of making few [page 2] remarks. —

Previous to my drawing any bill of the govern [ment] & c

In the course of the last autumn a Court of Oyer and terminur was held at St. Louis for the trial of a prisoner indicted of felony. the duty of presiding in the case Judge Lucas assigned himself. a few days previous to the trial the Judge made a formal application to me for certifyed copies of the Judiciary and criminal laws of the Territory declaring that unless the court was furnished with them he could not proceed with the trial of the prisoner; under those circumstances I did not hesitate to cause the copies of those laws to be made out and furnished him. The Secretary of the territory Mr. Bates previous to my drawing any bill on the government for publishing the laws of the territory had informed me that the expence of publishing or promulgating the laws of the territory in any shape could not be defrayed by the contingent fund placed under his control consequently I was compelled to take the course which I have or suffer a fellon to escape punishment. [page 3] I shall write more fully to the Secretary of State on this subject and inclose him my vouchers for the expenses which have been incurred in publishing the laws of the territory as I am imperitively directed by [Meriwether Lewis].

14. WILLIAM SIMMONS TO MERIWETHER LEWIS, JULY 15, 1809, WAR DEPARTMENT[14]

After the sum of seven thousand dollars had been advanced on the Bills drawn by your Excellency on account of your Contract with the St. Louis Missouri Fur Company for conveying the Mandan Chief to his Village; and after this Department had been advised that "for this purpose the Company was bound to raise, organize, arm & equip at their own expence one hundred and forty Volunteers and to furnish whatever might be deemed necessary for the Expedition, or to insure its success"—it was not expected that any further advances or any further agency would be required on the part of the United States. Seven thousand dollars was considered as competent to effect the object. Your Excellency will not be surprized that your Bill of the 13th of May last drawn in favor of M. P. Chouteau for five hundred dollars for the purchase of Tobacco, Powder, &c. intended as Presents for the Indians, through which this expedition was to pass and to insure its success, has not been honored. In the instance of accepting the volunteer services of 140 men for a military expedition to a point and purpose not designated, which expedition is stated to combine commercial as well as military objects, and when an Agent of the Government appointed for other purposes is selected for the command, it is thought the Government might, without injury to the public interests, have been consulted. As the object & destination of this Force is unknown, and more especially as it combines Commercial purposes, so it cannot be considered as having the sanction of the Government of the United States, or that they are responsible for the consequences. On another account it was desirable that this Government should have been consulted. Being responsible for the expenditure of Public money & made judges in such cases whether the Funds appropriated by the Legislature are applicable and adequate to the object, it is desirable in all practicable cases that they should be advised and consulted when expenditure is required. As the Agency of Mr. Chouteau is become vacant by his accepting the command of the Detachment it is in contemplation to appoint a suitable character to supply his place. Another bill of your Excellency's in favor of Mr. Chouteau drawn for materials for erecting an assaying Furnace has not been protected, there being no appropriation of this Department applicable to such an object.

The President has been consulted and the observations herein contained have his approval,—and your Excellency may be assured that they are dictated by a sense of public duty and are perfectly consistent with the great respect and regard with which I have the honor to remain, &c &c &c.

15. MERIWETHER LEWIS TO WILLIAM SIMMONS, AUGUST 18, 1809, SAINT LOUIS.[15]

Yours of the 15th July is now before me, the feelings it excites are truly painful. With respect to every public expenditure, I have always accompanied my Draft by Letters of advice, stating explicitly, the object of the expenditure: if the object be not a proper one, of course, I am responsible; but if on investigation, it does appear to have been necessary for the promotion of the public Interests, I shall hope for relief.

I have never received a penny of public Money, but have merely given the Draft to the person who had rendered the public service, or furnished articles for public use, which have been invariably applied to the purposes expressed in my Letters of advice.

I have made advances for the Public from time to time in small sums for recovering of public horses which were lost, for forage for them, expenses attending Sales &c. and have retained from the sales of those horses the sum of eighty five Dollars, for which I have ample vouchers. In these transactions, I have drawn no draft, calculating on going forward long since and settleing my Accounts with the Public.— The balance of the Sales in Money and Bonds have been lodged with Gen. Clark by the Vendue-Master: —to the correctness of this statement, I call my God to witness.

I have been informed Representations have been made against me,—all I wish is a full and fair Investigation. I anxiously wish that this may reach you in time to pr[e]vent any decision relative to me.

I shall leave the Territory in the most perfect state of Tranquility which I believe, it has ever experienced. I find it impossible at this moment, to explain by letter, and to do away by written explanations, the impressions which I fear, from the tenor of your letter, the Government entertain with respect to me, and shall therefore go on by the way of New Orleans to the City of Washington with all dispatch—Thursday next I have appointed for my departure from Saint Louis. I shall take with me my papers, which I trust when examined, will prove my firm and steady attachment to my Country, as well as the Exertions I have made to support and further it's interests in this Quarter.

I do most solemnly aver, that the expedition sent up the Misoury under the Command of Mr. Pierre Chouteau, as a military Command, has no other object than that of conveying the Mandane Chief and his Family to their Village—and in a commercial point of view, that they intend only, to hunt and trade on the waters of the Misoury and Columbia Rivers within the Rockey-Mountains and the Planes bordering those Mountains on the east side—and that they have no intention with which I am acquainted, to enter the Dominions, or do injury to any foreign Power—

Be assured Sir, that my country can never make "A Burr" of me— She may reduce me to Poverty; but she can never sever my Attachment from her.

Those protested Bills from the Departments of War and Treasury, have effectually sunk my Credit; brought in all my private debts, amounting to about $4000, which has compelled me, in order to do justice to my Creditors, to deposit with them, the landed property which I had purchased in this Country as Security.

The best proof which I can give of my Integrity, as to the use or expenditure of public Monies, the Government will find at a future day, by the poverty to which they have reduced me—still, I shall do no more than appeal to the Generosity of the Government by exposing my Claims.

I had sooner bear any pecuniary embarrassment, than attempt, in any manner, to wound the Feelings, or injure in the public Opinion, the present Executive, or either of the Heads of the Departments, by complaining of Injuries done me, other than in friendly Expostulations.

I am convinced that the Motives expressed in the latter part of your Letter, are those which have actuated you; but at the same time, I trust that the Motives that induced me to make the Expenditure, will be found equally pure.

Some weeks after making the Contract with the Misoury-Fur-Company, for taking the Mandane Chief to his Village, I received information, ~~that~~ through the Sous and Mahas that the Chyenns had joined the Aricaras and were determined to arrest all Boats which might ascend the River, I conceived it necessary, in order to meet the additional Force and to insure the success of the Expedition conveying the Mandane Chief, to make the further advance with a view, that should it become necessary to engage an auxiliary force among the friendly Nations through which they would pass, that Mr. Chouteau, the Commanding Officer, might be enabled to acquire such aid by means of those supplies.

You will find from the enclosed Document, that if Mr. Chouteau does not expend the articles for the purposes mentioned, that he is still held responsible to the Government for such part thereof as may remain unexpended.

With respect to the assaying Furnace, I did conceive that such an Estabishment was necessary; but, as there is no Appropriation for such objects, arrangements have been made by me, to meet the protested Bill—and no claim will hereafter be made for that object.

I have reason to believe that sundry of my Letters have been lost, as there remain several important Subjects on which I have not yet received an Answer.

I still hope that Mr. Chouteau will not be removed, he is ordered to return this Fall, or as soon as the military Expedition is at an end, which you will recollect, ceases as soon as he arrives at the Mandane Nation.

Col. August Chouteau of this place, his brother, has agreed with me to act in his place Pro. Tem. The Osage Treaty not having been ratified, would, in my opinion, recommend this arrangement.

I have the honor to be with much rispect Your Obt. Servt.

—Meriwether Lewis

N.B. The reasons for wishing Mr. Chouteau not to be displaced is that if the event takes place before one or the other of the Osage treaties ar ratifyed there will in my opinion be War with that nation.

16. WILLIAM CARR TO CHARLES CARR, AUGUST 25, 1809, SAINT LOUIS[16] (EXCERPT)

Good lands must greatly increase in value here in the course of a few years—I shall certainly purchase if I can do so without involving myself—They are offered to me every day on a long credit, by paying a little cash in hand. I expect Mr. Bates our Secretary will join me in some purchases we contemplate making in a short time— If therefore you think proper to vest any of your money in property of that kind & can trust it with me I flatter myself I could employ it to a great advantage for you.

I have made more important contracts in six months past than I ever made in all of my life before—I have bought two negro fellows, one last spring—another a few weeks since for $333.33 part on a credit of 12 months—This last I sold again directly for one of those land warrants issued by the late Secy of War to the followers of Lewis and Clark for 320 acres each—payable at the land office at $2 an acre . . . .

Our Governor left us a few days since with his private affairs altogether deranged. He is a good man, but a very imprudent one—I apprehend he will not return—He has drawn on the general government for various & considerable sums of money which have not been paid: of course his bills have been protested—He has vested Judge Stuart of Kaskaskia, Gen. Clark and myself with full powers to adjust and liquidate all demands against him & left in my hands all his land titles, to be sold for that purpose. . . . Neither Nancy nor myself have been very well lately. . . . Some of these lands situated about 10 miles from this place near a little village called St. Ferdinand will be sold [this was the tract that Meriwether Lewis bought for his mother—see his letter to Lucy Marks, December 1, 1808]. The title is complete & the quality of the land excellent. It is also situated on the bank of the Missouri—If I had the money I would give it for the land instantly. . . .

17. Meriwether Lewis to Pierre Chouteau, September 2, 1809, Saint Louis[17]

I would thank you to furnish me with the following articles by two o'clock this evening in order that the same may be delivered to the Chiefs and warriors of the Great Osages of the River Arkansas who did on the 31st sign the treaty entered into by the great and little Osages of the Osage River on the tenth day of November last; as well as to chiefs and warriors of the last mentioned land who have accompanied them to this place. I presume that all the articles in this list can be furnished by the time mentioned except the chiefs coats and pantaloons which when completed will be delivered to Sherman (Clermont) and Big-Track the principal chief of the bands of the Arkansas. 2 chief coats. 2 pr pantaloons, 2 hats decorated with band cocadis and feathers, 2 fusils, 50th of balls, one piece of Indian common calico, 8 yards of scarlet—cloath of second quality, 10 yards of blue strouding, 4 1/2 vermillion, 5 dozen common Indian knives, 4 Gorgets, 2 pr. of armbands, 100 flints, 1 piece of red ribbon, 17 blankets—3 points. The Indians will be dispatched to their respective villages the day after tomorrow with some trusty interpreter to conduct them beyond the settlements with provisions until they pass the inhabitants.

I am with much respect your obed. Servant M.L.

[his signature] recorded September 30, 1809

18. WILL: SEPTEMBER 11, 1809, NEW MADRID[18]

I bequeath all my estate real and personal to my Mother Lucy Marks of the County of Albermarle and State of Virginia after my private debts are paid of which a stateant will be found in a small minute book deposited with

—Meriwether Lewis

Pernia my Servant
September 11, 1809
In the presence of F. S. Trinchard

Geau Peaeny

At Albermarle March Court 1810
   The within instrument of writeing purporting to be the last will and testament of Meriwether Lewis deceased was produced into Court and the hand writeing with the Signature hereto was proven to be the hand writeing of said Lewis by the oathes of Dabney Carr. Thomas W. Maury and Dabney Minor and ordered to be recorded

—Teste

—John Nicholas CC

Copied from page 66, Will Book No. 5 at the Albermarle County Clerk's office.

A copy—Erato Maupin, clerk

19. MERIWETHER LEWIS TO JAMES MADISON, SEPTEMBER 16, 1809, FORT PICKERING, CHICKASAW BLUFFS

Dear Sir,
   I arrived here yesterday about ~~2 OCk~~ P.M. ~~yesterday~~ very much exhausted from the heat of the climate, but having taken medicine feel much better this morning. my apprehension from the heat of the lower country and my fear of the original papers relative to my voyage to the Pacific ocean falling into the hands of the British induced me to change my route and proceed by land through the state to Tennisse to the City of washington. I bring with me duplicates of my vouchers for public expenditures &c. which when fully explained, or reather the general view of the circumstances and which they were made I flatter myself ~~that~~ they will receive both sanction & approbation ~~and~~ sanction.

Provided my health permits no time shall be lost in reaching Washington. My anxiety to pursue and to fulfill the duties incident to the internal arrangements incident to the government of Louisiana has prevented my writing you more frequently. ~~Mr. Bates is left in charge.~~ Inclosed I herewith transmit you a copy of the laws of the territory of Louisiana.—I have the honour to be with the most sincere esteem your Obt. ~~and very humble~~ Obt. and very humble Servt.

20. MERIWETHER LEWIS TO AMOS STODDARD, SEPTEMBER 22, 1809[19], FORT PICKERING, CHICKASAW BLUFFS

Dear Majr:

I must acknowledge myself remiss in not writing you in answer to several friendly epistles which I have received from you since my return from the Pacific Ocean, continued occupation in the immediate ~~disc~~ discharge of the duties of a public station will I trust in some measure plead my apology.

I am now on my way to the city of Washington and had contemplated taking Fort Adams and Orlianes in my rout, but my indisposition has induced me to change my rout and shall now pass through Tennessee and Virginia, the protest of some bills which I have lately drawn on public account form the principal inducement for my going forward at this moment. an explanation is all that is necessary I am sensible to put all matters right, in the mean time the protest of a draught however just has drawn upon me at one moment all my private debts which have excessively embarrassed me. I hope you will therefore pardon me for asking you to remit as soon as is convenient the sum of $200 which you have informed me you hold for me I calculated on having the pleasure to see you at Fort Adams as I passed, but am informed by Capt Russel the commanding officer of this place that you are stationed on the West side of the Mississippi.

You will direct to me at the City of Washington untill the last of December after which I expect I shall be on my return to St. Louis.

Your sincere friend, & Obt. servt.

21. JAMES HOWE TO FREDERICK BATES, SEPTEMBER 28, 1809, NASHVILLE, TENNESSEE

I arrived here two days ago on my way to Maryland—yesterday Majr Stoddart of the army arrived here from Fort Adams, and informs me that in his passage through the indian nation, in the vicinity of Chickasaw Bluffs he saw a person, immediately from the Bluffs who informed him, that Governor Lewis had arrived there (some time previous to his leaving it) in a state of mental derangement, that he had made several attempts to put an end to his own existence, which this person had prevented, and that Capt. Russell, the commang officer at the Bluffs had taken him into his own quarters where he was obliged to keep a strict watch over him to prevent his committing violence on himself and had caused his boat to be unloaded and the key to be secured in his stores.

I am in hopes this account will prove exaggerated tho' I fear there is too much truth in it—As the post leaves this tomorrow I have thought it would not be improper to communicate these circumstances as I have heard them, to you.[20]

22. *Missouri Gazette*, October 4, 1809, Wednesday

A report prevailed here last week, that his Excellency Governor Lewis was much indisposed at New Madrid, we were informed yesterday by a person direct from that palce, that, he seen him off in good health for New Orleans, on his way to the Federal City.

23. Major James Neelly to Thomas Jefferson, October 18, 1809, Nashville, Tennessee[21]

It is with extreme pain that I have to inform you of the death of His Excellency Meriwether Lewis, Governor of Upper Louisiana who died on the morning of the 11th Instant and I am sorry to say by Suicide.

I arrived at the Chickasaw Bluffs on or about the 18th of September, where I found the Governor (who had reached there two days before me from St. Louis) in very bad health—It appears that his first intention was to go around by water to the City of Washington; but his thinking a war with England probable & that his Valuable papers might be in danger of falling into the hands of the British, he was thereby induced to change his route, and to come through the Chickasaw nation by land; I furnished him with a horse to pack his trunks &c. on, and a man to attend to them; having recovered his health in some degree at the Chickasaw Bluffs, we set out together. And on our arrival at the Chickasaw nation I discovered that he appeared at times deranged in mind, we rested there two days & came on, one days

Journey after crossing the Tennessee River & where we encamped we lost two of our horses, I remained behind to hunt them & the Governor proceeded on, with a promise to wait for me at the first houses he came to that was inhabited by white people; he reached the house of a Mr. Grinder about sun set, the man of the house being from home, and no person there but a woman who discovering the governor to be deranged gave him up the house & slept herself in one near it. his Servant and mine slept in the stable loft some distance from the other houses. The woman reports that about three o'clock She heard two pistols fire off in the Governors Room: the servants being awakened by her, came in but too late to save him. he had shot himself in the head with one pistol & a little below the Breast with the other— when his servant came in he says: I have done the business my good Servant give me some water. he gave him water. he survived but a short time. I came up some time after. I had him as decently Buried as I could in that place—if there is any thing wished by his friends to be done to his grave I will attend to their Instructions.

I have got in my possession his two trunks of papers (amongst which is said to be his travels to the pacific Ocean) and probably some Vouchers for expenditures of Public Money for a Bill which he said had been protested by the Secy. of War; and of which act to his death, he repeatedly complained. I have also in my Care his Rifle, Silver watch, Brace of Pistols, dirk & tomahawk: one of the Governors horses was lost in the wilderness which I will endeavour to regain, the other I have sent on by his servant who expressed a desire to go the governors Mothers & to Monticllo: I have furnished him with fifteen dollars to Defray his expenses to Charlottesville. Some days previous to the Governors death he requested of me in case any accident happened to him, to send his trunks with the papers therein to the President, but I think it very probable he meant to you. I wish to be informed what arrangements may be considered best in sending on his trunks &c— I have the honor to be

With Great respect

Yr. Ob Sevt

James Neely

U.S. Agent to the Chickasaw Nation

The Honble Thomas Jefferson late President of the United States
Monticello near Charlottesville Va—

24. JOHN BRAHAN TO THOMAS JEFFERSON, OCTOBER 18, 1809, NASHVILLE, TENNESSEE[22]

It is with painful sensations that I announce to you the death of His Excellency Meriwether Lewis Governor of Upper Louisiana which took place on the morning of the 11th Instant; the following circumstances attending this unhappy affair I have obtained from Maj. James Neelly agent to the Chickasaw nation—he informs me that he left the Chickasaw Bluffs in Company with the Governor the last of Sept– on their way to this place—that the Governor appeared some days thereafter while on their journey to be some what deranged in mind; after crossing the Tennessee River and traveling one day of the Governor's & one of Maj. Neelly's horses got away from the place where they had encamped. The Governor proposed to the Majr to remain behind and find the horses, & that he would proceed on his Journey and wait for him at the first house from there inhabited by white people to which the Majr agreed & the Governor proceeded on with his Servant & Majr Neelly—to the house of a Mr. Grinder. When he arrived about sun set—no person being at home but the wife of Mr. Grinder—the woman discovering the governor to be deranged gave him up the house, and slept herself in another house near it—the two servants slept in a stable loft some distance off: about three o'clock the woman heard two pistols fire off. Being alarmed she went & waked the servants when they came in they found him weltering in his blood. He had shot himself first it was thought in the head. The ball did not take effect. The other shot was a little below his breast, which proved mortal. He lived until sun rise & expired. The Majr had him decently buried. Majr Neelly informs me that he has got his two trunks with his valuable papers, amongst which is his journal to the pacific Ocean, & perhaps some vouchers for Public Money expended in the Territorial Government of Upper Louisiana—he has also got his silver watch—his Brace of pistols, his Rifle & Dirk—one of his horses was lost in the wilderness which may probably be got again, the other horse John Purney the Governors Servant will ride on, who will leave here early in the morning for Monticello: Majr Neelly has given him fifteen dollars to take him on; and I was fearful that he might be short of money & have furnished him with five dollars more which will be sufficient—I would have given him more but was fearful it might cause him to drink as discover he has a propensity at present, but perhaps it may be from distress of mind at the death of the Governor. I shall remain in this place some time and will with great pleasure attend to any instruction you may think necessary either in sending on the trunks of papers or the other articles of his property wherever directed—which will probably be to Monticello—I feel great distress at the premature death of the Governor he was a very particular friend of mine, being intimately acquainted, and one for whom I had the Greatest respect.

Ps: I am told that Governor Lewis left two trunks & some other articles with Capt. Gilbert C. Russell Commanding officer at the Chickasaw Bluffs.

25. JOHN BRAHAN TO SECRETARY OF WAR, OCTOBER 18, 1809, NASHVILLE, TENNESSEE.[23]

Dear Sir: It is with great concern that I announce to you the death of His Excellency Meriwether Lewis Governor of Upper Louisiana, which took place on the Morning of the 11th Instant at the House of a Mr. Grinder about seventy five miles from this on the Natchez Road—and what renders this unhappy affair more melancholy it is stated from a correct source that he committed Suicide. Majr. James Neelly agent for the Chickasaws had traveled with the Governor from the Chickasaw Bluffs until they got within a days Journey of the place where the unfortunate affair took place—they had lost two horses & the Majr. remained behind to hunt them, & the governor proceeded on to get to a house where a white man lived. he reached there before night, & about three oclock in the morning shot himself with two pistols: the first ball it is said wounded him in the head the other entered a little below his breast which caused his death in about three hours—majr. Neeley had him intered as decently as he could—and he informs me that he has in his Care two trunks of the Governors containing his Valuable papers, probably his Journal to the Pacific Ocean & perhaps vouchers for money expended in his Territorial Government; but I have not seen them: Maj. Neeley informs me that he has his Brace of Pistols Rifle gun & watch—which will remain in his hands until he learns what he is to do with them—he has communicated to Mr. Jefferson late president this unfortunate affair, & has informed him what he has got in his hands belonging to the Estate of Governor Lewis—Majr. Neeley informs that he discovered some days previous to the death of the Governor strong proofs of a derangement in his mind —

I have the honor to be
With Great Respect Yr. Obt.
John Brahan, Capt.
2nd Regt. US. Infy.

26. *MISSOURI GAZETTE*, OCTOBER 19, 1809[24]

Col. Bissell politely favored us with the following extract of a letter from Maj. Stod-dard dated Nashville, Sept. 8 [probably 18th]—We sincerely hope that the next communication may bring the agreeable news of Gov Lewis' health being perfectly restored.

> I have some unhappy intelligence to give you. I saw a gentleman in the Chickasaw nation, directly from the Bluffs, who informed me, that Governor Lewis was at that place much indisposed. That he was so for several days previous to his arrival. Capt. Russell received him into his quarters and stored his property.
>
> He was under the hands of the surgeons mate, Dr. Smith, but no alteration for the better had taken place when my informant left the bluffs. This affair has given me much pain, and I leave it with you to divulge it to the Governors friends, in such manner as you may think proper.

27. *DEMOCRATIC CLARION*, OCTOBER 20, 1809, NASHVILLE, TENNESSEE[25]

To record the untimely end of a brave and prudent officer, a learned scholar and scientific gentleman this column of the Clarion is ushered to the world in black.

On the night of the 10th instant Meriwether Lewis, esq. governor general of Upper Louisiana, on his way to washington city, came to the house of Mr. Grinder near the Indian line in this state—called for his supper and some spirits of which he partook and gave some to his servants. Mr. Grinder not being at home, Mrs. Grinder retired to the kitchen with her children, and the servants (after the governor went to bed, which he did in good order) went to a stable about three hundred yards distant to sleep—no one in the house with the governor—and some time before mid-night Mrs. Grinder was alarmed by the firing of 2 pistols in the house—she called to the servants without effect—and at the appearance of day light the servants came to the house when the governor said he had now done for himself—they asked what, and he said he had shot himself and would die, and requested them to bring him water, he then laying on the floor where he expired about 7 o'clock in the morning of the 11th—he had shot a ball that grazed the top of his head and another through his intestines, and cut his neck, arm and ham with a razor. when in his best senses he spoke about a trunk of papers that he said would be of great value to our government. He had been under the influence of a deranging malady for about six weeks—the cause of which is unknown, unless it was from a protest to a draft which he drew on the secretary at war, which he considered tantamount to a disgrace by government.

In the death of governor Lewis the public beheld the wreck of one of the noblest of men—he was a pupil of the immortal Jefferson—by him he was reared—by him he was instructed in the tour of the sciences—by him he was introduced to public life, when his enterprising soul, great botanical knowledge, acute penetration, and personal courage soon pointed him out as the most proper person to command a projected exploring party to the north west coast of the American continent—he accepted the arduous command on condition that he might take Mr. Clark with him—they started, the best wishes of the American people attended them. After an absence of two years, to us of anxious solicitude, we were cheered with the joyful return of our countrymen. A new world had been explored—additional knowledge in all the sciences obtained, at a trifling expence of blood and treasure. The voice of fame echoed the glad tidings thro' the civilized world—the name of Lewis was the theme of universal praise.— The national legislature voted a complimentary donation to the brave little band.

Scarcely had the governor time to pay his respects to a widowed mother, before he was again called into public service. The territory of Upper Louisiana had been torn to pieces by party feuds, no person could be more proper to calm them—he appeared and all was quiet.

The limits assigned this notice do not admit of a particular detail of his executive acts—suffice it to say that the parties created by local circumstances and Wilkinson were soon united—the Indians were treated with [presents] and large purchases of valuable land made of them—the laws were amended, and judicious ones adopted—to the securing the citizens of the territory from a renewal of the scenes of 1806.

During the few leisure moments he had from his official duties, he was employed in writing the particulars of his celebrated tour up the Missouri—to complete which appears to have been the wish nearest his heart—and it gives us much pleasure, if we can feel pleasure in the present melancholy instance, to state that we have it from a source which can be depended upon, that he had accomplished the work in three very large volumes, with an immense number of paintings—& all was ready for the press. We hope these volumes may be the means of transmitting to posterity the worth of a man whose act cast a gloom over the fair pages of his early life.

> "The boast of heraldry, the pomp of pow'r,
> And all that beauty, all that wealth e'er gave
> Await alike th' inevitable hour———
> The path of glory lead but to the grave."[26]

28. James Madison to Thomas Jefferson, October 30, 1809[27]

We just learn the melancholy fate of Governor Lewis which possibly may not have travelled so quickly into your neighborhood. He had, it seems, betrayed latterly symptoms of a disordered mind; and had set out under the care of a friend on a visit to Washington. His first intention was, to make the trip by water; but changing it, at the Chickasaw Bluffs, he struck across towards Nashville. As soon as he had passed the Tennessee, he took advantage of the neglect of his companion, who had not secured his arms, to put an end to himself. He first fired a pistol, at his head, the ball of which glancing, was ineffectual. With the 2d. he passed a Ball thro' his body, wch. being also without immediate effect, he had recourse to his Dirk with wch he mangled himself considerably. After all he lived till the next morning, with the utmost impatience for death.

29. John Breck Treat to Frederick Bates, October 31, 1809, Washington City[28]

My Dear Friend

This moment the Secretary of War has mentioned to me his having by this days Mail received an account of the extraordinary death of Governor Lewis: for which no one here undertakes to account for—& certainly the short acquaintance I had with him at St. Louis in June last wholly precludes my having any reason to offer for his committing an act to any extraordinary & unexpected—It is already ask'd here who will become Govr of the Territory. . . .

30. *Missouri Gazette*, November 2, 1809, Thursday

By last mail we received the melancholy account of the premature death of his Ex'y Governor Lewis; he landed at the Chickasaw Bluffs much indisposed, and shortly after set out on his way to the Federal City via Nashville; about 40 miles east of the river Tennessee, the party stopped for the night and became much alarmed at the governor's behavior, he appeared in a state of extreme mental debility, and before he could be prevented, discharged the contents of a brace of pistols in his head and breast, calling to his servant to give him a basin of water; he lived about two hours and died without much apparent pain. The governor had been of late very much afflicted with fever, which never failed of depriving him of his reason. . . .

31. *ARGUS OF WESTERN AMERICA*, NOVEMBER 4, 1809, FRANKFORT, KENTUCKY[29]

Nashville, October 20—It is with extreme regret we have to record the melancholy death of his excellency Meriwether Lewis, Governor of Upper Louisiana, on his way to the City of Washington. The following particulars, are given us by a gentleman who travelled with him from the Chickasaw Bluffs.

The governor had been in a bad state of health, but having recovered in some degree, set out from the Chickasaw Bluffs and in travelling from that to the Chickasaw nation, our informant says, he discovered that the governor appeared at times deranged, and on their arrival in that nation, having lost two horses, the governor proceeded on, and the gentleman detained with a view of hunting the horses. The governor went on to a Mr. Grinder's on the road, found no person at home but a woman: she observed something wild in his appearance, become frightened and left the house to sleep in another near it, and the two servants that was with him went to sleep in the stable. About three o'clock the woman says she heard the report of two pistols in the room where he lay, and immediately awakened the servants, who rushed into the house, but too late! he had shot himself in the head and just below the breast, and was in the act of cutting himself with a razor. The only words he uttered, was "It is done, my good servant give me some water," and expired in a few moments after.

He was as decently intered as the place would admit.

32. FREDERICK BATES TO RICHARD BATES, NOVEMBER 9, 1809, SAINT LOUIS[30]

You have heard no doubt, of the premature and tragical death of Gov. Lewis. Indeed I had no personal regard for him and a great deal of political contempt; Yet I cannot but lament, that after all his toils and dangers he should die in *such a manner.*

At the *first*, in *Washington* he made to me so many friendly assurances, that I then imagined our mutual friendship would plant itself on rocky foundations. But a very short acquaintance with the man was sufficient to undeceive me. He had been spoiled by the elegant praises of Mitchell & Barlow, and over whelmed by so many flattering caresses of the *high* & *mighty*, that, like an over-grown baby, he began to think that everybody about the House must regulate their conduct by his caprices.

'*De mortuis nil nisi bonum*' is a good old maxim; but my character has been assailed, as respects our late Governor, and I owe to those I love some little account of myself.

I never saw, after his arrival in this country, anything in his conduct towards me, but alienation and unmerited distrust. I had acquired and shall retain a good portion of the public confidence, and he had not generosity of soul to forgive me for it. I was scarcely myself conscious of my good fortune; for the still voice of approbation with which I was favored by the People, was, as yet drowned in the clamours of my enemies. As soon as I was seen in conflict with my associates in business, my friends came forward with a generous and unexpected support.—I bore in silence the supercilious air of the Governor for a long time; until, last summer he took it into his head to disavow certain statements which I had made, *by his order* from the Secretary's Office. This was too much—I waited on him,—told him my wrongs— that I could not bear to be treated in such a manner—that he *had* given me the orders, & as truth is always eloquent, the Public *would believe* it on my assurances. He told me to take my own course—I shall, Sir, said I, and I shall come, in future to the Executive's Office when I have *business* at it.

Some time after this, there was a ball in St. Louis, I attended early, and was seated in conversation with some Gentlemen when the Governor entered. He drew his chair close to mine—There was a pause in the conversation—I availed myself of it—arose and walked to the opposite side of the room. The dances were now commencing.—*He* also rose—evidently in passion, retired into an adjoining room and sent a servant for General Clark, who refused to ask me out as he foresaw that a Battle must have been the consequence of our meeting. He complained to the general that I had treated him with contempt & insult in the Ball-Room and that he could not suffer it to pass. He knew my resolutions not to speak to him except on business and he ought not to have thrust himself in my way. The thing *did pass* nevertheless for some weeks when General Clark waited on me for the purpose of inducing me to make some advances. I replied to him 'NO, the Governor has told me to take my own course and I shall step a *high* and a *proud* Path He has *injured* me, and he must *undo* that injury or I shall succeed in fixing the stigma where it *ought to rest*. You come' added I 'as *my* friend, but I cannot separate you from Gov Lewis— You have trodden the *Ups* & the *Downs* of life with him and it appears to me that these proposals are made solely for *his* convenience.'

At last, I had business at the Executive Office—He pressed me to be seated and made very handsome explanations. I told him that they *sounded* well; but that I could not accept them unless with the approbation of my friend Wm. C. Carr—*He*, with some other Gentlemen were then called in, & *this* particular misunderstanding adjusted to the entire satisfaction of Carr and myself.

33. GILBERT RUSSELL TO THOMAS JEFFERSON, JANUARY 4, 1810, FORT PICKERING, CHICKASAW BLUFFS[31]

Concerning it a duty encumbered upon me to give the friends of the late Meriwether Lewis such information relative to his arrival here his stay and departure, and also of his pecuniary matters as came within my knowledge which they otherwise might not ascertain and presuming that as you were once his patron, you still remain'd his friend, I beg leave to communicate it to you and thru you to his mother and such other of his friends as may be interested.

He came here on the 15th of September last from whence he set off intending to go to Washington by way of New Orleans. His situation I tho't rendered it necessary that he should be stoped until he would recover, which I done & in a short time by proper attention a change was perceptible and in about six days he was perfectly restored in every respect & able to travel. Being placed then myself [page 2] in a similar situation with him by Bills being protested to a considerable amount I had made application to the General & expected a leave of absence every day to go to Washington on the same business with Governor Lewis. In consequence of which he waited six or eight days expecting that I would go on with him, but in this we were disappointed & he set off with a Maj. Neely who was going to Nashville.

At the request of Governor Lewis I enclose the land Warrant granted to him in consideration of his services to the Pacific Ocean to Bowling Robinson Esq., Secy of the Treasury at Orleans with instructions to dispose of it at any price above $2 an acre & to lodge the money on the Bank of the United States or any of the branch banks subject to his order.

He left with me two Trunks a Case and a bundle which will now remain here subject at any time to your order or that of his legal representatives. Enclosed is his memo respecting them but before the Boat in which he directed they might be sent got to this place I recd. a verbal message from [page 3] him after he left here to keep them untill I should hear from him again.

He set off with two trunks which containing all his papers relative to the expedition to the Pacific Ocean, Genl Clarks Land Warrant a Port-Folio, pocket Book, Memo, and note Book together with many other papers of both a public & private nature; two horses two saddles, & bridles a Rifle gun pistols pipe Tommy hawk & dirk, all ellegant & perhaps about two hundred & twenty dollars of which $99 58/100 was a Treasurer's Check on the U.S. branch Bank of Orleans endorsed by me. The horses and saddle and this Check I let him have. Where or what has become of his effects I do not know but presume they must be in the care of Major Neelly near Nashville.

As an individual I very much regret the untimely death of Governor Lewis whose loss will be great to his Country & severely felt by his friends. When he left this I felt much satisfaction for indeed I tho't I had been the means of preserving the life of one (?) valuable man, and as it has turn'd [page 4] out I still have the consolation that I discharged those obligations towards him that man is bound to do to his fellow.

It is probable that I shall go to the City of Washington in a few weeks—if so I shall give you a call and give you any further information you may require that has come within my knowledge.

Having had the pleasure of knowing Mr. Randolph, I pray you to tender my respects to him.

I remain Sir with the utmost veneration & respect
your Obt Servant

Meriwether Lewis's handwriting:

Capt. Russell will much oblige his friend Meriwether Lewis by forwarding to the care of William Brown Collector of the port of New Orleans, a Trunk belonging to Capt. James House addressed to M. Donald and Ridgely Merchants in Baltimore. Mr. Brown will be requested to forward the trunk to it's place of destination.—

Capt. R. will also send two trunks as packages and a case addressed to Mr. William C. Carr of St. Louis unless otherwise instructed by M. S. by letter from Nashville.—

M. Lewis would thank Capt. R. to be particular to whom he confides these trunks & a Mr. Cabbini [Cabanne] of St. Louis may be expected to pass this place in the course of the next month to him [page 6] they might be safely confided.—

Memorandum

Sent Capt. Hous's Trunk by Benjamin Wilkinson on the 29th Sept 1809
    Russell
Govr. Lewis left here on the morning of the 29th Sept—[32]

34. GILBERT RUSSELL TO THOMAS JEFFERSON, JANUARY 31, 1810, FORT PICKERING, CHICKASAW BLUFFS

I have lately been inform'd that James Neely the Agt to the Chickasaws with whom Govr. Lewis set off from this place has detain'd his pistols & perhaps some other of his effects for some claim he pretends to have upon his estate. He can have no just claim for any thing more than the expenses of his interment unless he makes a charge for packing his two trunks from the Nation. And for that he cannot have the audacity to make a charge after tendering the use of a loos'd horse or two which he said he had taken from the Nation & and also the aid of his servant. He seem'd happy to have it in his power to serve the Govr & but for his making the offer which was accepted I should have employed the man who packed the Trunks to the Nation to have taken them to Nashville & accompanyed the Govr. Unfortunately for him this arrangement did not take place or I hesitate not to say he would this day be living. The fact is which you may yet be ignorant of that his untimely death may be attributed solely to the free use he made of liquor which he acknowledged verry candidly after he recovered & expressed a firm determination never to drink any more spirits or use snuff again both of which I deprived him of for several days & confined him to claret & a little white wine. But after leaving this place by some means or other his resolution left him & this agt being extremely fond of liquor, instead of preventing the Govr from drinking or putting him under any restraint advised him to it & from every thing I can learn gave the man every chance to seek an opportunity to destroy himself. And from the statement of Grinder's wife where he killed himself I cannot help believing that Purney was rather aiding & abetting in the murder than otherwise.

This Neely also says he lent the Govr. Money which cannot be so for he had none himself & the Govr had more than one hund. $ in notes & specie besides a check I let him have of 99.58 none of which it is said can be found. I have wrote to the Cashier of the branch bank of Orleans on whom the check was drawn in favour of myself or order to stop payment when presented. I have this day authorized a Gentleman to pay the pretended claim of Neely & take the pistols which will be held sacrad to the order of any of the friends of M. Lewis free from encumbrance.

35. Thomas Jefferson to Gilbert C. Russell, April 18, 1810[33]

Sir

I have to acknowledge the reciept of your favors of Jan. 4. & 31. the last of which did not reach me till two days ago; and with my own, to express the thankfulness of all the friends of the late unfortunate governor Lewis for your kind attentions to him. we have all to lament that a fame so dearly earned was clouded finally by such an act of desperation. he was much afflicted & habitually so with hypochondria. this was probably increased by the habit into which he had fallen & the painful reflections that would necessarily produce in a mind like his. his loss to the world is a very great one, as it is impossible that any other can paint to them the occurencies of his journey so faithfully as he who felt them. I have duly handed on whatever you have communicated to me respecting his pecuniary interests to Capt. William Meriwether, his relation, his intimate friend & one of his executors, and pray you to accept the assurances of my esteem & respect.

—Th. Jefferson

36. Alexander Wilson to Alexander Lawson, May 18, 1810 (excerpt)[34]

Next morning (Sunday) I rode six miles to a man's of the name of Grinder, where our poor friend Lewis perished. In the same room where he expired, I took down from Mrs. Grinder the particulars of that melancholy event, which affected me extremely. This house or cabin is seventy-two miles from Nashville, and is the last white man's as you enter the Indian country. Governor Lewis, she said, came there about sunset, alone, and inquired if he could stay for the night; and, alighting, brought his saddle into the house. He was dressed in a loose gown, white, striped with blue. On being asked if he came alone, he replied that there were two servants behind, who would soon be up. He called for some spirits, and drank very little. When the servants arrived, one of whom was a negro, he inquired for his powder, saying he was sure he had some powder in a canister. The servant gave no distinct reply, and Lewis, in the mean while walked backwards and forwards before the door, talking to himself. Sometimes, she said, he would seem as if he were walking up to her; and would suddenly wheel round, and walk back as fast as he could. Supper being ready he sat down, but had not eat but a few mouthfuls when he started up speaking to himself in a violent manner. At these times, she says, she observed his face to flush as if it had come on him in a fit. He lighted his pipe, and drawing a chair to the door sat down, saying to Mrs. Grinder in a kind tone of voice, "Madam this is a very pleasant evening." He smoked for some time, but quitted his seat and traversed the yard as before. He again sat down to his pipe, seemed again composed and casting his eyes wishfully towards the west, observed what a sweet evening it was. Mrs. Grinder was preparing a bed for him; but he said he would sleep on the floor, and desired the servant to bring the bear skins and buffaloe robe, which were immediately spread out for him; and it being now dusk the woman went off to the kitchen, and the two men to the barn, which stands about two hundred yards off. The kitchen is only a few paces from the room where Lewis was, and the woman being considerably alarmed by the behaviour of her guest could not sleep but listened to him walking backwards and forwards, she thinks for several hours, and talking aloud, as she said, "like a lawyer." She then heard the report of a pistol, and something fall heavily on the floor, and the words "O Lord!" Immediately afterwards she heard another pistol, and in a few minutes she hear him at her door calling out "O madam! Give me some water, and heal my wounds." The logs being open, and unplastered, she saw him stagger back and fall against a stump that stands between the kitchen and room. He crawled for some distance, raised himself by the side of a tree, where he sat about a minute. He once more got to the room; afterwards he came to the kitchen-door, but did not speak; she then heard him scraping the bucket with a gourd for water, but it appears that this cooling element was denied the dying man! As soon as day broke and not before, the terror of the woman having permitted him to remain for two hours in this most deplorable situation, she sent two of her children to the barn, her husband not being at home, to bring the servants; and on going in they found him lying on the bed; he uncovered his side and shewed them where the bullet had entered; a piece of the forehead was blown off, and had exposed the brains, without having bled much. He begged they would take his rifle and blowout his brains, and he would give them all the money he had in his trunk. He often said, "I am no coward, but I am so strong, so hard to die." He begg'd the servant [John Pernier] not to be afraid of him, for that he would not hurt him. He expired in about two hours, or just as the sun rose above the trees. He lies buried close by the common path with a few loose rails thrown over his grave. I gave Grinder money to put a post fence round it, to shelter it from the hogs, and from the wolves; and he gave me his written promise he would do it. I left this place in a very melancholy mood, which was not much allayed by the prospect of the gloomy and savage wilderness which I was just entering alone.

My thoughts dwelt with sad, but unavailing regret, on the fate of my unfortunate friend; and I endeavoured to give vent to the despondence of my mind in the following verses, which I wished to dedicate to his memory.

37. STATEMENT OF GILBERT RUSSELL, NOVEMBER 26, 1811, FREDERICKTOWN, MARYLAND

Governor Lewis left St. Louis late in August, or early in September 1809, intending to go by the route of the Mississippi and the Ocean, to the City of Washington, taking with him all the papers relative to his expedition to the pacific Ocean, for the purpose of preparing and putting them to the press, and to have some drafts paid which had been drawn by him on the Government and protested. On the morning of the 15th of September, the Boat in which he was a passenger landed him at Fort pickering in a state of mental derangement, which appeared to have been produced as much by indisposition as other causes. The Subscriber being then the Commanding Officer of the Fort on discovering from the crew that he had made two attempts to Kill himself, in one of which he had nearly succeeded, resolved at once to take possession of him and his papers, and detain them there untill he recovered, or some friend might arrive in whose hands he could depart in Safety.

In this condition he continued without any material change for five days, during which time the most proper and efficatious means that could be devised to restore him was administered, and on the sixth or seventh day all symptoms of derangement disappeared and he was completely in his senses and thus continued for ten or twelve days. On the 29th of the same month he left Bluffs, with the Chickasaw agent the interpreter and some of the Chiefs, intending to proceed the usual route thro' the Indian Country, Tennessee and Virginia to his place of distination, with his papers well secured and packed on horses. By much severe depletion during his illness he had been considerably reduced and debilitated, from which he had not entirely recovered when he set off, and the weather in that country being yet excessively hot and the exercise of traveling too severe for him; in three or four days he was again affected with the same mental disease. He had no person with him who could manage or controul him in his propensities and he daily grew worse untill he arrived at the house of a Mr. Grinder within the Jurisdiction of Tennissee and only Seventy miles from Nashville, where in the apprehension of being destroyed by enemies which had no existence but in his wild immagination, he destroyed himself, in the most cool desperate and Barbarian-like manner, having been left in the house intirely to himself. The night preceeding this one of his Horses and one of the Chickasaw agents with whom he was traveling Strayed off from the Camp and in the Morning could not be found. The agent with some of the Indians stayed to search for the horses, and Governor Lewis with their two servants and the baggage horses proceeded to Mr. Grinders where he was to halt untill the agent got up.

After he arrived there and refreshed himself with a little Meal & drink he went to bed in a cabin by himself and ordered the servants to go to the stables and take care of the Horses, least they might loose some that night; Some time in the night he got his pistols which he loaded, after every body had retired in a Separate Building and discharged one against his forehead not making much effect—the ball not penetrating the skull but only making a furrow over it. He then discharged the other against his breast where the ball entered and passing downward thro' his body came out low down near his back bone. After some time he got up and went to the house where Mrs. Grinder and her children were lying and asked for water, but her husband being absent and having heard the report of the pistols she was greatly allarmed and made him no answer. He then in returning got his razors from a port folio which happened to contain them and Seting up in his bed was found about day light, by one of the Servants, busily engaged in cutting himself from head to foot. He again beged for water, which was given to him and as soon as he drank, he lay down and died with the declaration to the Boy that he had killed himself to deprive his enemies of the pleasure and honour of doing it. His death was greatly lamented. And that a fame so dearly earned as his should be clouded by such an act of desperation was to his friends still greater cause of regret.

—(Signed) Gilbert Russell

The above was received by me from Maj. Gilbert Russell of the [blank] Regiment of Infantry U. S. on Tuesday the 26th of November 1811 at Fredericktown in Maryland.

—J. Williams

38. ALEXANDER WILSON, TRIBUTE TO MERIWETHER LEWIS, CIRCA 1810–1813[35]

For a more particular, and, doubtless, a more correct account of this, and the two preceding species,* the reader is referred to General Clark's History of the Expedition, now preparing for the press. The three birds I have here introduced, are but a small part of the valuable collection of new subjects in natural history, discovered, and preserved, amidst a thousand dangers and difficulties, by those two enterprising travellers, whose intrepidity was only equaled by their discretion, and by their active and laborious pursuit of whatever might tend to render their journey useful to science and to their country. It was the request and particular wish of Captain Lewis, made to me in person, that I should make some drawings of such of the feathered tribes as had been preserved, and were new. That brave soldier, that amiable and excellent man, over whose solitary grave in the wilderness I have since shed tears of affliction, having been cut off in the prime of his life, I hope I shall be pardoned for consecrating this humble note to his memory, until a more able pen shall do better justice to the subject.[36]

*Wilson here alluded to Clark's Crow, and the Louisiana Tanager, both of which are figured in the same plate with Lewis's Woodpecker.[37]

39. THOMAS JEFFERSON TO PAUL ALLEN, AUGUST 18, 1813, LATE GOV. OF LOUISIANA

Biographical Letter of Meriwether Lewis (excerpt):[38]

In 1792. I proposed to the A.P.S. [American Philosophical Society] that we should set on foot a subscription to engage some competent person to explore that region in the opposite direction that is, by ascending the Missouri, crossing the Stony mountains, and descending the nearest river to the Pacific. Capt Lewis being then stationed at Charlottesville on the recruiting service, warmly sollicited me to obtain for him the execution of that object. I told him it was proposed that the person engaged should be attended by a single companion only, to avoid exciting alarm among the Indians. this did not deter him. but mr. André Michaux a professed botanist, author of the Flora Boreali-Americana, and of the Histoire des chesnes d'Amerique, offering his services, they were accepted. he recieved his instructions, and when he had reached Kentucky in the prosecution of his journey, he was over-taken by an order from the minister of France then at Philadelphia to relinquish the expedition, & to pursue elsewhere the Botanical enquiries on which he was employed by that government; and thus failed the 2d attempt for exploring that region.

~~When in 1803. Louisiana was ceded to the U.S. a knolege of the Missouri was no longer an object of mere geographical curiosity, but was become highly inter-esting to the nation, all the country covered by the waters running into the Misipi constituting the extent of their new acquisition in the upper country. Capt. Lewis was now become my private Secretary, and on the first mention of the subject he renewed his solicitations to be the person employed. My knolege of him, now become more intimate, left no hesitation on my part. I had now had opportunity of knowing his character intimately.~~

In 1803 The act for establishing trading houses with the Indian tribes being about to expire some modifications of it were recommended to Congress by a confidential message of Jan. 18. and an extension of it's views to the Indians on the Missouri. In order to prepare the way the message proposed the sending an exploring party to trace the Missouri to it's source, to cross the highlands and follow the best water communication which offered itself from thence to the Pacific ocean. Congress approved the proposition and voted a sum of money for carrying it into execution. Captain Lewis who had then been near two years with me as private secretary, immediately renewed his sollicitations to have the direction of the party. I had now had opportunities of knowing him intimately. of courage undaunted, possessing a firmness & perseverance of purpose which nothing but impossibilities could divert from it's direction, careful as a father of those committed to his charge, yet steady in the maintenance of order & discipline, intimate with the Indian character, customs & principles, habituated to the hunting life, guarded by exact observation of the vegetables & animals of his own country, against losing time in the description of objects already possessed, honest, disinterested, liberal, of sound understanding and a fidelity to truth so scrupulous that whatever he should report would be as certain as if seen by ourselves, with all these qualifications as if selected and implanted by nature in one body, for this express purpose, I could have no hesitation in confiding the enterprize to him. to fill up the measure desired, he wanted nothing but a greater familiarity with the technical language of the natural sciences, and readiness in the astronomical observations necessary for the geography of his route. to acquire these he repaired immediately to Philadelphia, and placed himself under the tutorage of the distinguished professors of that place, who with a zeal & emulation, enkindled by an ardent devotion to science, communicated to him freely the information requisite for the purposes of the journey. while attending too, at Lancaster, the fabrication of the arms with which he chose that his men should be provided, he had the benefit of daily communication with mr. Andrew Ellicot, whose experience in Astronomical observation, and practice of it in the woods, enabled him to apprise Capt. Lewis of the wants & difficulties he would encounter, and of the substitutes & resources offered by a woodland and uninhabited country.

~~It was deemed necessary, also to provide an Associate properly qualified to succeed to the direction of the enterprize, in the event of accident to Capt. Lewis. He proposed William Clarke of Ohio, brother to Gl. Geo. Rogers Clarke, who was approved without hesitation~~.

Deeming it necessary he should have some person with him of known competence to the direction of the enterprise, & to whom he might confide it, in the event of accident to himself he proposed William Clarke, brother of Genl. Geo. Rogers Clarke, who was approved, and with that view recieved a commission of Captain.

In April 1803. a draught of his instructions was sent to Capt. Lewis & on the 20th of June they were signed in the following form. I here insert the instructions verbatim.

While these things were going on here, the country of Louisiana, lately ceded by Spain to France, had been the subject of negotiation at Paris between us & this last power; and had actually been transferred to us by treaties executed at Paris on the 30th of April. this information, recieved about the 1st day of July, increased infinitely the interest we felt in the expedition, & lessened the apprehensions of interruption from other powers. every thing in this quarter being now prepared, Capt. Lewis left Washington on the 5th of July 1803 and proceeded to Pittsburg where other articles had been ordered to be provided for him. the men too were to be selected from the military stations on the Ohio. delays of preparation, difficulties of navigation down the Ohio & other untoward obstruction retarded his arrival at Cahokia until the season was so far advanced as to render it prudent to suspend his entering the Missouri before the ice should break up in the succeeding spring. from this time his journal, now published, will give the history of his journey to and from the Pacific ocean until his return to St. Louis on the 23d of Sep., 1806.

He reached Washington accompanied by Capt. Clarke, about the middle of Feb. 1807. Congress being then in session never did a similar event excite more joy thro' the United States. the humblest of it's citizens had taken a lively interest in the issue of this journey, and looked forward with impatience for the information it would furnish. their anxieties too for the safety of the corps had been kept in a state of excitement by lugubrious rumors, circulated from time to time on uncertain authorities, and uncontradicted by letters, or other direct information, from the time they had left the Mandan towns, on their ascent up the river in April of the preceding year, 1805, until their actual return to St. Louis.

It was the middle of Feb. 1807. before Capt. Lewis, with his companion Clarke, reached the city of Washington, where congress was then in session.[39] that body granted to the two chiefs and their followers, the donation of lands which they had been encouraged to expect in reward of their toil & dangers. Capt. Lewis was soon after appointed Governor of Louisiana, and Capt. Clarke a General of it's militia, and agent of the U.S. for Indian affairs in that department.

A considerable time intervened before the Governor's arrival at St. Louis. he found the territory distracted by feuds & contentions among the officers of the government, & the people themselves divided by these into factions & parties. he determined at once, to take no side with either; but to use every endeavor to conciliate & harmonize them. the even-handed justice he administered to all soon established a respect for his person & authority; and perseverance & time wore down animosities and reunited the citizens again into one family.

Governor Lewis had from early life been subject to hypocondriac affections. it was a constitutional disposition in all the nearer branches of the family of his name,

& was more immediately inherited by him from his father. they had not however been so strong as to give uneasiness to his family. while he lived with me in Washington, I observed at times sensible depressions of mind but knowing their constitutional source, I estimated their course by what I had seen in the family. during his Western ~~enterprize~~ expedition, the constant exertion ~~of body & mind to which he was favored~~ which that required of all the faculties of body and mind, suspended these distressing affections; but after his establishment at St. Louis in sedentary occupations they returned upon him with redoubled vigor, and began seriously to alarm his friends. he was in a paroxysm of one of these when his affairs rendered it necessary for him to go to Washington. he proceeded to the Chickasaw bluffs, where he arrived on the 16th of Sep. 1809. with a view of continuing his journey thence by water. mr. Neely, agent of the US. with the Chickasaw Indians arriving there two days after, found him in ~~ill health~~ extremely indisposed, and betraying at times some symptoms of a derangement of mind. the rumors of a war with England, & apprehensions that he might lose the papers he was bringing on, among which were the vouchers of his public accounts, and the journals & papers of his Western expedition, induced him here to change his mind and to take his course by land thro' the Chickasaw country. altho' he appeared somewhat relieved, mr. Neely kindly determined to accompany & watch over him. unfortunately, at their encampment a day's journey, ~~on this side of the tennissee~~ after having passed the Tennessee one day's journey, they lost two horses, which obliging mr. Neely ~~being obliged~~ to halt for their recovery. the Governor proceeded under a promise to wait for him at the house of the first white inhabitant on his road. He stopped at the house of the first white inhabitant on his road. he stopped at the house of a mr. Grinder, who not being at home, his wife ~~discovering~~ alarmed at the symptoms of derangement she discovered, gave him up the house, and retired to rest herself in an out house [outbuilding]; the Governor's and Neely's servants lodging in another. about 3. oclock in ~~that~~ the night he did the deed which plunged his friends into affliction and deprived his country of one of her most valued citizens whose valour & intelligence would have been now employed in avenging the wrongs of his country and in emulating by land the splendid deeds which have honored her arms on the ocean. it lost too to the nation the benefit of recieving from his own hand the Narrative now offered them of his sufferings and successes in endeavoring to extend for them the boundaries of science, and to present to their knoledge that vast & fertile country, which their sons are destined to fill with arts, with science, with freedom & happiness.

   To this melancholy close of the life of one whom posterity will declare not to have lived in vain I have only to add that all the facts I have stated are either known to myself, or communicated by his family or others for whose truth I have no hesitation to make myself responsible: and I conclude with tendering you the assurances of my respect & consideration.

Appendix B

MERIWETHER LEWIS'S COURT-MARTIAL PROCEEDINGS, NOVEMBER 6–11, 1795

Cantonment Greene Ville November 6th 1795—[1]

At a General Court Martial this day convened pursuant to a General Order of yesterday "for the trial of such prisoners as may be brought before them"—

Maj. Shaylor—President—

Members

Capt. H. Lewis -	Capt. Marts
Lieut. Polhemus	Lieut. Steele
Lieut. Bissell—	Lieut. Sterett
Lieut. Webster -	Lieut. Strugh
Ensign Johnson -	Ensign Swain
Ensign Rand	Ensign Dodd

The following proceedings were had—Ensign Meriwether Lewis of the 4th-SubLegion in arrest appeared for trial, and challenged Capt. Marts, Lieutenants Bissell Sterett and Webster from setting as members on his trial—[2]

Ensign Rand, challenged on the part of this United States—Capt. McRea, Lieutenants Devin and Freemer, and Ensigns Richmond Scott—returned vice those challenged appeared Capt. McRea, Lieut. Devin, Lieut. Freemer, and Ensign Richmond challenged by Ensign Lewis.

[page 2]
A Letter received by the Judge Marshall and Advocate General from the Adjutant General of which the following is a copy

—Greene Ville 6th Nov. 1795

251

Sir

I recieved your note of this date acquainting me that Ensign M. Lewis had objected to four members of the General Court Martial appointed to try him, viz Capt. Marts, Lieut. Sterett, Lieut. Webster and Lieut. Bissell—The Commander in Chief was made acquainted with the circumstance and directed that four other members should be detailed to supply their places on the Court—The second objection made by Ensign Lewis to four of his judges viz to Capt. McRea Lieuts Devon and Freemer and Ensign Richmond, is not approved of the General nor can it be admitted unless Ensign Lewis gives reasons for his objections. The Court are to judge other reasons given and in case they are deemed sufficient, new members will be warned, otherwise not—

This you will be please to make known to the Court—

I am Sir your obedt serv

John Mills

Adjt Genl

Lt E Smith Ind. Mat. & Adv. Genl to the Legion—

[page 3]
which being read Ensign Lewis offered to them the following objections—

"I hope none of the gentlemen I have objected to have felt themselves hurt on the occasion—I also feel myself disagreeably situated to be obliged to make my objections known which respect the last members which I have objected to—But I trust they will excuse me knowing my reputation is at stake and the obligation is from the order of the Commander in Chief and not from myself"—

"I object to Capt. McRea because he has exhibited charges which savour of his personality and such as I now appear before the Court for, against Capt. William Lewis"—

"I object to Mr Diven for having exhibited charges which the Commander in Chief has thought similar to those just mentioned, as is made known by his order pursuant to a Court Martial held at Hobson's Choice"[3]—

"I object to Mr Freemer and Mr Richmond for not having understood their own sentiments or rather for infirmness in matters in business as made known by their having withdrawn their signatures after having firmly affixed them to a price signed by a number of Officers of the Legion"—

Which being submitted to the other

[page 4]
members it was determined as their opinion that the reasons assigned are sufficient to preclude those challenged from sitting on the trial of Ensign Lewis—

Members dismissed by the President til tomorrow morning—

November 7th 1795 —

The members assembled pursuant to appointment.

A letter of the 6th instant from the Adjutant General to the Judge Martial and Advocate General was read stating that the objections of Ensign Lewis as reported yesterday had been handed to the Commander in Chief and that other members were ordered to be detailed to supply the place of those objected to—

Capt. Prior, Lieut. Jones, Lieut. Buttes and Cornett Ball returned members vice those challenged appeared—

The Court being now complete were sworn on the trial of Ensign Lewis on the following charges exhibited against him by Lieutenant Elliot—viz—

1st Charge—A direct, open and contemplative violation of the 1st and 2nd Articles of the 7th Section of the Rules and Articles of War—

Specification 1st—in presuming on or about the 24th September last to use provoking speeches and gestures to Lieutenant Elliot

[page 5]
in his own house—

Specification 2nd—In presuming on the same day to send Lieutenant Elliot to a Challenge to fight a duel—

2nd Charge—Conduct unbecoming an officer and a gentleman to Lieut. Elliot on the 24th of September—

Specification—In abruptly and in an ungentlemanlike manner, when intoxicated, entering his, (Lieut Elliot's) house on the 24th September last and without provocation insulting him and disturbing the peace and harmony of company of officers of whom he had invited there—Which being stated to him he pleads that he is not guilty thereof—

Whereupon the Court proceeded to the examination of the following witnesses—

Lieutenant Sterett, on oath says On the 24th of September last, Doctor Carmichael, Lieut Diven and Judge Smith dined with Mr Elliot and myself—soon after dinner Mr Smith went out—soon after this Mr Lewis and another gentleman Mr Rand came in and Mr Lewis asked Mr Diven

[page 6]
Diven saying "Mr Diven I wish to speak to you"

—they stepped aside, opened a door which leads to a platform projecting towards the Park—they left the door on a jar perhaps about half open—Doctor Carmichael got up and pushed too the door with his foot—Mr Elliot replied,—that was perfectly right, as he or they (alluding to the Company) did not wish to hear their conversation—in a short space of time the conversation of the gentlemen on the platform became so loud that we heard the sound of their voices.—Mr Elliot rose saying "this is wrong" and opened the door and addressed himself to Mr Diven "Sir you are my guest you were invited here pray do take your seat gentleman (addressing himself to the others) I am sorry that you came to my house to settle your disputes"—Mr Lewis turned into the house and appeared to be very much hurt and answered Mr Elliot "that he did not come to his house to settle his disputes nor had he any dispute with Mr Diven that he wished to settle"—more conversation of this kind perhaps past on both sides, but it was all nearly equal to that—and Mr Elliot mentioned that he wished them to sit down and take a glass of brandy and water and say no more on the Subject—I rose to help the gentleman and found no water—and handed the pitcher

[page 7]
to one of the Boys to bring some water—previous to its being brought—the conversation or the subject of the gentlemen's coming in was removed and conversation similar to the first took place—Mr Elliot warmly said that his house should be sacred that he would not suffer any disputes to be settled in it while he was master of it or something to that effect—but that his favor would be open to any gentleman officer at any time in a respectable decent way—Mr Lewis and Mr Rand in consequence of the second conversation immediately went down stairs—In a few minutes Mr Lewis came up the stairs again—the company were seated round the table—Mr Lewis stepped up towards Mr Elliot and addressed himself to him, "Sir I am now perfectly cool I consider myself to have been insulted in your house and by you Sir— as an officer and a gentleman I wish for Satisfaction, in two hours I will see you"— Mr Elliot replied "Very well Sir"—Mr Lewis then descended the stairs again—soon after Doctor Carmichael and Mr Diven left the house—Mr Elliot requested me to stay untill the two hours would elaspe [elapse]—in about half an hour after that perhaps,—an officer came in—he asked Mr Elliot and they went down stairs and remained a few minutes and returned—Mr Elliot mentioned

[page 8]
to him that he need not be backward in speaking before me as I was privy to what had passed before—the gentleman then addressed me saying "this is an unfortunate dispute that has took place between Mr Lewis and Mr Elliot, as a friend of Mr Lewis I wish to know who Mr Elliot's friend is—I have asked him who he is and he won't tell me—he says he has no friend—if I knew his friend I think I could have the business accommodated—Mr Sterett you are his friend, as you and he are mess mates he has surely mentioned the business and his determination to you"—I declared to him that Mr Elliot had even hindered me from speaking a word to him on the subject

nor he had spoken to me—Mr Elliot then said "No Sir, Mr Sterett knows nothing of the ~~matter~~ business I have no friend nor do I think that I need a friend in this case—I don't know you as a friend to Mr Lewis nor do I know Mr Lewis as a challenger untill he sends a challenge in writing"—the gentleman then said "He must have misunderstood" Mr Lewis for he had told him that he had challenged him (meaning Mr Elliot)—but I shall go to Mr Lewis you will please to wait half an hour—I shall return in half an hour—he did return in less than half an hour—Mr Elliot was sitting at the end of the table, and he handed him a piece of paper—

[page 9]
Mr Elliot opened it and apparently read it—then Mr Elliot asked him "Sir what does this mean"—the gentleman smiled and said "Mr Elliot you seem to be a strange man, you surely can see that he means to fight you"—"what (said Mr Elliot) does the gentleman mean to fight with, is it with a six pounder or with a five and a half inch horwitz," smiling at the time—"No Sir (said the gentleman) he means to fight you with pistols powder and ball as is usual on such occasions, as the place and time & has been left to me I make choice of tomorrow morning at gun firing within a hundred yards of old Number 6—he expects your answer"—Mr Elliot rose and stepped towards a table where some books were lying and took up the Articles of War, and said "Sir this is the way I will fight him—I will arrest him for a breach of certain articles of War naming them"

Ques. Did you read the paper handed by the gentleman to Mr Elliott!—
Answer—Yes

A paper here produced by the Judge Advocate signed Meriwether Lewis of which the following is a Copy—

Sir:
  Your treatment to me as an officer and a gentleman obliges me to call on you for satisfaction; the terms will be left to my

[page 10]
  from Capt. Marschalk—
  Yours
    Meriwether Lewis
    Ensign 4th SubLegion

Lieut Elliot
  Question to Mr Sterrit—Is this the paper handed by the officer to Mr Elliot?
  Answer—It looks like the paper—

Ques. Do you believe it to be the same—

Answer—I do—

Ques. Was Mr Lewis at the time of his coming into Mr Elliot's house as mentioned intoxicated?

Answer—My acquaintance with him will not enable me to say whether he was or was not.

Ques. How far was you from Mr Diven and Mr Lewis when you heard the sound of their voices?

Answer—Perhaps about fifteen feet and a door shut between them—

Ques. Was this paper out of your sight between Mr Elliot's receiving it and your reading it?

Answer—It was—

Ques. What was the reply of Mr Elliot to the gentleman who handed the paper to him when he said he was sorry there had been a difference between him and Mr Lewis

Answer—He said he did not consider it a

[page 11]

dispute as worthy of so much ado about it—he had a good deal of conversation in which he held out the idea that there had been no disputes between them—

Ques. Did Mr Elliot make use of any provoking language to Mr Lewis?

Answer—No I think not—

Ques. Did Mr Lewis use any provoking or menacing gestures towards Mr Elliott?

Answer—Not more than I have related

Ques. by Mr Lewis—Was I at the time of entering the house of Mr Elliot guilty of a breach of any forms of Decorum—

Answer—I believe he wrapped at the Door, befors and walked up stairs—I supposed they were asked to walk up—they did not take off their hats—otherwise they came in in the usual way—and Mr Lewis walked up and spoke to Mr Diven apparently in a hurry—

Ques. by the Court—Had these gentlemen ever been in the house before?

Answer—Mr Rand had frequently—and I believe once before—

Ques. by Mr Lewis—Did not Mr Elliot when I left the room the last time and mentioned the time of his giving me satisfaction with an assenting tone say "I will" or "I will Mr Lewis"?

Answer—He said "very well Sir"—bowing as I thought—

[page 12]

Ques. Did you know if the paper came from me or if the gentleman alluded to was authorized by me to wait on Mr Elliot with it?

Answer—No otherwise then by the gentleman's own words as before mentioned—

Ques. Did you hear me say anything to Mr Elliott about fighting or arms—

Answer—I did not—

Doctor Carmichael on oath says—I dined on the day alluded to in the charge with Mr Elliot—after dinner Mr Lewis and Mr Rand came into the room and called Mr. Diven from the table. They and Mr Diven went out of the room leaving the door half open behind them—some interesting conversation appeared likely to take place between them: and, to prevent my hearing it, I shut the door—for which Mr Elliot thanked me and observed that he never wished to hear any thing like disputes or controversies and was surprised if that was the business of the gentlemen that they should come to his quarters—he soon afterwards got up and went to the door and invited the gentlemen to walk in and requested Mr Diven to take his seat—he observed to the gentlemen that he should be happy to see any gentlemen in his house but that it was not the place for settling disputes or to that amount—that they could be settled else where—that he wished his guests and such

[page 13]

such gentlemen as came to his house to enjoy themselves. During this conversation Mr Elliot invited the gentlemen to take some brandy and water—Mr Lewis made some apologies—that he had no intention of quarrelling or disputing in his house— he appeared much agitated and withdrew—a few minutes after he returned to the room and addressed Mr Elliot "Sir I am now cool, I consider myself insulted in your house—I therefore call upon you for satisfaction as a gentleman—I will call upon you in two hours." He made a slight bow and withdrew—Mr Elliot answer'd "very well"—

Question—was Mr Lewis intoxicated at this time—

Answer—I am not sufficiently acquainted with him to determine—he appeared agitated but I did not then know the cause—previous to his leaving the room the first time, he appeared to have some difficulty in expressing himself and shed tears—

Ques. Had Mr Elliot made use of any provoking language or gestures to Mr Lewis—

Answer. Not more than I have related—

Ques. Did Mr Lewis when he returned and spoke to Mr Elliot make use of any provoking gestures to him?—

Answer—There was nothing provoking in his

[page 14]

gestures, his manner appeared interesting—

Ques. In what manner did Mr Lewis first enter the room and call Mr Diven out—

Answer—They both came into the room—I had not heard them knock or Mr Elliot invite him in before they came up stairs—one or both of them immediately called upon Mr Diven from the table. I did not know that they were come in untill I saw Mr Elliot speak to them—Adjourned til tomorrow morning—

November 8th 1795—
Court met pursuant to adjournment—

Lieutenant Diven, on oath says—on the day we dined at Mr Elliot's, Mr Lewis and Mr Rand came there and took me out, told me that they had some business with me—we went out on the platform—the door was a little open and was put to by some person—we staid there about a minute—Mr Elliot opened the door asked me saying "Mr Diven you are my guest I will thank you to walk in and take your seat" at the same time asking Mr Lewis and Mr Rand and take some Brandy and water—and said if we had any disputes he hoped they would not be settled in his house or something to that amount—I told him there was no dispute between them and me—Mr Lewis seemed very much hurt though I did not see him

[page 15]

treated improperly—Mr Lewis and Mr Rand went down stairs and as they were going down Mr Rand said he would never trouble Mr Elliot's house again or to that amount—they were gone but a few minutes when Mr Lewis returned and addressed himself to Mr Elliot and said—"I am now cool Sir I conceive that I have been insulted in your house by you" and I believe said he was an officer and a gentleman and demanded gentlemanly satisfaction and said Mr Elliot would hear from him in two hours—Mr Elliot said "Very well Sir"—

Ques. Was Mr Lewis intoxicated at this time—

Answer. I cant say that he was—he might have been drinking a little—

Ques. In what manner did Mr Lewis and Mr Rand enter the room—

Answer. I cant tell—I thought it was one of the boys coming up—and when I looked round I saw the gentlemen coming in—I dont know that they knocked at the door—I heard Mr Elliot say as soon as they were up—"Walk forward gentlemen"—

Ques. Did you conceive any part of Mr Lewis conduct merited a rebuke from Mr Elliot in the first instance?

Answer—I did not see Mr Lewis treat him improperly in the first instance unless by coming in the room in the manner in which he did.

[page 16]

Ques. by Mr Lewis. Was the conversation between you and me very loud—

Answer—The latter part of it was pretty loud—

Ques. by the Court—Was his conversation above the normal tone of Mr Lewis's voice?

Answer—I dont know he talked so that they might hear him in the room—thought he was not in a passion

Capt. Marschalk sworn—The paper before mentioned again produced.

Ques. Did you ever see that paper before—

Answer—I believe I have—

Ques. Do you know who wrote it—

Answer. I think I can Mr Lewis write it—

Ques. Did you see it delivered to Mr Elliot—

Answer. I did—

Ques. Did you know if it was delivered as a challenge to fight a duel—This question overruled by the Court and the witness not permitted to answer it—

Ques. Do you know of Mr Lewis having challenged Mr Elliot to fight a duel—This question also overruled by the Court and the witness not permitted to answer it—

Ques. by Mr Lewis—Did you see me intoxicated on the day alluded to in the charge?

[page 17]

Answer. I did not think he was intoxicated with liquor—Lieutenant Elliot, called as a witness and excepted to by some of the Court as an interested witness—then objection overruled by the Court—

Lieut. Elliot—sworn—confirmed the testimony of Lieut. Sterett circumstantially—the paper again produced here—

Ques. Do you know this paper—

Ans. Yes—

Ques. Was it delivered to you as a challenge from the day mentioned to fight a duel

Answer—Yes

Ques. Was it for the express purpose of fighting or for any other kind of satisfaction—

Answer—I do know that it was delivered for the express purpose of fighting because the gentleman who delivered it told me so—and the weapons and materials were named—and the time and place—he said the terms were left to him—that it was delivered as a challenge—that he saw Mr Lewis write it—no other satisfaction than fighting was asked—

Ques. Do you know that no other satisfaction than fighting would have been received?

Answer—I dont know but suppose other satisfaction would have been received—such as if I had asked his pardon after he challenged

[page 18]

me when I had given him no provocation—I was asked for no other—

Ques. by Mr Lewis—Has the ~~previous~~ papers produced been out of your possession before it was produced to the Court?

Answer. No.

Ensign Rand, called by Mr Lewis, sworn says,—

On the 24th September, I believe, Mr Lewis and I went into Mr Elliots chamber—Mr Lewis wanted to speak to Mr Devin who was dining with Mr Elliot—Mr Devin was asked to go step to the door—he, Mr Lewis and I went to the door—while we were there Mr Elliot came to the door and asked Mr Devin if he was his guest that day at dinner—Devin said he was—Mr Elliot desired him to take a seat—Devin went in and set down at the table—Mr Elliot observed to Mr Lewis that his house was an improper place for him to settle his disputes—Mr Lewis observed that he had no disputes with Devin—that he only wished to ask him a question—which he did not wish to ask before the company—some words such between Mr Lewis and Mr Elliot which I don't recollect—Mr Lewis's feelings appeared to be very much hurt he shed tears, and we went down stairs shortly afterwards—we stopped at Mr Whipple's and Mr Lewis returned to the chamber by himself—

Ques. by Mr Lewis—Did you not go with me to the quarters of Mr Diven in order to see him previously to our going to Mr Elliot's—Answd Yes—

[page 19]

Ques. Did we not stay until we conceived the Company of Mr Elliot had dined and were at leisure

Answer'd Yes—

Ques. Did we not use the ceremony of knocking at the Door before we went in and wait till we were invited before we ascended the stairs?

Answer—I knocked at the door and was on the stairs when we were invited it—

Ques. Was not Mr. Elliot abrupt conduct to me such as to hurt my feelings, before I had spoke to him and did you conceive yourself also hurt—

Answer. I conceived Mr Elliot to be rather hasty in the beginning of the business—

Ques. Did not Mr. Elliot when he first spoke address himself to Mr. Diven and me with warmth—

Answer—Yes—I conceive it to be so—

Ques. by the Court—Did Mr Lewis make use of any provoking words or gestures—

Answer—I don't conceive that his language was positivly provoking—

Ques. by Mr Lewis—Did not Mr. Elliot, addressing himself particularly to me, observe that no gentleman would come to his house to settle his disputes, after being informed by me that it was no dispute I came to settle—

Answer—Mr Elliot observed that his house was not a proper place for any gentleman to settle his disputes

Ques. by the Court—Do you know of Mr Lewis having challenged Mr. Elliot to fight a duel that day?

Answer I do not—

[page 20]

Ques. Was Mr Lewis intoxicated that day—

Answer I did not conceive him to be in in the least—

Ques by Mr. Lewis—Were you not with me from the forenoon of that day until we entered the house of Mr. Elliot when the conversation happened—

Answer. I was with him from 10' O' Clock I believe until the conversation happened

Defence to be heard on the 11th instant

Court adjourned till tomorrow—

[page 21]

Court adjourned till tomorrow—

November 11th 1795—Court met pursuant to adjournment and resumed the trial of Ensign Lewis—

Ensign Scott, on oath says—I have known Mr Lewis since Christmas last and have been on a most intimate footing with him ever since—I never saw him the least intoxicated but conceive that he has always conducted himself with the utmost propriety—

Ensign Lewis then read to the ~~following Defence~~
Court a Defence of which the following is a Copy—

Mr President and Gentlemen of the Court

I can but blush at the occasion which has obliged me to appear before you this day, an location as singular as ridiculous, as trivial as personal and as designed as it is ridiculous; Also an occasion which has turned the design and intention of the noble institution of Courts Martial, into a Tribunal only calculated to settle the private controversies of Officers. Were I capable of being the author of this original Scham, I should not have the effrontery to offer a word in vindication of myself, but patiently await your condemnation and the sensure of the world, with which I should be deservedly marked. But the character in which I appear is a sufficient demonstration of its not being a voluntary act of my own and therefore relieves me of having conscientiously deserved the one or other—

[page 22]

That this business is entirely personal is evidently shown by the charges and specifications themselves—I beg leave for the last time to repeat the charges and specifications which the gentleman for the ~~last time~~ good of the service has thought proper to exhibit against me—

1st Charge—For a direct, open and contentious vilation of the 1st & 3nd Article of the seventh Section of the Rules and Articles of War—

1st Specification—in presuming on the 24th of September last to use provoking speeches to me In my own house—

2nd Specification—In presuming on the same day to send me a Challenge to fight a duel—

2nd Charge—unofficer and ungentlemanly Conduct to me this day—

1st Specification—In abruptly and in an ungentlemanly manner, when intoxicated. Entering my house on the 24th of September last, and without provocation insulting me, and disturbing the peace and harmony of a Company of Officers whom I had invited there—

The rigor with which the Rules and Articles Of War treat all persons concerned in challenging either as principles or seconds makes it a business of the utmost consequence to all accused therewith, and had this charge been substantiated I know too well the sacred bonds by which the members of this tribunal are bound to recco[mend]

the awful sentence already passed and enjoined upon them by a superior power, (against which

[page 23]

there is no recrce [recourse] not to be well assured of the inevitable consequence—But I trust the contrary will be the result of the present inquiry. That in an army there will be private disputes and controversies is as evident, as the consequence of fire is smoke. That the most speedy method of settling them is best is as evident as that Military Law is the most valuable in proportion to its energy and force—That custom has ever derided and condemned the practice of settling private controversies in a public manner, as is evident as that custom has pointed out a method better calculated for the practice of military men. Perhaps it may not be amiss before I proceed further to recite a fin sintencer which it has pleased the Commander in Chief to deliver at several different times for the better regulation of the conduct of Officers who may be unfortunately engaged in any private controversies. They are first his observations pursuant to a Court Martial held at Legionville the 22nd of January 1792. When he mentions that such charges as these which had been exhibited by the Complanent against the Defendant when not supported, savored reather of private resentment than an inclination to promote military disciplin.

We also find his detestation more strongly Marked on this subject in his observations hersuant to a Court Martial held at Hobson's Choice the 9th of May 1793 which had been

[page 24]

produced at the instance of the same two gentlemen first refured to, who now appear in reverced order.—He here observes that the charges exhibited by the Complanent against the Defendant appear to be the counterpart of those exhibited by the at present Defendant against the Complanant at a former Court Martial, neither having for its basis the honor or dignity of the Legion, or the benefit of service, but evidently founded on Mallice and personal resentment and had better settled by some other method than that of a Court Martial. The Commander in Chief further observes that he hopes in future the times of the Officers will not be taken up, or their feelings tortured by hearing and recording charges and proceedings, which only tend to disgrace the orderly books of the Legion.[4] Can any doubt, but what the Commander in Chief, was induced to make those observations from the most noble motives truly worthy of himself viz the good of the service.—The reputations of the Officers of his Corps. An anxiety that they should distinguish themselves as gentlemen, men of honor, men who are ever as willing to unsheath the sword in redress of private injuries, as public rongs. Also that the records of this noble Tribunal, a Tribunal which ought to be held sacred

[page 25]

to honor and justice among military men, should not be disgraced with charges fostered by malice and dictated by spleen—

But I must here beg leaf to recall your attention for a moment from the past to view the matter which more intimately concerns me, the one now before you. This shall be discussed with as much brevity and precision as I am capable of—I am happy that the business has been so thoroughly investigated—

I rely with patient resignation on the superior judgment of the Court, with whom it rests to determan how far the testimony or the note adduced as testimony amounts to a violation of the Article refered to in the first charge—I have been accused of having directly and pointedly challenged Mr. Elliot, I deny it from this presumption, that a challenge should both mention fighting and the implements of War with which to fight, before it can amount to a direct challenge, such as the Rules and Articles of War take cognizance of—We find nothing decisive or printed as having come from me contained in the testimony either of fighting or arms, which I conceive as the only principe constituant parts of deweling [dueling]. Mr. Elliot has informed you in his testimony that he received that note as a challenge to fite a diewel [duel], provided that note had come from me,

in his construction of that note, or an explination

[page 26]

of it by another to be a proof of my intentions? by no means I conceive—

If the gentleman from his frantic immagination has construed the vague word Sattisfaction into a loaded pistol intended for his execution; without having any other resources, am I to be accountable, or punished for his frenzy? I trust not or perhaps my stripes might be many. Is any presumtive proof, or the mear opinion of any person as to the intention of the note to justify so harsh a sentence as that of dismissing me from the service of my country—Has it not appeared from the testimony of the several gentlemen, that I first waited on Mr Diven at this own Quarters found him not at home, was informed he was a guest of Mr. Elliot's—That I proposed by waited some time in order not to disturb him, or any other guest of Mr. Elliot's, it being about the time of dining. That I entered the house of Mr Elliot in the form generally observed in Camp. That Mr Diven did at my request, retire for a few minutes from the company. That my business with Mr. Diven was entirely friendly. That Mr Elliot interrupted us when in private conversation, that he spoke with warmth, when he first addressed me—previous to my speaking to him—

And that Mr. Rand the Gentleman who was with me, although not in particular addressed as myself, felt himself as much hirt at Mr. Elliot's expressions and manner, as to reply to him—

[page 27]

as he left the room, that he would not ever again ~~ever~~ trouble his quarters—

As far as a contracted bow, a stern countenance, or a menacing tone, can express, a cool, deliberate, and dispationate, manner of speaking so far Mr Elliot acted consistent with what he has endevoured to prove—

It appears evident that a demand has been made of restitution for injuries done, and that this demand was suited to the nature of the injury done, an injury done my feelings my reputation and my honour—Now I should be much obliged to any Gentleman to shew me any law, either Civil or Millitary, Divine or Human, that does debar a man from a demand of his rights, no it would be a vain attempt to unmar every principle of equity

and justice, on which is evidently founded the intention, the support, and the spirit of all Law—

So far from being debared this priviledg, Law directs that a demand shall be made, Justice that restitution shall be given; Can it then be either unlawfull or unjust to make such demand? I answer not—Is, or ought not justice to be the intention of Law? is, or ought not Law to be handmaid of Justice? moste certainly; for by Law as the instrument are the mandates of Justice inforced—

That it is both lawfull and just to demand

[page 28]

restitution for an injury done, and that, that demand should be the anticident of the injury, cannot be demur?—That is if my property is injured, protection requires of the aggressor a like sacrifice to reinmburse me; if this is not obtained, so far law must be deficient—If any outrage be commited on my person, justice requires a restitution similar to the injury, if this is not done, the deficiency must be in Law—If my feelings, or more my reputation and honour, are wontonly spoorted with to flatter the vanity, or swell the ambition of my self important aggressor. Justice cry is allowed for restitution, and Law is evidently deficient, that does not amply satisfy her demands—

It is an undoubted truth, and yet a misfortune ever to be lamented, that law is not fully addiquate to this task, notwithstanding the numerous coads [codes] which our virtuous legislature have laboured to compile—Were law to arrive at this perfection, that is, were law justice and justice law, those Hippocrits, would be more cautious, how they under the suspicions of defending the law, trample with impunity on every principle of justice—The deficiency of Law that barters reputation for goald [gold] or that so far deviates from the dictates of justice as protection to virtue, must be sincerely lamented by every sensible feeling mind—He who acts agreeable to the dictates of Justice, acts against

[page 29]

to what is or ought to be law, and is therefore justified by every principle of both—
I have in every instance paid the greatest deference to Law of my country neither
have I lost site of equity and justice—My conduct to this Gentleman has not been
improper in any one instance, but justified me in treating him as such, The simi-
larity of conduct not only of himself, but every officer in the Legion situated as I
was justified it—The exemplary conduct of the officers of all armies that have
heretofore served the United States, further countenances me. Custom Justifies me
And Custom when founded on Justice, and sided by time, in a measure, rises superior to Law, and justified a breach in the eye of the world whos good opinion is the
magnet of all our actions—

I was Justified from a still more pleasing principle, a conscientious nolege of
having discharged my duty to my country, to the gentleman, and to myself—I ask
you Mr President and Gentlemen of the Court wherein I have erred—Is it a crime
to comply with the simplest dictates of equity and justice?—Is it a crime to
comply with the law? Is it a crime to protect your person or reputation against an
assailent? Or is it a crime to settle personal

[page 30]

disputes in a private manner? If you answer in the affirmative, sentence me accordingly for they are crimes if necessary I will daily and hourly commit. If you answer
in the negative, I must further ask why I have been like a criminal dragged before
the bar of justice to answer crimes which you determan virtues. If this be the case
you will answer the fault mus not be in Law but from who procicutes [prosecutes],
and loudly calls in question his judgment—Can virtue and vice be here in strongly
contrasted, in their simple truths, that any gentleman should mistake the one for
the other? no matter of surprise then that he who can be such strainge impropri-
eties, should act widly different from all others of his profession—as to equity and
justice. I presume the gentleman did not dwell long on their good properties as the
more he did so the more he found them discountenance Injuries wantonly commited—as to law perhaps he might have dwelt with more pleasure on it than the
former as its dificiencies better suited the hue of his heart as to that first principle
of mature self defence, he must have seen a strainge inconsistency in it, one never
never discovered before by any but men of his passive turn of mind, to justify his
conduct, for when he was injured, as he assures you he was, he did not defend himself, neither did he put

[page 31]

my plain honesty to the test as far as even demand sattisfaction—But this inconsistency dose not account for the contradiction you find that he was not first
injured, but that felt myself hirt at his abrupt and warm address in the first instant;

therefore his supposed injury was no other than a retalliation for an outrage he had himself previously commited—

Were that Gentleman no fonder of altercation than myself he would not contend as much before a Publick Trybunal of Justice for sattisfaction, which he mite easily have obtained of me privality in a few minutes—What mus be the reflection of our Countrymen when they find the men whom they singled out from among thousands, as men of firmness and resolution, and those best calculated to defend their country fight its battles and aveng its rongs? when they find these very men, so far sacreficed their good oppinion, as to protect individuals? Will they not do you suppose, with poignant regret acknoledg their error, and with every true hearted soldier acknoledg them a disgrace to the profession of arms,

[page 32]

a profession honorable to themselves and ucefull to their country—

As to the business of settling personal disputes in a private manner I conceive it is intimately connected with the former (viz—Self Defence) for he who is willing to settle his own private disputes, need not call upon the Publick for her protection in the one cace, or pester trybunals in the other—He who acts differently sets up in opposition to the oppinions of all that vallue their reputations as millitary men, as well as the customs of all armies that have exhisted to the remotest ages, and will no doubt, for his unexampled vanity be rewarded with their contempt—

Any gentleman who will act from such principles must not have set an high estimate on his reputation, or otherwise cannot reflect an instant on the impropriety of such conduct, to act incongruous to every principle of honor and justice—

Any gentleman who can undervalue his own reputation so far, is reather, more excusable in undervaluing the reputation of another, it being the most equitable criterian to judg others by ourselves—

That my Posicutor sets a low estimate on my reputation is obvious an expression, which (from the goodness of his heart) he has made several times since my ~~trial~~ arrest, viz. that he had arrested me mearly for an experiment;

[page 33]

A noble sentiment indeed, one truly worthy of his great and magnanimous soul, that can at ease wantonly sport with the reputation of another for mear information—Or that can to add to his diar [dire] idol experience unfeelingly sacrifice the reputation of one he has already doubly injured; Doubly injured I say fore for in addition to the grosest insult he has laboured under with all invention of a malignant heart to add the greatest of misfortunes, to deprive me of my reputation—I had much reather he had of indulged his favorite, experience with an attempt on my life an object better calculated to serve the experience of a millitary man—But those unfounded arguments, or vague equivocations, cannot delude the vigilant mind which must discover that they were not the motives by which the gentleman was actuated; Or the passions under whos influence he is unfortunately laboured.—

I can not finally conclude this subject without some further comment on the word sattisfaction—I mus remind you that gentlemanny sattisfaction ~~what~~ was what I demanded, it is certainly not a gentleman but an assassin who can not be satisfied with any thing less than the life of his adversary, altho he may have been injured in a variety

[page 34]

of instances—I have endeavoured to prove that a demand of sattisfaction was both lawful and just, I must further urge that it is also necessary to wach your reputation with all the eyes of Argus—[hundred eyes of Argus]

Will you not believe no better than he is said to be, when he suffers another to tell him to his face, either by a direct or an indirect expression that he is no gentleman, and dos not resent it or call the person who may be so impurtinent to account for such impurtinence. You will answer that it is the general received oppinion.— now as it is very disagreeable to hobble through life with a broken reputation, I conceive the duty of every man to connect intimally, their life and reputation by all possible ties, to the end. that when the one makes its exit the other may also.—Had I received a billet which demanded gentlemanny sattisfaction, (as Mr Elliot has informed you he conceived he did from me) I should of thought it a compliment, as none but a gentleman is expected to give gentlemanny sattisfaction—

If he had punished the man ~~who has paid him~~ who has paid him a compliment how much more ought to be punished who can insult another in his own house— That the word sattisfaction is vague, and may be given in a variety of forms each sufficient to do justice to the feelings of a gentleman, cannot be denied—

[page 35]

I observed in the first instance that this business was designed and mallicous, in justification of which, I will observe to the Court, that immediately I was in confinment, proposals were made to the gentleman of leaving it to refferees, who should determan upon honor, who had been the aggressor, and how far, and also the method and manner of the accomidation. this might this mite have done justice to the feelings of both without the trouble of a Court Martial. But in order to put his favourit scheme in ~~execution~~ practice, or from a contintiencious knowledge of the ballance being much in my favour, he proved refractory as he has done in every other instance—The specification of my being intoxicated proves it malicious, for it has been proven by several that I was not in the least intoxicated either before or after visiting the house of Mr. Elliot.—It has also proven by a gentleman who has been intimate with me for many months that he never saw me intoxicated during his acquaintaince with me—

As to the second charge of unofficer and ungentlemany conduct—I defy not only my Prosicutor but the world to alledg any thing derogatory to the character of a gentleman

I wish the gentleman may see his faults, and that he never may on his imagination through this life meet with

[page 36]

an adversary so mallicious refractory or obserd [absurd] as he had proven to me— I also trust that my sword will not only be returned, but that it will be done in a manner which will do justice to the cause in which I have contended—

I am with due submission your most obedient
      Servent
      Meriwether Lewis
    Ensign 4th S. Legion

Which being read and heard, the Court in consideration on the testimony adduced are of opinion that Ensign Lewis is not guilty of the Charges exhibited against him, and sentence that he be acquitted with honor—[5]

Appendix C

EXCERPTS FROM THE LETTERS OF SAMUEL LATHAM MITCHILL, 1801–1808

S amuel Latham Mitchill's letters describe Meriwether Lewis, Thomas Jefferson, the ague, other interesting persons, and facts of interest to his wife, Catherine Akerly Mitchill. These excerpts are drawn from the Mitchill Collection, Museum of the City of New York.

1. DECEMBER 2, 1801—FOLDER 41.321.17

. . . just arrived in Philadelphia.

2. DECEMBER 4, 1801—FOLDER 41.321.18

. . . just arrived in Baltimore. Going to take tea with the Smiths.

3. DECEMBER 7, 1801—FOLDER 41.321.4

. . . to dine with Thomas Jefferson today.

4. DECEMBER 21, 1801—FOLDER 41.321.30

I have been to one of the Washington Balls. They are held alternately at Washington near the Capitol, and at Georgetown. Tho' the territory of these two places is contiguous or is joined together at their extreme parts by bridge over Rock-Creek, yet the compact part of Georgetown is distant from the Hill where the Capitol stands, and near which the assemblies are held, about three miles. . . . A Capt. Lewis— master of ceremonies.

5. JANUARY 2, 1802—FOLDER 41.321.7

Yesterday, New Year's Day, I dined again with President Jefferson. The Company was not numerous. . . .

6. JANUARY 10, 1802—FOLDER 41.321.36

I have had several opportunities of seeing and conversing with him [Thomas Jefferson] since my arrival at Washington. He is tall in stature and rather spare in flesh. His dress and manners are very plain. He is grave or rather sedate; but without any tincture of pomp, ostentation or pride. And occasionally can smile; and both hear and relate lively anecdotes or humorous stories as well as any other man of social feelings. At the moment he has a more press of care and solicitude because Congress and Senate are in Session and he is anxious to know in what manner the Representatives will act upon his Message and how the communications he expects soon to make to the Senate will be recd. . . . He has generally a Company of eight or ten persons to dine with him every day. Our Company were Eustis, Varnum, Randolph, Genl. Smith & Mitchill of NY, Baldwin, Brackinridge of Kentucky, the President and his secretary, Capt. Lewis made the party.

7. FEBRUARY 4, 1802—FOLDER 41.321.28 [PARAPHRASE]

[Mitchill appointed Professor of Chemistry and Natural History—January 1, 1802 to New York Hospital. He replied January 12, 1802, from Washington, thanking them.] My relations to scientific institutions are so various, and my correspondence with learned men so extensive . . . [Also dined with Jefferson].

8. FEBRUARY 8, 1802—FOLDER 41.321.35 [PARAPHRASE]

[Mitchill] to dine with Thomas Jefferson this afternoon.

9. FEBRUARY 10, 1802—FOLDER 41.321.40

On Tuesday, I dined with Thomas Jefferson. The company consisted of myself, & Captain Lewis, his Secretary, Gen Smith of Long Island, Brackenridge, Sumpter, Jones of Philadelphia, Varnum and one or two more. His cook is a Frenchman. . . . Ice-Creams are produced in the form of Balls of the Frozen materials in covers of warm pastry. . . . [He was on a Committee] on the Memorials concerning Perpetual Motion.

10. MARCH 17, 1802—FOLDER 41.321.48

It does not seem to be healthy here. . . . The Season for Agues has not arrived, or it is probable we should have many cases of that disorder. In 50 years it is predicted Washington will have 200,000 inhabitants—but there is a wide tract of low and marshy land between the River Potomack and Pennsylvania & New Jersey Avenues. In Autumn intermittents prevail over this Region. The circulation of the water is very slow & sluggish; it has no tincture of salt. . . . There seems to be something unwholesome in the fogs & damps which overhang situations on the east sides of the Rivers. . . . Washington built on the east side of the Potomac.

11. APRIL 28, 1802—FOLDER 41.321.9

Dining with Thomas Jefferson today.

12. APRIL 29, 1802—FOLDER 41.321.10

Thomas Jefferson's mansion is about a mile and three quarters from the Capitol. Dined with Thomas Jefferson yesterday. Took a Hackney Coach. The remoteness of Buildings renders it necessary to have many of those vehicles in Washington.

The party consisted of Thomas Jefferson, Mason, Mitchill, Baldwin, Macon, Stone, Eustis, Appeton, and Pichon.

I went into the President's Council Chamber with Captain Lewis his Secretary. There I saw two heads or Busts of Indian Hatuary, lately found near the Mississippi. I did not know until I saw these that sculpture had advanced so far among the Native red-men of North America. These are rude figures of men, considerably defaced but still bearing a nearer resemblance to the human form than you would suppose. There is another curious little stone image, as if of a man on his hands and knees. This is carved so oddly as to look considerably like a Tortoise, with his large head . . . a good way beyond his shell. Whether they were Idols, or likenesses, or Symbols, I do not know.

13. MAY 3, 1802—FOLDER 41.321.2

. . . leaving town.

14. DECEMBER 6, 1802—FOLDER 41.321.26

Arrived here last evening and stayed in Philadelphia and attended a lecture of Dr. Rush "on faculties of the Mind." Then went to Woodhouse's classroom. Rush escorted him to Dr. Caldwell's classroom and then to the Anatomical Theater where Dr. Wistar had invited him to attend his lecture on Osteology. Then had dinner and paid for passage for Baltimore.

During the recess, Washington has been very sickly. Dr. May informs me that not merely intermittent but remittent fevers of an obstinate kind had been very prevalent and in several instances fatal.

15. DECEMBER 8, 1802—FOLDER 41.321.8

Thomas Jefferson has not yet made his speech. This day I am to dine with Thomas Jefferson. His two daughters, Mr. Randolph and Mr. Eppes said to be with him.

16. DECEMBER 11, 1802—FOLDER 41.321.54

Dined with Gallatin and met for the first time the celebrated Thomas Paine. . . .

17. DECEMBER 15, 1802—FOLDER 41.321.53

Just heard the President's address which is full of peace and plenty. Our affairs are represented as very prosperous both at home and abroad. . . .

18. JANUARY 5, 1803—FOLDER 41.321.259

I send you a likeness of poor Tom Smith. Mrs. S. H. Smith gave it to me a few evenings when I called at their house and passed part of an evening in Chat by the fire-side. She has been tormented almost a year with the ague; and has more or less of it every day at this time. . . .

19. JANUARY 31, 1803—FOLDER 41.321.265

My Dear Kate

I write you from a secret conclave of Congress; for the House of Representatives is now setting with <u>closed</u> doors. The Galleries were cleared a little while ago to receive a <u>confidential</u> communication. After receiving it, a Debate arose whether it ought to be considered as a <u>secret</u> any longer or whether the Injunction of Secrecy should be <u>taken off</u>. And that discussion is now going on. So I thought I would write you, my dear, a few lines to let you know there was a considerable portion of <u>Free-Masonry</u> in Politics. Perhaps I might let you know something about this <u>Political Secret</u>, was I not restrained by my own decision because I have just set down after making a Speech against taking off the Injunction of Secrecy. You must however not imagine any thing about it, nor pretend to suppose that a secret expedition is meditated up the river Missouri to its source, thence across the Northern Andes and down the Western water-courses to the Pacific Ocean, and that the reason of keeping it secret is that the English and Spaniards may not find it out and frustrate it. . . .

20. FEBRUARY 3, 1803—FOLDER 41.321.263

Monroe departing for Europe in his ministerial mission. I have subscribed to it with many other Republican Members of Congress. . . . On Saturday I am to dine with Genl. Dearborn, the Secretary of War. . . .

21. FEBRUARY 9, 1803—FOLDER 41.321.85

Dinner at [unreadable] Tavern for Monroe—subscribers only—and some of the ministers. Burr not invited—Republicans have ceased to confide in him. . . .

22. FEBRUARY 11, 1803—FOLDER 41.321.272

. . . no ladies present. Dined with Thomas Jefferson and Monroe who will be leaving for France about the 1st March. . . .

23. FEBRUARY 14, 1803—FOLDER 41.321.257

Valentine's Day . . .

24. FEBRUARY 22, 1803—FOLDER 41.321.254

Several gentlemen have made an arrangement to return to Philadelphia by a route we never travelled before by way of Annapolis, Maryland.

After the House adjourns, I am to go and take my dinner with Mr. Jefferson who continues to give his elegant entertainments with as much regularity and agreeableness as ever. . . .

25. FEBRUARY 28, 1803—FOLDER 41.321.252

This day I have spent pretty much in Congressional Business, and this evening Judges Verplanck and I sallied out to Mrs. Dr. Thornton's.

26. MARCH 3, 1803—FOLDER 41.321.106

. . . close of Congress.

27. MARCH 3, 1803—FOLDER 41.321.248

The Committee of Ways and Means are making a grave report which I must listen to. All is anxiety and bustle.

28. OCTOBER 17, 1803—FOLDER 41.321.247

At Fredericktown I felt a little aguish and feared a return of my disease, but as it has not returned I hope to escape it. . . .

29. OCTOBER 18, 1803—FOLDER 41.321.249

Verplanck and I are living together. Verplanck and I are accommodated in the same Chamber. . . . My fever has not returned and I hope has left me entirely.

30. OCTOBER 25, 1803—FOLDER 41.321.245

After church I visited Gen. Dearborn. Met his son who, just out of college, had been ill of a fever, and nearly as they feared, at the point of death. The family was more comfortable knowing that one of its members is recovering from a dangerous fit of sickness. . . . I am to dine with Thomas Jefferson which I accepted on Saturday.

31. OCTOBER 27, 1803—FOLDER 41.321.244

The setting of the House did not adjourn until half past seven and did not arrive at Mr. Jefferson's until eight. Dinner was kept waiting until the Company came . . . . His late Secy. Capt. Lewis has gone on the public expedition through Louisiana, up the great River Missouri. . . . Congress passed the bill to take Louisiana voting 89 to 23. . . .

32. NOVEMBER 8, 1803—FOLDER 41.321.240

. . . horseraces at Washington. . . .

33. NOVEMBER 21, 1803—FOLDER 41.321.235

[Mitchill's] speech on the Louisiana Treaty published in the National Intelligencer this morning. . . .

34. NOVEMBER 23, 1803—FOLDER 41.321.234

Dining with Thomas Jefferson.

35. NOVEMBER 24, 1803—FOLDER 41.321.232

Among the remarkable things told of Louisiana is the existence of a Mountain of salt on the River Missouri. This extraordinary production of nature is mentioned in the Message sent to Congress on 15 November 1803. It is there stated to be 1000 miles above the place where that River falls into the Mississippi. Several respectable and enterprizing traders have visited it. They have brought several bushels of this natural salt down to the settlement of St. Louis. A sample of it has been forwarded to Marietta. The mountain or country of salt . . . is alledged to be 180 miles in length and 45 in width. . . .

Lest the account of such a body of Common salt should appear fabulous, I send you a specimen of the real article, which Mr. Jefferson received from the westward a few days ago; and which he presented to me. The arrival of the sample at the seat of government assists in dispelling the doubts which might exist and reduces the story to a certainty. . . . Mr. Shoto a respectable man is quoted as the witness that the sample I now lend you. . . .

I herewith also send you a piece of gypsum which came from Upper Louisiana. This was likewise given me by Mr. Jefferson. It is striated or crystallized form of plaster of paris and is very pure. It is very rare here & must be imported from Nova Scotia and France. In Louisiana, it appears that Plaster of Paris is one of the natural productions. . . . It comes from 450 miles up the Missouri.

36. November 25, 1803—Folder 41.321.231

[Mitchill goes on a long discourse on the length and breadth of Louisiana. He states that the Northern Andes (Rocky Mountains) are the western limit of Louisiana.]

I ought to mention to you also that part of my geographical information (besides Arrowsmith, John Mitchill, Pawnall's, and Carleton maps) is derived from 3 manuscript maps of which I obtained examination since I hade been at the seat of government. And from Manuscript Maps, has our Executive department also, derived no small part of the knowledge it possesses. An entire map of such an unknown and wild territory cannot be soon expected. . . .

In the course of two years, it may be expected we shall know more about this land of Curiousity. Under an appropriation of Money made for the purpose during the last Session of Congress, a Voyage of Exploration and discovery is now going on. Captain Meriwether Lewis late private Secretary to the President and W. Clark son of Genl. Clark accompanied by a select Corps of 12 Men, have departed on this fatiguing mission. They have already passed down the Ohio, and are expected to ascend the Mississippi as far as Kahokia, and there to pass the Winter. Tho' if the Autumn should be mild, they have the discretion given them of passing up the Missouri as far as they can and of finding winter-quarters on its banks. Next spring they are to start as early as possible and after tracing the Missouri or one of its streams to its source, they are to traverse the chain of mountains and transport themselves on one of the rivers running westward from it to the Pacific Ocean. This will be a Summer's work. They are to pass the next winter somewhere in that region, and set out on their homeward bound Voyage in the spring of 1805 and get back in the autumn of that year. They are to note the Rivers, Mountains, People, Port, and Productions, and in short every thing a rational Mind can seize and apprehend. I confess when I consider the hardships and dangers of such an undertaking, I tremble for the fate of the adventurers. On mentioning my fears to Mr. Jefferson, he said the Commanders and Crew were well selected and with great care for the purpose in view, and were uncommonly zealous to perform the service. I am sure I wish them success.

I may further assure you that Government has not published the entire volume of information on hand, relative to Louisiana. Some portion of the intelligence is so alluring that it was deemed improper to publish . . . it under governmental sanction or by public authority. It was feared the descriptions might be too romantic and that our citizens might be tempted to remove thither injuriously to themselves. . . .

37. NOVEMBER 29, 1803—FOLDER 41.321.72

Col. Varnum he knew a French gentleman who returned from a voyage of about 1500 miles up the Missouri, five years ago. This traveller, who was a general officer told him that on the bank of the river he saw a whitish mountain of great size . . . found to be an entire body of Common Salt.

Hoge of Pittsburgh relates that he has conversed with several persons who have seen the Mountain of Salt on the Missouri. An acquaintance of his examined separately 3 traders who had travelled upon the western expeditions along that river. They all agreed in the reality of the Salt-mountain.

[Mitchill spoke with other members of Congress] who affirmed the story of the Salt Mountain.

38. DECEMBER 8, 1803—FOLDER 41.321.280

I see that the editor of the American Citizen has published your specimen of Salt from the Missouri with your name. I find that General Collot a Frenchman who went up that River a few years ago, declares the reality of the Mountain. . . .

39. JANUARY 20, 1804—FOLDER 41.321.309

Now the microscope has taught us that these sparks of oceanic fire. . . .

40. JANUARY 22, 1804—FOLDER 41.321.311

Went to dine with Mr. Jefferson. I went early and had a good deal of conversation. He shewed me a new french Work on geology by Fanjas de Saint-Fond [naturalist].

41. FEBRUARY 26, 1804—FOLDER 41.321.328

Dr. Morse the Geographer has been kind enough to send me the half sheets of his new Edition of the American Gazeteer, which contains his Account of Louisiana. . . .

42. FEBRUARY 29, 1804—FOLDER 41.321.329

I have been reading O'Reilly's and Carondelet's Laws, to prepare for a speech on it today [regarding Louisiana].

43. MARCH 6, 1804—FOLDER 41.321.332

I have made a Review of the President Publication on Louisiana for the Med. Rep. [Medical Repository] and prepared various articles of intelligence for that work, which have been transmitted to my colleague.

44. MARCH 15, 1804—FOLDER 41.321.337

Today I enclose for you something on the propriety of having the unknown parts of Louisiana explored. You see that I sieze opportunities as they offer, of promoting Industry and Research. In this paper you will find stranger things than the Salt Mountain. Here is a <u>Salt River</u>, and Minerals of <u>Gold & Silver</u>. I might have added a <u>Volcano</u>, for you know you have in your collection, a fine parcel of the Pumice Stone, which is the evidence of a burning Mountain, that was found floating on the Missouri . . . corroborated by documents in my possession and by good parole evidence.

45. MARCH 19, 1804—FOLDER 41.321.339

Dined for the last time at the Presidents. . . .

46. MARCH 20, 1804—FOLDER 41.321.340

. . . retroceded parts of Maryland & Virginia to create the territory of Columbia.

47. MARCH 21, 1804—FOLDER 41.321.341

[Mitchill broke his arm.]

48. NOVEMBER 5, 1804—FOLDER 41.321.346

. . . just arrived in Washington.

49. NOVEMBER 6, 1804—FOLDER 41.321.347

Gen. Dearborn has left his family in Maine . . . Washington has been miserably sickly and is far from being entirely healthy at this Day. The Parts of Virginia which lie between the North & South Mountains and along the River Shenandoah have been dreadfully infected with a malignant distemper accompanied with Black Vomiting in various instances . . . I have put on one of my flannel shirts, and find it rather too warm but shall continue to wear it. [Rush and others thought that wearing flannel would reduce an attack of ague.]

50. NOVEMBER 10, 1804—FOLDER 41.321.348

Washington has been very sickly this season. Remitting fevers have been frequent and violent and numbers have been cut off by them. The inhabitants of the Capitol-Hill look very sickly and some of them are yet in their sick-beds. The unhealthiness of the situation seems to be owing to the noxious exhalations from a marsh which lies to the Southward of it and between it and the Potomack the Southwardly breezes waft these deleterious has in a direct line to the Capitol-Hill. Along New Jersey Avenue, where I use to live, the sickness has been very distressing and the people who survived look miserable yet. The fever has not been so prevalent at Georgetown. This unwholesomeness of its situation is a woeful impediment to the growth & prosperity in Washington.

51. NOVEMBER 26, 1804—FOLDER 41.321.357

A few days ago I dined with President Jefferson. He treated us with water from the Mississippi and Mammoth Cheese of Cheshire (Map?). . . . Thomas Jefferson shewed me various specimens of the Lead Ores from the great mines of Louisiana. They were Galenas [grades], with cubes of different sizes and surfaces of various splendor like those in your cabinet. He showed several other <u>Galenas</u> too, from the Osage-River. And he also exhibited two pieces of <u>Grey Silver Ore</u> from Mexico. He had "dates" on the Table among the fruits brought on with the Dessert. I mentioned to him the rarity of that fruit in our Country and even in Europe and asked him where he procured it. He said they were produced from Marseilles. . . .

52. DECEMBER 17, 1804—FOLDER 41.321.366

Dined at Jefferson's. He gave me a plural of Water and a Stalactite from the hot spring up the Washita River in Louisiana. This spring is nearly the temperature of boiling water and constantly emits a cloud of vapour. . . . From Mr. Dunbar who has gone to visit it, we may expect a very correct & scientific report.

53. DECEMBER 25, 1804—FOLDER 41.321.369

No session of Congress. . . .

54. DECEMBER 2, 1805—FOLDER 41.321.405

Samuel Smith, President of the Senate pro Tempore.

55. DECEMBER 5, 1805—FOLDER 41.321.407

Some Choctaw Indians have just arrived . . . the [?] man had a conversation with them and wished to know what God they worshipped. They said the Great Spirit.

56. DECEMBER 19, 1805—FOLDER 41.321.415

I send you the abstract I have made from Mr. Dunbar's Voyage into Louisiana. It is intended for the Medical Repository. But will not be wanted immediately. . . .

57. JANUARY 2, 1806—FOLDER 41.321.422

Yesterday being New Year's Day there was no sitting of Congress. . . . In the evening, I received the visits, at my lodgings of three Indian interpreters from the

Northwest and the Missouri. With them I discoursed on the geography of the remote regions west of us, on their Rivers & productions, on the manners of the savages, & & I gathered from them a considerable amount of information; and expect to procure an Osage Song on War. . . .

58. JANUARY 29, 1806—FOLDER 41.321.430

I have for several evenings been engaged in translating some french Manuscripts containing interesting intelligence from the upper country lying towards the head of the River Missouri: And I am getting a MSS map of some part of those Regions, copied. I put the Indians at work the other evening with Chalk to make me a delineation of their Country, on the floor. And I am exceedingly pleased with the correspondence there is between their rude marks and the fine strokes of a Surveyor.

59. FEBRUARY 10, 1806—FOLDER 41.321.435

I send you a map of another part of Louisiana. Some time ago I sent you a delineation of the Washita. Now I forward you a manuscript chart of the upper branches of the Arkansas River and of the Great and Little Osage Rivers with sketches of the Mississippi, Missouri, Maramec, Gasconade, and some others.

The great salines or natural magazines of salt, four in number are here specially delineated. These are all on the streams of the Arkansas; for it is now ascertained that the Mountain of salt on the Missouri does not exist! But vast beds of strata of Sal Gen or native rock salt exist on the plains and vallies marked on the map, as being in the vicinity of the upper streams of the Arkansas. The memoir which explains the map was translated from the French by myself.

You see how hard it is to get good information concerning that Western Country. Scraps and fragments of geography, are hitherto all we can obtain. But soon there will be sent to Congress a better Map of Louisiana than ever appeared, compiled under the eye of Mr. Jefferson and Mr. Dearborn from the communication of Capts. Lewis and Clark and other manuscript maps & documents of travellers. It is ascertained that there is no foundation for the story of Indians up the Missouri speaking the Welch language. The Welch descendants and the Mountain of Salt are both fabulous; tho' in favor of the latter, we may alledge that there are mines and plains of salt, which amount substantially to the same thing.

. . . a few nights ago I obtained a beautiful confirmation of the Matters solicited on the Map from several Osage Indians that invited me. I asked them to draw with chalke on the floor, villages, rivers and paths of their country. They performed this with great readiness and in a manner nearly corresponding with the present performance of Mr. Soulard, Surveyor General of Louisiana. The proficiency made by our Redmen in Geography, I mean of their own regions, is very remarkable.

60. FEBRUARY 19, 1806—FOLDER 41.321.440

I took a walk this morning between the hour of breakfast and prayer, to the Presidents House. There I saw an Indian curiousity—It is a map done by the Missouri natives, on a fine dressed Buffaloe skin. The skin is dressed after the manner of a Deer-skin, and it is of the same whitish on buff colour on this soft and clean hide which is as large as that of an Ox. There is a delineation by an Aboriginal hand of the vast River Platte & Missouri, and of the Principal streams, mountains, villages and minerals, lying between those prodigious water-courses. Among these remarkable things are marked four mines of Platina, several of copper, and a volcano. It is really a pleasing proof of the Geographical Knowledge of these self-educated People. It was a short time ago sent to Mr. Jefferson by Gov. Wilkinson of Louisiana.

61. DECEMBER 3, 1806—FOLDER 41.321.450

Saw Thomas Jefferson who had an accident. Arm in a sling—fingernail torn off.

62. DECEMBER 8, 1806—FOLDER 41.321.451

[Mitchill invited to dinner at Thomas Jefferson's.] Thomas Jefferson in fine health [told Mitchill that] Pike's map & Freeman's were in an engraver's hands at Philadelphia. And that Congress would soon have the printed copies laid before them.

63. DECEMBER 18, 1806—FOLDER 41.321.457

This morning I went to the War Office and saw Lieut. Pike's Map of the Mississippi. . . . We shall soon have the map and Memoir of Mr. Pike's laid before Congress. . . .

64. DECEMBER 21, 1806—FOLDER 41.321.458

The Osages who came with Capt. Lewis have arrived here. Last evening I saw them. They are tall and whitish like the rest whom we have seen. The Capt. has gone to Virginia to visit his relations after his journey to the Pacific Ocean and will probably be here in a few weeks. . . .

65. DECEMBER 23, 1806—FOLDER 41.321.90

Burr's expedition engrosses almost all of the intervals between the battles of Buonoparte; and the eyes of our Politicians are alternately directed to the Ohio and Principia [illegible].

66. DECEMBER 30, 1806—FOLDER 41.321.464

Capt. Lewis has reached this place after the performance of a journey across the Continent of North America, quite across to the Pacific Ocean, and back again. The distance is computed to be considerably more than three thousand miles across. He and his party went away from Washington in the Summer of 1803, and owing to the lowness of the water in the Ohio, got no farther than Kahokia on the Mississippi, and wintered there. The ensuing spring, he reached Mandane, near the great Bend of the Missouri and passed the cold season at that place [1804–1805]. Thence he proceeded westward, and crossing the Northern Andes, near some of the sources of the Missouri, travelled before the Vigorous Weather set in, as far as the Ocean, near the mouth of the Columbia River. Here he remained during the inclement part of 1805–6; and as soon as the spring was far enough advanced for marching, he started for home. And here, he is once in good health & spirits. I feel rejoiced on his own account; an account of Geography & Natural History; and on account of the Character and Honour of Country that this expedition has been successfully performed. They were so pinched for food while passing the snows of the Rocky Mountains that they fed upon their Horses and Dogs, until they arrived to more benignant [beneficial] regions.

67. JANUARY 1, 1807—FOLDER 41.321.74

New Year's Day is the time of the greatest exhibition that usually occurs in Washington. Both houses of Congress adjourned from Wednesday to Friday for the purpose of enjoying it the better. The Weather has been very fine, and pursuant to a standing custom during the present administration, all the great and fashionable folks went to pay their compliments to Mr. Jefferson at the President's House on the Palatine Hills. . . .

. . . While I was looking round and meditating what to do with myself, the Miss Johnsons . . . expressed a desire to be escorted to the side of the room where the newly arrived Indians were. I at once became their pioneer and showed them the King and Queen of the Mandanes, who with a child of theirs, have come a journey of about 1600 miles down the Missouri to see their great Father the President. His majests were gaily dressed in a regimental coat, &, but his Consort was wrapped in a blanket, and had not the smallest ornament about her. She resembled exceedingly one of our Long Island squaws. There was also another Mandane woman there, who was wife to a Canadian White man, that acted as interpreter. She had two children with her. We also looked at the five Osages and the one Delaware warriors of whom I wrote you before. . . .

68. JANUARY 7, 1807—FOLDER 41.321.75

I have just written a Note to Capt. Lewis to dine with me on Saturday.—In a late conversation I had with him, he gave me a description of the <u>burning plains</u> up the Missouri. . . .[1]

69. JANUARY 12, 1807—FOLDER 41.321.62

. . . this evening I am to call upon Capt. Lewis at the Presidents House & see his new Map of Louisiana and his specimens of Natural History. . . .

70. JANUARY 16, 1807—FOLDER 41.321.103

A few evenings ago, I went to the Presidents House to see the specimens of Natural History brought by Capt. Lewis from Louisiana, and his Map of the regions he has visited between the Mississippi and the Pacific. He has several non-descript animals, among which are five species of quails, partridges and grous that are probably new to naturalists; three or four sorts of squirrels besides those which are found in the Atlantic regions; and a white-coated quadruped of a character somewhat between the <u>Sheep</u> and Goat, having both hair and wool for a fleece; it is probably the Vir-

ginia sheep of Spanish America, now for the first time found in the Freedish dominions. He often saw the mountain-ram.

He has brought with him the seeds of many plants; and shewed me several
presses of dried plants in fine preservation. These make an instructive herbarium of
the Regions to which he passed.

Few of his minerals have arrived. But they are on their way hither.

But his Map of those parts of North America is the most instructive of his
bounties. It gives an enlarged and Comprehensive view River Missouri, and of the
vast streams, which under the names of Osage, Kanzas, Platte, &c. fall into it. Of
these the Platte alone is larger than the Mississippi above Kaskaskias. The distance
from the Source of the Missouri to its junction with the Gulf of Mexico is computed
to be more than 4000 miles and it runs the greater part of this distance without a
Cataract. The mountains whence the Head Waters issue are not high & continued
chains like the Andes, but Elevations of not perhaps more than 3000 feet, and so
broken & irregular that the streams which run eastward toward the Missouri inter
lock with those that run westward with the Columbia River. The Waters are more
precipitous on the other side of the Rocky Mountains. Their descent is too Great to
render them navigable by boats even in their passage downward. The travellers were
obliged to purchase horses from the Indians; for in those parts the Natives all have
these animals to ride. Here there are few inhabitants; but as soon as they arrived to
the Plains on the Columbia River, that are visited by the Tide-waters there is an
uncommon number of inhabitants. . . . The article of the highest value among these
people is the Blue-bead . . . blue ones will purchase their sea-otter skins, or any
thing they possess. This journey has not only enlarged our knowledge of Natural
History and Geography but dis dessed to our men of monied enterprize a view and
hitherto unexplored Country for Beaver skins and the fur-trade. For the beavers exist
on the upper waters of the Missouri in almost incredible numbers, and a long series
of Years will elapse before they are extin ported (exported). Hence our Merchants
have the encouraging prospect of large fortunes to be made by encouraging the
Indians and other hunters to kill them and bring their skins to market. . . .

71. JANUARY 31, 1807—FOLDER 41.321.112

Last winter my dear . . . I prepared for you two curious morsels of Aboriginal North
American Poetry. They were, you may remember, a War song and a Peace song of
the Osage Indians. I now send you another. It was translated from the original by
Mr. Chouteau, a different person from him who made a version of the former. He
performed this talk at the request of Mrs. Smith. To this lady, I am indebted for the

French manuscript and at her suggestion I have attempted to turn this third morsel of our native composition into English. Mrs. Smith is engaged in making another translation; and then she and I are to compare our performances and examine which has succeeded best. . . . [Mitchill then transcribes song of the Osage for his wife]

72. FEBRUARY 5, 1807—FOLDER 41.321.77

French Minister . . . General Turreau's dining Party yesterday was well attended . . . Capt. Lewis were the principal member of the Party [mentioned Vice-President Clinton], my colleague Smith and myself from New York, including Madison and Gallatin.

73. FEBRUARY 7, 1807—FOLDER 41.321.55

. . . 3 above zero. . . .

74. FEBRUARY 18, 1807—FOLDER 41.321.69

After the [congressional] adjournment, I went to dine with Mr. Jefferson. There I found Capt. Clarke the traveller to the Pacific Ocean. He is a fine-looking soldierly man, and very conversant with the North American Indians. My seat at the table was between the President and him. So of course I could converse, by turns, with each. I improved the opportunity to inquire of Capt. C. concerning the manners and Customs of the native tribes he had visited on the Missouri. He told me many things and among. . . . [following page missing]

75. DECEMBER 18, 1808—FOLDER 41.321.192

. . . the sickness of Mr. Madison has retarded the negotiation with Mr. Rose. He has been ill for several days.

Appendix D

NOTES ON MERIWETHER LEWIS'S REAL ESTATE TRANSACTIONS AND PERSONAL DEBTS

For private landowners who sold real estate in the Louisiana territory, the sale carried a provision that if the land could not be confirmed by the United States, "the money shall be returned with interest from the date of the decision."[1]

Meriwether Lewis, as governor of the Louisiana Territory, and residing in Saint Louis, was required under the Northwest Ordinance to have a freehold estate of one thousand acres.[2] By May 1808, Lewis had purchased about 6,300 acres of land for $1.14 an acre.[3] Then in the summer of 1808, he bought more land, with the plan of bringing his mother to the region because of his belief that the values of "lands are rising fast."[4]

There have been few studies on Lewis's personal finances, and these always revolve around criticism that Lewis spent too much time purchasing land, which ultimately led to his downfall when his governmental drafts were rejected.

In February 2002, *We Proceeded On* published L. Ruth Colter-Frick's, "Meriwether Lewis's Personal Finances," which was considered to include the most accurate information on the subject at that time. Ms. Frick relied upon several sources of information: the Grace Lewis Miller Collection, at the Jefferson National Expansion Memorial Library in Saint Louis; Meriwether Lewis's Account Book, 1807–1809, at the Missouri History Museum; and the Lewis/Marks Papers, located at the University of Virginia. However, the Grace Lewis Miller Collection is incomplete, while the other two are not comprehensive.[5]

Ms. Colter-Frick was one of several persons who prepared the "Finding Aid to the Grace Lewis Miller Papers, 1938–1971," which enabled her to author a book *Courageous Colter and Companions* and write the *We Proceeded On* article. While she took advantage of these three primary resources, she did not consult any legal documentation, which portrays the other side of the debts and expenses.

My work is based on the documentation taken from the accountant's ledgers (see appendix E) and the following:

Missouri State Archives, Territorial Court Records
Civil Court Archives, Lower Court Records
Recorder of Deeds, Property Transactions
Collet's Index, an inadequate real estate property index

The following pages list multiple transactions and descriptions of Lewis's real estate purchases. Individuals who may want to research Lewis's financial health will have to consult these records and not depend solely upon Lewis's Account Book or the Grace Lewis Miller Collection. Lewis's Account Book, while detailed, is missing much information.

The real estate transactions are quite complex, which is an indication that Lewis was interested in remaining in the territory for a long time. The volume of information contained in the following documentation was staggering, and I had to abridge much of it. What is represented here is a condensed presentation of the facts—a direct and unedited transcription of the research notes I generated while consulting the relevant source materials—along with citations that are intended to direct scholars to where the complete source information may be found. My selection and presentation represents my initial interpretation of those primary sources.

Lastly, the court records for the Missouri Fur Company are also listed here. There has been much speculation that Meriwether Lewis was a silent partner in the fur company, but it is evident that he was not a member. Furthermore, the transactions of the fur company throw new light on the expedition too.

Edward Hempstead, a lawyer, had been hired to represent the Missouri Fur Company. Hempstead was also Lewis's attorney. He had first arrived in St. Louis in 1808, and in March 1809, Governor Lewis appointed him attorney general of the Louisiana Territory. In September 1809, when Lewis departed Saint Louis, he empowered Hempstead to represent his personal affairs. Since Lewis had not been paid by the War Department for some of his drafts, individuals who had been promised payments by Lewis but had not received them were forced to sue him in Saint Louis. After Lewis's death, Hempstead represented the Lewis estate beginning in 1810 and ending on October 9, 1812.

Note, as you read this appendix, that a French arpent, abbreviated arps., measures 192 feet in width by 1.5 miles long, which amounts to .85 of an acre.

Meriwether Lewis's Court Cases, April 3, 2003
Civil Court Archives, 710 Washington Ave., Saint Louis, Missouri

Jacob Philipson v Meriwether Lewis—heirs William Clark foreclosure on mortgage; March 1810, #8

3 tracts of land ($400) ($65) ($100) = $565

Amount of decree $890; paid $360.41

Charles Sanguinette v. Edward Hempstead, adm of Meriwether Lewis estate

Debt to recover money due on bonds; November 1810, #16, Court of Common Pleas

details all debts of ML upon his death $2842.06

Lewis's estate was worth $1811.65

August 24, 1809—a writing obligation—"sealed with the seal or Scrawl of the said Lewis & by him signed"—owed to Sanguinette payable Oct 1, 1809

—William C. Carr, atty.

—Benjamin O'Fallon testified

—[not signed by Meriwether Lewis]—(copy of bond)

{page ripped here}

Debts:

Jacob Philipson	361.61
Alexander Stuart	750.00
James McFarlane	718.45
Pierre Provenchere	18.75
Antoine Saugrain	30.75
Auguste Chouteau	10.00
Sherrid Swaine	48.00
William H. Thomas	220.50
John Colter	559.00—plaintiff demand on this
Sanguinette	125.00

Total $ 2842.06

Sherred G. Swaine v. Edward Hempstead, adm. of Meriwether Lewis debt, account for services

Nov 1810, #31; Swaine kept mare and 20 head of cattle from Nov 1, 1809 to April 30, 1810
—court document Sherred G. Swain
—Samuel Hammond—presiding judge

John Colter v. Edward Hempstead, adm. of Meriwether Lewis estate
Nov 1810, #31 debt; services rendered (Corps of Discovery)
May 4, 1809 indebted $559; "Nevertheless the said Meriwether Lewis his promise and assumption in form aforesaid made not regarding, but contriving and fraudulently intending him the said John in this behalf craftily and subtilly to deceive and defraud, the aforesaid sum of $559. —J. A. Graham, atty
Money received by Meriwether Lewis from the War Department on acct of John Colter for wages due Colter $380 with extra pay allowed by Congress $179 = $559

Falconer and Comegys, merchants (Peregrine Falconer & John G. Comegys) v. Edward Hempstead, adm. of Meriwether Lewis
March 1811, #27; William Carr—atty
Aug 22, 1809, $331.45 1/2, also $23

Gilbert C. Russell, note against Lewis $379.58
Total debt $3452.59, 1/2 only
$2419.89, 1/2 came from sales

Pierre Chouteau v. Edward Hempstead, adm. of ML
Nov 1811, #67; William C. Allen—atty
$1061.65; demanded on Aug 10, 1809, $81
Bill of exchange June 16, 1809 denied by Eustis
case continued—Allen, atty.
March 1812, #30; July 19, 1809 $81, John Davidson presented to William Eustis—original bill
March 1812, #31; May 15, 1809 $440—Eustis (Simmons) refused to pay presented bill on Oct 16, 1809 and refused again

Deed Book Transactions
(Collet's Index—Missouri History Museum)
Meriwether Lewis as Grantor

Name	Date	Book/Page
John Mullanphy	?	A: 30
Cavalier & Fils, tr.	?	A: 30
Louis Lemonde	?	A: 37
Charles Simoneau, mgee	May 1806	? 86
John Mullanphy	May 1806	? 88, 92
Antoine Reynal	1805	? 198
Baptiste Molaire	May 1806	? 276
Antoine Bouis	Sept 28, 1807	? 504
David Delaunay	?	B: 10
Jacob Philipson, mgee	?	C: 17
Pre Chouteau, mgee	?	? 26
Wm C. Carr	?	? 39
Fredk Bates	?	? 186
Joseph Philipson	?	? 243 and 478
Bazil Bissonnet	?	? 580
Risdon H. Price	?	E: 18
Pierre Chouteau	?	? 24

Meriwether Lewis as Grantee

Name	Date	Book/Page	Description
John Bapt. Lorin	May 3, 1808	B: 18	1x40 arps. Prairie of St. Louis—$60
Francois Dunnegant	May 20, 1808	B: 24–5	4x40 arpents, Fontaines des Biches District—$120
Jos. Aubuchon	May 20, 1808	B: 25	2x32 arps—Prairie of St. Ferdinand, $120
John Mullanphy		B: 26	3.78 1/2 arps—$38
Hyacinthe St. Cyr, sr.	May 26, 1808	B: 40–1	400 arps—property confirmed or deed annulled—$300

Thos. Roy Musick	June 9, 1808	B: 62–3	7x2 acres or 85 arps—property confirmed or contract annulled, money returned—$170
Peter Chouteau	July 1, 1808	B: 95	tract in Portage des Sioux—property confirmed or contract annulled, money returned—$800
Peter Chouteau	Aug 3, 1808	B: 98	1370 arps in Portage des Sioux—property confirmed or contract annulled, money returned—$338
Peter Chouteau		B: 98	290 arps in Portage des Sioux—included in the same price as above
Peter Chouteau	Aug 3, 1808	B: 101	30 arps & 93 perches (ft) in Portage des Sioux—must be confirmed—$248
Peter Chouteau	Aug 3, 1808	B: 103	345 arps on the Missouri—a mile below Belle Fontaine—property confirmed or contract annulled—$517.50
Peter Chouteau	Aug 4, 1808	B: 106	4850 arps, six miles NW of the Town of St. Louis—property confirmed or contract annulled—$1500
Articles of Association		B: 373–77	co-partnership Benjamin Wilkinson, P. Chouteau, Sr., Manuel Lisa, Augustus Chouteau, Jr., Reuben Lewis, William Clark, and Sylvester Labbadie and Andrew Henry of Louisiana Terr., also Pierre Menard and William Morrison of the town of Kaskaskia, Indiana Terr.

Jacob Philipson, mgee	Aug 3, 1808	C: 17	Land of Hortiz—Marais Castor (from B/106)—must be confirmed . . .—$1000
John Mullanphy	Aug 18, 1808	?	224 arps
J. Hortiz	Aug 18, 1808	??	
Abraham Musick ML's	1 April 1809		400 arps on Bon Homme
Administrators William C. Car	19 Aug 1809	C: 39	Lorin's land (May 3, 1808)—40 arps—$160
Frederick Bates		C: 186–7	Court problem (Philipson)
Frederick Bates	Oct 25, 1811		30 arps, P. Chouteau (B: 101) $248 sold to Risdon Price $759 (Price then sold 18 arps in 1817 for $2986.66 (Frederick Bates Papers, MHM, St. Louis)
John McKnight	?	C: 558	
Thomas Brady	?	C: 558	
Leduc auctioned lands	Oct 4, 1812	?: 473	ML's lands—345 arps (B: 103)—$325
William Clark	Oct 25, 1812	?: 500	4x40 arps (B: 24–5)—$40 highest bidder
William Preston	Oct 25, 1812	?: 501	400 arps from St. Cyr (B-40-1)—$110
Risdon Price	?	I: 224	
Wm. Clark	?	I: 224	
M. Leduc	?	I: 224	
Wm Preston	?	I: 224	
Thos Brady	?	I: 224	
John McKnight	?	I: 224	
Hempstead to Benjamin Howard	July 7, 1813	H2: 255	sale of lands $900
Peter Chouteau & Meriwether Lewis		H2: 289	Conveyance July 31, 1808: land in Portage des Sioux (Aug 3, 1808, B: 98, land disposed of on April 19, 1839 for $800.

Deed Books, St. Louis Recorders Office
Land Warrants,   15 Nov 1808   B: 152–7

Warrants for 7 members of the expedition: Patrick Gass, John Collins, Hugh
McNeal, John B. Thompson, Alexander Millard, Joseph Whitehouse, George
Drouillard (320 acres each). John Collins assigned warrant to Drouillard on 29
June 1806 and then assigned it to Riddick and McNair on 28 June 1808. Hugh
McNeal to George Gibson on 9 March 1807 who assigned it to Bates on 4
October 1808.

B: 153	Bates paid Gass $300 for the warrant on 2 April 1808
B: 155	John B. Thompson to Gibson on 12 August 1808

On Sept 3, 1809, Meriwether Lewis gave McFarlane a bond in the amount of
$800.08 since he was indebted to McFarlane previously for $718.45.

William Clark Papers, June-Sept 1809, Missouri History Museum
Lewis bought a medicine chest from Dr. Saugrain on August 24, 1809 for
$30.75
Clark's notebook, lists Lewis's private debts, top of p. 6:

John G. Commegys	$331.45 ½
Benjamin Wilkinson	151.60

[bottom half of p. 6]:

Col. Aug. Chouteau	$10.00
James McFarlane	657.95
d——d by Dubville	66.50

Issac Miller in favor of 202.87 ½
whom a note Capt. with Genl C.

Judge Stewart	$500.00
Wm. Basern a note	$150.00

for the ~~dention~~ detention of my bill

Grace Lewis Papers, JNEM, Box 3, Folder 1
Conditional deed to Alexander Stuart, August 19, 1809
Lands in Portage des Sioux, $750
St. Charles County Deed Records, Book B: 137

Lewis Marks Papers, #4730, Alderman Library, University of Virginia,
Charlottesville, VA
June 20, 1810, John Marks to William Clark, Albermarle

Dear Sir: In compliance with your request to [William] Meriwether I send you the following list of recepts, Where several recpts. have been given by the same persons. I have only noticed the latest

E. S. Piere	August 22, 1809	
Peter Prim	July 18, 1809	
Nathaniel Green	August 28, 1808	
Rodolphe Tillier	March 23, 1809	Rifle also for Acct. settled
Augt. Choteau	August 23, 1809	Merchandize
Prim & Davis	July 26, 1809	
B. Prat		Merchandize bought of Mr. Ranier
A. Woolfort	July 9, 1809	
A. Woolfort		money paid on R. L. (Reuben Lewis) order
Charles Bosseron	June 28, 1808	payment for rifle
Joseph Block & Co.	September 4, 1808	Account not receipted
J. Philipson	Dec 31, 1808	per [?]

Nov 15, 1806	ML paid taxes on land on Miller's Creek in Clark County
Dec 1806	Lewis in Albermarle County
Oct 1807	Albermarle (Woodson)
Nov 15, 1807	William Gertner paid ML $40 (on demand)
July 12, 1808	ML lent Ishmael Lewis $30. James McFarlane testified to the indenture.
Oct 14, 1808	ML sent Nathan Hart money on land

TERRITORIAL SUPREME COURT RECORDS, COURT CASES (ABRIDGED)

Date	Names	Box	Fol.	Instructions
1809				
Apr 3	John B. Treat v. Perley Wallis	29	8	Habeus Corpus
Apr 3	John B. Treat v. Perley Wallis	29	9	Certiorari—Lewis
May	William Thomas v. M. Lewis	23	14	draft

Oct	Rufus Easton v.	25	2	
1810				
Oct	Wm. Thomas v.	29	7	damages (23-14)
	Edward Hempstead			
1811				
May	E. Hempstead v.	30	22	sale of land
	Admr of M. Lewis	48	2&3	
May	Alexander Stuart	31	15	damages
	v. E. Hempstead			
1812				
May	E. Hempstead	34	23	petition
	admr of M. Lewis			
May	Andrew McFarland	34	32	Summons case of damages
	v. E. Hempstead			for $700
May	McFarlane v Chouteau	34	34	Case # 32
May	Wm. Thomas v.	35	17	Summons debt
	Edward Hempstead			
1818				
March	Wm. Clark & others v. Price Arnold	45	4	Capias

General Court, May 1811, Case No. 35: March 25, 1811
Alexander Stuart v. E. Hempstead adm of M. Lewis: an action of debt to recover the amount of a bond from M. Lewis to the Plaintiff for $1500.

—Carr representing the Plaintiff

On August 19, 1809: Lewis borrowed $750 from Stuart and promised to repay on or before October 1, 1810 with interest. The court paid Stuart $1234.50

Owed Jacob Philipson, paid him through sale of land for $809.00
Box 29: Jacob Philipson, July Term, Court of Common Pleas, St. Louis, 1809

Money owed:
James McFarlane $718.00: gave this amount on. . . .
a judgment rendered in the Court of Common Pleas on August 25, 1810.

Charles Sanguinet	135.50
John Colter	375.60
William H. Thomas	263.49

August Chartran	10.00
Peter Provenchere	18.75
Fergus Morehead	48.00
Gilbert C. Russell	379.58
Falconer & Comegys	331.45
Wilkinson & Price	153.60
James McFarlane	718.00

William Thomas v Lewis: Box 29, Folder 7, 1810

Jacob Philipson	890.00
Antoine Saugrain	30.75
August Chouteau	10.00
John Colter saying	559.00 awarded $375.60

Edward Hempstead—Admn. of Lewis Estate, October 9, 1812: Box 48, Folders 2&3
War Dept on Oct 20, 1809—Mr. Walter Smith—bill would not be paid
"Mr. Lewis not being authorized to draw." (Box 29—Folder 7, Oct Term 1810)
Judgment in General Court for $263.49—original bill was $220.50

Andrew McFarland v. Edward Hempstead: Box 34, Folder 32
Walter Smith, Notary Public in War Dept.
John Smith—Chief Clerk in War Dept.
$500 to Pierre Chouteau: Box 34, Folder 34

Doctor William Thomas: Box 35, Folder 17

Missouri Fur Company: Box 45, Folder 4, Superior Court: New Series—T 11/4
March, 1818: William Clark & others v. Price Arnold
William Clark, Pierre Chouteau, August P. Chouteau, Manuel Lisa, Silvestre
Labbadie, William Morrison, Pierre Menard, Samuel Bridge, Andrew Henry, and
Reuben Lewis—heretofore trading and doing business together under the name,
firm, and style of "The Missouri Fur Company."

On April 10, 1813, Price Arnold at Fort Manuel now County of Howard—then
County of St. Charles owed $196—did not pay suing now for $500. filed Sept 8,
1817 & Dec 10, 1817.

See Territorial Supreme Court Records: Box 23, Folder 14; Box 29, Folder 7; Box 30,
Folder 22; Box 31, Folder 15; Box 34, Folder 23; Box 34, Folder 32; Box 35, Folder

17; Box 48, Folder 2 and 3. Missouri State Archives, Jefferson City, Missouri.

Record Books in the City of Saint Louis, Recorder of Deeds, under M. Lewis:

M. Lewis claims under Antoine Baccane	A: 1273
M. Lewis claims under Chalifour	B:
M. Lewis claims under Alex Clark	B: 1
M. Lewis claims under David Eshborough	B: 5
M. Lewis claims under Jacques Godfroy	B: 3
M. Lewis claims under Capt. McDonald	B: 2

MISSOURI FUR COMPANY LAWSUITS

Clark Court Cases, Civil Court Archives, 710 Washington Ave., Saint Louis, Missouri
William Clark v. Joseph Richard # 1108
November 1809, #8: to recover money due on note of hand

William Clark, agent for the Missouri Fur Company
July 13, 1809 promised to pay Clark $84.75
Silas Bent—judge; Thomas Riddick—clerk; Jerimiah Connor—sheriff
We, Joseph Richard, Pelagie, Peletier, Vive, Morin, Wm. Morin—Francois Labeau—signed in presence of Benjamin Wilkinson, James Anderson, Charles Bourguion, Francois Labeleau, plaintiffs—Missouri Fur Company

Henly Donnolson v. William Clark (St. Louis Missouri Fur Company), William Morrison, Peter Menard, Pierre Chouteau, August P. Chouteau, Manuel Lisa, Benjamin Wilkinson, Andrew Henry, Reuben Lewis, Silvestre Labbadie
Nov 1810, #48—Russell E. Hicok (Hicock) his atty., April 19, 1809
A. P. Chouteau, agent for $500 for hunting and trapping for a term of one year

William Clark (use of the United States) v. Horrace Austin
July 1812, #18; Clark sued Austin for $148
George Casner (Carmer) v. William Clark, Manuel Lisa and Sylvestre Labbadie—directors of the Missouri Fur Company, money owed—hereby commanded John Gill & Antoine Roncourte
B. Wash—atty

William Clark v. James Beatty
March 1813, #9
Dardenne Township, St. Charles, June 18, 1812; $75.30 pay Clark
John W. Honey—clerk; Marie P. Leduc—clerk

William Clark v. Jeduthan Kendall
foreclosure; March 1813, #13
Maj. Jaduthan Kendall given by Christian Wilt to Gen. William Clark for $90,
Dec 1, 1812, St. Louis
$138.57 on November 5, 1811

William Clark v. Samuel Hammond
March 1813, #12; $1300 Hammond did not pay
Easton was Hammond's atty; Carr was Clark's atty
March 1813, #14; $200

William Clark v. Charles Latour
October 1817, #63
William Clark, William Morrison, Peter Menard, Pierre Chouteau, August P.
Chouteau, Manuel Lisa, Andrew Henry, Reuben Lewis, Silvestre Labbadie, Samuel
Bridge

"Fort Recovery on the Missouri River," Sept. 18, 1811 at a place called Fort Ricaras
on the Missouri River in the County of St. Charles now County of Howard. Manuel
Lisa, Factor and Agent: $431.92 beaver fur at a rate of $1.50 per lb "in an equipment for the chase."

Thomas James v. St. Louis Missouri Fur Company
Nov 1810, Book B : cited from Bk A: 71

William Clark v. Thomas James—March 9, 1811
Bk A: 103: John G. Heath, merchant; Salt Manufacturer under the name William
Christy & Co.
Bk A: 144–5: Thomas James dropped suit (Nov 6, 1811)

Missouri Fur Company v. Thomas James
Oct 1814, #29 (On Oct 7, 1809 for $400)

Appendix E

NOTES ON WARRANTS, DRAFTS, AND BILLS OF EXCHANGE ISSUED FROM THE ACCOUNTANT'S OFFICE

This body of research, copied directly from the accountant's ledgers, spanned the years from 1796 to 1811 and skipped the expedition almost entirely.[1]

My intent was to digitally photograph the entries in order to save time instead of writing out each one. In that respect, it worked well, however in 2005 the resolution of my camera was pitiful, and some of the entries today are difficult to read. Be that as it may, when I started to photograph the pages I soon realized that I would need to transcribe what I was photographing in order to use the information for publication purposes. This appendix consists of those unedited notes, which I generated while conducting research using the primary source material.

Many of the accountant's books are missing today. While I spent three days at National Archives II, College Park, Maryland, there were other books and ledgers that I could have perused—for instance, the settlement of Governor Lewis's account after his death by orders of the comptroller of the Treasury.[2]

Abbreviation: BOE = Bill of Exchange

ENTRY 353, SET NO. 1, LEDGER B, VOLUME 2, ACCOUNTANT'S OFFICE

p. 574   Dec. 8, 1796   William Clark, Warrant 2062, bounties to soldiers $168
p. 578   Dec. 8, 1796   William Clark, expenses for recruiting $30

ENTRY 353, SET NO. 1, LEDGER C, VOLUME 3, ACCOUNTANT'S OFFICE

p. 1155	Mar. 1, 1801	Warrant 4305, $123.10
p. 1553		Seth Hunt, Mjr by Brevet & Commander of the Troops, District of Louisiana.
p. 1555		Return J. Meigs, Lt. Col. Commander, St. Charles district, Upper Louisiana.
p. 1558		John B. Scott, Col. Commander in Louisiana.
p. 15701805		Capt. John McClellan, July and Dec bounties for soldiers

ENTRY 353, SET NO. 1, LEDGER D, VOLUME 4, ACCOUNTANT'S OFFICE

p. 1771	Dec. 17, 1805	John McClellan, $16	recruiting
p. 1796	Aug. 5, 1807	Meriwether Lewis, paid $3053.31	Indian Department
p. 1796	Feb. 22, 1808	William Clark, $91.50	Indian Department
p. 1810	Aug. 5, 1807	Meriwether Lewis, $6210.06	subsistence of the Army
p. 1929	May 13, 1808	Governor Lewis, draft $300.55	
	June 21	Governor Lewis, draft $636.57	
	June 25	Governor Lewis, $319.50	
	July 12	Governor Lewis, $1380.20	
	Aug. 17	Governor Lewis, $1277.33	
	Sep. 29	Governor Lewis, $319.00	
	Dec. 1	Governor Lewis, $50.00	Nicholas Boilvin
	Feb. 21, 1809	Governor Lewis, $140.00	
	Apr. 24	Governor Lewis, $156.00	
	Sep. 7	Governor Lewis, $43.25	
	Oct. 7	Governor Lewis, $1488.76	
	Aug. 22, 1811	Governor Lewis, $908.68	
	June 1, 1812	Governor Lewis, $69.49	Indian Dept.
p. 1966	July 8, 1807	William Clark, $2000	
	July 20	William Clark, $589.66	
	July 24	William Clark, $300	
p. 1969	Apr. 30, 1807	Lt. John Newman to Constant Freeman, $136	
p. 1988	Aug. 5, 1807	Capt. M. Lewis	

ENTRY 366, VOLUME 5, JOURNAL E
FEBRUARY 14, 1797–MAY 22, 1798

[Nothing]

ENTRY 366, VOLUME 9, JOURNAL K,
JULY 31, 1803–OCTOBER 31, 1804

p. 4959	July 20, 1803	Capt. Meriwether Lewis $1000 receipt dated June 1803 for the purpose of providing suitable stores for the expedition under his direction.
p. 4962	Aug. 9, 1803	
p. 5175	Jan. 1, 1804	Meriwether Lewis paid Joseph Stretch, $136
p. 5242	March 1804	Meriwether Lewis disbursements $1357.60
p. 5332	May 21, 1804	Meriwether Lewis, for provisions $1703.53
p. 5340	May 31, 1804	Meriwether Lewis to John Hay $159.81 and to Charles Gregoire $1500.00
p. 5388		Chouteau led a deputation
p. 5394	May 3, 1804	Meriwether Lewis wrote seven BOE's for Indian deputation
p. 5441		William Simmons finding small errors with ML's accounting

ENTRY 366, VOLUME 10, JOURNAL L,
NOVEMBER 1, 1804–DECEMBER 31, 1805

p. 5799	July 29, 1805	Meriwether Lewis paying for lumber to build a boat
p. 5863	Aug. 31, 1805	Meriwether Lewis
p. 5866		Stoddard going to Fort Massac, attending a court martial from November 20, 1804 to January 14, 1805
p. 5891	May 28, 1805	Meriwether Lewis
p. 5917	July 28, 1805	Meriwether Lewis paying boatmen
p. 5921	July 28, 1805	Meriwether Lewis paying Rivet
p. 5928	Aug. 20, 1805	Meriwether Lewis Newman
p. 6002	May 20, 1804	Meriwether Lewis's payment to a soldier or worker
p. 6034	Apr. 4, 1805	Meriwether Lewis at Fort Mandan
p. 6035	Nov. 11, 1805	Stoddard's deputation

ENTRY 366, VOLUME 11, LETTERBOOK M,
JANUARY 1, 1806–DECEMBER 31, 1806

p. 6059   Jan. 18, 1806   Stoddard's deputation

p. 6069   Stoddard's dinner expenses at St. Louis

p. 6226   Apr. 30, 1806   Pierre Chouteau, warrant 9084 to James Davidson
bill of exchange dated June 7,1806, in favor of P. Dorion on account of
expenses of Indians sent to St. Louis by Capt. Lewis.

p. 6227   Apr. 30, 1806   Seth Hunt, moving back to Keene, N.H.
May, 1805 Lewis, $50.

p. 6231   May 5, 1806   Lewis Morin

p. 6240   Scott

p. 6285   May 31   Morin & Chouteau

p. 6304   June 19, 1806   Chouteau & Indian Department

p. 6305   June 20, 1806   Chouteau & Indian Department

p. 6306   June 20, 1806   Meriwether Lewis

p. 6305   June 20, 1806   Pierre Dorion for 2 boats for the use of Indians sent to
St. Louis by Capt. Lewis in May 1805, $50.

p. 6306   June 20, 1806   Meriwether Lewis, for amount of payments made by
him on account of expenditures exploring Louisiana to Henry K.
Mullin for keeping 4 Magpies, 1 Prairie Hen & 1 Prairie Dog which
were sent by Capt. Lewis to The President of the U. States, $5. to
Charles Gratiot for 6 shirts and 2 Pieces of handkerchiefs delivered to
the Sioux and Pancora Indians accompanying Capt. Lewis, $26.to
Hunt and Hankinson for tin cups, $6.

p. 6307   June 20, 1806   Meriwether Lewis, payment to J. B. Ortes for
boarding 2 interpreters, 1 month accompanying Capt. Lewis, $25.
J. B. Belen for ferriage of sundry Indians accompanying Capt. Lewis at
St. Charles, $15. Charles Hebert? for services while employed by Capt.
Lewis & his letter on file dated October 11, 1804 at Ricara Village,
$157.83.

p. 6317   June 30, 1806   Morin

p. 6451   Oct. 11, 1806   Tillier

p. 6452   Oct. 11, 1806   Tillier

p. 6507   Nov. 30, 1806   Meriwether Lewis

p. 6508   Nov. 30, 1806 for warrant No. 9465 transmitted to John Shee (Super-
intendent of Indian Affairs) at Philadelphia for so much due to the
Factory at Bellefontaine for sundry Goods furnished Capt. Lewis for a
Mandan Chief, two squaws & 3 children, $65.55

p. 6509   Nov. 30, 1806   Meriwether Lewis

p. 6511   Nov. 30, 1806   Chouteau and Soulard
p. 6575   Dec. 29, 1806   Meriwether Lewis
p. 6576   Dec. 29, 1806   Meriwether Lewis
p. 6577   Dec. 29, 1806   Meriwether Lewis
p. 6580   Dec. 31, 1806   Nicholas King

ENTRY 366, VOLUME 12, LETTERBOOK N, JANUARY 1, 1807–JANUARY 23, 1808

p. 6611   Jan. 19, 1807   Meriwether Lewis, Rene Jessomme, Indian Interpreter, $94.44,
p. 6619   Jan. 31, 1807   Meriwether Lewis, a bunch of warrants
p. 6620   Jan. 31, 1807   Meriwether Lewis, a bunch of warrants
p. 6621   Jan. 31, 1807   Meriwether Lewis, a bunch of warrants
p. 6622   Jan. 31, 1807   Meriwether Lewis, a bunch of warrants
p. 6634   Jan. 31, 1807   Jessomme & Labiche
p. 6653   Feb. 16, 1807   Chouteau and Wilkinson, interpreter & annuities
p. 6654   Feb. 16, 1807   Chouteau and Wilkinson, interpreter & annuities
p. 6671   Feb. 23, 1807   Indian Department, Louisiana Territory
p. 6672   Feb. 23, 1807   Indian Department, Louisiana Territory
p. 6675   Feb. 28, 1807   Meriwether Lewis
p. 6676   Feb. 28, 1807   Meriwether Lewis
p. 6685   Feb. 28, 1807   Lewis Morin
p. 6686   Feb. 28, 1807   Peter Provenchere
p. 6687   Feb. 28, 1807   Nicholas Boilvin
p. 6715   Mar. 17, 1807   Meriwether Lewis & Paul Chouteau
p. 6736   Mar. 31, 1807   Capt. Meriwether Lewis: for amount paid by Lt. Kimball at St. Louis for 65 yards Russia Sheeting procured on the order of said Lewis for making 2 Tents for the services of the U. States, $65.
p. 6740   Mar. 31, 1807   William Clark, compensation Louisiana Territory
p. 6789   Apr. 30, 1807   Meriwether Lewis
p. 6790   Apr. 30, 1807   Meriwether Lewis & Chouteau
p. 6791   Apr. 30, 1807   Lewis Morin
p. 6793   Apr. 30, 1807   Meriwether Lewis
p. 6890   June 30, 1807   Meriwether Lewis
p. 6964   Aug. 5, 1807   Meriwether Lewis
p. 6965   Aug. 5, 1807   Meriwether Lewis
p. 6966   Aug. 5, 1807   Meriwether Lewis
p. 6967   Aug. 5, 1807   Meriwether Lewis

p. 6968   Aug. 5, 1807   Meriwether Lewis, subsistence of the Army 1804, $228.51. For subsistence of Lt. Wm. Clarke & his black waiter for same time $228.51. Subsistence of the Army 1805, $273.75. For subsistence of Lt. Clarke & his black waiter for same time, $273.75. Subsistence of the Army 1806, $244.77. For subsistence of Lt. Wm. Clarke & his black waiter for same time $244.68. For payment made the non commissioned Officers & Privates of his Detachment for balance of Subsistence made on May 14, 1804 the time they entered the Missouri to October 1, 1806 the day they were discharged, together with an allowance for traveling home,—a proportion of the Subsistence furnished by the public having been deducted from them on settlement, $5458.63. Deduct George Drewyer an Interpreter for Subsistence, which payment is carried to the expences of the Expedition.

p. 6969   Aug. 5, 1807   Meriwether Lewis and William Clark, subsistence of the Army 1806, continued for this amount being that part of the Rations &c furnished by the Public & charged to Capt. Lewis in this account which he considered as intended for the Soldiers of the party, & which he deducted from them on settlement—the residue being for the support of Boatmen, Interpreters &c & carried to the expences of the expedition, $459.69. Subsistence of the Army from January 1 to March 2, 1807, the date of his resignation, $31.11. For Subsistence of Lt. Clarke & his black waiter from January 1 to Feb. 28, 1807, the day he resigned, $27.44.

p. 6970   Aug. 5, 1807   Meriwether Lewis

p. 6971   Aug. 5, 1807   Meriwether Lewis and Expedition to the Pacific Ocean, Indian Department 1806. For disbursements made for the purchase of Horses & other articles incident to the outfit & for the expences of conducting a party of Mandan Indians from St. Louis to Washington City between Sept. 23 and Dec. 31, 1806, $3009.31

p. 6972   Aug. 5, 1807   Meriwether Lewis

p. 6957   Aug. 31, 1807   Meriwether Lewis, warrant # 10145, balance of his acct. while employed to the P. O., $814.20

p. 6995   Aug. 31, 1807   William Clark

p. 7068   Nov. 30, 1807   Frederick Bates

Entry 366, Volume 13, Letterbook O, January 29, 1808–November 30, 1808

p. 7207   Feb. 22, 1808   Accountant's Office, Item 6577, entry 1878, William Clark, Indian Department 1807, For disbursements made by him in the Indian Department in 1807. Articles purchased—for payment made to the Mandan Chief to enable him to purchase sundry articles for his use in St. Louis, $30. Paid P. Dorion for sundry articles purchased by him for the use of the Sioux & Teton Indians on their way from their Towns to St. Louis, including purchase of a Barge & Oars & for hire of 4 men to navigate the same down the Missouri, $329. Paid Falconer and Comegys for 102 ½ of Carrotted Tobacco for the Mandan Chief, $9.23. Paid ditto for scalping knives, strouds, blankets &c for Indians & sundry articles for a command to escort the Mandans and Sioux Indians to their Nations, $220.67. Paid John McClallen & Co. for 1 double Barreled Gun for the Indians, $23. Paid V. Camis for 6 bushels meal, $3.

p. 7208   Feb. 22, 1808   William Clark, Indian Department 1807, Entry 1878.

#10—For this sum expended by Wm Clark in discharging sundry small purchases made by the Sioux chief at St. Louis, $21.

#11—Paid Wm. Christy Jr. for 12 yards Russia Sheeting &c to make bags for Mandan Indians ascending the Missouri, $12.50.

#12—Paid Ens. N. Prior (Nathaniel Pryor) to enable him to purchase provisions for Indians passing to the Upper Settlements, $10.

#13—John Lowry for a Boat Sails &c to convey the Mandan Chief to his Nation, $194.25.

#14 & 15—Paid R. Tillier U.S. Factor for Sundry articles furnished the Mandan Chief & Sioux Indians, $589.66.

#16 & 17—Paid Auguste Chouteau for sundry articles furnished the Sioux & Mandan Indians, $640.68.

#18 & 19—Paid Hunt & Hankinson for sundry articles furnished the Sioux Indians, $202.

#20—Paid Peter Chouteau for sundry articles furnished for Indians at St. Louis, $103.97.

#21—Paid B. Delauney for Russia Sheeting for bags, $40.

#22—Paid A. Chouteau for sundry articles, as Specimen of goods suitable for the Indian trade, $70.00.

p. 7209   Feb. 22, 1808   William Clark, #'s 24–27 more expenses for the voyage, $450.

p. 7210   Feb. 22, 1808   William Clark

p. 7373   May 31, 1808   Meriwether Lewis, Warrant #338 to Wm. Whann for BOE dated March 31 and drawn in favor of D. Delauney on acct. of Indian Department $300.55.

p. 7411 May 31, 1808   Joseph Lambert—Gunsmith for Osage; Aug 1 to Oct. 31, 1807; May 1 to July 31, 1807; Dec 1807.

p. 7453 June 30, 1808   Meriwether Lewis, Warrant #486 to N. Lufborough for 2 BOE's; No. 2 for $568.60 in favor of P. Dorion dated April 13, 1808 and No. 9 for $68.77 in favor of Wilkinson & Price dated May 7, 1808 on acct. of Indian Department.

p. 7456 June 30, 1808   Meriwether Lewis, BOE April 27, 1808, $319.50

p. 7478 June 30, 1808   Jeremiah Connor, Wilkinson appointed him October 1805

p. 7560 July 31, 1808   Meriwether Lewis, BOE's

p. 7584 Aug. 31, 1808   Meriwether Lewis

p. 7585 Aug. 31, 1808   Meriwether Lewis

p. 7631 Sept. 30, 1808   William Clark

p. 7633 Aug. 13, 1808   Meriwether Lewis, BOE in favor of James McFarlane, $319. This comprised two bills: one for hiring persons to explore the saltpeter caves and the other as a reward for bringing in four horses stolen from the Shawnee that belonged to residents in the territory.

Entry 366, Volume 14, LetterBook P, December 1, 1808–February 24, 1810

p. 7716 Oct. 29, 1808   Gov. Lewis, receipt $50 to Nicholas Boilvin

p. 7863 Jan. 31, 1809   William Clark

p. 7864 Jan. 31, 1809   William Clark

p. 7933 Feb. 28, 1809   Meriwether Lewis, Warrant #1231 to John Rice Jones for a BOE in favor of Edward Hempstead dated September 24, 1808 for services in presenting sundry Indians with murder, $140

p. 7996 Apr. 11, 1809   Chouteau

p. 7997 Apr. 11, 1809   Chouteau

p. 8000 Apr. 11, 1809   William Clark, Indian Agent, for warrant no. 1391 to Thomas T. Tucker for a bill of exchange in favor of Wm. Croghan dated December 24, 1808 drawn on account of the Indian Department, $200.

p. 8007 Apr. 30, 1809   William Clark

p. 8009 Apr. 30, 1809   ML and WC, Andrew and James McFarlane, 7 October and 26 August 1808.

p. 8030 May 31, 1809   William Clark

p. 8048 June 22, 1809   Entry 1929 Govr. Meriwether Lewis, a bill of exchange in favor of Andrew McFarlane dated August 26, 1808 and drawn on account of the Indian Dept., $156.

2103   William Clark, Indian Agent, bill of exchange no. 21 in favor of James McFarlane dated October 7, 1808 drawn on account of the Indian Dept., 851.42.

1032   William Clark, Indian Agent, bill of exchange in favor of Manual Leeza dated St. Louis, October 17, 1808 drawn on account of the Indian Dept., $500.

1992   Frederick Bates, acting Supt. of Indian Affairs for the following warrants standing to the debit of F. Bates now transferred to the debit of Wm. Clark:
Warrant No. 10321 dated November 9, 1807—$300
Warrant No. 10348 dated January 15, 1808—$200
Warrant No. 10313g dated March 5, 1808—$500

1994   Nicholas Boilvin for this sum of J. G. Comegys, Agent for Boilvin receipt February 18, 1809 as the balance of his account, $38

2103   Sundries Dr. to William Clarke, Indian Agent, his account closed this day.

1842   Indian Department 1806, paid William Lorimier for his services as Interpreter to the Delaware and Shawnee Indians from Sept. 1 to Dec. 31, 1806, $122

1879   Indian Department 1807, Pay of Interpreters
Paid William Lorimier Interpreter from Jany. 1 to Dec. 31, 1807, $365
Paid Baptiste Saucier Interpreter from July 1 to Sept. 30, 1807, $50
Contingency
Paid M. P. Leduc for translating sundry papers, $4
Paid John McClallen & Co. for sundry articles for an Otto chief at St. Louis, $47

p. 8051   June 22, 1809

1902   Services of George Shannon as a Hunter accompanying the escort of the Mandan chief to the Ricara Village from April 18, 1807 to November 30, 1808. Payment to Dr. Farrar for medical services to said Shannon. Indian Dept., Articles purchased: Paid sundry persons for merchandize for Indians of different nations & generally for the use of the Indian Department between February 5 & October 20, 1808 including articles furnished the Great and Little Osage Nations in conformity to a Treaty made with them by Governor Lewis at Fort Clark on November 10, 1808, $4968.78. (Governor Lewis was in St. Louis for the treaty signing on November 10, 1808)

p. 8145   Sept. 30, 1809   Meriwether Lewis, Warrant #1871 to Renner and Bussard for a BOE #30 in favor of Wm. Christy dated July 6, 1809 drawn on acct. of a detachment of the militia of Lousiana called into actual service in 1809, $43.25.

p. 8171   Oct. 31, 1809   Gov. Lewis, Warrant #1957 to P. Ferrall for a BOE dated St. Louis June 26, 1809, in favor of Wm. Christy on account of expenditures of a detachment of the militia of Louisiana in the service of the United States, $1488.76.

p. 8231   Jan. 31, 1810   Gov. Lewis, Warrant # 2265 to William Whann for a BOE # 64 in favor of Toussant Charbono dated Mandan Village, August 17, 1806 drawn for the services of said Charbono as Interpreter on the expedition to the Pacific Ocean, $136.33.

p. 8231   Jan. 31, 1810   Meriwether Lewis, late Gov., Warrant # 2280 to James McFarlane for expenditures made by him in the Indian Dept. On the orders of Lewis, $800.80.

ENTRY 366, VOLUME 15, LETTERBOOK Q, FEBRUARY 20, 1810–JANUARY 6, 1820

p. 8289   Feb. 20, 1810   F. Bates, Secretary of Louisiana

p. 8450–1 William Ewing—Sak Indians, October 1805–March 1806; employed several persons to accompany him and build an establishment (11): O'Bannon, Walker, Dickson, Tompson, Shapel, Squires, Gold, Gondaines, Richardson.

p. 8619   Aug. 22, 1811   Meriwether Lewis

p. 8620   Aug. 22, 1811   Meriwether Lewis

p. 8620   Meriwether Lewis paid J. Van Bibber and Nathan Boone for 5 days services as spy, sent to ascertain the position of a party of Osages reported to be in arms on the frontiers of Louisiana Territory, $15.

p. 8622   Aug. 22, 1811   Meriwether Lewis—Indian Department. Expenditures made in exploring the Salt Petre Caverns in Louisiana in conformity to directions from the Secy of War dated March 28, 1808—paid J. McFarlane for 5 pack horses & other articles for the above purpose, $459.54. Paid J. McDonald & others for wages while employed in searching for Salt Petre Caverns, $271. Paid Pierre Chouteau for Bricks & Lime to be used in erecting at St. Louis a small furnace calculated for the investigation of Salt & Minerals, $81. For expenses incurred in conducting the Mandan Chief to his Village—viz. paid P. Dorion Interpreter & Sub Agent, $313.70. Paid J. McFarlane for expenditures on an Expedition to the Indian Tribes on the Rivers St. Francis, & Arkansas & to the Osage Town on the Arkansas, $800. Paid

John Mullanphy for 6 Check Handkerchiefs purchased for the Mandan Chief, $2.25.

p. 8624   Aug. 22, 1811   Capt. Meriwether Lewis—Expedition to the Pacific Ocean. For the extra pay of Capt. M. Lewis, Lieut. Wm. Clark & the Interpreters, non commissioned Officers & privates of the party who accompanied him to the Pacific Ocean from the date of their engagements, to the termination of the Expedition in pursuance of an Act of Congress, March 3, 1807, entitled an Act making compensation to Messrs. Lewis & Clark & their companions, $9014.35.

Deduct amount of balance of pay due John Colter, $54.19.
Deduct amount of pay of J. B. LaPage, no receipt, $116.33
Total $8843.84.

ENTRY 366, VOLUME 16, JOURNAL NO. 1, ACCOUNTANT'S OFFICE, APR 15, 1811–MAR 16, 1812

p. 971   Mar. 7, 1809   Gov. Lewis—Indian Department
p. 1289   Mar. 5, 1812   Meriwether Lewis
p. 1290   Mar. 5, 1812   Meriwether Lewis
p. 1291   Mar. 5, 1812   Meriwether Lewis

ENTRY 374, VOLUME 5, NO. 8, 1809–1810, ACCOUNTANT'S OFFICE [*MANY VOLUMES MISSING*]

p. 4   Jan. 3, 1809   William Clark BOE #32 in favor of Jacob Phillipson, $1500
p. 21   Mar. 7, 1809   Meriwether Lewis, 2 BOE's, #21 for $1000 & #23 for $1500, Ben. Wilkinson, agent of the St. Louis Missouri Fur Company
p. 27   Apr. 11, 1809   William Clark BOE to James Morrison, $1300
p. 37   May 11, 1809   William Clark BOE in favor Falconer & Comegys, $1500
p. 38   Mar. 25, 1809   William Clark BOE in favor of Robt. Heath, $700
p. 60   June 8 1809   William Clark BOE #44 in favor of John Mason, $235
p. 61   May 10, 1809   William Clark BOE #40 in favor Falconer & Comegys, $379.20
p. 67   July 4, 1809   William Clark BOE #49 in favor Falconer & Comegys, $1318.71

p. 67   July 8, 1809   William Clark BOE #51 in favor of P. Chouteau, $285.03

p. 71   June 30, 1809   William Clark BOE #48 in favor of J. Phillipson, $750.00

p. 71   July 6, 1809   William Clark BOE #50 in favor of J. Phillipson, $1000.00

p. 78   May 29, 1809   William Clark BOE #42 in favor of Toussant Dubois, $100.00

p. 105   Oct. 1, 1809   William Clark BOE #104 in favor of J. Phillipson by P. Chout. Fils., $382.79

p. 106   Oct. 25, 1809   William Clark BOE #56 in favor of E. & J. H. Clark, Louisville, $375.00

p. 131   James McFarlane, $235.50: Being for his pay as special agent of Indian Affairs for the District of New Madrid and Arkansas, from June 1, 1809, the date he was last paid by William Clark, Indian Agent, to the September 2, 1809 inclusive the date on which his services ceased—per report on file.

ENTRY 493, BOX 3; LETTERS RECEIVED BY THE ACCOUNTANT FOR THE WAR DEPARTMENT

Oct. 23, 1807	William Clark in Louisville, Ky (C-1807)
Feb. 12, 1807	P. Chouteau, drafts totaling $1104.00
May 18, 1808	William Clark drawn on the War Dept. by F. Bates in favor of Falconer & Comegys for $200 dated October 20 and November 26, 1807. Comegys on behalf of Boilvin, October 20, 1808 recd, November 28, 1807. Boilvin left this place a few days since, going up the Mississippi.
June 10, 1808	P. Chouteau, enclosing his accounts
Nov. 10, 1808	William Clark expenditure in Indian Dept., vouchers No. 70 to 115 inclusive "please to inform me if you have received the public vouchers which I sent from this place last August. The distance and uncertainty of the mail, creates some anxiety on this subject."
Dec. 10, 1808	P. Chouteau claims against the U.S. to be $1775.35. "His excellency the Governor has no doubt informed you of my last journey among the Osage nation & of the conclusion of the treaty with which I was charged; I think it therefor useless to enter upon any detail on this subject. . . ."

ENTRY 493, BOX 1

Nov. 7, 1807	Russell Bissell
Sept. 22, 1808	Army officers lodging complaints against Simmons through Paymaster General Robert Brent's office.
Oct. 8, 1808	Meriwether Lewis had some errors in his accounts, which were rectified by "His Excellency Govr. Lewis . . ." both Lewis and Clark endorsed Boilvin to take Campbell's place.

ENTRY 496, VOLUME 1, LETTERBOOK A, APRIL 14, 1795–FEBRUARY 25, 1796

p. 1	Apr. 24, 1795	Lieut. John McClallen of Art. Engineers	Albany, New York
p. 80	June 5, 1795	Lieut. John McClallen of Art. Engineers	West Point
p. 171	Aug. 3, 1795	Lieut. John McClallen of Art. Engineers	West Point

ENTRY 496, VOLUME 1, LETTERBOOK B, FEBRUARY 27, 1796–APRIL 7, 1797

p. 408	Mar. 10, 1797	Capt. James Bruff, commanding at Niagara

ENTRY 496, VOLUME 3, LETTERBOOK C, APRIL 7, 1797–OCTOBER 31, 1797

[No Meriwether Lewis]

p. 190	Aug. 11, 1797	Wm. McFarlane, Lt. Col. of militia at Carlisle

ENTRY 496, VOLUME 4, LETTERBOOK D, NOVEMBER 1, 1797—SEPTEMBER 5, 1798

p. 8:	William McFarlane of Carlisle—Lt. Col. of militia, Aug thru Nov. 1797
p. 116	Dec. 19, 1797 Ensign Meriwether Lewis: Charlottesville, Virginia, for pay and subsistence up to the 31st for $325.38.

ENTRY 496, VOLUME 5, LETTERBOOK F, MAY 16, 1799–FEBRUARY 27, 1800

ENTRY 496, VOLUME 6, LETTERBOOK G, FEBRUARY 27, 1800–JUNE 11, 1801

ENTRY 496, VOLUME 9 OF 95, LETTERBOOK K, FEBRUARY 24, 1804–OCTOBER 3, 1805

p. 241   Ferdinand Claiborne and John Sappington
p. 347   Mar. 18, 1805   James B. Wilkinson
p. 423   Dr. Antoine Saugrain
p. 319   John Sappington

ENTRY 496, VOLUME 8, LETTERBOOK I, DECEMBER 31, 1802–FEBRUARY 24, 1804

p. 252   July 7, 1803   Amos Stoddard
p. 277   July 15, 1803   Capt. Meriwether Lewis

ENTRY 496, VOLUME 7, LETTERBOOK H, JUNE 11, 1801–DECEMBER 28, 1802

p. 89   August 27, 1801   Lt. Meriwether Lewis and Caleb Swan, Commanding officer at Charlottesville, Virginia from January 1, 1798 to April 30, 1799

ENTRY 496, VOLUME 10, LETTERBOOK L, OCTOBER 4, 1805–MAY 11, 1805

p. 90   Amos Stoddard, Indian deputation, William Christy overcharged him.
p. 381   Dec. 30, 1806   Meriwether Lewis to William Taylor, merchant—you will receive $220.36 in favor of Capt. Lewis draft in favor of John Kelly.
p. 492   Apr. 15, 1807   Meriwether Lewis in Philadelphia

ENTRY 496, VOLUME 11, LETTERBOOK M, MAY 12, 1807–JULY 22, 1808

p. 42   Governor Meriwether Lewis
p. 79   July 20, 1807   William Clark, in Jackson
p. 95   July 31, 1807   William Clark, in Jackson

ENTRY 496, VOLUME 12, LETTERBOOK N, JULY 22, 1808–MAY 5, 1808

Daniel Bissell	pp. 398 and 522
Nicholas Boilvin	pp. 53 and 179
William Clark	pp. 209 and 427 (March 17, 1809)
Pierre Chouteau	p. 475

ENTRY 496, VOLUME 13, LETTERBOOK O, JULY 5, 1809–NOVEMBER 12, 1809

[Meriwether Lewis]	[none]	
p. 60	May 16, 1809	William Simmons to William Clark
p. 61		William Clark starting with new SD card
p. 162	Feb. 22, 1809	William Clark's letter recd. June 22, 1809
p. 354	July 22, 1809	William Clark's letter recd. Sept. 2, 1809

ENTRY 496, VOLUME 14, LETTERBOOK P, NOVEMBER 8, 1809–JULY 24, 1810

[Meriwether Lewis]	[none]	
[William Clark]	[none]	
p. 286	March 19, 1810	Simmons writing a personable letter to Chouteau and Gen. William Clark

ENTRY 57, VOLUME 1, 1801–1842, 1ST COMPTROLLER'S OFFICE

[Four handwritten letters written between 1801–1809, none present]

ENTRY 57, VOLUME 4, 1801–1833, ACCOUNTANT

John Brahan	October 9, 1811
Gabriel Duvall	March 7 and November 23, 1805, Sept. 29 and Oct 6, 1805
William Ewing	October 9, 1811
Albert Gallatin	October 6, 1806
Moses Hooke	November 28, 1810
Territory of Louisiana	January 19, 1811
Benjamin Price	October 6, 1806

ENTRY 515, VOLUME 1, REPORT BOOK A,
APRIL 1795–JULY 1797

p. 323   Dec. 5, 1796   Ensign Meriwether Lewis

ENTRY 515, VOLUME 2, REPORT BOOK B,
JULY 1797–MAY 1798

p. 29   Sept. 30, 1797   John McClallen, stationed at Fort Niagara, Bruff commander

p. 71   Dec. 19, 1797   Ensign Meriw. Lewis paying for his subsistence from Nov. 1 to Nov. 30, 1797.

p. 102   Feb. 14, 1798   John McClallen, Quartermaster

p. 179   June 6, 1798   John McClallen stationed at Governor's Island, New York

p. 232   Sept. 10, 1798   Paid. Owed Lewis from Dec 1 to July 31, 1798. Edward Carrington to pay him at Richmond.

p. 247   Oct. 16, 1798   John McClallen stationed at Governor's Island, New York

Nov. 13, 1798   John McClallen stationed at Governor's Island, New York

Feb. 16, 1799   John McClallen stationed at Governor's Island, New York

p. 355   Mar. 4, 1799   John McClallen stationed at Fort Jay

p. 363   Mar. 15, 1799   Meriwether Lewis

p. 387   July 24, 1798   John McClallen promoted Capt.

ENTRY 515, VOLUME 3, REPORT BOOK C,
MAY 1799–DECEMBER 1801

p. 10   May 16, 1799   Lt. Meriwether Lewis, transmittal to Edward Carrington

p. 13   May 16, 1799   stationed at Charlottesville, Virginia, under the command of Meriwether Lewis, Lieut. in the 1st Reg of Infantry.

p. 44   June 19, 1799   detachment of the 1st Reg. of Infantry stationed at Camp near Staunton, Virginia under the command of Capt. Alexander Gibson and to pay Lt. M. Lewis.

p. 204   May 21, 1800   William McFarlane, Lt. Col. of militia, in the regiment of Cumberland County militia ordered into service in the year 1794 to suppress an insurrection in the western counties of Pennsylvania.

ENTRY 515, VOLUME 4, REPORT BOOK D, JANUARY 1802–NOVEMBER 1805

p. 60   Apr. 22, 1802   Lewis to pay Dr. Alexander Humphrey's of Staunton, Virginia, $105 for supplies of barracks.

p. 515   Sept. 20, 1805   deputation sent by Lewis

ENTRY 515, VOLUME 5, REPORT BOOK E, NOVEMBER 1805–FEBRUARY 1809

p. 6   Dec. 6, 1805   Capt. John McClallen at Fort McHenry

p. 25   Jan. 25, 1806   Nicholas King

p. 25   Meriwether Lewis

p. 125   Meriwether Lewis

p. 137   Jan. 3, 1807   Frederick Bates

p. 142   Meriwether Lewis

p. 146   Meriwether Lewis

p. 150   Meriwether Lewis

p. 167   Paul Loise

p. 169   Feb. 26, 1809   Peter Provenchere

p. 244   Meriwether Lewis

ENTRY 515, VOLUME 5, REPORT BOOK G, 1811–1813

p. 172   March 4, 1812   Due to the estate of Meriwether Lewis for the conveyance of the Mandan Chief and his family to his village on the Missouri River—including the damages, interest and cost of protest of three bills of exchange drawn by him on this Department in May 1809, for said purposes, which were protested for non-payment now admitted in conformity to the decision of the Secy. of War which sum is to be transmitted by the Treasurer of the United States to Edward Hempstead, administrator, $636.25.[3]

Appendix F

MERIWETHER LEWIS'S ACCOUNT BOOK, 1807–1809

Meriwether Lewis's account book is divided into three sections. The first section details general debts, the second section includes medicinal recipes, and the third section lists draughts (drafts). In order to differentiate between the first section and the last two, Lewis used a simple technique of flipping the book over and turning it around. The debt section is thirty pages, the medicinal section is five pages, and the draft section numbers thirty-three pages.

Some of the line items are not dated by year or day but are chronologically listed. There are line items that are crossed out, and it appears that they were crossed out as Lewis paid them.

The account book is small, about four by five inches, and I inserted page numbers within brackets. The length of the description of the line items will not follow the margins of the book. Wherever possible, Lewis's writing is copied verbatim. The date and the number of a draft on some line items were reversed for uniformity.

FIRST SECTION—GENERAL DEBTS

[page 1]
To this sum paid John Ordway from his journal which is to be charged to the experiences of my journal, $150.
To this amount paid for paper to print prospectus of my voyage &c to be charged as above, $20.
To this amount paid Mr. Varnum for distributing prospectus to the Post Masters to be charged as above, $10.
Inclosed to William Woods this sum by Majr. Randolph which was to pay the balance of Acct to Clarkson & to purchase a horse for my mother, $100.

[page 2]
To this amount paid St. Memin for likeness of the Indians &c necessary to my publication to be charged to the expences of said work, $83.50.
To expences from the 6th to the 9th of Sept 1807 from Washington to Baltimore, $10.

April 14, 1807   arrived in Philadelphia
April 18   pd. John Ordway $150 agreeable to contract of his journal
18   pd. Dorion for gratuity allowed by Congress, $266.58

[page 3]
May 3rd   pd. Mr. Hessler $100 celestial observations charged to the expense of my work
10   gave Pursh, the botanist, preparing drawing & specimen of plants for my work
9th   Henry Baldwin for the uce of his ward, Mr. Bates
13   gave this sum to Amy a mulatto woman, nurse of Mrs. Madison

[page 4]
Gave Mrs. Wood the following sum of money
April 20 a dozen of porter, $5 to Mrs. Wood
May 5   1 dozes of ale, $10
8th   to cash lent her $40
13   received money from Mr. Baldwin on order of Mjr. Craig of Pittsburgh, $134.22
          balanced due me by Mr. Baldwin $15.78

[page 5]
May 13   money paid to Mr. Varnum distributing prospectus
18   received money from Mr. McKennan for Baldwin $15.78
21   sent sum for a doz of ale, went pd for 2 doz, $3
29   paid Mrs Wood for board &c, $14 more than was due, $50

[page 6]
May 20   purchased pistols of Mr. Boot, $87
26   paid Pursh for drawing of plants, $40

[page 7]
June 21   Sent Mrs. Wood on account of board, $20
July 8   paid Mrs. Wood for board, $28.58 in full

15   paid Mr. Barrellet for drawing the Falls of Missouri, $40
Oct 8   drew money from salary
20   satisfied a debt in Richmond threw Mr. Wirt (3 bills satisfied)

[page 8]
          [explanation of bills]

[page 9]
25   Reuben Lewis paid Maupin—3 entries
Dec 26, 1806   expences to Georgia
Oct 28   paid Mr. Wood for services as steward

[page 10]
27   gave draft to Anderson—4 entries

[page 11]
Nov 23   paid to John Garrison in presence of John Marks
Dec 4   drew draft for salary as governor

[page 12]
14   draught in favor of Wm. King, $188
Feb 15,   draught in favor of Thomas Prather, $150
1808

[page 13]
17   Louisville—pd. John Clark $20.67—a case of wine for Wm Clark
March 13 St. Louis—Hunt & Hankinson, $200
April 2   drew in favor of John Higbee, $150

[page 14]
24   draught Jacob Phillipson, $400, part of his salary
29   drew one draft No. 10 on the Bank of the United States in favor of
          Joseph Charless for the sum of $100 in full of my quarter salary note
          the same inclosed (said draught together with 95 dol. in bank bills
          and an order on Genl Clark) to Mr. Fitzhugh to be paid to Mr. Char-
          less as a loan for establishing a paper at this place, the same being the
          amount subscribed by myself and others on 225 dollars to said Char-
          less for that purpose.

[page 15]
Dec. 20,   examined & measured a natural bridge near a Mr.
1807   Pain's on Stock Creek a northern branch of Clinch.

[page 16] [continuation of measurements]

[page 17] [continuation of measurements]

[page 18]
Sept 30,   drew a draft for Andrew McFarlane, $500, quarter salary
1808
April 13, drew a draft for Jacob Phillipson, $500
1809

[page 19]
  April 2,   ~~lent Mrs. Pike money in a letter enclosed by Dr. Sograin~~
    1808   [Saugrain]
      15   ~~sum for Mr. Jarrott, $17~~
      30   ~~Joseph Charless, per subscription, $20~~
          ~~Col. Chouteau, $25~~
          ~~M. Ledue, $6~~

[page 20]
  May 6   ~~sum pd. by me for shot for the Mandan Chief, $1.50~~
    2   ~~P. Chouteau lent me $10~~

[page 21]
   17   ~~borrowed the sum of $20 of Mr. F. Bates~~
       ~~(November 5, 1808)~~
   17   ~~P. Chouteau lent me $10~~
   19   ~~Peter Chouteau paid for a tract of land, $128, payable July 19~~
   25   ~~borrowed of Peter Chouteau, $10~~
   26   ~~land transaction, note of demand to Hyacinte St. Cyr, $200~~
   26   ~~land transaction, note of demand to Francis Dunegant, $25~~
   28   ~~borrowed this sum of P. Chouteau, $95~~
   28   drew a draft for $600 on Alexander Steward of Richmond, Virginia
  June 7   paid Chouteau $1600 for a tract of land on the Missouri
    7   Ludwell Bacon $50 via Steward
   18   borrowed money from Mr. McFarlane to buy Musick's land, $100
       and still indebted to Musick $70

[page 22]

July 12	drew draft on Steward for $225 land purchased
August 3	~~Peter Chouteau, expences for chartering a masonic lodge at St. Louis, $20~~
30	~~to be repaid by the lodge (settled with Chouteau but not with the lodge)~~

[page 23]

~~Borrowed this sum of Genl. Clark which I lent to Reubin Lewis, $6~~

30	~~Gave York this sum to bear his expences when he went in search of a negroe man of Genl. Clark's in St. Charles dist~~, $4
July	~~Paid this sum for the rent of the house in which Genl. Clark resides, $125~~
Sept 24, 1808	Purchased of Comegys for Reubin Lewis for certain merchandize for which Said Reubin is accountable this amount as per bill, $62.25

[page 24]

1808

Oct 7th	~~borrowed of Genl Clark this sum, $50~~
28th	then obtained from Genl. Clark his order for the amount on John Clark of Louisville Ky. which is to be paid to Issac Miller for that sum received by me on acct of Said Miller from Nicholas Boilvin for two barrels of whisky of 33 Gls each belonging to said Miller, $49.50

[page 25]

1808

Dec 27th	borrowed of Genl. Clark this sum which was paid to Solomon on act. of G. Dreuilliard [Drewyer or Drouillard] who has undertaken to arrest Doct. Dunlop, $20
Jany 29th	Received of Mr. John Sappington Snr. this sum of nine dollars on account of certain mairs put by him to a horse of Reubin Lewis's which, I have promised to account for to the said R Lewis.

[page 26]

Jny 31st	Received of Mr. Andrew Kincade by the hand of his son this sum on account of certain mares which were put to the hors . . . which

was kept by said Kincade for Reubin Lewis on shares—which sum I am to account for to Said R. Lewis, $31

1809

April 6th   Gave Swain this sum to purchase some tools for the side of my plantation near St. Louis, a handsaw . . . $4

[page 27]
1809

Apl. 11th wain the Overseer, do. To this sum given him to purchase a cowbell, $1.25

Do. to this sum lent Hugh Hall which was to be by promise of said hall returned to me on the same evening, $2

Nov. 20, 1808   Then drew a draught No. 12 for this amount in favor of Sydall Manley the bank of the U'States the same being for my quarter salary ending the 31st December 1808, $500
March 10th   3 & 4 in favor of the same for the same
July 8, 1809   5 & 6 in favor of K [ink stain] same for the same

[page 28]
1809
    Jue 15th   ~~On settlement with Mr. Peter Chouteau this day he falls on my debt—$450~~
    Isaac Miller's account with me for 14 Barrels of whiskey which he sent to St. Louis for sale
    Paid him through John Clark for 2 barrels of 33 Gls. each—$49.50
    Paid by Genl. Clark to him for 4 Brls. by Boilvin —$102
    I owe him for 5 bls— $123.75
    I have settled 3 bls with No. 14 Mr. Webster, $79.12 ½
    owe Mr. W. N., $202.87 ½
    23rd .1809 Then drew a draught in favor of Falconer & Comegys for this sum on bank of US in part of my sallary ending the 30th June 1809, $344.11

[page 29]
1809

    May 22nd   Reubin Lewis—do.

                This sum paid George Boume as pr. his draught and said
                Boume's receipt.—$300

    July 14th   No. 15 then drew draft for this sum being the balance due by the
                bank of the UStates for my salary ending the 31st of June 1809 in
                favor of Jacob Phillipson —$421 & $86

[page 30]
1809

    July 17th   Judge Alext. Stewart [Stuart]—do.

                To this sum paid you in cash, $100

    24th   To this sum is a duebill on Webster, $35
                [description is crossed out and illegible] ~~purpose of producing~~
                ~~lands~~

                John Pernia—do.

                To cash paid Peter Prim [Primm] the taylor for you, $10

Second Section

[1808–1809, flip side of account book]

[page 1]

    Reciept for the best stomachic

    1/4 oz of cloves

    1/4 oz of Columbo, 1 oz Peruvian bark, 1 quart of port wine—the ingredients
to be well pounded and shook when taken—a wine glass twise or twise a day may
be taken with good effect, it is an excellent restorative

[page 2]

Recipe for making wine

[page 3]

Method of treating bilious fever when unattented by Typhus or nervous symptoms—Let the patient take a strong puke of tartar emetic: the second day after a purge of Calomel and Jallop, which should be repeated after two days more, to be taken in the morning, and no cold water to be used that day.—a pill of opium and tartar to be taken every night and after the purgatives. ten grains of Rhubard and 20 grains of Barks should be repeated every morning and at 12 O'clock.

Emetic—4 grs Tartar to be disolved in 3 Table spoonfuls of water warm one spoonful to be taken every five minutes to procure at least five pukes or motions

[page 4]

pills of Opium & tartar

9 grains of tartar emetic, 12 grs of opium made into 18 pills—one every night at bed time

doze of Calomel and Jallap

6 grs of Calomel and 15 of Jallop

antibilious pills

20 grs. of vitriolated tartar

& 40 of Jallop made into 12 pills

3 to be taken at night, to which if they do not operate by morning two others are to be taken to facilitate their operation

[page 5]

alloe Pill

the size of an English pea ~~made up with molasses and flour~~ to be given at night at bedtime

[page 6]

1808

List of draughts on the War dept. for the expences incurred in the indian department of Louisiana—

May 7th 1808

~~No. 7 in favor of George Shannon for wages and expences in hospital,~~ $[illegible]

No. 1. March 13th D. Delauny for Indian supplies, $300.55

No. 2 Apl. 13th 1808 in favor of Peter Dorion for expenditurs in the indian dept., 568.60

No. 3. April the 15th do. for do., 179.66 2/3

do.

No. 4 do. do. for do.—313.70

Mr. Dorion is paid for his monthly wages by Genl. Clark to the 30th of September 1807 his pay is $.50 per day—

[page 7]

Aprl 25th 1808 No. 5 in favor of Renie Jussome or order for his wages as interpreter of the Mandan language to 30th of Apl. 1808 inclusive, $213

27th No. 6 in favor of Peter Dorion or order for his wages as Sub-Agent of the Missouri to the 30th Apl. 1808 inclusive—$319.50

May 1st No. 7 in favor of Nicholas Boilvin or order for his wages as Indian Agents to the 30th of April 1808 inclusive—$275

No. 8 in favor of do. do. for the wages of three men under his direction to now paid to the 30th of April 1808 incl., $220

[page 8]

May 7th	No. 9 in favor Wilkinson & Price supplies to Shannon while in the hospital, $68.27
12th	No. 10 in favor of Peter Dorion for expenditurs in the indian dept., $184
17th	No. 11 in favor of Baptist Dorion for transporting certain Soos, $75
18th	No. 12 in favor John Riffle for this sum on account of a horse which the Sacs killed the same to be deducted from the Sac annuity, $50

[page 9]

1808

| May 20th | No. 13 in favor of James Reid or order for this sum it being the pay of Baptiste Sausier [Saucier]—interpreter of the Arkansas from the 1st of Sept. 1806 to June 30th 1807 and from October the 1st to March 31st, 1808. at $200 pr. annum. |
| 28th | then drew a draught No. 1 on the Secretary of State for this sum in favor of P. Provenchere for his services in translating and transcribing certain laws of this U'States territory and a proclamation |

[page 10]

1808

~~June 24~~

~~No. 14 then drew a draft for this sum on the department of war in favor of Wilkinson & Price being the amount of two orders given by Lieut. Pike to certain persons for the hire of Pack horses while in his rout to Mexico in 1806.—$29~~

~~No. 15 in favor of the same for this sum it being an account of articles delivered the Sacs by Robert Dixon by order of Peter Dorion—$106.50~~

[page 11]
1808
June 21st

~~No. 16 Then drew on the war department for this sum in favor of Wilkinson & Price for this sum for supplies made to the Ioways and Sacs by Mesrs. Crawford and Dixson by order of N. Boilvin for &284.33 1/3 cents~~

June 24th No. 14 then drew a draught in favor of Wilkinson and Price on the department of war for this sum for sundry expenditurs in the indian department $419.83 1/3

[page 12]
July 1st 1808
No. 15   Then drew a bill of exchange for this sum in favor of James McFarlane on the Secretary of War—for the outfit of exploring salt peter caves—$459.54

July 22nd No. 2 in favor of Joseph Charless or order on the Secretary of State—it being an advance to said Charless for furnishing paper and publishing the laws of the territory—250 copies in English & 100 in French—$500

[page 13]
August 13th 1808
Then drew on the Secretary of War in favor of James McFarlane order for this sum the same being the wages of the persons employed in exploring saltpeter caves—$271

Also included in this same draught this sum as a reward to the Shawnies for delivering four horses taken by them in battle from the Osage Indians, which said horses belonged to the citizens of this territory. $48

total draught $319

[page 14]

August 19th 1808

~~Then received of Nicholas Boilvin for Isaac Miller for two barrels of whiskey~~
~~of 33 gals each at 75-6 pr. gln, the above discharged by Genl. Clark by way of order~~
~~on John Clark his nephew, $49.50~~

August 26th

No. 17 then drew a draught in favor of Andrew McFarlane for this sum it
being the pay of Morris Blondeau as sub Agent from the 19th of July to the 30th
October 1808 inclusive $156

[page 15]

September 24th 1808

No. 18 Then drew a draught for this amount in favor of Edward Hempstead
for his services as deputy Attorney Genl. for the prosecuting certain inditements
against Ioways & Saucs for murder, $140

November 5th then borrowed of Genl. Clark this sum, $100

November 5th Paid Music (Musick) in full for lands purchased from him and
other accounts

[page 16]

November 1808

9th Then borrowed of Genl. Clark this sum to pay Doctor Farrar for his attendance on my servant Pernia, an account which I conceive exorbitant, but which my
situation in life compels me to pay—$49

Borrowed also from Genl. Clark, $1   Amount $50

15th Borrowed of Genl. Clark this sum of which I paid Mipho 37 dof [doz?]
for dish &c, $40

[page 17]

Dec. 20th To this sum borrowed of Genl. Clark to ~~pay~~ loan to the [Masonic]
Lodge of this place. $15

Dec. 28th No. 3 Then drew a draught on the Secty of State for this sum in
favor of Francis V. Bouis for transcribing certain laws of the territory, $18

"No. 4 Then drew a draught for this amount on the Secty of State in favor of
Joseph Charless for printing certain laws of the territory necessary for immediate
distribution, $88.75

[page 18]
1809
Jany 1st Paid Pernia, $15
1808
Dec
31st U'States—Cnt.
received this sum for one public horse sold at public sale, $32
USt.   do
To Bell ringer, $3
26th   To paid for hunting horses of public, $5
25th   To paid for hire of a horse for one man to hunt public horses this sum, $4.50
~~All other sales amounts of sales in notes and money lodged with Genl Clark I also of $55 dols received for those public horses~~.
Paid at sundry times for care for public horses, $19.75

[page 19]
1809   Genl. Clark Cnt.
Jany 6   By this sum paid Philipson for me, $70
16th   Then rented the three small farms which I purchased of Mr. P. Chouteau to Alexander Eastwood until the 25th of December 1809. conditions—Eastwood to give me 20 barrels of corn on the 1st of November 1809 or to secure the same if I was not ready to receive it and to make up the fences of the two small farms nine logs high and lock them also that of the large or center farm seven logs high staked and ridered.—he is to have the privilege of the shuger [sugar maple] orchard, but is not to tap the trees but with an augur and not to bore

[page 20]
more than two holes in a tree in this same season—to cut cole [coal] wood and timber necessary for the shops of Blacksmith and waggonmaker and to clean what land he may think proper in the river bottom provided this same be adjoining the lower part of the center farm &c &c—this instrument signed in the hand of Thomas Musick near Florissant.
Jany 12th To paid this sum to Noele Mograin [Noel Mongrain, Indian interpreter] it being his travling expenses when hunting public horses, $1.10
Apr. 3rd Paid ferriage for express

[page 21]
1809
   January 25th
   Borrowed of Genl. Clark this sum at a card party in my room, $1
   Febr. 6th   No. 5 Then drew a draught on the Secty of State in favor of P.
               Provenchere for that sum for transcribing certain laws of the terri-
               tory, $18.70
   12th paid this sum at sundry times as express hire on public account, $6
   Peter Chouteau   do.
   To the purchases of public horses, $55

[page 22]
   U'States   Cnt.
   To this amount received of Peter Chouteau for one public horse, $55
   6th March Paid Pernia eight dollars on his own account, $8
   7th ~~Paid Joseph Charles for printing genl. orders to be charged to the publick,~~
~~$8~~
March
   7th No's. 19. 20. 21. 22. 23 & 24 were drawn in favor of Benjamin Wilkinson
as the agent of the Missouri fur company, on the War department for this sum the
bills were in the following proportions—$7000

[page 23]
No. 19	$1,000
No. 20	$1,500
No. 21	$1,000
No. 22	$1,000
No. 23	$1,500
No. 24	$1,000
amounting to	$7,000

April 19th 1809 Then received of James McFarlane this sum which he recieved of
Mr. Hays of Cahokia and receipted for in my own name; the same being the sum
which I expended in an attempt to apprehend Dunlop.—this order of Govr. Harrison on this Treasur of In. T. [Indiana Territory]

[page 24]
was for 90 dollars only though the full amount of the sum paid is due me from the
territory yet I hold myself responsible to Mr. Hays for the fifty dollars should the
account not be allowed in full by the I. Territory, $140

May 1st 1809 No. 25 Then drew a draught for this amount in favor of Dr. William Thomas on the War Department which he furnished for the expedition destined to conduct the Mandan Chief and family to his village, $220.50

[page 25]

Reubin Lewis   do
~~To Cash lent~~————————————~~$30~~
~~To do——— do~~————————————~~$10~~
~~To do by order on Philipson——$193.50~~
~~May 10th To paid Hatter for you——$10~~
~~US do~~

May 2nd   Paid Bell ringer this sum for giving notice for the sale of public horse, $1

May 5th   Then drew a draught No. 6 on the Secretary of State in favor of Joseph Charless for printing the laws of the

[page 26]

Territory genl. orders blanks for returns of Militia &c &c, $822

1809

May 13th No. 26 Then drew a draught in favor of P. Chouteau on the Secretary of War for this amount it being in part for ammunition furnished the Mandan Expedition to be given in case of necessity to the Auxillaries should it become necessary to Cut off the Aricares, $500

May 15th 1809 By settlement with Reubin Lewis this day he is indebted to me this Sum, $260

[page 27]

May 15th then drew draught (No. 27) for the same purposes as that of (No. 26) for $440

May 18th Then recieved this sum from James McFarlane which is in part of 31 dollars paid for wintering recovering one of his horses, $20.75

June 16th No. 28 Then drew a draught on the department of war for 81 dollars in favour of Peter Chouteau for Brick and lime to build a furnace to make experiment

[page 28]

on salt peter earth and other minerals of the country, $81

June 26th No. 29 Then drew a draught for this sum on the War department in favor of William Christy Q.M. Genl. for furniture made by him in his depart for the Use of the troops called into public service for the defence of the territory against the Indians, $1488.76

July 6th No. 30 The same for the same, $43.25

[page 29]
1809

July 17th William Christy—do.

~~To this sum paid R. Webster for a horse purchased for the public, which sum was allowed you in the settlement of your public account, $40~~

Augt. 20 To your duebill on settlement left with Genl. Clark, $81

—except the sum of eighty five dollars Genl. Clark has all the bonds notes on money arrising from the sales of public horses sold at St. Louis.

[page 30]
August 21st

final settlement made this day between Genl. Clark and myself he paid me this sum, $53

Enquire of Brown at Orleans for the bones of the Mamoth sent him by Genl. Clark for the president of the U'States.

[page 31]
1809 August 22nd St. Louis

A list of private debts due

To John G. Comegys, $331.45 ½

To Benjamin Wilkinson, $151.60

To Col. August Chouteau, $10

~~To James McFarlane, $657.95~~

~~To do by Dubill, $60.50~~

[Lewis tallies the amounts at $728.45]

[Lewis subtracts $10]

To Issac Miller for which a note is left with Genl. Clark, $202.87 ½

Settled with Chouteau by 4,355 [acres]

returning lands—next is redeem and if the money is paid by May

~~Ludwell Bacon payable on demand given for disappointment as a sum of money paid 7th June 1808 to be first paid. $150~~

[page 32]

I owe John Colter this sum having recieved the sum for him at the War office as the gratuity allowed by thus government of the U'States for his services on a tour to the Pacific Ocean, $320

August 24th 1807

John Coltr—Do.

To paid your order in favor of Charles Sanganet [Sanguinette], $125

I have agreed to pay Mr. L. Bacon the sum of one hundred dollars next spring or to his order in full for the inconvenience sustained by him in not recieving the amount of a note given him for 450 dollars agreeable to contract, $100

[page 33]

Settle with McFarlane when I meet him.

Gave Judge Stewart (Stuart) a deed for 708 acres of land at portage DeSous [Portage des Sioux]—condition that if I return him $750 with interest thereon before the 10th of October 1810 then the deed to be voyd.

Directed my letters to be returned to the City of Washington—

[page torn out]

[page 34]

deliver a receipt from Mr. McFarlane to Capt. Russell at Chickasaw Bluffs.

Sept. 1st 1809

Gave James McFarlane my note payable on demand for $718.44.—which is in full of all our private transactions—

Sept. 3rd

gave James McFarlane my bond for $800.08 cts for his vouchers & account for expences on a trip to the St. Francis [Francois River] and the Osage Village of Arkansas when bringing in the chiefs of that band to sign the treaty.—

[page 35]

1809

Sept. 17th

Then inclosed my land warrant for 1600 acres to Bomby [Thomas Bolling] Robertson of New Orleans to be disposed off for two dollars per acre or more if it can be obtained and the money ~~sent~~ deposited in the branch of the New Orleans or the City of Washington subject to my order or that of William D. Meriwether for the benefit of my creditors.—M. Lewis

[page 36]
September 27th

Then borrowed of Capt. Gilbert C. Russell a check on the Branch Bank of New Orleans for this sum, for which I gave him my note, $99.58

Do to the same for two horses, $280

left the trunk of Capt. House with Capt. Russell to be sent to the care of Mr. Brown of Orleans Collector—

[page 37]
[continued] to be by him forwarded to McDonald and Ridgely of Baltimore as addressed.

Also left with Capt. Russell two trunks one containing papers or a case for liquor and a package of blankets sheets and coverlid to be sent to William Clarr [Clark] of St. Louis for me—unless I shall otherwise direct.

[page 38]
February 28, 1810

~~tten~~ then taken by me from this Book 2 papers being statements of the situation of John Marks, land in Ohio, on one of which there is a recpt. by the Auditor to Reuben Lewis for $17.295 for which the heirs of John Marks are indebted to Reuben Lewis.—John H. Marks

taken also the will of Brother M. Lewis which I shall have proved at March Court.—J. H. Marks

Appendix G

GEORGE HUXTABLE'S INTERPRETATION OF MERIWETHER LEWIS'S SEXTANT CALCULATIONS

from "The Homeward Bound Journey"

On October 4, 2010, George Huxtable, who lives in the United Kingdom, sent an e-mail to the Missouri State Archives in Jefferson City, Missouri, inquiring about specialized and arcane information concerning latitude and longitude in 1803–1804, the time period of the Lewis and Clark Expedition. He wrote:

> In the course of some research into Lewis and Clark's wintering at Fort Dubois, 1803–4. I'm interested in the following question—
>
> At or about the time of the handover to the US, in March 1804, was there any knowledge, in St. Louis, of the town's geographical position, latitude and longitude, particularly longitude?
>
> It might possibly have been established by a military surveyor attached to the expeditionary force when St. Louis was founded 30 years earlier. After all, the French were the world experts, at that time, in such land-survey, with longitude based primarily on timed observations of satellites of Jupiter.
>
> I wonder if there might have been, in the town prior to 1804, a resident savant, amateur astronomer, surveyor, geographer, clockmaker, schoolteacher, who might have taken an interest in such observations (French or Spanish). Or whether the US sent an official who was capable of delineating the position of the new Gateway, as part of the junketings associated with Three Flags Day.
>
> And if the answer isn't known, what's the earliest date for the position of St. Louis to be recorded? I am aware that Lewis and Clark themselves noted coordinates for Fort Dubois, but I am trying to discover whether they might have been assisted in this by the prior knowledge of the St. Louis citizenry.

A few days later, Huxtable's e-mail was forwarded to me, and during our correspondence over the next few months, I gave him the information he sought. To return the favor, he provided the "back office" information on Lewis's trip to the Cumberland Gap explained in chapter 5 of this book.

Lewis had used several instruments at the Cumberland Gap that were utterly foreign to me, but when I mentioned them to Huxtable, he easily expounded on what they were. This led to a larger discussion, which is detailed below. As an expert on early survey techniques, Huxtable observed that

> throughout the expedition, Lewis & Clark made a consistent mistake in correcting for the index error of their sextant or octant when measuring reflected altitudes in an artificial horizon. Instead of correcting the sextant reading for index error, and then halving to allow for the doubled angle due to reflection, as they should have, they would halve the reading and then correct it for index error. The result was that measured altitudes were always in error by half of the index error of the instrument. When the sextant was used, for which the measured correction was normally 8' 45" (to be subtracted), the erroneous procedure caused the deduced altitude to be too low by 4' 22".
>
> When used to obtain a latitude from a meridian altitude, that latitude would always be too high by a corresponding amount, 4' 22". The effects of this problem became much more serious when the sun's altitude exceeded 60°, as it did at summer noons. In that case their octant, in back-observation mode, had to be used, and in this mode the index correction was as great as 2° 11' 40" (to be added). As a result, altitudes calculated in this erroneous way from an observation would be too high by 1° 05' 50", and latitudes derived from such a meridian altitude would be too low by nearly that same amount.

Huxtable also provided much information about reading a sextant, which he said

> is capable of looking in two directions at once, and precisely measuring the angle between the two views. For measuring latitudes at sea, the sun appears in view in one mirror, and the sea-horizon in the other. The sextant itself does not need to be precisely aligned with anything though its frame needs to be kept in a vertical plane. The altitude, the angle by which the sun is above the horizon, reaches a maximum near noon, and that maximum value is noted, before the sun starts to fall again. All that's needed is for both the sun and the horizon to be seen, clearly and sharply, for a few minutes around noon. No timepiece is required.
>
> The land-navigator has no sea-horizon to measure up from, so his procedure has to be different. Instead, he measures the angle between the sun up in the sky, and the sun's reflection seen looking down into the horizontal surface of a bowl of liquid; which was often simply water, but which could be mercury. The angle between those two views of the sun is exactly twice the sun's altitude, so the angle, as measured, has to be halved. This works well, as long as the surface can be

shielded from being ruffled by wind. However, the standard mariner's sextant could measure only up to an angle of 120°, which meant that it could not tackle noon sun altitudes greater than 60°; which they were, over the months of high summer, throughout the United States. In that case, a different instrument, or another technique, was called for.

In either case, there are important corrections to be made to the sun's measured altitude, and it was these corrections that Lewis and Clark tended to get wrong, rather than the basic measurement of angle. The largest correction allowed for the sun's slowly changing declination as it moved north of the equator in northern summer and south in northern winter, which was readily available from an almanac.

After those corrections had all been made, an experienced observer, with a good instrument, could reliably determine land-latitudes within rather better than a minute of arc, or within about one land-mile of the true position.

The sextant was the instrument favoured by travelers as, being hand-held, it needed no elaborate setting-up, so latitude could be determined at a short pause in a journey, around noon. Surveyors, on the other hand, were under less time pressure and sought greater accuracy, so in preference to a sextant they would employ a theodolite, or a zenith sector, and might well use observations of stars rather than the sun. But these instruments would call for a firm base, such as the stump of a felled tree, and needed precise orientation and levelling beforehand.

Huxtable gave a detailed explanation for Lewis's readings using what Lewis called Ellicott's "much approved Zenith Sector." Lewis had to take a crash course in surveying and taking latitude and longitude measurements using celestial bodies in order to prepare for the expedition in 1803. Huxtable explained that Lewis's instruction "was aimed at sea-navigation, not the special aspects of navigating on land. But nobody should be sent off with only a few weeks of instruction under his belt, without some expert on hand to turn to." Huxtable continued:

I understand that Ellicott had two zenith sectors made for him by David Rittenhouse, the larger of which could be transported only by water. A zenith sector, which measures the altitudes of stars that lie nearly overhead, is indeed a very precise instrument for determining latitude. Ellicott's observation of the position of the Ohio-Mississippi junction may have taken place on December 18, 1796, on his way to establish the border between Spanish and U.S. America. Lewis doesn't quote Ellicott's results, but the modern reckoning of that point, south of modern Cairo, between the two rivers, puts it at 37° 00' N. Nor has Lewis's deduced latitude for that point survived, in his journal for November 14–20, 1803, though we can make deductions from his equal-altitude observations (that were beyond him), and obtain good agreement with the modern latitude. However, any meridian altitude observation made by Lewis would always have produced a deduced latitude that was too high by more than 4' (nearly 5 land-miles too far north), because of his incorrect procedure in subtracting his sextant's index error after (rather than before) halving the altitude. I am, then, surprised that he found such agreement with Ellicott's observations at that same spot. As he provides no numbers, neither his nor Ellicott's, we are not in a position to assess for ourselves whether (and to what extent) he did.

Huxtable also talked about the zenith sectors, which "have little relevance to a study of Lewis and Clark, as they never used such an instrument, as far as I know. The only way they enter into the discussion is Lewis's claim, a doubtful one to me, that at the same spot as modern Cairo, Lewis obtained the same latitude with his sextant as Ellicott had previously measured with his zenith sector."

Huxtable also provided information on Ellicott's instruments, which can be found at the Smithsonian Institution's Website. "Both Ellicott's instruments, made by David Rittenhouse . . . seem to be beautifully made, in two very different sizes. The smaller one, much more portable, was probably the one used by Ellicott in 1796." To view these instruments, consult the following Web addresses.

Zenith telescope (19 inches long): http://americanhistory.si.edu/collections/surveying/object .cfm?recordnumber=758696

Zenith telescope (5.5 feet long): http://americanhistory.si.edu/collections/surveying/object .cfm?recordnumber=758697

Huxtable's Website, "Lewis and Clark on the Mississippi: Commentary on Their Celestial Navigation," provides much information on what he calls the "Index mixup," section 1.11.2.http://www.hux.me.uk/lewis02.htm. For Huxtable's own work, see George Huxtable and Ian Jackson, "Journey to Work: James Cook's Transatlantic Voyages in the Grenville 1764–1767," *Journal of Navigation* 63 (2010). Huxtable also recommended Lawrence A. Rudner and Hans A. Heynau, "Revisiting Fort Mandan's Longitude," We Proceeded On 27, no. 4 (November 2001): 27–30. This article also describes other aspects of sextant calculations on the Lewis and Clark Expedition.

APPENDIXES H–I: FICTION WEAVED INTO NONFICTION

Appendix H

THE ETIOLOGY OF
THUNDERBOLTS/THUNDERCLAPPERS

In 1969, historian Paul Russell Cutright applied a nickname to Dr. Benjamin Rush's medicinal pills:

> [A] product of the genius of Dr. Benjamin Rush, [the pills] were well-known in those days and alluded to, often with some feeling, as Rush's "thunderbolts." Each consisted of 10 grains of calomel and 10 of jalap and consequently was a powerful physic.[1]

Calomel, derived from mercury, was a metallic substance with an alluring name. It was first manufactured in an alchemist's workshop in the fourteenth century.

In 1996, the thunderclapper nickname caught the attention of the general public with the publication of Stephen Ambrose's *Undaunted Courage*. "Those pills were under Dr. Rush's patent known as 'Rush's pills' but generally referred to as 'Thunderclappers,'" intoned Ambrose in the text. This single addition to the Lewis and Clark lexicon galvanized historians and amateurs, and two years later in another publication, Ambrose amplified the description:

> Rush's specific for nearly all the ills of mankind were purging pills composed of calomel, a mixture of six parts mercury to one part chlorine, and jalap. Each drug was a purgative of explosive power; the combination was so awesome the pills were called Rush's Thunderclappers.[2]

Neither Cutright nor Ambrose cited their source for Thunderbolts or Thunderclappers, and historians today use the terms with wild abandon, as if they were common names during the time of Lewis and Clark.[3] David J. Peck, a physician and an author on the topic of wilderness medicine, stated that Lewis packed fifty dozen of Rush's pills known as "Thunderclappers" for the expedition, but did not list a citation for the term.[4] One would assume that such a popular name would have an easily discoverable source in the secondary source literature since it is cited in multiple publications, yet there are almost no such references.

The first use of the term "Rush's Thunderbolts" was published in 1933 when Dr. Morris Fishbein described the pills in his book on the frontiers of American medicine:

> A favorite prescription of the doctors of an earlier day in this country was Benjamin Rush's combination of ten grains of calomel and ten grains of jalap, given at a single dose as a strong purgative. It was known as Rush's thunderbolt.[5]

Rush's pills were actually another doctor's prescription. Dr. Benjamin Rush had learned of the pill from Dr. Thomas Young, senior surgeon in the military hospitals during the Revolutionary War. Rush modified Young's formula to fifteen grains of jalap and ten of calomel and prescribed it three times a day.[6] He reported that "the effects of this powder, not only answered, but far exceeded my expectations."[7] In September 1793, he "imparted the prescription" to the College of Physicians as a cure for yellow fever, although today it is known that it has the power to cure nothing, and twentieth century medical textbooks discourage the internal use of calomel entirely.[8]

US patents for bilious pills were approved for several persons with the last name of Lee from 1796 through 1800. Benjamin Rush never filed a patent on a mercury pill or formula.[9] However, there is some evidence on the etiology of a mercury thunderbolt or bolus in the annals of British naval medicine, but the author of the article describing it does not list a source for his information.

> Treatment of all kinds of fever with large doses of mercury in the form of boluses of calomel was commonly practised by naval surgeons in the eighteenth century. They called it the 'calomel plan'; their patients knew it as the 'thunderbolt cure' and the boluses as 'thunderbolts' because of the force with which they passed through the human body.[10]

A bolus is a "rounded mass, or a large pill," usually applied internally.[11]

To borrow a phrase from Mark Twain, this term is "the most majestic compound fracture of fact," or as Dr. Thomas Szasz has stated, this "misattribution" is another "bogus Benjamin Rush quote," which completely ignores and at the same time pokes fun at a frightful and archaic treatment in the dark ages of medical history.[12] The term cannot be traced back to Lewis's time through the secondary literature, nor have I seen a contemporary reference by Lewis or any other eighteenth- or early ninteenth-century person to "thunderbolts" in the primary source literature.

Appendix I

A FICTIONAL ROMANCE

Meriwether Lewis and Theodosia Burr Alston never knew one another because they lived and died in separate parts of the country. Lewis was born and raised in Charlottesville, Virginia, and entered the US Army in May 1795 at the age of twenty-one. Lewis was stationed at Detroit in 1801, and on February 23, newly elected president Thomas Jefferson invited him to be his private secretary.[1] On March 7, 1801, Lewis arrived in Pittsburgh and with much haste closed his accounts and departed for Washington, arriving on April 1. Expecting to meet with Jefferson, Lewis found that the president had already departed for Monticello and so he followed a few days later. Lewis's tenure as Jefferson's secretary began on April 30, 1801, and continued until March 3, 1803, which was at the close of the congressional session. During this time, there was never a moment when the two may have met, as we shall see. Lewis then went to Philadelphia to meet with various members of the American Philosophical Society who could enhance his training in the sciences for the expedition. Lewis finally departed for the west about the end of July 1803.

Theodosia Burr, daughter of Aaron Burr, spent her premarried life in New York and married Senator Joseph Alston of South Carolina on February 2, 1801, in Albany, New York.[2] They visited Baltimore on February 28, where they met her father, Aaron Burr, and stopped in Washington on March 4, 1801, where they witnessed his swearing-in ceremony as vice president. The couple then departed for South Carolina. Her son was born in the spring of 1802, and she returned to New York on June 16, 1803, to visit her family, and then met with her father and husband in Washington on October 16, 1803.[3] Six years later, Theodosia was still living with her husband in Chiraw, South Carolina. Certainly by the time of Burr's trial in August 1807, political animosity would have kept them apart if not the fact that she was a married woman.

The stories of the romance between Lewis and Burr Alston are bunk and complete fabrications, unsupported by primary accounts. The first story originated with *Munsey's Magazine*, which published Emerson Hough's "The Magnificent Adventure" in April and May of 1916.[4]

Compared to other New York magazines, *Munsey's* was known for its active, timely, and "juicy" articles.[5] After the publication in *Munsey's*, I. J. Cox, a professor of history at the University of Cincinnati, wrote to Stella Drumm at the Missouri Historical Society:

> On a recent brief railway trip I devoted some time to Hough's "Magnificent Adventure." It is a magnificent distortion of historical facts, where he mentions facts. He does not seem to care for historic sequence at all and to be utterly regardless of time. His main theme is a rather audacious conception, but I think it very poorly executed. . . . Many of its passages intended to be striking are more bathos.[6]

Delbert E. Wylder, professor at Murray State University, wrote Hough's biography and related some interesting facts about the "fictional creation" of the romance.

> The relative success of *Out of Doors* led to the publication of another group of the *Post* (*Saturday Evening Post*) in 1916. That year also saw the publication of his first novel in three years, *The Magnificent Adventure*, a historical novel about the Lewis and Clark Expedition into the Far West complicated by a fictional creation of a love affair between Lewis and Theodosia Alston, daughter of Aaron Burr.[7]

In 1941, Anya Seton endorsed the romance with an emotional burst, supposedly from Meriwether Lewis, that was lacking in Hough's creation:

> I am going to die, Theodosia, I cannot tell you how I know it but I do. I might tell you a vision I had, the second-sight of my Scotch forbears. I might tell you of the prophecy of the Mandan woman. . . . For me, I know that the trail is nearly ended. . . . I want to see you once again first. I shall be with you in mid-October. I shall not embarrass you; it will be but for a few hours. I am on my way to clear my name. President Madison has seen fit to question my expenditures out here. He questions my honor. It seems that I have made many enemies, who do not scruple to slander me.[8]

A year later, Fillmore Norfleet fanned the fictional flames.

> [S]ent by Jefferson to Richmond sometime during the Burr trial, during which time he saw Theodosia Burr Alston, for whom his love had never waned despite her marriage and her father's antipathy for him; from St. Louis, Merne, as Theodosia called him, wrote September 1, 1809, I am going to die, Theodosia, I cannot tell you how I know it but I do. I might tell you a vision I had, the second-sight of my

Scotch forbears. I might tell you of the prophecy of the Mandan woman. . . . For me, I know that the trail is nearly ended. . . . I want to see you once again first. I shall be with you in mid-October.[9]

The romance was kept alive in Eldon Chuinard's book in 1980 on the medical aspects of the Lewis and Clark Expedition. Why Chuinard included the romance in this fine book is a mystery. In 1994, David Chandler waded in with his *Jefferson Conspiracies*.[10] Reimert Ravenholt, an epidemiologist, believed that Lewis had succumbed to venereal disease and included Seton's banter:

That Lewis was aware what was happening to him during 1809 is revealed by a letter to his old flame Theodosia Burr Alston, written shortly before he left St. Louis for the East: I am going to die, Theodosia, I cannot tell you how I know it but I do. . . . For me, I know that the trail is nearly ended. . . . I want to see you once again first. I shall be with you in October.[11]

Seton added verve to a later passage, which would have prevented Ravenholt altogether from copying her work: "She read the letter again, then, leaning over the fire, put it on the embers, where it flared up brightly, and was gone."[12]

At the end of her book, Seton stated that her credibility was sound "with the exception of the Meriwether Lewis romance for which there are three separate sources." Ms. Seton does not cite any sources.

Lastly, Emerson Hough created a new nickname for Meriwether, Merne, when "Widow Lewis" (Lucy Marks, his mother) writes to Meriwether.

I am always waiting for you, Merne, said she. She used the Elizabethan vowel, as one should pronounce "bird," with no sound of "u"—Mairne, the name sounded as she spoke it. And her voice was full and rich and strong, as was her son's; musically strong.[13]

In 1934, Charles Morrow Wilson in *Meriwether Lewis of Lewis and Clark*, took the bait, broadened the scope of the name, and brought it to life. Wilson wrote that William Clark protested when Lewis decided to go to Washington to clear up his financial affairs in person: "It's tomfoolery, Merne, and if you weren't sick, you'd know it."[14]

NOTES

PREFACE

1. Bernard DeVoto, "An Inference Regarding the Expedition of Lewis and Clark," *Proceedings of the American Philosophical Society* 99, no. 4 (August 1955): 186.

ACKNOWLEDGMENTS

1. Jeanne M. Serra is the author's spouse.

2. John Danisi is an assistant professor and chair of the Department of Philosophy and Religious Studies at Wagner College, Staten Island, New York. He received his PhD in philosophy at New York University. Professor Danisi is the author's brother.

3. W. Raymond Wood is a Missouri River historian and professor emeritus of anthropology at the University of Missouri-Columbia.

4. Caesar A. Cirigliano is a practicing attorney in Tennessee. Mr. Cirigliano is the author's nephew.

CHAPTER 1: DEMANDING SATISFACTION: THE PERILOUS TRIAL OF ENSIGN MERIWETHER LEWIS

1. "General Anthony Wayne's General Orders," *Michigan Pioneer Collections* 34 (1905): 635.

2. Ibid., p. 581.

3. Historian Richard Dillon, in his biography of Lewis, introduced the battalion colors stating that Lewis exchanged the red of the Second Sub-Legion for the green of the Fourth. He then launched into his exaggerated version that "Lewis, drunk, had burst into [Elliot's] room, uninvited and abruptly and in an ungentlemanly manner." According to Dillon (whose book does not contain footnotes and has no references), Lewis insulted Elliot "without provocation and offered to duel to the death with him." Richard Dillon, *Meriwether Lewis: A Biography* (Santa Cruz, CA: Western Tanager Press, 1965), p. 21. Colors of the four battalions were white, red, yellow, and green ("Wayne's General Orders," 385), but there's more:

"Soldiers of the first sub-legion were to wear white bindery and white plumes on their hats. The second sub-legion was to be identified by red binding and red plumes, the third by yellow, and the fourth by no binding and black plumes. Officers were to wear plain hats with the plumes of their respective legions." Harry M. Ward, *The Department of War, 1781–1795* (Pittsburgh: University of Pittsburgh Press, 1962), p. 149.

4. Lieutenant John Boyer, "Daily Journal of Wayne's Campaign," *Michigan Pioneer Collections* 34 (1905): 651–52.

5. The term courts-martial, now called court-martial, is the military equivalent of a criminal court trial.

6. Eldon Chuinard, "The Court-Martial of Ensign Meriwether Lewis," *We Proceeded On* 8, no. 4 (November 1982): 13–15.

7. Ibid., p. 14; Stephen Ambrose, *Undaunted Courage* (New York: Simon & Schuster, 1996), p. 45; Dillon, *A Biography*, pp. 20–21.

8. Anthony Wayne Papers, General Orders of Court Martial, May 1793–October 1796, vol. 50, fol. 49–91, Historical Society of Pennsylvania, Philadelphia, PA.

9. Ibid., transcribed page 35.

10. Meriwether Lewis to Lucy Marks, October 4, 1794, Meriwether Lewis Collection, Missouri History Museum.

11. Landon Y. Jones, *William Clark and the Shaping of the West* (New York: Hill & Wang, 2004), p. 79. On April 6, 1795, Lewis wrote his mother and said he had been stricken with a serious illness that may have either been malaria or dysentery. Meriwether Lewis to Lucy Marks, Meriwether Lewis Collection, Missouri History Museum.

12. Ibid., pp. 75, 84.

13. Ambrose, *Undaunted Courage*, pp. 45–46. Historian William Foley stated that "immediately following the verdict . . . Wayne reassigned Lewis" to Clark's company. Other historians also agree on this scenario. William Foley, *Wilderness Journey: The Life of William Clark* (Columbia: University of Missouri Press, 2004), p. 40.

14. "Wayne's General Orders,"p. 480.

15. Wayne Papers, General Orders of Court Martial, transcribed p. 1.

16. Boyer, "Daily Journal of Wayne's Campaign," p. 643. Lt. Joseph Elliot was an officer in the light artillery unit.

17. Bradley J. Nicholson, "Courts-Martial in the Legion Army: American Military Law in the Early Republic, 1792–1796," *Military Law Review* 144 (Spring 1994): 103–104.

18. Wayne Papers, General Orders of Court Martial, transcribed pp. 24–25.

19. Nicholson, "Courts-Martial in the Legion Army," p. 101.

20. Wayne Papers, General Orders of Court Martial, transcribed p. 1.

21. See Amos Stoddard Company Book, p. 210, Louisiana Territory, Military Command, Adjutant's Record, 1803–1805, Missouri History Museum, Saint Louis, MO; George B. Davis, *A Treatise on the Military Law of the United States: Together with the Practice and Procedure of Courts-Martial and Other Military Tribunals* (New York: John Wiley & Sons, 1915); William C. Hart, *Observations on Military Law and the Constitution and Practice of Courts-Mar-*

tial (New York: Appleton, 1864), pp. 244–45. In addition to general courts-martial there were regimental, garrison, or company courts-martial that were composed of three commissioned officers and heard cases of a noncapital nature. They could inflict corporal punishment but could not fine a soldier more than one month's pay or imprison or "put to hard labor" a soldier for over one month.

22. Wayne Papers, General Orders of Court Martial, transcribed p. 3.

23. Ibid., transcribed p. 6.

24. Ibid., transcribed p. 7.

25. Ibid., transcribed pp. 12–13.

26. Ibid., transcribed p. 13.

27. Ibid., transcribed p. 9.

28. Ibid., Lewis's note ends abruptly at the bottom of the transcript. The following page begins with "from Capt. Marschalk."

29. Ibid., transcribed p. 34.

30. Ibid., transcribed pp. 25–26.

31. Ibid., transcribed p. 32.

32. Ibid., transcribed p. 35.

33. Ibid., transcribed p. 35.

34. Ibid., transcribed pp. 19–21.

35. Ibid., transcribed pp. 35–36.

36. Ibid., transcribed p. 36.

37. See appendix B, note 5: locating the Meriwether Lewis courts-martial case.

CHAPTER 2: LEWIS AND CLARK'S ROUTE MAP: JAMES MACKAY'S MAP OF THE MISSOURI RIVER

*Copyright 2004 by the Western History Association. Reprinted by permission. Thomas C. Danisi and W. Raymond Wood, "Lewis and Clark's Route Map: James MacKay's Map of the Missouri River, *Western Historical Quarterly* 35, no. 1 (Spring 2004): 53–72. The essay has been updated since its 2004 publication.

1. A. P. Nasatir, *Before Lewis and Clark: Documents Illustrating the History of Missouri, 1785–1804*, 2 vols. (Saint Louis: Saint Louis Historical Documents Foundation, 1952), 1: 80–83. Many of the MacKay, Finiels, and Soulard papers are to be found in the Papeles de Cuba Collection of the Archivo General de Indias in Seville, Spain. We thank Nancy Durbin of Lindenwood University and Anna Price for their French and Spanish translations of the MacKay, Soulard, Finiels, and Trudeau documents.

2. H. T. Beauregard, "Journal of Jean Baptiste Truteau among the Arikara Indians in 1795," *Missouri Historical Society Collections* 4 (Saint Louis: Missouri Historical Society, 1912): 22.

3. W. S. Wallace, ed., *Documents Relating to the North West Company* (Toronto: Champlain Society, 1934), p. 14.

4. Marilyn MacKay Ballard Rabakukk, *The Mackays of Arichliney* (Coral Springs, FL: Llumina Press, 2006), pp. 105–106. James MacKay had two brothers, John and William, who also traveled to the United States. John married Elizabeth Michau from Staten Island and remained in New York for the rest of his life. William went to Petersburgh, Virginia, and raised a family there.

5. "Narrative of Donald McKay," transcribed by John C. Jackson, December 1995, E.223/1, Hudson's Bay Company Archives, Winnipeg, Manitoba; *Manchester House Journal*, April 17, 1786/87, B121/a/1, Hudson Bay Company Archives; *Cumberland House Journal*, May 30, 1786, B49/a/16, 34, Hudson Bay Company Archives.

6. Rabakukk stated in her book that James and John were in England in August 1788, possibly because the North West Company had an office there. Rabakukk, *Mackays of Arichliney*, p. 105.

7. Nasatir, *Before Lewis and Clark*, 1: 130–31.

8. Perrin Collection, 1737–1809, St. Clair County Circuit Court, Case File 114 (1792), Illinois Regional Archives Depository, Illinois State Archives, Archives Building, Springfield.

9. John B. C. Lucas, "Notes of J. B. C. Lucas on the Custom of Selling Slaves by Paper," interviewing landowners: Charles Gratiot, Antoine Soulard, and James MacKay, John B. C. Lucas Papers, box 20–21, folder 1, p. 3, Missouri History Museum, Saint Louis, Missouri.

10. Nasatir, *Before Lewis and Clark*, 1: 181.

11. Charles Theodore Greve, *Centennial History of Cincinnati and Representative Citizens*, 2 vols. (Chicago: Biographical Publishing, 1904), 1: 360–61.

12. W. Raymond Wood, *Prologue to Lewis and Clark: The Mackay and Evans Expedition* (Norman: University of Oklahoma Press, 2003), pp. 190–93.

13. Nasatir, *Before Lewis and Clark*, 1: 97.

14. Gwyn A. Williams, *Madoc: The Making of a Myth* (New York: Oxford University Press, 1987), p. 153.

15. Francois Vallé to Zenon Trudeau, March 6, 1794, Letter 22, AGI-PC 209: 598; microfilm copy in Missouri History Museum.

16. Pierre Charles Delassus de Luziéres to Francisco Louis Hector Carondelet, April 16, 1794, AGI-PC 208a: 480, Missouri History Museum.

17. Henry Peyroux to Francois Vallé, December 26, 1793, AGI-PC 208a: 490; Trudeau to Carondelet, January 28, 1794, AGI-PC 209: 634, AGI-PC 208a: 480, Missouri History Museum.

18. Saint Louis Recorded Archives, vol. 2, bk. 2, instrument 625, p. 388, Jefferson National Expansion Memorial Library, National Park Service, Saint Louis, Missouri.

19. Manuscript ca. 1804, notes on Indian tribes in James MacKay's hand, note 4. Clark Family Collection, Missouri History Museum. We cannot help but be curious as to where Rhys had obtained his Mandan vocabulary.

20. Aubrey Diller, "Maps of the Missouri River before Lewis and Clark," in *Studies and Essays in the History of Science and Learning*, ed. Ashley Montagu (New York: Schuman, 1946), p. 507.

21. Nasatir, *Before Lewis and Clark*, 1: 96, n. 61; A. P. Nasatir, "Anglo-Spanish Rivalry on the Upper Missouri," *Mississippi Valley Historical Review* 16, no. 4 (March 1930): 507.

22. Jacques Clamorgan to Jean Baptiste Truteau, June 30, 1794, box 2, folder 34, Louis Houck Collection, Document 66, Missouri History Museum.

23. Nasatir, *Before Lewis and Clark*, 1: 257, n. 6.

24. Zenon Trudeau to Francisco Louis Hector Carondelet, August 8, 1794, AGI-PC 197: 707; De Luziéres to Carondelet, September 17, 1794, AGI-PC 209: 663, October 17, PC 209: 666, Missouri History Museum.

25. Antoine Soulard to Manuel Gayoso de Lemos, December 15, 1797, AGI-PC 213: 833, Missouri History Museum; US Congress. Senate. Substance of an Argument, 21st Cong., 2nd sess., 1830. S. Doc. 12, Serial 203, p. 27.

26. Diller, "Maps of the Missouri River," p. 508.

27. This map is illustrated in W. Raymond Wood, "Native American Tribes Inhabiting Villages on the Missouri River," in Thomas C. Danisi and W. Raymond Wood, "Lewis and Clark's Route Map: James MacKay's Map of the Missouri River," *Western Historical Quarterly* 35, no. 1 (Spring 2004): 55.

28. Diller, "Maps of the Missouri River," pp. 507–8.

29. Antoine Soulard to Manuel Gayoso de Lemos, December 15, 1797, AGI-PC 213: 833–35, Missouri History Museum.

30. William Dunbar to Thomas Jefferson, March 18, 1806, document 27579, reel 35, Thomas Jefferson Papers, Library of Congress. In this letter, Dunbar speaks of "Mackay's treatise on longitude," but this is not our James MacKay from Saint Louis. John Garnett, *Tables Requisite to Be Used with the Nautical Ephemeris, for Finding the Latitude and Longitude at Sea* (London: Commissioners of Longitude, 1806).

31. Ibid.

32. Nasatir, *Before Lewis and Clark*, 1: 97.

33. Ibid. 1: 86, 2: 452, 520; Deposition of James MacKay, March 7, 1817, Saint Charles Papers, Missouri History Museum; Francisco Louis Hector Carondelet to Jacques Clamorgan, October 26, 1796, Clamorgan Collection, Missouri History Museum.

34. Nasatir, *Before Lewis and Clark*, 2: 410–11.

35. Ibid.

36. Ibid.

37. Ibid., 2: 416–17.

38. Ibid.

39. Ibid., 2: 410–14.

40. Bernard DeVoto, *Course of Empire* (Boston: Houghton Mifflin, 1952), p. 377.

41. Nasatir, *Before Lewis and Clark*, 2: 461–62, 500.

42. A. P. Nasatir, "Anglo-Spanish Rivalry in Iowa," *Iowa Journal of History and Politics* 28 (July 1930): 359; Nasatir, *Before Lewis and Clark*, 2: 520 (quote).

43. MacKay's Table of Distances, Nasatir, *Before Lewis and Clark*, 2: 485–99.

44. Nasatir, *Before Lewis and Clark*, 2: 520, n. 6.

45. Ibid., p. 545.

46. Zenon Trudeau to Manuel Gayoso de Lemos, March 5, 1798, AGI-PC 49: 822, Missouri History Museum.

47. Ibid. A condensed version of the letter is in Nasatir, *Before Lewis and Clark*, 2: 545, n. 3.

48. Frederick Teggart, "Notes Supplementary to any Edition of Lewis and Clark," *American Historical Association Annual Report* 1 (1908): 186. Reuben Gold Thwaites edited and published the letter in the *Original Journals of the Lewis and Clark Expedition*, 8 vols. (New York: Dodd, Mead & Company, 1904), 7: 291, but did not comment on it.

49. A. P. Nasatir, "John Evans, Explorer and Surveyor," *Missouri Historical Review* 25 (July 1931): 591, n. 29.

50. Ibid., p. 608.

51. Ernest Staples Osgood, ed., *The Field Notes of Captain William Clark, 1803–1805* (New Haven, CT: Yale University Press, 1964), p. 25, n. 8.

52. William Wesley Woolen, Daniel Wait Howe, and Jacob Piatt Dunn, eds. *Executive Journal of Indiana Territory 1800–1816* (Indianapolis: Bowen-Merrill, 1900), p. 95, n. 3. Jones had been appointed attorney general on January 29, 1801, and resigned on July 31, 1804. English Collection, M-98, box 31, folder 7, July 31, 1804, Vincennes, Indiana Historical Society, Indianapolis, Indiana. Jones supported two residences in Kaskaskia and Vincennes during this time. On December 28, 1802, he wrote that he had to travel 160 miles from his home to the seat of the territorial government at Vincennes. On that same day he also sent a letter to Thomas Jefferson, asking if he could be appointed a judge of the territory, since he was not paid a salary or compensated for the position of attorney general. Logan Esarey, ed., *Governor's Messages and Letters: Messages and Letters of William Henry Harrison 1800–1811*, 2 vols. (Indianapolis: Indiana Historical Commission, 1922), pp. 66–67.

53. Donald Jackson, *Letters of the Lewis and Clark Expedition with Related Documents, 1783–1854*, 2nd ed., 2 vols. (Urbana: University of Illinois Press, 1978), 2: 689.

54. Nasatir, *Before Lewis and Clark*, 2: 718–19.

55. Jackson, *Letters*, 1: 163.

56. Nasatir, "Anglo-Spanish Rivalry in Iowa," pp. 366, 369. De Finiels's wife, Marie Anne Riviere, gave birth to Marie Susann-Adele de Finiels on July 13, 1797, in Saint Louis (Oscar Collet, Index to Saint Louis Cathedral and Carondelet Church Baptisms, p. 66, Missouri History Museum).

57. Nicolas de Finiels, "Notice sur la Louisiane Supérieure," p. 89, box 41, folder 20, John Francis McDermott Collection, Lovejoy Library, Southern Illinois University, Edwardsville.

58. Reproduction de la carte du Mississippi de Nicolas de Finiels, Recueil, 69 carte 34, Marine Nationale, Service historique de la Marine, Château de Vincennes, B. P. n-2-00300 Armées, France; W. Raymond Wood, *An Atlas of Early Maps of the American Midwest*, Part II, Illinois State Museum, Scientific Papers 28 (2001): plate 13.

59. Finiels, "Notice sur la Louisiane Supérieure," p. 62.

60. Map can be found in M-M 508, box 5, #516, MSS, Bancroft Library, University of California, Berkeley. The Spanish word *apeadas* or *afseadas*, is unknown.

61. Ibid.

62. MacKay was appointed commandant of Saint André, the Bon Homme settlement, in 1798. See Nasatir, *Before Lewis and Clark*, 2: 587.

63. *American State Papers, Public Lands*, 2: 495.

64. Nicolas de Finiels, *An Account of Upper Louisiana*, ed. Carl J. Ekberg and William E. Foley (Columbia: University of Missouri Press, 1989), p. 72, n. 118. MacKay produced a rough "plan" in October 1802 of Femme Osage, Daniel Boone's settlement. See James MacKay to Charles Dehault de Lassus, October 29, 1802, AGI-PC 219: 559, Missouri History Museum.

65. Nasatir, *Before Lewis and Clark*, 2: 605, 545, n. 3.

66. Manuel Gayoso de Lemos to Charles Dehault de Lassus, May 12, 1799, AGI-PC 134a: 387, Missouri History Museum.

67. Annie H. Abel, "Trudeau's Description of the Upper Missouri," *Mississippi Valley Historical Review* 8 (June–September 1921): 154.

68. Frederick Teggart, "Notes Supplementary to Any Edition of Lewis and Clark," *American Historical Association Annual Report* 1 (1908): 188; Annie H. Abel-Henderson, "Mackay's Table of Distances," *Mississippi Valley Historical Review* 10 (March 1924): 428–46; Milo M. Quaife, "Extracts from McKay's Journal and Others," *Wisconsin Historical Society Proceedings* 63 (1916): 186–210; Annie H. Abel, "A New Lewis and Clark Map," *Geographical Review* 1 (May 1916): 329–45; De Voto, *Course of Empire*, 372–79; David Williams, "John Evans' Strange Journey," *American Historical Review* 54 (January 1949): 277–95 and (April 1949): 508–29; Aubrey Diller, "James Mackay's Journey in Nebraska in 1796," *Nebraska History* 36 (June 1955): 123–28; John Logan Allen, *Passage Through the Garden* (Urbana: University of Illinois Press, 1975), pp. 141–42; Jackson, *Letters*, 1: 135–36.

69. Jackson, *Letters*, 1: 104–105, 142–43.

70. James Holmberg, ed., *Dear Brother* (New Haven, CT: Yale University Press, 2002), p. 61.

71. "Meriwether Lewis to Thomas Jefferson, December 28, 1803," in Jackson, *Letters*, 1: 163, 148–55.

72. James MacKay to Charles Dehault de Lassus, July 10, 1800, AGI-PC 217b: 180, Missouri History Museum; Finiels, *An Account of Upper Louisiana*, pp. 72–73.

73. Jackson, *Letters*, 1: 131, 137.

74. Gary E. Moulton, ed., *The Journals of the Lewis and Clark Expedition*, 13 vols. (Lincoln: University of Nebraska Press, 1983–2001), 2: 134, 140–41.

75. Ibid., 2: 154. When Soulard surveyed MacKay's land on Bon Homme Creek on March 5, 1798, he stated that it was about thirty-one miles west of Saint Louis. See *Pintado Papers*, bk. IX and bk. P: 141, Louisiana State University, Baton Rouge. De Finiels gauged the distance at thirty miles. See Finiels, *An Account of Upper Louisiana*, pp. 70–71.

76. James MacKay to John Fowler, September 24, 1803, Box 24, Breckenridge Family Papers, Library of Congress.

77. Osgood, *Field Notes*, p. 16. Various historians have agreed on this date to suggest that MacKay's meeting on January 10 had been planned.

78. W. Raymond Wood, *An Atlas of Early Maps of the American Midwest*, plate 13.

79. Saint Louis Recorded Archives, vol. 4, bk. 1, instrument #1128 and 1132, pp. 53–55, Jefferson National Expansion Memorial Library, Saint Louis; RG 952, Series 5, US Surveyor General for Missouri, Outgoing Correspondence 1816–1863, box 32, bk. Q: 315, Missouri State Archives, Jefferson City.

80. Moulton, *Journals*, 2: 154.

81. Osgood, *Field Notes*, pp. 14, 19–23.

82. Ibid., p. 27; Donald Jackson, "A New Lewis and Clark Map," *Missouri Historical Society Bulletin* 17 (January 1961): 119–26; Jackson, *Letters*, 1: 198–203; Thomas Jefferson to Albert Gallatin, July 12, 1804, document 24594, reel 30, Thomas Jefferson Papers, Library of Congress.

CHAPTER 3: INTRIGUE, MAYHEM, DECEPTION

1. *Philadelphia Daily Advertiser*, January 7, 1804, p. 3.

2. Louis Pelzer, "The Spanish Land Grants of Upper Louisiana," *Iowa Journal of History and Politics* 11 (1913): 20; Eugene Morrow Violette, "Spanish Land Claims in Missouri," *Washington University Studies* 8, no. 2 (1921): 176–77; Paul Gates, *History of Public Land Law Development* (Washington, DC: Public Land Law Review Commission, 1968), p. 93; Gerald T. Dunne, *The Missouri Supreme Court* (Columbia: University of Missouri Press, 1993), p. 24; Dick Steward, *Frontier Swashbuckler* (Columbia: University of Missouri Press, 2000), pp. 33–34; Walter A. Schroeder, *Opening the Ozarks: A Historical Geography of Missouri's Ste. Genevieve District, 1760–1830* (Columbia: University of Missouri Press, 2002); William E. Foley, *The Genesis of Missouri* (University of Missouri Press, Columbia, 1989), pp. 99–100, 143–44; William Thomas Farnan, "Land Claims Problems and the Federal Land System in the Louisiana-Missouri Territory," (PhD diss., Saint Louis University, 1971): pp. 23–26; LeRoy Hafen, ed., *The Mountain Men and the Fur Trade of the Far West* (Glendale, CA: Arthur H. Clark Company, 1966), pp. 198–99, 204–205.

3. *Kentucky Gazette*, February 15, 1803.

4. Jerry W. Knudson, "Newspaper Reaction to the Louisiana Purchase," *Missouri Historical Review* 63, no. 2 (January 1969): 188. Also known as the Pinckney Treaty of 1795.

5. Ibid., p. 97

6. "Memorial to Congress by Inhabitants of St. Clair and Randolph Counties, October 26, 1803," Clarence Edwin Carter, ed., *The Territorial Papers of the United States*, 28 vols. (Washington, DC: Government Printing Office, 1934–962), 7: 131.

7. War Department to John Rice Jones, August 12, 1802, RG107, M370, roll 1, p. 348, frame 0200, National Archives and Records Administration; Jones had been appointed attorney general on January 29, 1801, and resigned on July 31, 1804. English Collection, M-98, box 31, folder 7, July 31, 1804, Vincennes, Indiana Historical Society, Indianapolis, Indiana.

8. Thomas Cushing to Amos Stoddard, December 25, 1802, RG 94, M565, roll 1, page 385, frame 0201, National Archives and Records Administration; Secretary of War to Amos Stoddard, February 19, 1803, Carter, *Territorial Papers*, 7: 85–86.

9. Everett S. Brown, *Constitutional History of the Louisiana Purchase, 1803–1812* (Berkeley: University of California Press, 1920), pp. 98, 136, 144; Everett S. Brown, ed., *William Plumer's Memorandum of the United States Senate, 1803–1807* (New York: Da Capo Press, 1969), p. 110.

10. Thomas Jefferson to DeWitt Clinton, December 2, 1803, document 23594, reel 27, Thomas Jefferson Papers, Library of Congress.

11. "Petition to Congress by Inhabitants of Knox, St. Clair and Randolph Counties, October 26, 1803," in Carter, *Territorial Papers* 7: 140–43.

12. "Judge Thomas Davis to John Breckinridge, October 17, 1803," in Carter, *Territorial Papers,* 7: 124. Davis also wrote to James Madison, the secretary of state, the following day and communicated the same points. Carter, *Territorial Papers,* 7: 125.

13. "Extract of a letter from Kaskaskias, Indiana Territory, October 18, 1803," in *American State Papers, Public Lands*, 1: 173. The original document was reproduced on microfilm: http://memory.loc.gov/ammem/amlaw/lwsp.html (accessed November 15, 2010).

14. "Issac Darneille to John Breckinridge, October 22, 1803," in Carter, *Territorial Papers*, 7: 131–32.

15. James Robertson, *Louisiana under the Rule of Spain, France and the United States, 1785–1807*, 2 vols. (Cleveland: Arthur H. Clark Company, 1911), 2: 54, n. 38.

16. *Philadelphia Daily Advertiser*, January 7, 1804, p. 3.

17. Thomas T. Davis to John Breckinridge, November 25, 1803, Breckinridge Family Papers, Box 25, p. 81, Manuscript Division, Library of Congress.

18. "John Rice Jones to Judge Davis, January 21, 1804," in Carter, *Territorial Papers,* 7: 169.

19. "Amos Stoddard to Thomas Jefferson, January 10, 1804," in *American State Papers, Public Lands*, 1: 193.

20. "Frederick Bates to Josiah Meigs, November 20, 1816," *Report of the Commissioner of the General Land Office in Relation to Lead Mines and Salt Springs*, 18th Cong., 1st sess., 1824, H. Rep. 98, serial 98, p. 120; "Petition to Congress by Moses Austin and John Rice Jones, January 21, 1811," Annals of Congress, Senate, 11th Congress, 3rd Session, pp. 99–100.

21. Carter, *Territorial Papers*, 13: 524.

22. Charles Dehault de Lassus, the lieutenant governor of Upper Louisiana, had received correspondence from his superiors in New Orleans sooner than previously thought. New information from the Spanish Archives in Seville now gives a definitive timeline of those events. "Juan Manuel de Salcedo to Charles Dehault Delassus, May 3, 1803," *Papeles de Cuba Collection of the Archivo General de Indias* 78, stamped pp. [Archivo de las Indias Numbers] 161, 162, 163; "Salcedo to Delassus, May 11, 1803," pp. 121–24; "Salcedo to Delassus, May 20, 1803," stamped pp. 344–45 [Archivo de las Indias Numbers]; "Delassus to Salcedo, August 1, 1803," stamped pp. 352–54 [Archivo de las Indias Numbers]; "Salcedo to Delassus, September 3, 1803," stamped pp. [Archivo de las Indias Numbers], copies at the Jefferson National Expansion Memorial Archives, Saint Louis, Missouri.

23. *American State Papers, Public Lands*, 1: 206, 208.

24. Ibid., 8: 836.

25. Amos Stoddard, *Sketches, Historical and Descriptive of Louisiana* (Philadelphia: Mathew Carey, 1812), p. 252.

26. Henry Williams, a Saint Louis land trial lawyer, stated that Frederick Bates, Saint Louis recorder, reported eleven complete titles, which was found in First American Title # 32507 Saint Louis, pp. 3–5, Missouri History Museum. Austin's grant passed all the necessary qualifications to complete title and was recorded in 1802.

27. Louis Houck, *History of Missouri*, 3 vols. (Chicago: Donnelly & Sons, 1908), 3: 44; Robert R. Archibald, "Honor and Family: The Career of Lt. Gov. Carlos de Hault de Lassus," *Gateway Heritage* 12, no. 4 (Spring 1992): 37; Floyd C. Shoemaker, *Missouri and Missourians*, 5 vols. (Chicago: Lewis Publishing, 1943), 1: 197; Lemont K. Richardson, "Private Land Claims in Missouri," *Missouri Historical Review* 50, no. 2 (January 1956): 134–35, and no. 3 (April 1956): 280; Robert R. Archibald, "From La Louisiane to Luisiana, the Imposition-Spanish Administration in the Upper Mississippi Valley," *Gateway Heritage* 11, no. 1 (Summer 1990): 28; Jeff Patridge, "The Legacies of Conflict in Missouri Land Grants," *Record* 4, no. 4 (Spring 1994): 6–8.

28. Lewis, Stoddard, and Jones were Masons, which may have been the unifying link.

29. Thomas C. Danisi, "Land Fraud in Upper Louisiana: A Misconception," Missouri Conference on History (April 2008), Columbia, MO; Thomas C. Danisi, "What Conspiracy?" *We Proceeded On* 35, no. 1 (February 2009), 30–31. This was a reply to a writer in a previous issue of *We Proceeded On*.

30. James Gardner, *Lead King: Moses Austin* (Saint Louis: Sunrise, 1980), p. 42; W. A. Burt Jones, "John Rice Jones—A Brief Sketch of the Life and Public Career of the First Practicing Lawyer in Illinois," *Chicago Historical Society's Collection* 4 (1890): 236.

31. Gardner, *Lead King*, p. 42. Austin claimed that Jones, a Kaskaskia resident, had to disband their partnership. Supposedly, aliens could not own land in Upper Louisiana, but Jones had dual citizenship. He had taken an oath of allegiance in June 1794 at New Madrid (AGI-PC 2363: 300). The Spanish archives documented a land transaction whereby John Rice Jones sold a farm in Saint Louis to Manuel Lisa on September 29, 1799. Saint Louis Recorded Archives, vol. 2, bk. 3: 467–69, instrument # 783A, Missouri History Museum, Saint Louis, Missouri; "Minutes of the Board of Commissioners," 7: 1, Missouri State Archives, Jefferson City, Missouri.

32. *John Rice Jones v. Moses Austin*, Articles of Partnership, File # 18, Sainte Genevieve, September 11, 1812. The case file was transferred to the Chancery Court at Saint Louis: *John Rice Jones v. Moses Austin*, October 1813, Civil Court Archives, Saint Louis, Missouri. The articles of partnership were recorded in Deed Book Record A, 1804–1809, pp. 246–51, Sainte Genevieve County Courthouse, Sainte Genevieve, Missouri, and in Deed Book F, p. 392, Saint Louis Recorder of Deeds, City Hall, Saint Louis, Missouri.

33. James A. Gardner, "The Life of Moses Austin: 1761–1821," (PhD diss., Washington University, 1963), p. 173.

34. Charles Dehault de Lassus succeeded Zenon Trudeau as the lieutenant governor of Upper Louisiana on July 28, 1799.

35. Gardner, *Lead King*, p. 93.

36. Carter, *Territorial Papers*, 13: 524–25.

37. Ibid, 13: 524.

38. Ibid, 13: 525.

39. James Alexander Gardner, "Moses Austin in Missouri: 1789–1821" (master's thesis, Washington University, 1951), p. 51.

40. Eugene Barker, *The Austin Papers*, 2 vols. (Washington: Annual Report of the American Historical Association, 1919), 1: 91.

41. John Rice Jones to Thomas Jefferson, February 11, 1804, document 23900, reel 29, Thomas Jefferson Papers, Library of Congress.

42. *American State Papers, Public Lands*, 1: 206–209.

43. Barker, *Austin Papers*, 2: 97–98; Moses Austin to Rufus Easton, August 14, 1805, p. 3, Rufus Easton Papers, Missouri History Museum.

44. Jones sued Austin for failing to pay him a profit for the entire time they were partners. *American State Papers, Miscellaneous*, 1: 362; *Jones v. Austin*, October 1813, Civil Court Archives, Saint Louis, Missouri.

45. "List of Appointments and Removals, May 8, 1807," in Thomas M. Marshall, ed., *The Life and Papers of Frederick Bates*, 2 vols. (Saint Louis: Missouri Historical Society, 1926), 1: 320; "August 26, 1807," 1: 325.

46. "Frederick Bates to Richard Bates, March 24, 1808," in ibid., 1: 315.

47. "Frederick Bates to Moses Austin, September 12, 1807," in ibid., 1: 186–87; "Frederick Bates to James Madison, September 25, 1807," in ibid., 1: 194–95; and "Moses Austin to Frederick Bates, August 27, 1809," in ibid., 2: 77–79.

48. "A Journal of the Proceedings of the Legislature of the Territory of Louisiana Commencing June 3, 1806, and ending October 9, 1811," Special Collection M-61, Mercantile Library, University of Missouri-Saint Louis. Judges Lucas and Schrader first met with Lewis on Monday, June 13, 1808. Lewis also wrote that he wanted "to revise the laws of the Territory and will most probably originate others . . ."; Meriwether Lewis to William Clark, May 29, 1809, William Clark Collection, Missouri History Museum.

49. *Laws of the Territory of Louisiana* (Saint Louis: Joseph Charless, 1809).

50. "Meriwether Lewis to John Perry, October 10, 1808," in Marshall, *Frederick Bates*, 2: 34–35; "Frederick Bates Appointment of John Perry, October 3, 1807," 1: 329.

51. Ibid., 1: 320, n. 16.

52. "Meriwether Lewis to James Austin, November 10, 1808," in ibid., 2: 38–39.

53. Ibid, 2: 39. It was no surprise when Bates reported to his brother that he abhorred Lewis's style of maintaining order: "How unfortunate for this man that he resigned his commission in the army: His habits are altogether military & he never can I think succeed in any other profession." Ibid., 2: 69.

54. Bates was paid $2,700 a year: invoices 21407, 21409, 21410, RG217, M235, roll 65, frames 1191, 1195, 1201, National Archives and Records Administration. (Secretary of

the territory, $1,000; Recorder of land titles, $500; Land commissioner, $1,200.) Governor Lewis was paid $2,000 annually. Bates rationalized that he was not interested in the governorship because his combined salaries and "my present Offices were nearly equal to the government and greatly superior in *emolument*. . . ." Ibid., 2: 69.

55. "Moses Austin to Frederick Bates, August 27, 1809," in ibid., 2: 78.

56. "Albert Gallatin to Frederick Bates, April 18, 1812," in Carter, *Territorial Papers,* 14: 546.

57. "Albert Gallatin to Clement Penrose, March 24 and 26, 1812," *American State Papers, Public Lands,* 2: 378–79.

58. "Rufus Easton to Thomas Jefferson, January 17, 1805," in Carter, *Territorial Papers,* 13: 85; Anton Pregaldin, "Introduction," in *Missouri Land Claims* (New Orleans: Polyanthos, 1976), p. v.

59. US Congress, Senate, Substance of an Argument, 21st Cong., 2nd sess., 1830. S. Doc. 12, serial 203, 24–25.

60. US Congress, Senate, Report from the Commissioner of the General Land Office, 24th Cong., 1st sess., 1835. S. Doc. 16, serial 280, 3–4.

61. Ibid.

62. Congress confirmed Austin's Spanish land grant in 1873, but in 1884 the present owners of the land grant were sued by claimants that Austin had swindled years earlier. US Congress, House, "An Act," 42nd Cong., 3rd sess., 1873, Bills and Resolutions 3731, Report No. 489; *Bryan v. Kennett* (1884), 113 US 179; *Bryan v. Kennett*, RG 21, United States Circuit Courts, Eastern District of Missouri, Eastern Division, Saint Louis, Missouri: Law, Equity, Criminal (1838–1912), Case Number: 4746, Row 48, Unit 01, Shelf 13, Box 246, National Archives—Central Plains Region, Kansas City, Missouri.

CHAPTER 4: THE MISSING JOURNAL ENTRIES: FACT OR FICTION

1. "Jefferson's Message to Congress, January 18, 1803," in Donald Jackson, ed., *Letters of the Lewis and Clark Expedition with Related Documents, 1783–1854,* 2nd ed. 2 vols. (Urbana: University of Illinois Press, 1978), 1: 12–13.

2. Thomas C. Danisi and W. Raymond Wood, "James MacKay: International Explorer," *Missouri Historical Review* 102, no. 3 (April 2008): 154–55.

3. "Jefferson's Message," p. 13.

4. Ibid.

5. Thomas Jefferson to Henry Dearborn, August 13, 1803, document 23157; and Henry Dearborn to Thomas Jefferson, August 28, 1803, document 23219, roll 28, Thomas Jefferson Papers, Library of Congress.

6. Alexander Wilson, *American Ornithology: or The Natural History of the Birds of the*

United States, 3 vols. (New York: Collins, 1828), 2: 46–47. The full quote is printed in appendix A, no. 38.

7. Jefferson's Instructions to Meriwether Lewis, June 20, 1803, document 22884–87, reel 28, Thomas Jefferson Papers, Library of Congress.

8. A complete transcription of the instructions are printed in Jackson, *Letters,* 1: 61–66.

9. Ibid, 1: 64–65.

10. Ibid, 1: 16, 17, 21.

11. George Huxtable, an on-land navigation scholar who resides in England, inquired if there was any knowledge, in Saint Louis, of the town's geographical position, latitude, and longitude, particularly longitude in March 1804. "It might possibly have been established by a military surveyor attached to the expeditionary force when Saint Louis was founded thirty years earlier. After all, the French were the world experts, at that time, in such land-survey, with longitude based primarily on timed observations of satellites of Jupiter. I wonder if there might have been, in the town prior to 1804, a resident savant, amateur astronomer, surveyor, geographer, clockmaker, schoolteacher, who might have taken an interest in such observations (French or Spanish)." He was also interested in the person who gave Meriwether Lewis this information in 1803–1804. E-mail from Robyn Burnett, Missouri State Archives, to Michael Everman, October 5, 2010. Huxtable's Website contains much information concerning "Lewis and Clark on the Mississippi: Commentary on Their Celestial Navigation," http://www.hux.me.uk/lewis02.htm (accessed February 3, 2011).

12. *New-England Palladium,* December 30, 1803, Boston. Stoddard did not have the appropriate information to make correct calculations. George Huxtable, reporting on Lewis and Clark as navigators on the expedition, wrote: "We can tell, from his reference to the equivalence between 1,437,976 square miles and 920,304,640 acres, that he is referring to land-miles, as a square land-mile corresponds to 640 acres. One degree of latitude corresponds to 60 nautical miles or 69 land-miles. When he refers to the 'Rio del Nord, or North River,' this is the Rio Grande, rising in the Rockies to the southwest of modern Denver. In which case, we can go along with his width of the territory, 692 miles, as a reasonable guess. Then when he says that Upper Louisiana (from that southern boundary to the Shining Mountains, wherever they were, or to the sources of the Mississippi and Missouri) is 2,078 miles by 692 miles in width, and that this corresponds to 1,437,976 square miles, he is considering a plane rectangle of 2,078 by 692, which multiply together to give exactly that area. So we deduce that he must be referring to straight-line distances, as the crow flies, northing and westing, and not to distances measured along the course of a winding river. Indeed, such an area calculation, that can be made on a plane surface, is far from legitimate for such large tracts on a sphere. All this leads up to an attempt to understand his figure for the north–south extent of Upper Louisiana, of 2,078 land-miles, which seems crazy. At 69 land-miles per degree, it corresponds to a separation between its northern and southern boundaries of 2,078 / 69, or 30° of latitude. As we can accept his figure for the southern boundary to be 36°, that would put the northern boundary of Upper Louisiana to be at 66° north, within 30 miles of the Arctic Circle, and close to the northern limit of the Canadian mainland."

13. Amos Stoddard to Adjutant General's Office, November 1, 1806, RG94, M566, roll 1, frame 0797, p. 48, National Archives and Records Administration.

14. Amos Stoddard, *Sketches, Historical and Descriptive of Louisiana* (Philadelphia: Mathew Carey, 1812).

15. Reuben Gold Thwaites, ed., *Original Journals of the Lewis and Clark Expedition, 1804–1806*, 8 vols. (New York: Dodd, Mead & Co., 1904), 1: xxxv, n. 2, American Journeys Website: http://content.wisconsinhistory.org/cdm4/document.php?CISOROOT=/aj& CISOPTR=762 (accessed June 22, 2011).

16. Gary Moulton, "The Missing Journals of Meriwether Lewis," *Montana: The Magazine of Western History* 35, no. 3 (Summer 1985): 28–39; Paul Russell Cutright, "The Journal of Captain Meriwether Lewis (Some Observations Concerning the Journal Hiatuses of Captain Lewis)," *We Proceeded On* 10, no. 1 (February 1984): 8–9; and "Meriwether Lewis: Zoologist," *Oregon Historical Quarterly* 69 (March 1968): 5.

17. Moulton, "Missing Journals," p. 30.

18. Stephen Ambrose, *Undaunted Courage* (New York: Simon and Schuster, 1996), p. 431.

19. Paul Russell Cutright, "The Journal of Captain Meriwether Lewis," *We Proceeded On* 10, no. 1 (February 1984): 8; Ambrose, *Undaunted Courage*, p. 110.

20. Gary E. Moulton, ed., *The Journals of the Lewis and Clark Expedition*, 13 vols. (Lincoln: University of Nebraska Press, 1983–2001), 2: 18.

21. Paul Russell Cutright, "Meriwether Lewis: Botanist," *Oregon Historical Quarterly* 69 (June 1968): 159.

22. See the online "Fort Mandan Miscellany," in Moulton's *Journals*, for a daunting itemization of Lewis's work when shipping the diversity of specimens in April 1805. His work runs into hundreds of typed pages. When scrolling to the bottom of each page, click on "next." See http://lewisandclarkjournals.unl.edu/read/?_xmlsrc=1804-1805.winter.introduction .xml&_xslsrc=LCstyles.xsl (accessed October 6, 2011).

23. Moulton, *Journals*, 3: 450–72; Velva E. Rudd, "Botanical Contributions of the Lewis and Clark Expedition," *Journal of the Washington Academy of Sciences* 44 (November 1954): 354.

24. Ibid., 3: pp. 472–78.

25. See online, Moulton, *Journals*. Lewis recorded astronomical data on November 1, 2, and 11, 1804, http://lewisandclarkjournals.unl.edu/read/?_xmlsrc=1804-11-01.xml&_xslsrc =LCstyles.xsl (accessed October 6, 2011).

26. Velva Rudd gives an accounting of the botanical shipment. "The shipment included two bundles of dried plants, one with numbers 1–60, the other 1–67. It is not known whether the two bundles represent duplicates, or a total of 127 collections. . . . The material at Philadelphia is distributed on about fifty herbarium sheets and represents about thirty-six collections." Rudd, "Botanical Contributions," 354.

27. Henry Setzer, "Zoological Contributions of the Lewis and Clark Expedition," *Journal of the Washington Academy of Sciences* 44 (November 1954): 356–57.

28. "Meriwether Lewis Astronomy Notebook, 1805," microfilm C1074, Manuscripts Collection, State Historical Society of Missouri, Columbia, Missouri.

29. "Meriwether Lewis, April 7, 1805," in Moulton, *Journals*, 4: 7–10. See appendix A, no. 3.

30. "Meriwether Lewis, August 18, 1805," in Moulton, *Journals*, 5: 117–18, or see appendix A no. 4. Lewis wrote many journal entries that are filled with succint descriptions of wonder, humility, grace, sudden joy, happiness, and sadness. The phraseology that he employed transcends any negative appraisal of his ability when simply conveying new scenes or ideas on the expedition. While historians have harshly judged his writing in some of these passages, it needs to be viewed in the spirit in which it was conceived and written—as an observation in the middle of awe and majestic grandeur. Lewis defended that position when he wrote on June 13, 1805, "I could not perhaps succeed better than pening the first impressions of the mind." On April 7, 1805, he wrote that "the colouring to events, when the immagination is suffered to wander into futurity, the picture which now presented itself to me, was a most pleasing one." Describing the Rocky Mountains on May 26, 1805, "in some measure counterballanced the joy I had felt in the first moments in which I gazed on them." In his May 31 entry he wrote that "the hills and river Clifts which we passed today exhibit a most romantic appearance." Lewis also traversed tiny emotions when conveying the sublime on June 1, 1806: "I met a singular plant today in blume of which I preserved a specemine." See Moulton, *Journals*, 4: 200–202, 224–27, 283–87; 6: 151–52.

31. Ibid., 8: 262–66.

32. Ibid., 8: 333–35 and 335, n. 1.

33. Ibid., 3: 450–55, 6: 258–60, 362–65, 7: 42–46, 191–94, 318–21, 8: 70–72, 142–44.

CHAPTER 5: THE HOMEWARD BOUND JOURNEY

*This essay was originally published in the journal of the Lewis and Clark Trail Heritage Foundation. Thomas C. Danisi and John C. Jackson, "Homeward Bound," *We Proceeded On* 33, no. 2 (May 2007): 16–19. It has been updated and rewritten since its 2007 publication.

1. *Connecticut Herald*, November 4, 1806, p. 3.

2. "Rufus Easton to President Jefferson, October 19, 1806," in Clarence E. Carter, ed., *The Territorial Papers of the United States*, 28 vols. (Washington: Government Printing Office, 1934–1962), 14: 45.

3. On April 18, 1796, Congress authorized the "factory system" to trade fairly and without profit with Native Americans using "factors" appointed by the president as official agents of the government. Factories were embedded in military forts on the edges of the frontier.

4. George Sibley to Samuel H. Sibley, October 25, 1806, Sibley Papers, Lindenwood Collection Transcripts, Missouri History Museum.

5. Pierre Chouteau said that he departed Saint Louis with the Osage on October 21, 1806, C194, M22, roll 3, p. 45, frame 0292, National Archives and Records Administration.

6. Pierre Chouteau to Henry Dearborn, October 14, 1806, Pierre Chouteau Letter-book, pp. 108–109, Missouri History Museum.

7. James Holmberg, *Dear Brother* (New Haven, CT: Yale University Press, 2002), p. 115.

8. Ibid., p. 122, n. 1.

9. Pierre Chouteau to Henry Dearborn, November 16, 1806, C203, M22, roll 3, p. 46, frame 0292, National Archives and Records Administration.

10. Pierre Chouteau to Henry Dearborn, December 7, 1806, C209, M22, roll 3, p. 46, National Archives and Records Administration.

11. "Thomas Jefferson to Thomas Mann Randolph, November 3, 1806," in Andrew A. Lipscomb and Albert Ellery Bergh, eds., *The Writings of Thomas Jefferson*, Library ed., 20 vols. (Washington, DC: Thomas Jefferson Memorial Association of the United States, 1903), 18: 249.

12. Abraham Bradley Jr., *Map of the United States: Exhibiting the Post-Roads, the Situations, Connexions & Distances of the Post-Offices, Stage Roads, Counties & Principal Rivers* (Philadelphia: F. Shallus, 1804). The Wilderness Road equates to today's US-25. Bradley's map can be found at http://en.wikipedia.org/wiki/Abraham_Bradley,_Jr. (accessed January 26, 2011).

13. Kerry Oman, "Serendipity," *We Proceeded On* 27, no. 4 (November 2001): 8. Ordway accompanied Lewis and the Mandan to the Cumberland Gap. Letter dated November 20 from Campbell explaining Ordway's presence with the group.

14. "Arthur Campbell to Governor Charles Scott, January 31, 1810," in *Journal of the House of Representatives of the Commonwealth of Kentucky: Begun and Held in the Town of Frankfort, on Monday the Fourth Day of December, 1815* (Frankfort, KY: Gerard & Berry, 1816), pp. 111–12.

15. See appendix G for George Huxtable's explanation on early survey techniques.

16. Ibid.

17. Lowell Hayes Harrison and James C. Klotter, *A New History of Kentucky* (Lexington: University Press of Kentucky, 1997), p. 22.

18. Arthur Campbell to Christopher Greenup, November 24, 1806, *Early American Imprints*, second series, no. 37990, p. 107. See appendix G for Huxtable's elaboration of what Lewis called Ellicott's "much approved Zenith Sector."

19. "Meriwether Lewis to Colonel Arthur Campbell, November 23, 1806," in *Journal of the House of Representatives of the Commonwealth of Kentucky*, pp. 89–92, 107–111; H. W. Flournoy, ed., *Calendar of Virginia State Papers and Other Manuscripts Preserved in the Capitol at Richmond, 1799–1807*, 11 vols. (Richmond: R. F. Walker, 1875–1893), 9: 504–506. In Arthur Campbell's letter dated February 23, 1807, to Gov. William G. Cabell of Virginia, he showed Lewis's certificate to General Clark. Historian James Holmberg says this was most likely Jonathan Clark, who was on his way to Virginia in February 1807. The Diary of General Jonathan Clark (1750–1811), February 14–27, 1807, bk. 16 (January 1, 1806–June 30, 1809), microfilm, Filson Historical Society, Louisville, Kentucky.

20. Meriwether Lewis to Henry Dearborn, December 22, 1806, bill of exchange #121 to James Gilmer for $52.16, Reproductions, 1806–May 1808, box 2, folder 2, Meriwether Lewis Collection, Missouri History Museum.

21. Samuel Latham Mitchill to Catherine Mitchill, December 21, 1806, folder 41.321.458, Samuel Latham Mitchill Collection, Museum of the City of New York, New York.

22. Thomas Jefferson to Wolf Indian Chief, December 30, 1806, document 28642-44, reel 37, Thomas Jefferson Papers, Library of Congress; President Jefferson to the Mandan Nation, December 30, 1806, RG75, M15, roll 2, pp. 269–70, frame 0124; Thomas Jefferson to Osage Chiefs, December 31, 1806, document 28645-46, reel 37; National Archives and Records Administration.

23. Samuel Latham Mitchill to Catherine Mitchill, January 1, 1807, folder 41.321.74, Samuel Latham Mitchill Collection, Museum of the City of New York.

24. *New-York Gazette & General Advertiser*, January 22, 1807, p. 2. The banquet was held at Stelle's Hotel. William Clark finally arrived in Washington on January 18. William E. Foley, *Wilderness Journey: The Life of William Clark* (Columbia: University of Missouri Press, 2004), p. 157.

25. *The Sun* (Washington, DC), February 7, 1807, p. 4.

26. Ibid. In February 1803, Meriwether Lewis was a member of the American Board of Agriculture and served on the committee of correspondence for the territory of Columbia. *Republican Watch-Tower* (Washington, DC), March 9, 1803, p. 2.

27. *The Sun*, February 7, 1807, p. 4.

28. "We proceeded on" was a favorite phrase often repeated by Lewis and Clark during the expedition.

29. US Congress, House Journal, 9th Cong., 2nd sess., December 2, 1806.

30. "Henry Dearborn to Willis Alston, January 14, 1807," in Donald Jackson, ed., *Letters of the Lewis and Clark Expedition with Related Documents, 1783–1854*, 2nd ed. 2 vols. (Urbana: University of Illinois Press, 1978), 1: 363.

31. US Congress, *Annals of Congress of the United States, 1789–1824*, 42 vols. (Washington, DC, 1834–1856), 9: 591–92.

32. "The Act Compensating Lewis and Clark, March 3, 1807," and "Messrs. Lewis & Clarke's Donations Lands, March 6, 1807," Jackson, *Letters*, 2: 377, 380.

33. US Congress, Senate Journal, 9th Cong., 2nd sess., March 3, 1807.

34. Carter, *Territorial Papers*, 13: 97–98, 383, 504; Thomas Jefferson to James Monroe, May 4, 1806, document 27777-78, reel 35, Thomas Jefferson Papers, Library of Congress. See letters 179 and 190, Thomas Jefferson to James Monroe correspondence, Gawalt, Manuscript Division, Library of Congress; Thomas Jefferson to Samuel Smith, October 15, 1806, document 28352, and Albert Gallatin to Thomas Jefferson, October 25, 1806, document 28381, roll 36.

35. Thomas M. Marshall, *The Life and Papers of Frederick Bates*, 2 vols. (Saint Louis: Missouri Historical Society, 1926), 1: 17–18. Frederick Bates (1777–1825) was a long-term public servant in Missouri who was elected the second governor of the state in 1824. Born in Goochland County, Virginia, Bates studied law in Virginia, then joined the army in 1797 and served as a paymaster in Detroit, where he may have met Meriwether Lewis. In 1800 Bates resigned from the army and became a merchant in Detroit, but a fire in 1805 destroyed

most of his possessions. Holding a series of government positions such as postmaster, judge, and land commissioner in the Northwest Territory paved the way for Bates to be appointed by President Jefferson as secretary of the Louisiana Territory at the same time that Lewis was appointed governor. Awaiting Lewis's arrival, Bates was acting governor for nearly a year, from April 1, 1807, until March 8, 1808. During that time Bates organized the territorial militia and served as US Indian agent with the assistance of William Clark. After Lewis's death, Bates once more became acting governor in 1809, and served in the position for another year in 1812 and 1813. Bates did not want the territorial governorship for himself (it was offered to him) because his job as secretary, combined with the position of recorder of land titles, was more lucrative. Bates married Opie Ball in 1819, and they had four children. He died suddenly of pleurisy in 1825 while in office as governor of the State of Missouri.

36. "Lewis's Estimate of Expenses, 1803," and "Financials of the Expedition, August 5, 1807," in Jackson, *Letters*, 1: 8–9 and 2: 419–28.

37. "Observations and Reflections on the Subject of Governing and Maintaining a State of Friendly Intercourse with the Indians of the Territory of Louisiana," in Thomas C. Danisi and John C. Jackson, *Meriwether Lewis* (Amherst, NY: Prometheus Books, 2009), pp. 349–73.

38. Thomas Jefferson to Charles Willson Peale, March 29, 1807, document 29235, reel 38, Thomas Jefferson Papers, Library of Congress. Jefferson reminded Peale that Lewis was bringing money to reimburse him for the inkholders.

39. Alexander Wilson, *American Ornithology: or The Natural History of the Birds of the United States*, 3 vols. (New York: Collins, 1828), 2: 46–47. The full quote is printed in appendix A, no. 38.

40. "Conrad's Estimate of Publishing Costs, April 1807," in Jackson, *Letters*, 2: 392–94.

41. "The Conrad Prospectus, April 1, 1807," in Jackson, *Letters*, 2: 394–97.

42. *Philadelphia Aurora*, June 16, 1807, p. 1.

43. "The Mahlon Dickerson Diary, June 16, 1807," in Jackson, *Letters*, 2: 682.

44. The original letter reads A– R–ph., November 3, 1807, MG31, box 2, folder 38, Statesman Collection, New Jersey Historical Society, Newark, New Jersey.

45. James R. Bentley, "Two Letters of Meriwether Lewis to Major William Preston," *The Filson Club History Quarterly* 44, no. 2 (April 1970): 174, n. 8; "Meriwether Lewis to Mahlon Dickerson, November 3, 1807," in Jackson, *Letters*, 2: 720.

46. Grace Lewis Miller Collection, Jefferson National Expansion Memorial Archives. John Pernier, a mulatto free man, had worked for Thomas Jefferson since the beginning of October 1804. Massachusetts Historical Society, Thomas Jefferson's Account Book, March 25 to May 1805, p. 18. Lewis hired him in July 1807.

47. *National Intelligencer and Washington Advertiser*, February 22, 1808, p. 3.

48. Meriwether Lewis to Lucy Marks, February 15, 1808, Meriwether Lewis Collection, Missouri History Museum.

CHAPTER 6: PRESERVING THE LEGACY OF
MERIWETHER LEWIS: LETTERS OF
SAMUEL LATHAM MITCHILL

*This essay was originally published in the journal of the Lewis and Clark Trail Heritage Foundation. Thomas C. Danisi, "Preserving the Legacy of Meriwether Lewis: The letters of Samuel Latham Mitchill," *We Proceeded On* 36, no. 1 (February 2010): 8–11.

1. Frederick Bates had attended the banquet at Stelle's Hotel on January 14, 1807, and witnessed the plethora of toasts, as well as Barlow's oration. I thank Bates for his comments toward Lewis: they enriched my understanding of his wily character. It was no mistake that Clark described Bates as a "little animale." James Holmberg, *Dear Brother* (New Haven, CT: Yale University Press, 2002), p. 248.

2. "Frederick Bates to Richard Bates," in Thomas M. Marshall, *The Life and Papers of Frederick Bates*, 2 vols. (Saint Louis: Missouri Historical Society, 1926), 2: 108.

3. Joel Barlow, "On the Discoveries of Lewis, January 14, 1807," in Richard Dillon, *Meriwether Lewis, A Biography* (Santa Cruz, CA: Western Tanager Press, 1965), pp. 269–70.

4. In January 1804, James MacKay met with Meriwether Lewis and William Clark at Camp River Dubois and lent them his map of the first 1,500 miles of the Missouri River. Thomas C. Danisi and W. Raymond Wood, "Lewis and Clark's Route Map: James MacKay's Map of the Missouri River," *Western Historical Quarterly* 35, no. 1 (Spring 2004): 53–72.

5. Samuel L. Mitchill, ed., *Medical Repository*, 12 vols. (New York: 1804–1812), 4: 27–36; Mitchill, "Descriptive Observations on Certain Parts of the Country in Louisiana," *Medical Repository* (1806), 3: 309. Mitchill, as chairman of the special committee established to investigate the possibility of exploring the Louisiana Territory, introduced the bill that authorized Lewis and Clark to explore the country to the Pacific Ocean. Alan David Aberbach, *In Search of an Identity: Samuel Latham Mitchill, Jeffersonian Nationalist* (New York: Peter Lang, 1988), pp. 69–70.

6. The Samuel Latham Mitchill letters are located at the Museum of the City of New York. In July 2004, the Lewis and Clark Trail Heritage Foundation awarded me a small research grant, which helped fund this important trip. I also visited the New Jersey Historical Society during the same trip and was able to uncover several gems by Mahlon Dickerson for the biography *Meriwether Lewis*.

7. The first date was December 1806, then 1807, 1805, the rest of 1806, 1804, 1808, 1801, and 1802.

8. Stephen Ambrose, *Undaunted Courage: Meriwether Lewis, Thomas Jefferson and the Opening of the American West* (New York: Simon and Schuster, 1996), p. 409.

9. Samuel Latham Mitchill to Catherine Mitchill, December 30, 1806, folder 41.321.464, Samuel Latham Mitchill Collection, Museum of the City of New York. See appendix C, no. 66.

10. Aberbach, *In Search of an Identity*, p. 70.

11. *The Congressional Journals of the US Senate: Thomas Jefferson Administration*, 8 vols.

(reprint, Wilmington, DE: Michael Glazier, 1977), 3: vii; Alan D. Aberbach, "Samuel Latham Mitchill: A Physician in the Early Days of the Republic," *Bulletin of the New York Academy of Medicine* 40 (July 1964): 508. Mitchill was founder of the New York Academy of Sciences and served as its president from 1817–1823.

12. "Samuel Latham Mitchill to Catherine Mitchill, January 10, 1802," quoted in "Dr. Mitchill's Letters from Washington: 1801–1813," *Harper's New Monthly Magazine* 58, Issue 347 (April 1879): 743–44. Mitchill arrived in Washington on December 7, 1801. See appendix C, no. 6.

13. Ibid., 740. A digital reproduction is available through Cornell University Library: "The Making of America," http://dlxs2.library.cornell.edu/cgi/t/text/pageviewer-idx?c=harp ;cc=harp;rgn=full%20text;idno=harp0058-5;didno=harp0058-5;view=image;seq=0750 ;node=harp0058-5%3A13 (accessed May 14, 2011).

14. Copied verbatim from an online exhibit at the Library of Congress titled, "Religion and the Founding of the American Republic: The State Becomes the Church, Jefferson and Madison, Part II." Incident at Congressional Church Services, Catherine Akerly Mitchill to Margaret Miller, April 8, 1806, Manuscript Division, Library of Congress (document 167), Washington, DC, http://www.loc.gov/exhibits/religion/rel06-2.html and http://www.loc .gov/exhibits/religion/f0609s.jpg (original letter) (accessed May 14, 2011).

15. Catherine Mitchill to Margaret Miller, August 17, 1807, Mitchill manuscript, Manuscript Collection, New York Historical Society, New York, New York. Carolyn Hoover Sung, "Catherine Mitchill's Letters from Washington 1806–1812," *Quarterly Journal of the Library of Congress* 34, no. 3 (July 1977): 171–89.

16. "Dr. Mitchill's Letters," p. 740.

17. Courtney Robert Hall, *A Scientist in the Early Republic, Samuel Latham Mitchill 1764–1831* (New York: Russell & Russell, 1962), pp. 13–14.

18. "Samuel Latham Mitchill to Catherine Mitchill, January 10, 1802," quoted in "Dr. Mitchill's Letters," p. 744.

19. Samuel Latham Mitchill to Catherine Mitchill, April 29, 1802, folder 41.321.10, Museum of the City of New York.

20. Samuel L. Mitchill, "Lewis's Map of the Parts of North America," *Medical Repository*, 3: 315–18; Samuel L. Mitchill, "Review: Message from the President of the United States Communicating Discoveries Made in Exploring the Missouri," *Medical Repository*, 4: 165–74; Amos Stoddard, "The Greatest Lead Mines in Upper Louisiana," *Medical Repository*, 3: 87–88.

21. US Congress, House Journal, 7th Congress, 2nd session, January 18, 1803; US Congress, Senate Journal, 7th Congress, 2nd session, January 18, 1803; "Jefferson's Message to Congress, January 18, 1803," in Donald Jackson, ed., *Letters of the Lewis and Clark Expedition with Related Documents, 1783–1854*, 2nd ed. 2 vols. (Urbana: University of Illinois Press, 1978), 1: 13; US Congress, House Journal, 7th Congress, 2nd session, February 26, 1803.

22. Samuel Latham Mitchill to Catherine Mitchill, January 31, 1803, folder 41.321.265, Museum of the City of New York.

23. Samuel L. Mitchill, *Discourse on Thomas Jefferson, More Especially as a Promoter of Natural & Physical Science* (New York: G & C Carvill, 1826), p. 28; Samuel Latham Mitchill to Catherine Mitchill, January 7, 1807, folder 41.321.75, Museum of the City of New York.

24. Samuel Latham Mitchill to Catherine Mitchill, January 16, 1807, folder 41.321.103, Museum of the City of New York. See appendix C, no. 70.

25. Samuel Latham Mitchill to Catherine Mitchill, February 18, 1807, folder 41.321.69, Museum of the City of New York. See appendix C, no. 74.

CHAPTER 7: OBSERVATIONS AND REMARKS FROM LEWIS TO DEARBORN IN 1807: AN UNKNOWN LETTER REVEALS AN *IN ABSENTIA* GOVERNOR IN CONTROL

*This essay was originally published in the journal of the Lewis and Clark Trail Heritage Foundation. Thomas C. Danisi, "Observations and Remarks from Lewis to Dearborn in 1807," *We Proceeded On* 35, no. 3 (August 2009): 32–38.

1. Clarence Edwin Carter, ed., *The Territorial Papers of the United States*, 28 vols. (Washington, DC: Government Printing Office, 1948). *Microfilm Resources for Research, A Comprehensive Catalog* (Washington, DC: National Archives and Records Administration, 2000). Today this guide is online and as helpful as the printed version.

2. Carter, *Territorial Papers*, pp. 13, 14; General Records of the Department of State, Denis Fitzhugh to James Madison, August 15, 1808, RG59, M179, roll 22, p. 88, National Archives and Records Administration.

3. I thank Susan Saxton of Saint Louis, Missouri, for suggesting and implementing this novel idea.

4. Records of the Office of the Secretary of War, Meriwether Lewis to the Secretary of War, RG107, M222, 1807, S1807, roll 2, frames 0952-54, National Archives and Records Administration.

5. *Letters Received by the Secretary of War, Unregistered Series, 1789–1861*, Microcopy M222, (Washington, DC: National Archives and Records Service, 1963), pp. 2–3.

6. Roll 2 piqued my interest more than roll 1 because of the dates, 1805–1807. Roll 1 includes the dates 1789–1804 and contains letters from Captain Amos Stoddard describing some of Lewis's requests.

7. RG107, M222, L1806, roll 2, frames 0657–81, National Archives and Records Administration.

8. General Dearborn arrived in New York on July 11 and returned to Washington by August 7. Henry Dearborn to Thomas Jefferson, July 12, 1807, document 29710, roll 38, and August 7, 1807, document 28318, reel 39, Thomas Jefferson Papers, Library of Congress, http://memory.loc.gov/ammem/collections/jefferson_papers/ (accessed May 20, 2011).

9. William Clark to Secretary of War, May 18, 1807, C280, and June 1, 1807, C282, RG107, M221, roll 5, frames 1326–36; Frederick Bates to Secretary of War, May 15, 1807, B245, M221, roll 4, National Archives and Records Administration.

10. Lewis was appointed governor of the Louisiana Territory by Congress on March 3, 1807, and returned to Saint Louis to assume the role of full-time governor almost one year later, on March 8, 1808.

11. Meriwether Lewis Account Book, 1807–1809, Meriwether Lewis Collection, Missouri History Museum; "William Simmons to Meriwether Lewis, July 31, 1807," Jackson, *Letters*, 2: 419.

12. Samuel Latham Mitchill visited Philadelphia in 1802 and attended a few lectures at the American Philosophical Society. He wrote to his wife when he departed Washington and again when he arrived in Philadelphia. The time lapse was two days. Samuel Mitchill to Catherine Mitchill, December 6, 1802, folder 41.321.26 and December 8, 1802, folder 41.321.8, Samuel Mitchill Collection, Museum of the City of New York. The time varied by coach or horseback. Henry Adams, *The History of the United States of America during the Administration of Thomas Jefferson*, 9 vols. (New York: Charles Scribner's Sons, 1891), 1: 11–14; Abigail Adams to her sister, November 21, 1800, Stewart Mitchell, ed., *New Letters of Abigail Adams, 1788–1801* (New York: Houghton Mifflin, 1947); Cliff Sloan and David McKean, *The Great Decision: Jefferson, Adams, Marshall, and the Battle for the Supreme Court* (New York: Public Affairs, 2009), p. 6.

13. Meriwether Lewis Account Book, 1807–1809, Meriwether Lewis Collection, Missouri History Museum; Henry Phillips Jr., "Early Proceedings of the American Philosophical Society . . . from the Manuscript Minutes of Its Meetings from 1774 to 1838," *Proceedings of the American Philosophical Society* 22 (1884): 396–98; John Vaughan to Thomas Jefferson, November 21, 1803, document 23559, roll 29, Thomas Jefferson Papers, Library of Congress.

14. Jackson, *Letters*, 2: 696, n. (a); Thomas C. Danisi and John C. Jackson, *Meriwether Lewis* (Amherst, NY: Prometheus Books, 2009), 349–73.

15. For a transcription of the two letters, see "William Clark to Secretary of War, May 18, 1807," and "William Clark to Secretary of War, June 1, 1807," in Carter, *Territorial Papers*, 14: 122–25 and 126–27; http://digital.library.umsystem.edu/cgi/t/text/text-idx?sid=ebad2bc2458828beb40539b706811b94;g=;c=umlib;idno=umlc000005 (accessed May 20, 2011).

16. Danisi and Jackson, *Meriwether Lewis*, pp. 117, n. 13, 119, n. 53, and 128, n. 17.

17. Carter, *Territorial Papers*, 14: 122.

18. Ibid. The Mandan chief Sheheke-shote was invited by Lewis and Clark near the conclusion of their 1804–1806 expedition to leave his home in present-day North Dakota and travel back with them to meet the president in Washington. Because of a hostile outbreak among the Arikara, who blocked passage to all on the upper Missouri River, a military expedition to return Sheheke-shote failed in 1807 and was forced to return to Saint Louis. This was the topic of Clark's letter. Following this failed expedition, the Mandan chief and

his family languished in Saint Louis. Lewis and Clark had promised the chief and his people that he would return within a year of his departure and had failed to keep this pledge, which prompted the efforts of many to find a solution for his safe return in 1808 or 1809.

19. Since Clark mentioned that this incident took place "last fall," and Lewis mentioned Lts. Pike and Wilkinson, it is certain that the dispute arose from preparations for Zebulon Pike's Southwestern Expedition in 1806. On August 27 of that year, when Pike and his command were staying with the Osage in southwest Missouri, he recorded in his journal that they procured six horses from the Indians. Lt. James B. Wilkinson was Pike's second in command and may have been in charge of procuring the horses; he later led a detachment to explore the lower Arkansas River. Wilkinson split off from Pike's main party on October 28, 1806, and returned to Saint Louis later that year. See Donald Jackson, *The Journals of Zebulon Montgomery Pike* (Urbana: University of Illinois Press, 1962).

20. Carter, *Territorial Papers,* 14: 124.

21. Dorion wrote several letters pleading to be paid, but his requests went unanswered. Pierre Dorion to Secretary of War, November 19, 1807, D208, RG107, M221, roll 6, frame 1903. Lewis finally paid Dorion. Meriwether Lewis to Secretary of War, April 15, 1808, L67 and L68, M22, National Archives and Records Administration.

22. For a transcription of the letter see Thomas M. Marshall, *The Life and Papers of Frederick Bates*, 2 vols. (Saint Louis: Missouri Historical Society, 1926) 1: 119–22.

23. Danisi and Jackson, *Meriwether Lewis*, p. 195; "Frederick Bates to Secretary of War, September 28, 1809," Marshall, *Frederick Bates*, 2: 87.

24. Secretary of War to William Clark and Frederick Bates, August 17, 1807, RG107, M15, roll 2, frame 0147, p. 328, National Archives and Records Administration.

CHAPTER 8: MERIWETHER LEWIS'S LAND WARRANT: AN UNTIMELY REWARD

*This essay was originally published in the journal of the Lewis and Clark Trail Heritage Foundation. Thomas C. Danisi, "Meriwether Lewis's Land Warrant: An Untimely Reward," *We Proceeded On* 35, no. 4 (November 2009): 26–28.

1. Donald Jackson, ed., *Letters of the Lewis and Clark Expedition with Related Documents, 1783–1854*, 2 vols. (Urbana: University of Illinois Press, 1978), 1: 361.

2. Ibid., 1: 363.

3. Ibid., 1: 363–64; US Congress, House Journal, 9th Congress, 2nd session, January 2, 1807, p. 104.

4. Annals of Congress, 9th Congress, 2nd session, February 20, 1807, p. 591; US Congress, Senate Journal, 9th Congress, 2nd session, March 3, 1807, Vol. 4, p. 172.

5. Jackson, *Letters*, 2: 377.

6. Clarence Edwin Carter, ed., *The Territorial Papers of the United States*, 28 vols. (Washington, DC: Government Printing Office, 1948), 13: 536 and 15: 109.

7. Land Warrants, November 15, 1808, Record Deed Book B, pp. 152–157, City of Saint Louis, Recorder of Deeds, City Hall, Saint Louis, Missouri; *Missouri Gazette*, March 29, 1809, vol. 1, issue 43; William Carr to Charles Carr, August 25, 1809, William Carr Papers, Missouri History Museum.

8. Lillian Ruth Colter-Frick, *Courageous Colter and Companions* (Washington, MO: Colter-Frick, 1997), pp. 339–41; Carter, *Territorial Papers*, 14: 85–86 and 289–93; James J. Holmberg, ed., *Dear Brother* (New Haven: Yale University Press, 2002), pp. 201, 209–10, and 215.

9. Thomas M. Marshall, *The Life and Papers of Frederick Bates*, 2 vols. (Saint Louis: Missouri Historical Society, 1926) 2: 86; Meriwether Lewis Account Book, September 17, 1809, Meriwether Lewis Collection, Missouri History Museum.

10. Gilbert Russell to Thomas Jefferson, January 4, 1810, document 33616–17, roll 45, Thomas Jefferson Papers, Library of Congress. No mention is made of Clark's warrant, and when Lewis's trunks arrived in Washington, Clark portioned the contents to Jefferson, the War Department, Lewis's family, and himself. I can only speculate that Clark's warrant was returned by an unknown means—when James McFarlane arrived in New Orleans in November 1809, he could have picked it up or it was among Lewis's papers. In either case, Clark never raised concern about it. James McFarlane, microfilm F523, vol. 4, instrument 2990, French and Spanish Archives, City of St. Louis, City Hall, St. Louis, Missouri.

11. General Land Office to Scott Leavitt, House of Representatives, January 5, 1926, Grace Lewis Miller Collection, box 8, folder 15, Jefferson National Expansion Memorial Archives.

12. Richard Searcy to George Graham, Commissioner of the General Land Office, December 31, 1826, Arkansas Territory, Miller Collection, box 8, folder 15, Jefferson National Expansion Memorial Archives. In Danisi and Jackson's biography of Meriwether Lewis, the name Searcy was mistaken for Gearey. The Searcy document is nearly unreadable in the Grace Lewis Miller collection but a second letter (Richard Searcy to Major Reuben Lewis, April 3, 1820, box 1, folder 14) corroborates the spelling in the Meriwether Lewis Collection at the Missouri History Museum.

13. Bills and Resolutions, House of Representatives, 20th Cong., 1st sess., A Bill for the relief of the legal representatives of Meriwether Lewis, House Resolution 282, Journal of the Senate of the United States of America, 1789–1873, vol. 17, appendix, p. 506.

CHAPTER 9: WAS GOVERNOR LEWIS'S CORRESPONDENCE INTENTIONALLY DELAYED?

1. RG107, M22, *Registers of Letters Received by the Office of the Secretary of War, Main Series, 1800–1870*, and M221, *Letters Received by the Secretary of War, Main Series, 1800–1870*, National Archives and Records Administration.

2. Each letter of the alphabet ran its own course for number designations. For instance, the letter L, for the year 1806 extended to April 1, 1808, and totaled 247 letters before beginning again on April 14, 1808, and ending October 26, 1809, and totaling 347 letters (M22, roll 3, frames 0357–63 and roll 4, frames 0503–0510). The letter M, in 1808 began April 1 and ended December 1, 1809, and contained 635 letters (M22, roll 4, frames 0510–25).

3. Clarence Edwin Carter, ed., *The Territorial Papers of the United States*, 28 vols. (Washington, DC: Government Printing Office, 1948), 13: p. 74.

4. James Wilkinson to War Department, W14-20, RG107, M22, roll 3, National Archives and Records Administration.

5. William Clark to Secretary of War, June 8, 1807, C338, M22, roll 3, National Archives and Records Administration.

6. On his way to Julia's home, Clark stopped outside of Cincinnati at Big Bone Lick and performed an errand for President Thomas Jefferson by digging up mammoth bones. William Clark to Secretary of War, September 12, 1807, C321, M22, roll 3, p. 52, frame 0295; Donald Jackson, ed., *Letters of the Lewis and Clark Expedition with Related Documents, 1783–1854*, 2 vols. (Urbana: University of Illinois Press, 1978), 2: 442.

7. Meriwether Lewis to Secretary of War, August 20, 1808, Carter, *Territorial Papers*, 14: 212.

8. Pierre Chouteau to Secretary of War, February 12, 1808, C458, M22, roll 3, National Archives and Records Administration.

9. Meriwether Lewis to Secretary of War, April 15, 1808, L67, Pierre Dorion for $313.70; L68, Pierre Dorion for $168.73; L69, Baptiste Dorion for $45; L70, John Reffle $50, M22, roll 4, p. 238, frame 0504, National Archives and Records Administration.

10. Meriwether Lewis to Secretary of War, April 25, 1808, L97, M22, roll 4, p. 240, frame 0505, National Archives and Records Administration.

11. William Clark to Secretary of War, August 13, 1808, C411, Falconer and Comegys, $350, M221, roll 20, frame 6093, National Archives and Records Administration.

12. William Clark to Secretary of War, November 10, 1808, Entry 493, Box 3; Letters received by the Accountant for the War Department, College Park II, Maryland, National Archives and Records Administration. This letter bypassed the secretary of war because it related to expenditures. The November 18, 1808, letter on the list is not this one.

13. Meriwether Lewis, November 20, 1808, draft no. 12 in favor of Sydall Manley, Meriwether Lewis Account Book, Meriwether Lewis Collection, Missouri History Museum.

14. The July 8, 1809 letter is printed in appendix A, no. 13.

15. William Clark to Henry Dearborn, July 20, 1810, C193, RG107, M221, roll 35, frame 2577, National Archives and Records Administration.

16. "Frederick Bates to Richard Bates, March 24, 1808," in Thomas M. Marshall, *The Life and Papers of Frederick Bates*, 2 vols. (Saint Louis: Missouri Historical Society, 1926) 1: 315.

17. Meriwether Lewis to William Clark, May 29, 1808, Clark Family Collection, Missouri History Museum.

18. "Frederick Bates to Richard Bates, November 9, 1809," in Marshall, *Frederick Bates*, 2: 109–10.

19. "Frederick Bates to Gabriel Duvall, August 13, 1808," and "Frederick Bates to Albert Gallatin, August 28, 1808," in Marshall, *Frederick Bates*, 2: 11, 19. Before Bates departed on the circuit, he wrote a letter on May 26 to John Breck Treat, the Arkansas Indian agent, and said that he arrived on May 29 at Cape Girardeau. Marshall, *Frederick Bates*, 1: 344 and Carter, *Territorial Papers*, 14: 190.)

20. "Judge Lucas to the Secretary of the Treasury, January 4, 1806," in Carter, *Territorial Papers*, 13: 374; "Judge Lucas to the Secretary of the Treasury, January 4, 1807," in Carter, *Territorial Papers*, 14: 60.

21. This is a simplified story of Tillier's removal from office. For the deeper conflict, see Thomas C. Danisi, "George Champlain Sibley: Shady Dealings on the Early Frontier," *Confluence* 2, no. 1 (Fall/Winter 2010): 39–49.

22. George Mason to Rodophe Tillier, May 20, 1808, RG75, M16, roll 1, pp. 154–55; George Mason to George Sibley, May 24, 1808, M16, roll 1, frame 0069, p. 147; George Mason to Rodophe Tillier, May 27, 1808, M16, roll 1, p. 158; Rodophe Tillier to George Mason, June 30, 1808, T1808, RG107, M222, roll 3, frames 1404–1405; George Mason to Rodophe Tillier, May 19, 1809, M16, roll 1, p. 381; Rodophe Tillier to George Mason, May 27, 1809, T1809, M222, roll 4, frame 1628; George Mason to Rodophe Tillier, June 21, 1809, M16, roll 2, p. 13; Danisi, "George Champlain Sibley," pp. 46–48.

23. Ernest Staples Osgood, ed., *The Field Notes of Captain William Clark, 1803–1805* (New Haven, CT: Yale University Press, 1964), p. 25, n. 8.

24. Andrew Todd of Montreal, Canada, vol. 5, no. 3, pp. 427–514, Saint Louis Recorded Archives, Jefferson National Expansion Memorial Library, National Park Service, Saint Louis, Missouri; Abraham P. Nasatir, ed., *Before Lewis and Clark: Documents Illustrating the History of the Missouri, 1785–1804*, 2 vols. (Lincoln: University of Nebraska Press, 1990), 2: 443

25. Nasatir, *Before Lewis and Clark*, 2: 437.

26. Gary E. Moulton, ed., *The Journals of the Lewis and Clark Expedition*, 13 vols. (Lincoln: University of Nebraska Press, 1983–2001), 2: 126; Will of Andrew Todd, Saint Louis Recorded Archives, vol. 5, no. 2, 427–514; Power of Attorney at Saint Louis, June 2, 1798, and May 4, 1799, Saint Louis Recorded Archives, WPA Subject Matter Index; Nasatir, *Before Lewis and Clark*, 2: 571–73, 578.

27. There has been extensive discussion over the identity of John Hay, Cahokia postmaster, and John Hays, Cahokia sheriff, who both lived in Cahokia at the same time. To verify their identities, one can look at the petitions to the US Congress and compare their signatures against other documents of the time. Postmaster Hay wrote to the US postmaster general on many occasions and always signed his letters. He also wrote extensively to Auguste Chouteau, and his letters can be viewed at the Missouri History Museum. As Sheriff, John Hays signed numerous documents that would easily differentiate the two men. Lastly, we have Lewis's word about the two men and how he was able to tell them apart. See

James and Andrew McGill & Co. to Auguste Chouteau, Saint Louis, October 8, 1802, in care of Mr. John Hay, Postmaster, Cahokia, Indiana Territory, microfilm reel 3, frame 0603, Chouteau Collection, Missouri History Museum; Account with Todd, Chouteau, reel 1, Chouteau Collections, Missouri History Museum.

28. Kevin C. Witte, "In the Footsteps of the Third Spanish Expedition: James Mackay and John T. Evans's Impact on the Lewis and Clark Expedition," *Great Plains Quarterly* 26, no. 2 (Spring 2006): 93–94.

29. "Meriwether Lewis to an Unknown Correspondent, October 14, 1806," in Jackson, *Letters*, 1: 335, n. 43. The only other copy of this letter is in David Thompson's hand in the Vancouver, British Columbia, Public Library.

CHAPTER 10: GOVERNOR MERIWETHER LEWIS'S FISCAL HOUSE OF CARDS: A CLOSER LOOK

1. Donald R. Kennon and Rebecca M. Rogers, *The Committee on Ways and Means: A Bicentennial History, 1789–1989* (Washington, DC: US House of Representatives, 1989), pp. 38–39; Alexander Balinky, *Albert Gallatin: Fiscal Theories and Policies* (New Brunswick, NJ: Rutgers University Press, 1958), p. 104.

2. US Statutes at Large 1 (1792): 279–80, http://memory.loc.gov/cgi-bin/ampage ?collId=llsl&fileName=001/llsl001.db&recNum=403 (accessed February 10, 2011); Ezekial Bacon to William Simmons, April 18, 1814, p. 2, Series 1: General Correspondence, reel 16, James Madison Papers, Library of Congress.

3. Harry M. Ward, *The Department of War, 1781–1795* (Pittsburgh: University of Pittsburgh Press, 1962), p. 144.

4. George Washington to the Senate, June 12, 1795, Nominations, Letterbook 27, Series 2 Letterbooks, Library of Congress; Records of the Accounting Officers of the Department of the Treasury, RG217, M235, roll 67, frame 1202, National Archives and Records Administration.

5. US Statutes at Large 1 (1798): 563–64.

6. William Clark to War Department, October 30, 1808, C284, M221, roll 20, frame 5964, National Archives and Records Administration.

7. Peter Hagner's Statement: Confrontation between Captain Samuel Vance and William Simmons, February 20, 1799, p. 41, Papers of the War Department, 1784–1800, Alexander Hamilton Papers, Library of Congress. Hagner was the principal clerk in Simmons's office; http://wardepartmentpapers.org/docimage.php?id=30526&docColID=33485 (accessed February 11, 2011).

8. William Simmons paid Meriwether Lewis on December 19, 1797, March 10 and March 22, 1798, and June 19, 1799.

9. Thomas and Cuthbert Bullitt of Louisville, Kentucky.

10. Gabriel Duvall to C. & T. Bullitt, November 10, 1810, D81, RG107, M221, roll 36, frame 3109, National Archives and Records Administration. Duvall, the Comptroller of the Treasury, was also a lawyer—a requisite demanded by President Jefferson. Thomas Jefferson to Gabriel Duvall, November 5, 1802, document 21939, roll 27, Thomas Jefferson Papers, Library of Congress.

11. The Latin legal term "ex parte," means from or by one side only, and with the other side absent or unrepresented.

12. "William Simmons to Meriwether Lewis, July 31, 1807," and "Financial Records of the Expedition, August 5, 1807," in Donald Jackson, ed., *Letters of the Lewis and Clark Expedition with Related Documents, 1783–1854*, 2 vols. (Urbana: University of Illinois Press, 1978), 2: 419–31. Jackson simplified this part of the accounting, which gives the appearance that Lewis had little work to accomplish when meeting with Simmons. On the contrary, Simmons recorded the expedition expenses in more than thirty ledgers (partially filled with expedition information). The ledgers measured about 24 x 30 inches. If Lewis was required to produce paper in support of Simmons's line items, the expedition would have failed to return any scientific discoveries.

13. "William Simmons to Meriwether Lewis, June 17, 1807," in Jackson, *Letters*, 2: 416–17.

14. "William Simmons to Meriwether Lewis, July 31, 1807," Jackson, *Letters*, 2: 419.

15. "Thomas Jefferson to Meriwether Lewis, July 4, 1803," Jackson, *Letters*, 1: 105–106; *Early American Imprints*, second series, no. 21675, pp. 4 and 14, and no. 24153, p. 6.

16. James Wilkinson to Albert Gallatin, September 5, 1807, document 77, Albert Gallatin Papers, 1807, reel 14, New York Historical Society, New York.

17. Opinion of the Honorable C. A. Rodney on the claim of Genl. Wilkinson for extra rations and quarters, December 1809, R275, M221, roll 29, frame 9791–92, National Archives and Records Administration.

18. Extra Allowances to the Commander-in-Chief of the Army, *American State Papers, Finance* 2: 339.

19. Ibid., 2: 340–41.

20. "Public Plunder: Letters from William Simmons, Accountant of the War Department to Brigadier General Wilkinson regarding Unauthorized Expenditures," *An American Time Capsule: Three Centuries of Broadsides and Other Printed Ephemera*, Library of Congress, http://lcweb2.loc.gov/cgi-bin/query/r?ammem/rbpe:@field(DOCID+@lit(rbpe22702700)) (accessed March 11, 2011).

21. In 1803, Gilbert C. Russell was a captain in the Tennessee militia. *Annals of the Congress of the United States, 1789–1824*, 42 vols. (Washington: Gales & Seaton, 1834–1836), 15: 183, 197, 210, 224–25, http://memory.loc.gov/cgi-bin/ampage?collId=llac&fileName=015/llac015.db&recNum=0 (accessed February 15, 2011).

22. Gilbert Russell to Secretary of War, March 15, 1808, R133, RG107, M221, roll 12, frame 3623, National Archives and Records Administration. William Anderson and Joseph P. Anderson were brothers.

23. Ibid.

24. "Gabriel Duvall to William Simmons, January 9, 1809," in *American State Papers, Finance* 2: 339.

25. Statutes at Large 2 (1807): 451–52. On June 22, 1807, a British warship fired upon an American naval vessel off the American coast and impressed several seamen. The Embargo Act was passed in an act of protest and retaliation at the end of 1807.

26. "Secretary of War to William Clark, March 9, 1807," in Carter, *Territorial Papers*, 14: 108–109.

27. Ibid, p. 109.

28. John B. C. Lucas to James Mountain, March 3, 1808, Lucas Collection, Box 3, Missouri History Museum. Lucas was also a commissioner on the land board and wrote to Gallatin on a regular basis. They were also friends from former times in Congress and having been on the same committee in the Pennsylvania legislature in the 1790s. Hugh G. Cleland, "John B. C. Lucas, Physiocrat on the Frontier," *Western Pennsylvania Historical Magazine* 36, no. 2 (June 1953): 92–100.

29. "William Clark to Secretary of War, June 1, 1807," in Carter, *Territorial Papers*, 14: 126; "William Clark to Secretary of War, May 18, 1807," in Carter, *Territorial Papers*, 14: 122. Clark's June 1 letter was more comprehensive than the one on May 18 as to the total number of persons on the voyage.

30. William Clark to Henry Dearborn, December 3, 1807, C378, RG107, "Kimball's Report," M221, roll 5, frame 1563, National Archives and Records Administration; Thomas C. Danisi and John C. Jackson, *Meriwether Lewis* (Amherst, NY: Prometheus Books, 2009), pp. 191–92.

31. "Nathaniel Pryor to William Clark, October 16, 1807," and "William Clark to Henry Clay, September 11, 1816," Jackson, *Letters*, 2: 432–38, 619–21. René Jesseaume said that 700 Arikara warriors were armed. Stan Hoig, *The Chouteaus: First Family of the Fur Trade* (Albuquerque: University of New Mexico Press, 2008), pp. 39–41. The attack was in response to an Arikara chief who had been part of an Indian delegation to Washington and had suddenly died on the return trip. The death had not been properly explained to the Arikaras, and traders who had come up the river before the party presented a view that maddened the Arikaras, who felt deceived by the Americans.

32. Thomas Hunt to Secretary of War, November 20, 1807, H327, RG107, M221, roll 8, frame 2601; Marie Philipe Leduc to Secretary of War, May 5, 1810, L62, M221, roll 38, frame 4860, National Archives and Records Administration. Ensign Nathaniel Pryor headed the party and George Shannon and Robert Frazer went as hunters; all three were members of the Lewis and Clark expedition. René Jesseaume, the Mandan interpreter, accompanied the expedition for part of 1804.

33. The total cost included medical expenses for six of the wounded. "Frederick Bates to Denis Fitzhugh, December 16, 1807," and "Frederick Bates to William Clark, December 1807," in Thomas M. Marshall, *The Life and Papers of Frederick Bates*, 2 vols. (Saint Louis: Missouri Historical Society, 1926), 1: 237, 247–48; William Simmons, Accountants Office,

entry 353, set no. 1, ledger D, vol. 4, p. 1966: July 8 for $2000, July 20 for $589.66, and July 24 for $300. Other expenses were accounted for in February 1808, entry 366, vol. 13, letterbook O, January 29, 1808–November 30, 1808, pp. 7208–7209, nos. 10–22 and 24–27. For more information, see appendix E.

34. Carter, *Territorial Papers*, 14: 125. Wilkinson had advanced $200 to Dorion when he was appointed.

35. Pierre Dorion to Secretary of War, November 19, 1807, D208, RG107, M221, roll 6, frame 1903, National Archives and Records Administration.

36. In his letter to the secretary of war, Clark stated that Dorion's services had not been approved through official channels: "Two of his accounts (which you will find enclosed) for articles which he was not positively ordered to expend in his instructions, I have refused to pay, altho' I think that it might be necessary to give such things." "William Clark to Secretary of War, May 18, 1807," in Carter, *Territorial Papers*, 14: 125.

37. "Frederick Bates to Meriwether Lewis, January 16, 1808," in Marshall, *Frederick Bates*, 1: 265.

38. "Frederick Bates to Timothy Kibby, March 22, 1808," in Marshall, *Frederick Bates*, 2: 314.

39. On April 13, Lewis paid Dorion $568.60 and two days later handed over two more drafts that completed the obligation. Accountant's books, January 29, 1808, to November 30, 1808, entry 366, vol. 13, letterbook O, p. 7453, National Archives, College Park, Maryland; Lewis's Account Book, 1808–1809, drafts nos. 3 and 4, Meriwether Lewis Collection, Missouri History Museum.

40. *Laws of the Territory of Louisiana* (St. Louis: Joseph Charless, 1809).

41. "William Clark to Henry Dearborn, April 29, 1809," in Carter, *Territorial Papers*, 14: 266.

42. Ibid., 2: 41.

43. James R. Bentley, "Two Letters of Meriwether Lewis to Major William Preston," *Filson Club History Quarterly* 44, no. 2 (April 1970): 173. In this letter, Lewis said that he had purchased 7,440 arpents of land, or 6,300 acres, which converts at .85 to an acre, but in a later letter to his mother, he claimed to have bought 5,700 acres. Meriwether Lewis to Lucy Marks, December 1, 1808. See appendix A, no. 11.

44. Meriwether Lewis to William Clark, May 29, 1808, appendix A, no. 9. Lewis obtained $95 in banknotes from other citizens and added a bill of exchange for $100 drawn upon the War Department. He authorized Denis Fitzhugh to add an additional $30 of his funds, amounting to $225. Having a newspaper in Saint Louis was crucial for attracting new citizens to the territory.

45. When examining Jackson's records in *Letters of the Lewis and Clark Expedition* and Colter-Frick's records in L. Ruth Colter-Frick, "Meriwether Lewis's Personal Finances," *We Proceeded On* 28, no. 1 (February 2002): 16–20, their documentation is lacking. For a more comprehensive account of Lewis's lost income, see appendixes D–F.

46. Printing territorial and national laws was a federal requirement for a new territory.

US Statutes at Large 1 (1804): 283–84. Peter Provenchere was also known in Saint Louis as Pierre Provenchere.

47. Meriwether Lewis Account Book, July 22, 1808, Meriwether Lewis Collection, Missouri History Museum; *Early American Imprints*, second series, no. 15451, *The Laws of the Territory of Louisiana* (Saint Louis: Joseph Charless, 1808).

48. US Statutes at Large 1 (1804): 302.

49. Secretary of War to Meriwether Lewis, March 28, 1808, RG107, M370, roll 3, frame 0118, item 647, p. 209.

50. Robert Brent, the army paymaster, was not immune to Simmons's practices. In September 1808 he received complaints from officers in the field because Simmons hadn't paid their accounts. Robert Brent, Paymaster General, September 22, 1808, Records of the Accounting Officers of the Department of Treasury, Letters Received by the Accountant of the War Department, Unbound Records, entry 493, box 1, National Archives II, College Park, Maryland. See appendix E, p. 313.

51. Kate L. Gregg, ed., *Westward with Dragoons: The Journal of William Clark on His Expedition to Establish Fort Osage, August 25 to September 22, 1808* (Fulton, MO: Ovid Bell Press, 1937).

52. William E. Foley, *Wilderness Journey: The Life of William Clark* (Columbia: University of Missouri Press, 2004), p. 173.

53. William Clark to Henry Dearborn, August 20, 1808, C197, RG107, M221, roll 19, frame 5842–43, National Archives and Records Administration.

54. "Secretary of War to William Clark, April 29, 1809," in Carter, *Territorial Papers*, 14: 264. This is the last letter that Dearborn wrote to Clark, which he received on November 17, 1808.

55. James J. Holmberg, ed., *Dear Brother* (New Haven, CT: Yale University Press, 2002), p. 154; Landon Y. Jones, *William Clark and the Shaping of the West* (New York: Hill and Wang, 2004), pp. 168–69. Expenses related to the treaty included presents to the Osage totaling $4,968.78.

56. William Clark to War Department, February 20, 1810, C48, M221, roll 35, frames 2307–2311, National Archives and Records Administration. "Louisiana" in this case referenced the Louisiana Territory, the land given up being specifically within the bounds of modern-day western Missouri.

57. Meriwether Lewis to Lucy Marks, December 1, 1808, appendix A, no. 11.

58. *American State Papers, Indian Affairs* 1: 767.

59. Clark wrote that the Saint Louis lodge opened on November 8, but Bates reported November 9, 1808. Holmberg, *Dear Brother*, p. 161. Western Star Lodge, No. 107, was established in Kaskaskia in December 1805; Louisiana Lodge No. 109 was established in Sainte Genevieve in 1806. Everett R. Turnbull, *The Rise and Progress of Freemasonry in Illinois, 1783–1952* (Illinois: Pantagraph Printing, 1952), pp. 8–24 and insert on p. 24; James W. Skelley, "Some Early History of Freemasonry in Missouri," paper read before the Missouri Historical Society, November 26, 1943, Missouri History Collection, Missouri History

Museum, Saint Louis; Ray V. Denslow, *Territorial Masonry: The Story of Freemasonry and the Louisiana Purchase, 1804–1821* (Washington, DC: Masonic Service Association of the United States, 1925). The first worshipful master of Saint Louis No. 111 was Meriwether Lewis. Thomas F. Riddick (Thomas Fiveash Riddick) was senior warden, Rufus Easton (Saint Louis postmaster) was junior warden. Signers for the petition were Meriwether Lewis, Thomas F. Riddick, J. V. Garnier, Joseph Kimball, Rufus Easton, Benjamin Wilkinson, Major James Bruff, John Coons, John Hay, John Hays, and Michael E. Immell. Others who belonged to the lodge were Frederick Bates, Silas Bent, William C. Carr, Joseph Charless, Major William Christy, William Clark, Dr. Bernard G. Farrar, Alexander McNair, Risdon Price, Alexander Stuart, and a number of US Army officers stationed at Bellefontaine. Skelley, "Early History of Freemasonry," pp. 8–10. Frederick Bates delivered the oration at the lodge's opening. *Early American Imprints*, no. 16954: Frederick Bates, Oration delivered before Saint Louis Lodge No. 111.

60. See chapter 13 on Dr. Saugrain's treatment of Meriwether Lewis.

61. Copy of a letter from "Governor M. Lewis to the President of the United States, Relative to the Treaty Concluded with the Osage Indians, December 15, 1808," in *American State Papers, Indian Affairs* 1: 766–67. Donald Jackson claims that Lewis did not write to Jefferson after June 27, 1807, but as a matter of efficiency his letters to the secretary of war were shared by the two and noted by Jefferson. The letter takes into account Lewis's arrival from March 8, 1808, to December 15 and includes treaties and letters from Clark, Bates, and other officials. RG107, M222, roll 3, L1808, frames 1260–88. Lewis wrote another letter dated August 27, 1809, that was forty-six pages long and described events beginning in late 1808. RG107, M221, roll 38, L101, frames 4907–31.

62. Stephen Ambrose, *Undaunted Courage* (New York: Simon & Schuster, 1996), p. 430.

63. There are two separate copies of this long letter, as well as some treaty information. The manuscript copy, which is eleven pages, was printed in the *American State Papers* while the draft copy, which is seven pages, was included in a William Clark document. The etiology of the two documents originated with Lewis, and it appears that Lewis sent the manuscript copy in December 1808. However, Chouteau's letter dated October 3, 1808, was missing by the time it reached Washington. The draft copy, among Lewis's papers after his death, was given to Clark when he arrived in Washington in December 1809. The manuscript copy is detailed and can be found in its entirety in RG107, M222, roll 3, L1808, frames 1260–88, while the draft copy is part of William Clark to War Department, February 20, 1810, C48, M221, roll 35, frames 2307–2317, National Archives and Records Administration. Much of the content of this William Clark letter can be found in *American State Papers, Indian Affairs* 1: 763–66. Included in this file is the draft copy of the letter that Lewis wrote to Pierre Chouteau dated October 3, 1808. The preservation of this information bodes well for other primary documentation presumed to be lost or missing, specifically Lewis and Clark's Indian vocabularies, printed in *American State Papers, Indian Affairs* 1: pp. 705–721. There is hope that Lewis and Clark recorded more Indian vocabularies than what was printed in *American State Papers* and that these may still be preserved in a National Archives file;

http://memory.loc.gov/cgi-bin/ampage?collId=llsp&fileName=007/llsp007.db&rec
Num=764 (accessed May 20, 2011).

64. Albert Gallatin to the Committee of Ways and Means, December 10, 1808,
RG233, M1268, roll 7, frame 0081, p.180, National Archives and Records Administration.

65. US Statutes at Large 2 (1809): 528–33. Dearborn believed that the Embargo Act
would start a war; since he felt inadequate to head the War Department during hostilities,
he tendered his resignation, but Jefferson persuaded him to not resign. Henry Dearborn to
Thomas Jefferson, December 29, 1807, document 30676, reel 40, Thomas Jefferson Papers,
Library of Congress.

66. Albert Gallatin to the Committee of Ways and Means, December 10, 1808,
RG233, M1268, roll 7, frame 0084, p.185, National Archives and Records Administration.

67. House Representative John Rhea of Tennessee wrote Gen. James Robertson of
Nashville and announced Madison's election on January 25, 1809. Madison took office on
March 3, 1809. James Robertson, 1742–1814, microfilm Mf. 801, box 3, folder 9, frame
0944, Tennessee State Library and Archives, Nashville, Tennessee.

68. Henry Dearborn to Thomas Jefferson, February 16, 1809, reel 10, document 5985
¼, James Madison Papers, Library of Congress. Or see http://memory.loc.gov/cgi-bin/
ampage?collId=mjm&fileName=10/mjm10.db&recNum=1047&itemLink=r?ammem/mj
m:@FIELD(DOCID+@BAND(@lit(mjm015257))) (accessed August 10, 2011).

69. "John Fanning to the Public," in *Early American Imprints*, second series, no. 11805,
p. 2.

70. Albert Gallatin to Thomas Jefferson, December 18, 1812, document 35020, reel
46, Thomas Jefferson Papers, Library of Congress. "It is to be hoped that Mr. Eustis's resignation will open brighter prospects . . . yet his incapacity and the total want of confidence
in him were felt through every ramification of the public service."

71. RG94, M565, roll 2, p. 51, frame 0276, National Archives and Records Administration.

72. The point on the trail ended at Cahokia, and mail for Saint Louis and Fort Bellefontaine had to be ferried across the Mississippi River.

73. "Postmaster General to Governor Lewis, March 29, 1809," in Carter, *Territorial
Papers*, 14: 256–57.

74. Ibid., p. 257.

75. Jackson, *Letters*, 2: 436; Accountant's Office, entry 366, vol. 14, letterbook P,
December 1, 1808–February 24, 1810, p. 8051, entry 1902; René Jussome (Jesseaume),
April 25, 1808, Meriwether Lewis's Account Book, Meriwether Lewis Collection, Missouri
History Museum.

76. "Meriwether Lewis to Henry Dearborn, March 7, 1809," in Jackson, *Letters*, 2:
450–51.

77. William Clark to Secretary of War, 1810, C221, M221, roll 35, National Archives
and Records Administration. Document contains sketch of building.

78. William Clark to War Department, January 26, 1809, C456, RG107, M221, roll

20, frame 6133; William Simmons to William Clark, May 11, 1809, RG75, M15, roll 2, p. 436, frame 0190, National Archives and Records Administration.

79. Ibid. Clark, unafraid of Simmons, responded that he had been instructed by the secretary of war to pay the accounts as necessary. "I do not recolect to have exceeded what appeared to be necessary." William Clark to William Simmons, July 1, 1809, C581, M221, roll 20, frame 6275, National Archives and Records Administration.

80. Tillier fired Sibley because Sibley had caught Tillier stealing from the factory. Thomas C. Danisi, "George Champlain Sibley: Shady Dealings on the Early Frontier," *Confluence* 2, no. 1 (Fall/Winter 2010): 39–49.

81. Carter, *Territorial Papers,* 13: 239.

82. Rodolphe Tillier to John Mason, April 20, 1809, T266, RG107, M221, roll 32, frame 0270; Rodolphe Tillier to John Mason, April 27, 1809, T1809, RG107, M222, roll 4, frames 1628–29; Rodolphe Tillier to John Mason, May 12, 1809, T273, M221, roll 32, frame 0719, National Archives and Records Administration. An abridged version of the April 27 letter is printed in, Robert A. Rutland et al. ed., *The Papers of James Madison: Presidential Series*, 5 vols. (Charlottesville: University of Virginia Press, 1984), 1: 141–42.

83. Rodolphe Tillier to John Mason, April 27, 1809, T1809, RG107, M222, roll 4, frames 1628–29, National Archives and Records Administration.

84. Rodolphe Tillier to John Mason, May 12, 1809, T273, M221, roll 32, frame 0719, National Archives and Records Administration.

85. John Mason to James Madison, June 9, 1809, M1809, M222, roll 4, frames 1582–84.

86. "Secretary of War to Governor Lewis, July 15, 1809," in Carter, *Territorial Papers,* 14: 285–86.

87. Chouteau received $940 from Lewis to distribute presents on May 15, 1809: 400 lbs. of gunpowder for $600; 100 guns for $100; 1250 lbs. lead for $100; 20 lbs. vermillion for $50; and 600 lbs. of tobacco for $90.

88. Lewis sent a draft of $18 on December 28, which was refused and returned on March 14, 1809. The refusal letter explained that funds of this kind were to be paid by Territorial Secretary Bates. When Lewis submitted the bill to Bates, he refused to pay, stating that there was not enough money in the account. Marshall, *Frederick Bates*, 2: 73–74.

89. Lewis's delayed payments are discussed in chapter 9 of this book.

90. William Clark to William Simmons, July 1, 1809, C581, M221, roll 20, frame 6275, National Archives and Records Administration.

91. "William Clark with Estimate of the Expenditures in the Indian Department under His Superintendence in Louisiana for the Quarter Ending 31st Dec. 1809." When Clark departed St. Louis in September 1809 and arrived at the War Department in December, he spoke for Lewis and himself on the complexities of the Louisiana Territory. The department reimbursed him for those salaries, "for the amount of pay due them . . . from their last settlement entitled dismissed from the service of the U.States." William Clark to War Department, December 31, 1809, C8, M221, roll 35, frames 2247–49, National Archives and Records Administration.

92. "William Simmons to William Clark, August 7, 1809," in Carter, *Territorial Papers,* 14: 289.

93. Meriwether Lewis to William Simmons, July 8, 1809, appendix A, no. 13. Lewis, Anderson, and Marks Families Papers, 1771–1908, microfilm M668, Albert and Shirley Small Special Collections Library, University of Virginia, Charlottesville, Virginia.

94. Pierre Chouteau to War Department, June 14, 1809, C562, M221, roll 20, frame 6255, National Archives and Records Administration. See appendix A, no. 12. Bates wrote other letters for Chouteau's son, August 12, 1809, C612, M221, roll 20, frame 6310; September 1, 1809, C625, from Carter, *Territorial Papers,* 14: 312–19. Chouteau's son wrote in French on October 2 to the War Department, and upon receipt his letter was translated there: "I am continually apprehensive that the reports of ill-intentioned persons may have given you some prejudices against my Father. . . ." Auguste Chouteau to War Department, October 2, 1809, C650, M221, roll 20, frame 6364, National Archives and Records Administration.

95. July 15, 1809, appendix A, no. 14. "William Simmons to Meriwether Lewis, July 15, 1809," in Carter, *Territorial Papers,* 14: pp. 285–86 or Jackson, *Letters,* 2: pp. 456–57.

96. August 18, 1809, appendix A, no. 15.

97. William Thomas L340: $220; Pierre Chouteau L341: $440, L295: $500, L303: $1, and L302: $81. Dearborn had made provisions for Indian presents. L340 had not been included in the original recommendation.

98. August 18, 1809, appendix A, no. 15.

99. Meriwether Lewis to William Simmons, August 18, 1809, L328, RG107, M221, roll 23, frame 8501, National Archives and Records Administration.

100. Appendix A, no. 15. Donald Jackson omitted this paragraph in his transcription of the letter.

101. Correspondence that did not arrive or arrived too late added to Lewis's frustration.

sent	received	doc. #	description
Oct. 3, 1808	Mar. 20, 1809	L-250	draft, missing
Nov. 28, 1808	Jan. 19, 1809	L-199	contents missing, $500
May 1, 1809	Oct. 7, 1809	L-340	William Thomas, $220
May 13, 1809	Oct. 7	L-295	Pierre Chouteau, $500
May 15, 1809	Oct. 7	L-341	Pierre Chouteau, $440
June 26, 1809	Oct. 6	L-339	William Christy, $1,488.76
July 6, 1809	Sept. 5	L-326	William Christy, $43.25
July 8, 1809	undelivered		William Simmons
Aug. 18, 1809	Sept. 8	L-328	William Simmons
Aug. 26, 1809	Apr. 14, 1810	L-264	James McFarlane, $156

102. Frederick Bates had refused to withdraw funds from a contingent account to help pay for the printing. "Frederick Bates to Albert Gallatin, July 16, 1809," in Marshall, *Frederick Bates,* 2: 73–74.

103. A Journal of the Proceedings of the Legislature of the Territory of Louisiana Commencing June 3, 1806 and Ending October 9, 1811, Special Collection M-61, Mercantile Library, University of Missouri–Saint Louis. In the July 7, 1807, entry, the legislature

approved that the "Governor be hereby authorized to enter into a contract with an Printer for printing two hundred copies of the Militia Law and three hundred of the Laws of a public nature . . . to employ some fit person to translate such Laws of the Territory as he shall think proper into the French language: provided that the expences for printing and translating shall not exceed . . . Five Hundred Dollars . . . ."

104. Peter Provenchere to his father, July 29, 1809, Provenchere Family Papers, Missouri History Museum. Historian Grace Lewis Miller contended that Lewis was never paid, but this figure does not come up in his account book or in his estate settlements. What is clear is that he paid out the money from his own pocket and was not reimbursed for the duration of his governorship.

105. Peter Provenchere to his father, December 21, 1809, Provenchere Family Papers, Missouri History Museum. Lewis recognized Provenchere's talents and he appointed him judge of the probate court and notary public on July 8, 1808, box 2, folder 4, Reproductions, July 1808–October 1809, Meriwether Lewis Collection, Missouri History Museum.

106. John Moncure Daniel to Secretary of War, July 12, 1809, RG107, M6, roll 4, p. 170, and December 26, 1809, D345, M221, roll 21, National Archives and Records Administration.

107. James Wilkinson to Secretary of War, December 18, 1809, RG233, M1268, roll 12, p. 281, frame 0399, National Archives and Records Administration.

108. Correspondence between Thomas Van Dyke and William Simmons, V87, February 3 1809; V-97, July 27, 1809; V-104, October 17, 1809, RG107, M221, roll 32, National Archives and Records Administration.

109. Appendix A, no. 10. See also appendixes D–F for a detailed description of those expenses.

110. Meriwether Lewis, November 20, 1808, draft no. 12 in favor of Sydall Manley, Meriwether Lewis Account Book, Meriwether Lewis Collection, Missouri History Museum. Taken out of Lewis's payment for the quarter ending December 1808.

111. This $440 was absolutely necessary to the success of returning the Mandan chief. The presents were used to placate the other tribes along the Upper Missouri. Chouteau stated that he "distributed . . . Sixty pounds of powder . . . one hundred & Twenty pounds of the Ball . . . ten pounds of Vermillion, and one hundred and fifty Pounds of tobacco, which seemed to restore harmony amongst them." Carter, *Territorial Papers*, 14: 346.

112. Ibid. This payment totaled $940.

113. See appendix E, Lewis's Drafts and Warrants, entry 366, vol. 14, letterbook P, and vol. 15, letterbook Q in back of this book.

114. John Armstrong to James Madison, June 29, 1814, Series 1: General Correspondence, reel 16, p. 1, James Madison Papers, Library of Congress.

115. Ibid.

116. Ibid., pp. 1 and 2.

117. Ezekiel Bacon to William Simmons, April 18, 1814, Series 1: General Correspondence, reel 16, James Madison Papers, Library of Congress, http://hdl.loc.gov/loc.mss/mjm.16_0187_0191 (accessed March 11, 2011).

118. Ibid., p. 2.

119. William Simmons, "A Letter to the Senate and House of Representatives of the United States, Shewing the Profligacy and Corruption of General John Armstrong in His Administration of the War Department" (Georgetown: Robert Alleson, 1814) in *Early American Imprints*, second series, no. 32773, p. 11.

120. John Armstrong to James Madison, June 29, 1814, Series 1: General Correspondence, reel 16, p. 3, James Madison Papers, Library of Congress.

121. Simmons, *Early American Imprints*, p. 13.

122. Ibid, pp. 3, 5.

123. Ibid, p. 5.

124. James Madison to John Armstrong, July 6, 1814, "Notes on the Return of Papers Accompanied by a Letter from the Secy. of War of June 29, 1814," Series 3: Madison–Armstrong Correspondence, reel 27, p. 4, James Madison Papers, Library of Congress, http://hdl.loc.gov/loc.mss/mjm.27_0151_0156 (accessed August 10, 2011).

125. James Madison to William Simmons, July 6, 1814, *Early American Imprints*, second series, no. 32773, p. 6.

126. Simmons's written statements of refusal and settlement pervade thousands of documents in the National Archives. William F. Sherman and Craig R. Scott, *Records of the Accounting Officers of the Treasury Department*, inventory 14, rev. (Lovettsville, VA: Willow Bend Books, 1997). See record groups RG217 and RG107 for further details.

127. William Simmons has been described as patriotic because he served in the War of 1812, but this does not absolve him for his insufferable treatment toward War Department personnel. Walter Lord, *The Dawn's Early Light* (Baltimore: Johns Hopkins University Press, 1972), pp. 116, 152–53; Robert B. Lechter, "William Simmons, Accountant: Unsung Hero at the Battle of Bladensburg, MD, War of 1812," *MACPA Statement* 36, no. 9 (May/June 2001): 16.

CHAPTER 11: FROM FORT PICKERING TO NASHVILLE, TENNESSEE: THE FINAL CHAPTER

1. Robert Grinder's name has also been thrown into doubt, some claiming that the last name was Griner. A Williamson County Court document spelled the name Grinder, which was also corroborated by a Franklin, Tennessee, merchant's store. Glen O. Hardeman Collection C3655, Account Books, Franklin, Tennessee, box 3, folder 85, Journal, p. 63, and folder 86, Ledger with Index, p. 17, State Historical Society of Missouri, Columbia, Missouri.

2. Secretary of War to James Neelly, July 7, 1809, M15, roll 3, p. 112, and Secretary of War to James Neelly, June 4, 1812, M15, roll 3, p. 134. The secretary of war wrote the letter to Neelly on June 4 and Neelly tendered his account to Gen. James Robertson July 31, 1812. M22, N48, roll 6, p. 349, frame 0915, National Archives and Records Administration.

3. *Brad Meltzer's Decoded*, December 9, 2010, "Secret Presidential Codes," History Channel, http://www.history.com/shows/brad-meltzers-decoded/episodes/episodes-guide (accessed January 28, 2011).

4. Robert S. Cotterill, "The Natchez Trace," *Tennessee Historical Magazine* 7, no. 4 (April 1921): 27.

5. Ilene J. Cornwell and Deborah K. Henderson, *Travel Guide to the Natchez Trace Parkway* (Nashville, TN: Southern Resources Unlimited, 1984), p. 1.

6. Arrell Morgan Gibson, *The Chickasaws* (Norman: University of Oklahoma Press, 1971), p. 97.

7. Cornwell and Henderson, *Travel Guide*, p. 2.

8. Dawson A. Phelps, "The Natchez Trace, Indian Trail to Parkway," *Tennessee Historical Quarterly* 21, no. 3 (September 1962): 216.

9. Cotterill, "The Natchez Trace," pp. 30–31; Dawson A. Phelps, "The Chickasaw Agency," *Journal of Mississippi History* 14, no. 2 (April 1952): 120.

10. Henry Dearborn to Silas Dinsmoor to the Choctaw, May 8, 1802, RG75, M15, roll 1, pp. 207–208, frame 0094, National Archives and Records Administration. This letter was also addressed in the margin to Samuel Mitchell, the Chickasaw agent. Phelps, "The Chickasaw Agency," p. 132. The Phelps article printed the Dearborn letter but did not provide a citation.

11. Cornwell and Henderson, *Travel Guide*, p. 49.

12. Phelps, "The Chickasaw Agency," p. 125. Thomas McCoy was the weaver and instructor for the Chickasaws. Malcolm McGee to Secretary of War, December 16, 1808, M363, M221, roll 26, frame 8904, National Archives and Records Administration.

13. Samuel Mitchell, William Hill, Thomas Wright, James Neelly, James A. Robertson, and William Cocke. Dearborn to Robertson, February 27, 1806, box 4, folder 10, frame 1143, and Thomas Wright, April 17, 1807, box 4, folder 21, frame 1274, James Robertson, 1742–1814, microfilm Mf. 801, Tennessee State Library and Archives, Nashville, Tennessee. In 1816, William Cocke affirmed Neelly's reputation "for candor, probity, and good morals." *American State Papers, Indian Affairs* 2: 106.

14. Malcolm McGee to Secretary of War, September 27, 1808, M234, M221, roll 26, frame 8765, National Archives and Records Administration.

15. Dawson A. Phelps, "Colbert Ferry and Selected Documents," *Alabama Historical Quarterly* 25, nos. 3–4 (Fall and Winter 1963): 205; Malcolm McGee to Secretary of War, September 27, 1808, M234, RG107, M221, roll 26, frame 8765; George Colbert to Secretary of War, C469, February 18, 1809, roll 20, frame 6146, National Archives and Records Administration.

16. Phelps, "The Chickasaw Agency," p. 125; Robert S. Cotterill, "Federal Indian Management in the South 1789–1825," *Mississippi Valley Historical Review* 20, no. 3 (December 1933): 342–43, n. 23.

17. Guy B. Braden, "The Colberts and the Chickasaw Nation," *Tennessee Historical Quarterly* 17, no. 3 (September 1958): 227.

18. Cotterill, "The Natchez Trace," p. 31. A resident of Florence, Alabama, recalled

George Colbert as "tall, slender, and handsome with straight black hair that he wore long . . . down to his shoulders. His features were that of an Indian but his skin was lighter than that of his tribe." Braden, "The Colberts and the Chickasaw Nation," p. 229. Cherokee Indian Agent Return Meigs described George Colbert's business acumen: "[T]ho, not highest in rank in the Chickasaw Nation, yet from his ambition & interest, very much influences the affairs of that Nation. He is extremely mercenary . . . when not awed by the presence of the Officers of Government takes upon himself great airs." Return J. Meigs to Secretary of War, March 1, 1809, M448, M221, roll 27, frame 8964, National Archives and Records Administration.

19. The Chickasaw king's name, usually referred as the Mingo chief, was pronounced differently, and his name was spelled in various ways. Two of the most common spellings were: Chenubbee Mingo (Chinubbee Mingo) or Chinumba Mingo. M221, August 12, 1809, roll 27, frame 9074, and RG75, T58, roll 1, frame 0102, National Archives and Records Administration; US Statutes at Large 7 (1805): 89–90; John Sugden, "Early Pan-Indianism: Tecumseh's Tour of the Indian Country, 1811–1812," *American Indian Quarterly* 10, no. 4 (Autumn 1986): 291.

20. Chinumba Mingo to Secretary of War, June 27, 1809, M535, M221, roll 27, frames 9052–53, National Archives and Records Administration. This letter was composed and written by Malcolm McGee, the Chickasaw Indian interpreter in the presence of George Colbert and Chief O'Koy (Tishumastabbe).

21. Return J. Meigs to Secretary of War, June 12, 1809, M510, RG107, M221, roll 27, frames 9021–23, National Archives and Records Administration.

22. Return J. Meigs to Secretary of War, October 26, 1809, M595, M221, roll 27, frame 9010, National Archives and Records Administration.

23. Secretary of War to James Neelly, July 8, 1809, RG75, M15, roll 3, p. 1, frame 0019, National Archives and Records Administration.

24. Secretary of War to James Neelly, July 7, 1809, M15, roll 2, p. 442, frame 0192; James Neelly to Secretary of War, August 9, 1809, N91, M221, roll 27, frame 9211, National Archives and Records Administration.

25. Williamson County Record, County Courthouse Minutes microfilm, roll 45, vol. 1, 1800–1815, pp. 1, 86, 200, and 207, Tennessee State Archives and Library, Nashville, Tennessee.

26. Secretary of War to James Neelly, July 7, 1809, M15, roll 3, p. 1, frame 0019. "Having no Agent with the Chickasaws at the time orders were given to forward their Annuities for the present year, they were directed to be sent to Mr. David Hogg U.S. Factor at Chickasaw Bluff, on whom you will call with the enclosed order, receive them from him & duly distribute them to the Nation . . . ."

27. Secretary of War to David Hogg, July 7, 1809, M15, roll 3, p. 1, frame 0019, National Archives and Records Administration. "Please to deliver to Jas. Neeley, U.S. Agent to the Chickasaws, such goods as you may or have received on Acct. of the Annuity due that Nation for the present year, taking duplicate receipts therefor, one of which is to be transmitted to the superintendent of Military Stores at Philadelphia."

28. Secretary of War to Chinumba Mingo, George Colbert, and O'Koy, July 21, 1809, M15, roll 3, p. 3, frame 0019, National Archives and Records Administration.

29. Secretary of War to James Neelly, July 21, 1809, M15, roll 3, p. 3, frame 0019, National Archives and Records Administration. Henry Knox to the Chickasaws, "Supply for the Chickasaws," April 27, 1793, box 4, folder 11, frame 1174, James Robertson, 1742–1814, microfilm Mf. 801, Tennessee State Library and Archives. The Chickasaw annuity in 1795, agreed by treaty, was perpetual and included the following: 500 stands of arms, 2,000 lbs. powder, 4,000 flint, 4,000 lbs. lead, 500 bushels of corn, 50 lbs. vermillion, and 100 gallons of whiskey. See RG75, T58, roll 1, frame 0102, National Archives and Records Administration. The 1795 treaty amounted to $3,000 in specie, but the 1805 treaty soared to $20,000 and gave additional payments to certain chiefs, granted free schooling for select Chickasaw children, and presented other gifts and concessions. See US Statutes at Large 7 (1805): 89–90 for details.

30. The Chickasaw Agency was located at milepost 241.4 and Duck River was located at milepost 430. F. Lynne Bachleda, *Guide to the Natchez Trace Parkway*, 2nd ed. (Birmingham, AL: Menasha Ridge Press, 2011), pp. x–xi; Cornwell and Henderson, *Travel Guide*, p. 75.

31. James Neelly to Secretary of War, August 27, 1809, N94, M221, roll 27, National Archives and Records Administration. The frame numbers on the microfilm are unreadable after frame 9204.

32. James Neelly to Secretary of War, August 30, 1809, N97, M22, roll 4, frame 0528, National Archives and Records Administration.

33. Samuel Cole Williams, *Beginnings of West Tennessee: In the Land of the Chickasaws 1541–1841* (Johnson City, TN: Watuga Press, 1930), p. 68.

34. James Neelly to Thomas Jefferson, October 18, 1809, document 33522-23, roll 44, Thomas Jefferson Papers, Library of Congress; John Brahan to Thomas Jefferson, October 18, 1809, document 33520–21, roll 44, Thomas Jefferson Papers, Library of Congress; John Brahan to Secretary of War, October 18, 1809, B589, RG107, M221, roll 18, frame 5632, National Archives and Records Administration. See appendix A, nos. 16, 17, 18.

35. Meriwether Lewis to James Madison, September 15, 1809. See appendix A, no. 12.

36. Gilbert Russell to Secretary of War, May 19, 1809, R219, M221, roll 29, frame 9736, National Archives and Records Administration. Simmons had protested another account from Russell in the amount of $2,276 and Russell had sent a request in May 1809 to travel to Washington to explain the protested bill. Russell was not reimbursed until 1811.

37. The War Department wrote to Russell on September 25 about the repair of the buildings at the fort and being paid for those repairs by the military agent at Pittsburgh. There was no mention of his correspondence with William Simmons, the accountant, because Simmons handled all of those matters separately. War Department to Gilbert Russell, September 25, 1809, RG107, M6, roll 4, p. 209, frame 0118, National Archives and Records Administration.

38. Captain Gilbert Russell mentioned that there were some Indians who accompanied

the entourage. It is uncertain whether they were present at Fort Pickering on September 29 or the group met them along the way. Statement of Gilbert Russell, appendix A, no. 37.

39. We already know that it took Major Neelly about eighteen days to travel from the Chickasaw Indian village, Big Town, to Fort Pickering, which shows that Dawson Phelps assumed too much in his article. Phelps claimed that the distance from the fort to the Chickasaw Agency was "not much more than one hundred miles—a two-and-one-half or three days' journey." James Neelly to Secretary of War, August 27 and August 30, 1809, N94 and N97, M221, roll 27 and M22, roll 4, frame 0528; Dawson A. Phelps, "The Tragic Death of Meriwether Lewis," *William and Mary Quarterly, Series 3* 13 (July 1956): 314.

40. Rhea's Tennessee map of 1834 shows the road from Memphis intersecting the Natchez Trace near Waynesboro. Bachleda, *Natchez Trace Parkway*, p. xi.

41. Capt. Gilbert Russell had lent Lewis two horses and Neelly, as the Indian agent, was required by law to recover them. Russell describes the transaction in an 1813 letter. "From the tenor of a letter written to me in 1810 by Genl. Wm. Clark on the subject of the affairs of the decd. Gov. Lewis, I felt myself authorized to draw on him for the amount the Estate owed me for two horses & about one hundred dollars which I let the Govr. have to enable him to prosecute his journey to Washington. Under the impression that Genl. Clark would pay it I did draw on him for the amount of $379.58 with interest and bound myself in double the sum, if the Bill should be refund. Genl. C. refused to pay it, and my Agent at Sainte Genevieve instituted a suit against the administrator which has only had the tendency of incurring additional expense to me. . . ." Gilbert Russell to William D. Meriwether, April 18, 1813, New Orleans, Lewis, Anderson, and Marks Families Papers, 1771–1908, microfilm M668, Albert and Shirley Small Special Collections Library, University of Virginia, Charlottesville, Virginia. Russell also loaned Lewis a saddle, and Lewis promised to pay him by January 1, 1810. Gary E. Moulton, "New Documents of Meriwether Lewis," *We Proceeded On* 13, no. 4 (November 1987): 6.

42. Dawson A. Phelps, "Stands and Travel Accommodations on the Natchez Trace," *Journal of Mississippi History* 11, no. 1 (January 1949): 40. Phelps believes that Grinder's Stand opened sometime between January 18, 1808 and October 11, 1808. He may be right, but the minutes of the Williamson County Court prove that new roads were opened on Grinder's property between 1805 and 1809. Williamson County Record, County Courthouse Minutes microfilm, roll 45, vol. 1–2, 1800–1815, July 11, 1809, p. 412, Tennessee State Library and Archives, Nashville, Tennessee. In 1805, the Williamson County court ordered a landowner near Neelly's and Grinder's property to oversee and clear a new road: "Ordered that Elijah Hunter oversee the clearing out and keeping in repair the Public road from where the Natchez road leaves Maj. Neelly's road to where it intersects the road cut by the Federal troops at or near the Big Bridge and that all those hands resident in the following bounds to wit: Beginning at the forks of said road, then to William Hicks then to Robert Grinders, then to Mrs. Thompsons, then to Henry Inmans, then to Joel Hobbs, then to John Hunters from thence to the beginning." Williamson County Record, County Courthouse Minutes microfilm, roll 45, vol. 1–2, 1800–1815, July 9, 1805, p. 139, Franklin, Tennessee.

43. James Neelly to Thomas Jefferson, October 18, 1809, document 33522–23, roll 44, Thomas Jefferson Papers, Library of Congress.

44. *Brad Meltzer's Decoded*, December 9, 2010, "Secret Presidential Codes," History Channel, http://www.history.com/shows/brad-meltzers-decoded/episodes/episodes-guide (accessed January 28, 2011).

45. Tony Turnbow claims that the distance from the town of Franklin, Tennessee, to Grinder's Inn was about fifty-five miles, which made it impossible for Neelly to be there on October 11, 1809.

46. Williamson County Record, County Courthouse Minutes microfilm, roll 45, vol. 1, 1800–1815, p. 421, Tennessee State Archives and Library, Nashville, Tennessee.

47. Today this practice is still alive and well in both the Supreme Court of Tennessee and the Appeals Court of Tennessee; it is the normal mode of operation for many cases. Also, the waiver of appearance is common practice in debts court, chancery court, arraignments in criminal court, and motion dates.

48. Williamson County Record, County Courthouse Minutes microfilm, roll 45, vol. 1–2, 1800–1815, pp. 136 and 173, Tennessee State Archives and Library, Nashville, Tennessee.

49. Thomas C. Danisi and W. Raymond Wood, "Lewis and Clark's Route Map: James MacKay's Map of the Missouri River," *Western Historical Quarterly* 35, no. 1 (Spring 2004): 54.

50. There were other Neelly account holders, too: Maj. William Neelly, William Neelly, William Neelly Jr., Robert Neelly, George Neelly, George Neelly Sr., George Neelly Jr, Jean Neelly, John Neelly Sr., and Samuel Neelly. Glen O. Hardeman Collection, C3655, Account Books, Franklin, Tennessee: box 2, folder 80, pp. 35, 53, 65, 122; box 2, folder 81, p. 201; box 3, folder 84; box 3, folder 85, Journal, pp. 44, 49, 82, 84, 169, 174, 407, 412, 417; box 3, folder 86, State Historical Society of Missouri, Columbia, Missouri.

51. Williamson County Record, County Courthouse Minutes microfilm, roll 45, vol. 1, 1800–1815, pp. 243 and 245, Tennessee State Archives and Library.

52. I thank Caesar Cirigliano for initially raising the idea that there might have been more than one James Neelly living near Franklin, Tennessee. I also have to thank Tony Turnbow for informing me that Major James Neelly was from Duck River. Mr. Cirigliano had pointed out that because there were *no* identifiers within the James Neelly court document, the person named in the suit was ambiguous, which cast reasonable doubt upon the identity of the James Neelly involved in the suit.

53. Cotterill, "The Natchez Trace," p. 32.

54. In 1810 Alexander Wilson, the ornithologist, remarked on the width of the Harpeth River. Clark Hunter, ed., *The Life and Letters of Alexander Wilson* (Philadelphia: American Philosophical Society, 1983), p. 360; Cotterill, "The Natchez Trace," p. 32.

55. Nashville had been established as a trading post in 1716 and was the capital of the state. Historical Information Relating to Military Posts and Other Installations, 1700–1900, RG94, M661, roll 5, frame 0398, p. 10, and see also successive installations in Nashville on roll 5, frame 0401–0402, pp. 13–14, National Archives and Records Administration; Albert

C. Holt, "The Economic and Social Beginnings of Tennessee," *Tennessee Historical Magazine* 7, no. 4 (January 1922): 268. On May 4, 1810, Alexander Wilson departed Nashville and arrived at Grinder's Stand the following Sunday, May 10. This timeline coincides with Major Neelly's account. Hunter, *Alexander Wilson*, p. 360.

56. James Wilkinson to Secretary of War, June 28, 1809, W616, RG107, M221, roll 33, frame 1497, National Archives and Records Administration. Brahan was interested in continuing as the receiver of public monies but did not want to lose his captaincy commission in the army. At the end of September, he wrote to the secretary of war and explained his position. John Brahan to Secretary of War, September 30, 1809, B595, M221, roll 18, frame 5638, National Archives and Records Administration.

57. James Neelly to Thomas Jefferson, October 18, 1809, document 33522-23, roll 44, Thomas Jefferson Papers, Library of Congress; John Brahan to Thomas Jefferson, October 18, 1809, document 33520–21, roll 44, Thomas Jefferson Papers, Library of Congress; John Brahan to William Eustis, October 18, 1809, B589, RG107, M221, roll 18, frame 5632, National Archives and Records Administration. The two letters that Brahan wrote to Thomas Jefferson and the secretary of war have different content. See appendix A, nos. 23 and 24.

58. Neelly did not write the letter on October 18, but signed it *after* he returned from Nashville. At the top of the page of this letter, the year is misdated. Instead of 1809 it is written 1089, and whoever wrote it intentionally held the letter until Major Neelly returned so that he could sign it. James Neelly to War Department, October 18, 1089 [1809], N105, RG107, M221, roll 27, frame 9226, National Archives and Records Administration. The frame numbers on the microfilm are partially cut off after 9204. Major Neelly sent two other letters to the War Department on October 20 and October 28, and both arrived in Washington on November 16, 1809. The letter from the Chickasaw Agency dated October 18, 1809, arrived in Washington on November 24, eight days after the others. James Neelly to War Department, October 20 and October 28, 1809, N102 and N103, M221, roll 27, National Archives and Records Administration. There are also discrepancies with Neelly's letters dated September 24, 1809 (N99), and October 3, 1809 (N110), written from the Chickasaw Agency. On both dates Neelly was nowhere near the agency. Rather, he was at Fort Pickering (N99) and traveling to Nashville (N110) with Meriwether Lewis.

CHAPTER 12: THE GILBERT RUSSELL STATEMENT

1. Statement of Gilbert Russell, November 26, 1811, appendix A, no. 37.
2. Jonathan Williams Manuscript, box 6, Lilly Library Manuscript Collections, Indiana University, Bloomington, Indiana.
3. John D.W. Guice, ed., *By His Own Hand? The Mysterious Death of Meriwether Lewis* (Norman: Oklahoma University Press, 2006), p. 33.
4. David Leon Chandler, *The Jefferson Conspiracies: A President's Role in the Assassination

of Meriwether Lewis (New York: William Morrow and Company, 1994), p. 322; Jonathan Daniels, *The Devil's Backbone: The Story of the Natchez Trace* (New York: McGraw-Hill, 1962), p. 69; J. Frederick Fausz and Michael A. Gavin, "The Death of Meriwether Lewis: An Unsolved Mystery," *Gateway Heritage* 24 (Fall 2003–Winter 2004), p. 70; Larry E. Morris, *The Fate of the Corps: What Became of the Lewis and Clark Explorers after the Expedition* (New Haven, CT: Yale University Press, 2004), p. 73; James E. Starrs and Kira Gale, *The Death of Meriwether Lewis: A Historic Crime Scene Investigation* (Omaha, NE: River Junction Press, 2009), p. 229.

5. Gilbert Russell to Thomas Jefferson, January 4, 1810, document 33616–18, and Gilbert Russell to Thomas Jefferson, January 31, 1810, document 33657–59, reel 44, Thomas Jefferson Papers, Library of Congress.

6. Some writers have claimed that Wilkinson wrote the Russell Statement. To view samples of his handwriting, see the Library of Congress Website for correspondence of the Thomas Jefferson and James Madison Papers. James Wilkinson to Thomas Jefferson, September 15, 1807, Thomas Jefferson Papers, Library of Congress, http://memory.loc.gov/cgi-bin/ampage?collId=mtj1&fileName=mtj1page039.db&recNum=424&itemLink=/ammem/collections/jefferson_papers/mtjser1.html&linkText=7&tempFile=./temp/~ammem_HkGq&filecode=mtj&itemnum=1&ndocs=1 (accessed November 8, 2011).

7. Gilbert Russell to Secretary of War, June 24, 1809, R235, RG107, M221, roll 29, National Archives and Records Administration. The secretary of War promoted Russell to captain in April 1808, to major in April 1810, and appointed lt. colonel on December 31, 1811.

8. In November 1809, Russell placed the surgeon, Dr. William C. Smith, under house arrest because he refused to give out medicines and hospital stores and kept a mistress in quarters. Gilbert Russell to Secretary of War, January 2, 1810, RG107, R14, M221, roll 39, frame 6095, National Archives and Records Administration. Smith disagreed with Russell: W. C. Smith to Secretary of War, November 5, 1809, S743, M221, roll 31, frame 0463, National Archives and Records Administration.

9. Gilbert Russell to Secretary of War, August 26, 1809, RG107, R244, M221, roll 29, frame 9756, National Archives and Records Administration.

10. Thomas C. Danisi, "The 'Ague' Made Him Do It," *We Proceeded On* 28, no. 1 (February 2002): 12–13.

11. Secretary of War to James Neely, July 7, 1809, RG75, M15, roll 2, p. 442 and roll 3, p. 2, National Archives and Records Administration. Neely received the commission on August 8. James Neely to Secretary of War, August 9, 1809, RG107, N91, M221, roll 27, National Archives and Records Administration; "James Neely to Thomas Jefferson, October 18, 1809," in Donald Jackson, ed., *Letters of the Lewis and Clark Expedition with Related Documents, 1783–1854*, 2 vols. (Urbana: University of Illinois Press, 1978), 2: 467.

12. Gilbert Russell to Thomas Jefferson, January 4, 1810, document 33616, reel 44, Thomas Jefferson Papers, Library of Congress; see appendix A, no. 33. Russell had asked permission to leave his post for Washington before Lewis had arrived and was expecting a reply.

Russell had an ongoing dispute with the accountant of the War Department for expenses related to moving his company to Fort Pickering.

13. Gen. Henry Dearborn resigned from the Jefferson administration on February 16, 1809, and Madison took office on March 3. Henry Dearborn to Thomas Jefferson, February 16, 1809, document 33040, reel 42, Thomas Jefferson Papers, Library of Congress.

14. RG107, M221, R244, roll 29; RG217, M235, roll 67, document 22209, frame 0636; Gilbert Russell to Secretary of War, March 15, 1808, RG107, M221, R133, roll 12, frame 3623; RG94, M566, roll 2, frame 0322, National Archives and Records Administration.

15. Letters typically took four weeks to reach New Orleans. Russell would not have received any communication from Gen. Wilkinson in so short a time.

16. Gilbert Russell to War Department, November 23, 1810, R79, RG107, M22, roll 5, p. 337, National Archives and Records Administration. Simmons had protested another account from Russell in May 1809 for the amount of $2,276, and creditors had appeared at the fort at the end of August ready to confiscate Russell's property. In 1811 he finally had closure on the account. Gilbert Russell to Secretary of War, May 19, 1809, R219, M221, roll 29, frame 9736; Gilbert Russell to Secretary of War, August 26, 1809, R244, M221, roll 29, frame 9756; Gilbert Russell to Secretary of War, May 16, 1811, R144, M221, roll 39, frame 6199, National Archives and Records Administration.

17. James Howe to Frederick Bates, September 28, 1809, Frederick Bates Papers, Missouri History Museum.

18. Wilkinson did not receive those orders until June 14. Wilkinson commanded about 2,300 soldiers. James Wilkinson to Secretary of War, August 19, 1809, RG107, W658, M221, roll 33, frame 1564, National Archives and Records Administration; James Ripley Jacobs, *The Beginning of the US Army* (Princeton, NJ: Princeton University Press, 1947), p. 352.

19. Secretary of War to James Wilkinson, April 30, 1809, RG94, M1094, roll 1, p. 176, National Archives and Records Administration.

20. Mary C. Gillett, *The Army Medical Department, 1775–1818*, 3 vols. (Washington, DC: Government Printing Office, 1981), 1:142; RG 94, M1136, National Archives and Records Administration. Records of 1811 and 1815 Courts-Martial of Gen. James Wilkinson are on rolls 1 and 2 respectively. The first roll contains hundreds of pages of testimony and evidence, a staggering amount of information related to Wilkinson's duties during the time period from April to November 1809.

21. Testimony of Dr. Robert Dow interrogated by General Wilkinson, August 5, 1811, RG94, M1136, roll 1, frame 0840, p. 49, National Archives and Records Administration.

22. Testimony of 2nd Lt. Samuel McCormick interrogated by General Wilkinson, August 23, 1811, RG94, M1136, roll 1, frame 0870, p. 83, National Archives and Records Administration.

23. Testimony of Dr. Robert Dow, frame 0837, p. 45.

24. Testimony of Dr. William Hood interrogated by General Wilkinson, RG94, M1136, roll 1, frame 0841, p. 49, National Archives and Records Administration. Hood, a veteran of the New Orleans climate, first arrived in the city on November 29, 1799.

25. The Louisiana and Orleans territories experienced a malarial epidemic in the summer and autumn of 1809 that could not have been foreseen. Malaria was incurable until 1826, when quinine was chemically extracted from the Peruvian bark, cinchona. Wilkinson oversaw the building and repair of boats from July to the end of August 1809 and then was confined to his bed with malaria until the end of September. Conspiracy theorists claim that it was during this time that he was plotting to murder Lewis. Gillett, *Army Medical Department*, 1: 140–42.

26. United States Military Philosophical Society, Original Minutes and Records, Membership Lists, Correspondence and Papers, 1802–1813, 4 vols., microfilm, New York Historical Society, New York, New York.

27. Records relating to the 1811 and 1815 Courts-Martial of Maj. General James Wilkinson, Gilbert Russell's testimony on the 49th Day, 56th Day, and 58th Day, RG94, M1136, roll 1, pp. 70–72, frames 0226–27, National Archives and Records Administration. Russell remained in the Washington area until February 1812, RG107, M221, roll 48, R22, frame 2741, National Archives and Records Administration.

28. The Wilkinson pretrial and court-martial trial papers number into thousands of pages. The scriveners, with thick and thin quills, wrote fast, slow, and sometimes with patient handwriting that varied from page to page. The scrivener who wrote the Russell letter also had varied handwriting based on what was daily expected.

29. The murder theorists have portrayed Wilkinson as disliking Meriwether Lewis for unknown reasons, but actually the two were friends. Both were in the US Army, members of the prestigious American Philosophical Society, and members of the United States Military Philosophical Society. Lewis knew Wilkinson from his very earliest days in the army, during the Ohio campaign of the 1790s, and had sided with Wilkinson and against Anthony Wayne in the squabbles between those two generals during that period. Lewis met Wilkinson at the Burr Trial in 1807 and discussed the Louisiana Territory, where Wilkinson had been the governor and Lewis was going to be the governor. Henry Phillips Jr., "Early Proceedings of the American Philosophical Society . . . from the Manuscript Minutes of Its Meetings from 1774 to 1838," *Proceedings of the American Philosophical Society* 22 (1884): 266, 342–43; John Vaughan to Thomas Jefferson, November 21, 1803, document 23559, roll 29, and James Wilkinson to Thomas Jefferson, September 15, 1807, document 30145, roll 39, Thomas Jefferson Papers, Library of Congress.

30. Ralph R. Shaw and Richard H. Shoemaker, *American Bibliography: A Preliminary Checklist for 1806* (New York: Scarecrow Press, 1961), United States Military Philosophical Society files 11747, 14109, 16607, and 30385. President Jefferson appointed Jonathan Williams the first superintendent of the United States Military Academy in December 1801—Williams was also chief of engineers of the Army Corps of Engineers. Williams was always trying to promote the academy at West Point, and upon learning that Madison would succeed Jefferson as president, he wrote an impassioned letter hoping to further the aims of the academy: "I have been labouring to produce a national establishment, upon a scale worthy of the Government & honourable to our Country; but owing to the confined limits

of the Law, it is yet no more than an obscure mathematical School. . . . It is in my mind a settled principle, that a military academy can only flourish at the Seat of Government, and if this want is not to take place, it cannot be an object for my ambition to have any concern in it; my Duties as chief Engineer are equally arduous & pleasing those of Superintendent of the military academy are not less so; but it is really tedious to labour like Sissyphus in rolling a Stone up Hill." Jonathan Williams to James Madison, February 23, 1809, document 24.147–49, reel 10, James Madison Papers, Library of Congress.

31. Arthur P. Wade, "A Military Offspring of the American Philosophical Society," *Military Affairs* 38 (October 1974): 104.

32. Sidney Forman, "The United States Military Philosophical Society, 1802–1813: *Scientia in Bello Pax*," *The William and Mary Quarterly*, 3rd series, vol. 2 (July 1945): 278–82. Jonathan Williams cited the phrase "Scientia in Bello Pax," as the society's motif.

33. Samuel Lathan Mitchill to Jonathan Williams, December 31, 1806, United States Military Philosophical Society, vol. 2, p. 40, New York Historical Society, New York, New York.

34. Col. Jonathan Williams was stationed at West Point.

35. Jonathan Williams, "Notes Taken in the General Court Martial on the Trial of Brigadier General James Wilkinson Commencing September 2, 1811," Jonathan Williams Manuscripts, box 6, Lilly Library Manuscript Collections, Indiana University, Bloomington, Indiana.

36. "Thomas Jefferson to Gilbert Russell, April 18, 1810," in Jackson, *Letters*, 2: p. 728. See appendix A, no. 35.

37. "Rough Minutes of My Draft and of Major Amos Stoddard's for the Letter to the President of the United States Which Was Afterwards Composed by Me from These Notes," December 2, 1811, Jonathan Williams Manuscripts, box 7, Lilly Library Manuscript Collections, Indiana University.

CHAPTER 13: DR. ANTOINE SAUGRAIN'S TREATMENT OF GOVERNOR MERIWETHER LEWIS

1. Meriwether Lewis to Lucy Marks, April 6, 1795, Meriwether Lewis Collection, Missouri History Museum.

2. John H. Buell, "Fighting the Indians in the Northwest," *American History Illustrated* 3, no. 9 (January 1969): 35. The Battle of Fallen Timbers occurred on Wednesday, August 20, 1794. The name Fallen Timbers was derived from the location where a tornado had blown down hundreds of large hardwood trees. Ronald C. Hood, "The Battle of Fallen Timbers," *American History Illustrated* 3, no. 10 (February 1969): 9.

3. Fort Defiance, September 2, 3, 4, 1794, John Boyer, "General Wayne's Orderly Book," *Michigan Pioneer and Historical Collections* 34 (1904): 551–52. Joseph Gardner

Andrews, the surgeon's mate at Fort Defiance, reported in September 1795 that a large number of people at the fort had come down with the ague. On October 1, he reported that fifty-three soldiers were ill at Fort Defiance while "500 [were] sick at Greenville," with intermittent and remittent fevers. Andrews eventually fell ill and, short-handed, had to tend to the sick. Joseph Gardner Andrews, "A Surgeon's Mate at Fort Defiance; the Journal of Joseph Gardner Andrews for the year 1795," *Ohio Historical Quarterly* 66 (July 1957): 241, 247, 254. Other forts in the Ohio country were Fort Jefferson, Fort Washington, Hobson's Choice, Grand Glaize, Fort Wayne, and Fort Saint Mary's. The Ohio Historical Quarterly is online and is a valuable resource of documented information, http://ohsweb.ohiohistory.org/portal/historyjournal-p.shtml (accessed June 7, 2011).

4. Forts Greenville and Defiance reported cases of the ague in the summer and autumn of 1795. In September 1796, malaria struck again and Reverend David Jones, a chaplain in Wayne's army at Fort Greenville, "found the garrison very sickly . . . out of 350, 300 were sick." See "Extracts from the Original Manuscript Journal of the Reverend David Jones . . . Chaplain of the United States Legion, under Major-General Wayne, during the Indian Wars of 1794–5–6," *Michigan Pioneer and Historical Collections* 8 (1885): 393, 395, http://babel.hathitrust.org/cgi/pt?seq=9&view=image&size=100&id=mdp.39015071219458&u=1&num=393 (accessed January 24, 2011).

5. Peter Kendall, "History Unearthed in Greenville, Ohio," *Cube* 30, no. 1 (April 2009): 10; International Guild of Miniature Artisans, http://www.igma.org (accessed May 21, 2011).

6. "Anthony Wayne to Timothy Pickering, August 9, 1795," in Richard C. Knopf, ed., *Anthony Wayne: A Name in Arms* (Pittsburgh: University of Pittsburgh Press, 1960), pp. 442–45.

7. "Anthony Wayne to Timothy Pickering, September 2, 1795," Knopf, *Anthony Wayne*, pp. 447–51.

8. Ibid., p. 451.

9. Ibid.

10. "Anthony Wayne to Timothy Pickering, October 5, 1795," in Knopf, *Anthony Wayne*, pp. 465–65.

11. Eugene L. Huddleston, "James Elliot and 'The Garden of North America': A New Englander's Impressions of the Old Northwest," *Northwest Ohio Quarterly* 42, no. 3 (Summer 1970): 66.

12. "Anthony Wayne to Timothy Pickering, November 9 and 18, 1795," in Knopf, *Anthony Wayne*, pp. 470, 472.

13. Leonard J. Bruce-Chwatt, "Ague as Malaria," *Journal of Tropical Medicine and Hygiene* 79 (1976): 168.

14. Walther H. Wernsdorfer and Ian McGregor, *Malaria: Principles and Practice of Malariology*, 2 vols. (New York: Churchill Livingstone, 1988), 1: 4–6.

15. Margaret Humphreys, *Malaria, Poverty, Race, and Public Health in the United States* (Baltimore: Johns Hopkins University Press, 2001), p. 8.

16. Allan Saul, "The Role of Variant Surface Antigens on Malaria-Infected Red Blood Cells," *Parasitology Today* 15 (November 1999): 455.

17. Humphreys, *Malaria*, p. 8.

18. John Ball, *The Modern Practice of Physic* (London: A. Millar, 1762), p. 35.

19. Jean S. Alibert, *A Treatise on Malignant Intermittents* (Philadelphia: Fry and Kammerer, 1807), p. 30.

20. *Proceedings of the Celebration of the Three Hundredth Anniversary of the First Recognized Use of Cinchona* (Saint Louis: Missouri Botanical Garden, 1931), p. 149.

21. William Cullen Brown, *The Institutions of the Practice of Medicine*, 3 vols. (Edinburgh, 1801), 3: 354.

22. Since the 2002 publication of "The 'Ague' Made Him Do It," in *We Proceeded On*, the question has been asked many times, if both Lewis and Clark suffered from malaria, why did Lewis appear to be more sick than Clark? Reading about Clark's own bouts with the disease reveals that it was equally debilitating for him. Clark's journey up the Osage River to establish Fort Osage at Fire Prairie in August and September 1808 is a tacit reminder that malaria causes dysentery, which relentlessly afflicted him. See Kate L. Gregg, ed., *Westward with the Dragoons: The Journal of William Clark on His Expedition to Establish Fort Osage, August 25 to September 22, 1808* (Fulton, MO: Ovid Bell Press, 1937), pp. 28–32, 37, 39, 41, 42, and 45. For the first three days in September, Clark mistakenly wrote October, which is indicative that something was troubling him. On Sept. 13, 1808, Clark wrote, "I am verry unwell with a Desentary, which I have had for Some time and now become very Serios. No Sleep this Night."

23. See http://www.lexic.us/definition-of/relapse (accessed January 24, 2011).

24. Testimony of Dr. William Hood, RG94, M1136, roll 1, frame 0841, p. 49, National Archives and Records Administration.

25. Pierre Charles Delassus de Luziéres to Zenon Trudeau, September 28, 1793, AGI-PC 208a: 446 and 453; Zenon Trudeau to Francisco Louis Hector Carondelet, August 8 and September 8, 1794, AGI-PC 197: 707.

26. Once the bark is brewed into a tea, it is an extremely bitter substance, which usually induces vomiting. Adding brandy or wine dilutes the bitterness. "Meriwether Lewis, November 13, 1803," in *The Journals of the Lewis and Clark Expedition*, 13 vols., ed. Gary E. Moulton (Lincoln: University of Nebraska Press, 1983–2001), 2: p. 86, http://lewisandclarkjournals.unl.edu/ (accessed January 14, 2011).

27. *New-England Palladium*, December 30, 1803, p. 3.

28. Amos Stoddard to Colonel Thomas Cushing, November 8, 1806, RG94, M566, roll 1, frame 0800, National Archives and Records Administration.

29. John Breck Treat to Secretary of War, September 18, 1808, RG75, M271, Roll 1, frame 0488, National Archives and Records Administration.

30. Robert T. Boyd, "Another Look at the Fever and Ague of Western Oregon," *Ethnohistory* 22, no. 2 (Spring 1975): 135.

31. Center for Columbia River History, Exploring the Columbia Slough, Documents

Archive, section II: "Berries, Catfish, and Carp: Survival on the Slough, Descriptions of the Effects of Fever and Ague," http://www.ccrh.org/comm/slough/primary/descript.htm (accessed January 15, 2010).

32. Boyd, "Another Look at the Fever," p. 148.

33. Center for Columbia River History, "Berries, Catfish, and Carp."

34. Ibid.

35. *Wikipedia*, "Jesuit's Bark," http://en.wikipedia.org/wiki/Jesuit%27s_bark (accessed January 19, 2011); Catholic Encyclopedia, "Jesuit's Bark," http://www.newadvent .org/cathen/08372b.htm; Mark Honigsbaum, *The Fever Trail: In Search of the Cure for Malaria* (New York: Farrar, Straus, and Giroux, 2001), p. 89.

36. John Oldmixon, *British Empire in America*, 2nd ed., 2 vols. (London: 1741), 1: 429; "Rush's Observations on Yellow fever," *Medical Repository* 1, no. 1 (1798): 78; Benjamin Rush, *Medical Inquiries and Observations*, 4 vols. (Philadelphia: J. Conrad, 1805) 3: 417.

37. Francisco Guerra, "The Introduction of Cinchona in the Treatment of Malaria," part 2, *Journal of Tropical Medicine & Hygiene* 80, no. 3 (1977): 136.

38. John Redman Coxe, "Cinchona-Peruvian Bark," in *The American Dispensatory*, 5th ed., (Philadelphia: 1822), p. 193.

39. Dale C. Smith, "Quinine and Fever: The Development of the Effective Dosage," *Journal of the History of Medicine and Allied Sciences* 31, no. 3 (July 1976): 349. Quinine is a protoplasmic poison.

40. Ido Leden, "Antimalarial Drugs-350 Years," *Scandanavian Journal of Rheumatology* 10 (1981): 10; Coxe, "Cinchona-Peruvian Bark," p. 193; Guerra, "Introduction of Cinchona" part 1, *Journal of Tropical Medicine and Hygiene* 80, no. 6 (June 1977): 112–18; Friedrich A. Flückiger, *The Cinchona Barks* (Philadelphia: P. Blakiston, Son & Co., 1884), p. 195; Jackson, *Letters,* 1: 80. "Pulv. Cort. Peru" is *Pulvis Cortici Peruviana*, which meant powdered Peruvian bark.

41. William J. Fitzgerald, "Evolution of the Use of Quinine in the Treatment of Malaria," *New York State Journal of Medicine* 68 (March 1968): 801.

42. Brown, *The Institutions of the Practice of Medicine*, 3: 285; Coxe, "Cinchona-Peruvian Bark," p. 193.

43. J. Worth Estes, *Dictionary of Protopharmacology, Therapeutic Practices, 1700–1850* (Canton, MA: Science History Publications, 1990), p. 48; Flückiger, *Cinchona Barks*, p. 215.

44. Robert Desowitz, *The Malaria Capers* (New York: W. W. Norton, 1991), p. 202.

45. Drake W. Will, "The Medical and Surgical Practice of the Lewis and Clark Expedition," *Journal of the History of Medicine and Allied Sciences* 14 (July 1959): 282–83. Jefferson was a sufferer of diarrhea for most of his life and consulted with Benjamin Rush on May 5, 1803, when he also introduced Meriwether Lewis to the physician. Thomas Jefferson to Benjamin Rush, document 22673–74, reel 28, Thomas Jefferson Papers, Library of Congress.

46. "Benjamin Rush to Thomas Jefferson, June 11, 1803," and "Benjamin Rush's Rules of Health, June 11, 1803," in Jackson, *Letters*, 1: 54; Will, "Medical and Surgical Practice," p. 278. Jefferson transcribed Rush's rules and shortened the title to "Dr. Rush to Capt. Lewis

for Preserving His Health, June 11, 1803." Historians have emphasized that the instructions were for Lewis's men instead of Lewis, but this oversight minimizes Lewis's physical illness.

47. Jackson, *Letters*, 1: 55, 80.

48. Meriwether Lewis Account Book 1807–1809, Meriwether Lewis Collection, Missouri History Museum. See appendix F for details.

49. Capt. James House, Capt. E. B. Clemson, and Lieut. Alpha Kingsley to Secretary of War, January 12, 1808, C1808, RG107, M222, Roll 3, frames 1145–47. Capt. Russell Bissell, the commander of Fort Bellefontaine, succumbed to a malarial fever, and suffered for five days until he died on December 16, 1807.

50. John Boyer, "Daily Journal of Wayne's Campaign: General Wayne's Orderly Book," *Michigan Pioneer and Historical Collections* 34 (1904): 643; "Lt. William Clark's Report, November 12, 1795," Knopf, *Anthony Wayne*, p. 471.

51. Richard Allison was the senior surgeon in Wayne's Legion, along with Charles Brown, surgeon, and four surgeon's mates: John Gorham Coffin, John R. Lynch, Francis G. Brewster, and Richard Griffith. Dwight L. Smith, ed. "From Greene Ville to Fallen Timbers: A Journal of the Wayne Campaign" *Indiana Historical Society Publications* 16 (1952): 278; Boyer, "Daily Journal of Wayne's Campaign," p. 602; Virginius C. Hall, "Richard Allison, Surgeon to the Legion," *Bulletin of the Historical and Philosophical Society of Ohio* 9 (October 1951); James Holmberg, ed., *Dear Brother* (New Haven, CT: Yale University Press, 2002), p. 275, n. 6.

52. "William Clark to Meriwether Lewis, July 24, 1803," in Jackson, *Letters*, 1: 112–13.

53. Eldon G. Chuinard, *Only One Man Died: The Medical Aspects of the Lewis and Clark Expedition* (Glendale, CA: Arthur Clark, 1980), pp. 27, 264–65; Ronald V. Loge, "Illness at Three Forks," *Montana: The Magazine of Western History* 50, no. 2 (Summer 2000): 15; Ronald V. Loge, "Two Dozes of Barks and Opium: Lewis and Clark as Physicians," *We Proceeded On* 23, no. 1 (February 1997): 30; David J. Peck, *Or Perish in the Attempt: Wilderness Medicine in the Lewis & Clark Expedition* (Helena, MT: Farcountry Press, 2001), pp. 81, 103, 161; Drake W. Will, "Lewis and Clark: Westering Physicians," *Montana: The Magazine of Western History* 21, no. 4 (Autumn 1971): 14, 17.

54. Thomas C. Danisi and John C. Jackson, *Meriwether Lewis* (Amherst, NY: Prometheus Books, 2009), p. 309.

55. "Thomas Jefferson to Martha Jefferson Randolph, March 6, 1807," in Edwin Morris Betts and James Adam Bear Jr., eds., *The Family Letters of Thomas Jefferson* (Columbia: University of Missouri Press), pp. 298–99.

56. Frank Hawking, Michael J. Worms, and Kenneth Gammage, "Host Temperature and Control of 24-Hour and 48-Hour Cycles in Malaria Parasites," *Lancet* 7541 (March 1968): 506; Robert Thomas, *The Modern Practice of Physic* (New York: Collins, 1820), p. 5.

57. "Meriwether Lewis to William Clark, March 11, 1807," in Jackson, *Letters*, 2: 385.

58. "Thomas Jefferson to Martha Jefferson Randolph, March 16, 1807," in Betts and Bear, *Family Letters*, p. 302.

59. Humphreys, *Malaria*, p. 9; Abraham Rees, "Hemicrania," in Volumn 19 of *The Cyclopaedia*, 45 vols. (London: Longman, Rees, Orme & Browne, 1819).

60. "The symptoms which they exhibited were various. In some cases they assumed the character of periodical headache or sun-pain." Daniel Drake, "Report on the Diseases of Cincinnati in the spring of 1828 . . . for Ague and Fever," *Western Journal of the Medical and Physical Sciences* 2 (1828–1829): 217. Daniel Drake, *The Principal Diseases of the Interior Valley of North America*, 2nd ed., (Reprint. Philadelphia: Lippincott, Grambo & Co., 1854).

61. Thomas Jefferson, Recipe for the Head-Ach, document 41873, reel 16, Thomas Jefferson Papers, Library of Congress. Historians have debated Jefferson's headaches for a long time, but since 1984 they have come to the conclusion that it was a type of cluster headache brought on by tension. John Holmes came the closest to implying that it was malaria, noting that Jefferson had used the Peruvian bark "to treat fevers." Modern medical physicians, Battle, Cohen, and Rolak dismissed the malarial headaches in favor of ones caused by extreme tension. Kukla, another historian, also disagreed with Battle, Cohen, and Rolak, but did not herald the cause. By the fact that Jefferson had used the Peruvian bark when he experienced a periodical headache is enough proof to serve as an indication that Jefferson was a victim of malaria. For many years and under many circumstances Jefferson employed the use of the bark. On several occasions in 1790 and 1807 he wrote that the bark had failed to cure him. John H. Holmes, *Thomas Jefferson Treats Himself: Herbs, Physicke, & Nutrition in Early America* (Fort Valley, VA: The Loft Press, 1997), p. 62; John D. Battle Jr., "The 'periodical head-achs' of Thomas Jefferson," *Cleveland Clinic Quarterly* 51 (1984): 531–33; Gary L. Cohen and Loren A. Rolak, "Thomas Jefferson's Headaches: Were They Migraines?" *Headache: The Journal of Head and Face Pain* 46, no. 3 (March 2006): 492; Jon Kukla, *Mr. Jefferson's Women* (New York: Vintage Books, 2007), p. 227, n. 60.

62. Humphreys, *Malaria*, p. 29. President Jefferson wrote all of his letters, sometimes five or six in a day, but during this period in 1807 it was especially difficult to write when official letters demanded great concentration:

> March 6—to Martha Jefferson Randolph, his daughter: I have had a very bad cold, which laid me up with a fever one day. This indisposition will occasion me to be here some days longer than I expected.

> March 16—to Martha Jefferson Randolph: I am poorly myself, not at all fit for a journey at this time. The remains of a bad cold hang on me, and for a day or two past some symptoms of periodical headache. Mr. Coles and Capt. Lewis are also indisposed, so that we are but a collection of invalids.

> March 20—to Albert Gallatin, secretary of the Treasury: I have but a little moment in the morning in which I can either read write or think; being obliged to be shut up in a dark room from early in the forenoon till night with a periodical head-ach.

> March 20—to Martha Jefferson Randolph: I am now in the 7th day of a periodical head-ache, and I write this in the morning before the Fit has come on. The fits are by no means as severe as I have felt in former times, but they hold me very long from 9. or 10. in the morning till dark. Neither Calomel nor bark have as yet

made the least impression on them. Indeed we have quite a hospital, one half below and above stairs being sick.

March 21—to John Wayles Eppes: I am in the 8th day of periodical head-ach which threatens to be obstinate. . . . I write this under a fit of head-ach. . . .

March 21—to James Monroe, Ambassador to the United Kingdom: I am writing under a severe indisposition of periodical headache, with scarcely command enough of mind to know what I write.

March 23—to Martha Jefferson Randolph: My fits of head-ach have shortened from 9 hours to 5. but they have stuck some days at 5. hours, and when they will give further way cannot be divined. In our present situation it is impossible to fix a day of departure. It has always seemed to be about a week off; but, like our shadows, it walks before us, and still keeps at the same distance. I do believe however that Mr. Randolph will be able to travel within one week from the time of his getting on horseback. I write while a fit is coming on and therefore must conclude with my kisses to you all.

March 25—to Lt. Gov. of Massachussetts Levi Lincoln: I expected to have paid a short visit to Monticello before this, but have been detained by the illness of my son-in-law, Mr. Randolph, and now by an attack of periodical headache on myself. This leaves me but an hour & a half each morning capable of any business at all.

March 27—to Martha Jefferson Randolph: My fit of yesterday was so mild that I have some hope of missing it to-day.

March 30—to Martha Jefferson Randolph: I have no actual head-ach, yet about 9. oclock every morning I have a very quickened pulse come on, a disturbed head and tender eyes, not amounting to absolute pain. It goes off about noon, and is doubtless an obstinate remnant of the head-ach, keeping up the possibility of return. I am not very confident of it's passing off.

April 2—Martha Jefferson Randolph: Mr. Randolph is quite strong enough to begin his journey even now. I think that to-day for the first time I have had no sensation of any remain of my head-ach.

April 5—Martha Jefferson Randolph: We are all well here, My ever dear Martha, but I shall not be able probably to set out tomorrow, but shall on Tuesday. We shall be five days on the road.

March 6 and 16: Betts and Bear, *Family Letters*, pp. 298–99, 302; March 20 to Gallatin: document 29187, reel 38, Thomas Jefferson Papers, Library of Congress; March 20 to daughter: Betts and Bear, *Family Letters*, p. 304; March 21: document 29193 and 29195–6, reel 38, Thomas Jefferson Papers, Library of Congress, March 23: Betts and Bear, *Family Letters*, p. 304; March 25 to Levi Lincoln, the former attorney general of the United States: document 29214, reel 38, Thomas Jefferson Papers, Library of Congress; March 27 and 30: Betts and Bear, *Family Letters*, p. 305.

63. "Thomas Jefferson to Martha Jefferson Randolph, April 5 to June 1, 1807," Betts and Bear, *Family Letters*, pp. 306–307. In 1808 he succumbed again to the same illness beginning March 25 and ending April 12, 1808. He described his condition when writing to Ellen Wayles Randolph Coolidge (March 29), Cornelia Jefferson Randolph (April 3), and James Monroe (April 11).

64. Dr. Antoine Saugrain's Medical Ledgers, 1801–1817, 2 vols., Pettis County Historical Society and Museum, Sedalia, Missouri.

65. Jackson, *Letters*, 1: 192. See *Wikipedia*, "Antoine Saugrain," http://en.wiki pedia.org/wiki/Antoine_Saugrain; "Dr. Antoine Saugrain," National Park Service, http://www .nps.gov/archive/jeff/lewisclark2/circa1804/StLouis/BlockInfo/Block50DrAntoineSaugrain .htm; and Rootsweb, "Antoine Saugrain," http://freepages.history.rootsweb.ancestry.com /~earlystlouis/antoinesaugrain.html (accessed April 7, 2011).

66. Meriwether Lewis to Lucy Marks, April 6, 1795, Meriwether Lewis Collection, Missouri History Museum.

67. Antoine Saugrain, April 6, 1808, Medical Ledgers, vol. 1, p. 410, Pettis County Historical Society and Museum, Sedalia, Missouri.

68. S. Blumgarten, *Textbook of Materia Medica, Pharmacology and Therapeutics*, 7th ed. (New York: Macmillan, 1939), p. 228; John W. Fisher, *Medical Appendices of the Lewis and Clark Expedition* (Juliaetta, ID: John W. Fisher, 2006), p. 27. The Lewis and Clark Expedition carried six pounds of the salt and Lewis relied upon it often as a laxative to ease stomach and intestinal problems.

69. Antoine Saugrain, June 15 and 18, 1808, Medical Ledgers, vol. 1, p. 410, Pettis County Historical Society and Museum; Blumgarten, *Textbook of Materia Medica*, p. 189.

70. Antoine Saugrain, August 30, 1808, vol. 1, p. 410, Pettis County Historical Society and Museum.

71. Ira M. Rutkow, *Bleeding Blue and Gray: Civil War Surgery and the Evolution of Medicine* (New York: Random House, 2005), p. 48.

72. Saugrain abbreviated "cream of tartar." Blumgarten, *Textbook of Materia Medica*, p. 229.

73. See sppendix F. On November 9, Lewis paid Dr. Farrar (another physician in Saint Louis) $49 to take care of Pernia, Lewis's valet, who was also suffering from the ague. See Meriwether Lewis's account book, p. 16; Doctor Farrar's Ledger, Missouri History Museum.

74. Meriwether Lewis Account Book, 1808–1809, Meriwether Lewis Collection, Missouri History Museum.

75. Meriwether Lewis to Lucy Marks, December 1, 1808, Meriwether Lewis Collection, Missouri History Museum.

76. "Meriwether Lewis to Thomas Jefferson, December 15, 1808," in *American State Papers, Indian Affairs* 1: 763–67. The original letter and its contents totaled fifty-one pages.

77. Edward Kremers and George Urdang, *History of Pharmacy: A Guide and Survey* (Philadelphia: J. B. Lippincott, 1940), p. 401; Blumgarten, *Textbook of Materia Medica*, p. 232. Jalap produces results within an hour.

78. Clarence Edwin Carter, ed., *The Territorial Papers of the United States*, 28 vols. (Washington, DC: Government Printing Office, 1948), 13: 279.

79. Ibid.

80. Daniel Bissell to Secretary of War, September 28, 1809, B580, RG107, M221, roll 18, frame 5618, National Archives and Records Administration.

81. Meriwether Lewis to William Simmons, July 8, 1809, appendix A, no. 13. Lewis, Marks, Anderson Family: M668, University of Virginia, Alderman Library, Charlottesville, Virginia.

82. Thomas M. Marshall, *The Life and Papers of Frederick Bates*, 2 vols. (Saint Louis: Missouri Historical Society, 1926), 2: 24.

83. Carter, *Territorial Papers,* 14: 285–86.

84. Carter, *Territorial Papers,* 14: 290–93. The transcription does not identify the handwriting of the writer. Meriwether Lewis to War Department, August 18, 1809, L328, RG107, M221, roll 23, frame 8501, National Archives and Records Administration. This letter was not in Lewis's hand but was written by Jeremiah Connor, sheriff of Saint Louis, RG233, M1708, roll 6, frames 0497–99, National Archives and Records Administration.

85. Meriwether Lewis paid Dr. Saugrain to assemble a medicine chest for him, which amounted to $30.75. This was a costly expenditure due to the fact that there was a shortage of medicinal supplies in Saint Louis. William Clark's Account Book, June–September 1809, Clark Family Collection, Missouri History Museum.

86. Danisi and Jackson, *Meriwether Lewis*, p. 316.

87. Antoine Saugrain, Medical Ledgers, vol. 1, p. 410, Pettis County Historical Society and Museum. Saugrain's identification of "Porney" was Lewis's free mulatto valet, John Pernia or Pernier. Danisi and Jackson, *Meriwether Lewis*, pp. 190, 207, n. 2.

88. We should look at the expedition journals to verify when Lewis took Glauber's salts, which might indicate when he suffered from a malarial bout. Meriwether Lewis, August 1, 1805: "[T]o add to my fatigue in this walk of about 11 miles I had taken a doze of glauber salts in the morning in consequence of a slight desentary with which I had been afflicted for several days; being weakened by the disorder and the opperation of the medecine I found myself almost exhausted before we reached the river. I felt my sperits much revived on our . . . approach to the river at the sight of a herd of Elk of which Drewyer and myself killed two. we then hurried to the river and allayed our thirst. I ordered two of the men to skin the Elk . . . while myself and the other prepared a fire and cooked some of the meat. . . . [A]fter dinner we resumed our march and encamped about 6 m. above on the Stard side of the river." Meriwether Lewis, William Clark, et al., August 1, 1805, entry in *The Journals of the Lewis and Clark Expedition*, ed. Gary Moulton (Lincoln: University of Nebraska Press/University of Nebraska–Lincoln Libraries Electronic Text Center, 2005), http://lewisandclarkjournals.unl.edu/read/?_xmlsrc=1805-08-01&_xslsrc=LCstyles.xsl (accessed January 19, 2011).

89. The crew had reported that Lewis had made two attempts to kill himself while aboard the boat from Saint Louis. Chronic malarial patients have typically exhibited wild and erratic behavior, and persons unfamiliar with this pattern of the disease continually assign incorrect observations and judgments to those patients. While it may look suicidal, patients are attempting to alleviate long-standing pain of the head or simply to cool off in the river.

90. Gilbert Russell to Secretary of War, August 26, 1809, R244, RG107, roll 29, frame 9756, p. 1, National Archives and Records Administration. Capt. William Swan had been the commander of Fort Pickering until Russell's arrival.

91. Ibid., p. 2. It's somewhat of a mystery why six of his soldiers drowned, but the boats were in poor shape and laden with merchandise and tools. The drownings were likely the result of the soldiers' inadequacy at swimming.

92. William C. Smith, Surgeon's Mate of Fort Pickering, to William Eustis, November 5, 1809, S743, RG107, M221, roll 31, frame 0463, p. 1, National Archives and Records Administration. Capt. Russell wrote to the secretary of war on January 2, 1810, and referred to Smith as surgeon of the garrison: M221, R14, roll 39, frames 6095–6102, National Archives and Records Administration. Russell had charged Smith with conduct unbecoming an officer, and the secretary of war dismissed Smith on June 27, 1810. Francis Bernard Heitman, ed., *Historical Register and Dictionary of the United States Army from Its Organization, September 29, 1789, to March 2, 1903*, 2 vols. (Washington, DC: Government Printing Office, 1903), 1: 904.

93. RG107, M221, S743, roll 31, frame 0463, p. 1, National Archives and Records Administration.

94. Gilbert Russell to Secretary of War, August 26, 1809, RG107, R244, roll 29, frame 9756, p. 3, National Archives and Records Administration.

CHAPTER 14: REVISITING MERIWETHER LEWIS'S DEATH: A NEW PERSPECTIVE

*We have had lively discussions concerning the peculiar nature of Lewis's death for more than ten years. To understand its nature, we needed to do three things: (1) unravel Jefferson's remarks about Lewis's hypochondria; (2) provide an argument connecting Jefferson's remarks with Lewis's struggles as a malarial sufferer; and (3) establish that Lewis's death amounted to the alleviation of unbearable pain, and not to suicide, as traditional historians of Lewis maintain. The argument that we offer rests upon both an empirical and a nineteenth-century historical foundation; a foundation, moreover, that is radically different from that of the tradition, with its emphasis upon a more contemporary scientific, and thus speculative, foundation. We thus embarked on a journey centered upon the nature of hypochondria, malaria, depression, mind, death, and suicide, and upon their relation to Lewis—a journey that has its roots in our scholarship: "The 'Ague' Made Him Do It," "The Vanishing Consciousness," and *Meriwether Lewis*. In our view, Lewis did not commit suicide, and he should be restored to his rightful place among the great leaders of our nation.

1. Most physicians have taken the position that correlating a disease as it was understood and diagnosed in the past with a present-day equivalent is pointless because it cannot be medically confirmed that the diseases are one and the same using today's tests. Dr. Fis-

cher-Homberger, a historian of psychiatry, sums up the conundrum: "Medical history is qualified to further a historical understanding of medicine, but only on certain occasions is it capable of furthering a medical understanding of history." Esther Fischer-Homberger, "Hypochondriasis of the Eighteenth Century—Neurosis of the Present Century," *Bulletin of the History of Medicine* 46, no. 4 (July–August 1972): 401.

2. "Thomas Jefferson to Meriwether Lewis, February 23, 1801"; "Thomas Jefferson's Message to Congress, January 18, 1803"; "Thomas Jefferson to Benjamin Smith Barton, February 27, 1803"; and "Thomas Jefferson to the Senate, February 28, 1807," in Donald Jackson, ed., *Letters of Lewis and Clark Expedition with Related Documents, 1783–1854*, 2nd ed., 2 vols. (Urbana: University of Illinois Press, 1978), 1: 2–3, 10–13, 16–17, 376.

3. "Henry Dearborn to William Clark, March 9, 1807," in Jackson, *Letters*, 2: 382.

4. Gilbert Russell to Thomas Jefferson, January 4, 1810, document 33616–18, reel 45, Thomas Jefferson Papers, Library of Congress. See appendix A, no. 27.

5. Gary E. Moulton, ed., *The Journals of the Lewis and Clark Expedition*, 13 vols. (Lincoln: University of Nebraska Press, 1983–2001); Stephen Ambrose, *Undaunted Courage* (New York: Simon & Schuster, 1996); William E. Foley, *Wilderness Journey: The Life of William Clark* (Columbia: University of Missouri Press, 2004); John D. W. Guice, ed., *By His Own Hand? The Mysterious Death of Meriwether Lewis* (Norman: Oklahoma University Press, 2006); Jackson, *Letters*; Kay Redfield Jamison, *Night Falls Fast* (New York: Alfred A. Knopf, 1999); Clay Straus Jenkinson, *The Character of Meriwether Lewis: "Completely Metamorphosed" in the American West* (Reno, NV: Marmarth Press, 2000); Landon Y. Jones, *William Clark and the Shaping of the West* (New York: Hill and Wang, 2004); Larry E. Morris, *The Fate of the Corps: What Became of the Lewis and Clark Explorers after the Expedition* (New Haven, CT: Yale University Press, 2004); David J. Peck, *Or Perish in the Attempt: Wilderness Medicine in the Lewis & Clark Expedition* (Helena, MT: Farcountry Press, 2002); Paul Russell Cutright, "Rest, Rest Perturbed Spirit," *We Proceeded On* 12, no. 1 (March 1986); Howard I. Kushner, "The Suicide of Meriwether Lewis: A Psychoanalytic Inquiry," *William and Mary Quarterly,* 3rd series, 38, no. 3 (1981); Ronald V. Loge, "Meriwether Lewis and Malaria," *We Proceeded On* 28, no. 2 (May 2002); Dawson A. Phelps, "The Tragic Death of Meriwether Lewis," *William and Mary Quarterly* 13 (July 1956).

6. "Thomas Jefferson to Paul Allen, August 18, 1813," in Jackson, *Letters*, 2: 591–92.

7. "Thomas Jefferson to Gilbert Russell, April 18, 1810," in Jackson, *Letters*, 2: 728.

8. "Frederick Bates to Secretary of War, September 28, 1809," in Thomas M. Marshall, *The Life and Papers of Frederick Bates*, 2 vols. (Saint Louis: Missouri Historical Society, 1926), 2: 86.

9. September 11, 1809, New Madrid Courthouse, Lewis, Marks, Anderson Family, M668, Alderman Library, University of Virginia, Charlottesville, Virginia. We know some of Meriwether Lewis's circumstances at the time of his death: his brother Reuben had joined the expedition to return the Mandan chief Sheheke-shote to his family and then to accompany Manuel Lisa to trap furs on the Upper Missouri; Lewis was concerned regarding government reimbursements; Lewis was taking the original journals from his western expedition

with him, expecting to edit them while staying in Philadelphia; he was afraid that the British might confiscate the journals if he took a boat up the east coast of the United States, and was further disturbed by the news that an outbreak of malaria had seized New Orleans; as a consequence he decided to ride horseback from Tennessee to Washington; his malarial paroxysms were intensifying. Yet, despite what we know, we do not exactly know which of these circumstances, if any, may have precipitated the rewriting of his will. His life is shrouded in considerably more mystery than is commonly thought. Those historians who suggest definitive circumstances of Lewis's death are, in my opinion, speculating.

10. Jackson, *Letters*, 2: 573.

11. "James Neely to Thomas Jefferson, October 18, 1809," in Jackson, *Letters*, 2: 467–68.

12. Alexander Wilson, "Particulars of the Death of Captain Lewis," *Port Folio* 7 (January 1812): 37.

13. "James Neely to Thomas Jefferson," in Jackson, *Letters*, 2: 468.

14. Ibid., 2: 467.

15. James Holmberg, ed., *Dear Brother* (New Haven, CT: Yale University Press), p. 218.

16. John D. W. Guice, ed., *By His Own Hand? The Mysterious Death of Meriwether Lewis* (Norman: Oklahoma University Press, 2006). Guice claims that Thomas Danisi is a "suicide advocate." He is mistaken; Danisi clearly wrote in 2002 that he rejected "the notion that [Lewis's] death was a suicide." Thomas C. Danisi, "The 'Ague' Made Him Do It," *We Proceeded On* 28, no. 1 (February 2002): 10.

17. Moulton, *Journals*, p. 378.

18. Ambrose, *Undaunted Courage*, pp. 63, 431.

19. David J. Peck, "The Death of Meriwether Lewis," *We Proceeded On* 35, no. 4 (November 2009): 22.

20. Dawson A. Phelps, "The Tragic Death of Meriwether Lewis," *William and Mary Quarterly* 13 (July 1956): 317.

21. Paul Russell Cutright, "Rest, Rest Perturbed Spirit," *We Proceeded On* 12, no. 1 (March 1986): 9.

22. Jackson, *Letters*, 2: 575.

23. Ibid., p. 748.

24. Ibid., p. 728.

25. Ibid., p. 728, note below letter 452.

26. Jenkinson, *The Character of Meriwether Lewis*, pp. 97–98.

27. Ronald V. Loge, "Meriwether Lewis and Malaria," *We Proceeded On* 28, no. 2 (May 2002): 33.

28. Reimert T. Ravenholt, "Triumph Then Despair: The Tragic Death of Meriwether Lewis," *Epidemiology* 5, no. 3 (May 1994): 377.

29. "Meriwether Lewis, March 19 and January 27, 1806," in Moulton, *Journals*, 6: 239–40, 436.

30. John D. W. Guice, "Moonlight and Meriwether Lewis," *We Proceeded On* 28, no. 1 (February 2002): 21–23.

31. *Wikipedia*, "Photometry (Optics)," http://en.wikipedia.org/wiki/Photometry _(optics) (accessed May 26, 2011).

32. Howard I. Kushner, "The Suicide of Meriwether Lewis: A Psychoanalytic Inquiry," *William and Mary Quarterly*, 3rd series, 38, no. 3 (1981): 473.

33. Kay Redfield Jamison, *Night Falls Fast* (New York: Alfred A. Knopf, 1999), p. 229.

34. Ann Rogers, "Hypocondriac Affections: Letters Help Define Jefferson's Phrase," *We Proceeded On* 36, no. 1 (February 2010): 33, left column.

35. Ibid., p. 36

36. Thomas C. Danisi, "Keepers and Stewards Code Calls for Historical Facts," *We Proceeded On* 36, no. 2 (May 2010): 4–5, 7.

37. "Captain Lewis who had then been near two years with me as private secretary, immediately renewed his sollicitations to have the direction of the party. I had now had opportunities of knowing him intimately. Of courage undaunted, possessing a firmness & perseverance of purpose which nothing but impossibilities could divert from it's direction, careful as a father of those committed to his charge, yet steady in the maintenance of order & discipline, intimate with the Indian character, customs & principles, habituated to the hunting life, guarded by exact observation of the vegetables & animals of his own country, against losing time in the description of objects already possessed, honest, disinterested, liberal, of sound understanding and a fidelity to truth so scrupulous that whatever he should report would be as certain as if seen by ourselves, with all these qualifications as if selected and implanted by nature in one body, for this express purpose, I could have no hesitation in confiding the enterprize to him. "Thomas Jefferson to Paul Allen, August 18, 1813," in Jackson, *Letters*, 2: 589–90.

38. Ibid., pp. 591–92.

39. Thomas Jefferson to John Adams, April 8, 1816, document 36796–97, reel 48, Thomas Jefferson Papers, Library of Congress; Rogers, "Hypocondriac Affections," p. 33. Jefferson's letter to Adams can be read at http://memory.loc.gov/cgi-bin/query/P?mtj:1:./temp/ ~ammem_UjfM (accessed May 26, 2011).

40. Thomas Jefferson, "Thoughts on English Prosody," in Andrew A. Lipscomb and Albert Ellery Bergh, eds., *The Writings of Thomas Jefferson*, Library ed., 20 vols. (Washington, DC: Thomas Jefferson Memorial Association of the United States, 1903), 18: 417–51.

41. Thomas Jefferson to Joseph Priestly, January 27, 1800, document 18153–54, reel 22; and Thomas Jefferson to John Brazer, August 24, 1819, document 38550–51, reel 51, Thomas Jefferson Papers, Library of Congress; Stephen Fineberg, "The Music of Thomas Jefferson's Greek," *Classical Journal* 88, no. 4 (April–May 1993): 362–63, 368. Jefferson and John Adams held contests on who could implant more Greek quotes into their letters. Adams, who preferred Latin, finally lost.

42. Danisi and Jackson, *Meriwether Lewis*, p. 309.

43. Ibid., p. 308.

44. Robert Hooper and Samuel Akerly, *Lexicon Medicum*, 13th ed. (New York, Harper & Brothers, 1841), p. 443.

45. Stanley W. Jackson, *Melancholia and Depression* (New Haven, CT: Yale University Press, 1986), p. 274; Fischer-Homberger, "Hypochondriasis," pp. 391, 394, and 399; Daniel Drake, *The Principal Diseases of the Interior Valley of North America*, 2nd ed. (Philadelphia: Lippincott, Grambo & Co., 1854), p. 66.

46. Anthony Wayne Papers, General Orders of Court Martial, May 1793–October 1796, vol. 50, folio 49–91, transcribed page 25, Historical Society of Pennsylvania, Philadelphia, Pennsylvania.

47. "Essays on Postures," *North American Review* 5, no. 14 (July 1817): 170; "Miscellaneous Notes: Westminster Review," *North American Review* 18, no. 43 (April 1824): 424; "Lord Byron's Character and Writings," *North American Review* 21, no. 49 (October 1825): 302; William Hazlitt, "Lectures on the English Poets," *North American Review* 8, no. 23 (March 1819): 295. Capt. James House wrote an alternate form of the phrase in 1807 when describing Rodolphe Tillier's attitude toward George Sibley: ". . . he is extremely subject to gusts of passions and splenetic humours which renders it morally impossible for any young man to be connected with him. . . ." (Marshall, *Frederick Bates*, 1: 225.)

48. Bruce L. J. Chwatt, "Ague as Malaria," *Journal of Tropical Medicine and Hygiene* 79, no.8 (August 1976): 168–76; Walther H. Wernsdorfer and Ian McGregor, *Malaria: Principles and Practice of Malariology*, 2 vols. (New York: Churchill Livingstone, 1988): 1: 4–25.

49. Chwatt, "Ague as Malaria," p. 168.

50. There are hundreds of documents within the National Archives where soldiers have succumbed to the ague and fever, which was also called the ague.

51. Ronald Loge refutes this remark. "Scrutiny of the Lewis and Clark journals fails to uncover any such pattern of illness in any member of the expedition." The Rutmans (see below) argued this point: "How many physicians have seen an absolutely untreated case of malaria through its full course?" Disease was viewed in the past as "indistinct," yet the Rutmans believe that the historian can build an "inferential case for its prevalence," and combine "the available literary evidence with a contemporary understanding of the disease so that the two are consonant with each other." Basic medical observation in 1804 possessed its own reliable set of "demographic attributes" and must be considered as a factor in Lewis's time. Loge, "Meriwether Lewis and Malaria," p. 35; Darret B. Rutman and Anita H. Rutman, "Of Agues and Fevers: Malaria in the Early Chesapeake," *William and Mary Quarterly*, 3rd series 33, no. 1 (January 1976): 32–33.

52. Mark F. Boyd, *An Introduction to Malariology* (Cambridge, MA: Harvard University Press, 1930), pp. 21–24; Frank Hawking, Michael J. Worms, and Kenneth Gammage, "24- and 48-Hour Cycles of Malarial Parasites in the Blood; Their Purpose, Production, and Control," *Transactions of the Royal Society of Tropical Medicine and Hygiene* 62, no. 6 (June 1968): 731; Herbert S. Heineman, "The Clinical Syndrome of Malaria in the United States," *Archives of Internal Medicine* 129 (April 1972): 609.

53. Margaret Humphreys, *Malaria, Poverty, Race, and Public Health in the United States* (Baltimore: John Hopkins University Press, 2001), p. 8.

54. Barry S. Zingman and Brant L. Viner, "Splenic Complications in Malaria: Case Report and Review," *Clinical Infectious Diseases* 16 (February 1993): 227.

55. William Osler, *The Principles and Practice of Medicine*, 2nd ed. (New York: D. Appleton, 1895), p. 162; U. V. Gopala Rao and Henry N. Wagner, "Normal Weights of Human Organs," *Radiology* 102 (February 1972): 337; Julius P. Kreier, ed., *Malaria*, 3 vols. (New York: Academic Press, 1980), 1: 112.

56. Jean-Louis Alibert, *A Treatise on Malignant Intermittents* (Philadelphia: Fry and Kammerer, 1807), pp. 40, 44.

57. John Pringle, *Observations on the Disease of the Army* (Philadelphia: Fry and Kammerer, 1810), p. 157, in *Early American Imprints*, Second Series, no. 21145.

58. Ibid.

59. Jeffrey Goldberg, "Microbes on the Move," *New York Times Magazine* (October 10, 1999), p. 21. In November 1995, Mr. Goldberg, who initially visited Zanzibar, was "bit repeatedly by mosquitioes." In early December he traveled to Uganda and while hiking in the Bwindi forest succumbed to a malarial fever with accompanying "severe shakes." He writes that "a short while later, atop a mountain, I fell unconscious." He said that the paroxysm of fever had subsided for the moment and he "had to crawl down the mountain with the help of a very kind park official, who told me he would lose his job if I died on him." He was driven to a remote hospital and at one point in the night "a friend had to throw himself across my body to keep me from shaking myself off the bed." It took almost a week to recuperate, and Goldberg was "able to walk only on the fifth day."

60. John Macculloch, *Essay on the Remittent and Intermittent Diseases*, 2 vols. (London: Longman, Rees, Orme, Brown, and Green, 1828), 1: 250–51. Loge refuted this type of self-treatment by stricken malarial patients without taking into consideration that the patients observed by Dr. Macculloch were suffering from long-standing, untreated, end-stage malaria rarely, if ever, seen today. Loge asserts, "A survey of modern medical and infectious disease texts and an on-line search of the world's medical literature do not come up with any descriptions of such self-destructive idiosyncrasies in modern-day patients with proven malaria" (Loge, "Meriwether Lewis and Malaria," p. 35). Today, individuals diagnosed with malaria are cured within six months or less. Macculloch's patients were chronic, having had the disease for more than five years with *no* effective treatment to alleviate pain. They therefore presented with extreme, and what we would consider alarming, measures. Today, it would be surprising to find *any* journal articles reporting malarial patients with self-destructive tendencies given the fact that there is an effective treatment, and no cases progress to such a point.

61. Macculloch, *Remittent and Intermittent Diseases*, pp. 252–53.

62. Thomas C. Danisi, "Lewis's Death," *We Proceeded On* 28, no. 3 (August 2002): 2.

63. See the previous chapter, "Dr. Saugrain's Treatment," for details on Lewis's malaria.

64. "Benjamin Rush's Rules of Health, June 11, 1809," in Jackson, *Letters*, 1: 54–55.

65. "Meriwether Lewis, September 14, 1803," in Moulton, *Journals*, 2: 81.

66. "Meriwether Lewis, November 13, 1803," in Moulton, *Journals*, 2: 86.

67. Meriwether Lewis, November 13 and 14, 1803, Eastern Journal, August 30–December 12, 1803, film 214, reel 2, American Philosophical Society, Philadelphia, Pennsylvania.

68. "Meriwether Lewis, November 14, 1803," in Moulton, *Journals*, 2: 87.

69. Historians should not rely solely upon Moulton's transcriptions of the Journals of the Lewis and Clark Expedition. To completely understand the gravity of Lewis's illness from November 10 through November 27, one must examine the original journals, which have been microfilmed by the American Philosophical Society. In this seventeen-day period, the dates are crossed out, repeatedly, and Lewis's writing, while confusing, also continues to show crossed out words and large blank spaces. The transcriptions condensed all the blank spaces by simply omitting them, and the dates themselves do not show any distress.

70. Loge, "Meriwether Lewis and Malaria," p. 34.

71. William Allan Neilson, Thomas A. Knott, and Paul W. Carhart, eds., *Webster's New International Dictionary of the English Language*, 2nd ed. (Springfield, MA: G. & C. Merriam Company Publishers, 1960), p. 52 s. v. "ague."

72. Robert Hooper, *Lexicon Medicum*, 4th ed. (London: Samuel Wood and Sons, 1822), p. 351; Robert Hooper, *A Compendious Medical Dictionary* (Newburyport, MA: Wm. Sawyer & Co., 1809), p. 106; Robert Hooper and Samuel Akerly, *Lexicon Medicum*, 13th ed., 2 vols. (New York: Harper & Brothers, 1846), 1: 353.

73. John Elliotson, *The Principles and Practice of Medicine* (Philadelphia: Carey and Hart, 1844), p. 235.

74. Loge, "Meriwether Lewis and Malaria," p. 34.

75. Robert Desowitz, *Ova and Parasites* (Hagerstown, MD: Harper & Row, 1980), p. 188; George Miller Sternberg, *Malaria and Malarial Diseases* (New York: William Wood & Company, 1884), p. 25.

76. Danisi, "The 'Ague' Made Him Do It," p. 11.

77. Meriwether Lewis to James Madison, September 16, 2009, Meriwether Lewis Collection, Missouri History Museum.

78. James Wilkinson to William Eustis, August 19, 1809, W658, RG107, M221, roll 33, frame 1564–65, National Archives and Records Administration; Mary C. Gillett, *The Army Medical Department, 1775–1818* (Washington, DC: Center of Military History United States Army, 1981), pp. 140–43; RG233, M1136, roll 1, frames 0837–40, pp. 45–49, National Archives and Records Administration.

79. Wilson, "Death of Captain Lewis," p. 37.

80. Macculloch, "Remittent and Intermittent Diseases," p. 253.

APPENDIX A: DOCUMENTS FROM, TO, AND ABOUT MERIWETHER LEWIS, 1803–1813

1. November 13, 1803, Eastern Journal, August 30–December 12, 1803, film 214, reel 2, American Philosophical Society, Philadelphia, Pennsylvania. Transcribed directly from the Eastern Journal.

2. Ibid., November 14, 1803.

3. Gary E. Moulton, ed., *The Journals of the Lewis and Clark Expedition*, 13 vols. (Lincoln: University of Nebraska Press, 1983–2001), 4: 7–10.

4. Ibid., 5: 117–18.

5. Ibid., 6: 151–52.

6. Meriwether Lewis to Auguste Chouteau, February 11, 1807, City of Washington, Frederic Billon Papers, Missouri History Museum.

7. James Wilkinson to Thomas Jefferson, September 15, 1807, Richmond, document 30145, reel 39, Thomas Jefferson Papers, Library of Congress.

8. Meriwether Lewis to Mahlon Dickerson, November 3, 1807, Statesman Collection, MG31, box 2, folder 38, New Jersey Historical Society. The file for this letter is labeled *Lewis Meriwether*. Donald Jackson, ed., *Letters of Lewis and Clark Expedition with Related Documents, 1783–1854*, 2nd ed., 2 vols. (Urbana: University of Illinois Press, 1978), 2: 720. Jackson had miscopied the letter, and the original reads "A—n R—ph."

9. James R. Bentley, "Two Letters of Meriwether Lewis to Major William Preston," *Filson Club History Quarterly* 44, no. 2 (April 1970): 171–74.

10. Letitia Breckinridge, married June 2, 1808. Lewis admired her.

11. This letter is considered to be the last one that he wrote to his mother, but because of the delay of mail, and sometimes loss of letters, Lewis may have written others.

12. This is one of the oddest letters because it was written right before Chouteau departed for the Mandan village. It is doubtful that Chouteau completely understood what Bates had written. It was composed by Frederick Bates and signed by Pierre Chouteau. Pierre Chouteau to Secretary of War, June 14, 1809, C562, M221, roll 20, frame 6255, National Archives and Records Administration. Grace Lewis Miller is the only historian who speaks about it.

13. Draft of the letter. Lewis, Anderson, and Marks Families Papers, 1771–1908, microfilm M668, Albert and Shirley Small Special Collections Library, University of Virginia, Charlottesville, Virginia.

14. Carter, *Territorial Papers*, 14: 285–86.

15. Lewis was addressing Simmons in response to Simmons's letter of July 15 talking exclusively about expenses. Simmons's letter can be found in RG107, M6, roll 4, p. 177, frame 0104, National Archives and Records Administration. For reference, see Carter, *Territorial Papers*, 14: 290–93 or the original in RG107, M221, L328, roll 23, frame 8501, National Archives and Records Administration.

16. William Carr Papers, Missouri History Museum.

17. Deed Record Book B, p. 378, City of Saint Louis, Recorder of Deeds, Saint Louis, Missouri.

18. Francois Trenchard (F. S. Trinchard) was the clerk at the New Madrid Courthouse in 1809. Louis Houck, *A History of Missouri from the Earliest Exploration and Settlements until the Admission of the state into the Union*, 3 vols. (Chicago: R. R. Donnelly & Sons, 1908), 2: 161, n. 81.

19. The first part of this letter, "Extract of a letter from Governor M. Lewis," was printed in the *New-York Commercial Advertiser* on November 30, 1809, p. 2.

20. James Howe to Frederick Bates, September 28, 1809, Frederick Bates Papers, Missouri History Museum. Kira Gale wrote that the writer to Bates was James House. Capt. James House was the interim commanding officer at Fort Bellefontaine until Lt. Col. Daniel Bissell arrived on June 26, 1809. House remained at the fort until October 1809. He was granted a furlough in August, but could not leave until a minimum of troops arrived at the fort. RG94, M565, roll 2, pp. 64, 85, 86, 120, 131, 145–46, and 154, National Archives and Records Administration; James E. Starrs and Kira Gale, *The Death of Meriwether Lewis* (Omaha, NE: River Junction Press, 2009), p. 233.

21. James Neelly to Thomas Jefferson, October 18, 1809, document 33522–23, roll 44, Thomas Jefferson Papers, Library of Congress.

22. John Brahan to Thomas Jefferson, October 18, 1809, document 33520–21, roll 44, Thomas Jefferson Papers, Library of Congress.

23. John Brahan to William Eustis, October 18, 1809, B589, RG107, M221, roll 18, frame 5632, National Archives and Records Administration. Postmarked October 20, Nashville to Washington City, Received November 3, 1809.

24. "Daniel Bissell, October 19, 1809," *Missouri Gazette,* p. 3, col. 1, vol. 2, no. 65.

25. *Democratic Clarion,* Friday, October 20, 1809, vol. 11, no. 111, p. 3, cols. 1 and 2, published by Thomas G. Bradford, Nashville, Tennessee.

26. Amos Stoddard was a Masonic orator and he may have written the poetry.

27. Robert A. Rutland et al., *The Papers of James Madison,* 5 vols. (Charlottesville: University of Virginia Press, 1984), 2: 48–49. Madison read this embellished account from a newspaper. For original document see website, James Madison to Thomas Jefferson, October 30, 1809, Series 2, roll 25, document 1701, p. 2, James Madison Papers, Library of Congress, http://lcweb2.loc.gov/master/mss/mjm/25/2100/2100.jpg

28. "John Breck Treat to Frederick Bates, October 31, 1809," in Thomas M. Marshall, *The Life and Papers of Frederick Bates,* 2 vols. (Saint Louis: Missouri Historical Society, 1926), 2: 103. Marshall states that Treat's middle name was Burke, but the Arkansas Indian agent signed documents as *John Breck Treat.*

29. *Argus of Western America,* November 4, 1809, Frankfort, Kentucky, vol. 2, no. 89.

30. Marshall, *Frederick Bates,* 2: 108–12.

31. Gilbert Russell to Thomas Jefferson with memorandum, January 4, 1810, document 33616–18, roll 44, Thomas Jefferson Papers, Library of Congress.

32. Lewis's personal effects were opened and catalogued on November 23, 1809, by two army officers at Hiwassee Garrison, Tennessee. For an accounting of Lewis's personal effects, see Jackson, *Letters,* 2: 470–74.

33. Thomas Jefferson to Gilbert Russell, April 18, 1810, document 33748, reel 44, Thomas Jefferson Papers, Library of Congress.

34. Clark Hunter, ed., *The Life and Letters of Alexander Wilson* (Philadelphia: American Philosophical Society, 1983), pp. 360–62. The account of Lewis's death can also be found in Alexander Wilson, "Particulars of the Death of Capt. Lewis," *Port Folio* 7 (January 1812): 34–47. The *Port Folio* misprinted the date of the letter (May 28, 1811, instead of May 18, 1810).

Wilson wrote a eulogy to Meriwether Lewis in the form of a poem, comprised of nineteen stanzas, four lines of verse per stanza, which was included in the *Port Folio* article. Some of those verses were printed in the front of each chapter of Thomas C. Danisi and John C. Jackson, *Meriwether Lewis* (Amherst, NY: Prometheus Books, 2009). On May 4, Wilson departed Nashville and encountered the Great Harpeth, a stream, fifty yards wide, and eleven miles from his place of departure. He arrived at Grinder's Stand on Sunday, May 10. Wilson, "Death of Capt. Lewis," pp. 35–36.

35. Alexander Wilson, *American Ornithology: or The Natural History of the Birds of the United States*, 3 vols. (New York: Collins & Co., 1828), 2: 46–47. Alexander Wilson (1766–1813), known as the father of American ornithology, was a friend of Meriwether Lewis. He was working on his eighth volume of *American Ornithology* when he became ill and died. He had worked for the printer Bradford and Innskeep, who had published his series on birds and also went bankrupt because of it. Laura Rigal, "Empire of Birds: Alexander Wilson's *American Ornithology*," *Huntington Library Quarterly* 59, no. 2/3 (1996): 241.

36. The last sentence may have been written between May 10 and May 18, 1810, when Wilson travelled to Grinder's Stand and conversed with Priscilla Grinder about Lewis's death. Alexander Wilson, *American Ornithology*, 2: 46–47.

37. Species 9, *Picus Torquatus*, Lewis's Woodpecker (Plate XX—Fig. 3), Peale's *Museum*, no. 2020: Wilson, *American Ornithology*, 2: 46; Species 3, Tanagra Ludoviciana, Louisiana Tanager (Plate XX—Fig. 1), Peale's *Museum*, No. 6236, Wilson, *American Ornithology*, 2: 219. "This bird, and the two others that occupy the same plate, were discovered, in the remote regions of Louisiana, by an exploring party under the command of Captain . . . Merriwether Lewis, and Lieutenant, now General, William Clark, in their memorable expedition across the continent to the Pacific Ocean. They are entitled to a distinguished place in the pages of *American Ornithology*, both as being, till now, altogether unknown to naturalists, and as natives of what *is*, or at least *will be*, and that at no distant period, part of the western territory of the United States." Wilson, 2: 219; Species 61, *Corvus Columbianus*, Clark's Crow (Plate XX—fig. 2): Alexander Wilson and Charles Lucien Bonaparte, *American Ornithology: or The Natural History of the Birds of the United States*, 4 vols. (Edinburgh: Constable and Co., 1831), 1: 249. "In conversation with different individuals of the party,* I understood that this bird inhabits the shores of the Columbia, and the adjacent country, in great numbers, frequenting the rivers and sea-shore, probably feeding on fish; and that it has all the gregarious and noisy habits of the European species, several of the party supposing it to be the same. . . ." * "The exploring party, under Captains Clark and Lewis, mentioned at p. 168, by which this bird was discovered." [Same verbiage as Wilson, *American Ornithology*, 2: 219]

38. Thomas Jefferson to Paul Allen, August 18, 1813, document 35390–95, reel 46, Thomas Jefferson Papers, Library of Congress; Jackson, *Letters*, 2: 590–93.

39. Lewis arrived in Washington on December 28, 1806, and Clark arrived on January 18, 1807.

APPENDIX B: MERIWETHER LEWIS'S COURT MARTIAL PROCEEDINGS, NOVEMBER 6–11, 1795

1. The archivist at the Historical Society of Pennsylvania (HSP) reported that the court-martial case was fifty-two handwritten pages but upon examination, there had been a day's recess and another court-martial was heard and embedded within the Lewis case. The entire page count for the Lewis trial was about forty handwritten pages. This is not a strict transcription—where words were crossed out and then corrected in the manuscript, the crossed out ones were omitted. The sentences were short—typically seven words a line and thus I chose to lengthen the line. Words in the transcript were hyphenated at the end of a sentence and I deleted the hyphen when necessary. Where a word was unreadable, I marked it as illegible.

2. Ensign Meriwether Lewis was arrested on or about September 24. It is not apparent if he remained under house arrest or put in jail. The maximum amount of time soldiers remained in jail was typically eight days.

3. Hobson's Choice was the name of an Ohio fort.

4. Bradley J. Nicholson, "Courts-Martial in the Legion Army: American Military Law in the Early Republic, 1792–1796," *Military Law Review* 144 (Spring 1994): 103–104.

5. Finding the 1795 Meriwether Lewis courts-martial case proved to be especially protracted and difficult. It was my belief that it was buried in some forgotten place, and in April 2008 after sending the Lewis biography manuscript to Prometheus Books, I decided to embark on an extravagant hunt, which was to attempt to locate the court-martial case. It was reasonable to assume that the case had been stored in an undisclosed location of the National Archives, but the person who found the court-martial summary for Eldon Chuinard, Charles A. Shaughnessy of the Navy and Old Army Branch, Military Archives Division, had probably opened every drawer looking for it. In 2005, I spent a week at the National Archives, College Park campus, examining many of the documents that Donald Jackson had chosen for *Letters of the Lewis and Clark Expedition*, and I did not come across a hint of the court-martial files.

Shaughnessy sourced the citation for the summary to Record Group 94 and the *Guide to the National Archives of the United States* contained a detailed description of the "Records of the Adjutant General's Office, 1780s–1917. . . . There are 38,107 cubic feet of records dated ca. 1783 and 1917 in this record group." Details of those records followed in terse descriptions: returns, muster rolls, military posts, etc. etc., but nothing that indicated courts-martial from 1795. I chose to ditch that trail and began acclimating myself with the time period by reading hundreds of publications.

A year later my research had narrowed the field to General Anthony Wayne, commander of the Legion of the United States, whose career spread over Lewis's court-martial. There were several US repositories with massive collections of Wayne documents as well as numerous Ohio historical societies with enough information to make a paper river that extends the length of the state.

During 2009 it occurred to me why no one had found the case—the search was absolutely overwhelming. In the process I became quite familiar with Wayne, Wayne's army (officers and enlisted men), Wayne's forts, Wayne's personal family, and with the power of the Internet, the many online descriptions of Wayne collections. Some of them were pages long, but in the summer of 2009, when scrolling an untapped Website for information, my eye caught a glimpse of a description that mirrored the right combination of words: Courts-Martial 1792–1799. It was embedded in an obscure paragraph detailing a facet of a specific Wayne collection in Pennsylvania. I bought the *Guide to the Manuscript Collections of the Historical Society of Pennsylvania*, and upon receiving it, feverishly went to the index and looked up Anthony Wayne. While his name circulated in eight collections, number 699 stated on the fifth line: ". . . men active in colonial affairs, 1765–79, 47 vols.; records of court-martial, 1776–96, 3 vols. . . ."

In the fifteen months since I had begun looking, this was the first citing that confirmed my search, and I excitedly began to compose a letter of inquiry. But I had also encountered a serious challenge, which revolved around this question: How much to tip my hand? A few years earlier, I had discovered some new Meriwether Lewis material and, without thinking, requested photocopies. Within the year, that material had been published and all of my hard work had not only disappeared, but was credited to others. Keeping that experience in mind, on September 11, I asked for information on the General Anthony Wayne Papers, specifically the part dealing with "records of courts-martial, 1776–96, 3 vols." There was an eight-week wait, and I promptly forgot about the e-mail due to the upcoming Lewis bicentennial.

On January 4, 2010, I sent another e-mail requesting an update and quickly received a response that what I was looking for appeared to be in large, bulky volumes. I responded with more exacting information, hoping it was the long lost file.

On February 3, I received an e-mail stating that the "Court-Martial Record of Meriwether Lewis," was indeed at the Historical Society of Pennsylvania. The archivist wrote that the handwritten documents had been pasted into large, folio-size ledgers and could not be reproduced by traditional photocopying without ruining the ledger. He suggested a visit to Philadelphia, which I was able to undertake on April 27, 2010.

APPENDIX C: EXCERPTS FROM THE LETTERS OF SAMUEL LATHAM MITCHILL, 1801–1808

1. "Dr. Mitchill's Letters From Washington: 1801–1813," *Harper's New Monthly Magazine* 58 (April 1879): 740–55.

APPENDIX D: MERIWETHER LEWIS'S REAL ESTATE TRANSACTIONS AND PERSONAL DEBTS

1. "Meriwether Lewis to William Preston, July 25, 1808," in James R. Bentley, "Two Letters of Meriwether Lewis to Major William Preston," *Filson Club History Quarterly* 44, no. 2 (April 1970): 173.

2. Clarence Edwin Carter, ed., *The Territorial Papers of the United States*, 28 vols. (Washington, DC: Government Printing Office, 1934–1962), 2: 41.

3. Bentley, "Two Letters," p. 173. Lewis purchased 7,440 arpents of land for $5530. The ratio for the surface measurement of a French arpent was .85 of an acre of land, which equated to 6,324 acres at $1.14 an acre.

4. Ibid.

5. L. Ruth Colter-Frick, "Meriwether Lewis's Personal Finances," *We Proceeded On* 28, no. 1 (February 2002): 16–20.

APPENDIX E: WARRANTS, DRAFTS, AND BILLS OF EXCHANGE ISSUED FROM THE ACCOUNTANT'S OFFICE

1. William F. Sherman and Craig R. Scott, *Records of the Accounting Officers of the Treasury Department, Inventory 14* (Lovettsville, VA: Willow Bend Books, 1997), pp. 19, 95–96, 98, 124, 129. There is a minimum of document duplication from Donald Jackson, ed., *Letters of Lewis and Clark Expedition with Related Documents, 1783–1854*, 2nd ed., 2 vols. (Urbana: University of Illinois Press, 1978).

2. RG 217, Records of the General Accounting Office, reel 14, #85, Missouri History Museum.

3. Ibid., not copied verbatim: Jackson, *Letters*, 2: p. 576.

APPENDIX H: THE ETIOLOGY OF THUNDER-BOLTS/THUNDERCLAPPERS

1. Paul Russell Cutright, *Pioneering Naturalists* (Lincoln: University of Nebraska, 1969), p. 175. Lewis had written his own formula for Rush's pills, which was composed of six grains of calomel and fifteen of jalap. Meriwether Lewis Account Book, Meriwether Lewis Collection, Missouri History Museum.

2. Stephen E. Ambrose, *Undaunted Courage* (New York: Simon & Schuster, 1996), p. 89;

Stephen E. Ambrose, *Lewis & Clark: Voyage of Discovery* (Washington: National Geographic Society, 1998), p. 37.

3. James Holmberg, *Dear Brother* (New Haven, CT: Yale University Press, 2002), p. 65, n. 4; David Lavender, *The Way to the Western Sea: Lewis and Clark across the Continent* (Lincoln: University of Nebraska Press, 2001), p. 234.

4. David J. Peck, *Or Perish in the Attempt, Wilderness Medicine in the Lewis & Clark Expedition* (Helena, MT: Farcountry Press, 2002), p. 51; Ronald V. Loge, "Meriwether Lewis and Malaria," *We Proceeded On* 28, no. 2 (May 2002): 34; Ronald V. Loge, "Illness at Three Forks," *Montana: The Magazine of Western History* 50, no. 2 (Summer 2000): 5, 9.

5. Morris Fishbein, *Frontiers of Medicine* (Baltimore: Williams & Wilkins Company, in cooperation with the Century of Progress Exposition, 1933), p. 179. Fishbein was the editor of the *Journal of the American Medical Association*, which published a series of articles on quack and patent medicines from 1913 to 1925 with the assistance of Dr. Arthur Cramp.

6. Lyman H. Butterfield, ed., *Letters of Benjamin Rush, 1793–1813*, 2 vols. (Princeton, NJ: Princeton University Press, 1951), 1: 149, n. 2; 2: 649, n. 2.

7. Benjamin Rush, *An Account of the Bilious Remitting Yellow Fever* (Philadelphia: Thomas Dobson, 1794), p. 200.

8. Ibid., p. 202; Oliver T. Osborne, *The Principles of Therapeutics* (Philadelphia: W. B. Saunders, 1922), p. 339; Benjamin Rush to Doctor Belleville, September 3, 1793, Philadelphia, ID: PACV92-A30, Record Group No. MSS 2/0146–02, College of Physicians of Philadelphia, Philadelphia, Pennsylvania.

9. John Parascandola, "Patent Medicines in Nineteenth Century America," *Caduceus: A Museum Quarterly for the Health Sciences* 1, no. 1 (Spring 1985): 1–41; James Harvey Young, *The Toadstool Millionaires: A Social History of Patent Medicines in America before Federal Regulation* (Princeton, NJ: Princeton University Press, 1961), pp. 32–34; Lyman F. Kebler, "United States Patents Granted for Medicines during the Pioneer Years of the Patent Office," *Journal of the American Pharmaceutical Association* 24 (1935): 486–87.

10. William N. Boog Watson, "Two British Naval Surgeons of the French Wars," *Medical History* 13, no. 3 (July 1969): n. 222.

11. John R. Christopher, *School of Natural Healing* (Provo, UT: Christopher Publications, 1976), p. 478; Louise Tenney, *Today's Herbal Healing*, 2nd ed. (Provo, UT: Woodland Health Books, 1983), p. 1.

12. Thomas Szasz, "A Bogus Benjamin Rush Quote: Contribution to the History of Pharmacracy," *History of Psychiatry* 16, no. 1 (2005): 89. The Mark Twain quote (1882) was taken from page 90 of this article.

APPENDIX I: A FICTIONAL ROMANCE

1. "Thomas Jefferson to Meriwether Lewis, February 23, 1801," in Donald Jackson, ed., *Letters of Lewis and Clark Expedition with Related Documents, 1783–1854*, 2nd ed., 2 vols. (Urbana: University of Illinois Press, 1978), 1: 2–3.

2. Charles Felton Pidgin, *Theodosia: The First Gentlewoman of Her Time* (Boston: C. M. Clark, 1907), p. 236.

3. Charles Burr Todd, *Life of Colonel Aaron Burr: Vice-President of the United States* (New York: S. W. Green, 1879), pp. 236, 290.

4. Emerson Hough, "The Magnificent Adventure: A Romance of the Lewis and Clark Expedition," *Munsey's Magazine* 57 (April–May 1916).

5. Theodore P. Greene, *America's Heroes: The Changing Models of Success in American Magazines* (New York: Oxford University Press, 1970), p. 68.

6. I. J. Cox to Stella Drumm, October 9, 1916, Missouri Historical Society, Saint Louis, Missouri. Ms. Drumm pasted Cox's letter to the inside back cover of Emerson Hough's *The Magnificent Adventure*.

7. Delbert E. Wylder, *Emerson Hough* (Boston: Twayne, 1981), p. 55. Professor Wylder recommended an excellent dissertation on the colorful Emerson Hough. Carole McCool Johnson, "Emerson Hough and the American West: A Biographical and Critical Study," (PhD dissertation, University of Texas at Austin, 1975).

8. Anya Seton, *My Theodosia* (Boston: Riverside Press, 1941), p. 386.

9. Fillmore Norfleet, *Saint Memin in Virginia: Portraits and Biographies* (Richmond: Dietz Press, 1942), p. 183.

10. Eldon G. Chuinard, *Only One Man Died: The Medical Aspects of the Lewis and Clark Expedition* (Glendale, CA: Arthur H. Clark, 1980), p. 113; David Leon Chandler, *The Jefferson Conspiracies: A President's Role in the Assassination of Meriwether Lewis* (New York: William Morrow, 1994), pp. 140–41, 259.

11. Reimert Therolf Ravenholt, "Triumph Then Despair: The Tragic Death of Meriwether Lewis," *Epidemiology* 5, no. 3 (May 1994): 378.

12. Seton, *My Theodosia*, p. 388.

13. Hough, "The Magnificent Adventure," p. 526.

14. Charles Morrow Wilson, *Meriwether Lewis of Lewis and Clark* (New York: Thomas Y. Crowell, 1934), p. 262.

BIBLIOGRAPHY

MANUSCRIPT COLLECTIONS

Bancroft Library, University of California
    Louisiana Papers, 1767–1816
The College of Physicians of Philadelphia, Philadelphia, Pennsylvania
    Benjamin Rush Papers
Historical Society of Pennsylvania, Philadelphia, Pennsylvania
    General Anthony Wayne Papers, General Orders of Court-Martial, May 1793–October
    1796
Hudson's Bay Company Archives, Archives of Manitoba, Winnipeg
    Donald McKay Collection
    Cumberland House Journal
    Manchester House Journal
Illinois Regional Archives Depository, Illinois State Archives, Springfield, Illinois
    Perrin Collection
Indiana Historical Society, Indianapolis, Indiana
    English Collection
    William Henry Harrison Papers
    Mitten Collection
    Northwest Territory Collection
Jefferson National Expansion Memorial Library, National Park Service, Saint Louis, Missouri
    Grace Lewis Miller Papers, 1938–1971
    Saint Louis Recorded Archives
Kentucky Historical Society, Frankfort, Kentucky
    Field Notebook of William Peters, 1794–1795
Library of Congress, Washington, DC
    John Breckinridge Papers
    Thomas Jefferson Papers
    James Madison Papers
Library of Congress, Geography and Map Division, Washington, DC
    James MacKay's Map of the Missouri River
Lilly Library, Indiana University, Bloomington, Indiana
    Jonathan Williams Papers
Lovejoy Library, Southern Illinois University, Edwardsville, Illinois
    John Francis McDermott Collection
Louisiana State University Library, Baton Rouge, Louisiana
    Pintado Papers

Mercantile Library of Saint Louis
    Journal of the Proceedings of the Legislature of the Territory of Louisiana
    General Daniel Bissell Papers
Missouri History Museum, Saint Louis, Missouri
    Army Collection
    Frederick Bates Collection
    William Carr Papers
    Chouteau Family Papers
    Clark Family Collection
    Oscar Collet, Index to Saint Louis Cathedral and Carondelet Church Baptisms
    Rufus Easton Papers
    First American Title Abstracts
    Fur Trade Ledgers, 1804–1871
    Louis Houck Collection
    Kaskaskia Collection
    Meriwether Lewis Collection
    Lindenwood Collection
    Lucas Papers
    Louisiana Territory, Military Command, Adjutant's Record, 1803–1805
    Mines Envelope
    Missouri Gazette
    Mullanphy Family Papers
    Provenchere Family Papers
    Saint Charles Papers
    George C. Sibley Papers
    Amos Stoddard Company Book
Missouri State Archives, Jefferson City, Missouri
    Territorial Supreme Court Records, 1809–1812
    General Court Records, 1810–1812
    Missouri Supreme Court Records
    Minutes of the Board of Commissioners
    Surveyor General for Missouri, Outgoing Correspondence 1816–1863
Museum of the City of New York
    Samuel Latham Mitchill Papers
National Archives, Central Plains Region, Kansas City, Missouri
    RG21 United States Circuit Courts, Eastern District of Missouri
    Bryan v. Kennett: Case Number 4746
National Archives, Archives II, College Park, Maryland
    RG217, Records of the Accounting Officers of the Department of the Treasury
    Entry 57: Letters Received from the Accountant for the War Department
    Entry 353: Ledgers of the Accountant for the War Department (Set 1)

Entry 366: Journals of the Accountant of the War Department
Entry 374: Register of Warrants
Entry 493: Letters Received by the Accountant for the War Department
Entry 496: Miscellaneous Letters Sent by the Accountant for the War Department
Entry 515: Audit Reports on Military Accounts and Claims
New York Historical Society, New York, New York
  US Military Philosophical Society Papers
  General Anthony Wayne's Orderly Book, 1795
  Miscellaneous military manuscripts
New York Public Library, New York, New York
  Gansevoort-Lansing collection, 1650–1919
Pettis County Historical Society and Museum, Sedalia, Missouri
  Dr. Antoine Saugrain's Medical Ledgers, 1801–1817
Recorder of Deeds, City of Saint Louis, Saint Louis, Missouri
  Deed Books
Saint Louis Circuit Court, Civil Court Archives, City of Saint Louis, Saint Louis, Missouri
  Saint Louis Circuit Court Case Files
  Chancery Court Files
  Sainte Genevieve County Courthouse Files
State Historical Society of Missouri, Columbia, Missouri
  William Clark Notebook, 1798–1801
  Glen O. Hardeman Collection, C3655
  Meriwether Lewis Astronomy Notebook, 1805, C1074

MICROFILM

City of St. Louis, Archival Library, City Hall, Saint Louis, Missouri
  French and Spanish Archives of Saint Louis, Early Litigation
Emory University, Atlanta, Georgia
  The Review, 1809: Microfilm 3940
Filson Historical Society, Louisville, Kentucky
  Diary of General Jonathan Clark (1750–1811)
Jefferson National Expansion Memorial Library, National Park Service, Saint Louis, Missouri
  Papeles de Cuba (78) Collection, Archivo General de Indias, Seville, Spain
Missouri History Museum
  Chouteau Collections
  Clark Family Papers
  Albert Gallatin Collection
  Louis Houck Collection
  Meriwether Lewis Collection
  Papeles de Cuba Collection, Archivo General de Indias, Seville, Spain

National Archives, Washington, DC
  RG28: Records of the Post Office Department
      M601, Letters Sent by the Postmaster General, 1789–1836
  RG59: General Records of the Department of State
      M418, Letters of Application and Recommendation during the Administration of Thomas Jefferson, 1801–1809
  RG75: Records of the Bureau of Indian Affairs
      M15, Letters Sent by the Secretary of War Relating to Indian Affairs, 1800–1824
      M16, Letters Sent by the Superintendent of Indian Affairs, 1807–1823
      M271, Letters Received by the Office of the Secretary of War Relating to Indian Affairs, 1800–1823
      T58, Letters Received by the Superintendent of Indian Trade, 1806–1824
  RG94: Records of the Adjutant General's Office, 1780s–1917
      M565, Letters Sent by the Office of the Adjutant General (Main Series), 1800–1890
      M566, Letters Received by the Office of the Adjutant General, 1805–1821
      M661, Historical Information Relating to Military Posts and Other Installations, 1700–1900
      M1136, Records Relating to the 1811 and 1815 Courts-Martial of Maj. Gen. James Wilkinson
  RG107: Records of the Office of the Secretary of War
      M6, Letters Sent by the Secretary of War relating to Military Affairs, 1800–1889
      M22, Registers of Letters Received by the Office of the Secretary of War, Main Series, 1800–1870
      M220, Reports to Congress from the Secretary of War, 1803–1870
      M221, Letters Received by the Secretary of War, Main Series, 1801–1870
      M222, Letters Received by the Secretary of War, Unregistered Series, 1789–1861
  RG217: Records of the Accounting Officers of the Department of the Treasury
      M235, Miscellaneous Treasury Accounts of the First Auditor (Formerly the Auditor) of the Treasury Department, September 6, 1790–1840
  RG233: Records of the US House of Representatives
      M1268, Transcribed Reports and Communications Transmitted by the Executive Branch to the US House of Representatives, 1789–1819
      M1404, Unbound Records of the House of Representatives for the Eighth Congress, 1803–1805
New York University (NYU), Bobst Library, New York City
  Albert Gallatin Papers

Tennessee State Library, Nashville, Tennessee
Williamson County Clerk Minutes, Vols. 1–2, February 1800–October 1815, Roll 45
James Robertson, 1742–1814, Accession #801–1
Nashville Clarion and Tennessee Gazette, 1809, Roll 113
University of Virginia, Alderman Library, Charlottesville, Virginia
The Argus of Western America or *The Frankfort Argus*, 1809: N-US, Ky-4
The Frankfort Palladium, 1809: N-US, Ky-10, Reel 2.
University of Virginia, Albert and Shirley Small Special Collections Library, Charlottesville, Virginia
Lewis, Anderson, and Marks Family Papers, Microfilm M668.
State Historical Manuscripts Collection, Columbia, Missouri
William Clark Memorandum Book, 1809
Meriwether Lewis Astronomy Notebook, 1803–1805

MICROFICHE

Early American Imprints: First Series (Evans)

No. 18178: Saunders, William. Observations on the Superior Efficacy of the Red Peruvian Bark, in the Cure of Agues and Other Fevers. Boston, 1783.
No. 21777: Currie, William. A Dissertation on the Autumnal Remitting Fever. Philadelphia, College of Physicians, 1789.
No. 36370: Stoddard, Amos. An Oration Delivered before the Citizens of Portland, Maine and the Supreme Judicial Court of the Commonwealth of Massachussetts on July 5, 1799.
No. 36371: Stoddard, Amos. An Oration Delivered before the First Parish of Portland, Maine, June 24, 1799. Portland Lodge of Free and Accepted Masons in Celebration of the Festival of Saint John the Baptist.
No. 37604: Hemenway, Samuel. Medicine Chests, with Particular Directions. Salem: Thomas C. Cushing, 1800.
No. 45776: Lee's Genuine Bilious Pills, or Family Physic. Prepared by Samuel Lee, of Windham, in the State of Connecticut; for which Discovery He Obtained a Patent Signed by the President of the United States, 1799.

Early American Imprints: Second Series (Shaw-Shoemaker)

No. 11747: United States Military Philosophical Society, Extracts from the Minutes . . . 1806 (not as complete as 14101).
No. 11748: United States Military Philosophical Society, Extracts from the Minutes . . . 1806 (not as complete as 14101).

No. 11805: Watson, John Fanning. To the Public . . . Washington: 1806.

No. 14101: United States Military Philosophical Society, Extracts from the Minutes . . . October 6, 1806.

No. 15451: The Laws of the Territory of Louisiana. Saint Louis: Joseph Charless, 1809.

No. 16607: United States Military Philosophical Society, Extracts from the Minutes Held at Washington, January 30, 1808.

No. 16954: Bates, Frederick. Oration Delivered before Saint Louis Lodge No. 111. Saint Louis: Joseph Charless, 1809.

No. 18893: Simmons, William. To Inquire Whether Any Advances of Money Have Been Made to the Commander-in-Chief of the Army by the Department of War . . . Washington: 1809.

No. 21145: Pringle, John. Observations on the Disease of the Army . . . with Notes by Benjamin Rush. Philadelphia: Fry and Kammerer, 1810.

No. 21675: Letter from the Comptroller of the Treasury Transmitting a Statement of the Accounts in the Treasury, War, and Navy Departments. William Simmons. Abstract of accounts on the books of the Accountant for the Department of War which were unsettled on 30 September 1807 and which still remain unsettled. Washington: 1810.

No. 24153: Duvall, Gabriel. Letter from the Comptroller of the Treasury Transmitting a Statement of the Accounts Prior to 30 September 1808. Washington: 1811.

No. 30385: United States Military Philosophical Society, Minutes of a Meeting Held at Washington Hall, New York City, November 1, 1813.

No. 32773: Simmons, William. A Letter to the Senate and House of Representatives of the United States, Shewing the Profligacy and Corruption of General John Armstrong in His Administration of the War Department. Georgetown: 1814.

No. 37990: Journal of the House of Representatives of the Commonwealth of Kentucky: Begun and Held in the Town of Frankfort, on Monday the Fourth Day of December, 1815.

NEWSPAPERS

American Citizen (NY)

American Watchman (DE)

Argus of Western America (KY)

Bridgeport Herald (CT)

Connecticut Courant (Danbury, CT)

Connecticut Herald (CT)

Democratic Clarion or Nashville Clarion (TN)

Democratic Press (PA)

Kentucky Gazette (Lexington, KY)

The Frankfort Palladium (KY)

Louisiana Gazette (Saint Louis, MO)

Missouri Gazette (Saint Louis, MO)

National Intelligencer and Washington Advertiser (Washington, DC)

New-England Palladium (Boston, MA)

New York Gazette & General Advertiser (New York, NY)

Philadelphia Aurora (Philadelphia, PA)

Philadelphia Daily Advertiser (Philadelphia, PA)

Republican Star or Eastern Shore General Advertiser (MD)

Republican Watch-Tower (Washington, DC)

The Review (Nashville, TN)

The Sun (Washington, DC)

US CONGRESSIONAL SERIAL SET

US Congress. Senate. *Petition to Congress by Moses Austin and John Rice Jones*, 11th Cong., 3rd sess., 1811.

US Congress. House. *A Bill for the Relief of the Legal Representatives of Meriwether Lewis*, 20th Cong., 1st sess., H. Rep. 282 (1828).

US Congress. Senate. *Substance of an Argument*, 21st Cong., 2nd sess., 1830. S. Doc. 12, serial 203, 24–25.

US Congress. House. *Thirty-One Inhabitants of Old Mines*, 18th Cong., 1st sess., 1831, H. Rep. 98, serial 128, 120.

US Congress. House. *Old Mine Concession*, 23rd Cong., 1st sess., 1833. H. Doc. 79, serial 255, 55.

US Congress. House. *An Act*, 42nd Cong., 3rd sess., 1873. Bills and Resolutions 3731, Report No. 489.

WEBSITES

American Journeys: Eyewitness Accounts of Early American Exploration and Settlement http://www.americanjourneys.org (accessed June 22, 2011)

American State Papers
http://memory.loc.gov/ammem/amlaw/lwsplink.html (accessed May 20, 2011)

American Time Capsule: Three Centuries of Broadsides and Other Ephemera http://lcweb2 .loc.gov/cgi-bin/query/r?ammem/rbpe:@field(DOCID+@lit (rbpe22702700)) (accessed February 14, 2011)

Ancestry.com: Dr. Antoine Saugrain
  http://freepages.history.rootsweb.ancestry.com/~earlystlouis/antoinesaugrain.html
  (accessed April 7, 2011)
Annals of Congress, General
  http://memory.loc.gov/ammem/amlaw/lwac.html (accessed February 14, 2011)
Annals of Congress, Senate, Ninth Congress
  http://memory.loc.gov/cgi-bin/ampage?collId =llac&fileName=015/llac015.db
  &recNum=0 (accessed February 15, 2011)
Catholic Encyclopedia
  http://www.newadvent.org/cathen/08372b.htm (accessed January 19, 2011)
Center for Columbia River History
  http://www.ccrh.org/comm/slough/primary/descript.htm (accessed January 15, 2011)
Century of Lawmaking for a New Nation
  http://memory.loc.gov/ammem/amlaw/lawhome.html (accessed November 15, 2010)
Cornell University Library: The Making of America
  http://dlxs2.library.cornell.edu/m/moa (accessed January 22, 2011)
Garst Museum
  http://www.garstmuseum.org/ (accessed November 30, 2010)
Geography and Map Division, Discovery and Exploration, Library of Congress
  http://lcweb2.loc.gov/ammem/gmdhtml/dsxphome.html (accessed December 5, 2010)
George Huxtable: Lewis and Clark as Navigators
  http://www.hux.me.uk/lewis02.htm (accessed April 11, 2011)
George Washington Papers
  http://memory.loc.gov/ammem/gwhtml/gwhome.html (accessed March 11, 2011)
Hathi Trust Digital Library: Michigan Pioneer and Historical Collections
  http://babel.hathitrust.org/cgi/pt?view=image;size=100;id=mdp.39015071219458;pa
  ge=root;seq=9;num=i (accessed January 24, 2011)
History Channel, "Secret Presidential Codes"
  http://www.history.com/shows/brad-meltzersdecoded/episodes/episodes-guide
  (accessed January 28, 2011).
House Journal
  http://memory.loc.gov/ammem/amlaw/lwhj.html (accessed November 15, 2010)
James Madison Papers, Library of Congress
  http://memory.loc.gov/ammem/collections/madison_papers/index.html (accessed
  November 15, 2010)
The Journals of the Lewis and Clark Expedition, University of Nebraska Press/University
  of Nebraska-Lincoln Libraries, Electronic Text Center
  http://lewisandclarkjournals.unl.edu/ (accessed November 15, 2010)
Legion Ville (Fort Greenville), the Legion Ville Historical Society,
  http://www.legionville.com/ (accessed April 11,2011)
Lexicus Online Dictionary

http://www.lexic.us/definition-of/relapse (accessed January 24, 2011)

Library of Congress, "Religion and the Founding of the American Republic"
http://www.loc.gov/exhibits/religion/rel06-2.html (accessed January 22, 2011)

National Park Service, Dr. Antoine Saugrain
http://www.nps.gov/archive/jeff/lewisclark2/circa1804/StLouis/BlockInfo/
Block50DrAntoineSaugrain.htm, (accessed April 7, 2011)

Ohio Historical Society, Ohio Archaeological and Historical Society Publications,
http://publications.ohiohistory.org/ohstemplate.cfm?action=intro (accessed November
17, 2010)

Papers of the War Department, 1784–1800
http://wardepartmentpapers.org/index.php (accessed February 11, 2011)

Senate Journal
http://memory.loc.gov/ammem/amlaw/lwsj.html (accessed November 15, 2010)

Senate Journal, 20th Congress, 1st sess., HR 282, For the Relief of the Legal
Representatives of Meriwether Lewis
http://memory.loc.gov/cgi-bin/ampage?collId=llhb&fileName=009/llhb009.db&rec
Num=741 (accessed January 26, 2011)

Statutes at Large
http://memory.loc.gov/ammem/amlaw/lwsl.html (accessed November 15, 2010)

Thomas Jefferson Papers, Library of Congress
http://memory.loc.gov/ammem/collections/jefferson_papers/ (accessed November 15,
2010)

US Serial Set
http://memory.loc.gov/ammem/amlaw/lwss.html (accessed November 15, 2010)

US Supreme Court cases
http://supreme.justia.com/us/113/179/index.html (accessed November 15, 2010)

Wikipedia

Abraham Bradley's Map of the United States, 1804, http://en.wikipedia.org/wiki/Abraham
_Bradley,_Jr. (accessed January 26, 2011)

Dr. Antoine Saugrain, http://en.wikipedia.org/wiki/Antoine_Saugrain (accessed April 7,
2011)

Jesuit's Bark, http://en.wikipedia.org/wiki/Jesuit%27s_bark (accessed January 19, 2011)

Photometry, http://en.wikipedia.org/wiki/Photometry_(optics) (accessed December 22,
2010)

PRIMARY AND SECONDARY SOURCES

Abel, Annie H. "Trudeau's Description of the Upper Missouri." *The Mississippi Valley Historical Review* 8, nos. 1–2 (June-September 1921): 149–79.

———. "A New Lewis and Clark Map." *Geographical Review* 1, no. 5 (May 1916): 329–45.

Abel-Henderson, Annie H. "Mackay's Table of Distances." *The Mississippi Valley Historical Review* 10 (March 1924): 428–46.

Aberbach, Alan David. *In Search of An American Identity: Samuel Latham Mitchill, Jeffersonian Nationalist*. New York: Peter Lang, 1988.

———. "Samuel Latham Mitchill: A Physician in the Early Days of the Republic." *Bulletin of the New York Academy of Medicine* 40, no. 7 (July 1964): 501–10.

Ackerknecht, Erwin. *Malaria in the Upper Mississippi Valley, 1760–1900*. Baltimore: Johns Hopkins Press, 1945.

———. "Aspects of the History of Therapeutics." *Bulletin of the History of Medicine* 36 (September–October 1962): 389–419.

Adams, Henry. *The History of the United States of America during the Administration of Thomas Jefferson*. 9 vols. New York: Charles Scribner's Sons, 1891.

Alibert, Jean Louis. *A Treatise on Malignant Intermittents*. Philadelphia: Fry and Kammerer, 1807.

Allen, John Logan. *Passage Through the Garden*. Urbana: University of Illinois Press, 1975.

Ambrose, Stephen E. *Lewis & Clark: Voyage of Discovery*. Washington, DC: National Geographic Society, 1998.

———. *Undaunted Courage: Meriwether Lewis, Thomas Jefferson and the Opening of the American West*. New York: Simon and Schuster, 1996.

American State Papers. 38 vols. Washington: Gales & Seaton, 1832–1861.

Andrews, Joseph Gardner. "A Surgeon's Mate at Fort Defiance; the Journal of Joseph Gardner Andrews for the year 1795." *Ohio Historical Quarterly* 66 (January 1957): 57–86; (April 1957): 157–86; (July 1957): 238–68.

Annals of the Congress of the United States, 1789–1824. 42 vols. Washington, DC: Gales and Seaton, 1834–1836.

Archibald, Robert R. "From La Louisiane to Luisiana, the Imposition Spanish Administration in the Upper Mississippi Valley." *Gateway Heritage* 11, no. 1 (Summer 1990): 24–35.

———. "Honor and Family: The Career of Lt. Gov. Carlos de Hault de Lassus." *Gateway Heritage* 12, no. 4 (Spring 1992): 32–41.

Bachleda, Lynne F. *Guide to the Natchez Trace Parkway*. 2nd ed. Birmingham, AL: Menasha Ridge, 2011.

Balinky, Alexander. *Albert Gallatin, Fiscal Theories and Policies*. New Brunswick, NJ: Rutgers University Press, 1958.

Ball, John. *The Modern Practice of Physic*. London: A. Millar, 1762.

Barker, Eugene C. *The Austin Papers*. 2 vols. Washington, DC: Annual Report of the American Historical Association, 1919.

Battle, John D. Jr. "The 'periodical head-achs' of Thomas Jefferson." *Cleveland Clinic Quarterly* 51 (1984): 531–39.

Beauregard, H. T. "Journal of Jean Baptiste Truteau among the Arikara Indians in 1795." *Missouri Historical Society Collections* 4 (1912): 9–48.

Benson, T. B. "A Court-Martial Trial." *Virginia Law Register*, New Series 5 (May 1919): 37–46.

Bentley, James R. "Two Letters of Meriwether Lewis to Major William Preston." *Filson Club History Quarterly* 44, no. 2 (April 1970): 170–75.

Betts, Edwin Morris, and James Adam Bear Jr., eds. *The Family Letters of Thomas Jefferson.* Columbia: University of Missouri Press, 1966.

Blair, Bryce Dixon Jr. "The Battle of Fallen Timbers and the Treaty of Fort Greenville: Why Did Anthony Wayne Win Both and Could He Have Lost?" Master's Thesis, The University of Toledo, 2005.

Blanton, Wyndham. *Medicine in Virginia in the 17th Century.* Richmond, VA: William Byrd Press, 1930.

Blumgarten, A. S. *Textbook of Materia Medica, Pharmacology, and Therapeutics.* New York: Macmillan, 1939.

Boyd, Mark F. *An Introduction to Malariology.* Cambridge, MA: Harvard University Press, 1930.

Boyd, Robert T. "Another Look at the Fever and Ague of Western Oregon." *Ethnohistory* 22, no. 2 (Spring 1975): 135–54.

Boyd, Thomas. *Mad Anthony Wayne.* New York: Charles Scribner's Sons, 1929.

Boyer, John. "Daily Journal of Wayne's Campaign: General Wayne's Orderly Book." *Michigan Pioneer and Historical Collections* 34 (1905): 539–733.

Braden, Guy B. "The Colberts and the Chickasaw Nation." *Tennessee Historical Quarterly* 17, no. 3 (September 1958): 222–49.

Bradley, Abraham Jr. *Map of the United States: Exhibiting the Post-Roads, the Situations, Connexions & Distances of the post-Offices, Stage Roads, Counties & Principal Rivers.* Philadelphia: F. Shallus, 1804.

Brown, Everett S. *Constitutional History of the Louisiana Purchase, 1803–1812.* Berkeley: University of California Press, 1920.

———, ed. *William Plumer's Memorandum of Proceedings in the United States Senate 1803–1807.* New York: Da Capo Press, 1969.

Brown, William Cullen. *The Institutions of the Practice of Medicine.* 3 vols. Edinburgh, 1801.

Bruce, Marian C., and Karen P. Day. "Cross-Species Regulation of Malaria Parasitaemia in the Human Host." *Current Opinion in Microbiology* 5, no. 4 (August 2002): 431–37.

Brugger, Robert J., Robert A. Rutland, Robert Rhodes Crout, Jeanne K. Sisson, and Dru Dowdy, eds. *Papers of James Madison.* Secretary of State Series. 8 vols. Charlottesville: University Press of Virginia, 1986.

Bryan v. Kennett, 113 U.S. Reports 179 (1885).

Buckley, Jay H. *William Clark: Indian Diplomat.* Norman: University of Oklahoma Press, 2008.

Budka, Metchie J. E. "Minerva Versus Archimedes." *Smithsonian Journal of History* 1, no. 1 (1966): 61–64.

Buell, John H. "After the Battle of Fallen Timbers." *American History Illustrated* 4, no. 1, part 2 (April 1969): 32–35.

———. "Fighting the Indians in the Northwest." *American History Illustrated* 3, no. 9 (January 1969): 23–35.

Buley, R. Carlyle. *The Old Northwest: Pioneer Period, 1815–1840.* 2 vols. Indianapolis: Indiana Historical Society, 1950.

———. "Pioneer Health and Medical Practices in the Old Northwest Prior to 1840." *The Mississippi Valley Historical Review* 20 (March 1934): 497–520.

Burton, C. M. "Anthony Wayne and the Battle of Fallen Timbers." *Michigan Pioneer and Historical Collections* 31 (1901): 472–89.

Butterfield, Lyman H., ed. *Letters of Benjamin Rush, 1793–1813.* 2 vols. Princeton, NJ: Princeton University Press, 1951.

Calendar of the Correspondence of James Madison: Bulletin of the Bureau of Rolls and Library of the Department of State. Washington, DC: Department of State, 1894.

Calendar of the Correspondence of Thomas Jefferson. 3 vols. 1894. Reprint, New York: Burt Franklin, 1970.

Carter, Clarence E., ed. *The Territorial Papers of the United States.* 28 vols. Washington, DC: Government Printing Office, 1934–1962.

Carter, Ellerbe. "Courts Martial." *Virginia Law Review* 5 (February 1918): 329–35.

Chandler, David Leon. *The Jefferson Conspiracies: A President's Role in the Assassination of Meriwether Lewis.* New York: William Morrow, 1994.

Christopher, John R. *School of Natural Healing.* Provo, UT: Christopher Publications, 1976.

Chuinard, Eldon G. "The Court-Martial of Ensign Meriwether Lewis." *We Proceeded On* 8, no. 4 (November 1982): 12–15.

———. *Only One Man Died: The Medical Aspects of the Lewis and Clark Expedition.* Glendale, CA: Arthur H. Clark, 1980.

Chwatt, Bruce Leonard J. "Ague as Malaria." *Journal of Tropical Medicine and Hygiene* 79 (August 1976): 168–76.

Clark, Sanford. "Observations on the Peruvian Bark." *Medical Repository* 3 (1812): 241–46.

Cleland, Hugh G. "John B. C. Lucas, Physiocrat on the Frontier." *Western Pennsylvania Historical Magazine* 36, no. 2 (June 1953): 92–100.

Cohen, Gary L., and Loren A. Rolak. "Thomas Jefferson's Headaches: Were They Migraines?" *Headache: The Journal of Head and Face Pain* 46, no. 3 (March 2006): 492–97.

Colter-Frick, L. Ruth. *Courageous Colter and Companions.* Washington, MO: Colter-Frick, 1997.

———. "Meriwether Lewis's Personal Finances," *We Proceeded On* 28, no. 1 (February 2002): 16–20.

Congressional Journals of the United States House of Representatives: Thomas Jefferson Administration. 8 vols. Reprint, Wilmington, DE: Michael Glazier, 1977.

Congressional Journals of the United States Senate: Thomas Jefferson Administration. 8 vols. Reprint, Wilmington, DE: Michael Glazier, 1977.

Cooke, John. "Captain John Cooke's Journal of General Wayne's Campaign in 1794 & 1795." *American Historical Record* 2 (1873): 311–16, 339–45.

Cornwell, Ilene J., and Deborah K. Henderson. *Travel Guide to the Natchez Trace Parkway.* Nashville: Southern Resources Unlimited, 1984.

Cotterill, Robert S. "Federal Indian Management in the South 1789–1825." *Mississippi Valley Historical Review* 20, no. 3 (December 1933): 333–52.

———. "The Natchez Trace." *Tennessee Historical Magazine* 7, no. 4 (April 1921): 27–35.

Coxe, John Redman. "Cinchona-Peruvian Bark." In *The American Dispensatory.* 5th ed. Philadelphia: Thomas Dobson and Son, 1822.

Creecy, Donald B. "Courts-Martial." *Journal of the American Institute of Criminal Law and Criminology* 10 (August 1919): 202–207.

Cunningham, Noble E. *The Process of Government under Jefferson.* Princeton, NJ: Princeton University Press, 1978.

Cutright, Paul Russell. "I Gave Him Barks and Saltpeter." *American Heritage: The Magazine of History* 15 (December 1963): 58–61, 94–101.

———. "The Journal of Captain Meriwether Lewis (Some Observations Concerning the Journal Hiatuses of Captain Lewis)." *We Proceeded On* 10, no. 1 (February 1984): 8–10.

———. *Lewis and Clark: Pioneering Naturalists.* Urbana: University of Illinois Press, 1969.

———. "Meriwether Lewis: Botanist." *Oregon Historical Quarterly* 69 (June 1968): 148–70.

———. "Meriwether Lewis's 'Coloring of Events.'" *We Proceeded On* 11, no. 1 (February 1985): 10–17.

———. "Meriwether Lewis: Zoologist." *Oregon Historical Quarterly* 69 (March 1968): 5–28.

———. "Rest, Rest Perturbed Spirit." *We Proceeded On* 12, no. 1 (March 1986): 7–15.

Daniels, Jonathan. *The Devil's Backbone: The Story of the Natchez Trace.* New York: McGraw-Hill, 1962.

Danisi, John J. "The Vanishing Consciousness." *International Philosophical Quarterly* 29, no. 1 (March 1989): 3–16.

Danisi, Thomas C. "The 'Ague' Made Him Do It." *We Proceeded On* 28, no. 1 (February 2002): 10–15.

———. "George Champlain Sibley: Shady Dealings on the Early Frontier." *Confluence* 2, no. 1 (Fall/Winter 2010): 39–49.

———. "'Hypocondriac Affections' Revisted." *We Proceeded On* 36, no. 3 (August 2010): 4–5.

———. "James MacKay (1759–1822)." In *Dictionary of Missouri Biography*, edited by Lawrence O. Christensen, William E. Foley, Gary R. Kremer, and Kenneth H. Winn. Columbia: University of Missouri Press, 1999.

———. "John Evans (1770–1799)." In *Dictionary of Missouri Biography*, edited by Lawrence O. Christensen, William E. Foley, Gary R. Kremer, and Kenneth H. Winn. Columbia: University of Missouri Press, 1999.

———. "Keepers and Stewards Code Calls for Historical Facts." *We Proceeded On* 36, no. 2 (May 2010): 4–5, 7.

———. "Land Fraud in Upper Louisiana: A Misconception." Paper presented at the 50th annual Missouri Conference on History, Columbia, Missouri, April 2–4, 2008.

———. "Lewis's Death." *We Proceeded On* 28, no. 3 (August 2002): 2.

———. "Meriwether Lewis's Forecast of the Western Fur Trade." Paper presented at the 9th

North American Fur Trade Conference & 12th Rupert's Land Colloquium, Saint Louis, Missouri, May 24–28, 2006.

———. "Meriwether Lewis's Land Warrant: An Untimely Reward." *We Proceeded On* 35, no. 4 (November 2009): 26–28.

———. "Observations and Remarks from Lewis to Dearborn in 1807." *We Proceeded On* 35, no. 3 (August 2009): 32–38.

———. "Preserving the Legacy of Meriwether Lewis: The Letters of Samuel Latham Mitchill." *We Proceeded On* 36, no. 1 (February 2010): 8–11.

———. "What Conspiracy? Another Look at the Evidence Involving Lewis's Death." *We Proceeded On* 35, no. 1 (February 2009): 30–31.

Danisi, Thomas C., and Emily Troxell Jaycox. "A St. Louis River Map Guides the Lewis and Clark Expedition." *Gateway Heritage* 24, nos. 2 & 3 (Winter 2004): 6–17.

Danisi, Thomas C., and John C. Jackson. "Homeward Bound." *We Proceeded On* 33, no. 2 (May 2007): 16–19.

———. *Meriwether Lewis*. Amherst, NY: Prometheus Books, 2009.

———. "Was Meriwether Lewis the Godfather of the Fur Trade?" *Rocky Mountain Fur Trade Journal* 4 (2010): 1–19.

Danisi, Thomas C., and W. Raymond Wood. "James MacKay: International Explorer." *Missouri Historical Review* 102, no. 3 (April 2008): 154–64.

———. "Lewis and Clark's Route Map: James MacKay's Map of the Missouri River." *Western Historical Quarterly* 35, no. 1 (Spring 2004): 53–72.

Dary, David. *Frontier Medicine: From the Atlantic to the Pacific, 1492–1941*. New York: Alfred A. Knopf, 2008.

Davis, George B. *A Treatise on the Military Law of the United States: Together with the Practice and Procedure of Courts-Martial and Other Military Tribunals*. New York: John Wiley & Sons, 1915.

Denslow, Ray V. "Meriwether Lewis: Missouri's First Royal Arch Mason." In *Proceedings of the 95th Annual Convocation of the Grand Chapter of Royal Arch Masons of the State of Missouri* (April 1941): 72–97.

———. *Territorial Masonry, The Story of Freemasonry and the Louisiana Purchase, 1804-1821*. Washington, DC: Masonic Service Association of the United States, 1925.

DeRegnaucourt, Tony. *Archaeology of the Fort at Greenville, Ohio*. Arcanum, OH: Upper Miami Valley Archaeological Research Museum, 2007.

Desowitz, Robert. *The Malaria Capers*. New York: W. W. Norton, 1991.

———. *Ova and Parasites*. Hagerstown, MD: Harper and Row, 1980.

DeVoto, Bernard. *Course of Empire*. Boston: Houghton Mifflin, 1952.

———. "An Inference Regarding the Expedition of Lewis and Clark." *Proceedings of the American Philosophical Society* 99, no. 4 (August 1955): 185–94.

Diller, Aubrey. "James Mackay's Journey in Nebraska in 1796." *Nebraska History* 36 (June 1955): 123–28.

———. "Maps of the Missouri River before Lewis and Clark." In *Studies and Essays in the History of Science and Learning*, edited by M. F. Ashley Montagu. New York: Schuman, 1946.

Dillon, Richard. *Meriwether Lewis: A Biography.* Santa Cruz: Western Tanager Press, 1965.

Drake, Daniel. *The Principal Diseases of the Interior Valley of North America.* 2nd ed. Reprint. Philadelphia: Lippincott, Grambo and Co., 1854.

———. "Report on the Diseases of Cincinnati in the Spring of 1828 . . . for Ague and Fever." *Western Journal of the Medical and Physical Sciences* 2 (1828–1829): 216–19.

Dunne, Gerald T. *The Missouri Supreme Court.* Columbia: University of Missouri Press, 1993.

Elliotson, John. *The Principles and Practice of Medicine.* Philadelphia: Carey and Hart, 1844.

Esarey, Logan, ed. *Governor's Messages and Letters: Messages and Letters of William Henry Harrison, 1800–1811.* 2 vols. Indianapolis: Indiana Historical Commission, 1922.

"Essays on Postures," *North American Review* 5, no. 14 (July 1817): 164–74.

Estes, J. Worth. *Dictionary of Protopharmacology, Therapeutic Practices, 1700–1850.* Canton, MA: Science History Publications, 1990.

Evans, Charles. *American Bibliography.* 2nd Series. New York: Peter Smith, 1941.

Farnan, William Thomas. "Land Claims Problems and the Federal Land System in the Louisiana-Missouri Territory." PhD diss., Saint Louis University, 1971.

Fausz, Frederick J., and Michael A. Gavin. "The Death of Meriwether Lewis: An Unsolved Mystery." *Gateway Heritage* 24 (Fall 2003–Winter 2004): 66–79.

Fineberg, Stephen. "The Music of Thomas Jefferson's Greek." *Classical Journal* 88, no. 4 (April–May 1993): 359–74.

Fishbein, Morris. *Frontiers of Medicine.* Baltimore: Williams & Wilkins Company, 1933.

Finiels, Nicolas de. *An Account of Upper Louisiana.* Edited by Carl J. Ekberg and William E. Foley. Columbia: University of Missouri Press, 1989.

Fisher, John W. *Medical Appendices of the Lewis and Clark Expedition.* Juliaetta, ID: Fisher, 2006.

Fisher, Vardis. *Suicide or Murder? The Strange Death of Meriwether Lewis.* Denver: Alan Swallow, 1962.

Fitzgerald, William J. "Evolution of Use of Quinine in Treatment of Malaria." *New York State Journal of Medicine* 68, no. 6 (March 1968): 800–802.

Flournoy, H. W. ed. *Calendar of Virginia State Papers and Other Manuscripts Preserved in the Capitol at Richmond.* 11 vols. Richmond: R. F. Walker, 1875–1893.

Flückiger, Friedrich A. *The Cinchona Barks.* Philadelphia: P. Blakiston, Son & Co., 1884.

Foley, William E. *The Genesis of Missouri.* Columbia: University of Missouri Press, 1989.

———. *Wilderness Journey: The Life of William Clark.* Columbia: University of Missouri Press, 2004.

Foley, William E., and Carl J. Ekberg, eds. *An Account of Upper Louisiana by Nicolas de Finiels.* Columbia: University of Missouri Press, 1989.

Forman, Sidney. "The United States Military Philosophical Society, 1802–1813: Scientia in Bello Pax." *William and Mary Quarterly*, Third Series (July 1945): 273–85.

Gaff, Alan D. *Bayonets in the Wilderness: Anthony Wayne's Legion in the Old Northwest.* Norman: University of Oklahoma Press, 2004.

Gardner, James Alexander. "The Business Career of Moses Austin in Missouri, 1798–1821." *Missouri Historical Review* 50, no. 3 (April 1956): 235–47.

————. *Lead King: Moses Austin.* Saint Louis: Sunrise Publishing, 1980.

————. "The Life of Moses Austin: 1761–1821." PhD diss., Washington University, 1963.

————. "Moses Austin in Missouri: 1789–1821." Master's Thesis, Washington University, 1951.

Garnett, John. *Tables Requisite to Be Used with the Nautical Ephemeris, for Finding the Latitude and Longitude at Sea, First Published in London by Order of the Commissioners of Longitude to Which Are Now Added the Most Useful Astronomical Tables by Maskelyne, La Lande, Robertson, Vince, Mackay, Mendoza Rios, De Borda, &c With Many New Problems Explaining Their Use.* London, Commissioners of Longitude, 1806.

Garrison, George P. "A Memorandum of M. Austin's Journey from the Lead Mines in the County of Wythe in the State of Virginia to the Lead Mines in the Province of Louisiana West of the Mississippi," *American Historical Review* 5, no. 3 (April 1900): 518–23.

Gates, Paul. *History of Public Land Law Development.* Washington, DC: Public Land Law Review Commission, 1968.

"General Anthony Wayne's General Orders." *Michigan Pioneer Collections* 34 (1905): 341–501.

Gibson, Arrell Morgan. *The Chickasaws.* Norman: University of Oklahoma Press, 1971.

Gillett, Mary C. *The Army Medical Department, 1775–1818.* 3 vols. Washington, DC: Center of Military History United States Army, 1981.

Goldberg, Jeffrey. "Microbes on the Move." *New York Times Magazine* (October 10, 1999): 21–22.

Gracy, David. *Moses Austin: His Life.* San Antonio: Trinity University Press, 1987.

Greene, Theodore P. *America's Heroes: The Changing Models of Success in American Magazines.* New York: Oxford University Press, 1970.

Gregg, Kate L., ed. *Westward with Dragoons: The Journal of William Clark on His Expedition to Establish Fort Osage, August 25 to September 22, 1808.* Fulton, MO: Ovid Bell Press, 1937.

Greve, Charles Theodore. *Centennial History of Cincinnati and Representative Citizens.* 2 vols. Chicago: Biographical Publishing, 1904.

Guerra, Francisco. "The Introduction of Cinchona in the Treatment of Malaria." Part 1. *Journal of Tropical Medicine & Hygiene* 80, no. 6 (June 1977): 112–18.

————. "The Introduction of Cinchona in the Treatment of Malaria." Part 2. *Journal of Tropical Medicine and Hygiene* 80, no. 7 (July 1977): 135–40.

Guice, John D. W., ed. *By His Own Hand? The Mysterious Death of Meriwether Lewis.* Norman: Oklahoma University Press, 2006.

————. "Moonlight and Meriwether Lewis." *We Proceeded On* 28, no. 1 (February 2002): 21–23.

Guide to the Manuscript Collections of The Historical Society of Pennsylvania. 2nd ed. Philadelphia: The Historical Society of Pennsylvania, 1949.

Guide to the National Archives of the United States. Washington, DC: National Archives and Records Service, 1974.

Hafen, LeRoy, ed. *The Mountain Men and the Fur Trade of the Far West.* Glendale, CA: Arthur H. Clark, 1966.

Haggis, A. W. "Fundamental Errors in the Early History of Cinchona." *Bulletin of the History of Medicine* 10 (October 1941): 417–59, 568–92.

Hall, Courtney Robert. *A Scientist in the Early Republic, Samuel Latham Mitchill 1764–1831.* New York: Russell and Russell, 1962.

Hall, Virginius C. "Richard Allison, Surgeon to the Legion." *Bulletin of the Historical and Philosophical Society of Ohio* 9 (October 1951): 283–98.

Haller, John S. Jr. *American Medicine in Transition, 1840–1910.* Urbana: University of Illinois Press, 1981.

———. "Samson of the Materia Medica: Medical Theory and the Use and Abuse of Calomel in 19th-century America." *Pharmacy in History* 13 (1971): 27–34, 67–76.

Harrison, Lowell Hayes, and James C. Klotter. *A New History of Kentucky.* Lexington: University Press of Kentucky, 1997.

Hart, William C. *Observations on Military Law and the Constitution and Practice of Courts-Martial.* New York: Appleton and Co., 1864.

Hawking, Frank. "Circadian and Other Rhythms of Parasites." *Advances in Parasitology* 13 (1975): 123–82.

Hawking, Frank, Michael J. Worms, and Kenneth Gammage. "Host Temperature and Control of 24-Hour and 48-Hour Cycles in Malaria Parasites." *Lancet* 7541, no.1 (March 1968): 506–509.

———. "24- and 48-Hour Cycles of Malaria Parasites in the Blood; Their Purpose, Production and Control." *Transactions of the Royal Society of Tropical Medicine and Hygiene* 62, no. 6 (June 1968): 731–65.

Hay, Thomas Robson. "Some Reflections on the Career of General James Wilkinson." *Mississippi Valley Historical Review* 21, no. 4 (March 1935): 471–94.

Hazlitt, William. "Lectures on the English Poets." *North American Review* 8, no. 23 (March 1819): 276–322.

Heineman, Herbert S. "The Clinical Syndrome of Malaria in the United States." *Archives of Internal Medicine* 129, no. 4 (April 1972): 607–16.

Heitman, Francis Bernard, ed. *Historical Register and Dictionary of the United States Army from Its Organization, September 29, 1789, to March 2, 1903.* 2 vols. Washington, DC: Government Printing Office, 1903. Reprint, Urbana: University of Illinois Press, 1965.

Hibbert, Wilfrid. "Major Amos Stoddard, First Governor of Upper Louisiana and Hero of Fort Meigs." *Historical Society of Northwestern Ohio Quarterly Bulletin* 2, no. 2 (April 1930): 1–12.

Hoig, Stan. *The Chouteaus: First Family of the Fur Trade.* Albuquerque: University of New Mexico Press, 2008.

Holmberg, James, ed. *Dear Brother.* New Haven, CT: Yale University Press, 2002.

Holmes, John H. *Thomas Jefferson Treats Himself: Herbs, Physicke, & nutrition in Early America.* Fort Valley, VA: The Loft Press, 1997.

Holt, Albert C. "The Economic and Social Beginnings of Tennessee." *Tennessee Historical Magazine* 7, no. 4 (January 1922): 252–313.

434   BIBLIOGRAPHY

Homberger, Esther Fischer, "Hypochondriasis of the Eighteenth Century—Neurosis of the Present Century." *Bulletin of the History of Medicine* 46, no. 4 (July–August 1972): 391–401.

Honigsbaum, Mark. *The Fever Trail: In Search of the Cure for Malaria.* New York: Farrar, Straus, and Giroux, 2001.

Hood, Ronald C. "The Battle of Fallen Timbers." *American History Illustrated* 3, no. 10 (February 1969): 4–11.

Hooper, Robert. *A Compendious Medical Dictionary.* Newburyport, MA: Wm. Sawyer & Co., 1809.

———. *Lexicon-Medicum, or Medical Dictionary.* 4th ed. London: Samuel Wood and Sons, 1822.

———. *Lexicon Medicum, or, Medical Dictionary.* 13th ed. New York, Harper & Brothers, 1841.

Hooper, Robert, and Samuel Akerly. *Lexicon Medicum, or, Medical Dictionary.* 13th ed. 2 vols. New York: Harper & Brothers, 1846.

Houck, Louis. *A History of Missouri from the Earliest Exploration and Settlements until the Admission of the State into the Union.* 3 vols. Chicago: R. R. Donnelly & Sons, 1908.

Hough, Emerson. *The Magnificent Adventure.* New York: D. Appleton and Company, 1916.

———. "The Magnificent Adventure: A Romance of the Lewis and Clark Expedition." *Munsey's Magazine* 57 (April–May 1916).

Huddleston, Eugene L. "James Elliot and 'The Garden of North America': A New Englander's Impressions of the Old Northwest." *Northwest Ohio Quarterly* 42, no. 3 (Summer 1970): 64–73.

Humphreys, Margaret. *Malaria, Poverty, Race, and Public Health in the United States.* Baltimore: Johns Hopkins University Press, 2001.

Hunt, Robert R. "The Blood Meal: Mosquitoes and Agues on the Lewis and Clark Expedition, Part 1." *We Proceeded On* 18, no. 2 (May 1992): 4–10.

———. "The Blood Meal: Mosquitoes and Agues on the Lewis and Clark Expedition, Part 2." *We Proceeded On* 18, no. 3 (August 1992): 4–10.

Hunter, Clark, ed. *The Life and Letters of Alexander Wilson.* Philadelphia: American Philosophical Society, 1983.

Huxtable, George, and Ian Jackson. "Journey to Work: James Cook's Transatlantic Voyages in the Grenville 1764–1767." *Journal of Navigation* 63 (2010): 207–14.

Index to the James Madison Papers. Washington: Library of Congress, 1965.

Index to the Thomas Jefferson Papers. Washington: Library of Congress, 1976.

Isselbacher, Kurt J., Eugene Braunwald, Jean D. Wilson, Joseph B. Martin, Anthony S. Fauci, and Dennis L. Kasper, eds. *Harrison's Principles of Internal Medicine.* 13th ed. 2 vols. New York: McGraw-Hill, 1992.

Jackson, Donald. "A Footnote to the Lewis and Clark Expedition." *Manuscripts* 24 (Winter 1972): 1–21.

———. *The Journals of Zebulon Montgomery Pike.* Urbana: University of Illinois Press, 1962.

———. "A New Lewis and Clark Map." *Missouri Historical Society Bulletin* 17 (January 1961): 119–26.

————. "On the Death of Meriwether Lewis's Servant." *William and Mary Quarterly* 21, no. 3 (July 1964): 445–48.

Jackson, Donald, ed. *Letters of the Lewis and Clark Expedition with Related Documents, 1783–1854.* 2nd ed. 2 vols. Urbana: University of Illinois Press, 1978.

Jackson, Stanley W. *Melancholia and Depression.* New Haven, CT: Yale University Press, 1986.

————. "Melancholia and Mechanical Explanation in Eighteenth-Century Medicine." *Journal of the History of Medicine and Allied Sciences* 38 (July 1983): 298–319.

————. "Melancholia and the Waning of the Humoral Theory." *Journal of the History of Medicine and Allied Sciences* 33 (July 1978): 367–76.

Jacobs, James Ripley. *The Beginning of the US Army, 1783–1812.* Princeton, NJ: Princeton University Press, 1947.

Jamison, Kay Redfield. *Night Falls Fast.* New York: Alfred A. Knopf, 1999.

Jarcho, Saul. *Quinine's Predecessor.* Baltimore: Johns Hopkins University Press, 1993.

Jenkinson, Clay Straus. *The Character of Meriwether Lewis: "Completely Metamorphosed" in the American West.* Reno, NV: Marmarth Press, 2000.

Johnson, Carole McCool. "Emerson Hough and the American West: A Biographical and Critical Study." PhD diss., University of Texas at Austin, 1975.

Jones, Burt W. A. "John Rice Jones: A Brief Sketch of the Life and Public Career of the First Practicing Lawyer in Illinois." *Chicago Historical Society's Collection* 4 (1889): 99–139.

Jones, David. "Extracts from the Original Manuscript Journal of the Reverend David Jones . . . Chaplain of the United States Legion, under Major-General Wayne, during the Indian Wars of 1794–5–6." *Michigan Pioneer and Historical Collections* 8 (1885): 392–95.

Jones, Landon Y. *William Clark and the Shaping of the West.* New York: Hill and Wang, 2004.

Journal of the Executive Proceedings of the Senate. 36 vols. New York: Johnson Reprint Corporation, 1969.

Journal of The House of Representatives of the Commonwealth of Kentucky: Begun and Held in the Town of Frankfort, on Monday the Fourth Day of December, 1815. Frankfort: Gerard & Berry, 1816.

Kebler, Lyman. "United States Patents Granted for Medicines during the Pioneer Years of the Patent Office." *Journal of the American Pharmaceutical Association* 24, no. 6 (June 1935): 485–89.

Kendall, Peter. "History Unearthed in Greenville, Ohio." *Cube* 30, no. 1 (April 2009): 10–13.

Kennon, Donald R., and Rebecca M. Rogers. *The Committee on Ways and Means: A Bicentennial History, 1789–1989.* Washington, DC: US House of Representatives, 1989.

Knopf, Richard C. *Anthony Wayne, A Name in Arms: Soldier, Diplomat, Defender of Expansion Westward of a Nation; the Wayne-Knox-Pickering-McHenry Correspondence.* Pittsburgh: University of Pittsburgh Press, 1960.

————. *Anthony Wayne and the Founding of the US Army.* Pittsburgh, University of Pittsburgh Press, 1960.

————. "Journal of Wayne's Last Campaign." *Proceedings of the American Antiquarian Society* 64 (October 1954): 273–302.

———. "Two Journals of the Kentucky Volunteers, 1793 & 1794." *Filson Club History Quarterly* 27 (January 1953): 247–81.

———. "Wayne's Western Campaign: The Wayne-Knox Correspondence, 1793–1794." *Pennsylvania Magazine of History and Biography* 78 (July 1954): 298–341.

———. "Wayne's Western Campaign: The Wayne-Knox Correspondence, 1793–1794, II." *Pennsylvania Magazine of History and Biography* 78 (Oct. 1954): 424–55.

Knudson, Jerry W. "Newspaper Reaction to the Louisiana Purchase." *Missouri Historical Review* 63, no. 2 (January 1969): 182–213.

Kreier, Julius P., ed. *Malaria.* 3 vols. New York: Academic Press, 1980.

Kreier, Julius P., and John R. Baker, eds. *Parasitic Protozoa.* New York: Academic Press, 1977.

Kremers, Edward, and George Urdang. *History of Pharmacy.* Philadelphia: J. B. Lippincott Company, 1940.

Kukla, Jon. *Mr. Jefferson's Women.* New York: Vintage Books, 2007.

Kushner, Howard I. "The Suicide of Meriwether Lewis: A Psychoanalytic Inquiry." *William and Mary Quarterly,* Third Series, 38, no. 3 (1981): 464–81.

Larremore, Wilbur. "American Courts-Martial." *North American Review* 177 (Oct. 1903): 607–14.

Lavender, David. *The Way to the Western Sea: Lewis and Clark Across the Continent.* Lincoln: University of Nebraska Press, 2001.

Lawson, Charles F. *Remote Sensing and Archeological Testing of the Meriwether Lewis Monument and Pioneer Cemetery and the Search for Grinder's Stand.* Tallahassee, FL: National Park Service, 2002.

Lechter, Robert B. "William Simmons, Accountant: Unsung Hero at the Battle of Bladensburg, MD, War of 1812." *MACPA Statement* 36, no. 9 (May/June 2001): 16.

Leden, Ido. "Antimalarial Drugs—350 Years." *Scandinavian Journal of Rheumatology* 10 (1981): 307–12.

Lentz, Gary. "Meriwether Lewis's Medicine Chests." *We Proceeded On* 26, no. 2 (May 2000): 10–17.

Lewis, Grace. "Financial Records—Expedition to the Pacific Ocean." *Missouri Historical Society Bulletin* 10 (July 1954): 465–89.

———. "The First Home of Governor Lewis in Louisiana Territory." *Missouri Historical Society Bulletin* 14 (July 1958): 357–68.

Lipscomb, Andrew A., and Albert Ellery Bergh, eds. *The Writings of Thomas Jefferson.* Library ed. 20 vols. Washington, DC: Thomas Jefferson Memorial Association of the United States, 1903.

Loos, John Louis. "A Biography of William Clark, 1770–1813." PhD diss., Washington University, 1953.

Loge, Ronald V. "Illness at Three Forks." *Montana: The Magazine of Western History* 50, no. 2 (Summer 2000): 2–15.

———. "Meriwether Lewis and Malaria." *We Proceeded On* 28, no. 2 (May 2002): 33–35.

———. "Two Dozes of Barks and Opium: Lewis and Clark as Physicians." *We Proceeded On* 23, no. 1 (February 1997): 10–15, 30.

"Lord Byron's Character and Writings," *North American Review* 21, no. 49 (October 1825): 300–60.

Lord, Walter. *The Dawn's Early Light*. Baltimore: Johns Hopkins University Press, 1972.

Macculoch, John. *An Essay on the Remittent and Intermittent Diseases*. 2 vols. London: Longman, Rees, Orme, Brown, and Green, 1828.

———. *Malaria: An Essay on the Production and Propagation of This Poison*. London: Longman, Rees, Orme, Brown, and Green, 1827.

Marshall, Thomas Maitland. *The Life and Papers of Frederick Bates*. 2 vols. Saint Louis: Missouri Historical Society, 1926.

Maynard, Walter Jr. "A Fragment from the Diary of Major John Hutchinson Buell, U.S.A., Who Joined the American Army at the Beginning of the Revolutionary War and Remained in Service until 1803." *Journal of the Military Service Institution of the United States* 40, no. 145 (January–February 1907): 102–13; (March–April 1907): 258–68.

McGrane, R. C. "William Clark's Journal of Wayne's Campaign." *Mississippi Valley Historical Review* 1, no. 3 (December 1914): 418–44.

Microfilm Resources for Research: A Comprehensive Catalog. Washington, DC: National Archives Trust Fund Board, 2000.

Miller, Grace Lewis. *Finding Aid to the Grace Lewis Miller Papers, 1938–1971*. Saint Louis: National Park Service, 1999.

"Miscellaneous Notices: Westminster Review," *North American Review* 18, No. 43 (April 1824): 419–27.

Mitchell, Stewart, ed. *New Letters of Abigail Adams, 1788–1801*. New York: Houghton Mifflin, 1947.

Mitchill, Samuel Latham, ed. *Discourse on Thomas Jefferson, More Especially as a Promoter of Natural & Physical Science*. New York: G. & C. Carvill, 1826.

———. "Dr. Mitchill's Letters From Washington: 1801–1813." *Harper's New Monthly Magazine* 58 (April 1879): 740–55.

———, ed. *Medical Repository*. 12 vols. New York: 1804–1812.

Moore, John H. "The Death of Meriwether Lewis." *American Historical Magazine* 9 (1904): 218–30.

Moore, Kathyrn. "The Lost Years of Meriwether Lewis." *Journal of the West* 42 (Summer 2003): 58–65.

Moore, Robert J. Jr. "A Corps of Discovery." *Nebraskaland Magazine* 80, no. 7 (August–September 2002): 14–29.

———. "Lewis and Clark and Dinosaurs: The Fossil Record of the Expedition." *We Proceeded On* 24, no. 2 (May 1998): 26–28.

———. "Pompey's Baptism: The Christening of Jean Baptiste Charbonneau." *We Proceeded On* 26, no. 1 (February 2000): 10–17.

Moore, Robert J. Jr., and Michael Haynes. *Tailor Made, Trail Worn: Army Life, Clothing, & Weapons of the Corps of Discovery*. Helena, MT: Farcountry Press, 2003.

Morris, Larry E. *The Fate of the Corps: What Became of the Lewis and Clark Explorers after the Expedition*. New Haven, CT: Yale University Press, 2004.

Moulton, Gary E. *Herbarium of the Lewis and Clark Expedition.* Lincoln: University of Nebraska Press, 1999.

———. *The Journals of the Lewis and Clark Expedition.* 13 vols. Lincoln: University of Nebraska Press, 1983–2001.

———, ed. *The Lewis and Clark Journals: An American Epic of Discovery: The Abridgement of the Definitive Nebraska Edition/Meriwether Lewis, William Clark, and Members of the Corps of Discovery.* Lincoln: University of Nebraska Press, 2003.

———. "The Missing Journals of Meriwether Lewis." *Montana: The Magazine of Western History* 35, no. 3 (Summer 1985): 28–39.

———. "New Documents of Meriwether Lewis." *We Proceeded On* 13, no. 4 (November 1987): 4–7.

Moulton, Gary E., and James J. Holmberg: "'What We Are About': Recently Discovered Letters of William Clark Shed New Light on the Lewis and Clark Expedition." *Filson Club History Quarterly* 65, no. 3 (July 1991): 387–403.

Nasatir, Abraham P. "Anglo–Spanish Rivalry in the Iowa Country 1797–1798." *Iowa Journal of History and Politics* 28 (July 1930): 337–89.

———. "Anglo–Spanish Rivalry on the Upper Missouri." *Mississippi Valley Historical Review* 16, no. 4 (March 1930): 507–28.

———. "John Evans, Explorer and Surveyor." Parts 1–3. *Missouri Historical Review* 25 (January 1931): 219–39; (April 1931): 432–60; (July 1931): 585–608.

———, ed. *Before Lewis and Clark: Documents Illustrating the History of Missouri, 1785–1804.* 2 vols. Saint Louis: Saint Louis Historical Documents Foundation, 1952.

Neilson, William Allan, Thomas A. Knott, and Paul W. Carhart, eds. *Webster's New International Dictionary of the English Language.* 2nd ed. Springfield, MA: G. & C. Merriam Company, Publishers, 1960.

Nelson, Paul David. "Anthony Wayne: Soldier as Politician." *Pennsylvania Magazine of History and Biography* 106 (October 1982): 463–81.

———. *Anthony Wayne: Soldier of the Early Republic.* Bloomington: Indiana University Press, 1985.

———. "General Charles Scott, the Kentucky Mounted Volunteers, and the Northwest Indian Wars, 1784–1794." *Journal of the Early Republic* 6 (Fall 1986): 219–51.

Nicholson, Bradley J. "Courts-Martial in the Legion Army: American Military Law in the Early Republic, 1792–1796." *Military Law Review* 144 (1994): 77–109.

Norfleet, Fillmore. *Saint Memin in Virginia: Portraits and Biographies.* Richmond, VA: Dietz Press, 1942.

Oldmixon, John. *The British Empire in America.* 2nd ed. 2 vols. London, 1741.

Oman, Kerry. "Serendipity." *We Proceeded On* 27, no. 4 (November 2001): 7–11.

Osborne, Oliver T. *The Principles of Therapeutics.* Philadelphia: W. B. Saunders Company, 1922.

Osgood, Ernest Staples, ed. *The Field Notes of Captain William Clark, 1803–1805.* New Haven, CT: Yale University Press, 1964.

Osler, William. *The Principles and Practice of Medicine.* 2nd ed. New York: D. Appleton and Company, 1895.

Parascandola, John. "Patent Medicines in Nineteenth Century America." *Caduceus: A Museum Quarterly for the Health Sciences* 1, no. 1 (Spring 1985): 1–41.

Patridge, Jeff. "The Legacies of Conflict in Missouri Land Grants." *The Record* 4, no. 4 (Spring 1994): 6–8.

Peake, Ora Brooks. *A History of the United States Indian Factory System, 1795–1822.* Denver: Sage Books, 1954.

Pease, Verne S. "The Death of Captain Merriwether Lewis." *Southern Magazine* 4 (February 1894): 17–24.

Peck, David J. "The Death of Meriwether Lewis." *We Proceeded On* 35, no. 4 (November 2009): 16–25.

———. *Or Perish in the Attempt: Wilderness Medicine in the Lewis & Clark Expedition.* Helena, MT: Farcountry Press, 2002.

Pelzer, Louis. "The Spanish Land Grants of Upper Louisiana." *Iowa Journal of History and Politics* 11 (1913): 3–37.

Phelps, Dawson A. "The Chickasaw Agency." *Journal of Mississippi History* 14, no. 2 (April 1952): 119–37.

———. "Colbert Ferry and Selected Documents." *Alabama Historical Quarterly* 25, nos. 3–4 (Fall and Winter 1963): 203–26.

———. "The Natchez Trace, Indian Trail to Parkway." *Tennessee Historical Quarterly* 21, no. 3 (September 1962): 203–18.

———. "Stands and Travel Accommodations on the Natchez Trace." *Journal of Mississippi History* 11, no. 1 (January 1949): 1–54.

———. "Tockshish." *Journal of Mississippi History* 13, no. 3 (July 1951): 138–45.

———. "The Tragic Death of Meriwether Lewis." *William and Mary Quarterly, Series 3,* 13 (July 1956): 305–18.

Phillips, Henry, Jr. "Early Proceedings of the American Philosophical Society . . . from the Manuscript Minutes of Its Meetings from 1774 to 1838." *Proceedings of the American Philosophical Society* 22 (1884): 1–874.

Pidgin, Charles Felton. *Theodosia: The First Gentlewoman of Her Time.* Boston: C. M. Clark, 1907.

Plaisance, Aloysius. "The Chickasaw Bluffs Factory and Its Removal to Arkansas River, 1818–1822." *Tennessee Historical Quarterly* 11, no. 1 (March 1952): 41–56.

Poser, Charles, and G. W. Bruyn. *An Illustrated History of Malaria.* New York: Parthenon, 1999.

Pregaldin, Anton. "Introduction." In *Missouri Land Claims.* New Orleans: Polyanthos, 1976.

Pringle, John. *Observations on the Disease of the Army.* Philadelphia: Fry and Kammerer, 1810.

Proceedings of the Celebration of the Three Hundredth Anniversary of the First Recognized Use of Cinchona. St. Louis: Missouri Botanical Garden: Saint Louis, 1931.

Quaife, Milo M. "Extracts from McKay's Journal and Others." *Wisconsin Historical Society Proceedings* 63 (1916): 186–210.

————. "General James Wilkinson's Narrative of the Fallen Timbers Campaign." *Mississippi Valley Historical Review* 16 (June 1929): 81–90.

Rabakukk, Marilyn MacKay Ballard. *The Mackays of Arichliney.* Coral Springs, FL: Llumina Press, 2006.

Rao, U. V. Gopala, and Henry N. Wagner. "Normal Weights of Human Organs." *Radiology* 102 (February 1972): 337–39.

Ravenholt, Reimert T. "Triumph Then Despair: The Tragic Death of Meriwether Lewis." *Epidemiology* 5, no. 3 (May 1994): 366–79.

Rees, Abraham. *The Cyclopaedia; or, Universal Dictionary of Arts, Sciences, and Literature.* 45 vols. London: Longman, Hurst, Rees, Orme & Browne, 1819.

Richardson, Lemont K. "Private Land Claims in Missouri." *Missouri Historical Review* 50, no. 2 (January 1956): 132–44; no. 3 (April 1956): 271–86.

Rigal, Laura. "Empire of Birds: Alexander Wilson's *American Ornithology.*" *Huntington Library Quarterly* 59, no. 2/3 (1996): 232–68.

Riley, Patrick R. "Legion Ville Rediscovered: A Forgotten Chapter in American History." Master's Thesis, University of Pittsburgh, 1993.

Robertson, James Alexander. *Louisiana under the Rule of Spain, France, and the United States, 1785–1807.* 2 vols. Cleveland: Arthur H. Clark, 1911.

Rogers, Ann. "Hypocondriac Affections: Letters Help Define Jefferson's Phrase." *We Proceeded On* 36, no. 1 (February 2010): 33, 36.

Rudd, Velva E. "Botanical Contributions of the Lewis and Clark Expedition." *Journal of the Washington Academy of Sciences* 44 (November 1954): 351–56.

Rush, Benjamin. *An Account of the Bilious Remitting Yellow Fever.* Philadelphia: Thomas Dobson, 1794.

Rutkow, Ira M. *Bleeding Blue and Gray: Civil War Surgery and the Evolution of Medicine.* New York: Random House, 2005.

Rutland, Robert Allen. *The Presidency of James Madison.* Lawrence: University Press of Kansas, 1990.

Rutland, Robert A., Robert J. Brugger, Jeanne K. Sisson, Thomas A. Mason, Susannah H. Jones, and Fredrika J. Teute, eds. *The Papers of James Madison: Presidential Series.* 5 vols. Charlottesville: University of Virginia Press, 1984.

Rutman, Darrett B., and Anita H. Rutman. "Of Agues and Fevers: Malaria in the Early Chesapeake." *William and Mary Quarterly,* Third Series, 33, no. 1 (January 1976): 31–60.

Sanford, Clark. "Observations on the Peruvian Bark." Third Hexade. *Medical Repository* 3 (1812): 241–46.

Saul, Allan. "The Role of Variant Surface Antigens on Malaria-Infected Red Blood Cells." *Parasitology Today* 15 (November 1999): 455–57.

Schroeder, Walter A. *Opening the Ozarks: A Historical Geography of Missouri's Ste. Genevieve District, 1760–1830.* Columbia: University of Missouri Press, 2002.

Seiler, Toni T. *The St. Clair and Wayne Trails.* Arcanum, OH: Darke County Historical Society, 1989.

Senac, Jean. *A Treatise on the Hidden Nature and the Treatment of Intermitting and Remitting Fevers.* Philadelphia: Conrad & Co., 1805.

Setzer, Henry. "Zoological Contributions of the Lewis and Clark Expedition." *Journal of the Washington Academy of Sciences* 44 (November 1954): 356–57.

Shaw, Ralph R., and Richard H. Shoemaker. *American Bibliography: A Preliminary Checklist for 1806.* New York: Scarecrow Press, 1961.

Sherman, William F., and Craig R. Scott. *Records of the Accounting Officers of the Treasury Department.* Inventory 14 (revised). Lovettsville, VA: Willow Bend, 1997.

Shoemaker, Floyd C. *Missouri and Missourians.* 5 vols. Chicago: Lewis, 1943.

Skelton, William B. *An American Profession of Arms: The Army Officer Corps, 1784–1861.* Lawrence: University Press of Kansas, 1992.

Sloan, Cliff, and David McKean. *The Great Decision: Jefferson, Adams, Marshall, and the Battle for the Supreme Court.* New York: Public Affairs, 2009.

Smith, Dale C. "Quinine and Fever: The Development of the Effective Dosage." *Journal of the History of Medicine and Allied Sciences* 31, no. 3 (July 1976): 343–67.

Smith, Dwight L., ed. "From Greene Ville to Fallen Timbers: A Journal of the Wayne Campaign." *Indiana Historical Society Publications* 16 (1952): 237–333.

Smith, James Morton. *The Republic of Letters: The Correspondence between Thomas Jefferson and James Madison, 1776–1826.* 3 vols. New York: Norton, 1995.

Stagg, J. C. A. "Soldiers in Peace and War: Comparative Perspectives on the Recruitment of the United States Army, 1802–1815." *William and Mary Quarterly*, Third Series 57 (January 2000): 79–120.

Starrs, James E., and Kira Gale. *The Death of Meriwether Lewis: A Historic Crime Scene Investigation.* Omaha, NE: River Junction Press, 2009.

Sternberg, George Miller. *Malaria and Malarial Diseases.* New York: William Wood & Company, 1884.

Steward, Dick. *Frontier Swashbuckler: The Life and Legend of John Smith T.* Columbia: University of Missouri Press, 2000.

Stoddard, Amos. *Sketches, Historical and Descriptive of Louisiana.* Philadelphia: Mathew Carey, 1812.

Sugden, John. "Early Pan-Indianism: Tecumseh's Tour of the Indian Country, 1811–1812." *American Indian Quarterly* 10, no. 4 (Autumn 1986): 273–304.

Sung, Carolyn Hoover. "Catherine Mitchill's Letters from Washington 1806–1812." *Quarterly Journal of the Library of Congress* 34, no. 3 (July 1977): 171–89.

Szasz, Thomas. "A Bogus Benjamin Rush Quote: Contribution to the History of Pharmacracy." *History of Psychiatry* 16, no. 1 (2005): 89–98.

Teggart, Frederick. "Notes Supplementary to Any Edition of Lewis and Clark." *American Historical Association Annual Report* 1 (1908): 183–95.

Tenney, Louise. *Today's Herbal Healing*, 2nd ed. Provo, UT: Woodland Health Books, 1983.

Thomas, Robert. *The Modern Practice of Physic.* New York: Collins & Co., 1820.

Thwaites, Reuben Gold, ed. *Original Journals of the Lewis and Clark Expedition, 1804–1806.* 8 vols. New York: Dodd, Mead & Co., 1904.

Todd, Charles Burr. *Life of Colonel Aaron Burr: Vice-President of the United States*. New York: S. W. Green, 1879.

"Transfer of Upper Louisiana—Papers of Captain Amos Stoddard," *Glimpses of the Past* 2 (May–Sept. 1935): 78–122.

Underwood, Thomas T. *Journal of Thomas Taylor Underwood*. Cincinnati: Society of Colonial Wars in the State of Ohio, 1945.

Urdang, George. "The Early Chemical and Pharmaceutical History of Calomel." *Chymia* 1 (1948): 93–108.

US Congress. *Annals of Congress of the United States, 1789–1824*. 42 vols. Washington, DC: 1834–1856.

Valencius, Conevery Bolton. *The Health of the Country: How American Settlers Understood Themselves and Their Land*. New York: Basic Books, 2002.

Violette, Eugene Morrow. "Spanish Land Claims in Missouri." *Washington University Studies* 8, no. 2 *Humanistic Series* 2 (1921): 167–200.

Wade, Arthur P. "A Military Offspring of the American Philosophical Society." *Military Affairs* 38 (October 1974): 103–107.

Wallace, W. S., ed. *Documents Relating to the North West Company*. Toronto, Champlain Society, 1934.

Ward, Harry M. *The Department of War, 1781–1795*. Pittsburgh: University of Pittsburgh Press, 1962.

Watson, William N. Boog. "Two British Naval Surgeons of the French Wars." *Medical History* 13, no. 3 (July 1969): 213–25.

Wayne, Anthony. *The West Point Orderly Books*. Columbus: Ohio State Museum, Anthony Wayne Parkway Board, 1954.

Wernsdorfer, Walther H., and Ian McGregor. *Malaria: Principles and Practice of Malariology*. 2 vols. New York: Churchill Livingstone, 1988.

Wilkinson, James. *Memoir of My Own Times*. 3 vols. Philadelphia: Abraham Small, 1816.

Will, Drake W. "Lewis and Clark: Westering Physicians." *Montana: The Magazine of Western History* 21, no. 4 (Autumn 1971): 2–17.

———. "The Medical and Surgical Practice of the Lewis and Clark Expedition." *Journal of the History of Medicine and Allied Sciences* 14 (July 1959): 273–97.

Williams, David. "John Evans' Strange Journey." *American Historical Review* 54 (January 1949): 277–95; (April 1949): 508–29.

Williams, Gwyn A. *Madoc: The Making of a Myth*. New York: Oxford University Press, 1987.

Williams, Samuel Cole. *Beginnings of West Tennessee: In the Land of the Chickasaws 1541–1841*. Johnson City, TN: Watuga Press, 1930.

Wills, Gary. *James Madison*. New York: Henry Holt, 2002.

Wilson, Alexander. *American Ornithology or The Natural History of the Birds of the United States*. 3 vols. New York: Collins & Co., 1828.

———. "Particulars of the Death of Capt. Lewis." *Port Folio* 7 (January 1812): 34–47.

Wilson, Alexander, and Charles Lucian Bonaparte. *American Ornithology; or the Natural His-*

tory of the Birds of the United States. 4 vols. Edinburgh, Scotland, UK: Hurst, Chance, and Co., 1831.

Wilson, Charles Morrow. *Meriwether Lewis of Lewis and Clark.* New York: Thomas Y. Crowell, 1934.

Wilson, Frazer E., ed. *Journal of Captain Daniel Bradley.* Greenville, OH: Frank H. Jobes & Son, 1935.

Witte, Kevin C. "In the Footsteps of the Third Spanish Expedition: James Mackay and John T. Evans' Impact on the Lewis and Clark Expedition." *Great Plains Quarterly* 26, no. 2 (Spring 2006): 85–98.

Wood, W. Raymond. *An Atlas of Early Maps of the American Midwest*, Part II. Illinois State Museum, Scientific Papers 29 (2001).

————. *Prologue to Lewis and Clark: The Mackay and Evans Expedition.* Norman: University of Oklahoma Press, 2003.

Woolen, William Wesley, Daniel Wait Howe, and Jacob Piatt Dunn, eds. *Executive Journal of Indiana Territory, 1800–1816.* Indianapolis: Bowen-Merrill Co., 1900.

Wylder, Delbert E. *Emerson Hough.* Boston: Twayne Publishers, 1981.

Young, James Harvey. *The Toadstool Millionaires: A Social History of Patent Medicines in America Before Federal Regulation.* Princeton, NJ: Princeton University Press, 1961.

Zingman, Barry S., and Brant L. Viner. "Splenic Complications in Malaria: Case Report and Review." *Clinical Infectious Diseases* 16 (February 1993): 223–32.

INDEX

Peruvian bark. *See* cinchona bark (Peruvian bark)
Phelps, Dawson A., 197, 387n42
Philadelphia Aurora (newspaper), 87
Philipson, Joseph, 290, 292, 294, 296, 297, 298, 330, 332
Pike, Zebulon, 97, 175, 283, 369n19
plants, Lewis's finding and identifying. *See* specimen collection, Lewis's responsibility for
Polhemus, Lieut., 251
Pony Express. *See* mail service
"Porney." *See* Pernier [Pernia], John
Portage des Sioux, 50, 51, 293, 294, 295, 334
Portell, Thomas, 38
Preston, William, 219–21, 294, 376n43
Price, Risdon, 292, 294, 377–78n59
Pringle, John, 203
Prior, Capt., 253
Prior, Ens. *See* Pryor [Prior], Nathaniel (Ens.)
"proof spirits" test of temperature, 74
Provenchere, Peter (son of Pierre), 382nn104–105
Provenchere, Pierre [Peter], 84, 136, 152, 382nn104,105
    financial records involving, 115, 136, 149, 150, 290, 298, 305, 318, 327, 331
Pryor [Prior], Nathaniel (Ens.), 142, 144, 217, 218–19, 307, 375nn31–32

Quina. See cinchona bark (Peruvian bark)
Quincy, Josiah, III, 141

Rand, Ens., 30, 31, 33–34, 251, 254, 257, 264–65
Randolph, Anne Cary, 87, 216
Randolph, Martha (Jefferson), 398–99n62
Randolph, Thomas Mann, Jr., 85, 185, 271, 273
Ravenolt, Reimert, 198, 346

real estate. *See* land grants in Louisiana Territory
Rees [Rhys], John, 39, 350n19
regimental court-martial, 29, 348–49n21
"reptile Spaniards," 54
requête, 58
retrocession of Louisiana Territory, 54, 58
Richmond, Ens., 251, 252
Riddick, Thomas, 295, 299, 377–78n59
Rittenhouse, David, 338–39
Riviere, Marie Anne, 352n56
Robertson, James, 158–59
Robertson, John, 39
Robertson, Thomas Bolling "Bomby," 105, 334
Rodney, Caesar, 130
Rogers, Ann, 199
Rolak, Loren, 398n61
Rudd, Velva, 360n26
Rush, Benjamin, 76, 183, 204, 210, 342–43, 396–97nn45–46
    Mitchill on, 273
Rush's pills. *See* calomel (powdered mercury) and jalap
Russell, Gilbert, 17, 105, 131, 152, 160–61, 193, 370n10, 386–87n38, 390n7
    asking for furlough, 160, 171, 390–91n12
    financial records involving, 291, 298, 335
    at Fort Pickering, 202, 390n8, 402n90, 402n92
    "Gilbert Russell Statement," 19, 168–77, 245–46
        pages from, *169, 174, 175*
    handwriting of, 170
    letters from Jefferson on death of Lewis, 197, 243
    letters to Jefferson, 197, 240–42
    and Simmons, 161–62, 171, 386nn36–37, 391n16
    as witness for James Wilkinson, 168, 173, 175